THE
SECRET
BARRISTER

THE SECRET BARRISTER

Stories of the Law and
How It's Broken

MACMILLAN

First published 2018 by Macmillan
an imprint of Pan Macmillan
20 New Wharf Road, London N1 9RR
Associated companies throughout the world
www.panmacmillan.com

ISBN 978-1-5098-4110-3

Typeset by Palimpsest Book Production Ltd, Falkirk, Stirlingshire
Printed and bound by CPI Group (UK) Ltd, Croydon, CR0 4YY

For the third pig,
who I begrudgingly concede is always right.
For your love, strength and continued inspiration:
as ever, that'll do.

Contents

Introduction:
My Opening Speech

'And so that is your defence, is it, Mr Tuttle?'

A pause. His eyes dart to his girlfriend in the public gallery and back to me – a micro-glance, no more – but enough, I'm hopeful, for the jury to have clocked. I turn my head just slightly, crossing gazes with the lady on the front row at the far end. She's noticed. She's folded her arms. In fact, several of them have. The elderly chap in the navy blazer and beige slacks nudges the gingham-shirted, fabulously bearded fellow to his left, and they trade conspiratorial grins.

The body language is not good for Mr Tuttle.

He digs his fingers into the sides of the witness box, groping for the right response, oblivious that there isn't one. As his cheeks flush and he shuffles his feet, he appears to look longingly at the dock at the back of court, stung with regret at his decision to leave the safety of its perspex confines and walk the long fifteen feet to give evidence in his own defence. He had to, of course. It is near-impossible to successfully run self-defence without giving your own account on oath as to why you brought fisty justice to bear upon the man next door. But it is obvious that, if Mr Tuttle could turn back time, he'd give serious consideration to exercising his right to silence.

The double doors to my right groan. The usher slides in cradling his clipboard, pursued by a crash of law students, who are silently urged towards the public gallery. The only thing a barrister enjoys more than an audience is a bigger, more impressible audience. So I wait for them to squeeze themselves into the narrow oak pews in the back right corner. The lengthy pause, as Mr Tuttle weighs up how to answer my semi-rhetorical question, helps build the suspense. I savour it. I calmly top up my plastic cup from the water jug, and take an insouciant sip of water.

As I do, I notice that all eyes in the courtroom are momentarily trained on a trailing undergrad who, having entered last, has managed to clout Mr Tuttle's partner with his manbag as he climbs over her to the last space on the front row.

She audibly mutters some choice expletives as the student removes himself from her lap. The clerk of the court, hitherto tap-tap-tapping away at her computer, looks up and stares.

'What? He hit me in the face! Could have had my fucking eye out.'

'Shhhh!' the clerk hisses, waving a gowned arm towards the usher, who duly trots to the public gallery to administer a further, entirely superfluous, shhhh.

I look up behind the clerk towards the judge, expecting some sort of judicial admonishment for these noises off, but Her Honour Judge Kerrigan QC is still leaning back in her chair and staring longingly at a fixed point on the ceiling. Now the casual observer may, quite wrongly, think this an indication that Judge Kerrigan is bored by the pedestrian advocacy of a twenty-something upstart apparently channelling an unholy trinity of the Jeremies Paxman, Clarkson and Kyle as they superciliously showboat their intellectual advantage over the bewildered Mr Tuttle. The same observer may, equally mistakenly, bolster this conclusion by reference to the way in which Her Honour appears to have been, at various stages during the twenty-six laboured minutes of questioning leading up to this point, closing her eyes and dropping her head, before jolting alert again with a quiet snort.

But I know better. The Learned Judge is, quite plainly, bowled over by my oratory skill; no doubt mentally formulating the letter of praise that she will be sending to my Head of Chambers immediately the trial concludes. *Advocacy,* she will surely write, *has a new champion. A golden age of justice is upon us.*

Everyone now seated and hushed, I can resume my sparring. Mr Tuttle again glances for reassurance to his girlfriend.

'You won't find the answer in the public gallery, Mr Tuttle.' I obnoxiously smile at him.

'It's a very simple question. What you have said is what you're honestly asking this jury to believe, yes?'

This is an appallingly phrased, and wholly improper, question. Questions in cross-examination should strictly only be aimed at eliciting facts, not providing an opportunity for the advocate to comment. Closing speeches are where we get to make plain how preposterous we think the other side's case is. And clearly Mr Tuttle is asking the jury to believe what he said, otherwise he wouldn't have said it. But I'm feeling good, this is my first jury trial, and no one yet has interrupted to stop me. So I wait for Mr Tuttle's response.

He delivers another flick of the eyes to the gallery, and back. 'Yes,' he nods, any defiance long since melted.

'How tall are you, Mr Tuttle?'

'Dunno.'

'Would you agree that you're over six foot?'

'Probably.'

'And how much do you weigh?'

It doesn't matter what his answer is. Mr Tuttle is, at a conservative estimate, roughly the size of a supertanker, and, by obligingly wearing a skinny fit, short-sleeved white shirt, is displaying to marvellous effect every square inch of his tattooed mega-roided biceps. These questions are simply to hammer home the point.

As he mutters estimates, I yank my black gown straight. Posturing with faux furrows, I turn to the jury and look towards crossed-arms woman. I catch her eye. She raises an eyebrow. She knows where we're going.

'And,' I say, looking straight at the jury so as to maximize my apparent disbelief, 'you are telling this jury that the blind man on crutches hit *you* first?'

I swivel to him at those last three words and release them as slowly as melodrama allows. An audible snigger from my left tells me that Mr Tuttle's goose is cooked.

There is nothing he can now say to make his position seem less ridiculous. At this point in a boxing match, he would be hurried out of the ring by minders to avoid him doing himself any more damage. No answer can improve his position. One response, however, could take the goose out of the oven, elegantly carve it and serve it to the grateful cheers of the prosecution. And Mr Tuttle obliges.

'It wasn't how you're making it sound, yeah?'

The joy. I hear a stifled snort from the Crown Prosecution Service paralegal sitting on the row in front of me. My cross-examination, as written out neatly in the standard-issue blue counsel's notebook perched on my lectern, was going to end on that last, over-gestated question. But now, not only is Mr Tuttle giving the jury an implausible story, he's trying to wriggle out of it. The one thing worse than a liar is a liar lying about being a liar. So I treat myself to an encore.

'It wasn't how I made it sound?'

'Nah.'

'Well, we know Mr Martins is blind, yes?'

'Yes.'

'And you agree he was on crutches?'

'Yes.'

4

'And you say that he hit you first?

'Yeah.'

'Right. So, let's try again. You're saying that the blind man on crutches hit you first, aren't you?'

'Umm . . . yeah.'

'Right.'

As I take a beat to work out how best to gracefully conclude, there's a frantic scrabbling noise from the end of Counsel's Row – the long wooden bench at the front of court, facing the judge – as Tuttle's defence barrister, Mr Rallings, a surly old hack of forty years' call, furiously scribbles something on a scrap of paper and thrusts it with force along the bench towards me. Up until this point, Rallings has done his best to maintain a rictus poker frown as his client merrily yanks pins out of grenades and stuffs them down his trousers. But now he's stirring.

I take it. This is unnerving. Why a note, mid-cross-examination? Have I done something wrong? Is he pointing out that I've said something that breaches a vital rule of evidence or court etiquette? The blood rushes to my face as the panic takes hold. I have not been doing this long. I don't know what I'm doing. I'm a Crown Court virgin – no, a baby, a zygote. What fatal sin have I committed? I've blown it. I must have. Lord knows how, but the look on Rallings' wizened face – that cocksure lip-curl-cum-snarl – tells me all I need to know. Carried away with the myth of my own brilliance, I have somehow fluffed it all up. I have flown too close to the sun on wings forged of a misplaced confidence in my plainly meagre ability. I've kicked off my Crown Court career by losing the unlosable trial, and this scrumpled grey leaf of A5 bears my epitaph.

I try to feign composure as I unscrunch the note. Whatever it is, I silently counsel, it will be OK. I have my *Archbold* – the criminal lawyer's bible – to extricate me from any legal problem. I have the warm embrace of a four-legged friend waiting at home if I'm ultimately disbarred. Things will be OK.

I glance down at what Rallings has to tell me.

On the paper is a really rather good drawing of a stick man in a wig. He's sobbing into his arms. He has a little goatee like Rallings. Below the impression, Rallings has simply written: THIS IS A FUCKING TURKEY SHOOT.

He nods grimly, leans back and looks at the jury. And, then, with an almost imperceptible glint in his eye – a comradely tell of shared ownership of a moment, a sinking defendant setting fire to his own lifeboat, that we'll both remember for years – he turns to me, angling his head out of the line of sight of the jury. And winks.

This, ladies and gentlemen, is the English and Welsh criminal justice system in action. I don't suggest it is the finest example, but it serves as a rough extract of how contested matters of criminal law are settled. And it probably broadly conforms to the picture most of us in the UK immediately summon to mind when we think about justice. Whether learned from first-hand experience or absorbed from pop culture, we all share a conception of criminal justice that we have come to accept as representing the way things are done, and the way things *should* be done. It's culturally embedded, like apologizing when someone else bumps into you, or avoiding eye contact in a lift.

For some of us – if my non-lawyer friends are a reliable barometer – this mental portrait of English criminal justice fuses Judge Judy unholily with *that* scene from *A Few Good Men*. Others fall back on the home-grown motifs of Rumpole, Kavanagh QC or, lord help us, *All Rise for Julian Clary*.[1] But whatever variants we visualize, we probably all agree on the basics: an adversarial battle – *adversarialism* being a loose term for the model pitting the state against the

6

accused in a lawyer-driven skirmish for victory played out before an impartial body of assessors – comprising a courtroom, judge, jury, accused, lawyers, witnesses, questions and speeches in some sort of configuration. And plenty of wigs.

That, for most people though, is possibly where contemplations on criminal justice end. I imagine few of us devote much, if any, time to thinking critically about our criminal justice system; to considering how and why we have this particular way of doing justice, or reflecting on the impact it has upon the hundreds of thousands of people – defendants, witnesses and victims – who pass through the system every year. Not in the way that most of us form and gladly share opinions on the way we administer or fund healthcare, say, or the merits or demerits of types of schools. And this I find odd; because criminal justice affects us all.

We are yet to find a society that does not have rules surrounding the behaviour of its members and sanctions for their transgression. Agreeing social imperatives and taboos, and enforcing them through shunning, appears to be instinctual behaviour in cooperative primates[2], and the notion of a codified criminal law can be traced back to Bronze Age Mesopotamia and the Code of Ur-Nammu in 2050 BC. The precise rules have since differed across time and geography, but a mechanism for administering criminal justice always exists. To commit a crime is to break a law that offends not just those directly affected, but strikes at the heart of our communal values so deeply that we agree that organized, coercive action is required to mark the affront. Crimes are marked as the gravest breaches of our social codes which, unlike civil wrongs such as breach of contract, the state cannot leave to individuals to privately arbitrate.

The criminal law establishes the boundaries of our humanity by identifying the no-go zones and endowing the state with unique powers of correction intended to punish, deter, protect and rehabilitate. Crimes are the legal disputes that evoke primeval, visceral reactions in people with no stake in the fight, intruding through screens and leaping off pages and into our core identity, pinching and testing the standards by which we define ourselves. If crimes are permitted to occur unaddressed, or are attributed to the wrong person, the harm extends beyond those directly involved. It means that our streets are less safe, our values are undermined and our personal liberty is at risk. A fundamental term of our social contract is that the rules are enforced fairly against us all; a breach of this term offends our innate sense of fairness like little else.

And it is not merely theoretical. While we may not wish to think about it, for most of us the impact of criminal justice will someday be immediate and all too tangible. It is certain that at one point in your life, you or someone you love will be in a criminal courtroom; whether it is as a juror, a victim of crime, a witness or locked behind that perspex screen at the back of court, screaming your innocence and flanked by bruising security guards dragging you down to the cells.

I can understand why people might only think of criminal justice in the abstract. Without first-hand experience of the system, it is easy to not give its impenetrable workings much of a second thought. But that first direct contact changes everything. At this point it is brought home, vividly and viscerally, what criminal justice means in practice; not abstract concepts in dusty textbooks, but a suffusion of humanity – tears, blood, anger, loss, redemption and despair. 'Dispensing criminal justice' means changing lives forever. The trial process and court's judgment can tear a life apart. Families can be broken, children separated from their parents and people locked up for decades. A miscarriage of justice can leave the aggrieved confined, metaphorically or literally, in a prison from which there appears to be no escape. While in the UK the state no longer has the power to kill at the end of a criminal trial, functioning justice can still ultimately be a matter of life and death.

Furthermore, until that first contact, you may take for granted that, much like other inscrutable fundamentals of our society such as intelligence-gathering, refuse collection or library cataloguing, when required the system will broadly, allowing for the margin of error common to all state-delivered services, work as it should, and that the right outcome will be delivered in the end. This entirely understandable complacency is, for many people I meet, what makes that first immersion in the criminal justice system so shocking, as they realize not only how strongly they disagree with the way in which our society prioritizes and dispenses justice, but how, quivering outside the courtroom door, it is now too late to do anything about it.

As someone immersed in the fog of the criminal courts, my fear is that the public's lack of insight into our secretive, opaque system is allowing the consecration of a way of dealing with crime that bears little resemblance to what we understand by criminal justice. That defendants, victims and, ultimately, society are being failed daily by an entrenched disregard for fundamental principles of fairness. That we are moving from a criminal justice system to simply a criminal system.

When you have sat in as many decrepit court cells or tired, coffee-stained witness suites as I have, looking into the eyes of someone whose most basic sense of what is 'fair' and what is 'right' has been entirely crushed by their exposure to the criminal justice system, you can either slink into jaundiced defeatism, or you can sound an alarm.

This is what I want to talk about: to explore why criminal justice matters, and to show how I think we are getting it so wrong.

*

But first, a bit about me. I'm a criminal barrister. Not a particularly special one. My cases, by and large, aren't the ones you'll see on the news. I am the kind of jobbing, workaday junior practitioner whom you may find representing you if you suffer the twin misfortunes of being accused of an everyday criminal offence, and of not having available to you someone a little bit better.

I'm a 'junior' barrister in a similar way that the term is applied to junior doctors. It is not a signifier of youth, rather a catch-all for any barrister, from trainee (or 'pupil', in the legalese) up to grizzled old warhorse, who has not been appointed Queen's Counsel (the honour bestowed upon the most impressive in our ranks).

Hopefully, our paths will never cross. But if they do, I can guarantee that, like an undertaker or a clinician at an STD clinic brandishing a cotton bud, it will be at one of the lowest points of your life. Ours is the trade in human misery; the grotty little cousin of the finer, more civilized, more commercial tributaries of the law.

The role of barristers in this misery is, I have learned, not widely understood. Mostly the fault for that lies with us. For professional advocates, we do a strikingly bad job of explaining what we do, or why it matters. In a nutshell, criminal barristers are first and foremost advocates, presenting cases in court, usually the Crown Court, on behalf of either the prosecution or the defence. In practice, the job also requires the skills of a social worker, relationship counsellor, arm-twister, hostage negotiator, named driver, bus fare-provider, accountant, suicide-watchman, coffee supplier, surrogate parent and, on one memorable occasion, whatever the official term is for someone tasked with breaking the news to a prisoner that his girlfriend has been diagnosed with gonorrhoea.

My daily fare is eclectic and erratic. Usually I will be prosecuting or defending in jury trials, but some days are peppered with other, shorter hearings: opposing a bail application for an alleged arsonist here; advancing mitigation at the sentence hearing of a heroin dealer there. Sometimes I'll be doing my own cases, sometimes covering for colleagues who are stuck elsewhere.

It is unpredictable, irrational, adrenaline-infused mayhem every second of every day, where the only certainty is uncertainty. Hearings and trials overrun, find themselves suddenly adjourned or are listed immediately without warning, making it impossible to say with confidence what you will be doing or where you will be in four hours' time. Your bones ache, your shoe leather disintegrates bi-monthly and your shoulder creaks from dragging your suitcase laden with papers, books, wig and gown between courts and cities. You can become inured to the blood-spattered underbelly of the human condition; unmoved by the mundanity of yet another 'bog standard' stabbing, or desensitized by the unending parade of sexual abuse. You are at best a part-time family member and a fair-weather friend, expected by the courts to abandon holidays, weddings and funerals at a judge's command. An early night sees me home at 8 p.m. A late night is the following morning. Throw in the industry-wide 'perks' of self-employment – the perennial insecurity, the fear of work drying up, the absence of sick pay, holiday pay or pension, the fact that legal aid rates can work out at below minimum wage – and the criminal Bar is in many ways an intolerable existence.

But it is also irresistibly special.

In an age where juries have all but disappeared from civil courtrooms, criminal law is the last vestige of the pure advocacy tradition, where the power of persuasion and force of rational argument, its significance augmented by the historical trappings – the mode of speech, the splendour of the courtroom, the ridiculous Restoration-hangover horsehair wigs – is the tool by which liberty is spared or removed. The attraction to an egotist with an insatiable desire to hold centre stage – a description applicable to the near-entirety of the Bar – is plain; but for me, and most criminal barristers I know, there is a greater, overarching reason for choosing this path: crime is where the stakes are highest.

The worst that happens if you lose a case in civil or commercial law is that you lose a lot of money, or fail to win money. If you lose a family law case, you might lose your children. In a repossession case, you could lose your home. These are all significant, sometimes life-changing events. But if you lost a criminal case, up until 1965, you could lose your life. And while we have left behind our tradition of sanctioned bodily violations, dismemberment and killing, we have supplanted it with the deprivation of liberty, a punishment capable of encompassing all of the losses above and far more beyond. Loss of the freedom to live with those you love, to work in your job, to provide for your family; the abrogation of the pursuit of happiness, the pausing of your existence, for a period determined by the overbearing power of a state largely uninterested in the consequences for you or your family, is a price whose value only those who have paid it truly know.

And those of us criminal hacks who hawk our wigs and gowns from court to court across the land do so, spending long hours sifting through the very worst of the human condition, because of a fervent, some might say naive, faith in the rule of law and our role in upholding it. If criminals avoid justice, the loss is not only felt by the victim. The danger created by harmful behaviours going uncorrected presents a significant threat to the individual liberty of us all. If there are too many wrongful convictions, or too few criminals getting their just deserts, the delicate social contract bonding us all to each other and to the state can swiftly disintegrate. Simply put, if enough people don't believe the state to be capable of dispensing justice, they may start to dispense it themselves.

It is for these reasons that it is not hyperbolic, I honestly believe, to suggest that working criminal justice, and our role prosecuting and defending criminal allegations, is essential to peaceable democratic society. It is when people feel that justice is denied that they are at their most indignant and rage-filled; it is in the gaps between justice that anti-democratic, subversive urges can take root.

This is why I consider what I do on a day-to-day basis to be not just a privilege but a civic responsibility. And it is for the same reasons that the current state of our criminal justice system should terrify us.

Because despite the noble principles underpinning the system, despite its international prestige, its intellectual craftsmanship and the very real blood, sweat and tears spilt in its ponderous cultivation, my still-tender years exposed to the grim reality have taught me that the criminal justice system is close to breaking point.

Access to justice, the rule of law, fairness to defendants, justice for victims – these fine emblems which we purport to hold so dear – are each day incarnated in effigy, rolled out in the Crown and magistrates' courts and ritually torched.

Serious criminal cases collapse on a daily basis because of eminently avoidable failings by underfunded and under-staffed police and prosecution services. The accused and the alleged victim can wait years for a trial, told their cases are 'adjourned for lack of court time' for a second, third or fourth time, notwithstanding the brand new courtroom, built at significant public expense, sitting empty down the corridor due to slashed court budgets. The wrongly accused wait until the day of trial, or perhaps for eternity, for the state to disclose material that fatally undermines the prosecution case. Defendants can find themselves represented by exhausted lawyers able to devote only a fraction of the required time to their case, due to the need to stack cheap cases high to absorb government cuts. Some defendants are excluded from publicly funded representation altogether, forced to scrape together savings or loans to meet legal aid 'contributions' or private legal fees, failing which they represent themselves in DIY proceedings in which the endgame is a prison sentence. The bottom line is that victims of crime are denied justice, and people who are not guilty find themselves in prison.

And what astounds me is that most people don't seem to care. Or even know.

On the day after a parliamentary report published in May 2016[3] began with those nine damning words – *the criminal justice system is close to breaking point* – not one single newspaper thought it more newsworthy than repetitive scare stories about migration or, in one case, a confected 'scandal' over *Britain's Got Talent*.

When Karl Turner MP tabled a parliamentary debate over the parlous underfunding of the Crown Prosecution Service (CPS) in January 2017, his litany of sobbing CPS staff and collapsing prosecutions – the things that we in the courts see every day – was attended by a meagre handful of MPs, and met by a virtual media blackout.[4] When the courts upheld government initiatives to deprive the wrongly accused of their legal fees,[5] there was no clamour. Just deafening silence.

If the criminal justice system were the NHS, it would never be off the front pages.

I find it impossible to reconcile this collective indifference, because it is plain that innately we all do care. We know that from the green ink letters to the editor when a paedophile gets a 'soft sentence' or 'early release' from prison, or the police fail to investigate serious allegations of sexual abuse or, worst of all, when the wrong person is convicted. We know from popular culture – from our *Serials* and *Making a Murderer*s and our Innocence Projects – that the ideal of justice, and in particular criminal justice, can be perhaps our greatest unifier. But something somewhere has clearly gone wrong.

I think it's traceable to the failure of the establishment – and us, the professionals in the system – to properly explain to the wider public how the criminal courts work, why they work the way they do, and why that is a good or bad thing, which has led to a catastrophic dissonance in public understanding. What a jury, or what the public, gets to see is but a pinhole view of the system. There is far more happening behind the scenes, or unreported in magistrates' and Crown courtrooms, closeted in comfortable anonymity and about which the people we serve simply don't know.

This is why I have written this book. I want to shine a light on what really goes on, to take you into the rooms you never get to enter; but more than that I want to explore why we should care, and to illustrate what happens when we don't.

I'm probably not the sort of barrister usually invited to publish a book. I am not reliving a CV bursting with the great and weighty cases of our time. I profess no particular specialism or expertise in my field. I am not an academic. I am not a jurist, a philosopher, an historian or a scholar. I am as much a stranger to the gilded upper echelons of the legal system as they are to me. But I have spent the best part of a decade prosecuting, defending and advising on behalf of my fellow citizens, and I wanted to write this book while I am still a relatively fresh face to this warped game, before the delicate balance between idealism and cynicism tips too far. I write anonymously because it buys the freedom to be candid; to call upon my own personal experiences, and those of others, to illustrate the first-hand tales of justice and injustice that play out every day in courts throughout the land.

This book is loosely structured following the life of a

criminal case, from the first appearance before a magistrates' court, through to trial in the Crown Court, sentence and appeal. And it considers, at each stage, how justice works, and, more importantly, how it often doesn't.

I will also do my best to explore some of the questions raised along the way; in particular common public concerns that we in the system should perhaps be better at answering. Why should the taxpayer fund legal aid for career criminals? How can you defend someone who you believe has raped their own child? Does our system of adversarial justice, pitting the state against the accused in a winner-takes-all war of attrition, do more harm than good? Is the sentencing of criminals just a giant con on the public? And the one overarching question of my own: how, if we truly value criminal justice, have we allowed our system to degrade to its current state?

Certain details of the cases that follow have been changed to preserve the identities of those concerned; however the core of each reconstruction – the incompetence, the error and the malice – is all too true. The examples cited are not special. They are not the stories that make the news. They are not the miscarriages of justice that engender Twitter storms or provoke magazine confessionals or inspire true-life cinema. They are the ordinary tales of injustice that stalk the criminal courts; the fleeting, repetitive diminishment of human dignity that crosses the path of the jobbing criminal hack.

My perspective is necessarily limited, and my role entirely incidental; but I hope it is nevertheless of value.

A working criminal justice system, properly resourced and staffed by dedicated professionals each performing their invaluable civic functions, for the prosecution and the defence, serves to protect the innocent, protect the public and protect the integrity, decency and humanity of our society. This should be a societal baseline. Not a luxury.

Most of you reading this will never expect to be plunged into a criminal courtroom – never expect to hear the constabulary knock on the front door, never expect to be a victim of crime, never expect to be accused of a crime you didn't commit. But the one thing I have learned about criminal justice is that it doesn't discriminate. Anyone can be reeled in. And if you are, whether you're giving evidence against the man who hurt your child, or swearing blind to a jury that that pedestrian stepped out in front of your car without looking, you want the system to work.

When it doesn't, the consequences can be unthinkable.

1. Welcome to the Criminal Courtroom

'It is a fair summary of history to say that the safeguards of liberty have frequently been forged in controversies involving not very nice people.'

Mr Justice Frankfurter,
United States Supreme Court, 1950[1]

To an extra-terrestrial touching down outside a city Crown Court, our way of resolving disputes where an individual is alleged to have breached our central social code would be unfathomable. Get two people with plummy accents, stick them in black capes, shove horsehair wigs on their heads, arm them with books of rules weighing as much as a grown pig and use them as proxies to verbally joust in front of a bewigged sexagenarian in a big purple gown, while twelve people yanked off the street sit and watch and try to make sense of it all and decide who's in the right. The winner gets nothing. The loser gets locked up in a concrete box.

To those earthlings not intimately acquainted with the English and Welsh criminal justice system, this spectacle is probably only marginally less bizarre. At this stage, it is therefore worth taking a moment to examine it a little closer. Before looking at how and why criminal justice may not be working, we need to explore how it *should* be working. Let's go back to that opening scene with our enormous-bicepped Mr Tuttle and quickly consider the elements within the courtroom. What exactly is taking place? How did we come to choose this ostensibly absurd routine as our vehicle for crime and punishment?

Let's start with the accused himself, slouched stony-faced in the dock.

The Accused

Mr Tuttle punched his neighbour in the face after a disagreement about a border between their properties, something that happens all over the world and has happened throughout history, and which means under current English and Welsh law he stands charged with 'assault occasioning actual bodily harm'. He was arrested by the police following the neighbour's complaint, interviewed in a police station with a solicitor and, after the police investigation produced sufficient evidence for the Crown Prosecution Service to authorize a charge, was charged. As he denies that he is guilty, he is being tried.

This particular offence can be tried in either a magistrates' court or a Crown Court. We'll come back to this distinction later, but what's important at this point is that Mr Tuttle has exercised his right to have his guilt determined in a Crown Court by an independent jury of his peers, who will know nothing of the case before coming to it. The twelve jurors will observe and listen to the evidence and arguments presented by the two competing sides, prosecution and defence, and will be directed by the judge on the applicable law, before retiring to consider one question: can they be sure that on the evidence the offence is proved beyond reasonable doubt? If guilt is proved, the maximum penalty the state can impose is a period of imprisonment, in this case up to five years.

As discussed, although culturally ingrained as the default mode of trying alleged crimes, this process is far from universal.[2] While we have exported our treasured form of adversarial, state-versus-defendant justice around the world, usually at the end of the barrel of a colonial musket, many other countries do things very differently. The most commonly cited distinction is the rough divide between Anglo-American adversarial proceedings, and Continental, Napoleonic-inspired inquisitorial proceedings.

If Mr Tuttle were being tried in Belgium, for example, he would find that he was party to what felt like an inquiry rather than a contest. As this is not a particularly serious allegation, he would fall under the jurisdiction of the middle 'tier' of the court system where the investigation is often placed in the hands of an investigating judge, who directs the police to gather evidence and then assesses it in a mostly paper-based trial process. Mr Tuttle's lawyer's role in challenging the prosecution witnesses would be minimal, with any questioning being conducted through the judge. There would be no jury, and he would have to wait a month following his trial for the judge's decision.[3]

If he were being tried in Saudi Arabia, he could expect to find himself in a closed courtroom, with no lawyer, charged with a *qisas* ('retaliation-in-kind') category of Sharia crime for which a judge might order an unpleasant form of physical retribution. Had Mr Tuttle's victim been unfortunate enough to lose an eye in the assault, the court could order that Mr Tuttle's eye be gouged out.[4] On the plus side, had this been a capital case of homicide, Mr Tuttle could evade execution by paying *diya*, or blood money, to the victim's family.

In our courts, Mr Tuttle could have avoided the stress of a trial by pleading guilty. Even if there was no other evidence against him, his confession to a criminal offence would be gladly banked by the English courts. However in

Japan, unless the state had corroborative evidence, Article 38 of the constitution would prevent him being convicted even if he gave a full and frank confession.

Put simply, without diving into a full-blown international comparative analysis, our familiar system is not the only way to deal with Mr Tuttle. Nor has it been the way our country has always tried the Tuttles throughout history.

In Anglo-Saxon England, the notion of trying a criminal allegation on the evidence simply did not exist. Until the tenth century there were no formal courts; instead wronged parties were encouraged to settle blood feuds with the accused by payment of *wergild* – blood money. From the mid-sixth century, the king handed down laws, or 'dooms', supplemented by local customary law. As Saxon kings gradually took a greater interest in enforcing the law, certain offences, such as treason, homicide and theft, were taken out of the scope of private settlement between the parties and into the hands of the king. Come the tenth century, if a citizen were accused of breaching either the king's law or local custom, he would be dragged by his accuser before a monthly community court and, unless he could find sufficient 'oath-swearers' to attest to his innocence, would have his guilt determined by trial by ordeal.

This would take either the form of trial by hot water, requiring Mr Tuttle to plunge his hand into a cauldron of boiling water to retrieve a stone; or trial by cold water whereby the accused would be trussed up and hurled into a lake. If his injuries healed within three days, in the case of the former, or if he sank, in the case of the latter, God had deemed him an innocent, if slightly burned/drowned, man. If his seared palm still appeared a bit bloody and charred, or if he floated (as many defendants did, simply because the way in which they were tied up created a buoyancy effect), this was God delivering a guilty verdict.

Following the Norman Conquest, Mr Tuttle would have

had the option of trial by combat (which from the looks of him, he would be sensible to take), with his accuser or their proxies; but it was not until the thirteenth century that something approaching a trial based on evidence, rather than wanton violence, emerged. We'll turn to that shortly.

In the meantime, before we move away from the accused, we should say a word about his fate upon (inevitable) conviction. A period of custody in one of Her Majesty's prisons is the most severe sentence the court can pass. Yet, the idea of deprivation of liberty as punishment is relatively modern. Anglo-Saxon and Norman sentencing offered a buffet of hanging, eye-gouging, testicle-extraction, nose-and-ear removal (a favourite of King Canute for female adulterers), fines, reparations and other creative facial and bodily mutilation. By the dawn of the Plantagenets and the reign of Henry II (1133–89), punishment for many crimes was standardized as the lopping off of the right hand and foot and banishment from the realm.[5]

Bodily mutilation of various grisly forms persisted through Tudor times, usually culminating in death. Public humiliation, including pillories and public whippings, were available for less serious matters until the late nineteenth century. Meanwhile prisons, first built in the twelfth century, were mainly used to hold prisoners awaiting trial or to detain debtors. From the early sixteenth century, houses of correction fell into fashion for vagrants, combining confinement with forced labour, but it was not until the 1800s that imprisonment took over from executions and transportation to the colonies as the favoured mode of punishing offenders. Although Mr Tuttle's offence would not then have cast him in the shadow of the noose, hanging remained for murder and treason until the abolition of the death penalty in 1965. Nowadays the courts also have an array of sentencing disposals aside from prison, including powers to impose, for example, a community order with unpaid work and an alcohol rehabilitation programme, and a compensation order. As was ultimately imposed upon Mr Tuttle back in twenty-first-century England by our possibly only semi-conscious judge, whom we should probably take a look at.

The Judge

Turning our heads away from Mr Tuttle and towards the raised bench at the back, we can see the judge. The first thing to note is that she does not have a gavel. Gavels have never been used in English and Welsh courtrooms. The one way guaranteed to provoke the pedant in a British lawyer is to illustrate a legal story with a stock photo of a gavel. What Her Honour Judge Kerrigan QC does have is a fetching black and purple robe with a red sash and a short, frizzy horsehair wig; the working court dress of a Circuit Judge. She also has a relatively fixed sense of what the law is and how that should impact upon the directions she gives the jury and the sentence she bestows, which as we'll see hasn't always been the case.

The term 'Circuit Judge' refers to the six legal circuits or regions into which England and Wales have been tradition-ally divided – Northern, North-Eastern, Western, Midlands, South-Eastern, and Wales and Chester. Prior to 1166, justice was mostly administered in London by the king and his advisors sitting in the King's Court (the *Curia Regis*) in Westminster, while out in the country justice was dispensed by smaller local courts, presided over by lords or stewards applying whatever kooky parochial customs took their fancy. It would mean that Tuttle would have received differ-ent treatment depending on where he lived. This created obvious inconsistencies in how the law was applied across the land, so at the Assize of Clarendon in 1166, Henry II sought to introduce a 'common law' applicable nationwide, by establishing a cadre of judges who roamed the circuits, sitting in pop-up courts ('assizes') and applying the new common law. A key feature of the so-called 'common law tradition' is that where legislation has gaps or ambiguities, or calls for clarifying interpretation by judges hearing cases, the rulings of the most senior courts (today the High Court, Court of Appeal and Supreme Court) have the force of binding law, and must be followed by lower courts. This means that if you want to know the law on a given topic, the statute alone only tells you half the story; you will need to know what gloss has been slapped over it by court precedents.[6]

In the criminal sphere, there gradually developed three tiers of court: the least serious matters were handled by non-legally qualified Justices of the Peace, or magistrates (about which more later); middling crimes were heard at Quarter Sessions, in which magistrates presided over jury trials; and the assizes, with their professional judges and juries, reserved for heavyweight felonies. In 1971, the Crown Court was created and absorbed the work of the assizes and the Quarter Sessions, leaving us with a two-tier court system for criminal trials – Crown Court and magistrates' court. There are now around ninety Crown Courts nationwide, the most famous of which sits at the Central Criminal Court in London – the Old Bailey.

Initially, knights, clergy, ealdormen and lords were appointed as judges by the king. By the thirteenth century, the judiciary began to professionalize as lawyers took up the robes. In the modern day, almost all judges are former practising solicitors or barristers, appointed through an independent selection process (the Judicial Appointments Commission).

When Henry II came to the throne there were eighteen judges. Now there are over 35,000,[7] including magistrates, District Judges, Circuit Judges, High Court judges, Lord

Justices of Appeal and Supreme Court Justices, and all manner of part-time and specialist tribunal judges in between.

The role of the judge in the Crown Court remains strictly legal; the judge directs the jury as to what the relevant law is, and the jury applies the law as directed to the facts as the jury finds them to be. Upon a guilty verdict, the judge will pass sentence, but otherwise the power lies with the jury. The judge is not supposed to express any views about the factual merits of a case, even one as obviously open and shut as Mr Tuttle's. So precious are we about the separation of functions that whenever an advocate wishes to argue a point of law during a trial – for example, to apply to ask a witness about their previous convictions – the jury is sent scurrying out of court so as not to be contaminated by anything that might be said during the legal argument between the advocates and judge.

The Jury

Craning our necks to the judge's left reveals two benches of six attentive citizens – our iconic jury. Mr Tuttle's jury, like any other, is a ragtag assortment of twelve randomly plucked justice-dispensers. Try as we always do to read the jury out of the corner of our eye, it is as reliable a science as tasseography. The only proven maxim for barristers is Beware the Nodding Juror, as a juror who bobs and smiles enthusiastically as you hammer out your closing speech will invariably be the one who delivers the verdict that crushes your case.

Every trial in the Crown Court[8] calls upon twelve randomly selected members of the public aged between eighteen and seventy-five to hear the evidence and to unanimously (or, in certain circumstances, by a majority of ten to two) agree on whether a defendant is guilty or not guilty. Unless you have a criminal record or are seriously mentally unwell, anyone is eligible,[9] and most of us will at some point be called to serve on a jury. However, notwithstanding its unchallenged position as the defining emblem of our justice system, the modern jury is also a product of a long process of evolution.

Around the same time as laying the foundations for the common law, Henry II also promoted the concept of a twelve-man jury to arbitrate land disputes, which in 1166 he extended into the criminal sphere in the guise of the 'grand' or 'presenting' jury. Despite the name, this jury per-formed a vastly different function to the modern jury; investigative rather than adjudicative. Whenever a judge rocked up on Circuit to preside over a pop-up court, twelve free men were summoned and charged with reporting, under oath, any felony (serious crime, including murder, robbery and theft) that they knew of or suspected. Having pointed the finger and presented inculpatory evidence, the squealing grand jury would then sit back as God rolled up his sleeves and mucked in with trial by ordeal.

This persisted until 1215, when Pope Innocent III and the Fourth Lateran Council belatedly realized the dubious godliness of trial by ordeal and forbade clerics presiding over it. Instead, local men likely to know the circumstances of a crime were engaged as a fact-finding band of invest-igators who would assemble at court, pool their knowledge and determine guilt. In this model, the 'grand' jury – which over time grew to twenty-three members – were still respon-sible for 'presenting' the accused – agreeing that there was a case for him to answer – with the smaller, 'petit' twelve-man jury then proceeding to hear the evidence at trial.

The idea of a grand jury acting as a filter to determine whether someone should face trial died out in England and Wales in 1933[10] (although is still alive in American criminal proceedings); but the twelve-strong jury remains our touchstone. Originally deployed to settle civil disputes as well, juries are now the near-exclusive property of the criminal courts. The nature of a jury has morphed over the centuries from a gaggle of local Poirots expected to have first-hand knowledge of the allegation they were trying, to a disinterested body of strangers receiving evidence from sworn witnesses. In stark contrast to the thirteenth century, today's jurors are expressly prohibited from conducting any investigations or having any prior knowledge of the parties involved in, or the circumstances of, a criminal case. None of these twelve know Mr Tuttle, or, prior to the start of the trial, knew how strongly he felt about the encroachment of his neighbour's weeping willow over the boundary fence.

As a juror, you can often feel like a spare part, waiting backstage for days, called into court hours after you arrive and shunted out again whenever a lawyer stands up to boom, 'Your Honour, a matter of law has arisen.' It would be easy to gain the impression that jurors are the least important people in the courtroom, rather than central to the entire process, so it is probably worth considering for a moment why we still cling to the ideal of the jury.

The first reason usually offered is the jury's independence from the state. The signing of Magna Carta at Runnymede on 15 June 1215 is often cited as fundamental in this regard. The best-known constitutional landmark in English and Welsh legal history marked the denouement of an entrenched dispute between King John I and some seditious land barons plotting his overthrow. In reaching an uneasy accord, the king agreed to cede the monarch's absolute power and become bound by common law. Among the sixty-three chapters initially enacted in the treaty, numbers thirty-nine and forty stand as the two with which people today will be most familiar:

No free man shall be seized or imprisoned, or stripped of his rights or possessions, or outlawed or exiled. Nor will we proceed with force against him except by the lawful judgment of his equals or by the law of the land. To no one will we sell, to no one deny or delay right or justice.

Popular re-telling of Magna Carta tends to gloss over the fact that within three months of it being signed both sides had reneged on their obligations and the king had persuaded Pope Innocent III to annul the charter altogether. It was only the following year, when John I died and was succeeded by nine-year-old Henry III, that Magna Carta was reissued as a sincere royal acknowledgement of the people's rights, sowing the seeds for democratic government, the rule of law and freedom of expression.

So, in chapters thirty-nine and forty, we see a grounding for jury trial, or 'lawful judgment by one's equals'. In reality, the land barons were keen on these clauses because injecting their own people into the adjudication process increased their chances of future land disputes with the king being settled in their favour. However, this self-interest should not detract from the underlying merit: in a battle with the state, the inclusion of an independent, non-state actor in the adjudication process is a necessary safeguard against oppression.

And so it has proved with criminal trials. No matter the perceived strength of the prosecution case, if the jury has a feeling that something is not quite right – if the prosecution seems oppressive or unjustified, or the jurors don't share the judge's apparent faith in the *bona fides* of the prosecution witnesses – no one can stop them acquitting the defendant. This was the take-home lesson from a famous 1670 Old Bailey trial of two Quakers, William Penn and William Mead, for 'unlawfully and tumultuously' preaching outside a church. When a rebellious jury led by a man called Edward

Bushel refused to return guilty verdicts in the face of a strong prosecution case, the judge's response was:

> Gentlemen, You shall not be dismissed till we have a verdict that the court will accept; and you shall be locked up, without meat, drink, fire, and tobacco; you shall not think thus to abuse the court; we will have a verdict, by the help of God, or you shall starve for it.[11]

Any modern juror forced to sit through an afternoon of interminably dull evidence, waiting pained for a judicially sanctioned smoking break, will no doubt sympathize. After the tobacco-and-fire-starved jurors were duly imprisoned for contempt of court, Bushel took his plight before Chief Justice John Vaughan, who ruled that jurors could not be punished for acquitting according to their conscience, thereby consecrating the jury's hallowed reputation as the bulwark of individual liberties. While the jury has to accept the judge's directions as to what the law is and how it applies, the verdict is entirely a matter for the twelve angry laypeople.[12] In the eighteenth century, many juries fought back against the widespread use of the death penalty by committing what was known as 'pious perjury', and returning verdicts deliberately designed to circumvent capital punishment (for example by undervaluing stolen goods to render an offence of theft a non-capital crime).[13] In the famous articulation of Lord Devlin: 'Trial by jury is more than an instrument of justice and more than one wheel of the constitution: it is the lamp that shows that freedom lives.'[14]

The second popular justification for juries is an appeal to democracy. Bringing the life experience and oft-acclaimed 'common sense' of twelve ordinary people to bear on the fact-finding process is important not just in adjudicating disputed matters of fact (i.e. which witness is lying), but also in determining questions of contemporary mores. If criminal law sets the boundaries of interpersonal behaviour, democracy arguably demands that the interpretation of those boundaries meets with public consent. For example, a key ingredient to proving offences under the Theft Act is dishonesty, the legal test for which requires that the defendant acted in a way that was dishonest 'according to the ordinary standards of reasonable and honest people', and that the defendant *knew* that his conduct was dishonest by those standards.[15] So pooling their respective experience and values, the jury firstly determines the moral question – what is dishonesty here? – and then the factual question – did young Steve McThief know he was being dishonest? A trial I prosecuted early on in my career centred on whether a young beauty therapist, Chantelle, who had picked up a mobile phone dropped in Asda and flogged it in the pub, had acted dishonestly. She insisted with wide eyes that it was not dishonest – finders keepers, losers weepers. The jury disagreed – this was blatantly dishonest by the standards of upstanding Bristolians, and it was clear from her unimpressive answers under cross-examination that Chantelle knew as much.

Mr Tuttle's case itself stands as a further case in point. He claimed that he had used reasonable force acting in self-defence. If the jury accepted that the blind complainant had indeed swung for the ginormous Tuttle, they would need to consider whether Mr Tuttle's response – two jabs to the mouth topped off with a slap – was 'reasonable' in the circumstances as Tuttle honestly perceived it to be. What is 'reasonable' in these cases is a value judgment entirely for the jury.

As it happened, the jury either disbelieved his account entirely, or believed it but were sure that he was not using reasonable force against his blind opponent. We will never know which; juries cannot be asked about their verdicts nor do they give reasons. When the jury finishes deliberating and returns to court to be asked by the court clerk for the verdict, the defendant hears the foreman deliver only a one- or two-word verdict sealing his fate.

Of course, the jurors could only reach their verdict having heard evidence from the various parties who witnessed the alleged crime.

The Witnesses

Opposite the jury stands the witness box. Each witness, including Mr Tuttle if he so chooses, will enter the witness box – they do not, in the American, 'take the stand' – swear an oath or affirmation to tell the truth and give their evidence orally in the form of answering questions put to them by the advocates for each side. The prosecution witnesses go first. The prosecution advocate examines the witness 'in-chief', asking the witness open questions to elicit their evidence, before the defence cross-examine the witness through a series of short closed questions designed to undermine the prosecution case and lead the witness to the desired answer. The prosecution is permitted to ask brief clarifying questions in 're-examination'. When it is time for the defence witnesses, the sequence is reversed.

The full spectrum of human behaviour is exhibited from this small, boxy wooden platform. Some witnesses are accomplished performers; others have to be reminded repeatedly, and in increasingly impatient judicial tones, to speak loud enough for the jury to hear. Some are captivating in their believability; one man I cross-examined looked towards someone in the public gallery before answering each question I put to him. When, for the benefit of the jury, I asked him why he kept glancing to his left before answering, and whether it was because his answers were being prompted, he unwittingly sparked hilarity among the jurors by looking to his left before replying, nervously, 'No.'

Save for exceptions, such as complainants in sexual allegations whom the judge can allow to testify over a video-link from outside the courtroom, it is from the witness box that live evidence in a trial emerges. Uncontroversial witnesses can have the witness statements that they made to the police read to the jury, saving them the hassle of attending court. But the main evidence will be given live. It will often be supplemented by exhibits, such as documents and photographs, and the parties may produce a list of 'agreed facts' to fill in the background, but the hallmark of criminal trials is the oral tradition.

Oral evidence is assumed to be intrinsically superior to written evidence. The idea is that a living, breathing, sweating witness standing a few feet away from the jury and testifying in their own words to what they have personally seen or heard affords the jurors the best chance to get the measure of a witness. It is far easier to embellish, lie or commit to a mistake in a written statement; having your words forensically jabbed and teased as they fall from your lips is apt, the theory runs, to bleed out the inconsistencies and half-truths.

The value attached to oral evidence is such that this alone can prove someone guilty. Unlike in Scotland, where the rule of 'corroboration' requires two independent sources of evidence before a jury can convict, the word of one witness will suffice (except, curiously, in prosecutions for perjury and speeding). Often defendants will complain that there is 'no evidence' against them. What they usually mean is that there is no evidence to corroborate what a witness says. A single sworn oral account is itself evidence, and if the jury are sure that it is true and accurate, it can be decisive.

It should be emphasized that all sworn evidence, whether given by prosecution witnesses, the defendant or defence witnesses, carries equal weight: just because the defendant stands accused, his evidence and that of his witnesses is not automatically worth any less (although it may be after it has been shredded in cross-examination).[16]

The CPS

Sitting at the long bench directly in front of me is Megan, the Crown Prosecution Service caseworker, who is the in-court representative of the prosecuting agency instructing me as their advocate to take down Mr Tuttle. Once upon a time this would have been a CPS lawyer, but repeated budget cuts mean that there is now usually a single administrative caseworker covering multiple courtrooms and rushing around to tend to the demands of multiple barristers and multiple judges.

The CPS is a relatively modern invention. Until 1880, there was no public prosecutor; a victim of a criminal offence seeking to prosecute had to either pay their own lawyers or present the prosecution case themselves, save for the most serious cases in which the Crown would take the lead and instruct counsel.[17] Between 1880 and 1986, the state took control of prosecutions, with nearly all decisions made by the local investigating police force. However, nationwide inconsistency and a succession of weak cases being booted out of court by judges raised questions over whether police officers were best placed to make fair and objective calls on whether cases they had painstakingly investigated and glued together should be prosecuted or binned. So it was that 106 years and two Royal Commissions later,[18] the Prosecution of Offences Act 1985 gave us the Crown Prosecution Service; an independent authority headed by the Director of Public Prosecutions, which would be split into geographical regions and provide independent, expert legal advice to the police, and take charging decisions – that is the decision whether to charge a suspect and, if so, with which offences – in all but the most straightforward, minor cases with which the police could be trusted. This would theoretically lead to uniformity of charging decisions, improve the quality of the decisions taken and ensure that prosecutions were prepared fully and efficiently for court. We'll look in due course at how those good intentions are playing out in practice.

The Solicitor

Further along the same row as the CPS caseworker, perched in front of Mr Rallings, a pin-striped young man with glasses and designer stubble takes notes. This is Mr Tuttle's solicitor. In most Crown Court trials, a defendant has a solicitor responsible for the conduct of litigation – trial preparation, management and client care, put very loosely – with the barrister instructed by the solicitor to provide specialist advice and present the case in court. The common, if slightly tortured, analogy of the solicitor–barrister relationship is that of the relationship between a general practitioner and a consultant surgeon. With which solicitors would probably agree, if the GP diagnoses the problem, tells the surgeon exactly what needs doing and sits forbearingly in silence as the surgeon brags to the patient about how his surgical skills have saved the day.

The distinction has existed since the fourteenth century, when lawyers were categorized as either behind-the-scenes 'attorneys' or courtroom advocate 'pleaders'. Today, barristers automatically enjoy full 'rights of audience', which permit us to appear in any court in the land, from magistrates' courts through to the United Kingdom Supreme Court. By contrast, solicitors are only permitted to appear in the 'inferior courts', as they are (supposedly non-pejoratively) called – magistrates' and county courts – unless they undertake specialist courses and qualify as 'solicitor-advocates'.

The importance of a good criminal solicitor cannot be oversold. Not just because their faith in my limited abilities pays my mortgage, but because their role, unlike the aloof barrister who will rarely even speak to you directly, except at intimidating 'conferences' in their chambers where you sit around an antique table sipping Assam tea from bone china, infiltrates every part of the criminal process. The solicitor will be squatting in your stinking police cell post-arrest, advising you on your rights, the nature and strength of the allegations against you and how you should approach the impending police interview, during which they'll sit dutifully alongside, barking at any sneaky trick questions from the officers. After you are charged, your solicitor will usually be the one representing you at the first appearance before the magistrates, advising you on the initial evidence, the appropriate plea and whether to opt for trial before magistrates or jury. If it's a Crown Court case, they will handle the heavy-duty defence evidence-gathering: taking witness statements, pursuing lines of inquiry, demanding undermining disclosable material from the CPS. They will instruct an expert to challenge the Crown's mistaken DNA evidence, prepare the various administrative documents that the court requires and ensure that you get as much face-to-face contact as you desire, whether at their offices or in one of Her Majesty's salubrious remand prisons. They will analyse the evidence and devise strategy, tactics and presentation with the barrister, or if the case is a magistrates' trial, they will usually do all the courtroom advocacy themselves as well. In the Crown Court, the best solicitors will attend throughout your trial to offer moral and practical support to you and your barrister. They will help you get your belongings back from the police if you win your trial, and will visit you in prison to advise on your appeal if you finish runner up. Good solicitors will be your first and last point of contact, on call twenty-four hours a day; their *raison d'être* being to protect you from the merciless swing of the prosecution scythe.

The Barrister

Standing up and engaged in polite, overly formalized exchanges with the judge are myself and Mr Rallings – the barristers. Our role is to present our respective clients' cases as persuasively as possible, by adducing evidence, arguing over the applicable law, questioning witnesses and persuading the jury of the virtue of our cause in chest-beating speeches. This is the nub of the adversarial criminal trial.

For many, an air of mystery hangs over what we actually do. Partly this is because many people's experience of lawyers will be limited to civil, as distinct from criminal, law. In its very loosest sense, civil law encompasses a broad range of legal services from non-contentious – such as the conveyancing when you buy or sell a property, or wills and probate – to contentious, including personal injury claims, contract disputes, employment law, divorce and commercial litigation. If this is all you have encountered of the legal system, you will invariably be dependent on second-hand accounts, TV shows and guesswork to cobble together an understanding of the alien world of criminal litigation. Public unfamiliarity may also be because the Bar is traditionally a 'referral profession'; individuals have to go through a solicitor to instruct a barrister, meaning most contact is at arm's length.[19]

But mostly, it's our fault that the public doesn't know what we do. We glide by, certain that our professional heritage gives us a self-evident importance requiring no introduction, with the result that not many ordinary people know much about us. No one needs a primer explaining the difference between a GP and a surgeon. But ask your average jury to delineate titles tossed around by the legal industry, and most would fumble in an indistinct haze of barristers, solicitors, lawyers, advocates, attorneys, paralegals and briefs, before volunteering a tentative jumble of words ending with a rising inflexion on the word 'Rumpole'.

Put into the criminal context, our adversarial justice system pits the state against the accused. A publicly funded prosecutorial office (usually the Crown Prosecution Service) instructs a barrister to prosecute those accused of criminal offences to persuade a jury that the case is proved on evidence beyond reasonable doubt. The prosecuting barrister will advise the CPS on what further evidence is required and on any complex legal matters arising, and will present the prosecution case at trial. The accused is in turn defended by (theoretically) equally competent legal counsel, instructed by defence solicitors, advising the client on the evidence against him and, if the client denies guilt, fighting to ensure that the law is applied in the client's favour, cross-examining the prosecution witnesses and trying to persuade the jury that the prosecution case has not been made out. If the client pleads guilty or is convicted, the defence barrister will present his mitigation at the sentence hearing before a judge.

Out of the 15,000 barristers in England and Wales, around 4,000 of us are criminal practitioners, assuming one of these diametric roles in Crown Court (and occasionally magistrates' court) cases across the country. Most of us are self-employed; hired guns, ethically obliged by the 'cab rank rule' to take the first case that comes calling to our clerks, regardless of its merit or our personal feelings about the parties or principles involved. And in crime, this means that most barristers both prosecute and defend (although not, obviously, in the same case). And my view has always been that doing a bit of both is good for the soul. It reinforces your independence. It sharpens your objectivity. And it helps you, in any given case, to know your enemy.

As for what causes a law graduate to swallow the red pill marked 'Barrister', we all have our official stock answers gathering dust from our days interviewing for pupillages. A *thirst* for justice. A *passion* for advocacy. A *need* to help the helpless, voice the voiceless and improve the unimprovable. (If you think that last one is particularly cringeworthy, you'd be right. But, believe it or not, for my first five interviews, I actually thought it sounded impressive.) Sentiments which are all, in their essence, both necessary and true. But most applicants are too timid to admit the core motivation that lures someone to the Bar: the cry for attention, the desperate need to be centre stage in the climactic scenes of people's lives. A combination of sated vanity and, buried deep below the affectations of brash nonchalance, a quiet but sincere desire to help people tends to be the unifier among most criminal hacks.

Up until the eighteenth century, however, Mr Tuttle would not have had the advantage of an advocate to plead his case to the jury.[20] Despite the legal profession having been recognized in law since 1275,[21] it was simply not the practice, until the 1700s, to sully us with the criminal process, with pleaders confined to civil proceedings. Instead, the 'altercation trial' that emerged in the sixteenth century pitted the alleged victim, who was also the prosecutor, directly against the defendant in a daytime TV-inspiring confrontation, while a jury determined guilt according to the defendant's often-inarticulate responses to the prosecution's allegations. It was something of a free-for-all, with no rules of evidence, and no lawyers.

Barristers first started traipsing into criminal courts towards the beginning of the eighteenth century, when the Crown, having up until now nominally prosecuted in the king's name but outsourced the grubby work to the complainant, decided to instruct lawyers to prepare and prosecute their cases in court. However, there persisted an institutional, judge-bolstered resistance to allowing the defendant to be legally represented. This was, rather splendidly, justified in terms of concern for the defendant, who, it was considered, would make a much better fist of telling a court about matters that he had witnessed first-hand than if he had some stuffed shirt distilling his words for him. The defendant's interests, it was said, could be adequately protected by the judge ensuring that the trial was conducted fairly.

Such was the 'disadvantage' of being legally represented, that, by the early seventeenth century, though it was not uncommon for defence lawyers to be permitted to act for people accused of trivial misdemeanours, judges insisted that their courtrooms remain defence-lawyer free in serious felony cases of life and limb, purely for the defendant's own benefit. Cynics of the age suggested that the prohibition on defence lawyers was simply to make it easy for a bumbling, vulnerable accused to unwittingly inculpate himself. It simply wouldn't do to have lawyers distracting the jury when the 'truth' could so easily be extracted from an unrepresented defendant.

To an extent, judges were right. Once the Treason Trial Act of 1696, which guaranteed the right to defence representation in treason cases, nudged the door ajar, beseeching lawyers persuaded judges to incrementally extend the right to representation in other, serious trials, until, by the end of the eighteenth century, defence advocates were a regular presence in the criminal courts. And, as feared, they ran riot over the settled production line of convicting miscreants. At first the barrister's role was strictly limited: he (for it was always 'he' until Helena Normanton smashed the glass ceiling in 1922) could address the court on matters of law. And he could cross-examine the prosecution witnesses. He was not permitted to assist in the presentation of the defence evidence, and was not allowed to address the jury. The theory was that defendants would continue to be obliged to speak in their own defence, from which the truth would emerge.

Inevitably, lawyers pushed the envelope. Matters of facts were spuriously recast as matters of law. They used cross-examination to indirectly address the jury. Some of them resorted to outrageous acts of intellectual – and actual – dishonesty to save their clients. But, most importantly, it was thanks to their ingenious arguments that courts found themselves railroaded into developing laws of evidence – such as the rule against hearsay (things said out of court being relied on as evidence in court), designed to protect defendants from being convicted on the basis of untested second-hand gossip.

In 1791, in a trial at the Old Bailey, celebrity barrister *du jour* William Garrow sternly told the judge that 'every man is presumed to be innocent until proved guilty'. This was the first formal articulation of what would, in 1935, be described by the Court of Appeal as 'the golden thread' running through the web of English criminal law[22] – the presumption of innocence, and the burden of proof. Its application in practice – that the prosecution must prove its case beyond reasonable doubt (or, as it is nowadays phrased for juries, proved so that they are 'sure' of guilt) – is without question, as you will hear in every defence advocate's closing speech to the jury, the greatest protection our system offers. No one shall have their liberty infringed on the basis of guesswork or supposition.

The Trials for Felony Act 1836 gave all prisoners on trial for felony the right to be represented by defence counsel, and granted defence counsel the same right as the prosecution to address the jury on matters of fact. That was the final piece of the jigsaw. Belatedly, we had arrived. Complainant-led altercation had given way to lawyer-dominated adversarialism.

It should be said that professional ethics have improved since the nineteenth century. Many people today might assume from popular culture that the famous complaint from the *Law Times* in 1844 that 'An Old Bailey Practitioner is a byword for disgrace and infamy' still holds true, and there undoubtedly persists a media-reinforced image of defence lawyers breaking whatever codes of morality or law are required to secure the acquittal of clients whom they know are guilty. But in reality, our professional obligations are strictly prescribed.

The Bar Code of Conduct imposes a duty on the barrister to 'promote and protect fearlessly and by all proper and lawful means his lay client's best interests and do so without regard to his own interests or to any consequences to himself or to any other person'; but the key is 'proper and lawful'. Our overriding duty is to the court. We cannot mislead the court by saying something that we know to be untrue. So, for example, if my client tells me he scrumped an apple, I can't stand up and suggest to a jury that he didn't, or that the witnesses who saw him scrumping are lying. But if he insists that, notwithstanding the compelling testimony of the two hundred witnesses in the orchard, he is an innocent man, I roll away my personal views on the veracity of his tale, put on my wig and get ready for battle. We do not judge. We don't know the truth of our clients' situations, and it's not for us to guess. All we can do is advise and advance their instructions as best we can, even where, as with Mr Tuttle, it might appear obvious that the client is as guilty as original sin.

This feeds into the core identity of the Bar: its independence. The majority of criminal barristers are self-employed practitioners operating out of clusters of offices known as 'chambers' (or 'sets'), originally in the fifteenth century housed in the Inns of Court in London, but nowadays spread throughout the country. The Inns of Court – Lincoln's Inn, Inner Temple, Middle Temple and Gray's Inn – are our professional associations. A barrister must be a member of one, and it is at the Inns' ceremonies that Bar school graduates are 'called to the Bar'. Standing in the heart of London's legal district, sweeping across the west boundary of the City of London from Holborn through to Temple, the Inns are, for the uninitiated, perhaps best described as a cross between an Oxbridge college and Hogwarts. Great vaulted gothic halls, libraries and chapels, and sprawling acres of rare, capital green squares have evolved from monopolistic providers of barristerial training and accommodation to a softer hybrid of continuing education and administering professional discipline. And, of course, dining. Which is important, because, believe it or not, in order to qualify as a barrister in this country, a condition is that, as a student on the postgraduate £20,000-a-pop Bar Practical Training Course (as it now is), you have to attend your Inn and eat twelve meals. I kid you not. A fundamental requirement of membership of the oldest advocacy tradition in our legal history is that having ploughed yourself into a £32k professional loan (including interest),[23] you must ingest heavily subsidized haute cuisine twelve times.[24] And people say we're out of touch with the modern world.

Chambers house anything from half a dozen to several hundred self-employed barristers, and are designed to allow sole practitioners to pool knowledge, wisdom and overheads, such as rent and staff. The most important of these are the clerks. Clerks are our pimps. They get the work in to chambers, schmoozing solicitors and prostituting barristers to ensure that everyone's diaries remain full, and that cases are covered. And the chambers system underpins that fulcrum of independence. The theory is that barristers are beholden to no one. Our advice to our clients can be objective and robust, and we are not dependent on favour or goodwill, least of all that of the state, in dispatching our duties. If you are accused of a crime, or if the state wishes to prosecute someone accused of a crime, there is a cadre of independent advocates and consultants always available to help.

Oh, and the horsehair wigs? They, like the black gowns which barristers adopted when mourning the passing of Charles II, are simply a relic of Restoration fashion. While wigs and gowns have been removed from civil and family courts and the Supreme Court in the name of modernity, the criminal courts cling on. For my part, I rather like court dress as a social leveller, a sort of school uniform. It also offers a veneer of disguise in those rare but unsettling cases where a defendant you have spent an afternoon dismantling in cross-examination decides to wait outside the court building to offer a review of your performance.

Taking a step back and surveying the courtroom from above, trying to be as disinterested as I can, when these constituent elements are all pieced together, I think we have something special. Lying beneath each fragment, each procedural development and each incremental extension of the accused's legal rights, is what, for me, the notion of justice is about. And that is fairness. To me, fairness is rooted intractably within what we mean when we talk about criminal justice. Fairness to the defendant. Fairness to the victim. Fairness to the witnesses. And fairness to the public. When we cry that an outcome or a procedure is unjust, we tend to mean that it's not fair. I shall neatly sidestep the approaching criticism that, in so defining, I am guilty of substituting one abstract, indefinable concept for another, by appealing to what I hope we would all agree are shared understandings of the overlapping terms.

The Rule of Law[25] is fairness. It is fair that, as declared by

Magna Carta, everybody from kings to gentry to peasants are equally bound by the law. It's fair that the rules are agreed by democratically elected representatives and not imposed arbitrarily by the monarch. It's fair to know the rules before you're punished for breaking them. It's fair that, if you're accused of breaking them, the procedure is the same fair procedure available to everyone else, and that you're judged independently and by the same standards as your peers. It's fair that you have access to an unbiased court, refereed by an independent, highly qualified judge, who ensures that the law is correctly applied. It's fair that those judging you are unbiased ordinary men and women, unconnected to the case, at liberty to return whatever verdict they see fit.

It's fair that a public prosecutor, shielded from the heat of the complainant's grievance, brings a case where law and public policy dictate that it should, not simply where an aggrieved party can afford to prosecute. It is fair that a defendant has access to legal advice and representation of equal calibre to the Crown, including a fearless, independent advocate to ensure that his case is not diminished for want of his own eloquence, education or other social capital; and, where he says that he is innocent, to fight using all lawful means to persuade a court that the case against that man is not proven.

It is fair, given the highest of stakes at play, that we presume that all persons accused are innocent, and do not convict, and subject them to life-changing punishment, unless we are sure that they committed the crime. It's fair that those who are convicted of causing harm to others are properly punished and, wherever possible, rehabilitated. It's fair that the jury should base their verdicts on sound evidential bases, rather than prejudice, speculation or rumour. It's fair, ultimately, that the guilty should be convicted, and the innocent acquitted, but, where doubt prevails, that we exercise it in favour of the accused.

Our adversarial system, when it works, is perhaps the greatest guarantor of individual liberty there is. The miscarriages of justice that have been avoided and righted over the last century have almost without exception been so as a consequence of fearless, independent advocates and litigators relentlessly challenging the power-laden assumptions of the state in the service of their client's cause: the barrister who exposes, through forensic cross-examination, the conspiracy of corrupt police officers fitting up their client; the solicitor who pursues the DNA analysis that proves the state has got the wrong man; the prosecutor who reviews the unused material during a trial and honourably discloses to the defence the key that sets the defendant free. There's a reason why ascending tyrants always round up the lawyers first.

I really can see why our criminal justice system, as curiously evolved a mongrel of a system as one might hope to find – one which, even the official website of the English and Welsh Judiciary admits, is 'contradictory', 'confusing' and which 'it is doubtful [. . .] anyone asked to design a justice system would choose to copy'[26] – is still widely regarded as one of the best in the world. When it works, I would tend to agree.

The problem is that often it doesn't. As we shall see, despite the grand principles at its heart, at nearly every stage of our prized system of criminal justice we see things going badly, and preventably, wrong.

Let's begin where all criminal prosecutions start their lives. To do so, we need to rewind from the Crown Court setting. For the first station in the voyage of every criminal case lies in a far less grandiloquent location: the Magistrates' Court.

2. The Wild West:
The Magistrates' Court

'There is, I verily believe, no people's court on either side of the Iron Curtain or anywhere in the world which is as representative of the responsible elements of society as the lay bench of England and Wales.'

Lord Hailsham, 1984 AGM
of the Magistrates' Association[1]

Kyle slumped amidst the swelling noise of the waiting area and impatiently banged the split rubber of his soles against the backrest of the chair in front. This had the unintended result of awaking its slumbering, but invisible, occupant, who, cuddling his tin of Special Brew in his anorak and reeking potently of urine, had been sprawled across three seats, apparently sleeping off the effects of the previous night.

Whether this man had a case listed before the magistrates that morning, or was accompanying a friend or simply enjoyed the hospitality of the one public space where society's unwelcome can pass a day, sheltered from the elements, without interrogation or risk of being moved on, was not immediately clear. At some point that morning, a harried usher would pop out of Court 4, ask the gentleman which case he was here for, and, upon getting no coherent reply, would swiftly move on under the assumption that, whoever he was, he was not her court's problem, and his implicit leave to doze would be extended.

Three police officers, their radios buzzing, strode past cradling polystyrene-clad coffee, negotiating the scores of recognizable ne'er-do-wells spilling out of the rows of screwed-down seating. One officer swerved to avoid a woman swinging a bulging Morrisons carrier bag over her head as she directed imaginary sky traffic with gusto, and the constables darted into the safety of the police room at the far end of the lobby, where they could sip Americanos in peace until troubled by the prosecutor to give evidence in their trial.

The hubbub of gathering souls was getting too loud for Kyle to think. An indecipherable tannoy directed someone of some name to go immediately to see someone else of another name at the cells. Solicitors bearing chunky files swept past the rows of chairs, calling out the familiar names, which were quickly matched to the familiar faces, that they would be representing that morning. These shouted names were harmonized by the chorus of the ushers, springing out of their respective courtrooms like cuckoos to summon the next unfortunate on the list.

A man with a gleaming head, zipped-up tracksuit and giant curved scar stretching from his forehead over his scalp and ceasing just below his nape, was accosting each suit that walked by: 'Are you the duty?' ''Scuze mate, are you the duty?' 'Love, you ain't the duty, are ya?' A probation officer, starting her delayed 9 a.m. appointments for pre-sentence reports, squeezed past him and into the Probation Office, followed by a candid youth bravely wearing a fashion T-shirt bearing the slogan, 'Weekend Offender'.

At the furthest corner of the lobby, an ostensibly more respectable crowd assembled outside the door to the traffic court; a businessman in Armani, flanked by his privately paid road traffic solicitors, fidgeted nervously, the soundness

48

of his multi-thousand-pound investment about to be tested to destruction before a foul-tempered District Judge.

Kyle gazed around for his solicitor and absent-mindedly dragged his bulging Adidas carrier bag back and forth along the floor by its drawcord. Inside were the bare essentials – tracky bottoms, T-shirt, underwear, deodorant, family photos – that his brothers said he would need at the Young Offender Institution to which he was heading after today's hearing. At only nineteen years old, Kyle now appeared at the magistrates' court with the same regularity as he had at the Youth Court up to the age of eighteen, and well knew the score. The magistrates had taken pity on him after his last car radio theft – the sixth of his career – and had imposed a community order with eighty hours of unpaid work six weeks ago. Having been found in the passenger seat of a 'borrowed' VW Golf barely a month later, Kyle was prepared for the spell in custody that was now looming. He just wanted the hearing over and done with, so he could check out of this human zoo, excuse himself from the present company of junkies, wife-beaters, drink-drivers and the otherwise socially dispossessed and meet up with his mates on the inside.

A man from British Gas flashed his identity card at the usher outside Court 2, and was promptly escorted straight inside, his application to the magistrates for warrants to disconnect the energy supplies of errant non-payers taking precedence as first order of business. As he stepped through the doorway, his escorting usher waved away a perspiring, onrushing barrister staggering under the weight of a dozen double-stuffed files, who was pleading to nil effect that they were the prosecutor allocated to this courtroom and simply had to get into court. Their desperation was palpable, as if they were being chased by a swarm of flying deathmonkeys, salvation from which lay just beyond the threshold.

This prosecutor was me. And I was desperate. I was the

49

junior gopher instructed to prosecute all the cases listed in Court 2 that day – the so-called 'prosecution list' – and, having had the four-foot stack of files comprising the papers for today's seven listed trials in my custody for less than ten minutes, was seeking refuge from the attentions of the seven defence solicitors vying for my attention and demanding answers which may, or, more likely, may not, lie within these unread, disordered Crown Prosecution Service files. I knew that, in fifteen minutes' time, I would be summoned into court before three magistrates expecting me to be in a position to start the first trial, and as yet I didn't even know what any of the cases were even about, let alone what my questions for the witnesses would be. With every pokey meeting room in the building either arbitrarily locked or occupied by defendants giving instructions to their briefs, the courtroom itself was my best and last bet for a few uninterrupted moments to read the damn files. Denied, I'd have to wing it. Somehow I was going to have to stand up in court and prosecute trial after trial, examining and cross-examining witnesses and making devastatingly persuasive arguments of fact and law, without knowing what the hell I was talking about.

I soon learned that I'd fit right in.

Welcome, ladies and gentlemen, to the magistrates' court. This, the lowest court on the criminal rungs, is where all[2] criminal cases start their lives. If you are charged with a criminal offence, this apparent replica of an inner-city A&E department on a Saturday night is where your journey begins. If your case is sufficiently serious, it will be dispatched from here to the more civilized and structured Crown Court to live out its days in front of a jury (assuming you do not plead guilty), and your sojourn before the magistrates will not extend beyond a single, brief 'first appearance'. Those offences deemed fit for summary (magistrates') trial – your low-level assaults, thefts and driving offences – remain in the lower court to be case-managed and, at some point in the future, tried before the magistrates, or, as they are referred to interchangeably, Justices of the Peace (JPs).

While most of us probably think of jury trial as our most common criminal tribunal, 94 per cent of the 1.46 million individuals brought before the magistrates each year[3] will never see the inside of a Crown Court. Their cases, from first appearance through to – if they plead guilty or are convicted after trial – their sentence, will be dealt with at one of approximately 150 magistrates' courts dotted across the land, and their fate determined most likely by three out of 17,500 serving magistrates;[4] volunteers with no formal legal qualifications but the power to determine both rulings of law and findings of fact, and to send their fellow citizens to prison for up to a year.

That last sentence may have taken you by surprise. Unqualified volunteers in charge of law and justice? A little history is probably needed for context.

In 1195, Richard I decided to commission good and lawful men to act as *custodes pacis* and keep the local peace. Since that time, volunteers from the landed gentry have sat in judgment over the lower orders, their office later formalized in law by the Statute of Westminster 1361. These Justices of the Peace were not expected to be learned in the law, in contrast to the judges who sat in the King's Court and the assizes on the Circuits and presided over serious criminal trials with juries; rather, JPs would knock heads together and dish out plain speaking and patrician over-bearing to the local riff-raff, as well as administering the smorgasbord of eclectic local governmental duties they accumulated over the centuries.

JPs' original peace-keeping obligations restricted their involvement in the criminal law to restraining, chastising and imprisoning 'offenders, rioters and all other barrators [frauds]' who in their judgment had disturbed the king's peace. But incrementally their powers increased.

From the fourteenth century, JPs began to preside over an emerging second tier of criminal court, known as Quarter Sessions (so-called because it sat in the locality four times a year). Quarter Sessions tried 'misdemeanours' – less serious offences – to alleviate the burden on professional judges sitting with juries in the assizes. Like the assizes, allegations in the Quarter Sessions were tried by a jury, but JPs, rather than professional judges, chaired proceedings. The assizes and Quarter Sessions were combined to form the modern Crown Court in 1971.

From around the 1730s, a third tier of criminal courts emerged: the Petty Sessions, where JPs formally sat to deal with, among other things, peace-breakers, fine-defaulters and bastardy examinations. 'Formally' is probably putting it a little strong; until the beginning of the nineteenth century it was not uncommon for the 'court' to be held in a magistrate's living room. It was at that time, however, that the extension of magistrates' powers kicked in. From the 1820s, magistrates found themselves subject to a procession of new laws formalizing, recording and regulating summary proceedings, and, in return, the jurisdiction of the Petty Sessions was expanded to take some of the work of the Quarter Sessions. Criminal offences that could only previously have been tried in front of a jury, such as larceny, could now be tried by magistrates alone, with the consent of the accused (consent would often be given due to the magistrates having lower sentencing powers than the Quarter Sessions).

Throughout the nineteenth century, as industrialization swept in and the volume of criminal work increased, the list of offences which could be tried swiftly and inexpensively by magistrates grew. In the twentieth century, not only were more offences reclassified as 'triable either way' – suitable for either summary trial or jury trial – but some were made mandatorily 'summary only' and so the defendant's right to elect trial by jury was removed altogether.

So it is that today, criminal offences are divided into three categories. The least serious 'summary only' offences – motoring offences, common assault, minor public disorder – can only[5] be tried in the magistrates' court. The most serious 'indictable only' offences – murder, rape, possessing firearms, serious violence and so forth[6] – can only be tried in the Crown Court. The meaty filling of 'triable either way' crimes in between those two extremes – your burglaries, drug transactions, semi-serious violence and garden-variety sexual offending – can be heard either in the magistrates' court or the Crown Court, and the first appearance is used to determine which venue is most suitable (the 'allocation' procedure). To do this, the magistrates look at the facts of the allegations and the relevant Sentencing Guidelines, and consider whether, if the defendant were to be convicted, the magistrates' powers of sentence (a maximum of six months' imprisonment for a single offence, or a maximum of twelve months' imprisonment for two or more 'either way' offences) would be sufficient. If so, they will deem the case suitable for summary trial. If not, or if the case is unusually legally or factually complex, they'll send it to the Crown Court.

The bottom line though is that, whatever view the magistrates take on venue, the defendant has the right in all 'triable either way' cases to elect to go before a jury in the Crown Court.

So that is the historical explanation for magistrates' courts. The justification for their continued existence takes us back a chapter to the feting of jury trial – Magna Carta, participative democracy and all that jazz. Magistrates' courts, it is submitted, root criminal justice in the community, satisfying our constitutional craving for judgment by our peers. The Kyles of England and Wales will be judged by unpaid locals who can empathize with their backgrounds while reflecting the diversity of modern society, in the same way that we trust that juries do. Of course, the cost of securing and accommodating twelve laypeople to decide every contested criminal allegation would be frankly astronomical. Only 1 per cent of criminal cases are resolved by jury trial,[7] and the cost of that, the Ministry of Justice insists, is already too high. Accordingly, for all but the most serious offences, the magistrates' court offers a compromise. Three volunteer JPs – an experienced 'chair' sitting in between two 'wingers' – assisted by a qualified 'legal advisor' to parse the relevant law, offer a scaled-down version of the judge-and-jury trial, preserving its essential democratic goodness, while diluting the formality, delay and expense of Crown Court proceedings. The law, trial procedure and rules of evidence are basically the same as in the Crown Court; the primary distinctions are the body determining guilt, the level of formality – there are no wigs, gowns or judicial robes, for example[8] – and the fact that solicitors, not just barristers, have rights of audience and so handle the bulk of the courtroom advocacy. Due to the dialled-down formality and absence of a jury, magistrates' trials are far quicker than Crown Court trials; trials last half a day in the mags, on average, compared to days, if not weeks, in the Crown. And, of course, there's the cost: £1,150 a day to run a magistrates' court, compared with an average £1,900 per day for a Crown Court.[9]

A further advantage is that magistrates are multipurpose, and as mini-judge-cum-juries are able to deal with matters of law which Crown Court juries are forbidden from touching. For instance, magistrates can run case management hearings, at which pre-trial issues – such as whether the parties are ready for trial, or defence applications for the prosecution to disclose relevant material – are thrashed out between the parties. They can determine legal applications, for example arguments over whether a piece of evidence is admissible at trial. Unlike juries, magistrates, having returned a guilty verdict, can go on to sentence the defendant. And there are scores of ancillary functions, including issuing search warrants to the police and authorizing utility companies to disconnect households defaulting on bills. Outside the adult criminal courts, magistrates can undertake special training to qualify to sit in the Youth Court, which deals with children aged between ten and seventeen, and the Family Court.

What we have, in summary, is a system designed to deliver affordable, speedy, summary justice for high-volume, less serious crime. Over the past ten years, various initiatives[10] have popped up to streamline proceedings, the aim now being that all magistrates' cases be reduced to two hearings – the first appearance and, as soon as possible thereafter, trial and/or sentence. Two hearings, boom. The best bits of the jury system, only a fraction of the cost. All topped off with an infusion of a near millennium of hardy English tradition, which in the law is nearly always A Good Thing.

That, I am afraid, is as favourable a gloss as I am able to put on magistrates' court justice.

I did my best over the previous pages. Honestly I did. I emptied out my bag of rhetorical tricks; I gave you statistics, forced whimsy, a whistle-stop history lesson and exploited the virtues of the jury system in the hope that you might overlook how poorly the same arguments transfer to magistrates.

The truth is that the entire case in favour of magistrates' courts, as we currently run them, is a sham. There is little sustainable rationale for their existence in principle, and no justification whatsoever for the way in which these courts operate in practice. There is no excuse for the amateur, sausage-factory paradigm of justice and 'that'll do' complacency that pervades 94 per cent of criminal cases, other than that most cynical political trinity: it's cheap, it's the way we've always done it and no one who votes either knows or cares. And the more you experience magistrates' court justice, and interrogate the base assumptions of this system, the less explicable the whole pantomime becomes.

Let's rewind to Kyle, kicking his heels in the lobby and waiting for his brief. Kyle's brief is Rachael, the same fearless, no-shit-taking solicitor who has represented Kyle from his early days in the Youth Court, and has watched with weary familiarity as, in spite of her best efforts, her thirteen-year-old client has carved out the same career path as his older brothers. Rachael also represented Kyle during his interview at the police station following his arrest, so is already familiar with his latest snafu, but this isn't always the case. Sometimes defendants will be represented at the police station by the duty solicitor, but select a different firm, or the court duty solicitor, to act for them at court. Assuming they satisfy a strict means test, defendants will usually be represented before the magistrates by solicitors from legal aid firms. Meanwhile the prosecution is handled either by in-house CPS lawyers, or by external solicitors or junior barristers, like me, instructed for the day as 'agents'.

When Rachael arrives, Kyle will confirm his instructions, admitting that he took a ride in the car knowing that it was nicked, and upon being advised on the sensible course will follow Rachael into court to enter his guilty plea.

The first thing to note is that the figures on the bench are unlikely to conform to Kyle's, or indeed many defendants', definition of peers or equals. The demographic of most defendants in these courts is homogeneous; society's lost boys and girls, a sorry parade of abused children turned drug-abusing adults. Sliding on and off the bottom rung of social functioning, in and out of homelessness, joblessness and wretched worthlessness, their histories are scabbed with violence, mental ill-health and chaos, and their present lies in a parallel universe where the middle-class ambition of the Good Life is replaced with a desperate scrapping for daily survival.

As I say, those sitting in judgment will invariably not be of the same stock.

For a start, it is possible that the 'mini-jury' in his courtroom won't even feature lay magistrates, but will instead comprise a single professional District Judge. DJs, as they're known in the trade, are legally qualified full-time judges who sit alone in magistrates' courts. Their powers and functions are largely the same as lay magistrates; they hear trials and case management hearings and pass sentence. The only formal difference is their professionalism. DJs first emerged around 1740 in the shape of 'stipendiary magistrates', salaried Justices of the Peace appointed as a response to rampant corruption among lay justices in London.[11] Now there are around 130 District Judges nationwide splitting the workload with around 100 part-time 'deputy' DJs and 17,500 magistrates. DJs are experienced legal practitioners – usually solicitors or barristers – appointed on the recommendation of the Lord Chancellor upon demonstration of, among other qualities, their knowledge and understanding of the law. Whatever the advantages of DJs (and we'll come to those shortly), a single legal expert appointed by the state is hardly a diverse, independent exemplar of participative democracy. If it's a scaled-down version of the jury, it's scaled down by 12:1. Where that 1 is a state-salaried solicitor. Given that Kyle has no say over whether his case is heard by a District Judge or by JPs, it is clear that the noble principle of lay participation is not inviolable.

But even if, as was the case on this day, Kyle found himself before a lay bench, it is obvious that magistrates too are anything but a mini-jury. Jurors are randomly selected from the electoral register, and anyone aged between eighteen and seventy-five (save for those with serious criminal convictions or severe mental illness) can be compelled to sit on a jury. Students, stay-at-home parents, police officers, judges, MPs, the employed, the self-employed, the unemployed, the retired, the obscenely wealthy, the desperately poor, big business owners, small business owners, zero-hours workers, conservatives, trade unionists, neoliberals, Marxists, the disabled, the abled and the full gamut of racial, cultural, class and religious identities are impanelled as jurors, whether they like it or not. Jurors do not self-select (and, unlike in the US, cannot be strategically chosen to suit the parties). Jurors don't put themselves forward as Solomons walking among us. It takes a certain type of character to volunteer to sit in judgment over one's fellow citizens as a hobby. And it so happens that, to the present day, that type of character has uniformly been white, middle aged and middle class, with a traditionally conservative leaning.

Geoffrey Robertson QC offered a withering description of magistrates in his evidence to the House of Commons Home Affairs Committee in 1995, painting them as:

> Ladies and gentlemen bountiful, politically imbalanced, unrepresentative of ethnic minority groups and women, who slow down the system and cost a fortune.[12]

In fairness, we have seen slight improvements since 1995, a time when JPs were recruited *sans* interview by a tap on the shoulder from an old chum. But the unsurprising legacy of an institution which, until 1906, jealously restricted membership to the landed gentry, and until the 1990s was still dominated by freemasons,[13] is that today with your average bench, you're not entrusting your liberty to the collective wisdom of twelve everymen; the butcher, baker, candle-stick emporium televangelist etc. You're often pitching to the admissions board of a 1980s country club.

While I have only once been treated to a demonstration of explicit magisterial racism – a white chairwoman musing, apropos of nothing, in front of me as prosecutor and her embarrassed colleagues: 'Mohammed is now the most popular boys' name, apparently. Isn't that terrifying?' – it is the subtler expressions of privilege and prejudice that pervade.

'We understand that your upbringing was difficult,' I've heard countless well-heeled chairs tell nineteen-year-old heroin addicts, graduates of the council-estate-to-care-home-to-streets pathway, moments before they're given eight weeks because (reading rote from the mags' pro forma sentencing remarks), 'You must learn that shoplifting is a very serious offence and you must stop committing serious offences of shoplifting.' More times than I can recall have I heard the same monotone chiding of homeless alcoholics who have breached a court order, usually obtained at great public expense by the local authority, banning them from begging for money. 'Breaching a court order is a very serious offence . . .', the chair's finger wags at the wretch in the dock, making little effort to hide his incredulity at why this man doesn't just stop begging, put on a decent suit and get a job.

This is not, I hasten to add, the attitude of all magistrates. A number bring to the bench invaluable, real-world experience of the underbelly of society. Community outreach workers, youth workers, social workers, teachers, medics and people who know the daily reality of the Kyles living hand-to-mouth, growing up in abject, abusive poverty and being trapped from a young age between disjointed education and peers and family members dragging them into criminal lifestyles. I've met these magistrates outside the courtroom, and their broad independent-mindedness and hunger for social justice represent beautifully the ideal to which the institution aspires.

But in my experience they remain a minority.

Despite a conscious push in the mid-2000s to diversify

the magistracy following a series of critical reviews and reports,[14] decreasing numbers of volunteers in recent years – a drop of nearly 50 per cent since 2006 – has in fact had the opposite effect. In 2016, 57 per cent of magistrates were over sixty, as opposed to 32 per cent in 1999. Anyone aged eighteen or over can apply to be a magistrate, but less than 1 per cent are under thirty. While 14.1 per cent of the population identify as Black and Minority Ethnic (BAME), the declared figure is only 10 per cent among magistrates, and some courts have no BAME representation at all. Only 4 per cent of magistrates identify as disabled, compared to 16 per cent of working age adults and 45 per cent of adults over state pension age. What official figures there are – and this will be supported qualitatively by any criminal practitioner – indicate that magistrates present as mostly middle class. And equal representation by sexuality, reports suggest, is also some way off.[15]

There is a longstanding, and often greater, chasm in representativeness visible in the judiciary too (although DJs are on average significantly younger than magistrates); however, judges don't justify their existence on the basis that they are the modern-day heirs to Magna Carta, drawn from the same stock as those upon whom they sit in judgment and enriching the criminal process with the breadth of their worldliness and unerring feel for the lot of the common man. When your official *raison d'être* is to reflect the local community, it becomes a problem if case after case looks to the outside world like old, white, middle-class people lording it over young, working-class, BAME defendants.

And it is not merely a matter of presentation. A socially, culturally and ethnically homogeneous lay judiciary leads inevitably to a narrower and more entrenched set of beliefs and presumptions, as betrayed by questions and off-the-cuff comments that we hear from the bench.

The decisions that are handed down in magistrates'

courts too rarely deviate from the predictable. This is demonstrated most glaringly by the statistically suggested pro-prosecution attitudes on display.

Earlier, we touched upon a defendant's right to elect jury trial in either-way offences. This decision is one of the earliest on which defence lawyers have to advise the client: do you stick in the magistrates' court, where the maximum sentence for a single offence is six months, or twist and go to the Crown Court, where the maximum sentence will be measured in years?

Why, you might ask, would a defendant opt for the Crown Court and the risk of a much higher sentence? The answer lies in the statistics. Trials in the magistrates' court are far more likely to result in a win for the Crown. In 2016/17, the Crown Prosecution Service prosecuted 52,140 trials in the magistrates' court. Of these, 33,371 resulted in conviction, a conviction rate of 64 per cent. Over the same period, the CPS prosecuted 14,967 trials in the Crown Court, of which 7,806 ended in conviction. A conviction rate of 52.2 per cent. That is a disparity of nearly twelve percentage points, or, put another way, you have a 23 per cent better chance of being acquitted in the Crown Court.[16]

Twenty-three per cent.

Possibly this can be explained as another vestige of history. In the sixteenth century,[17] JPs, who were not yet trying criminal cases by themselves, nevertheless played a vital role in prosecutions. As there was no police force or public prosecutor, and most prosecutions were brought by the complainant, magistrates were commanded to help investigate and build the prosecution case. They took depositions from prosecution witnesses (and stoutly refused to depose anyone who might assist the defence), and compelled those witnesses to attend trial. Through interrogation magistrates extracted 'confessions' from defendants, and then appeared at trial to give evidence for the prosecution, in the same way that a modern police officer in charge of a case gives evidence about the investigation. Don't mistake this for a balanced inquisitorial procedure such as we see on the Continent; these partisan mags were explicitly told that they should do everything in their power to secure 'anything material to prove the felony against [the defendant]'.[18]

Although by the twentieth century incremental recalibrations had tilted magistrates towards a disinterested judicial role, magistrates' courts were until 1949 formally referred to as 'police courts'. And that is what they were; the courts were (and many still are) physically attached to the local police station. The police guarded the doors, brought the prisoners to court, put prisoners in the dock and were the primary state prosecution agency until the Crown Prosecution Service was created in 1985.

Even now, you will still hear old-school mags occasionally slip into possessive determiners when referring to the prosecution: 'our officer' or 'our prosecutor'. Indeed, as I crash into court laden with my files, before I can catch my breath the chair peers up from behind her spectacles to score a double whammy: 'Ah finally, our prosecutor. Now, is our policeman here for the first trial?'

It's a cliché in legal circles, but no less true for so being, that if it's the word of a police officer against your client, it's usually game over before you've begun. You're normally facing a combination of General Melchett starting Captain Blackadder's trial by commanding, 'Pass me the black cap, I'll be needing that,' and Alan Partridge suggesting to a lawyer interviewee that 'with the greatest respect, the police are hardly likely to arrest a man if he's innocent, are they?' Or, in the historic words of the magistrates themselves:

Quite the most unpleasant cases that we have to decide are those where the evidence is a direct conflict between a police officer and a member of the public. My principle in such cases has always been to believe the evidence of the police officer, and therefore we find the case proved.[19]

Don't assume that the bias operates solely against the Kyles of our society. The angriest defendants I've seen at the magistrates' courts have been those of impeccable reputation from comfortable backgrounds who are charged with an offence based on the word of a police officer. Assaulting a police constable during a neighbourhood dispute by allegedly jabbing a finger in the officer's face, for instance. Or being accused of driving while using a mobile phone. They turn their heads, eyes wide in burning disbelief as the magistrates unquestioningly accept the hesitant officer's account, and reject the evidence of the defendant and his two witnesses.

'But . . . that police officer lied!' they splutter, purple-faced as they leave the courtroom. The family join in: 'How can the magistrates not see that?' And the defence lawyer can only nod as they fill out the appeal form. 'I know.'

Maybe the disparity in conviction rates is attributable to jury fallibility. They are less case-hardened than magistrates and DJs, ingrained cynicism at the 'usual defences' having not set in. They are perhaps overly cautious at branding someone with a criminal conviction. Perhaps even gullible. I have seen some ludicrous acquittals by juries. More than once have I enjoyed the post-trial scorn of the acquitted client whom I have advised throughout will almost certainly be convicted, or skulked out of court in shame having lost the unlosable prosecution.

But my fear is that it goes deeper. It is rooted in a recruitment and training system which not only continues to embed a lack of diversity, but permits a quality of decision-making which is too often inconsistent, irrational and, at times, plainly unlawful.

*

Let's start with the latter, as it is on its face the least justi-fiable dimension of the magistrates' court. In twenty-first-century criminal litigation where liberty is on the line, mat-ters of *law*, not just fact, are decided by volunteers armed with absolutely no formal legal knowledge or training.

The most complex legal principles and judgments, handed down by Lords, Ladies and Justices of Appeal over scores of pages ruminating on the most technical nuances of the application or meaning of the law, which will often have been argued before the Court of Appeal or Supreme Court (or its predecessor the House of Lords) over many days by the finest Queen's Counsel in the realm, and whose ambigu-ities and intricacies form the subject of ferocious academic debate among the most learned legal scholars, are inter-preted and applied by, using the term as neutrally as possible, amateurs. People who fancy a go. All the decisions taken in Crown Court proceedings by experienced judges – such as applications for bail, applications to adjourn hear-ings to obtain evidence, applications to admit or to exclude certain evidence (e.g. hearsay or previous convictions), applications to have prosecutions 'stayed' (struck out) for abusing the process of the court, submissions of no case to answer and sentencing convicted defendants – magis-trates can try their hand at the lot. Although particularly complex legal applications and argument will, wherever possible, be shoved under the beak of a District Judge, if none is available, or if a point of law arises mid-trial, magistrates get to roll up their sleeves and make rulings of law carrying exactly the same force and weight as DJs.

It's easy to understand why tension is reported between mags and DJs, arising in part out of magisterial umbrage at DJs being 'allocated the best work' and perceived as 'more highly rated'.[20] In order to become a District Judge, you need to have amassed a law degree, a postgraduate legal qualification, vocational training, at least five years' legal practice as a solicitor or barrister, plus usually two years of sitting as a deputy (part-time) District Judge. This adds up to at least ten to twelve years of experience in the law, which is vital; magistrates' court law and procedure is rammed full of quirks and technicalities – many of which, incidentally, don't apply in the Crown Court – and DJs are often drawn from the shrewdest, sharpest solicitors familiar with obscure legal technicalities that baffle day-tripper barristers visiting the magistrates' court. The application process for DJs is protracted and punishing, comprising an examination paper traversing the darkest, most technically fiendish plains of criminal law and procedure; a panel interview, where an experienced judge will mercilessly scrutinize your powers of critical reasoning, logic, deduction and legal analysis; and a role play simulating a courtroom environment to assess your temperament, judgment and ability to cope with the chaos of the unexpected. You will also require professional references attesting to how splendid a lawyer you are. Experienced solicitors and barristers often have to go through the process multiple times, over many years, before they are deemed ready to exercise the judicial responsibilities that accompany the office.

To become a magistrate, exercising the same powers in criminal cases, you need to fill in a form, attend an interview, demonstrate that you've done some charity work and show willing to sit for thirteen days a year. If you make it through the interview, you receive eighteen hours' 'induction and core training', during which the rudiments of magistrates' court procedure and the art of judging are explained, and then after three visits to watch a mags' court in action, you're away. Your performance will be appraised once every three years, and this appraisal is limited to a single day's observation, often by someone you know. This was unsurprisingly condemned by the House of Commons Justice Committee in 2016 as 'inadequate', and by magistrates themselves as 'woeful' and 'unfit for purpose'.[21] Continued 'essential training' applies once you've started sitting, albeit a minimum of only *six hours every three years*, and its quality is reportedly dubious. As budgets are shorn, the spending by the Judicial College on magistrates' training decreased from £110 per magistrate in 2008/9 to £36 in 2015[22] (as contrasted to £629 per District Judge). One magistrate told charity Transform Justice in 2014: 'As somebody who has been involved in education all her life, I am truly shocked by the lack of professional training in what should be a professional role.'[23]

The theoretical supplement to the legal anaemia on the bench is the magistrates' legal advisor, although this is only a recent, twenty-first-century development. Each local justice area has a justices' clerk, a qualified and experienced solicitor or barrister with responsibility for providing legal advice, support and training to magistrates. Their powers are delegated to 'assistant justices' clerks' or 'legal advisors', one of whom sits in each courtroom and provides legal advice to the magistrates. The legal advisor must be a qualified solicitor or barrister (although they do not need to have actually practised), and has various delegated powers of case management that they can exercise on the magistrates' behalf. Good legal advisors effectively run the courtroom. If you inveigle yourself into their good graces, they can make your day a lot easier, and shepherd the magistrates towards a sensible way of operating. But their powers are ultimately only advisory. By contrast, in the Crown Court legal decisions are made by the judge, and the jury is told it *has* to accept the judge's directions as to how the law applies. In the mags, JPs can – and often do – disregard or misunderstand the entreaties of their learned colleagues with abandon. I've lost count of the times I've locked eyes with a legal advisor and watched their eyebrows ascend to the heavens as a magistrate reads out a decision wildly ignoring the legal advice patiently explained to them just moments before.

In Kyle's court, for example, on just one morning we enjoy a parade of errors. The first trial on my list is prosecuting a man, John, who was stopped on the street late at night carrying a baseball bat, and has been charged with possessing an offensive weapon in a public place. His defence is that the bat was being carried only to scare off some youths who had been causing trouble outside his home. In law, a baseball bat only qualifies as an 'offensive weapon' if the holder intends to use it to cause injury – using it to *scare* is not enough. But one of the magistrates thinks he knows otherwise, and tries to persuade John's solicitor that John should be pleading guilty as 'that's definitely not a defence'. Fortunately, the solicitor and I stand our ground until the legal advisor checks the law, realizes the error and reins the magistrate in. But had John been unrepresented – as many people in the magistrates are due to severe restrictions on legal aid – a guilty plea might well have been extorted from him. He could have gone to prison for something that was simply not a crime.

At the other extreme, an unrepresented defendant attends and pleads guilty to a motoring offence. The legal advisor looks at the form that the defendant has filled out and wrongly muses that he may in fact have a defence in law. It falls on me to point out that the defence he is thinking of was repealed by Parliament over a year ago.

Another trial later in the day involves an assault on a girl in a nightclub. At the start of the trial, the defence solicitor applies to adduce evidence of, and question the complainant about, a caution that she was given for theft years ago. The legal test for introducing 'bad character evidence' of a complainant is stringent: the court must be satisfied either that it is *important explanatory evidence*, without which the court would find it impossible or difficult to understand other evidence in the case; or the evidence must have *substantial probative value* in relation to a matter which is of *substantial importance* in the context of the case. In other words, the evidence has to be especially relevant and especially important. The rationale is obvious – witnesses should not be cross-examined about matters having nothing to do with the instant allegation where there is minimal or no relevance. As I tell the magistrates, an aged caution for shoplifting falls several miles short of either of these tests. Nevertheless, as the bench huddle together to deliberate, an audible failed *sotto voce* leaks: 'It sounds interesting.' Thus, the carefully crafted legal criteria are supplanted by human curiosity, and the poor girl spends half an hour being wrongly and unnecessarily humiliated under cross-examination by a bullish defence solicitor.

And today is not unusual. It reflects, I'm afraid, common experience of the magistrates' court. On another day, when I'm prosecuting a trial, one of the wingers on the bench interrupts three questions into my opponent's cross-examination. 'That,' he says sternly, 'was a leading question.' The defence solicitor and I look at each other, and then to the legal advisor, who very gently reminds the magistrate that cross-examination is, since time immemorial, a series of leading questions. On a separate occasion, a defendant who turns up five minutes late to his trial due to rail delays is, entirely unlawfully, refused entry to the courtroom, forced to sit outside as he is convicted in his absence.

Magistrates would say that they are entitled to better service from their legal advisors or the lawyers in court. They may further point out that such errors in law as do occur can, if they lead to wrongful convictions or acquittals, be appealed to the High Court, and that statistically very few cases are successfully appealed. But the latter point overlooks that a route of appeal is only meaningful if you are aware of it; many unrepresented defendants are not even aware of the errors, let alone the means of redress. Often, because of the way in which cases are rushed through – which we shall turn to shortly – errors are missed by the lawyers too.

And while it is no doubt right that legal advisors, solicitors and barristers will on occasion be responsible for magistrates wandering off the beaten legal path, often they receive the right advice, but fail to apply it. And I understand – law is complicated. But that is the point. Like science or medicine, a comprehensive grounding in law is not something that you can absorb on a crash course. Many magistrates are talented and brilliant people in their individual fields; a friend once told me in chambers that after he had sat bemoaning the ineptness of his mags while they were out deliberating, the legal advisor had taken him aside and told him that the chair of the bench was a neurosurgeon, admonishing, 'Bet you feel pretty silly now.' But that misses the point. No doubt that gentleman's next patient would find little comfort in looking up on the operating table to see me brandishing a scalpel and cooing, 'It's fine, I'm a barrister. But I've done a weekend residential in Troon and there's a junior doctor in the corner whose advice I *might* listen to.'

The comparison, although flippant, bears consideration. In what other area of public life do we allow amateurs to carry out the functions of qualified and regulated professionals? No one sensibly suggests that we keep education cheap by using volunteer teachers. We don't allow have-a-go anaesthetists working in PFI hospitals, the cost of which has been helpfully suppressed by contracting DIY architects and someone who read the 'Engineering' page on Wikipedia.

But when it comes to criminal justice, we are happy to subcontract laypeople to perform a strictly legal function. What is more, experience suggests that the filtering and training process places insufficient emphasis on broader, but equally vital, skills of logical and critical reasoning.

Officially, the criteria that the Local Advisory Committees – the body of magistrates responsible for recruiting magistrates – are supposed to apply are listed as 'good character; commitment and reliability; social awareness; sound judgement; understanding and communication; maturity and sound temperament'. But there is no critical reasoning test, as is now common in most professional or managerial job applications, and those who have been through the process have commented that there is a fixation on how much 'voluntary work in the community' you've done. A criminal solicitor colleague who applied was rejected on the grounds that, due to her eighty-hour professional workload, she had not done enough 'non-legal voluntary work' in her non-existent free time.

Inevitably, when you have a recruitment system which prizes whether you ran a tombola over your capacity for legal analysis and critical thinking, you will end up with a disproportionate number of successful candidates whose ability to make correct inferences, recognize assumptions, make deductions, come to conclusions and interpret and evaluate arguments is lacking, to say the least.

It's an accepted, trite fact of criminal practice – if you spend a day before a lay bench, you will come away with a sack full of logical fallacies, streams of consciousness and contortions of rationality with which to regale your colleagues in chambers that evening.

Which brings us back to Kyle, who is eventually bundled in to my court to be dealt with. He pleads guilty to a charge of being carried in a vehicle taken without consent, and after I briefly outline the facts to the bench, Kyle's solicitor stands to mitigate. The submissions are frank: Kyle wants to go to prison. He has tried his best on his existing community order, but has fallen short. He doesn't feel he has the discipline to cooperate with probation and do unpaid work. He's the broken product of a broken society for whom there is no hope. He invites the court to send him to a Young Offender Institution.

The screaming subtext to those in the know is that, to Kyle, sitting around listlessly with his mates in a YOI for a few weeks appears far less onerous than dragging himself out of bed and getting the bus to the Probation Office to meet his supervisor twice a week for the next six months. The immediate horror of first-time prison would disabuse him of this, but having never tasted custody before, Kyle is sure that it's a doddle.

The magistrates, though, seemingly cottoning on to Kyle's masterplan, are not so quick to dismiss Kyle's pessimism in his own capabilities. 'Listen here,' the chair of the bench addresses Kyle directly, 'we don't want to lock you up. You're a young lad with a bad past, but we've read a lot about you in your previous probation reports, and we think you've got prospects. You're bright. You're intuitive. If you put the same level of commitment into bettering yourself as you do relieving motor vehicles of their satnavs, you could make something of your life. So we're going to ask you – please Kyle, say you'll accept Probation's help, do the unpaid work and we'll let this community order continue.'

Kyle is unpersuaded. He responds in person. 'I can't do it.' Not just won't – can't. It's beyond him.

'Nonsense, young man. Your probation officer in this report says . . . in fact, can we get the officer to court?' A relay of messages to the court Probation Office confirms that Kyle's supervisor can get here within the hour. The case is stood down for us to crack on with another trial. An hour later, the probation officer is in the witness box, joining hands with the mags as they all vainly coax Kyle into agreeing to do the work. But to no avail.

The mags are not to be defeated. Thinking on their feet, they yank out the big guns. Is your mum with you at court today, Kyle? Of course she isn't. The parents of the Kyles of this world never are. But could she get here, if we stood the case down for another hour?

Two hours later, Kyle's mother arrives in her pyjama bottoms. She is swiftly commandeered by the bench for their cause, and joins the chorus of pleas to her recalcitrant son. You're a good boy at heart. Don't be like your dad and your brothers. Make something of yourself. Come on, Kyle, they evangelize. We believe in you. We believe. We. Believe.

At 6 p.m., some four hours after the hearing started, Kyle's resolve slips. A 'maybe' quickly tumbles into a 'yes', and, to general astonishment, this truculent bulldog of a youth appears to transform into the scared, weeping, bruised child that the bench had seen hiding deep inside. 'I do want help,' he sobs. 'I don't want to spend my life in and out of prison. You're right, mum. You're right, your majesty [the best distortion of a magistrate's honorific that I've ever heard]. I'll do it. I'll do the work.'

The bench smile at each other. They smile at Kyle. Kyle smiles at mum, who smiles at the probation officer, who smiles at the solicitor. Had I a dancing partner, I'd smile at them too. This is what summary justice is about. Rolling up sleeves, solving problems and improving lives. 'We have to formally "retire" to consider our decision,' the chair winks at Kyle with a grandfatherly twinkle, 'and we'll be back in a moment.'

I still do not know, all these years later, what happened in that retiring room. Nor do any of us in court, least of all the incredulous legal advisor who had to get the chair to repeat twice what he was saying. But they return stony-faced and send Kyle down for nine weeks.

This was a particularly incomprehensible decision with which few magistrates reading would agree, which is why Kyle's case has stuck with me through a myriad of the merely semi-bizarre. But a much bigger, recurring problem relates to the most basic fundament of the criminal trial – the burden and standard of proof. The prosecution must prove their case (burden of proof) beyond reasonable doubt (standard of proof). They must make the fact-finders sure of guilt. Juries are directed that anything less than sure means they must acquit. This is hammered home remorselessly in every criminal trial, by every advocate and every judge; in every speech, in every summing up. Its centrality and pervasiveness cannot be overemphasized. If you think the defendant might have done it, the defence barrister hams it up for the jury, he's not guilty. If you think he probably did it, he's not guilty. If you're almost sure he did it, he's not guilty. Only sure will suffice for a guilty verdict, ladies and gentlemen.

Magistrates, unlike juries, are required to give reasons for their verdicts. And these reasons are instructive in observing how the magistrates' cogs are whirring as they grapple with this straightforward, unassailable principle of British justice.

The standard formulation you hear intoned by the chair upon a guilty verdict, which for its ubiquity I can only assume is instilled at gunpoint during training, is the classic: 'We preferred the evidence of the prosecution witness[es] to the evidence of the defendant.'

This I have never liked, 'preferring' being to my mind some distance short of 'being sure of'. But its vagueness at least disguises the cognitive rot that might be lying beneath. Unlike this candid descent into tautology: 'We preferred the evidence of the complainant, because she is the complainant.'

Or this departure from orthodoxy, from a friend's trial: 'We weren't sure whether to believe the defendant or the complainant. We find the defendant guilty.'

And, my personal favourite, which I took home with me from the heart of rural Wales and will treasure forever: 'Well, we've had a think about it, and we reckon you probably did it. You did, didn't you? Go on. No? Well we think you did.'

*

The quality of magistrates' court justice cannot, however, be attributed solely to the figures on the bench. They are but three of many players on a stage without director, script or functioning sound and light, blindly dancing to an increasingly shrill imperative that they must process more cases, more quickly, with far fewer resources. Between 2010 and 2016, the politically unimportant Ministry of Justice was required to implement budget cuts of over one third, the hardest-cut department second only to the Department of Work and Pensions.[24] As it slashed court staff and closed magistrates' courts with gay abandon – reducing the number of magistrates' courts from 330 to around 150[25] – the only clear route through has been to stack cases even higher, and sell 'em even cheaper. Court listing officers cram trials into the list with apparent disregard for the immutability of time and space, and with what can be most charitably characterized as dazzling optimism as to the speed of the magistrates. Because every decision has to be taken collectively by the three magistrates, the most straightforward, which a judge would make on the spot – such as calculating a fine using the Sentencing Guidelines – is subject to the same protracted choreography; the mags listen politely to the counsel of their legal advisor, rise, shuffle out to their retiring room, enjoy a cuppa, summon the legal advisor to remind them of what they've already heard, discuss their decision, summon the legal advisor to remind them how to fill in the relevant form and shuffle back into court any time between ten minutes and two hours later to hand down their decree. In 2011, an MoJ-commissioned report found that District Judges get through cases an average of 43 per cent quicker than lay benches; in the field, the discrepancy often feels much greater.[26]

It is not uncommon for trial lists to therefore contain twice or even three times as much work as can physically be accomplished, leaving only three possible conclusions. Some trials will 'naturally' resolve, through late guilty pleas or prosecutions collapsing for want of evidence/witness problems. The bulk of the remainder will be hurried through at breakneck speed, often regardless of whether the parties are ready. And those that simply can't be accommodated before the security staff go home to bed (I've been at magistrates' courts until 9 p.m. waiting for verdicts) will be adjourned, the witnesses sent home and commanded to return some months into the future, when the lottery starts afresh. If a trial goes part-heard – if it is started but not completed in a single day – it will be adjourned to resume not on the next day, as happens with Crown Court trials, but on the next day convenient to the magistrates and the court. Rather than insist that their assumed public function requires mags, like juries, judges and lawyers, to work around their personal or professional commitments, a lengthy diarising process ensues in which the court identifies a suitable date to reconvene. This date can be weeks, if not months, into the future, by which time basic science tells us that memories of the evidence heard on that first day will have faded or been corrupted.

The overloading of court lists contributes to the way in which many summary trials are prosecuted, as evidenced by my day with Kyle and the dreaded 'prosecution list'. This staple of the baby barrister diet involves being instructed by the CPS as an agent to prosecute their magistrates' caseload (which is usually handled by in-house staff) when they are short on numbers, or where they spot an iceberg looming in a case and wish to affix a non-CPS face to the bow as the ship dips beneath the waves. For reasons I have never understood, and can only attribute to resourcing, the files are only delivered to the agent on the night before or the morning of the big day. Whether on paper (as when I first started) or emailed (as now), they are guaranteed to be incomplete, disordered and missing the latest vital information, such as the letter sent a month ago by the defence solicitors informing the CPS that the defendant will be changing his plea to guilty, or the last-minute case review from a CPS lawyer decreeing that the case should be terminated. Now, a couple of badly prepared trials, you have a hope of rescuing. But if listing have shoved seven of the little bastards in your courtroom, that is seven lots of incomplete, incomprehensible and disordered bundles of evidence (at anything up to 200 pages each) that you have to re-order, interpret and somehow prepare for trial.

And those seven will not be your lot; once at court, cases will be swapped between courtrooms without notice, and unplanned hearings – such as a youth who has been arrested that morning for breaching the terms of his bail, or the sentence hearing that the CPS advocate can't do because they work condensed hours and have to leave early – will be dropped on you throughout the day. The magistrates' court is the accident and emergency department of criminal justice: any moment, a problem will walk through the door and the prosecutor will have to deal with it blind. Much prosecuting in the magistrates' court takes the form of someone getting to their feet and presenting a case they have never set eyes on before. The Director of Public Prosecutions rejected this claim when it was put to her by the House of Commons Justice Select Committee, stating that it had not been her experience,[27] but I can promise you that it happens every single day.

And while in the Crown Court we barristers commonly boast about our ability to rapidly master the facts of a spontaneously apparating case, and pulling an all-nighter to prepare a late-returned trial is standard fare, the notion of preparing *seven* at the drop of a hat – interposed with half a dozen impromptu hearings like Kyle's – would confound even the more senior in our number. Yet for those baby juniors learning their trade in the lower courts, it's entirely unexceptional. And, it goes without saying, dangerous.

You've been punched outside your house when confronting an irksome street punk? Got a black eye and soreness? That's assault by beating and suitable for magistrates' trial. That's one of the seven cases which, if it's in my prosecution list, I'll receive at, if I'm lucky, a few hours' notice, and to which I might get to devote a whole fifteen minutes' reading, preparing and sorting for trial. How confident are you that I'll know the ins and outs of the proceedings that have dominated your personal and professional life for the last year? Are you happy that, in between my relay of phone calls to faceless, office-based CPS lawyers and police officers to track down the missing evidence in my other six trials, I'll have crafted the exquisite cross-examination required to shred the credibility of that lying defendant who alleges that you hit him first? Are you satisfied that, while I'm darting to and from the witness suite and the courtroom, juggling the questions and demands of the fifteen witnesses who have attended and chasing the half-dozen who haven't, I'll have ensured that all the witness statements volunteered by you, your family and your neighbours have found their way into my brief, and have not been misfiled or lost by the police? As I glance through my list of seven trials, and mentally note the headlines – a youth court trial for sexual assault involving child witnesses; a burglary where the defendant is in custody; an affray with three defendants that has already had two aborted trial dates; a careless driving trial with a heavily pregnant witness who has just announced that she has to leave at lunch to pick up her son from nursery – where do you think your case is going to rank in importance in my list? And where do you think it is going to rank in the corresponding defence solicitor's trial list of one? In my best Dirty Harry voice, I invite you to ask yourself one question.

And if the trial is not properly prepared, if key witnesses

haven't been warned to attend or vital evidence hasn't been properly obtained, don't think for one moment that the court is going to happily grant the opportunity to put it in order. The past few years have overseen a procession of well-meaning initiatives with comforting management-speak titles – 'Criminal Justice: Simply, Speedy, Summary'; 'Stop Delaying Justice'; 'Transforming Summary Justice'; 'Better Case Management' – aimed at streamlining summary justice. The emphasis, magistrates have been commanded from on high, is on reducing the number of unnecessary hearings and 'doing it right first time'. No more sluttishly adjourning trials simply because one of the sides bats their eyelashes at you. Firm and robust judicial case management at the first appearance, and cultivating a culture of individual responsibility for cases in which both sides adhere to the Criminal Procedure Rules, should mean that a legitimate request for an adjournment on the day of trial is a rare bird.

No issue can be taken with that ethos. But the predicted output is false; the reasons for cases requiring additional hearings and parties seeking adjournments will not and cannot all be judicially managed away. Much of the cause, on the prosecution side, is resource-led. Evidence is often not served and disclosure not made because the CPS is hideously under-staffed after shedding a third of its staff.[28] Witnesses sometimes don't turn up for trial because the Witness Care Unit has given them the wrong date, or because they notified the CPS months ago that they would be out of the country on the week of the trial. Or, most frequently, because of the inherent chaos and complexity of the lives of most of the damaged protagonists and antagonists in criminal cases: the twisted dynamics exerted in violent relationships that make securing the attendance of the victim a messy, difficult task; the defendant's exhausted benefits meaning he can't afford the bus to court – essentially the near-impossibility of imposing order on the fucked up, timeless existences of society's most disordered. These are complexities that you don't solve by drilling magistrates to simply refuse adjournments.

For me as a baby prosecutor, the most difficult cases in this regard were always allegations of domestic violence. You'd open up the file to read a history of a battered, vulnerable woman making weekly 999 calls, none of which made it as far as a formal complaint until now. Having summoned the courage to provide a witness statement to the police, her nerve would then falter on the day of trial and, at the suspected behest of her brutish beloved, she would disappear underground. Domestic abusers know this routine; they bank on it by holding on to a not guilty plea until trial. If she shows up, they'll throw their hand in and admit guilt; if not, they'll rely on the court losing patience with the prosecution and kicking the case out. Sometimes I'd find that magistrates would permit the prosecution a chance to track the complainant down, but many times that single failure would signal game over. The 'no adjournments' ethos was stretched to absurd cruelty in a case in late 2017, in which a District Judge hearing a sexual assault trial was informed that five members of the complainant's family had been killed overnight in an accident and the complainant was, unsurprisingly, unable to attend court. The prosecution application to adjourn was refused.[29]

And it by no means only affects the prosecution; defendants often suffer worse. I have lost count of the times that material that we had been demanding from the prosecution for months was insolently dropped on me on the morning of trial: giant, four-inch-thick chunks of potentially crucial medical records or mobile phone data. I'd beg the magistrates for an adjournment so that I could properly take instructions from my client on this late disclosure, entirely the fault of the prosecution. Invariably the response was an offer of 'fifteen minutes, and then we're starting the trial'.

Once I was drafted in to defend a man of good character accused of harassing an alleged love rival after the solicitor defending collapsed minutes before the trial was due to start. Faced with a thick bundle of evidence I had never read, and a non-English speaking client I had never met, I applied in these exceptional circumstances to adjourn the trial to another date. 'You have fifteen minutes,' the chair tutted, as if the defendant was somehow to blame for his solicitor's incapacitation. Fortunately, after three long days of evidence, the man was acquitted, but others are not so lucky.

The bottom line is that there may well be fewer, quicker hearings. There may well be fewer adjourned trials. But to my mind, what is happening in these courts is not justice. It is not, as the Criminal Procedure Rules proudly proclaim to be their 'overriding objective', acquitting the innocent and convicting the guilty. It's getting numbers through the door and out again, as inexpensively and swiftly as possible. It's roulette framed as justice, where if the case does go the right way, its debt is to fate; occurring not because of the build of the system but in spite of it. And it is in these conditions that 94 per cent of our criminal justice is taking place.

Troublingly, far from asking whether it is right, in a modern, twenty-first-century democracy, to invest the unrivalled power to determine law, facts and sentence in unqualified, unrepresentative volunteers – to make lay magistrates judge, jury and executioner – and to embed a bargain basement retail model of summary justice, the establishment is planning a future where magistrates play an even greater role.

The mission creep is being achieved in three ways. Firstly, more either-way cases are being blocked from being tried in the Crown Court. Magistrates are now encouraged by official allocation guidelines to keep hold of more either-way offences, by deeming as suitable for summary trial serious cases that they previously would have sent to the Crown Court.[30] The second arm of the pincer, if Sir Brian Leveson's 2015 *Review of Efficiency in Criminal Proceedings* is implemented in full, will be that defendants lose the historic right to elect jury trial; the decision as to trial venue will be solely the court's. To cope with the increase in the volume of serious cases that would now be kept in the magistrates' courts, the bottom end of summary justice – criminal offences including rail fare evasion, motoring offences and fly-tipping – is being squeezed out of the courtroom and onto the internet. Defendants will log in to an automated system, view the evidence against them and click to plead guilty and generate their 'sentence'.[31] Justice, and a criminal conviction, will be served not just behind closed courtroom doors but behind closed bedroom doors, without any public scrutiny or independent judicial oversight at all. The 'Single Justice Procedure', whereby magistrates can now sit alone in private to deal with minor uncontested matters, is a new development with strong echoes of the eighteenth-century Petty Sessions convened in JPs' living rooms.

Secondly, and complementarily, magistrates' powers of sentence will be doubled to twelve months' imprisonment for a single offence. This change has been lying dormant on the statute book for fifteen years,[32] just waiting for an obliging government to accede to magistrates' pleas to bring it into force. When it does, an avalanche of either-way cases will suddenly be capable of being tried by magistrates, who will duly exercise their powers to send more people to prison for longer.

Thirdly, the right to appeal the decisions of magistrates is under threat. Presently, in all magistrates' cases there is an automatic right of appeal to the Crown Court, where a defendant's trial and/or sentence will be heard anew by a Crown Court judge sitting with two magistrates. Where the ground of appeal is solely a question of law, such as whether evidence was correctly admitted or whether a legal test was correctly interpreted, there is also an alternative route of appeal to the High Court, but this is only meaningful if you understand the law, or have access to someone who does. Many defendants in the magistrates' courts do not qualify for legal representation, and the automatic right to a re-hearing at the Crown Court is vital for those defendants, who may not appreciate that they have a legally nuanced ground of appeal. In the Crown Court, I have prosecuted many appeals from the magistrates' court against unrepresented defendants, and have lost count of the number of cases where there has been a conviction that is completely wrong in law, or completely wrong on the evidence, the fact of which only emerges upon close inspection of the papers. The automatic right of appeal to a professional Crown Court judge is the last bulwark against the anarchy of the a-professional lower courts. But the *Leveson Review* would have it removed.

The net result of these reforms should terrify: an enormous influx of serious criminal cases subjected to the second-class treatment of the magistrates' courts, hammered through the sausage factory of summary justice by our jolly, willing amateurs, and with enormous restrictions on the right to appeal. House burglaries, assaults causing grievous bodily harm, semi-complex frauds and sexual assaults presently deemed too serious to be dealt with summarily will routinely be the stuff of magistrates' lists. Prosecutions warehoused and unprocessed until tardily dumped on agent prosecutors the night before trial; defendants – innocent men and women – wrongly convicted due to failures to review cases or complete statutory disclosure. For the latter, no guarantee of a re-hearing. And, for the vast majority of all concerned, no hope of a qualified judge overseeing the case to spot the errors and put things right.

Magistrates, and the quality of justice that their courts engender, are very much The Future. This hangover of thirteenth-century parochial peace-keeping, far from being gently put out to pasture, is re-engineered as our turbo-charged, armoured vehicle of justice for the new millennium. And, try as I might, I cannot accept that the arguments in favour withstand the slightest scrutiny. Why is our focus in summary proceedings not on the quality of justice or the fairness of the trial procedure, but trained remorselessly on turnover of cases? Why is ours the only legal system in the world that empowers volunteers to send their fellow citizens to prison? Why do we not only accept but *prize* the resolution of pure matters of law by non-lawyers? I accept that in straitened times – even in good times – we probably can't afford to universally apply the Crown Court model of a legally qualified judge directing a lay jury; but the next best thing surely isn't to have a self-selecting, homogeneous lay jury one quarter of the size and give them the judge's function of deciding complex arguments of law. Rather, should we not just concede the facade of lay participation and wholly professionalize summary justice, either by hiring District Judges for all cases, or, alternatively, enlisting trained, professional lay assessors, selected for their tested and proven skills of critical analysis and logical reasoning rather than their public spirit?

The answer, I fear, is because 800 years ago the state wanted low-level trouble and strife dealt with quickly and cheaply. It mattered not at that time, when individual rights and the presumption of innocence were half a millennium away from public consciousness, whether justice was being administered fairly, so long as it was being administered. In the twenty-first century, when no government worth its political salt will voluntarily pledge expenditure on something as headline-unworthy as the lowest criminal courts, the same attitude persists. It's just the underclasses who are affected. Except, of course, it isn't. It's anyone who is accused of a criminal offence. Anyone who witnesses an offence. Anyone who is a victim. And anyone who values liberty.

On liberty, it would be easy to assume that such weighty determinations only kick in after the formalities of a trial and a guilty verdict; but that would be mistaken. Whether your criminal case remains with the magistrates or is destined for the comparative luxury of the Crown Court, the issue of bail – of your immediate freedom – will often be addressed at that very first appearance before the magistrates, in those same conditions of maniacal disorder.

Let's look at how we deal with the decision of whether you spend the months awaiting trial in your own bed, or bunking up with a new friend in one of Her Majesty's festering prisons. Let's take a quick peek at applications for bail.

3. Imprisoning the Innocent: Remand and Bail

'Those on remand . . . are not inside for long enough for [work and education] programmes to make a difference – but they are there long enough to lose their jobs, their family relationships, and even their homes. This can push someone off the straight and narrow for good.'

Home Secretary David Blunkett,
Observer, 3 February 2002[1]

The first question fired at you as you enter the yellow-stained cells in the bowels of the magistrates' court to meet a seasoned client for his first appearance is invariably the same: am I getting bail? That this is often the opening gambit ahead of any protestation of innocence is an indicator of the premium placed upon this decision by veteran defendants. And for good reason. Whether you spend the 182 nights preceding your trial in the comfort of your own bed, or count them locked in a bottom bunk with your head next to an open steel toilet blocked with the shit of the top bunk's incumbent is a meaningful dichotomy no matter how many times you've suffered a remand in custody before.

Of course, not all defendants are produced via the cells for their first appearance. Most arrive under their own steam, having been charged and bailed at the police station or summonsed by post to attend, and will in all likelihood leave through the same door at the end of the morning, bail notice in paw commanding their voluntary surrender at the next hearing. But, as a general rule, if the police thought the allegations serious enough to detain you at the station overnight pending your first court appearance, they, and the Crown Prosecution Service, are probably going to be asking the magistrates that you be escorted from court in handcuffs to await your fate at one of Her Majesty's less opulent guesthouses.

The decision on whether to grant bail will initially be taken by magistrates at the end of the first appearance, which will usually be held within a few weeks of being charged, unless the police remand you in custody post-charge in which case your first appearance will take place the following day. Often the prosecution will assent to bail, either unconditionally or on agreed conditions, and the court is merely rubber-stamping. If bail is opposed, the prosecutor stands up and regales the bench with their grave misgivings over bailing this dangerous flight risk of a man with an appalling record and evidence against him strong enough to suplex a blue whale. And the defence solicitor or barrister then humbly submits that the prosecution's concerns are entirely ill-founded, or, alternatively, can be assuaged by the imposition of 'stringent bail conditions' (a stock legal phrase – bail conditions are *always* stringent, in the same way that any lawyer in the news is always a 'top lawyer').

The magistrates then huddle together to discuss in stage whispers to what extent the accused – who, we must remember, is at this stage innocent – should have his liberty infringed. Will he be one of the 70,000-odd people remanded in custody each year, at an estimated cost of £429 million?[2] Or will he be bailed with a curfew, electronically tagged and monitored, on the condition that he report thrice-weekly to his local nick, in order that his good behaviour and continued presence in the jurisdiction be maintained? If he's unhappy with the magistrates' decision, he can appeal to a Crown Court judge,[3] but if the Crown Court judge says nay, then barring a significant change in circumstances he's staying in prison until trial. This period can be up to seventy days if a magistrates' trial[4] or 182 days – six months – if a Crown Court trial, and can be extended further in certain circumstances.

The concept of bail stretches back to the Middle Ages, the word being derived from the old French for 'custody' or 'jurisdiction', and the verb *bailler* – to take charge of. The presumption in law today is that a defendant will be bailed. Our venerated tradition of *habeas corpus* – Latin for 'you may have the body' – ensures, through permitting individuals to challenge in court the legality of their detention by the state, that liberty is only deprived in accordance with the law. Notwithstanding the efforts of various monarchic rogues to insist that the say-so of the king was sufficient cause for detaining those falling out of his favour, Parliament acted to prohibit, through a succession of landmark legislation – notably the Habeas Corpus Acts of 1640 and 1679, and the Bill of Rights 1689 – the arbitrary detention of people accused of crimes. Although not reasoned as such at the time (the presumption of innocence being an articulation of the late eighteenth century), this principle dovetails neatly with our modern golden rule that the accused is innocent until guilt is proven. Innocent people should only be locked away where it is justified – which put loosely is where a court finds substantial grounds for believing they will fail to attend court, re-offend or interfere with prosecution witnesses. The importance of bail decisions is easy to underestimate in the abstract; in the flesh and blood of criminal cases, its significance can become horribly tangible.

One of the very first defendants I met when training as a pupil was Rio. I was in my second week of my 'first six', the first half of pupillage in which you obediently follow your pupil supervisor like a duckling, greedily absorbing knowledge and experience from their daily court grind. Alan, my pupilmaster (as he, a weathered refusenik to anything that might be perceived as political correctness, insisted on being called), had a conference at the local prison with a new client. 'Conference' is the industry term for a meeting. By referring to it as a conference (or 'con' for short), we succeed in our twin aims of linguistically alienating outsiders and making what we do sound more impressive than it actually is. It was thus that, in the blustery October twilight following a fruitless day at court waiting in vain for Alan's trial to be called on, I had the pleasure of meeting Rio.

Rio was charged with multiple counts of rape, alleged to have been committed against his long-term partner, Lori, over a period of several years. She had fled their dysfunctional, alcohol-sustained relationship with their infant son the previous spring, and, upon finding refuge at a friend's home, had recounted in lurid detail the variety of physical and sexual abuse she had suffered at Rio's hands. Following charge, Rio had been refused bail, both by the magistrates and, upon appeal, by a Crown Court judge, and this, along with a series of other perceived slights, lay behind his decision to dispense with his previously instructed counsel and direct his solicitor to 'find me some other cunt'. Alan, with me as his willing lackey, was that cunt.

Perhaps surprisingly to the uninitiated, Rio would not have known exactly what happened at his Crown Court bail application. He would have been present at the magistrates' court, watching forlornly from the dock as the magistrates, having sent his case to the Crown Court, took all of ten seconds to consider his solicitor's submissions and refuse bail, but a bail appeal to the Crown Court usually takes place in private, without the defendant. As a barrister, this represents most of my involvement with bail applications.

Occasionally, if there's an important client with a juicy-looking Crown Court case who's up for his first appearance, the solicitors will ask that the barrister go along to the mags to make a good impression, but mostly I am prosecuting or defending applications before a Crown Court Circuit Judge, in his or her chambers. 'Chambers', in the judicial context, refers to a judge's private room where he robes and reads his papers. At one time the bail application would actually take place in those quarters, but nowadays the court clerk simply announces, 'Court as chambers,' which means the court is cleared of everyone save the advocates and the judge, who then all take off our wigs and pretend that we're not in court at all. If there were a less strange way to explain this, I promise I'd do so.

The absence of the defendant from his own hearing has a strange effect. On the one hand, it makes your job a little easier when defending. Unlike in the magistrates' court, where you may be trying to persuade an unimpressed bench of your client's bailability, punctuated by helpful yelps from the dock ('Tell 'em I'll go on tag. I'll do fucking anything!'), no such distractions prevail here. The judge is forced to imagine how unappealing your client is, rather than have the proof of the pudding shouting racial epithets from the back of court.

But it also means that the defendant is shielded from the reality of the cursory treatment that his bail application may receive. An observer might suppose that bail apps carry the lowest consequence in the court list: up to half a dozen hearings are squeezed into the top of the daily list, to be rattled through in succession at 10 a.m. before the court starts its proper, meaningful business. Although they can take hours to prepare, the hearings are usually short, sometimes no more than a few minutes a pop – often rightly so, because of the straightforwardness of the argument, occasionally less rightly, because of a trigger-happy judge shooting from the hip or an advocate implicitly (or explicitly) conceding his client's cause. The fees are low (£46.50 plus VAT if you're prosecuting, slightly more if defending), meaning that the barristers involved will need to take on several bail apps – or other types of case – if they're going to turn a profit that day, diluting further the significance of a given application.

And this all contributes to a feeling of remoteness, of insubstantiality, which, I sometimes think, can make it easy to forget the importance of what we're dealing with. I am guilty of it. I know from experience that others are. Often, particularly when prosecuting, you will be instructed to appear on the bail application alone, and will never see the case again. The defendant is just a transient name, never to be matched to a face. Our submissions, our pleas on his behalf or against his right to liberty, are delivered in the formulaic legal standard – 'grave concerns' tutted by the prosecutor, 'stringent bail conditions' proffered by the defence – from the comfort of an oak-panelled courtroom many miles from the crumbling Victorian prison in which the subject being discussed is bricked up, waiting desperately for the screws to tell him when the fateful fax from the Crown Court has landed. His destiny is determined by the application of abstract concepts in an academic analysis of 'competing interests', by strangers cloaked in black, noses in their weighty textbooks or against the screens of their iPads.

It's easy to understand how alienation and frustration can set in. It had for Rio. He had been remanded for nearly five months by the time Alan and I pulled through the prison gates in Alan's 'vintage' Vauxhall Vectra, and he would serve another month or so until trial. The grounds for the court refusing bail appeared, to my barely trained eye, reasonable enough. Rio's previous record made for concerning reading. Domestic violence was his stock in trade. He had not only been convicted of assaulting two previous partners, but had in each case gone on to breach the restraining order that the court had imposed. In unrelated criminal proceedings, he had failed to surrender to bail on three occasions. Having regard to this background, and the double-figure prison sentence that Rio was looking at if convicted of the rapes, the court had little trouble in finding substantial grounds for believing that if bailed Rio would either interfere with witnesses – by tracking down and exerting his toxic influence upon Lori – or fail to surrender to court for his trial.

As for the recent allegations, they were all lies, I had learned from Rio's written instructions in Alan's brief. He never forced Lori into sex. He wouldn't. He didn't need to; he got all the action he wanted, from all manner of local lovers. (Upon meeting Rio, his missing teeth and impressive, two-seat encompassing girth cast this strand of his instructions into dubious relief, but I suppose the heart wants what it wants.) In fact, it was one of these lovers, and specifically her presence in Rio's bed when Lori returned home early, that lay behind the outpouring of false allegations from the conniving, scorned complainant, well aware that Rio's disreputable history would bolster the credibility of her false allegations.

As we were escorted across the various levels of prison security – passports scrutinized, fingerprints recorded, outer clothing removed and bodies frisked – and trudged through a succession of giant, steel-wrapped locked doors, leading ultimately to the meeting cubicle, I prepared myself to hear Rio repeat these denials ad nauseum and in detail. After all, I thought, that's what I would do in his shoes when meeting my new barrister.

But that wasn't what Rio wanted to talk about. Instead, he wanted to use his permitted forty-five minutes to talk – and at times shout and scream and bang emphatically on the screwed-down table – about his life outside. And of the unjustness of being sequestered away from it for something he hadn't done 'this time'. He wanted to tell Alan about his new girlfriend, Jade, who, aside from the three-month over-lap with his relationship with Lori, had pointed him towards the straight and narrow. Because of her strict edicts about drugs around her three kids, Rio had packed in the Colom-bian marching powder, and cut back significantly on his drinking, and had unsurprisingly found that the familiar sudden urge to violence at the slightest provocation was dimming. Plus, he hadn't grafted (stolen) the whole time he'd been with her. Most importantly, she had stood by him through the allegations, through the lies, because she knew that, whatever his faults, he would not do the things that Lori claimed. She believed in him.

And he was worried because, although Jade had visited him every week for the first three months, the visits had lately become irregular. When she did come, she appeared distant. And he had become paranoid, and she resistant at his suspicious questioning, and round and round they span. And he was terrified that she was losing interest; losing faith. And he missed her. And he missed his three-year-old son, who he hadn't seen for months, 'cos he was in the care of that lying bitch Lori – 'Christ knows what she is telling him about me; about where I am, what I've done.' He wanted to talk about his job, running deliveries for a mate's building supplies company. It wasn't much, but it was work. Work that he hadn't been able to do for most of the year. Work that had probably now gone to somebody else.

And as Rio vented, and as Alan, and the solicitor, Denise, listened, nodded, ummed and awwed in the right places, it struck me – and still strikes today, as an uncomfortable, wel-come reminder whenever I picture Rio and his earnest, angry indignation – just how inestimable the impact of losing your liberty on remand can be. Everything you have built over the course of a lifetime – your relationships, your family, your employment, your income, your home – is suddenly, without notice, snatched away from you and placed on a high shelf beyond your reach. There's usually no time to get your affairs in order. If you have been on bail before conviction, you will at least have been able to plan for your impending incarceration. Detention in remand effectively starts the moment you are arrested, when the police turn up unexpectedly one idle Tuesday afternoon while you're midway through hanging up the washing, or as you arrive home from a double shift. From that moment, your freedom is the property of the state. You can be detained at the police station overnight, taken to court from the police cells and then formally remanded until trial. It could be months, if not years, before you are returned to normality.

And every day that passes is another day that your life is continuing without you in it. Your partner going about their business. Your job still needing to be done. Your children hitting their developmental milestones. Rent accumulating and bills piling up, and the consequences of their neglect – dismissal, eviction, repossession, disconnection – awaiting you upon your release, or, more painfully, exacted upon your loved ones as you watch their suffering helplessly through the prison bars.

For the guilty, it is easy to dismiss this as the unpleasant, but not undeserved, consequence of committing a criminal offence. And, if you are convicted, any time spent remanded in custody will automatically count as time served on your ultimate sentence,[5] so you haven't lost anything. In fact, in such cases, you may have gained, as the privileges regime in prison is more favourable for remand prisoners than for the convicted, so you will have spent part of your sentence in more hospitable surroundings than had you been bailed and then required to serve your full sentence as a serving prisoner.

But for the not guilty, for the innocent forcibly removed from their homes and families and locked in a fetid cell for twenty-three hours a day for months, if not years, of their lives, there is nothing. No compensation. No assistance in piecing together, or even sweeping up, the fragments of your shattered existence. Not even an apology. The jury return with their not guilty verdict, your barrister asks the judge to discharge you from the dock and you are released into the big wide world without so much as a 'sorry about that, old bean'. You can't even, as some enterprising defendant argued before the Court of Appeal, ask a court to order that those wasted months count towards a prison sentence for a future offence.[6] Those six months of hell, and the consequent, irreparable destruction wrought on the lives of you and your beloved, are written off as the price we – you – pay as a citizen living in our justice system. If the procedure that led to your remand was correctly followed, then your substantive innocence is immaterial.

This is the position in which roughly one in seven remanded defendants – over 67,000 people in 2016 – find themselves.[7] Nearly 15 per cent of remand prisoners are acquitted or not proceeded against. And, among this number, as it happened, was Rio. He was acquitted. The jury did not accept Lori's claims, and Rio was found not guilty on every count. The time spent on remand was something he was just expected to accept, forgive and forget.

To me, this cannot be right. It can't be fair, on the most fundamental level, that the state can sweep in, turn your life upside down and waltz out again, like a remorseless, localized tornado, without so much as an apology. Not even a recognition, *post facto*, in depersonalized bureaucrat-speak that The State Regrets That You Were Imprisoned. I think of this when I meet those clients, like Rio, who are court regulars, livid at the world, spilling over with molten hate for the police, for the courts, for civil society. Their collected grievances and protestations of injustice are not always simply bywords for reflexive frustration at being caught, or a rootless, ingrained Fuck You, I Won't Do What You Tell Me. Part of their rage against the machine will be the – I think justified – sense of persecution inculcated by the regular, uncompensated loss of time, of liberty, in police cells, or on remand, for things they didn't actually do. And for many it's an increasingly vicious circle, because once you've had bail refused the first time, it's likely to be refused the next occasion you are accused. And the next.

The same argument pertains to the many more innocents subject to conditional bail prior to acquittal, whose liberty is curtailed by other means, such as a restrictive curfew preventing them from leaving the house every evening, or visiting friends or family at long distance, or going on holiday. Or those who are excluded from entering parts of their home town. Or who suffer the social embarrassment and physical discomfort of having a chunky electronic monitoring tag on their ankle visibly branding them a person of suspicion. No apology follows the not guilty verdict. No compensation. Just be grateful you weren't convicted, and be on your way, ma'am.

And if the state is unwilling to contemplate the notion of apology or compensation, arrogant in the assumption that those hit hardest are those for whom public sympathy will never register on opinion polls, it should at the very least ensure that the procedure by which bail decisions should be made is properly respected. I think we must accept that a properly working system will still inevitably result in the remand of some people who will be acquitted, but our focus should be on maximizing, as best we can, the quality of bail decisions, to minimize the risk of incarcerating the innocent who pose no significant risk, and directing limited prosecutorial, prison and police resources towards restricting the liberty of those defendants who are genuinely likely to upset the course of justice by abusing bail.

And yet, despite there being, for all concerned, an obvious imperative in ensuring that determinations of bail are treated with rigour and care, the courtroom reality reveals something markedly, shockingly different.

Before looking at the theory, the first imported misapprehension to dispel is that bail rarely has anything to do with money. We are not, contrary to what a client of mine ostentatiously whipping out his chequebook in court once assumed, concerned with a question of 'posting bail' American-style by handing over large wads of cash. In the Middle Ages that was very much the done thing, and much parliamentary effort was expended on stopping judges maliciously detaining suspects by deliberately setting the bail bond at an unaffordable level (a practice ultimately outlawed in the Bill of Rights).[8] Today, while the court still has the power to order as a condition of bail that a forfeitable security (money paid into court by a defendant) or surety (money paid into court by a third party) be paid, financial means are rarely determinative of a grant of bail.

Instead, the legal starting point is that every accused person has a general right to bail.[9] From there, the legislation lays down the process by which the court may disapply the presumption. For one, the right to bail doesn't apply if you're charged with murder, or are a convicted manslaughterer or rapist accused of a further, similar offence. In those cases, the law considers you something of a potential menace, and the onus is on you to persuade the court that you should, exceptionally, be granted bail.

For the remaining dishes on the criminal offence buffet, the right to bail is engaged unless certain exceptions apply. And it is argument over the applicability of these exemptions that forms the subject of most contested bail applications. The exact test varies depending on whether the alleged offence is indictable (triable at the Crown Court) or summary (only triable at the magistrates' court), but as an overview, if you are charged with an imprisonable offence and meet any of the following criteria, the court is generally entitled to withhold bail:

(a) Where there are substantial grounds for believing that the defendant, if bailed, would:
   — Fail to surrender to custody
   — Commit an offence while on bail
   — Interfere with witnesses or otherwise obstruct the course of justice
   — Cause injury or fear of injury to an 'associated person' (usually a partner in a domestic violence case)
(b) Where the defendant was already on bail at the date of (allegedly) committing the offence
(c) Where the defendant has already been granted bail in these proceedings and has failed to surrender or has breached his bail conditions
(d) Where the court is satisfied that the defendant should be kept in custody for his own protection
(e) Where the defendant is already a serving prisoner
(f) Where there has been insufficient time to obtain the information needed to make a decision on bail

When making an assessment under (a) above, the court can have regard (non-exhaustively) to the following:

— The nature and seriousness of the alleged offence (in Rio's case, plainly very serious)
— The likely sentence (for Rio, a prison sentence well into double figures)
— Character, including previous convictions and community ties (Rio was no stranger to the courts)
— The strength of the evidence (on its face, a credible account provided by Lori)
— The defendant's previous record of being granted bail

(Rio had failed to surrender when granted bail on
several previous occasions)
— The risk that the defendant will engage in conduct
likely to cause injury (the prosecution submitted that
Rio may seek to intimidate Lori into retracting her
complaint)

Finally, if we are still pre-trial and there is 'no real prospect' of a custodial sentence upon conviction – i.e. if the offence is really not that serious – then (a), (b) and (c) do not apply.

If, as mentioned previously, the magistrates' court refuses bail and an appeal is made to the Crown Court, the exact same framework applies again from scratch.

I set out the law in some detail to overwork the following point: the withholding of bail is a deliberately involved process. The use of remand is tightly regulated, and there is a statutory duty[10] upon the court to fully record the reasons why bail is refused, and why the various bail conditions provided for in the legislation – such as an electronically monitored curfew; 'signing on' at a police station X times a week; non-contact with prosecution witnesses; surrendering passports; paying a surety or security – can't allay the court's concerns. This deference to liberty is reflected in the careful drafting of the Bail Act, the associated Criminal Procedure Rules, centuries of High Court judgments, European Union law and the jurisprudence of the European Court of Human Rights.

It's a shame it's not reflected in practice.

The problems start in the magistrates' court at the first appearance. In keeping with the established theme of this venue, applications are made and decisions taken at speed on the basis of incomplete, and sometimes wholly inaccurate, information.

Despite the fact that the police will have obtained enough evidence to support a charge – i.e. sufficient evidence to establish 'a realistic prospect of conviction' – this available evidence will rarely be given to the defence at the first appearance. The rules instead require only that the prosecution supply the defence with a summary of the facts of the alleged offence, and a copy of the defendant's previous convictions.[11] This summary, known as an MG5, is prepared by the police. The first thing you are taught as a pupil is not to believe what the MG5 says. Because while it is *generally* accurate, quite often it is not. This is not through malice; rather it is usually an inevitable knock-on of the pressures of time and resources under which under-staffed police forces operate. Nevertheless, a close reading of the witness statements upon which the MG5 is based will often reveal a different composition from that painted by the police. Those witness statements, however, are rarely available at the first appearance.

A 2016 research report into pre-trial detention also found that lists of previous convictions provided were out of date, and in some cases the defence were not even given a charge sheet setting out exactly what offence the defendant faced. The defence solicitor discussing the case meaningfully with the prosecutor was often not an option due to the workload – up to thirty-five cases in a court day – placing 'a premium on speed rather than thoroughness, both in terms of preparation and court time'.[12]

So the Bail Act specifically requires the court to consider the strength of the prosecution evidence when assessing whether the prosecution's objections to bail are justified. But if the court has not seen the evidence, and is instead reliant solely on a police summary of dubious accuracy, it is impossible for this properly to be done. What happens instead, one finds, is that the magistrates' inherent pro-prosecution disposition kicks in, and they not only accept the accuracy of what the prosecution assert, but, particularly in cases involving serious allegations, turn the presumption in favour of bail on its head, and require the defence to convince the court why the defendant *should* have bail. Terrified, it seems, of being the ones to release a dangerous lunatic onto the streets, the very mention of a charge involving serious violence, drugs or sex is usually enough for the mags to render the law redundant. In the 2016 study, even a former prosecutor ruefully opined on the pro-prosecution attitudes that prevail at bail applications.[13]

It is perhaps unsurprising therefore that magistrates often fail to comply with their duty to give proper reasons for refusing bail. More times than my breaking heart can sustain have I heard the phrase, 'We refuse bail because this is a serious offence,' or 'We think there is a strong case against you,' both of which may be true, but neither of which suffices as a reason for withholding bail. The findings of the report conclude that, in failing to give adequate reasons for their decisions, magistrates 'routinely breached' the standards of the European Convention on Human Rights.[14]

Against this backdrop, if the case involves a serious allegation and is being sent to the Crown Court, some defence solicitors don't even bother making representations in the mags, saving their breath for an application to a Crown Court judge in chambers, by which time further, meaningful material may have emerged from the prosecution file.

I use 'may' with caution. In the Crown Court, while judges are usually, and quite properly, much more demanding of the prosecution, the problems with getting hold of prosecutorial information persist. When I am instructed to prosecute a Crown Court bail application and receive the brief (nowadays electronic, in the olden days you'd pick up the file at court), it is pot luck whether there is anything included beyond the defence's written application. And even that isn't guaranteed.

Because applications are made early on in proceedings, for obvious reasons – everyone wants bail as soon as possible – the evidence available is often little more than what the parties had at the magistrates' court, and submissions are still often largely premised on the assumed veracity of the MG5. If it later emerges that the evidence paints a different picture, you might, if lucky, be able to persuade a judge that there has been a 'change of circumstances' that permits you to make a renewed bail application, but that is entirely in the lap of the judge.

However, the most tired refrain, in both courts, laments the inexplicable blockages in the channels of communication between the CPS and the police. Bail applications in the Crown Court are usually made at twenty-four hours' notice, one of the purposes being to allow the police and CPS an opportunity to verify assertions made in the written bail application, such as proposed bail addresses. Often, a defendant cannot be bailed to his home address, as he shares it with the girlfriend who's saying that he beat her, or it's a hop, skip and jump from the pub he allegedly torched, and so the application will offer up a suitable bail address many miles away where he can patiently await trial in the law-abiding fashion to which he is accustomed.

The police will probe the availability and suitability of the proposed address with a good old-fashioned knock on. The bobbies go round, speak to the owner, check it's not a crack den crammed with malleable prosecution witnesses, and come back to the CPS with an aye or nay.

It is obviously vital that this be done, even if the police think there's no way on earth that the defendant is getting out on bail, because, if the judge grants bail in principle, the court will rightly expect the prosecution to immediately voice any objections to the proposed conditions and bail address. The court is mightily disappointed by the prosecutor standing there bleating, 'Your Honour, I am afraid I don't have that information available.'

But disappointed the court often is. An enormous proportion of bail applications that I prosecute start and end with me standing wordlessly, mouth agape like some nattily dressed pilchard as the judge intones the five words that comprise the bulk of every prosecutor's auditory diet – Why Hasn't This Been Done? The answer is rarely available, and even more rarely satisfactory. Sometimes the CPS don't notify the police of the bail application. Sometimes the police don't notify the CPS of the outcome of their enquiries. Sometimes they try to, but the computer system is down, or the fax is broken. Sometimes the police don't have the resources to carry out an address check at twenty-four hours' notice. Sometimes the occupant will have been out at work when the police called, and the officers haven't had the time to go back.

And while judges typically allow one, sometimes even two short adjournments for these checks to be completed, they will eventually lose patience with prosecutorial blunders, and one of two things will happen. The more pro-prosecution judges will find a way to blame the defence, and bail will be refused through no fault at all of the defendant. Or the more exasperated judges will simply grant bail on the defence's terms.

Which can be problematic. Because while most solicitors wouldn't dream of misleading the courts, some of their clients make a tidy living from it. A bail application putting up the defendant's old mum as a willing innkeeper does so on the defendant's instructions. If mum is unwilling to open the door to her errant, estranged offspring, or if she died five years ago and the address is now a Chicken Cottage, you have a defendant at large, who may be none too easy to locate.

A few years back, I prosecuted some bail applications

brought by a roaming group of youthful Albanians. They had been apprehended by a train guard for not having tickets, when he noticed that all of their tracksuit bottoms were taped around the ankles and bulging alarmingly. The explanation became plain when the police arrived, and recovered sixty phones, belonging to sixty dozing train passengers, from within the boys' trousers. A contemporary Fagin's gang, although the profit margins on sixty iPhones is obviously in wild excess of the Artful Dodger's most improbable fantasies.

Being, the youths claimed, ordinarily resident at the other end of the country, they wished to offer a bail address in that far-away city. The address hadn't been checked by the time the application first came before the Crown Court. Nor the second time. In the face of this unexplained prosecution slovenliness, the exasperated judge was urged by the defence to grant bail to the proposed address. The judge ummed and aahhed and appeared set to accede, before looking pitifully at my pathetic, plaintive face and grudgingly adjourning for yet another Last Chance.

And it's a good thing he did. Because hours before the third hearing was due to be called on, police officers belatedly knocked at the proffered address, only to be turned away by an irate elderly lady, who had no knowledge of or connection to any Albanian street gangs, but a despairing familiarity with her address being given by their members to unwitting courts. But for the judge's largesse in allowing us a final opportunity to do what we should have done months earlier, the defendants would have been bailed, no doubt never to be seen again, and a little old lady would have had to spend yet another evening explaining to G4S security staff why they couldn't install electronic monitoring equipment in her bungalow. We got lucky. It is not always so. Other judges would have lost patience, and rightly so. Too often, it seems, these are 'just' bail apps. In an age of straitened police resources, they're simply not a priority.

Notwithstanding the chaotic, slapdash handling of bail applications by the prosecuting authorities at the outset of proceedings, an entirely different mentality kicks in once a defendant has been safely remanded into custody. The one occurrence above all others guaranteed to trigger CPS internal inquiry and managerial recriminations is the Custody Time Limit Failure. All trials are listed within the Custody Time Limits (182 days in the Crown Court). If the trial, for whatever reason, has to be adjourned to a date beyond those limits, the prosecution must publicly apply to extend the CTLs to ensure that the defendant remains remanded until the new trial date. The legal test for extending the CTLs requires that the court be satisfied that the prosecution has acted with 'due diligence and expedition, and that there is good and sufficient cause for [extending the limit].'[15]

So if the need to adjourn the trial is due to CPS error – let's say they fail, despite repeated requests, to disclose vital material undermining their case until the eleventh hour and fifty-ninth minute – they are unlikely to satisfy the judge of their due diligence and expedition, and you have a 'CTL failure', resulting in the defendant being bailed and CPS heads rolling onto serving platters. I use that particular example because that's what happened to Rio. His trial, at which he was acquitted, ultimately took place a year after I first met him in that dank prison cubicle, all because vital material that assisted his defence was sat on by the prosecution and not disclosed until it was too late for Alan to do anything with it. So the judge granted Alan's application to adjourn the first trial. And refused the prosecution's pleas to extend the CTLs, observing darkly that this was a case 'where the statutory requirements are far from made out'. An ecstatically grateful Rio could be freed; no Jade waiting for him, alas, the strain of his incarceration too much for the long-distance relationship to withstand, but his liberty at least restored, bailed to his mate's flat to piece his life together again while he awaited his eventual acquittal.

I was not privy to the fall-out at the CPS, but from experience in my own cases, it would have been significant. A potentially dangerous rapist (as they believed him to be) out on the streets. Enquiries would have been made, reports generated and explanations brutishly extracted for this ugly red blotch on their internal statistics. A far cry from the absence of fuss where a remanded defendant is acquitted. Or where a lazy, borderline application to remand is granted by obsequious magistrates in circumstances that don't come close to the statutory test. Or even where the defendant gets bail, like my Albanian phone merchants, solely due to the prosecution not doing its job.

This contrast – the slovenliness of the initial bail application against the seismic import attached to custody time limits expiring – is difficult to explain, but I imagine, as with so much modern CPS policy, it is media-driven. Should a dangerous released suspect do something horrid, it is far juicier a story if the CPS had the bad guy locked up and let him go than if he was never remanded at all due to some woolly liberal judge. Notwithstanding that you will often find, if you scrabble deep enough into the origins of that woolly liberal decision, a prosecution failing lying at its heart.

Rio's face as he was granted bail will remain with me until the end of my career. The unrestrained happiness, the rolling tears of relief at being free. The high five he gave an awkward Alan after the hearing. A few months later, I was in my 'second six' of pupillage, on my feet and doing my own work, prosecuting bail applications in the Crown Court. On my first such day, I bumped into a senior colleague from chambers, Matthew, in the robing room, who politely asked me what I was up to. When I told him, with an affected insouciance that I thought belied my inexperience (but probably just made me come across as a twit), that it was 'just a bail app', Matthew admonished me. Bail apps, he said with a schoolmasterly tone, are the most undervalued hearings in the criminal process. There is no such thing as 'just' a bail app. Each is a determination on liberty that can have life-changing consequences for the parties involved. And I thought back to the day that Rio was released, to the intensity, the quality, of his joy at winning his freedom, and I understood.

And I continue to think back to Rio's smiling face from time to time. I can't profess that every one of my bail apps and CTL extensions is conducted with the weight of his memory borne on my shoulders, his visage looming in a cartoon thought-bubble above my head. But there are certain occasions – certain factually similar cases, for example – that fleetingly trigger a recollection of Rio leaving the courtroom. And of how that played out.

Because, contrary to the prosecution's fears, once released, Rio complied with his bail condition not to contact the complainant. He obediently attended his trial. And, contrary to their expectations, with Alan's assistance Rio was acquitted.

He only attended trial, though, because he was brought in a van. From prison. Where he was a serving prisoner. Because, two weeks after being granted bail, liberated from the moderating influence of the departed Jade, Rio got high on a cocktail of ecstasy, crack and vodka. He took a kitchen knife to the local pub, and plunged it thirty times into the chest, throat and back of a random punter. He was, by the time of his adjourned rape trial, serving life for murder.

As Matthew said, every decision affecting liberty matters. Life-changing consequences follow. Ensuring that the test for withholding bail is properly exercised is as crucial as ensuring that, once a dangerous individual has been remanded, the prosecuting authorities act expeditiously to bring the case to trial. The centrality of the prosecution obeying court orders and complying with its obligations to timeously serve evidence and disclose undermining material cannot be understated. Failure can have shattering consequences.

Unfortunately, in our modern, cash-starved and understaffed prosecuting authorities, failure does not start at the beginning of proceedings amid the chaos of the first appearance and finish in the fog of ramshackle bail applications. As serious cases progress to the Crown Court and start being prepared for trial, a culture of error can take root. And, as we shall see, when it does, the stakes can be devastatingly high.

4. Watching the Guilty Walk Free: Prosecuting on the Cheap

'The tipping point was reached in 2015, and it was one of the reasons why I decided that I didn't want to be part of the service, because I felt it was asking too much of the people that I have so much respect for – the people I work with . . . You're asking the more junior staff, less experienced staff, to do more with substantially less in a climate where they're constantly under scrutiny.'

Nazir Afzal, Former Chief Crown
Prosecutor for the North-West, 2015[1]

Amy Jackson was fourteen years old when she first met Rob McCulloch, then a brooding twenty-something fresh out of prison, at the bus stop round the back of her care home. She was fifteen years old when she moved in to his squat; a few months older when Rob, to 'break her in' on her sweet sixteenth, first injected her with heroin. She was sixteen years and one day old when he first pinned her against the sofa and tore clumps of hair out of her scalp – the penalty for her reluctance to have sex with Rob's dealer as part-payment for her birthday present. For her seventeenth birthday, she received a diagnosis of hepatitis C; whether as a consequence of the needle-sharing that had become her routine, or a souvenir of the many occasions she was traded by Rob to sate their collective addiction, she couldn't and didn't care to know; the only certainties lay in the knowledge that this, her life with Rob – and importantly her obedience – was what it was to be loved. And for every birthday thereafter, and most unbirthdays in between, she would know what it was not to be loved; to disappoint Rob by not pushing enough tenths (if it was crack or heroin that day), or grams (if it was coke); or, most unforgivably, to betray his indiscretions by exposing her mottled face and missing teeth to the world, and worse her mum, who, on rare occasions of sobriety, would issue indignant threats to call the police. And whether by dint of the rug of human hair that collected under the broken lamp by the sofa, or the recognition that her dependencies, both chemical and emotional, had no other means of satisfaction, Amy learned to be grateful for her lot, to embrace the protection of Rob's love – to remain dumb when police officers attended the squat on a concerned neighbour's alert, or when a hospital trip for sutures could not be avoided, to shake her head and mutely deny the undeniable – and accept the bruising of a good day as preferable to the snapped arm of a bad one.

She was twenty-two when Rob really lost his shit. A careless retort heralded a reign of punches, heavy thuds to the mouth that repeated for whole minutes, until she couldn't see or swallow for the blood. Dragged by her hair like a ragdoll out of the house and tossed into the front garden, lifting her head she could just make out the blurry figure of Rob taking a run up towards her head, like taking a penalty kick. And then everything went black.

Later she would learn that the intervention of a passing taxi driver had saved her from what might have followed, chasing Rob away before dialling for an ambulance. And when, lying prone in her hospital bed that night, the police asked if she wanted to tell them what had happened, Amy nodded. And then she did. The whole history. Half a lifetime of brutality distilled and poured for the attending police officer, each revelation forged with the acknowledgement that next time, in the absence of a good samaritan, Rob would probably kill her.

Rob was arrested. He was interviewed by the police. He answered each question about his involvement – from the soft-ball opener, 'How do you know Amy Jackson?' through to the, one might think, eminently answerable, 'Have you ever assaulted her?' – with a calm, 'No comment.' Rob was duly charged with inflicting grievous bodily harm with intent, the most serious offence of violence short of attempted murder, punishable with life imprisonment. His case was sent to the Crown Court, and I was the barrister instructed to prosecute the trial.

The competent prosecution of criminal offences is a fundamental term of our social contract. The power to investigate and prosecute alleged offences is, in all but the rarest cases, removed from the private individual and nationalized. The state investigates, arms the prosecutor, determines and provides the venue for litigation and hands down sentence on the guilty. In return, citizens are entitled to expect that criminal prosecutions are properly financed and capably litigated. I have been raised as a true believer in that arrangement – of ensuring that serious criminal allegations are professionally and independently litigated based on their objective merits, rather than, as in the past, on the wherewithal, whims or capital of the individual complainant. When you see first-hand the desperate vulnerability of so many victims of crime, predominantly drawn from the same poverty-stricken estates as their tormentors, you quickly become convinced of the advantages of forcibly subcontracting prosecutions to a competent, impartial state agency.

As someone regularly instructed to prosecute on behalf

of the state, however, I find it difficult to constrain my anger at how frequently and flagrantly that contract is breached; not for want of effort by the good men and women who devote their working lives to the creaking Crown Prosecution Service, but for a chronic lack of staff and funding abetted by successive cynical governments.

Walk into any criminal court in the land, speak to any lawyer or ask any judge, and you will be treated to uniform complaints of court deadlines being repeatedly missed, cases arriving underprepared, evidence being lost, disclosure not being made, victims being made to feel marginalized and millions of pounds of public money being wasted. And, as a consequence, every single day, provably guilty people walking free.

Before looking at my involvement with Rob McCulloch, it is worth revisiting how prosecutions are supposed to be handled. As we saw earlier, between 1880 and 1986 all prosecution decisions were made by the local investigating police force, who took responsibility for both investigating and prosecuting alleged crimes, until the creation of the CPS in 1985, designed to ensure higher quality, consistent prosecution decisions nationwide.

The past decade of budget cuts has seen an extensive handover of charging decisions from the CPS back to the police, and over the years various other public bodies have been vested with the power to initiate prosecutions,[2] such as local authorities, the Department of Work and Pensions, the Environment Agency and the Health & Safety Executive. There is also still a right for an individual to bring a private prosecution[3] (as is exercised by the RSPCA, for example, and as was used in the unsuccessful prosecution of the killers of Stephen Lawrence in 1996). But the overwhelming majority of prosecutions in England and Wales – 588,021 in 2016–17[4] – are brought by the CPS.

When someone, such as Rob McCulloch, is charged with

an offence, the typical life-cycle of the prosecutorial process should look something like this:

— The police receive a complaint about a criminal offence and investigate all reasonable lines of inquiry, including (usually) interviewing the suspect under caution. Investigative advice can be sought from a twenty-four-hour 'CPS Direct' helpline.

— Having investigated, the police apply the two-stage test set out in the Code for Crown Prosecutors[5] – the 'Full Code Test'.[6] Firstly, does the evidence establish a 'realistic prospect of conviction'? Secondly, is it in the public interest to prosecute?

— If the police believe the Full Code Test is met, they can either charge the suspect themselves if the allegation is a minor summary offence[7] or, for more serious cases, such as Rob's, the police must refer to a CPS lawyer for a charging decision (applying the same test).

— The suspect is charged.

— The CPS receives the police file, reviews the case and prepares a file for the first hearing before the magistrates' court.

— If the case is sent to the Crown Court, it should have allocated (i) a CPS caseworker to deal with the administrative aspect, to ensure that evidence is served, to liaise with the police and so forth; (ii) a CPS lawyer to review the case and manage the legal side, such as disclosure (about which more later) and drafting legal applications; (iii) a barrister or solicitor-advocate to advise on the evidence and present the case in court.

— The evidence should be provided by the police to (i), (ii) and (iii) above, and the components of this well-oiled machine should grind in harmony to ensure that everything is ready for trial.

— Finally we have a trial, at which all relevant evidence,

which has been served on the defence in good time, is put before the court, and a jury returns a fully informed verdict as to whether the allegation is proved beyond reasonable doubt.

We've already looked at the climatic chaos of the magistrates' court, but glitches arise even before the first appearance.

For starters, the file that arrives in the magistrates' court – nowadays a digital file accessed by the CPS magistrates' prosecutor on an electronic 'Case Management System' (CMS) – is often not only incomplete, but sometimes hasn't even been looked at prior to that first hearing. 'Why does this straightforward shoplifting of meat [it's *always* meat, usually steaks as these can be sold on down the pub for a few quid] also have a public order charge attached?' I'd be asked as an agent prosecutor juggling the list, and my response would frequently be a wide-eyed shrug as I waved my empty file at the bench and defence.

The Code for Crown Prosecutors and the Director's Guidance on Charging require that the CPS review all cases, in particular those where the charging decision was taken by the police, before the first hearing in the magistrates' court. The reason is self-evident – the police are not lawyers, and sometimes make mistakes in applying the law and the charging tests. Under-pressure CPS charging lawyers can and will also make errors in judgment that need nipping before some poor sod is standing up in court being asked to justify why a defendant has been charged with the long-repealed offence of assault with intent to stop the free passage of potatoes.[8] And mistakes are often made – an inspection in 2015 found that nearly one in five police charging decisions, and one in ten CPS lawyer charging decisions, were wrong. These were not just a bit wrong, or technically wrong on an esoteric application of complex legal principles – but fundamentally wrong about basic points of law:

> [S]ome failures related to very common offences, such as assaults, burglaries and robberies and a number arose from failure to apply the law properly to identification evidence, forensic evidence, self-defence and joint enterprise. These are offences and issues that lawyers deal with on a daily basis and should rarely result in errors.[9]

A later report in 2017 found that nearly half of CPS pre-charging advices sampled were still failing to fully meet expected standards, so that initial post-charge review is vital. But around one in six cases were called on in the magistrates' courts – that is to say defendants were brought into court and had criminal allegations put to them – without a CPS lawyer ever having read the file or considered the charge. Where there had been an initial review between charge and the first hearing, 39.4 per cent failed to meet the required standards.[10]

In other words, if you are accused of a crime, there is roughly a 50 per cent chance that the prosecution hasn't fully prepared for the first court hearing. And this sets the tone for what follows.

For years, many Crown Court cases didn't have an allocated CPS caseworker. The introduction of the digital case system in 2016, which aimed to take all Crown Court cases online as part of long-overdue efficiency reforms championed by Sir Brian Leveson, included a requirement that CPS caseworkers and lawyers be identified. In most cases this is observed, albeit the CPS Inspectorate notes 'there is limited evidence of true file ownership'.[11] Prior to 2016, at the time when Rob McCulloch's case flew into my pigeonhole, it was seldom that any individual would be identified as responsible, save for in particularly serious cases. So there was no caseworker named on the brief in Rob McCulloch's case.

A brief word about 'briefs'. The brief in a case was traditionally a paper bundle, wrapped in pretty ribbon (pink for defence briefs, white for prosecution) and provided to a barrister by the solicitor instructing them – in this case, the CPS lawyer. It should contain all the papers that the barrister needs to advise on the case and prepare it for trial. Since 2016, we receive briefs by email, with all the evidence in Crown Court cases uploaded to the digital Case Management System.

When prosecuting, your brief should include, first and foremost, the evidence – all the witness statements and exhibits that make the prosecution case, including, for example, photographs, CCTV footage, medical notes, transcripts of a defendant's police interview, mobile phone records and bank statements. It should contain the indictment – the official Crown Court document setting out the charges against the defendant. It should contain documentation from the police – including a summary of the allegations, the charging decision, the charging CPS lawyer's advice and views, and any correspondence. It should have been reviewed following the magistrates' court appearance, and the reviewing CPS lawyer's views should be included. There should be a Schedule of Unused Material – a document listing all material generated in the investigation of the case which is not relied on as prosecution evidence. The contents of the schedule should be reviewed by a CPS 'disclosure lawyer' to see whether there is anything there that might assist the defence or undermine the prosecution. If there is, the defence are entitled in law to have it.

Finally, and, you might feel, quite importantly, the brief should include instructions from the CPS lawyer, telling the barrister what the case is about, what issues they've identified and are in need of addressing, what evidence is still outstanding, what legal applications they anticipate we may need to make to the court, whether there are any difficulties with the case that may not be obvious – for example the police have learned that a witness has gone missing – and whether there is anything in particular on which the barrister's advice is required.

I can't speak for why no one had typed any instructions on my Rob McCulloch brief, but if pushed I'd venture that it's the same reason that charging decisions aren't reviewed: that evidence is served late in almost every case; that in less than 25 per cent of cases do the police and CPS fully comply with their statutory disclosure obligations (meaning that potentially exculpatory material is not given to the defence);[12] that court orders are regularly not met; and that Rob McCulloch's case would take the course it ultimately did. And that is down to the simple fact that over the last eight years, the CPS has lost almost a third of its workforce.[13] One quarter of prosecutors – many of them senior and experienced – have been sacrificed through voluntary redundancy schemes, which themselves have reportedly cost in excess of £50m,[14] in an aim to meet expenditure cuts of 27 per cent imposed since 2009–10.[15]

And this was far from an organization that ran like clockwork prior to 2010, nor some flabby public body from which giant globules of fat could easily and painlessly be liposuctioned by HM Treasury. The Royal Commission on Criminal Justice offered the observation:

> We have been told . . . that because of budgetary constraints, the police may decide not to send samples collected at the scene of a crime for scientific analysis . . . There are also complaints about the quality of service provided by the Crown Prosecution Service. No one disputes that at its inception the CPS was seriously under-resourced and even now individual prosecutors

may be required to undertake a heavier caseload than is consistent with the ability to prepare all cases thoroughly.[16]

That was in 1993.

Anyway, Rob McCulloch. Ordinarily, faced with an absence of contact details and instructions, and having learned from grim experience that the CPS switchboard will either ring out or reroute you through nameless call-handlers on a loop until you give up, I would either lazily ask my clerks to ring around the CPS to find someone who was willing to take ownership of the case and speak to me. Or I would call the caseworker whose direct dial I have saved in my phone for such an emergency; someone who had nothing to do with this case, but who I knew would obligingly take the time to do some digging and find some answers for me.

So I rang Megan. Megan had been a caseworker in the CPS for about fifteen years. She was undervalued, over-worked and almost certainly despicably underpaid for the quality and importance of what she did. We had worked on many cases together over the years, and, however tight the institutional manacles in which she was required to perform an increasingly onerous and underappreciated task, she remained dedicated, warm and professional. And she is far from alone. This is the paradox of the CPS, and why, in spite of my railing, I still fervently believe there is hope.

For while it is possible to caricature the CPS institutionally as the Peter Principle[17] in action, below the executive and senior management hierarchy there are many, many wonderful and hardworking men and women. Lawyers, caseworkers and administrators who do give a damn. Who recognize the constitutional magnitude of an operative prosecution service, who aspire to make a difference and who despair at the vicious circle of cuts and inefficiency that renders their working life a cruel pastiche of *Groundhog Day*, only inverted so that they are Ned Ryerson and the government is Bill Murray, punching them day after day after day in their stupidly optimistic faces.

I work alongside them daily. The caseworker who, battling with IT systems that don't function, is required to be in literally four courtrooms at once – each courtroom listed with several cases, each case marked with a dozen problems – valiantly attending to the cries of four judges and a gaggle of prosecuting barristers demanding answers to questions that should have been on the brief, which has been left blank by some other caseworker in the office with their own corresponding abomination of a workload. I've seen these good public servants break down in tears at court at the Sisyphean trials of their thankless job. I have shuffled through the grey CPS offices for conferences with lawyers and inhaled the sprawling, groaning misery piling up on the hot-desks of talented professionals who find themselves dumped with two new cases for every one they manage to clear.

I've seen some of the best people leave, seizing their golden ticket to another civil service post where there's a fighting chance of managing their caseload, without the stress of trying to realize the impossible dream of running a national prosecuting agency for less than it costs to give free television licences to pensioners.[18] And, inevitably, I've seen a few who are simply past caring. If it's not possible to do the job well, why bother trying?

Fortunately, Megan had not yet joined the queue for the door, although it is surely only a matter of time until she realizes how talented – and how wasted – she is. And she could see on the Case Management System that, while there hadn't yet been a caseworker or a lawyer allocated to Rob McCulloch's file, there were some notes providing a little case history that she could send me.

The history was somewhat tortured. I had suspected that this was one of those cases that might have spent a little time with the CPS in-house before they decided to instruct independent counsel, and so it proved. R v McCulloch – 'R' standing for 'Regina', as standard for all cases prosecuted in the Crown's name – had been bounced between the CPS's employed advocates over two pre-trial hearings already, and the defendant still hadn't even been arraigned (asked to plead guilty or not guilty). Presumably the CPS had hoped that the evident difficulties would dissipate and they might manage to squeeze a guilty plea out of a seemingly guilty defendant, before realizing how much trouble the case was in and frantically briefing it out to independent counsel; for muggins here to step into the breach with a tin hat foisted atop my wig, a paper captain to go down with this breached, doomed ship.

Why was this case in trouble? Well, for the prosecution to prove an allegation of inflicting grievous bodily harm with intent (to cause grievous bodily harm), three elements are required. Firstly, that the defendant unlawfully (i.e., not in self-defence) assaulted the complainant. Secondly, that the defendant caused grievous bodily harm – explained to juries as 'really serious harm'. And thirdly, that the defendant intended to cause really serious harm; that is to say he didn't, for example, throw a punch intending to cause minor harm, perhaps a black eye, and accidentally shatter the victim's jaw. And to prove these types of cases, you need, as the bare minimum, two types of evidence.

One, you require evidence that the defendant assaulted the complainant. This would usually be a witness statement from the complainant, but it might alternatively or additionally include statements from others who witnessed the attack, or sometimes CCTV footage. In this case, Amy was the only witness to the assault, the taxi driver having fled, untraceable, when the ambulance arrived. And two, you need medical evidence from a doctor setting out the injuries that were sustained.

Amy had sustained a multiplicity of injuries in the course of the assault. She had suffered a fracture to the left wrist, a fractured eye-socket, a broken jaw and extensive bruising and grazing where she had been dragged through the flat and out to the front garden. And she had given her account of what had happened to the police.

But I know this – and the details of the assault and Amy's history as set out at the beginning of the chapter – only because it all appeared on my brief in the MG5. This is the document we encountered earlier, composed by the police and (theoretically) containing a precis of what the evidence shows.

The problem was that the actual evidence itself – the statement presumably taken from Amy and the medical records from the hospital – was nowhere to be found on my brief. Now, evidence not appearing on a prosecution brief is far from unusual. Often it will exist on the CPS computer and will just have been missed off the brief. Other times it will still be in the possession of the police, who upon prompting will forward it to the CPS to pass to the barrister. But it became apparent upon reading the notes of the previous hearings by the in-house CPS advocates that, in this case, the evidence had simply . . . gone. It had never been served on the defence. It had never even reached the CPS.

And the Crown Court, or to be more precise two Crown Court judges, had granted the prosecution successive extensions of time for this evidence to be served on the defence. Twice the case had been listed for Rob to be arraigned (to enter his plea of guilty or not guilty), and twice it had been adjourned because the rudimentary evidence wasn't available. Christ knows where it had gone, or alternatively why it hadn't been obtained. Clearly Amy had given a lengthy account to *someone*, as the details appeared on the MG5. Likewise, someone somewhere – either the officer completing the MG5 or the person feeding that officer the information – had seen the medical records, or taken a statement from the hospital staff. Similarly, the MG3 – the document completed by the charging CPS lawyer – referred to the same material; although again, it was unclear whether the CPS lawyer had actually seen the evidence, or had simply assumed that the contents of the MG5 were correct. This stuff, I ranted to an entirely blameless Megan, doesn't just spontaneously appear.

So this evidence was available. It had to be. And this is presumably why judges had given the CPS several chances to get hold of it. Even though courts are nowadays required to resist indulging prosecution errors, in a serious case like Rob's, where it should simply be a matter of finding out who has a few documents, Crown Court judges will generally allow the Crown a little latitude. But tracing the history of the case through the hearing notes, it was clear that there was a blockage somewhere. It was suggested, in an internal email that Megan dug out and forwarded to me, that the police had in fact never taken a formal statement from Amy; that what appeared in the MG5 reflected the account she had orally given an officer from her hospital bed, but this had not been put into the form of an admissible witness statement. To compound matters, it appeared that the police pocket notebook (PNB) in which this first account had been recorded had gone missing.

Nevertheless, this should have been surmountable. All the police needed to do was allocate an officer to go to Amy's address and take a statement from her. And then, on their way back to the station, pop into the hospital and grab a copy of her medical records. And finally, scan those documents onto the police electronic 'tree', and ping them across to the CPS to serve on the defence.

Indeed, the notes suggested that the CPS advocate at the conclusion of each of the earlier hearings had sent reminders to (unidentified) caseworkers with clear instructions to tell the police to do just this. Yet, on each following occasion, the advocate had had to stand up in court and tell the judge that it had not been done. On the most recent occasion, the defence had indicated, at the invitation of the exasperated judge, that at the next hearing they would be making an application to dismiss the charges.

An application to dismiss can be made by a defendant at an early stage in proceedings, after the prosecution have served their evidence, and before the defendant has been arraigned – asked whether he pleads guilty or not guilty – to the indictment (the Crown Court charge sheet). If it appears to the judge that the evidence against the defendant would not be sufficient for him to be properly (i.e. safely) convicted, then the judge must dismiss the charges, and the case is over.[19] Theoretically, applications to dismiss should rarely succeed if the CPS has properly applied the evidential test when charging. It's worse than an acquittal after trial, where a jury may well feel there was a good case against the defendant, but not quite enough to make them sure beyond reasonable doubt. It's worse than a judge stopping a trial at the end of the prosecution case having found that there is 'no case to answer', where the prosecution can at least tell themselves that the problem lay with the live witness evidence. A judge ruling against the CPS on a dismissal is saying, 'Your evidence is on its face so weak that I'm not letting you take this case any further.' It is the courtroom equivalent of your boss not merely criticizing that report you submitted, but setting it on fire in public and taking a crowbar to your fingers to ensure you don't try to do it again.

It's for that reason that, I understand, successful applications to dismiss are viewed particularly dimly by CPS statisticians. And the fear of a dismissal in Rob's case is why, I assumed, the CPS had given up juggling this hot potato and batted it out to independent counsel to either find the solution or take the fall.

Here, as is common, the threat of an application to dismiss had been brandished by the judge as a cattle prod to spark the CPS into life. If you don't get the evidence, the judge was saying, I'll have no choice but to put this case in a rock-filled bag and toss it in the river. The judge had known that often the words 'possible application to dismiss' on the CPS record sheet have a miraculous stimulant effect on the internal whirrings of the prosecution engine, and had listed the case for the hearing of such an application, although the date of this hearing was missing from my brief.

'When,' I asked Megan, now the de facto caseworker and patiently picking up my third call of the afternoon, 'is this application to dismiss?'

'One moment,' as she scrolled through the CPS record sheets. Each court hearing is supposed to be attended by a caseworker to complete a record sheet of any court directions, dates of future hearings and other relevant information, which are uploaded to the CPS's case management system. Due to the current, financially mandated practice of allocating lone caseworkers to multiple courtrooms, commonly a caseworker will not in fact be in court to hear the case take place, and will be reliant on second-hand information from the advocate as to what directions have been made.

After twenty minutes of grappling with the system, Megan was able to discern that the hearing was in three days' time, and that a memorandum had been sent to the police. The copy memorandum on the system was blank – CMS is a temperamental beast – but *something* at least had been sent to the police, hopefully enjoining them to obtain the evidence.

I thanked Megan sincerely, and for completeness bashed out a short, direct email for Megan to forward directly to the police officer in charge of the case (OIC). We need, I curtly advised, by Monday: (i) a witness statement from Amy Jackson, setting out the details of the assault; and (ii) her medical records detailing her injuries, with a statement from a doctor explaining what the records show. I'd be grateful if the OIC rang me on the below number to discuss.

Email sent, there was little to do but wait for the OIC's call and see what Monday would bring. The call never came, so I arrived early at court on Monday and, having robed, headed to the CPS room at court. The CPS room is a dark, windowless box in which a row of paper-strewn desks host a trail of power sockets for caseworkers to plug their laptops into. A photocopier/printer sits at one end, a Blu-tacked A4 sheet cautioning against using tray 2 permanently affixed to the front. Next to it stands a fax machine, which a few years ago deputized as a printer for a week, when the photocopier jammed and the contractor couldn't send an engineer for seven days. For an entire working week, any documents that needed printing – including jury bundles for trials, which can stretch to dozens of pages – had to be printed at the central CPS HQ and faxed, page by page, to the CPS room at court. They were lucky. Another CPS room I once visited was deprived for a fortnight of working lights, and the damned inhabitants were forced to rely on tiny desk lamps brought from home to illuminate their underground cavern.

As I entered, a frazzled caseworker handed me an MG6 – a memo from the police. I exhaled with relief. Prematurely, it emerged. The memo read: 'PC Roberts attended AP ['aggrieved person' – shorthand for complainant] address. She is still willing to give evidence and is happy for hospital to release medical records.'

I read it twice. And then looked at the caseworker. 'And the complainant's witness statement? And the actual hospital records?'

He shrugged. 'Don't know, I'm afraid, I was just asked to hand you that. It's not my court; it's Aaron's but he's part-heard in the trial in Court 5 and is down in the witness suite dealing with that.'

A further interrogation of the system confirmed that this futile document was the only new material received from the police. The caseworker kindly took time out of his own morass of work to ring the central police hub to try to track down the OIC so that I could get some answers, but, fifteen minutes later, was informed that he, and the aforementioned PC Roberts, were working nights this week and were unavailable.

'In which case,' I mused, choosing my words delicately, 'I think we're fucked. I'll apply to adjourn this application to allow us yet another chance, but the judge is going to say that three tries is more than enough.' The case was going to be kicked before Amy got within a mile of the courtroom; the evidence that she was seemingly eager to give would go unheard.

The judge, as expected, did indeed say that three tries were more than enough for the prosecution to get evidence that should have been available three months ago. He did shout at me for my inability to provide any explanation as to why I still had nothing from Amy or the hospital. He did ridicule the pathetic memo I was forced to read to the court – *So the officer visited the complainant, asked if she would give a statement, and when the complainant said yes, the officer just left? Is that what you're telling me?* He did indeed say that the CPS did not deserve an adjournment. And he did indeed say that the defence was entitled, as they naturally did, to urge the court to deal with the application today and dismiss the prosecution case.

But, perhaps because, like I, he had read the MG5 and been hit with that visceral, abdominal instinct you develop over time that the description of what had taken place was, in the criminal hack vernacular, a true bill. And maybe because he had seen Rob's previous convictions, page after page of violence – usually against women – and had heard from me, probably naughtily, of the history of police call-outs to Amy's address where officers had found her crying, bruised and insistent that she had walked into a door; and because he knew that, whatever the failings of the state, this was a vulnerable woman in desperate need of protection, who, having finally turned to the state for help, shouldn't be required to suffer God-knows-what fate as payment for our institutional incompetence. Or perhaps for some other reason altogether, he acceded to my speculative, hopeless application to adjourn.

'You have seven days,' he intoned. 'If you appear this time next week without evidence, I *will* dismiss the case. Last chance. There is a willing complainant here. The police know where she is. This is not rocket science. Seven days.'

When I got back to chambers later that afternoon, I composed a further, entirely repetitive, advice to the CPS, setting out the history of the case, and the overriding importance of securing this bloody evidence. With Megan away, and the generic CPS email address printed on the brief containing the usual imperceptible error that means that all emails immediately bounce back as undeliverable, my best hope was to address the email to the duty caseworker and the duty lawyer. The duty lawyer's phone number rang out with no voicemail facility, and so I took on trust the 'read' receipt that dropped into my email account as assurance that my advice had been received, and was in the system. All I could do now was wait.

At this point I could take you through the minutiae of the next seven days. Of the reminder emails I sent when nothing had arrived by Thursday. Of the panicked calls I put in on the Friday when the evidence still hadn't appeared in my pigeonhole. Of the unshakeable foreboding when I walked into the CPS room that following Monday. Of what the caseworker told me, of the documents I wasn't handed, of the disgust on the face of the judge when I told him.

But you know where this is going. And you could probably replicate the judge's comments as he dismissed the charges, and capture the vitriol in his ruling as he surmised how, had the evidence been obtained, it might have provided a compelling case. How the prosecution had provided no good reason for failing, time and time again, to get the basics in place.

There was nothing. No evidence arrived. No explanation. And with the giant medical-and-complainant-shaped hole in the Crown's case, there was ruled to be no case against Rob McCulloch. He was free to go. An innocent man. And of course, he is. No case has been proven against him, and he is entitled to be treated as if no criminal act had taken place against Amy Jackson. If, however, he had been tried by a jury, who had heard Amy's evidence and found themselves unconvinced, and returned a verdict of not guilty, that would be one thing. The course of justice would have run. But for the trial to not even take place, due to unexplained state error, is not justice. Or rather, it is the type of justice you get if you stop caring about the quality of justice.

I still to this day do not know what happened in that case. To an extent, I am blindsided. I can only recount what I see from my ivory tower and cast partial judgment based on incomplete information. I don't know where the fault truly lay. Whether it was with the police or with the CPS. Whether there's another explanation entirely. I just know that something, somewhere, went very, very wrong. In a way that should never happen, but does. And not just as one-offs, but regularly, in cases just like McCulloch's, in cases far less serious, and in cases even more so.

The next week, I was defending a lady, Laura, accused of stealing money from an old man in her care. She had emptied his bank account of his life savings – close to £20,000 – and told police in interview the slightly unlikely tale that she had done so at the man's behest, to pay for his day-to-day pocket money. Unfortunately, in the complainant's video interview statement, the police had forgotten to elicit the vital evidence that the gentleman had not given Laura permission. Clearly something had been said to suggest he hadn't, as otherwise there wouldn't have been a criminal complaint. But the police had forgotten to actually get him to say it in *evidence*. Easily fixable though – you just re-interview him and ask him, *Did you give her permission to empty your bank account?* But no one did. When, after an inexplicable delay of three years, the case appeared in the Crown Court, the prosecution was afforded repeated opportunities to re-interview the complainant. And they did nothing. This time, I was the one making the application to dismiss, watching my poor colleague get a judicial thrashing for the failings of those instructing him as another viable case collapsed.

As I say, it is not news to those who see it every day. This happens. We all know it. And defendants know it, too. Practised criminals know that, even if the evidence against them appears strong, there is always the chance that the prosecution case will spin off the rails en route to trial and smash open an escape tunnel. One of the reasons that many defendants plead guilty only on the day of trial is that they will bide their time, hopeful that a prosecution error or a key witness losing their resolve – a crushingly prevalent problem in allegations of domestic violence – will free them at the last. Only when it is clear that the prosecution's house is in order will these practised criminals – usually the violent, predatory Robs of our world who try to exploit their malign hold over their victim to thwart her cooperation with the authorities – admit their guilt.

It is easy, seeing this every day, for the police, caseworkers, prosecutors, barristers and judges to become case-hardened; to see the collapse of viable prosecutions as inevitable collateral damage when resources are straitened. The humanity of a vulnerable, shaking, bleeding person howling impotently for rescue can be reduced to an unfavourable icon on a database, another disappointing statistic to be diluted in a sea of thousands. Or for us at the Bar, another cracked trial to add to the list, bill and forget.

But some, like Amy, jolt us back into reality. Her case stays with me because, as far as I knew, this was a woman we should have been able to help. I never met her, but I share in the shame; the unshakeable niggle of guilt at having no satisfactory explanation for what went wrong.

I have my theory, of course. For, while the clichéd woe of the public service professional decrying government cuts is quickly dismissible as self-serving protectionism, there can be no organization in any field that, from a starting position of being underfunded, then loses a third of its workforce and has its budget reduced by a quarter and still performs as it should.

When that organization depends on the investigative prowess of a national police force which, over the same period, has lost nearly 20,000 officers – a fall of 13 per cent – and has sustained budget cuts of 20 per cent, the window for error is opened even wider.[20]

And I wonder how CPS employees feel whenever the Director of Public Prosecutions, in whichever incarnation, has the evidence, statistical or anecdotal, put to them on the rare occasions the media take an interest, and they shake their head at the impossible naivety of the question, at the inquisitor's ignorance of the CPS's strategic objectives and quality standards and performance delivery systems, and how they *don't recognize that description of the CPS* or *don't recognize those statistics*. This, instead of admitting the struggle – the implausibility – of delivering justice at barely two pence per day per capita,[21] and telling Parliament, the media and the public, when asked, that the Crown Prosecution Service and local police forces are on their knees.

Digitization Will Save Us, the shout goes out. And it will make a difference; it already has in many positive ways. Things are better than they were only a few years ago at the time of Rob McCulloch. But it is not a panacea. Evidence and disclosure still need to be reviewed; documents still need to be obtained and uploaded; cases still need to be properly managed. Moving criminal cases online does not change their inherent nature. They are complex organisms that need careful attention if they are not to wither on the vine. This requires people. And money.

Notwithstanding the optimism of the CPS's senior management, HM Crown Prosecution Service Inspectorate, the CPS watchdog, concluded in its most recent five-year review that:

> The continuing reduction in resources has led to prosecutors handling increasing caseloads. This is undoubtedly making it more difficult to maintain effective oversight of cases as they progress to trial.[22]

CPS employees put it more bluntly:

> There will be miscarriages of justice down the road from here because there are some cases that are going through the system and people have not looked at disclosure properly and have not looked at what is going on behind the scenes. Things we simply would not have had ten years ago.[23]

Meanwhile, reviewing the CPS's specialist Rape and Serious Sexual Offences (RASSO) units in 2016, the Inspectorate warned darkly: 'The model has shown that the CPS is under-resourced for the current volume of work and even more so for anticipated future increases.'[24]

This is the iceberg ahead. For, while it is true that the overall number of cases processed by the criminal courts is falling, those coming before the Crown Court increasingly involve allegations of sexual offending, often historic, which are the most complex and time-consuming to prepare. It is estimated that more than *half* of cases before the Crown Courts now involve sexual allegations,[25] and the Criminal Bar Association warned in 2017 of a further 'tsunami of highly sensitive sex cases'.[26] The work involved is substantial: the complainants are often particularly vulnerable and require significant support; the law governing alleged sexual offences that occurred pre-2003 is inexplicably complicated and ridden with pitfalls for unwary prosecutors; the disclosure process can involve procuring and reviewing decades' worth of faded, handwritten Social Services and medical records; the trials, because of their nature, can take weeks, if not months; and the stakes, for victims, for the wrongly accused and for the public, could not be higher.

I don't know what happened to Amy. I was never instructed to prosecute Rob McCulloch again. I hope this is because, recognizing his incredible good fortune, he regarded Amy Jackson as a bullet dodged and kept his head down. I hope he didn't track her down, as perpetrators of domestic violence are wont to do, to seek reconciliation. Or revenge. I hope that the women's refuge helped resettle her somewhere far, far away, where she might have a hope of escaping a life of Rob McCullochs. And I hope that someone took the time to apologize. Because if Amy had, to use the ugly argot, cultural capital – if she had a good support network and family and friends and an education and wasn't hooked on heroin and wasn't fatally vulnerable to the violent charms of vicious, brutal men – she would have demanded answers, instead of settling, as I fear she may have, for the self-told assurance that this is just how the state treats people like her.

The mistreatment of victims in the criminal justice system is not, however, solely down to prosecution error. Amy's case is an example of how victims can be failed by mistakes at an early stage in the pre-trial process, but we will now look at how, as cases proceed towards trial, the criminal process can often feel as if it's designed to accommodate the needs of everybody but the person most directly affected by the (alleged) criminal offence. It is this perception that draws us to the siren calls of the politicians pledging to Put Victims First.

And crashes us straight onto the rocks.

5. The Devil's Greatest Trick: Putting the Victim First

'Victims must have more help navigating a confusing and often intimidating Criminal Justice System. Too often they tell us they feel they are treated as an after-thought or that the "system" made their already horrific experience worse . . . This total revamp of the Victims Code has been one of my main priorities and I have heard from victims just how important getting this right is . . . It is one of many measures I am introducing to make sure the "system" starts to put victims first.'

Helen Grant, Victims' Minister,
29 March 2013[1]

The witness box is a pulpit of human despair. From within this enclosed square metre of panelled oak, witness after witness, and victim after victim, has for centuries told a jury of strangers, seated opposite, their true-life stories of barely imaginable misery and suffering.

It is the witness box that plays centre stage in the theatre of the courtroom as captured in television and cinema. As the alleged victim gives evidence on oath of the wrong perpetrated against them, truths are revealed, lies are exposed, tears spill, hopes rise and fade and credibility crumbles.

The routine for each victim is usually the same. Having given their witness statement to the police, they wait months, if not years, to unburden themselves of the grievance that has plagued their every waking moment. They will be kept informed – or, depending on your viewpoint, at arm's length – by the Witness Care Unit, who provide piecemeal updates as the case preparation progresses behind closed office doors. The lucky may be treated to a 'court familiarization day' and a tour of the courtroom in advance, but for most the first trip to court will be on the day of trial. The victim arrives at court through a side entrance and into the arms of the volunteers staffing the court Witness Service. They enjoy a hot drink while the prosecutor makes introductions and brings a copy of their witness statement to read over, and then it's show time. The complainant blinkingly enters the bright stage lights of the courtroom and steps tentatively into the witness box to be sworn. Nerves occasionally cause them to stumble over the wording – although notably not as often as do jurors with their oath – and they glance around at their surroundings; purple judge sitting high to their left, jury straight ahead, be-wigged barristers to their right.

If it is my witness, I will start with the same scripted prompt – 'I know this will feel a bit strange, but even though the questions are coming from me over here, please direct all your answers to the jury over there.' And I point demonstratively. 'It's important that the members of the jury and Her Honour hear everything you say, so please keep your voice nice and loud' – and then we're away.

Not today, though. The witness box is empty. The courtroom, in fact, is empty. Closed, locked, bolted. The complainant, Matthew, is sitting in the witness suite buried in the bowels of the court, politely nodding and crunching his way through his fifteenth digestive of the day as I, the prosecutor, remove my wig and apologetically explain that his six-hour wait at court today has been in vain: no courtroom has become available to hear our trial, and the case is being adjourned off.

The jurors – and there are plenty of them, also sitting around in waiting rooms with equally unexciting biscuits passing the time until a court becomes free – will have to wait to hear the evidence of his mugging; the brief but terrifying grab from behind in the alleyway next to Matthew's gym, the freezing coldness of the blade pressed against his face and the draining feeling of helplessness – inexplicably *shame* – as his hooded assailant rummaged until he found what he came for, and ran away into the autumn mist, iPhone in paw.

No jury will ever hear it. Matthew will return in eight months for the re-fixed trial date, and will play out the same day in replica: the same biscuits, the same wait, the same denouement. By now it is some two years after the original offence, and Matthew is desperate to give evidence against the defendant who, caught red-handed with the stolen iPhone, is running the laughable, and easily disprovable, defence that Matthew voluntarily gave it to him, a complete stranger. But again, the case will not reach the front of the queue. It will be adjourned for lack of court time *encore*, and at the third time of asking, Matthew will lose heart, he will disappear, and I will be informing the court on the next occasion that the prosecution is throwing its hand in.

Matthew's experience is not unusual. Another week in another court, I'm defending, imagining my opponent in the witness suite. She's having to explain to a complainant in a knifepoint sexual assault case that the prosecution has failed to secure the attendance of the other witnesses who, unlike the blindsided complainant, were able to positively identify the defendant as her attacker. Without them, there is no case against this defendant, and the prosecution is being aborted at the eleventh hour.

It is such common recurrences that cause criminal lawyers to greet the repeated political sloganeering to Put

Victims First with a scathing snort. Not because victims are unimportant or undeserving of consideration; to the contrary, they occupy a uniquely important and invidious position in our system. Having suffered the indignity of a criminal violation, their redress is subject to a hostile take-over by the state, which will determine if, and how, they shall receive justice for their suffering, but the victim is still expected to man the barricades and sacrifice their time and emotional resilience to the prosecution cause. If our criminal justice system doesn't adequately protect victims of crime – if it fails to provide due process and respect for those reliant on it, and if it loses their and public trust – it is failing its first principles. Without the victim's goodwill, there is rarely a viable prosecution case. Protecting the victim's interests is both a matter of practical sense and a moral duty.

Rather, my scepticism towards the Put Victims First manifesto arises because we see the institutional callousness with which victims are treated in practice. Notwithstanding that we now have a Victims' Code (formerly Victim's Charter), Victims' Minister, Victims' Commissioner (succeeding the Victims' Champion), Victims' Taskforce (recommending the implementation of a Victims' Law enforcing the Victims' Code, as promised by all three main political parties at the 2015 General Election), Victims' Information Service, Victims' Contact Scheme, Witness Charter, Victim Support, Ministry of Justice's Commitment to Victims, CPS Victims' Right to Review Scheme, National Police Chiefs Council Victim Right to Review Scheme, a Victims' Services Commissioning Framework, Victim Liaison Units, Victim Personal Statements and the Victim Surcharge, one bald statistic stands out above all: only 55 per cent of people who have been a victim or a witness in criminal proceedings would be prepared to go through it again.[2]

It bears repeated emphasis. Nearly half of all witnesses surveyed said that they would not be willing to take part in criminal proceedings on a future occasion. If they witnessed your daughter being mugged, they would not assist in bringing her assailant to justice. If you were falsely accused of assault, they would not come forward to say that they saw you acting in self-defence. If they were themselves a victim, they would not entrust the justice of that crime to the state, preferring, one infers, that the miscreant go unpunished, or be subject to a more immediate, possibly divine, form of retribution.

This is raw failure on the most fundamental plane. And it's no secret. Politicians, at least, are well versed in the unhappy lot of the witness, their inboxes no doubt over-flowing with irate correspondence from constituents appalled at their brush with the criminal courts. But the solution, universal across the political spectrum, remains the same zygotic slogan: Put Victims First.

That is not to say that victims' rights initiatives are not worthy; they are absolutely vital. Much of the misery I encounter when meeting witnesses at court is born of a lack of meaningful information provided by the prosecution agencies, or an absence of support with practicalities – such as arranging childcare during the court hearing – and pledges to improve such basic services should be realized.

But many of the reasons lying behind that devastating statistic – *55 per cent* – are those not solved by a well-intended charter. Rather, the roots of victims' suffering – of their perceived re-victimization at the hands of the system – are multifaceted and deeply embedded, often visible only to those plunged into the process. Too frequently the sim-plest reason is the under-resourcing and under-staffing of the court system, but this lurks in the ministerial and media blind spot. For me, these deeper problems are rarely honestly addressed; forsaken instead for another rousing rendition of Put Victims First.

Just as often, other truths are too hard, too politically ugly, for all except despised defence lawyers to voice: that in many aspects of the criminal process, the inevitable clash, and necessary compromise, between victim and defendant rights, and the guiding principle of not convicting the innocent, mean that the victim can't – and *shouldn't* – be put first.

I think we desperately need an analysis of brutal honesty. Victims, for all the talk, are not put first. Their rights are presently, in my view, subjugated threefold: to the interests of the court; the interests of the prosecution; and the interests of the defendant. Let's have a look at what this means for victims in practice.

Victims v the Court

For many witnesses I meet, like Matthew our mugging victim, criminal proceedings must feel like a near-permanent suspension of time. They wait months for the police to investigate. They wait for a charging decision. They wait for the trial to be listed. They wait for the trial date to come around. They wait all day at court only for the trial to be adjourned. And they are then sent home to wait again until the next date. And repeat. Entering the criminal justice system as a victim will test your patience, often to destruction and beyond repair, as you stumble into a vortex of 'poor performance, delays [and] inefficiencies'.[3]

Identifying a major cause is not difficult. Between 2010 and 2016, spending on the criminal justice system as a whole fell by 26 per cent, with a further 15 per cent cut to take effect by 2020.[4] The courts, Her Majesty's Courts and Tribunal Service, have borne a 35 per cent cut in real terms, and more is to come.[5] By 2020, there will have been a further 40 per cent cut in the court staffing budget.[6]

Although as of 2016 slightly fewer cases were entering the system, the new cases were more complex and resource-intensive, due largely to the sudden increase in allegations of historical sexual offences, the legacy of Jimmy Savile et al. At the same time, in order to comply with the Treasury's diktats, the Ministry of Justice cut the number of days that courts could sit.[7] You can walk into any major city Crown Court complex and gaze in wonderment at how many gleaming, fresh-out-the-box courtrooms, festooned with hi-tech electronics and lovingly carved to ergonomic perfection, lie locked and unused. And it's not for want of cases to fill them; the inevitable effect of 35 per cent budget cuts and a concurrent increase in the complexity and length of criminal trials has been a soaring backlog of serious criminal cases.

The National Audit Office reported in 2016 that the backlog in Crown Court had soared to 52,000 cases, an increase of 34 per cent in two years, with roughly 100,000 cases passing through the Crown Courts each year. It has since dipped back down to just under 40,000.[8] The average waiting time between first appearance in the magistrates' court and trial at the Crown Court is 123 days, an increase of 23 per cent since 2010, and this does not factor in the delay between reporting a crime and the first appearance, which can be months, if not years.[9]

To tackle the backlog in the Crown Court, court listing officers have taken to shovelling more and more trials into courtrooms in the hope that *some* might 'crack' (resolve, in normal language), prioritizing listing 'targets' above all else. In essence, it is replicating the model of the magistrates' court. And it means that a victim turns up at court for what they have been told is the trial date, only to be informed by the prosecution barrister or the friendly volunteers at the Witness Service that their trial is fourth in a list of 'floating' trials, and holds as much prospect of realization as an email from a beneficent Nigerian prince.

The 'floating trial', for the uninitiated, is the official term for a trial listed in a Crown Court centre but not allocated to a specific courtroom. Instead, as the name suggests, it floats ethereally around the building in the hope that one of the other trials listed in court 'cracks', and a trial slot opens up. When no slot appears, the trial is adjourned, either to a date far, far away, or, at certain sadistic court centres, to return the following day as a 'priority floating trial'.

The rationale behind floating trials and 'warned lists' – where a working week, rather than a day, is identified and the parties are expected to be available to begin any day that week – is theoretically sound: it is wasteful to have a courtroom sitting empty, and a judge, jury, clerk, usher and security staff twiddling their thumbs at a cost of £1,900 a day, if a listed trial does not go ahead. The need for back-up trials ready-to-go is obvious. But the number of trials listed as floaters in a single building, where it is clear that most of them have no hope of finding a home, is a victory for listing statistics over basic human decency. I have seen seven floating trials listed in a single day, meaning that seven lots of witnesses and victims will be dutifully rearranging their lives around that sacred date only for most to be sent away empty-handed at the eleventh hour. This is treating human beings, many of whom have been victims of the most foul, dignity-stripping crimes, as chattels of the court, to be distributed and warehoused as the court sees fit.

When I prosecute, it is notable how little warning victims and witnesses are given of the realities of the day ahead. They are usually oblivious to the fact that their trial is floating and what this means, and unprepared for the likelihood of waiting all day for the slinkiest chance that they might get the ordeal of giving evidence over with. If I have a floating trial, I will explain the position to the (often astonished and angry) witnesses at the start of the day, and thereafter return to the witness suite as often as I can with any updates, but usually I'm in the dark as much as they are. The best I might get is a whisper in the robing room that the trial in Court 3 might be cracking, or that the listing officer is considering admitting defeat at lunchtime and arranging for all floaters to be adjourned off, but transmitting speculation and false hope is, I judge, worse than an informational void.

If the witnesses are particularly unlucky, they may be bounced out of the building altogether and nonchalantly advised that the trial will now be heard at another court centre. Sometimes in another city. Again, no regard will be given to the practicalities involved, or the inconvenience caused. The witnesses, like the advocates, are just expected to lump it. To make their way there somehow. The police might help out with transporting witnesses if there's an officer at court. I've even been asked when prosecuting if I could drive a complainant to a freshly allocated court (not having a car with me exculpated me from this awkward conversation). Otherwise, in the absence of their own wheels, the witness is pointed towards the local train station and expected to fork out for a ticket (reclaimable at a later date) for the privilege of travelling to another court.

One such case I prosecuted involved a nasty robbery of a grocery store where the young female shopkeeper, Hana, had been threatened with a rusty screwdriver by a balaclava'd heroin addict. Having closed her shop for the day to attend court, at significant (and non-refundable) personal expense, she waited at court from 9.30 a.m. to 3 p.m. to be told that her trial had floated to another court centre fourteen miles away. She spent £30 of her own money on a taxi to the station, a return train ticket and a taxi to court on the other side, and arrived breathless at our new home shortly before 4 p.m. Meanwhile, in court, the judge took one look at the file, assessed that the trial was likely to run longer than the court could accommodate, and promptly adjourned the case off to the next available slot in eight months.

If you were a criminal mastermind trying to design a system to deter victims of crime from engaging with the authorities, you would struggle to devise something better.

Although 'lack of court time', as we politely call this failure to properly resource the system, is the primary cause of ineffective trials, it is by no means the only. If your trial *does* find a courtroom, there is still a Wacky Warehouse full of obstacles primed to stop the trial going ahead. Two thirds of Crown Court trials do not progress as planned. In some areas of the country, the proportion of ineffective trials is as high as four in five.[10] Sometimes this is for 'good' reasons – namely that a defendant, told by his barrister that the prosecution witnesses have all turned up, agrees that the game is up and pleads guilty. But mainly it is for other reasons: the case being adjourned, or thrown out, because the prosecution barrister instructed the night before has realized that key evidence hasn't been gathered, or because witnesses haven't shown up; defendants on bail failing to surrender, or defence witnesses not attending; the trial being adjourned because crucial undermining material has not been disclosed by the prosecution to the defence; defendants in custody not being brought to court by private contractors – a problem that plagues every court in the land every single day of the year; technology not working, such as a DVD of CCTV being in the 'wrong' format for the court system; or a broken video-link preventing a witness appearing virtually in the courtroom.

Or, a particular favourite of lawyers and judges, the interpreter for a non-English speaking defendant or witness may not be present. Up until 2012, courts would book interpreters directly, using an approved register of qualified translators. Then the Ministry of Justice put out to tender all justice-related interpretation services, and the contract was awarded to a small company, Applied Language Solutions, who, before the contract had kicked in, were purchased by Capita Translation and Interpreting. Immediately 66 per cent of qualified interpreters refused to work under the contract due to the derisory pay rates and conditions.

Those who were prepared to work were, to put it mildly, a mixed bag. Some had no training in court procedure, and so could not translate basic terms of law (in one case, an interpreter did not know the difference between murder and manslaughter). Some were entirely unqualified in the language they claimed to interpret.[11] A serious rape trial in 2016 had to be stopped after a week when it emerged that the interpreter was mistranslating the evidence.[12] A 2015 trial at the Old Bailey into alleged war crimes had to be stopped for want of a qualified interpreter.[13] An independent quality review in 2014 found that less than half of Capita's interpreters were properly qualified.[14] But the most common problem is that interpreters simply don't turn up. Over the life of the ALS/Capita contract, 2,500 trials were adjourned due to lack of interpreters.[15] Capita was made subject to numerous orders for wasted costs by livid judges, and thousands of complaints per year. Surprisingly enough, Capita declined to bid for the new contracts starting in late 2016, but problems persist.

Now, some of the variables above, attributable to the disordered lives of troubled defendants and witnesses, are difficult to control. But many of them patently are not. They are within the power of mankind to minimize. Some progress is (slowly) being made through Sir Brian Leveson's 2016 efficiency reforms, which place heavy emphasis on the importance of proper case management, by judges and parties, to reduce last-minute hiccups or changes of plea. The belated introduction of modern information technology into the criminal courts in 2016 is likewise making it easier to identify problems with cases earlier. But to bang again on this rusty, perforated drum, the primary cause that is identified by every person in the system, every parliamentary report and every purse-lipped auditor remains lack of proper funding. Each bereft component of the system – the courts, the prosecution and the defence – has its own inefficiencies compounded by those of the others, a clanging vicious circle which cannot be tidily managed away for free. At best, those inefficiencies can be disguised from public view by shuttling high volumes of cases through the system as swiftly as possible, as we see currently in the magistrates' courts, and as, I fear, we are moving towards in the Crown Courts, where even more serious offences, and the scope for even graver injustice, lurk. Given the choice between doing it quick 'n' cheap and doing it right, the laws of political attraction will always favour the former.

And so, notwithstanding the curdling screams of the victims that it pretends are put first, the executive ploughs on with further cuts to the courts, blithely insisting that the forthcoming Digital Age will be the cure-all, each transient minister safe in the knowledge that his or her accountability for those pledges will never be tested.

Which means, for example, that despite Her Majesty's Crown Prosecution Service Inspectorate making plain that the CPS's Rape and Serious Sexual Offences units are 'under-resourced for the current volume of work and even more so for anticipated future increases',[16] and that this feeds into the CPS failing to follow their victim policies in one third of sex cases,[17] there will be no money made available to plug the gap. No funding to address the fact that, in two thirds of cases where the victim has alleged serious sexual abuse, the CPS can't even afford to send a proper Victim Letter of adequate 'quality, content and tone'.[18]

Victim Letters may not sound important, but to a victim they can be vital. One of the hardest conversations I've ever had at court was with a man who had received a Victim Letter informing him that the thug who had violently entered his home and stolen his treasured family heirlooms had pleaded guilty. The victim had turned up at court for the sentence hearing hoping that the burglar might reveal the whereabouts of the stolen goods, which included materially worthless but invaluable personal documents, certificates and photographs. I had to inform him that, to the contrary, the man for sentence today was a burglar in an entirely different case. My further enquiries then revealed that the CPS had in fact discontinued this victim's case for want of evidence without telling him, compounding the misery by sending out the wrong pro forma Victim Letter.

By itself, this minor bureaucratic error sounds minimal. But for this man, it was everything. He asked me to repeat myself as he struggled with tears in his eyes to compute how such a thing might happen – *why would you tell me that my crime is solved?* He visibly crumpled as the realization dawned that he was going home empty handed, to explain to his wife that their burglar remained at large, and her irreplaceable professional qualification certificates, hastily gathered as she fled her war-torn homeland, would not be found. Standing there, functionally useless in my ridiculous courtwear, I apologized over and over, my vicarious guilt multiplied by the man's downright decency. I recommended that he raise a formal complaint, and promised that I would do likewise on his behalf. But it's not enough. He shouldn't be an afterthought.

But victims often are. Not by the people on the ground, and certainly not by the kind souls who volunteer their time to victims' charities or to offering comfort and support in the Witness Service at courts. But by those running the system. As HMCTS merrily continues its spree of widespread court sell-offs, it inverts the principle of locally rooted criminal justice and renders it harder, more time-consuming and more expensive for victims to get to court. 'There will still be a court within an hour's travel for 97 per cent of people',[19] the Ministry disingenuously insists, ignorant of or uncaring about the practical needs of those without their own car and in rural areas poorly served by public transport. And so it is that I find myself in witness rooms asking teenage boys who have been attacked in the street by hardened thugs to re-attend their 'local' Crown Court, a four-hour round trip on public transport, for an adjourned trial smack bang in the middle of their school exam period. Knowing that such requests are reinforced with the implicit threat of a court order to compel their attendance, it is difficult to convince myself, on such occasions, that I am on the side of good. Whose interests are being served by a justice system that treats its most vulnerable as dots and digits on a spreadsheet?

Where there is a clash between short-term fiscal policy and the welfare of victims, the former always wins out. Free pro-victim slogans, inexpensive talking shops and circular expressions of intent will triumph over costly extra court sitting days, a better quality of private contractor or a properly resourced prosecution service. I do not pretend that in a reality of finite resources, the solution is easy; but it is at least obvious. Practical improvements of the victim's treatment in the courts are identifiable. Unlock the empty courtrooms. Pay for more judges or recorders (part-time judges) to sit and deal with the backlog. Resource the police, CPS and the Witness Care Unit so that proper attention can be given to cases and errors can be minimized. Hold private contractors to their obligations, and enforce sanctions for the delay and suffering that is caused when they take four hours to drive a prisoner four miles to court. These should be the basics.

Victims v the Prosecution

'So let me get this straight,' the judge growled at me, head in his hands. I exchanged wide eyes with my opponent perched at the opposite end of the desk. He grinned, leant back in his chair and leisurely surveyed the environs of the judge's chambers. He, and I, knew what was coming.

Going into a judge's chambers is a curious experience. It's like going backstage at the theatre. The actors all take off their wigs, the formality is dialled down – the judge becomes 'Judge' rather than 'Your Honour' – and matters can be discussed more freely. Some judges only invite counsel into chambers under strictly limited and formal conditions, when the barristers need to tell the judge about a confidential matter that can't be spoken in open court – such as where a convicted defendant has turned police informant and wants the judge to know this before sentencing. Other judges habitually summon barristers for a gossip, post-match analysis, or, as in this case, where they want to bash heads together.

'The defendant has already pleaded guilty to two serious offences of violence. We're here today simply for trial on a minor allegation that, around the same time as breaking one man's jaw and injuring another's arm – both of which the defendant admits – he also bit someone's hand in the scuffle, and caused a tiny scratch that I can't even see on these damn photos.' The judge looked up to toss the offending images across the desk towards me.

That was the measure of it. The defendant, Ryan, had a distinguished history of expressing himself with wordless violence when he saw other men talking to his girlfriend. One such man was a twenty-two-year-old called Samuel, who made this error one night in a local bar. Two uppercuts and three kicks later, Samuel was cradling a shattered jaw, and his buddy, and brave intervener, Colin, was lying on the floor with an immobile arm. Sensibly, Ryan had pleaded guilty at an early stage to battery and inflicting grievous bodily harm. What he wouldn't admit, however, and the reason for our presence at trial that day, was that, as the melee spilled out onto the street and into the gutter, Ryan had deliberately bitten Colin's hand and caused a tiny, 1cm cut, charged optimistically in a separate count as actual bodily harm.

The judicial monologue continued.

'Now you tell me that the aforementioned bite-ee has attended court today oblivious to the fact that the defendant has even been charged with biting him.' I nodded – *Yes, judge. He came because he'd been mistakenly told that the defendant was denying breaking the other complainant's jaw.* The judge waved away my interjection. 'And this witness has said firstly that he's not sure that the bite was even intentional.' Another nod from me. 'And secondly, he has expressly told you that he has no interest in pursuing this trivial, inconsequential, unprovable bite to trial.' *Yup.* 'And your instructions from the Crown Prosecution Service are to nevertheless insist that this man go into the witness box and that we have a three-day trial, at the cost of several thousand pounds to the taxpayer, litigating something which will not make a blind bit of difference to the overall sentence?' I nodded and twirled my wig in my hands.

What I could not say out loud, but had tried to hint to the judge through coy smiles, nods and 'uh-huhs' during his soliloquy, was that I had given this exact advice, on three occasions including today, to the CPS Divisional Prosecutor.

Hauling seven civilian witnesses and three police officers to court for a three-day ABH Crown Court trial where the evidence of actual bodily harm is limited, and where the defendant has already pleaded guilty to inflicting grievous bodily harm such that, even if convicted of the bite, it would not make a difference to his sentence, does not appear to be in the public interest.

I had set out the Sentencing Guidelines to show how little difference the 'bite' would make to Ryan's sentence even if we won, which of course was by no means guaranteed. I suggested that the CPS speak to Colin, explain the position and seek his views. In response to my lovingly crafted five-page advice – gratis, I don't get paid for these things – I received a two-line memo from the Divisional Prosecutor saying simply, 'This must proceed to trial.' When I tried again, re-formulating my advice and politely asking whether I'd missed anything in my application of the public interest test, I got an equally sphinx-faced reply: 'I disagree with your advice. Proceed to trial.'

When Samuel and Colin arrived at court and realized that Ryan had already admitted breaking their respective jaw and arm, they immediately stated that they both wanted nothing more to do with proceedings. Colin's response when I explained that the trial was over the bite was a thoughtful, 'Bite? Oh yeah. Y'know, I don't think he actually meant it.'

I spoke to my nemesis on the phone and tried for a third time. His response was candid, if nothing else: 'We're not dropping this. I've read your advices, and if the witnesses are there, you're pressing on.' I explained – doing my level best to minimize the passive aggression in my tone – that not only were the witnesses reluctant, but Colin was effectively agreeing the defence case that the bite was not so much wilful mouth-to-hand as accidental hand-in-mouth. I really have to advise, I said, in the strongest terms, that we knock this on the head.

His barked reply disclosed the root of our stalemate: 'What about our statistics?'

I am not privy to the mysterious workings of CPS statistics, but a lawyer once told me that taking a decision not to proceed on the day of trial sets off all sorts of alarm bells, triggers and internal reviews. Therefore, even if a case is doomed, if it has nevertheless limped to the door of trial, the senior decision-makers will insist you push it through and force the jury, or the judge at the end of the prosecution case, to acquit.

And so we found ourselves in the judge's chambers at an

impasse, no one at court, least of all the victim, thinking that a trial was a sensible idea, but our hands tied by an office-bound civil servant craven to his statistics. The judge's expletive-filled reaction when I mentioned that the word 'statistics' had arisen in my discussions with the CPS was most unjudicial, but entirely apt.

And this illustrates the irreconcilable tension that can arise between the state prosecutor and the victim whose complaint it litigates. While the desires of the state and complainant often converge – both, for example, will usually want a conviction – the state has its own multiplex of competing interests to manage, some of which will sit at odds with the desires of the complainant.

Finite resources, for instance, will inevitably dictate that only cases where there is sufficient evidence to realistically support a conviction will be pursued to trial; to do otherwise would result in a disservice to not only the taxpayer but other complainants with more meritorious cases lingering in the blocked court system. It is also of fundamental fairness to the accused that the state does not abuse its might by launching speculative prosecutions based on negligible or inherently unreliable evidence, no matter how sure a complainant professes to be of a defendant's guilt. Moreover, public policy will require that some prosecutions, where there is evidence to support a charge, nevertheless ought not to be brought – for instance, in certain heartbreaking cases of assisted dying, or cases where a defendant is so infirm that a prosecution would be oppressive.

Those considerations are properly reflected in the Code for Crown Prosecutors, which we looked at earlier, setting out the test for whether to prosecute: is there a realistic prospect of conviction? And is it in the public interest, considering among other things the interests and wishes of the complainant?

Interests and wishes, it should be noted, are not synonymous. Domestic violence cases expose the distinction; often the prosecution will proceed notwithstanding the best efforts of the complainant, with her (for it is usually her) manipulative other half pulling her strings from the wings, to retract her truthful allegations. Securing the best interests of these vulnerable, repeat victims of abuse may require compelling them to cooperate with a trial process they profess no desire to enter.

But on other occasions, such as with Colin, it is difficult to see how the Code for Crown Prosecutors is being satisfied. *What about our statistics?* reverberates in my head several years on, a quasi-state secret let slip by an immovable bureaucrat in a flash of frustration.

Because we see, both in the ordinary cases that make up my daily fare and in macrocosm splashed across the newspapers, this third, uncodified consideration slip into prosecutorial decisions: *the prosecutor's interest test.* What makes life more straightforward for the CPS in a culture of hypercritical reflexive media reporting and centralized targets? And while cases such as Colin's are not a new phenomenon, the growing influence of extraneous considerations has in recent years been demonstrated most forcefully by the surge of prosecutions for allegations of historical sexual offences.

It is easy to understand how we got here. Taking allegations seriously, investigating them fully and prosecuting where the code is met are pillars of the prosecution covenant; too often in the twentieth century, we have belatedly learned, these were disregarded. Complainants – many potentially victims of the most horrific sexual crimes alleged against high-profile public figures – were failed. A correction was plainly required. Part of the recalibration has taken the form of the CPS Victims' Right to Review Scheme, whereby as of 2013 a complainant has a right to seek a formal review of a prosecution decision to not bring charges or to terminate proceedings. A corresponding scheme exists in respect of police decisions not to refer cases to the CPS. This is clearly a good thing. As the person most affected by the state's decision not to litigate a complaint, it stands to reason that the complainant has the right to request a review by a second CPS lawyer.

But while conscious decisions *not* to prosecute are now rightly made answerable, slipping under the radar are cases which are being prosecuted where they don't meet the code. Under-resourced and terrified of letting slip another Jimmy Savile, CPS Rape and Serious Sexual Offences (RASSO) units, set up in 2013 to provide a specialist prosecuting service for sexual allegations, have been overcompensating for historic wrongs by pursuing cases where the evidence simply isn't there. A review in 2016 concluded that RASSO units were misapplying the evidential test even more frequently than general CPS lawyers. Cases where there was no realistic prospect of conviction were being erroneously charged and erroneously reviewed. It was observed, from interviews with judges, police and barristers, that there was a perception of 'considerable pressure on the CPS to improve on success rates and to prosecute more cases, which may lead to some cases being pursued even though there is little chance of obtaining a conviction after a trial.'[20] A case study charted the tale, all too familiar to practitioners, of a weak case being wrongly charged, and subsequent reviewing lawyers feeling unable to take a sensible decision to discontinue the case. In other instances, 'decisions on cases are rushed to achieve timeliness targets and then subsequently dropped when more thought is given to the detail of the case.'

I have genuine sympathy. The pressure on the CPS, it must be recognized, is enormous. The media squall surrounding Greville Janner in 2014 is instructive. When the Director of Public Prosecutions decided that it was not in the public interest to prosecute the eighty-seven-year-old demented Labour peer on charges of historical sexual abuse, the media reaction was venomous. And wrongly so. While serious errors had been made in the 1990s and 2000s, when Janner wrongly, in the view of an independent report,[21] escaped prosecution, the position in 2014 was markedly different. Stricken with dementia and agreed by four psychiatrists to be 'unfit to plead' in law, Janner could not be tried in the ordinary sense. He could certainly not, as a matter of law, be convicted; all that could happen was a 'trial of the facts' in which the ultimate outcome could only have been an 'absolute discharge' – i.e. nothing. The DPP thus concluded that it would not be in the public interest to engage in a resource-intensive show trial of a seriously unwell octogenarian, putting complainants through the strain of criminal proceedings.[22] In response, campaigners and commentators, few of whom had acquainted themselves with the law or facts, clamoured for the DPP's resignation for 'failing the victims' until the decision was overturned (only to be ultimately thwarted by Janner inconsiderately dying shortly afterwards).

Now, imagine you're a CPS lawyer who saw first-hand the abuse that the DPP received for taking a difficult decision, which could not be sensibly characterized as unreasonable, not to prosecute a high-profile sex case. And you have on your desk, awaiting review, an allegation of historical sexual abuse, which doesn't quite satisfy the evidential test. With all that swirling in the mix, do you stick your head above the parapet and put your name to a decision to terminate proceedings? Do you rigorously apply the code and risk sparking a firestorm? Or do you perhaps loosen the strictures and think that, well, the case is *probably* going nowhere, but . . . we could stick it in front of the jury and see? Let them make the decision.

Many CPS lawyers I've worked with would do the first. They are brave and principled and cognizant of the compelling reasons why the code exists. But others, as the statistics in the report show, would follow the second course. Keep the complainant happy. Avoid any media fallout. Don't spook the internal CPS statistics. Plus, you never know – a jury may even convict.

I understand the human temptation. When I take off my wig and sit down with a witness at court to break the news that their case has collapsed, it is indescribably horrid. Being faced with the weeping flesh-and-blood cost of the system's failings and having to find the words to say, 'Sorry, no justice for you,' is one of the hardest parts of what we do. I at least am usually able to truthfully – weaselly – exculpate myself from personal blame by pointing to a decision of the judge or jury, or an evidential cock-up by a faceless, nameless police officer. I am fortunate enough not to have ever had to look a complainant in the eye and say, 'I see your pain. I hear your story. And, like the many professionals before me in whom you trusted, I am taking the decision to do nothing about it.' That daily burden on CPS prosecutors must be at times unbearable.

But the harm caused by pursuing weak cases is real, and acute. It is horribly difficult prosecuting sex cases. They are often compounds of the most combustible elements in the prosecutorial spectrum: extremely serious and distressing allegations; usually limited evidence beyond the word of the complainant; the complainant themselves may well be vulnerable and damaged and may have a personal, criminal or medical history which impinges upon their credibility. These cases usually invite media attention, plus there is the historical weight of state failure to act in previous such cases, and there is enormous public pressure to improve upon conviction rates perceived as historically paltry.

For all those reasons, it is imperative that only viable prosecutions are pursued to trial. Giving a complainant 'their day in court' is not an abstract administrative process.

It means dragging a potential victim of child sexual abuse through the years of interminable delays of the court process. It means compelling them to re-live, in public, freshly uprooted agonies that they thought were buried. It means subjecting them, in full view of their loved ones, to hostile cross-examination into the most intimate spaces of their personal and sexual lives. It means tearing through families, forcing parents and grandparents and children to take sides in traumatic adversarialism from which there is no hope of reunion. It means risking the burning anguish of a not guilty verdict which, no matter how many times you reassure them otherwise, they will forever carry as 'proof' that they were not believed.

Doing that is only justifiable, as a matter of fundamental morality as much as policy, if there is a realistic prospect that the state will secure a conviction. Any consideration that dilutes or interferes with the primacy of that assessment is bogus. It is to appropriate the complainant as an instrument in pursuit of another aim for which the criminal courts are neither intended, nor suited.

The criminal courts are not, for example, about catharsis, or giving a victim their day in court, or providing closure. If those emerge as fortuitous by-products of the trial process, so much the better, but the likelihood, from experience, is that the overriding emotion at the conclusion of a complainant giving evidence will be relief or regret, not celebration. Counsel are not counsellors. Cross-examination is not therapy.

Nor is the court designed as a tool for engineering statistics pleasing to CPS senior managers, or the politicians and special interests who bring their own agendas to bear on the independence of the prosecution. It should not be filled with unfeasible cases to virtue-signal to an inherently anti-defendant media Just How Seriously We Treat This Type of

Thing. Not least as the one thing guaranteed to wash out conviction rates is a flood of weak cases.

The court's ultimate function is unitary. It is to test state accusations of guilt. That's all the apparatus is set up to do. It tests the credibility of the evidence that the state brings in support of its case, and it asks the tribunal of fact one single question: are you sure of guilt? If the prosecution does not consider that it has a realistic prospect of succeeding, or that it is not in the public interest to prosecute, that must trump all else.

And although I don't for a moment expect those truths to be delivered by prosecutors to complainants in such stark terms, I do think it right that they, particularly those setting policy, internalize and act on those basic truths, instead of compromising. Being a prosecutor, as a wise colleague once told me, isn't about being popular. Less still, in the words of an even wiser judge, is it about bloody civil service targets.

The judge's solution to our impasse was ingenious. He directed that the CPS District Prosecutor attend court to explain his decision in person. Sure enough, no sooner had those words left my lips and whizzed down the receiver did the curt reply spring forth: 'Look, just offer no evidence. Goodbye.' After months of head-thumping wrangling, sensible instructions were finally forthcoming. But it took the threat of having to leave the snug confines of his office, enter the den of the criminal courts and publicly justify his decision, to make that jobsworth apply his mind to the genuine interests of the victims and the public. This is far from an exceptional tale. And, I would come to learn, far from an exceptional course taken by the judge.

Not long after, a colleague was prosecuting an allegation of racially aggravated common assault. The defendant had already been convicted of a spree of violent armed robberies and was awaiting sentence, which couldn't go ahead until this new matter was concluded. In between relieving jewellers of tens of thousands of pounds' worth of bling, he had slapped his girlfriend and called her a 'white bitch'. He admitted the assault. He would not admit using those words. Racially aggravated offences being of particular importance to CPS statisticians (notwithstanding the nil effect it would have on sentence in light of the armed robberies), there was no way, my friend was told, this could be dropped. Not even if the complainant agreed.

As in Ryan's case, when the apoplectic judge was informed of the Crown's position, he demanded an in-person explanation from the regional CPS bigwig. And, again, no sooner had the request been communicated than, strangely enough, an 'ad hoc review' immediately concluded that maybe, just maybe, proceeding to trial wasn't in the public interest after all.

Victims v Defendants

The filthy little secret that we hide from victims is that the aspects of the criminal process that often trigger the greatest distress are those that arise not by accident, but by design of the adversarial trial system that pits state against defendant. And this dynamic is worth considering further. Because amid the thud-thud of the Victims First march, there will be vulnerable people believing that the source of this trauma can easily be moderated. And crowd-pleasing snake oil politicians emptily indulging those misapprehensions, or worse, seeking to crudely realize them, with little understanding of the damage that they thereby do.

The difficulty begins when the state appropriates what is to an individual an essentially private dispute. From that moment, the fate of the victim and the state are tightly bound – although as we have seen above, it is far from an equal relationship. The victim is formally stripped out of the litigation; the indictment is headed 'Regina v Jones', not 'Smith v Jones'. The state determines whether to initiate proceedings, the parameters of any litigation and whether, at any stage, to silently discharge two bullets into the case and bury it at sea. The victim is no longer a victim; she is, in the properly neutral language of the court, a complainant. The existence and extent of her suffering will be doubted, the subject of debate and analysis by strangers; her agonies reduced to writing and legally pasteurized into admissible, artificial evidence. Her involvement is both peripheral and central; she is not represented – the prosecution barrister is not 'her barrister'; she will not be permitted to watch any of the pre-trial proceedings nor the trial itself until she has given evidence; and her views on what should happen at sentence are immaterial. Yet she will personally carry the success or failure of the proceedings. Her evidence will usually be crucial; she will be compelled under pain of imprisonment to attend court to deliver it. And, if the verdict is not guilty, she will feel responsible. No matter how many times I or any other prosecuting advocate assures her that a not guilty verdict does not mean that a jury has disbelieved her – often the verdict is a reflection of other weaknesses or inconsistencies in the prosecution's case – I will see in her eyes, as I see in the eyes of hundreds of others, that she doesn't believe me.

'The threshold for a guilty verdict is so very high,' I try to console a complainant after her alleged stalker is acquitted. 'It's not a reflection on you; it's a reflection on us, the prosecution.' But as the formula falls from my lips, it is plain she is not buying it. My entreaties cannot and will not help her find peace, or help her sleep. I'm just the wigged babbling fool who failed to catch her tormentor.

But more than that, being bound to the state also means

that the victim is forced to play by the state's rules, which hold at their heart a fundamental commitment to individual liberty. The state retains the power upon conviction to deprive a defendant of his freedom for any period up to and including his whole life. The greatest risk in this litigation is therefore borne by the accused; hence the centrality of the burden and standard of proof. Unlike in civil proceedings where only money is at stake and the burden is on the claimant to prove their case 'on the balance of probabilities', the potential for loss of liberty demands that a higher standard be imposed on a criminal prosecutor. They must prove their – and the complainant's – case beyond reasonable doubt. The defendant has to prove nothing. We agree that guilty people should walk free rather than the innocent be convicted. That is why, if we know one of two people did the deed but cannot be sure which one, we let both go free, rather than locking up both knowing that it guarantees we get the right man.

The complainant has to share that burden, and its consequences, in deference to our first principles. It regrettably follows that genuine victims will exit the process feeling that justice has been denied. That the verdict was wrong. But, save for the cases where the case has not been prosecuted competently, the only way to improve this state of affairs for the complainant would necessitate an incursion into the rights of the accused. Which would mean more innocent people are convicted.

The same zero-sum equation applies to the adversarial trial process. The defence advocate, instructed that his client is innocent, will at every turn be trying to undermine the credibility of the prosecution evidence, and therefore the complainant. Her honesty, accuracy and integrity will be questioned. If her evidence contrasts to the slightest degree with other evidence in the case, she will be accused of unreliability, or lying. If her evidence is wholly consistent with the others, it will be because she has connived with her fellow witnesses. If she mis-speaks, or contradicts herself, it will be held up to the jury as proof positive of her inherent uselessness as a witness of truth. If she breaks down in sobs, these are crocodile tears; a cynical performance for the jury.

It is this part of the process that understandably holds the greatest fear for witnesses. And it is the part that is guaranteed to see a defence barrister's face plastered across the tabloids when her guilty client is convicted and her earlier cross-examination of the distraught complainant is held up as the cynical effort of her client to evade justice for his sick acts. But while often the witness will be truthful, and the defendant a lying guilty scoundrel, on occasion the witness will be lying. Or genuinely mistaken. Improving the experience of the witness by softening the edges of the adversarial process may mean that those lies or mistakes go unexposed. And that innocent people are locked up.

There are of course proper limits on the way in which witnesses, and in particular complainants, may be challenged in court. Questions must be relevant. Advocates are barred, both by law and professional ethics, from pursuing lines of questioning or adopting demeanours designed to intimidate or humiliate witnesses. Vulnerable witnesses are eligible for 'special measures', allowing them to give evidence in court from behind a screen, or in certain cases over a video-link, to improve the quality of their evidence. Defendants cannot themselves cross-examine complainants in sex cases; if they are self-representing, a lawyer will be appointed by the court to act for them for that purpose.

But where we stray beyond that and interfere with the ability of the defendant to properly challenge the complainant's evidence, we are impeding him from challenging the prosecution. It sounds like a circumlocutory way to make a simple point, but I fear this self-evident truth has been relegated, if not forgotten completely, in the stampede to Put

Victims First. Testing a witness' evidence can sometimes not be done without robust challenge by the defence barrister. It is in those testy courtroom exchanges, as the sweaty witness becomes panicked, tied up in their own lies, that the jury sees the glint of truth escaping.

If, as we often hear suggested, certain lines of relevant questioning were prohibited in sensitive cases to spare the complainant's distress, the defendant would be deprived of challenging the prosecution evidence with the same vigour as he will no doubt be challenged by the prosecution barrister. Imbalance would result, and vital defence points, key to an acquittal, may not emerge in the evidence.

An illustration of this clash of interests made front pages in 2016, in the case of the professional footballer Ched Evans. His original conviction for rape was quashed on appeal after fresh evidence emerged relating to previous sexual behaviour of the complainant, and with the assistance of this evidence he was acquitted at his retrial. Questions about a complainant's sexual history are only allowed in tightly controlled circumstances following a change in the law in 1999,[23] and only where to *not* allow the evidence would result in the jury reaching an 'unsafe conclusion'. The Court of Appeal ruled that, in the exceptional circumstances of the case, the evidence and questions should be permitted. The reaction, from media, commentators and politicians, was as fevered as it was uninformed. This decision was falsely, but repeatedly, cited as establishing a dangerous precedent that women could be gratuitously asked about irrelevant matters of sexual history solely to discredit them in the eyes of the jury. The complaints were made almost entirely by people who didn't understand how the law operated, or why it was applied in the way it was in this particular case, and who didn't seem to care. Rather, they perceived a victim who had suffered an (undoubtedly) unpleasant and invasive experience in a sex trial, and decreed that Something Must Be Done. This Something, in the mind of Labour MP Harriet Harman, amounted to preventing defendants from ever applying to rely on evidence of a complainant's previous sexual history, a measure proposed as an amendment to a Bill in 2017.[24] It hadn't occurred to her to ask *why* the law allows such evidence in exceptional circumstances. She hadn't paused to consider, for example, that some of the grimmest cases involve sexual allegations made by very young children who have previously been abused. When, say, a troubled, confused seven-year-old girl makes a complaint against her teacher in the horrific detail that can only be gleaned from direct sexual experience, the prosecution will suggest to the jury that the allegation *must* be true; how else would a child so young know so much? But if the child was appallingly abused by her uncle at the age of five, this would provide the innocent teacher with an answer. Harman's Law however would strip him of this vital evidence. The complainant's comfort would be paramount. The impact upon the fairness of proceedings to the defendant, and the real risk of an unsafe conviction, would simply not matter.

And I fear that this captures the spirit of the times. Much of what has developed in recent years to accommodate witnesses – particularly the toolkits and training provided to advocates questioning child witnesses or witnesses with learning needs – is sensible, humane and proportionate. But when Putting Victims First means rebalancing adversarialism in the complainant's favour, and tilting the scales away from the defence, I worry. The test I think, in all such cases, is to put yourself in the shoes of the falsely accused. What restrictions on your ability to mount your defence are you content to accept to permit your accuser an easier ride? But as with so much when it comes to these debates, the underlying assumption is that *it will never be me*.

6. Defenceless and Indefensible

'To be an effective criminal defence counsel, an attorney must be prepared to be demanding, outrageous, irreverent, blasphemous, a rogue, a renegade, and a hated, isolated, and lonely person – few love a spokesman for the despised and the damned.'[1]

Clarence Darrow (1857–1938)

The Bar, and the criminal Bar in particular, invests its members with the glorious illusion of self-importance and gritty, doughty glamour. The role of the trial lawyer evokes the romantic myth of those historical and literary crusaders for justice whose swashbuckling advocacy and fearless derring-do capture the imagination of every popular retelling of a criminal case. Being a defence barrister satisfies that needy compulsion to take centre stage, to play the action hero in the story of somebody else's life. To be a defence barrister is to let the taste of the improbable acquittal linger coquettishly on the senses, before turning to your grateful, innocent client in the dock with the wink that says, Told You It'd Be Fine. It is to be greeted outside the swinging courtroom door by the ecstasy of vindicated relatives, patting you vigorously on the back and telling you that your voice, your *genius*, alone was the difference between the service of justice and its miscarriage. It is to tip your wig, and wryly reply to raucous, dizzy laughter: *In the nicest possible way, I hope I don't see any of you ever again*; and sweep into the embers of sundown with the misattributed words of Clarence Darrow playing against the swell of a John Williams soundtrack.

The daily reality is obviously nothing of the sort. You're more likely to be sitting in a urine-soaked cell with a career burglar demanding to know why his fucking co-defendant got unpaid work while he got three years, and listening politely at how the last fucking brief he had would've fucking got him off and what do you fucking mean there's no chance on a fucking appeal? But that is the story we spin for ourselves. We justify the neglect of our families and the ruin of our social lives with the soothing reassurances to our ego, bolstered by pop culture, that we Rumpoles, and what we do – trial advocacy – are what justice is all about.

Except, of course, it's not. Not remotely. Because the vast bulk of the work in most criminal cases will be done not by the advocate creaming the credit at the end of the trial, but by the litigator. The solicitor. If you are charged with a criminal offence, your solicitor will be your guiding light from dawn until dusk.

Their existence is critical to ensuring that the adversarial system functions as it should. And they are often under-appreciated as much by the Bar as by the public. I couldn't do what criminal solicitors do. I am fortunate to operate at several degrees of separation from the flesh and blood of my subject; by the time the brief reaches the barrister, the immediate horror of the allegations has been sanitized and packaged into a neat, dehumanized index of typed statements and two-dimensional photographs. The client will have had a few weeks to process his situation before he meets me; while he may still be distressed, the white-hot emotion of his visceral response to his predicament, often fizzing through the transcript of his police interview, has had time to cool. In that regard, much as I'd like to pretend otherwise, my services cannot really be described as front line. Whereas solicitors, like the police, very much are. They are the ones figuratively and literally rooting around in the dankest corners of the lives of those involved. It will be the solicitor who is roused at 3.30 a.m. to scurry to the police station to attend to the foaming, screaming crack addict caked in his girlfriend's warm blood; to inhale the foul mingling of bodily fluids and take those first harrowing instructions as to what manner of depravity he acted out upon her and exactly how he delivered the fatal blow. It will be the solicitor parking her car on the city's toughest estate as she trawls the neighbours for potential defence witnesses and returning to find her windows bricked in. She will be the one fielding hourly calls from the defendant's traumatized family bellicosely demanding answers that she cannot provide. Not me. I just read about her efforts in dispatches.

When defence solicitors are able to do their often grim and thankless job properly, it makes us all safer. The chances of the innocent being convicted, perhaps while the real culprit remains at large, are decreased. Good defence litigators keep the prosecution honest. And they keep the system honest.

A good example of this relates to one of the central planks of the grand efficiency reforms that kicked in in 2016: the drive to increase early guilty pleas.

As we saw earlier, one of the causes of scheduled trials not going ahead is defendants changing their pleas from 'not guilty' to 'guilty' at the last minute, often once they've learned that the prosecution witnesses have turned up for trial and conceded that the game is up. Tweaking the system to encourage such defendants to admit their guilt earlier, and spare the prosecution, courts and witnesses the cost of the matter proceeding to trial, is an ostensibly sensible way of smoothing those inefficiencies.

To achieve this, courts require a defendant to indicate his plea – guilty or not guilty – at the earliest stage in the proceedings before the magistrates, and penalize those who delay entering a guilty plea beyond that date. Again, on its face not an objectionable course: pragmatic sentencing policy has long rewarded those who admit their crimes with a 'discount' of up to one third off their sentence, and incentivizing this to occur at the earliest stage of the criminal process should generate the greatest savings.

But. But but but. We saw when discussing bail how little information is available to the defence at the first appearance. It often takes place within days of the alleged offence, while the prosecution case is still being built. The evidence against the defendant – the witness statements, photographs, medical reports and so forth – will often not have been passed to the CPS. All that the prosecution is required to provide at the first appearance is the often inaccurate MG5 police summary of the allegation; it is within the CPS's discretion as to whether other evidence is 'relevant to plea' and should therefore be handed over. And all the observations made when discussing bail apply here, only instead of a temporary restriction of liberty, the solicitor is expected to advise on the potentially life-changing issue of plea.

The justification is the tired mantra of the magistrates (and, increasingly, as a result of the 'efficiency reforms', judges) fired at the defence lawyer: 'Your client knows whether he's done it.' Which in straightforward cases may be correct ('Did you steal that apple, Dougal?' 'Yes ma'am, I did.') but in others will be a fallacy. Sometimes, it will simply not be possible to advise a client on whether the prosecution case is made out in law, without seeing the evidence supporting the charges. Saying 'a defendant knows what he's done' is like saying to a man in a GP's office: 'You know what's wrong with you.' He may know that his knee hurts, but how is he to say whether it is bruising, swelling, cartilage damage, pulled ligaments, a tear, sprain, twist, tweak or fracture without expert input? Now imagine the expert is asked to advise and diagnose without examining the knee. And then confidently recommend a life-changing course of action. That's what solicitors are being asked to do every day.

Let's take an example. A drunk yahoo on an adjacent barstool shouts something threatening in your direction and moves as if he's about to swing for you. You instinctively and pre-emptively hit him once to the face. He falls and thwangs his head on the floor. He later tells the police that he's suffered a fractured jaw, and you are charged with inflicting grievous bodily harm, carrying a prison sentence of up to five years. At the first appearance, your solicitor only has your instructions – which amount to, 'It all moved so fast, I thought he was going to hit me and I lashed out' – and the police MG5 summary based on the complainant's witness statement.

The issue here is whether you were acting in *reasonable* self-defence. The key word is 'reasonable': if a court finds that you were honestly acting in self-defence, but went *beyond* what is reasonable, you would be guilty. Cue your question: what is reasonable? The assessment of 'reasonableness' is the type of intangible value judgement on which a legal expert's opinion would be really quite useful. It would be invaluable, you might think, for a hardened veteran of such cases to advise on whether a court is likely to find for you or against you, before you admit guilt to a serious criminal offence.

If it were me advising, I would be enormously uncomfortable recommending a plea based on the MG5 and your hazy, speculative recollection. I would want to see the complainant's statement in full. I would want the statements of the other witnesses in the bar. I would want statements from your friends and family who saw what happened. I'd want the CCTV from the pub. I'd want to know a bit more about the complainant – let's see if he's the kind of brooding brute who would reasonably inspire terror, or if he's a five-foot, eight-stone string bean. I would want every perspective on that split-second flashpoint before I advised you on whether, in my professional opinion, you are likely to succeed running self-defence, or whether you are best off by pleading guilty on the basis that you intended self-defence but went a bit far, and thereby maximizing your discount on your sentence. I'd also want, for good measure, the medical evidence supporting the yahoo's claim of a fractured mandible, because if he's being untruthful and it's simply bad bruising, that ain't grievous bodily harm, sunshine.

But here's the rub – if I want that extra material, we're going to need an adjournment. And the new orthodoxy, as we saw when discussing magistrates, is No Adjournments. While we have already illustrated how this can operate against the prosecution, it operates equally as viciously against the defence. Whereas in the past a measure of judicial common sense was encouraged, and you could persuade a court to adjourn without indicating your plea to allow for that further, crucial evidence, now you will be forced to pin your colours to the mast. Plead guilty immediately, and get the lightest sentence. Or plead not guilty now, and then if you change your plea to guilty once the evidence has been served, take your punishment in the form of reduced credit on your sentence.[2]

The consequence of strong-arming defendants into early decisions is that people who may not be guilty of the charge – or of *any* charge – may feel pressured into pleading guilty. It is not merely a theoretical risk: the Court of Appeal has had to overturn convictions arising out of 'early guilty pleas' when the evidence has subsequently emerged and been shown to contradict the prosecution allegation.[3] And the only discernible explanation for the inflexibility of the policy is to save the court and prosecution costs involved in producing the evidence. Early guilty pleas equal cheap guilty pleas. It does not follow, of course, that early guilty pleas equal *correct* guilty pleas. The forsaking of the latter maxim in favour of the former is, in my view, repugnant. The courts, and the senior judiciary tasked with bringing in the new age of reform, trumpet an increase in guilty pleas as a self-evident good. I wonder whether they ever ask themselves how many guilty pleas would be too many.

But this all emphasizes the importance of good solicitors. Because solicitors have been central to challenging the operation of this policy, both at a higher level and at the coalface standing up to intransigent magistrates. Despite extreme pressure from courts to force solicitors to extract early pleas from their clients – for example, one London magistrates' court in 2016 operated a policy whereby any solicitor who wanted to apply for an adjournment would be made to wait all day until the end of the court list – good solicitors have stood firm and made plain, in person and through their professional bodies, that they will not collaborate in this parody of justice.[4] They have been relentless in resisting the state's efforts to save costs by diminishing the core principles of our justice system. They defy the prevailing judicial orthodoxy that more convictions and more guilty pleas, rather than the *quality* of justice, are the benchmarks by which our system should be appraised. And they are succeeding in winning incremental changes to the procedural rules that permit the present imbalance.

The importance of good, brave defence solicitors is further manifested at each stage of the criminal process. They take your instructions, apply for your legal aid, advise on the evidence, instruct the right barrister, instruct expert witnesses, take witness statements, visit you in custody if you're not on bail, chase the CPS endlessly for vital disclosure and handle an ever-growing Everest of paperwork on your behalf. And they do their damnedest to gather evidence to persuade the prosecution to discontinue. One of my solicitors visited fourteen houses to obtain fourteen witness statements from punters who confirmed that, contrary to what two police officers had claimed, my client Nathan, the landlord of The Old Goat, had in fact been in a different room of the pub entirely when the violence at the bar broke out, and far from being the instigator was trying to keep his old mum out of harm's way. The mistaken identification by the police officers was accepted by the CPS, who dropped the case before trial. Without his solicitor's efforts, there might have been a very different outcome. He was a magistrates' bench away from wrongful conviction, revocation of licence, and loss of home and livelihood. Such what-ifs often give me serious pause for thought.

However. There is an iceberg ahead.

The ability of publicly funded defence solicitors to do their job is under increasing peril. Prosecutorial and systemic inefficiencies and the correctives devised to address them together conspire to load resource-sapping burdens onto the plates of small and medium firms. In a sinister pincer, the relentless slashing of legal aid rates renders it near-impossible for many solicitors to remain financially viable. Meanwhile, their client base is under threat from a particular breed of unscrupulous vulture solicitor lurking in the shadows of the system. These crooks care not a jot for professional reputation nor the welfare of the defendant; they are parasites. They are the minority whose contempt for ethical and moral norms regrettably often defines the public perception of criminal defence lawyers. These firms poach unwitting clients with empty promises of guaranteed acquittals, cash payments and gifts. Once the client is signed up, they sit and wait to cash the legal aid certificate without doing any work on the case, either forcing the defendant to plead guilty or leaving him to swing in the breeze at trial. Their business model is stack 'em high and sell 'em cheap, maximizing the number of cases and minimizing the work actually done – a repugnant, but hideously rational, consequence of meagre fixed legal aid rates.

While presently this rabble is in the minority, if good local firms, caught between an indifferent system and unregulated pirates, find themselves unable to stay afloat, a lacuna will emerge which may be filled by exactly the wrong type of outfits. The unwary first-time defendant reliant on publicly funded criminal defence will be in very real danger.

Let's look at how the unsustainable pressures on defence solicitors are operating in practice.

Doing the Prosecution's Job

We've already visited the inefficiencies of the system in earlier chapters, and seen their impact upon the prosecution, courts and witnesses. But what we have not yet explored is how over recent years these have been reimagined not as the problem of the prosecution, nor of the court, but of the defence.

Walk into any case management hearing – where pre-trial issues are thrashed out – in any criminal courtroom, and you will usually observe two phenomena. First, the prosecution being castigated for failing to serve or disclose crucial material many months ago, in repeat defiance of multiple iterations of court directions. And second, the exasperated judge or magistrates, having listened to the prosecutor's predictable homilies ('It's a regrettable oversight, Your Honour'; 'I'm afraid I don't have a satisfactory explanation to put before the court'; 'Your Honour is aware of the straitened resources under which the Crown is operating'), recalibrating their artillery to take aim at the defence advocate and demanding to know what the defence have done to fix the problem.

Why so, you ask? The prosecution brings the proceedings

against the defendant; if it can't get its act together and comply with basics such as serving the evidence on which the case relies, what concern is it of the defendant? Why does he not just silently sit back and, if the prosecution's house is in disarray on the day of trial, take advantage by escaping lithely through a window? Why should he be under any obligation to mop up the Crown's spillages?

The answer lies in a cultural shift that has taken place over the last fifteen years or so, which has been codified in the Criminal Procedure Rules that since 2005 reign over criminal proceedings. Back in the mid- to late twentieth century, the burden of proof was not merely sacrosanct but absolute. The prosecution had to prove its case. The defendant was entitled to say nothing, do nothing, and simply wait until trial to see if there was a chink in the prosecution chainmail through which a cunning solicitor or barrister could fire a silver bullet. Often, the silver bullet would be a highly obscure and technical point of law; other times, it would be a point so crashingly obvious that the prosecution had assumed it was agreed and so had not adduced any evidence on it. Most commonly, these 'ambush defences' were deployed in the magistrates' courts, often in trials of motoring offences, where the general lack of order and scrutiny proved fertile ground for such tactics to thrive.

In the post-Criminal Procedure Rules world, things are very different. The 'overriding objective' of the Rules is that cases be dealt with 'justly', a proposition that includes:

> Acquitting the innocent and convicting the guilty, dealing with the prosecution and the defence fairly, respecting the interests of witnesses, dealing with the case efficiently and expeditiously, and also [. . .] dealing with the case in a way that takes into account the gravity of the offence, the complexity of what is in issue, the

severity of the consequences to the defendant and others affected and the needs of other cases.[5]

Additionally, both prosecution and defence are now under a duty to actively assist the court in that objective. A key component of this is that, after centuries of not being so required, the defence must clearly identify the disputed issues at the outset of proceedings. In a series of High Court decisions from 2006 onwards, cherished totems of the cunning defence lawyer were demolished one by one, held to be contrary to the spirit and letter of the New World Order. Defence lawyers were sternly warned:

> Criminal trials are no longer to be treated as a game, in which each move is final and any omission by the prosecution leads to its failure. It is the duty of the defence to make its defence and the issues it raises clear to the prosecution and to the court at an early stage.[6]

And so, at the first appearance before the magistrates, the defence will be expected to specify what is disputed: the correctness of an identification, or the accuracy of scientific evidence, self-defence, the drugs weren't mine and so forth. Attempting to obscure the issues, or raising an issue at the last minute in a nostalgic ambush, will attract not just censure but cost penalties against the lawyers. Plus the prosecution will be given the opportunity to reopen their case and fill the gap you've so cleverly spotted, so you gain no advantage whatsoever. If you fail to identify the issues in a Defence Statement in Crown Court proceedings, the jury can be told that they can hold that against the defendant when considering the issue of his guilt. Defence engagement is now key.

There are conflicting schools of thought among professionals and academics. Traditionalists would argue, and have argued (normally unsuccessfully before the High

Court), that this sea change offends basic founding principles of adversarialism, such as the burden of proof and the right to silence. No one chooses to be prosecuted; why should a defendant 'identify the issues' and give the prosecution a chance to build a stronger case against him?

For my part, I'm a little less militant (or less principled, depending on your view). While recognizing the eminence of the burden of proof, I see no offence in trying to ensure that cases are determined on their evidential merits, rather than on the sharpness of the lawyer. If the prosecution evidence is weak, or if, despite multiple opportunities, the Crown has omitted to address holes in its case, a defendant should plainly be entitled to the benefit of the state's failure. But where gamesmanship is deployed to catch the prosecution off-guard on a technical point of procedure, I struggle to accept that this is just part and parcel of the adversarial procedure. I think that the old way of operating was premised on a conception of justice as requiring solely the avoidance of the conviction of the innocent. Whereas I would submit, perhaps to howls of anguish from purists, that while that must be the most important principle, it is not the *only* one. As the Criminal Procedure Rules, and first principles, provide, the conviction of the guilty is of obvious secondary importance. And while I would never advocate a system that prioritized that over the acquittal of the innocent (for that way tyranny lies), requiring that the 'game' – even a game to which one participant is dragged rather than invited – be played by common rules designed to ensure a just outcome seems to me to be right. Rules that allow the court and the parties to engage with the real issues, and ensure that the proceedings are played cleanly by both sides, appear to be a proportionate means of achieving it. And if, as the Bar Code of Conduct tells me, my duty is to assist the court in the administration of justice, identifying the issues for trial does not strike me as anathema.

The rub comes when we look at how that principle has evolved in the courtroom. Because in practice, the defence are expected to do far more than simply identify the issues. Many solicitors would reflect that they are often expected to do the CPS's job for them. 'Assisting the court in fulfilling the overriding objective of the Rules' means that, if the court has directed that the CPS serve key evidence or a legal application (say an application to rely on the defendant's previous convictions) by a given date and the CPS has defaulted, the defence should be chasing the CPS to remind them to serve the incriminating evidence against their client. Rather than assume that the CPS's indolence will be their downfall, defence solicitors must in the spirit of the Rules chivvy the prosecution along and bring its failure timeously to the court's attention. Chasing the CPS has always comprised a thankless portion of the defence solicitor's diet. As we have seen, the disclosure of material in the prosecutor's possession that might reasonably assist the defence or undermine the prosecution and which the Crown are legally obliged to provide to the defence has long been abominable in both magistrates' and Crown Courts, and it is not uncommon for dozens of requests to be faxed, emailed and deposited on CPS answering machines, never to be addressed. But that, although unacceptable, can at least be chalked up as a job foreseeably within the remit of the defence representatives. When the same effort again has to be expended chasing material that doesn't assist your client but *assists the prosecutor*, solicitors are carrying a burden which, aside from the obvious objection from principle, has a cumulative consequence on defence resources. Put simply, the more time a firm spends chasing the CPS, the less time it has to prepare its clients' defences. And as the CPS budget has decreased, and its inefficiencies have increased, the volume of additional unpaid chasing that the defence are expected to undertake is going up and up and up.

I slipped in the word 'unpaid' advisedly. Because here lies the kicker. In police stations, magistrates' courts and 'volume' Crown Court cases (the bulk of the Crown Court's everyday work, excluding the super-serious or important cases), which make up the bulk of solicitors' work, and where the prosecution disorder is greatest, solicitors are paid a fixed fee per case. This system has been in place in the magistrates' court since 1993, and as of the latest round of 'reform efficiencies' in 2016, this has been extended so that litigators are now paid a modest fixed fee for police station, magistrates' court and Crown Court cases involving up to 500 pages of evidence (i.e. most Crown Court work). The fixed fee is intended to reduce spending on legal aid, but often does not reflect work actually done. If the idiosyncrasies of a case – the vulnerabilities of the defendant or the complexity and volume of the evidence – render it more time-consuming, much of the solicitor's work is unpaid. Or, if you like, all of it is paid, but at an economically unviable rate.

This may surprise you. The stereotype holds that lawyers are fabulously well off. You may well know a lawyer, or of a friend of a friend who's a lawyer, who is fabulously well off. If so, I offer you an iron-clad guarantee that they are not a criminal lawyer. We'll look a little more at the myths of barristers' earnings later, but suffice to say that the rates that your defence solicitor will be paid on legal aid can be astonishingly low.

What is Your Solicitor Being Paid?

Let's take a worked example, from police station through to trial. To borrow from a case I once defended: let's imagine that your marriage sadly dissolves, and you leave the family home to live elsewhere whilst the acrimonious legal process takes its course. On the eve of an important business trip, you realize in a panic that your passport is in a drawer in the study of your former abode. Your spouse is herself away on holiday and the house is locked and empty. Fortunately, you know that by jimmying a screwdriver in the conservatory back door, you can spring the mechanism, let yourself in, retrieve your passport and skip away into the starlight, with no harm or damage caused. Unfortunately, a nosy neighbour, knowing the occupiers to be in Spain, spies you fiddling with the rear door and calls the police, who arrive in a blaze of sirens moments later. When the police telephone your vengeful spouse in Malaga, she throws her weight behind a tactical prosecution, claiming that your true purpose in breaking in was to help yourself to certain valuable trinkets that were the subject of dispute in the divorce proceedings.

Your explanation cuts little ice with the uniformed officers, and you are arrested on suspicion of burglary and escorted to your local police station, arriving shortly before midnight. At this point, your solicitor kicks into action. They will clamber out of bed and head across town to join you. They will advise you during your police interview, which can last, depending on the seriousness of the allegation and the skill of the interviewer, up to several hours. In an ideal world, your explanation would suffice for the police to take no further action. But given what the police are inclined to believe in this case, they persist. You are bailed pending further enquiries, and, a month later, are charged with burglary.

That sounds like a straightforward enough process, but in that period between arrest and charge your solicitor will be beavering away for hours, if not days, trying to head off the prosecution. They will be writing letters to the police custody sergeant trying to relax that ridiculous condition on your police bail that prevents you from seeing your children.

They will be liaising with your divorce solicitor to obtain any paperwork from those proceedings that might help in proving your *bona fides* to the police. If you had been required to attend an identification procedure at the police station, they would accompany you, scrutinize the procedure to ensure its lawfulness and deal with the paperwork, which might take close to a full day. If further evidence emerges and the police wish to interview you again, back you and the solicitor go. You may have two years' worth of confrontational emails and social media correspondence with your estranged spouse, which your solicitor will read to ascertain whether anything might help you. There will be phone calls with you and written correspondence and every effort made to put together enough to dissuade the police from charging you.

For all that work, the solicitor will be paid a single fixed 'police station attendance' fee of roughly £170. If that sounds a low gross figure for what might amount to twenty hours' work, it's because it is. In the words of a solicitor I know, *every police station attendance is now considered a loss-leader*. Solicitors do it because they hope firstly that they will succeed in heading off a prosecution, and you will recommend the firm to your less fortunate friends, and, secondly, if you are charged, that you instruct them to represent you for the court proceedings, which may pay slightly better.

Not always, though.

Having been charged, you are now facing trial for burglary, an either-way offence that can be heard either before the magistrates or a jury. Let's say you qualify for legal aid and instruct the same solicitor's firm to prepare your defence for trial. Now a litigator might typically carry out the following work:

— Read and analyse the evidence (one hour)
— Examine the prosecution Schedule of Unused Material

and assess what unused prosecution material might be of help to your case (thirty minutes)
— Hold a conference with you to take your instructions (two hours)
— Prepare your Defence Case Statement to serve on the court (one hour)
— Draft your 'proof of evidence' (your witness statement, which is not served on the court or prosecution, but is used by your advocate when examining you in evidence to ensure that all relevant questions are asked) (one hour)
— Attend case management hearings at court (anything between half a day to a full day)
— Contact and take statements from your two defence witnesses (two hours)
— Accompany you to a conference with your trial advocate (two hours)
— Arrange the instruction of a defence expert to challenge the prosecution expert fingerprint evidence (two hours)
— Obtain the tapes of your police interview and check the accuracy of the prosecution transcript (three hours)
— Respond to your queries over telephone and email (two hours)
— Correspond with the prosecution in writing and over the phone regarding disclosure requests (one and a half hours)
— Attend court for a two-day trial (either as your advocate in the magistrates' court, or to support you and the advocate in the Crown Court)

On this rough calculation, we're looking at about twenty-two hours' preparation pre-trial, and then two days at court – so sixteen hours – for the trial itself. Now let's look at what, on current fixed legal aid rates, the litigator would expect to be paid.

In the magistrates' court, depending on geographical location the fee would be between £650 and £720. So between £17.10 and £18.95 an hour. In the Crown Court, it's even lower: the same case would attract a fixed litigator's fee of £352.72, giving a gross hourly rate of £9.28. The London living wage is £9.75 an hour. Even if we forgo the attendance at Crown Court, which for obvious reasons many solicitors nowadays do, the hourly rate lingers around £16. That is gross – out of that, the firm must pay staff salaries, National Insurance contributions, pension contributions, rent, rates, administrative costs, practising certificates for each solicitor, training costs, insurance and tax. Regardless of size, firms must employ a Compliance Officer for Legal Practice and a Compliance Officer for Finance and Administration. They must also pay to hold a quality mark authorizing them to carry out criminal legal aid work, and for IT costs to work on the court digital platform.

Imagine the quality of tradesman you would get offering that net rate. If on the day of trial the defendant pleads guilty, or the prosecution drops the case, the solicitor's fee will plummet to £233. Studies of the similar fixed fee regime in Scotland showed that, following its introduction, lawyers dramatically increased the number of cases they undertook, and correspondingly significantly reduced the time they spent preparing each one.[7] Such behaviour, while terrifying if yours is one of those cases, is the only rational response to such fee models. Although not the time for special barrister's pleading, this is perhaps an appropriate place to remark that, if you have elected a Crown Court trial – i.e. if the magistrates deem your case suitable for summary trial, but you sensibly prefer your chances in front of a jury – and you end up pleading guilty on the day of trial – perhaps because the prosecution make an offer that you can't refuse (let's say they offer to drop the burglary if you plead guilty to causing £15 worth of criminal damage to the conservatory door) – your barrister will be paid a flat fee of £194 for all her efforts on the case. All her appearances at court, all her trial preparation, all her conferences with you. The gross hourly figure, if it bears calculation, can be less than £3. Again, consider the perverse incentives deliberately engineered by the system which shouldn't, but which may, be influencing how much time your barrister decides to devote to preparing your case, or what advice they may give you when the prosecution dangle an offer in front of you. I will say, hand on heart, that my perennial 'impostor syndrome' and terror of looking foolish propels me to put as much effort into my cases as the laws of time and space allow; but I know several barristers who, faced with the prospect of making a loss on a case – of literally paying to work – will wing it and hope for the best.

If you are wondering how we came to a position where our betters decided that criminal defence representation was worthy of an hourly rate one tenth of an electrician's,[8] you will as ever find the answer embedded in a morass of institutional incompetence and botched money-saving. The Ministry of Justice's grand plan announced in 2013 was to slash the number of criminal legal aid firms by two thirds, from around 1,600 to 527, through a complex contracting scheme.[9] In short, only 527 firms would be contracted to carry out police station work, thereby excluding the remaining 1,100 from a valuable source of clients. The theory was that this would force a 'market consolidation' – i.e. the financial collapse of hundreds of small- and medium-sized businesses – which would result in fewer, larger criminal firms handling far more work. The economies of scale that it was assumed would follow would allow the MoJ to cut solicitors' fees, which had already been significantly reduced in real terms by inflation since their last adjustment in 2007, by a further average of 17.5 per cent, split into two staggered reductions of 8.75 per cent. It was another cheerful hurrah for the 'stack 'em high and sell 'em cheap' model beloved in the mags' courts, with no regard for quality of or access to justice. The fact that, for example, the contracting model would result in 'deserts' in rural areas, with a lack of local firms forcing defendants to travel several hours just to see a solicitor, was not germane to the MoJ's contemplations.

Nor, it transpired, was a grasp of economics. Because the base assumption of the model – that criminal firms could, through consolidation, absorb further significant cuts to legal aid rates – was false. The precarious finances of most criminal firms, even big firms, meant that very few could sustain the cuts, nor could they afford the upfront cost of restructuring into the larger organisms that the MoJ assumed would materialize. This was the conclusion of an independent report[10] that the MoJ itself commissioned in conjunction with the Law Society to analyse its proposed reforms. Before the government had acted on its proposals, the report warned that there were serious problems with the MoJ's modelling. It was noted that criminal legal aid firms operated on a tiny net profit margin – an average of 5 per cent – and their finances were 'fragile'. The bigger firms, perhaps counter-intuitively, reported the slimmest profit margins. Most did not have significant cash reserves or high excess bank facilities. The report cited research indicating that 50 per cent of solicitors' firms were at medium or high risk of financial difficulty, with their reliance on legal aid income a relevant 'risk factor'. Firms indicated that they had already made every cost saving they could, and there was little scope to reduce overheads further.[11]

What's more, the above calculations did not reflect a *previous* round of legal aid cuts that took place in 2010, including a 37 per cent real-term cut in Crown Court advocacy fees. Although this cut was aimed mainly at barristers, many solicitors' firms employ their own barristers or solicitor-advocates to conduct Crown Court advocacy and rely on the advocacy fees to cross-subsidize the lower-paid litigator rates. So the already gloomy assessment was in fact unduly optimistic. With all this in mind, the report implored the government not to implement any fee cuts with the market in its present condition.

Within a month, on 20 March 2014, the government went ahead with the first round of 'average' 8.75 per cent cuts to fees anyway, and the imposition of fixed fees for the bulk of the Crown Court litigation work.

Fortunately, shortly after the second tranche of cuts came into force, and following organized industrial action sparked by firms in the north-west refusing to take on cases under the new scheme, then-new Justice Secretary Michael Gove recognized his predecessor's folly and quickly abandoned the entire new contracting model in January 2016, reversing and suspending the second cut in the process. Less fortunately, he elected to leave that first 8.75 per cent cut in place, which, for firms operating on a net profit margin of 5 per cent, has not been easy to absorb. And that second cut remains hanging in abeyance; a Damoclean threat as the MoJ seeks to negotiate further cuts by other means.

And, of course, in the fixed fee model, each phone call made to the CPS chasing evidence, each fax repeating a disclosure request, each letter containing polite reminders to comply with court directions, each case management hearing and each futile adjournment represents an added expense for which the solicitor is not reimbursed. While streamlining proceedings and reducing the number of unnecessary court hearings will in the long term help to reduce the burden on defence firms, in the meantime it is they who are expected to shoulder more and more of the problems caused by the court and CPS inefficiencies.

This can't be right. Recent ministerial announcements appear to consider publicly funded law as a virtue; as something that can be done below cost or pro bono, subsidized by a firm's lucrative commercial law practice.[12] But aside from the offensive assumption that there is no value in criminal specialists, that this tortuous, complex legal behemoth can be tamed and mastered in the spare time of a Savile Row-embossed mergers and acquisitions associate, it cannot be right as a matter of principle that a decision on liberty is viewed as a loss leader. If you were wrongly accused of an offence, how confident would you be of the quality of your representation if you knew that their hourly rate was below minimum wage? Criminal cases should be paid properly in their own right. If they are not, if solicitors are paid peanuts, we know what will be proverbially swinging through the branches to defend you.

Fixers and Vultures

I first met Darius in the cells of the local Crown Court. The brief for his preliminary hearing had been hurled at me by the senior clerk at 6.25 p.m. the previous evening; an added bonus to my growing collection of 'returns' from senior, busier members of chambers. A 'return' is Bar lingo for covering somebody else's work; as court listings take little account of barristers' availability (and on the occasions that they do, the climate of chaos, delay, trial overruns and adjournments often conspires to make you unavailable), we frequently have diary clashes that prevent us from appearing at hearings for one or more of our cases, and call upon a colleague to step into the breach. A key part of the clerks' jobs is to keep an eye on the roving carousel and ensure that all hearings for the following day are covered when the music stops; thus, when they get a phone call from a ragged barrister at 5.05 p.m. reporting that her three-day trial is going into its fourth day, all hands leap to the pump to ensure that there is someone else in chambers who can pick up whatever other hearings that barrister has in her diary. As a junior paddling at the bottom of the food chain, returns make up a significant chunk of your practice until you have developed enough of a name that solicitors start instructing you in your own right. So it was that I, as chief bottomfeeder, had Darius enter my life.

The brief, even for a preliminary hearing, was alarmingly lightweight to the touch. While this, the first hearing in the Crown Court, was usually conducted without the full prosecution papers, which would be served some weeks later, the solicitors should have made efforts to scrape together more than just the police summary. There should also be some basic instructions from the solicitors, providing essentials such as the client's instructions to date, what he says about the allegations and any particular information that the barrister might need to know before meeting the client.

Such as the fact that the client has severe, crippling learning difficulties. That he is the abused product of a drinker (Mum) and a heroin addict (Dad), and, like many such children falling through the systemic cracks has disabling, belatedly diagnosed mental health problems. That, after Mum walked out when he was three, he had been raised single-handedly by ineffectual, addled Dad and had received no formal education, and was barely able to communicate. That his was therefore a world of perpetual silence and frustration, governed by a malign host of psychological, behavioural and psychiatric disorders that had culminated, since the age of fourteen, in a procession of Youth and magistrates' court appearances for the various petty offending – mostly criminal damage and public disorder – in which his frustration was manifested. And that, as his condition deteriorated, he had spent his nineteenth birthday in a secure unit, having been sectioned under the Mental Health Act, until upon his recent release returning to live with his dad.

All this I learned at court when, desperately searching for information and thwarted by the solicitor's refusal to pick up the phone, I resolved to pester the court probation officer, Martin, to dig out an earlier pre-sentence report from Darius' last appearance before the courts. Combined with the MG5, this enabled me to piece together the ghastly tableau of Darius' existence.

The clue to the informational void on my brief lay in the name of the solicitor typed unassumingly on the backsheet: Keres & Co. I use the term 'solicitor' loosely, because proper criminal solicitors are nothing like the amoral charlatans pretending at law that Keres represented. It is difficult to describe their malevolence without it reading like the character biography for 'Bad Lawyer 1' in a treatment for a 1990s screenplay. Every aspect of their existence – their *modus operandi*, the people they employ, the values they embody – was unyieldingly foul. The one positive is that such firms are fortunately a tiny minority, but nevertheless, exist they do, and for a first-time entrant to the criminal courts, your unwariness is their gain.

Their model for getting clients through the door relied not on a reputation for quality of service, but on 'fixers'. While it would be naive to ignore the reality that solicitors have to cultivate good relationships with the type of people that most of us would rather pretend didn't exist, the use of fixers is a particularly ugly proposition. Fixers are themselves not qualified lawyers – although they may occasionally brand themselves 'legal associates' or some other such semantically null title – and are often far closer to the roots of organized crime than a professional relationship should involve. They know people who know people, and when there's an arrest for a serious offence, the fixer is the one dripping honeyed words into the ears of the criminal community elders to secure the opportunity to tout the defendant's right to representation to the highest bidder.

If, for example, there's a giant drugs bust that looks likely to lead to a lucrative trial, the fixers and the Keres solicitors will be sniffing around the pubs, courts and prisons for an opportunity to lure the defendants away from their instructed solicitors and towards the brilliant wolfish smile of Mr Keres. The means of persuasion are often material – new trainers, contraband cigs in prison, a nice cash deposit in the girlfriend's bank account – but just as frequently fall back on the simple device of false advertising. Keres & Co. were peddling post-truth back before it was popular. *We guarantee to get you a not guilty*, they ooze. *We'll get you the best barrister – we have all the best barristers*, they spin like a poor Donald Trump parody. Sometimes they will indeed instruct very good barristers – the individuals in my chambers whose returns I was covering were excellent advocates. I don't know how on a human level they could bear to associate with Keres, but they seemingly accepted his malignancy as the price to pay for work. Other times, however, the Keres of this world will not instruct good counsel. They will keep the brief in-house, and instruct their own, lowly paid and even lower-ability employed advocates; barristers and solicitor-advocates tarnishing the brand with Ratner-style recklessness. These advocates barely know the law. They barely know the facts. When they know the facts, they think nothing of lying outright – be it to the client, their opponent or the judge. On numerous occasions, faced with one of these clowns as my opposite number, I have had to correct something said to the judge which directly contradicted what they had told me moments earlier. Everyone in the robing room and no doubt everyone in the judges' dining hall rolls their eyes at the mention of these names.

Alternatively, they might instruct an 'independent' barrister whose independent commitment to professional ethics is not a bar to him slipping Keres a tasty percentage of his brief fee in return for his instructions. Advocates' fees are paid separately to litigators' fees and directly to the advocate, to avoid the market distortion and dirty race to the bottom that would ensue if solicitors instructed barristers based not on ability but on how much of the advocacy fee they were willing to shovel the solicitor's way. And the vast majority of solicitors and barristers observe this strict separation. But every robing room will echo with whispers over that one barrister whose steady influx of high-quality work from a single, Keres-esque firm belies his modest talents, and in less-sober moments at Christmas parties, confessions will slip from mulled lips as to the existence of the informalized, forbidden referral fee lying at the heart of that arrangement.

Once the client is snared and the legal aid certificate is transferred, Keres' work on the case ends. They may *occasionally* venture to court or to prison for a quick PR visit with the client, but nothing constructive will be done on the case. If a decent barrister has been instructed, she will usually compensate for the solicitor's dereliction of duty by effectively doing the litigation herself. Otherwise, if it is a magistrates' case handled by Mr Keres himself, or a Crown Court case kept in-house or briefed on a referral fee, Keres & Co. will force the client to plead guilty, or proceed to trial and wing it. If the client is potted, they hope that he's too vulnerable or dim to identify their culpability. If he is acquitted, Mr Keres' reputation is enhanced. While I would usually say that the market in criminal litigation operates effectively – heavyweight crims are usually sufficiently long in the tooth to recognize a decent firm – the Keres buck the trend. Somehow, by hook or, more aptly, crook, they manage to trap some repeat clients for years.

Such as Darius, I would come to learn. As I stepped into the cell conference room and squeezed myself behind the table into the screwed-down seat closest to the wall (by the panic button, as my pupilmaster always taught me, 'Just in case the little bugger gets frisky'), I refreshed my memory of the allegations from the single-page police summary.

One evening a few weeks previously, Darius had asked his dad for some money to buy cigarettes. Dad said no. The argument escalated, and Darius picked up a plastic tray and threw it towards Dad, missing him by a good few feet. As Dad and Darius squared up to each other, Darius pushed Dad onto the sofa, before grabbing a fiver from Dad's wallet on the side and running out. Dad called the police, and Darius was charged with robbery.

His first phone call at the police station, or rather the call placed on his behalf, was to Keres & Co. Solicitors. And their craftsmanship was evident. As Darius' home address was his dad's house, he was remanded into police custody. The magistrates, with no alternative bail address sought by Mr Keres, remanded him at the first appearance, where he had remained for the best part of a month until I met him. I would learn that the bastard Keres hadn't bothered to visit Darius in prison, let alone tried to secure his vulnerable young client a place at a bail hostel. He hadn't spoken to the CPS to try to persuade them against prosecuting in the very sad circumstances. Darius, who had been advised to give a 'no comment' interview, had not been asked to give Keres any instructions as to what had happened that evening. Nothing of relevance, such as psychiatric or medical records, had been obtained. The prison had not been informed about Darius' medications. No intermediary had been arranged to help Darius communicate with me or the court. Keres had just left this boy to rot in his world of perpetual silence.

The question I was restraining myself from asking as a red-eyed Darius sloped into the seat opposite me was *Why them?* But more pressing matters were at hand. Over the next hour, we fumbled through speech and gesture as I learned about his life, taking what instructions I could. As

I led him through his previous convictions, the explanation for his dependency on Keres started to transpire. He'd always gone with them, since they approached his dad outside the Youth Court after one of his teenage appearances and successfully peddled their snake oil. He trusted that nice Mr Keres, who had always told Darius to plead guilty before the magistrates, whether he'd done it or not, 'as it's better for everyone'. Keres would never arrange for an intermediary at court – Darius would just rely on Mr Keres telling him at the end of the hearing what had been said and admitted in his name. The communication channels were obviously imperfect: for an offence of criminal damage earlier this year, Darius had been given a suspended sentence, of which he was now potentially in breach. When I mentioned this to him, it came as a complete surprise.

As the cell staff started banging on the door to alert me to the frantic loudspeaker announcements – *All counsel to Court 4, immediately. IMMEDIATELY. All counsel, IMMEDIATELY* – it was plain that we were not going to make any progress in court today. I, or rather instructed counsel, needed a lengthy conference with Darius, with an intermediary and the prosecution papers, before he could be properly advised on his plea. As I tumbled into court, spitting my profuse apologies for keeping everybody waiting, I tried to mentally formulate a form of wording that would not only secure the adjournment, but would impress upon the judge just how horrendously negligent Keres had been, in the hope that he would say something – I don't know what – that I might be able to feed back to Keres in my furious attendance note. Sadly, the judge was disinclined to hear Darius' tale. As I started to set out the bail position, the judge cut me off: 'I see there is no intermediary. Presumably you want an adjournment?' I nodded, but before I could qualify my agreement with further detail, the judge snapped up straight, said, 'You can agree a date with the clerk,' and marched off, stage right.

I asked the CPS prosecutor if it was possible to get a copy of the papers earlier than usual, explaining the position, and she was most helpful. Due to the CPS's photocopier being broken, she was unable to give me a copy at court, but assured me that if my solicitors rang the office, a copy would be posted or emailed to them.

Having arranged a new date for a fortnight later, which I assessed gave plenty of time for trial counsel to have a conference with Darius and for Keres to do something about his bail, I said my goodbyes down in the cells, and set about drafting a lengthy, irritable attendance note, setting out in bullet-point, moron-proof form what Keres had to do in the month between now and the next hearing. Get the papers, visit your client, try to get the kid bail, speak to the prison to make sure he's got his meds, arrange for an intermediary, have a proper conference with trial counsel. The fucking basics. The phrasing was politer than that, but only slightly. I emailed a copy to instructed counsel so that he could see the position, and suggested that he start chasing Keres straight away.

That, I thought, was the end of my association with Darius. Two weeks later, we were reunited. His instructed barrister again ended up being stuck in a trial that overran, and again the case found its way into my diary. When the clerks handed me the papers the night before, I noticed with a plunging heart that they appeared as devoid of content as they had a fortnight earlier. When I got to court early the next day, Darius was still in the cells. He still hadn't been visited. No one had applied for bail for him. He'd been off his meds for a month now. There was no intermediary arranged. He still didn't really understand why he was in prison. There had to be another adjournment. When I got back to chambers I kicked a wastepaper bin across my room in boiling, impotent rage.

I later found out that instructed counsel had, following that adjournment and my second, even less temperate note, bashed heads together and persuaded the CPS to speak to Dad and reconsider the public interest in the prosecution. And, a few weeks later, the proceedings were discontinued, precipitating Darius' release. But he had served close to two months in custody in conditions of the utmost inhumanity – deprived of contact, medication and information – as a direct consequence of the professional negligence of his solicitors.

And while Darius' was the first case to reduce me to tears – gulping undignified sobs in a rusting cubicle in the court toilets for the sadistic lottery of life that had bestowed the vampiric Keres upon this broken boy – his was far from the only Keres special to cross my path. Every 'brief' that entered chambers from this firm was predictably grim.

There was Adam, a gentleman I met on the day of trial who had spent three months on remand in custody awaiting his magistrates' trial for a minor assault. Keres had poached him from another firm a month before trial, but had not obtained *any* of the prosecution papers from the previous firm, nor had Adam been visited in prison. Had Keres done so, he would have learned that Adam suffered from severe psychiatric difficulties, as was immediately plain when, upon seeing me in the cells, he accused me of being a government apparatchik sent by the Labour Party to assassinate him, before dispensing with my services.

There was the case of Elizabeth, a young college student who had never been in trouble, accused by security staff of disorderly behaviour at a gig. She swore blind that it was mistaken identity, and had told Keres the night that she was arrested that the entire area was crawling with CCTV that would exonerate her. Keres did nothing to obtain it. By the time I met her at trial four months later, it was too late. The CCTV footage had long been deleted. And, notwithstanding my protests to the magistrates about the unfairness of a trial without such vital evidence, Elizabeth was convicted, despite being quite probably innocent.

The list could become a litany. The inaction of Keres and the paucity of his work was a running joke in chambers, although levity was far from anyone's mind. I told the clerks that I was refusing to do any further work for Keres after Darius, and several similarly disillusioned juniors joined me. But looking back, I see that I could, and should, have done more. I shouted loud to the senior members of chambers, but I could have shouted louder. After my very first Keres case, I should have recognized their service for what it was – professional negligence – and reported them to the Solicitors Regulation Authority. I could have confronted Keres directly, and told him exactly what I thought of him and his squalid ensemble, and that I would strongly advise all his clients to seek alternative representation.

I would like to think that now, with a few years under my belt, I would. But back then, I did not. I was complicit in the conspiracy of silence that allows the Keres of this world to prosper. I attribute it to naivety and weakness rather than self-interest or financial preservation; one of the many joys of working for Keres in magistrates' trials was that you would never be paid. Magistrates' work, unlike Crown Court advocacy, is paid directly to the solicitor for them to pass on to the advocate. Keres never did pass on the fees to the juniors. He knew that our chambers was too dependent on the big Crown Court work he sent in to kick up a fuss about baby barristers not being paid for magistrates' cases.

A few months after Darius' case, as I was still wrestling with my conscience over what to do, Keres went into liquidation. They went down owing me close to £3,000 for the work I'd done over the years. As far as I'm concerned, if that's the price to pay for no more Dariuses, it is worth every penny.

But the sorry affair highlights a significant problem in the regulation of these firms. The Solicitors Regulation Authority (SRA) is often accused of doing too little to step in to address the various misdeeds of Keres-style outfits – for example, poaching – to the constant frustration of legitimate firms.[13] But, in fairness to the SRA, it can only act on reports. And all too often, misbehaviour is unreported.

While forthright defendants are not shy to complain about perceived failings by their solicitors and barristers, the most vulnerable clients may lack the wherewithal to recognize incompetent representation. Judges, tasked now with prioritizing 'outcomes' – i.e. guilty pleas – ahead of process, are not required, and don't have the time, to scrutinize the quality of advice or service that a defendant has received. Solicitors may be nervous about reporting a fellow professional. And it would be remiss not to acknowledge our own fault, at the Bar. Too many of us look the other way. Or find excuses. Some prize their income stream over their professional duties. Some, like me, rely on youth and naivety as an excuse. But we should do more. I, personally, should have done more.

It cannot be stated loudly enough that Keres & Co. are in the tiny minority of publicly funded defence solicitors. Most firms are staffed by dedicated professionals who fight unyieldingly to safeguard the interests of their clients in the face of appalling systemic conditions. But the very real risk is that in increasing their workloads and decreasing their derisory fees, the good defence solicitors are going to fall by the wayside. I have seen more solicitors than I can count flee criminal legal aid work for the financial security of wills,

probate and private civil law. Some of the best are still cling-
ing on, but only just. If they lose their grip and slip away
into the financial abyss, the figures lurking in the shadows
will swoop in and sweep up, relying on volume, and not
quality or earned reputation. Unless they can afford to pay
for private legal representation, those accused of crimes
who depend on legal aid, including first-time entrants like
you, or your partner, or your child, will be at Keres' mercy.
Presently, I would say unhesitatingly that the best legal aid
firms provide, against all odds, a service equal to if not
better than that of their higher-remunerated private-client
counterparts. But if they fall and the Kereses rise, two-tiered
justice will become an embedded, accepted feature of our
criminal system.

In fact, speaking of two-tiered justice is not quite right.
Because presently there is a third tier, squashed between the
legally aided and privately funded, representing one of the
greatest hidden scandals of all. This is a stratum of middle-
income defendants who do not meet the criteria for legal
aid, and who cannot afford to pay privately. And who, as a
result of a silent but devastating government reform, find
themselves victims of what I call the innocence tax.

7. Legal Aid Myths and the Innocence Tax

'Upon taking office [in 2010] we had the most generous legal aid system in the world; but even after the spend and scope reductions we still have the most generous system in the world. To give you a comparator, France and Germany spend about £5 per head on legal aid, whilst we were spending £38 per head.'

Jonathan Djanogly MP, former
Minister for Legal Aid and Courts,
Address to Cambridge Union,
16 March 2015[1]

Something you may not have ever given any thought to is how you would fund a criminal defence. But you should.

Anyone can be wrongly accused of a criminal offence. You'd be surprised at how error or malice or awful, unthinkable twists of fate can convince the police and the Crown Prosecution Service that you have broken the law.

Perhaps you're driving home from school having picked the children up one idle Thursday afternoon. It's late autumn, so the light is already ebbing away at 3.30 p.m. and the conditions are blustery, wet leaves slapping against your windscreen as you crawl through the throng of 4×4s clogging your route. Although strapped in the back with an iPad for distraction, your dynamic duo are squabbling over whose go it is to play Minion Rush. The screams are wholly unbecoming, and so, while stationary, handbrake firmly on, you turn to administer a firm verbal caution, and confiscate the divisive device. Placing the iPad next to you on the front passenger seat, quietly satisfied by your military skills of discipline, you resume.

You notice that although the road ahead is clear, the Range Rover immediately in front has stopped, illegally, and put on its hazards, obviously waiting for somebody. You check your mirrors, indicate and pull out to go around. As you slide into second, the stiff gearstick causes you to reflexively glance down to your left; only for the splittest of seconds, but it's enough. As the five-year-old boy sprints in front of you, you look up only in time to see the blue flash of his cagoule. Your emergency stop comes precious seconds too late.

The boy's mother swears that you were fiddling with the iPad that the police find nestled on the seat next to you. Another witness agrees, adding that they recall that your car was still moving as you turned around to admonish your children. A third heard the revving of your vehicle, and assumed that you were impatiently accelerating around the motionless Range Rover. Yes, says the grief-stricken mother. Your burst of speed was wildly dangerous for the location and the conditions. Put together, the police, and the Crown Prosecution Service, are satisfied that there is a case to charge you with causing death by dangerous driving.

They're wrong, of course. You did nothing that came even close to 'dangerous' – defined as driving to a standard 'far below that of the careful and competent driver'. The traumatized witnesses are, understandably, wrong in their shaken recollections. The unbearable tragedy was caused by the little boy, as little boys are wont to do, darting into the road without looking. There is no moral or legal culpability; but the prosecution want to find some, with a prison sentence of up to fourteen years the potential price for you to pay.

You sensibly assess that you need legal representation for the court proceedings that follow; however there's a snag. Due to your family income, you are informed that you are not eligible for legal aid. Not a penny. And so you are compelled to beg, borrow and remortgage in order to afford the private fees of a large firm that specializes in these cases, and the private fees of the experienced barrister they recommend to you. Your total bill, at these private commercial rates, runs well into six figures.

The case proceeds to trial eighteen months later, and, thankfully, the jury accepts your evidence, aided by a vehicle accident reconstruction expert who demonstrates that your speed was far lower than the witnesses suggested. You are acquitted. The door to the dock is unlocked, and you step outside the glimmering glass facade of the Crown Court savouring your freedom. Your reputation saved and your liberty spared, you can begin the process of rebuilding your life. Starting with reclaiming the tens or hundreds of thousands of pounds paid out in successfully securing your acquittal.

But there is a postscript. Because, even though you have been found not guilty, and even though you had no choice but to instruct a privately paid legal team, the state refuses to reimburse you. It will give you a modest contribution towards your legal costs, but the rest you will have to foot yourself. Take it out of your pension pot. Or your children's inheritance. Or sell your house and move into rented accommodation.

You've been hit by the Innocence Tax.

It bears repeating. You can be prosecuted by the state. You can be refused legal aid and forced to pay privately. You can be found not guilty of any criminal offence. And the life savings that you have exhausted in the process of defending yourself will not be refunded.

The practical consequence of reforms snuck onto the statute book by stealth in 2012 is to financially punish innocent people for the 'crime' of being wrongly accused. When I explain this to non-lawyers, they assume I'm joking, or exaggerating for effect. How, they ask, could such a base affront to fairness come to pass without becoming headline news? Where was the opposition when this came to be? Where was the fourth estate? Where was the hue and cry from those caught in the snare? Even now, why is redressing this wrong not a matter of priority for any political party with a passing respect for the justice system?

To understand how we've arrived here, we need to first take a brief stroll through the recent, tarnished history of legal aid and access to justice. Because the way in which the government purchased cover for this reform – and the reason you were probably unaware of it – lay in a sustained and dishonest public campaign telling the public bare-faced lies about legal aid, who it is for and what it costs. As is encapsulated beautifully in the misleading quote from Jonathan Djangoly MP at the beginning of the chapter.

So let's deconstruct the myths, piece by piece.[2]

A Brief History of Legal Aid

As the state prosecution machinery professionalized in the nineteenth and twentieth centuries, and prosecution counsel took over the reins from citizen prosecutors, equality of arms demanded that a defendant be similarly advised and armed for battle. And it still does. Even for a career criminal who has long ago forfeited his right to public sympathy or patience, his right to receive competent legal advice and representation is vital to the system working. A common pub-bore suggestion I hear is that legal aid be allowed 'only for the first however many offences', after which these dirty lowlifes should be entitled to suckle on the public teat no longer. Which is all well and good to the Disgusteds of Tunbridge Wells until the state cottons on to how suddenly easy it is to cheaply improve conviction rates by pinning unsolved burglaries capriciously on to known repeat offenders who aren't protected by those pesky defence lawyers poking around in the prosecution's business, rather than putting in the investigative graft to track down the real villain who kicked your back door down. Defence legal aid, and the effective adversarialism that it permits, doesn't simply protect the defendant; it protects the public by keeping the prosecution, and the court system, honest. It also saves money. Any lawyer or judge will attest that the one way to guarantee that a hearing or trial overruns is to take out a lawyer. Special pleading and counter-intuitive though I accept it may sound, lawyers, particularly in crime, keep costs lower. Litigants-in-person (LiPs) – that is, defendants who are representing themselves – are untrained in law and procedure, and will in every single case cause costs to spiral, as witnesses are unnecessarily required to attend court, regular breaks are taken to remind the LiP of the basics and his questioning of witnesses takes ten times longer than would a lawyer's. Furthermore, legal representation for defendants avoids victims of serious crime being subjected to amateur, degrading questioning in public by their tormentors. Universal criminal legal aid therefore ensures that no one is denied justice – a fair trial and competent legal advice – for lack of means, keeps proceedings shorter and avoids the moral outrage of innocent people being out of pocket for having defended themselves.

Publicly funded legal assistance for people accused of criminal offences is a relatively modern concept. Up until the nineteenth century, whether a defendant was permitted to be represented by counsel at all was a matter within the discretion of the trial judge, and when the right to a defence barrister was enshrined by the Trials for Felony Act 1836, the accused needed either private funds or someone willing to act pro bono. In the early twentieth century, discretionary judicial and statutory schemes provided for payment to solicitors and counsel, but it was the Legal Aid and Advice Act 1949 that formally enshrined civil and criminal legal aid.

We'll put civil legal aid – which has traditionally covered legal proceedings concerning housing, welfare, debt, family law, clinical negligence, employment, immigration, mental health and public law – to one side for now, and focus on criminal legal aid. When criminal legal aid became commonplace in the 1960s, it was subject to a dual testing system – a means test and a merits-based 'interests of justice' test. From the 1970s onwards, the percentage of criminal cases that were publicly funded soared, and the introduction in 1984 and 1986 of statutory duty solicitor schemes for the magistrates' courts and police stations pushed the criminal legal aid budget even higher.

By the 1990s the issue of the cost of legal aid was squarely on the political map. Fee structures governing the work of solicitors and barristers were revised, tweaked, torn up and re-engineered by successive governments. Alternative models of legal provision were envisaged and consulted upon. In 1999, a statutory cap on total legal aid expenditure was introduced. But still the criminal costs kept creeping upwards, peaking in 2005/6 at just under £1.2 billion, where it hovered until dipping slightly such that, by 2010, the annual cost of criminal legal sat at £1.12 billion, with civil legal aid at a similar figure.

2010 was a significant year. With a new coalition government resolved to address the national deficit through a campaign of austere spending cuts, the Ministry of Justice, and in particular its juicy legal aid budget, was a sitting duck. There was, in the eyes of the government, a mandate for a radical re-imagining of the limits of publicly funded services, starting, uncontroversially, with the legal system.

What we have here, the public was solemnly told by ministers, represents the most expensive and generous legal aid system anywhere in the world. And it's getting more and more expensive. Fat-cat solicitors and swaggering ruddy-nosed barristers are gorging on taxpayer cream, cackling as they speed away from court in their open-top BMWs to quaff legally aided Dom Pérignon 1966 after a half-day spent pulling the wool over a jury's eyes in the service of some child rapist. And it is only right, the ministers and their tame tabloid nodding lapdogs echoed, that in straitened times, we take sensible steps to address this imbalance by reducing expenditure while ensuring that those who need legal aid still have access to it. This we can achieve by making those fat cats squeal.

In 2011, the Ministry of Justice prepared for battle. Identifying legal aid as a politically vulnerable target for some quick savings, it fumbled in its knapsack and withdrew what would come to be its most potent weapon in keeping the public onside against the inevitable wails from lawyers. From that day forth, every single Ministry of Justice pronouncement was squired by the same mantra: 'We have the most expensive legal aid system in the world.' As the title quotation demonstrates, so potent was it that, long after leaving ministerial office, MoJ alumni cannot help themselves from telling anyone who will listen that the per capita cost of legal aid in the UK is the highest in the world.

The only problem is that this claim was entirely, provably untrue.

The Most Expensive Legal Aid System in the World

So where did this claim come from?

It was first made in 2011, following the publication by the Ministry of Justice of a report entitled 'International comparison of publicly funded legal services and justice systems'.[3] This was a broad comparative report, prepared in 2009 from data collated between 2001 and 2007, in which the authors considered the costs of justice systems, with particular focus on legal aid provision, in eight countries – England and Wales, France, Netherlands, Germany, Sweden, Australia, New Zealand and Canada. You may, if counting is your strong suit, have noticed that 'eight' falls somewhere short of 'all the countries in the world'. But in any event, the comparison did indeed show that, per capita, England and Wales spend considerably more on criminal legal aid (€33.50 per capita) than any of the other seven countries.

Delighted at this headline figure, the MoJ proceeded to bury the deeply dull, but vital, explanation behind it: the legal systems of the eight candidate countries differed so vastly, they were almost impossible to directly compare. The selection contained a mix of civil law and common law jurisdictions. Some, such as France and the Netherlands, were inquisitorial systems in which court-based adversarial proceedings were a rarity. Some, such as Sweden and Australia, had an established 'public defender' model, in which state-employed lawyers provided criminal defence, leaving limited scope for legal aid payable to private providers. The English and Welsh adversarial common law system results in the bulk of the costs of criminal proceedings being borne by the protagonists – the prosecution and defence – with far lower costs falling on the courts' budget; in the other jurisdictions, costs which are met here by legal aid are allocated to different departmental accounts. Isolating and comparing legal aid in the UK with legal aid in, say, France, is therefore not only misleading but utterly pointless, for while our legal aid budget may be comparatively high, our courts' budget is comparatively minuscule. The report, or at least the MoJ's interpretation of it, did not compare like with like.

A true comparison, if a comparison is indeed helpful

(and for reasons we'll come to, I'd suggest it probably isn't), should therefore consider the overall cost of criminal justice in the comparator nations. This exercise was, as luck would have it, undertaken in a subsequent, but, for the MoJ, far less enthusiastically greeted, report by the National Audit Office in 2012, 'Comparing International Criminal Justice Systems',[4] which looked at the total annual costs of the criminal justice systems of every country in Europe. The report concluded that the average total annual public budget allocated to all courts, prosecution and legal aid as a percentage of GDP per capita was 0.33 per cent. The figure for England and Wales? 0.33 per cent. Bang on average. More than Lithuania, but less than Monaco.

But in any event, the figures alone only tell a fraction of the story. The per capita cost of criminal proceedings is driven, for example, by the number of per capita prosecutions that a state brings. And if you assumed that this will be broadly similar among developed nations, you would be much mistaken. In that first 2009 report, one of the many statistics suppressed by the MoJ was that per capita, England and Wales brought twice as many prosecutions as any other country.

A further point to note is that the legal aid figures relied upon in both reports, which were cited by the MoJ extensively as recently as 2014, only included data up to 2007 and 2008 respectively. In 2007, there were significant changes to legal aid fees paid to barristers, the effects of which would not have been reflected in those statistics, and as of 2010, the number of prosecutions started to decline. Indeed, by the time the government announced in 2013 that it was introducing further reductions (such as the cuts to solicitors' fees that we considered earlier) in order to tackle the 'out of control' legal aid budget, the spend had dropped by around £200 million, from £1.17 billion in 2010/11 to £975 million in 2012/13, and was forecasted by the MoJ to keep falling, even without further cuts. In the year to March 2017, expenditure was down to £858 million.[5] It should also be kept in mind that the Treasury dictates that VAT is chargeable and payable on all legal services, including legal aid. Therefore around one sixth of the headline cost of legal aid is VAT being paid by one branch of government (the MoJ) to another (the Treasury) via solicitors and barristers. The MoJ of course knows this. But it still likes to include VAT in the headline 'expenditure' figures to bolster its tutting at how much of YOUR money is pocketed by those vile CRIMINALS.

The 'most expensive legal aid system' memes are demonstrably, palpably false. They are post-truths, engineered and spun before post-truth became fashionable. But let's say for argument's sake that they were right. Does that of itself establish the MoJ's case? Is the 'fact' that we spend more on legal aid than anyone else a justification for reducing it? If this were true, is this not something we should celebrate? In its robust response to a government consultation in 2014 setting out further proposed fee cuts, the Bar Council made the following submission:

> Statistics published by the World Bank state that in 2011 the United Kingdom spent 9.3 per cent of its GDP on health, whereas Romania spent only 5.8 per cent. The government does not use those statistics to argue that England and Wales must reduce its health spending to match that of Romania. Rather, there is pride that an excellent health service is provided; there should be equal pride in relation to the provision of excellent access to justice.[6]

Pursuing this line of argument exposes the barrenness of the comparative exercise. Plainly, if we were outspending every developed nation on earth by a statistically significant margin, that *may* be an indicator that our model of criminal justice provision is inefficient, but as that premise is demonstrably not correct, where does that leave us? Is 0.33 per cent of GDP per capita for a criminal justice system too high or too low? Should we be aiming to join Albania down at 0.2 per cent? Or chasing Slovenia and busting the 0.4 per cent mark? Abstract percentages tell us little about the efficiency of the system, and even less about its quality.

The key to the success of the government's PR strategy is that by focusing on raw, contextless figures, it successfully obscures what criminal legal aid actually means to real people. The clichéd tabloid legal aid splash will shriek that child murderers have 'pocketed' a six-figure sum in legal aid – overlooking that this gross, VAT-inclusive figure, of which defendants do not personally receive a penny, may represent a year's work for a dozen people – but fail to mention the individually modest sums that have saved innocents from irredeemable injustice.

They don't tell you, for example, of the £1,000 legal aid bill that meant that my client of impeccable character, Marvin, was acquitted of a damaging allegation of stealing iPads from his employer, a canard which arose due to incompetent internal record-keeping. That gross figure, representing over 100 hours of pre-trial preparation and a full week at the Crown Court, would at private fee rates have been simply unaffordable for him.

They don't tell you of Jane, a police officer wrongly accused of harassing a man she had never met, but who, having noticed her car on several occasions passing through the small village in which they lived, became convinced that she was stalking him. The few hundred quid in legal aid that covered that – surprisingly complicated – magistrates' court trial and acquittal saved Jane's entire career.

No space is ever made alongside the outrage for a balanced reminder of our extended tradition of wrongful convictions that trip off the tongue – the Birmingham Six, the Guildford Four, the Cardiff Three – which were only overturned, and innocent people freed, thanks to the availability of legal aid.

And, of course, no comment is ever offered by the itinerant minister of the hour to explain that, where significant sums have been expended on convicting a guilty child rapist who does not have the means to repay it, this is still public money well spent, representing as it does the cost of ensuring that a fair trial has been held, and that we are as sure as we can be that the right man has been safely convicted.

This essential purpose of legal aid expenditure, to protect the innocent and safely convict the guilty, is the truth that government tries to keep at arm's length from the public, no doubt out of fear at the swell of resistance that would surface against cuts if legal aid's true worth was honestly discussed and made known. It is far politically smoother to obfuscate with distorted figures and snappy 'fat cat' jibes than meet the subject on its merits. Which brings us, neatly, to the next part of the myth.

Fat Cats and Skinny Kitties

Here, things get a little gauche. Because I'm afraid we need to consider the grubby subject of what barristers get paid, due to the recurring implication that the main driver of rising legal aid costs has been leeching lawyers. Again, the facts debunk the spin.

While total expenditure on criminal legal aid did until the mid-2000s continue to rise, peaking at £1.19 billion in 2004/5, this was largely attributable to the surge in criminal prosecutions coming to court. Between 1997 and 2008, the Labour government created over 3,600 new criminal offences – roughly a new offence every day.[7] The complexity of criminal law and proceedings increased staggeringly over that period, as the government legislated reflexively in shameless obeisance to every distorted tabloid commentary on 'soft judges' and 'broken laws'. As proceedings became more numerous, complicated and lengthy, both the legal aid and Crown Prosecution Service budgets increased, the latter by more than the former.[8] In 2007, the House of Commons Constitutional Affairs Committee heard evidence that the significant rise in Crown Court legal aid costs was largely down to increase in volume of cases, propelled by the creation of more criminal offences, and concluded that 'the average cost per claim did not and has not significantly increased'.[9] Legal aid had therefore increased not because of fat-cat lawyers exponentially milking the taxpayer, but because the state was increasing the volume of cases.

And the figures, it has to be repeated, are always gross. They always include a fat wodge of VAT and tax that is recycled back into public coffers. Legal aid firms grossing millions of pounds a year are not pocketing that as profit – they are using it to pay staff, rent and the everyday costs of running a business. Those eye-popping numbers in the tabloids – where they print pictures of QCs in their ceremonial wigs with accompanying tables of their whopping incomes – usually represent several years' worth of work, which, due to the delays in criminal cases and the inefficiencies of the Legal Aid Agency, can take years for payment to come through.

In fact, at the time the government was making its case for cuts in 2011, the fat cats were to the contrary becoming rapidly scrawny. Which brings us to the question: what do criminal barristers earn?

We should start with full disclosure: it would appear right to say that back in the 1980s, criminal legal aid was a bit of a gravy train. I say 'it would appear' as I cannot speak from first-hand experience, but senior colleagues fight back tears as they reminisce over the old days when you would bill by the hour, and assessors would wave through excessive guesstimates like a bored teenage car park attendant. 'Time was,' my very learned opponent in a trial once grumbled to me as he worked out his daily fee, 'that on a piddly little case like this, you'd pluck a number out of the air, stick it on a bill and then go and buy a little terraced house somewhere in the north to let out to students.' He was not alone in sharing such fond memories. While still the poor relations to commercial and civil brethren at the Bar, crime did use to pay, and very well. To the extent that my forebears milked, some might go as far as to say abused, the largesse of legal aid, the legal profession is to blame for its reputation.

But criminal practice in the twenty-first century is vastly different.

Hourly rates have gone. As of 1997, the bulk of defence cases have been paid on a reduced 'graduated fees' scheme, where the fee is worked out using a complicated formula factoring the type of case, the number of pages of evidence and the length of the trial in days. It is immaterial how much work you *actually* do. So if you have a difficult or vulnerable client who requires many hours of contact time before and after court sitting hours, or if an esoteric point of law arises requiring days of research and many hours spent drafting and honing written legal argument, that extra work is gratis. And of course, as the law and procedure becomes more complex, the volume of extra gratis work involved in straightforward cases increases. If the court decides that it wants to suddenly hold an impromptu hearing because the CPS hasn't served a piece of evidence, I either attend court the next day for free, giving up whatever other paid work I might have had in my diary that day, or I pay a colleague to go in my stead. Some days, therefore, we earn nothing. Other days, when our train ticket for a far-flung case costs £200, we literally pay to work. I don't say any of this expecting sympathy – I chose this career with my eyes open, and others toil harder in far more unpleasant conditions for even less reward – but I share a little of the reality as a counterweight to the government line.

Of course some days pay better for relatively little work. And some cases, serious, complex cases, pay very well. If you are, unlike me, excellent at the job, you can still earn a very good living from crime. If, as a society, we want to catch the biggest, slipperiest criminals, usually white collar, complex tax frauds or international drug cartels, it is not cheap. The evidence is usually voluminous; hundreds of thousands of pages. You need very good lawyers to get to grips with the complexities of the case, and present it to a jury. And equally good lawyers for the defence. And these, the very best QCs and experienced juniors, will receive an attractive headline figure for their experience and talent. A teensy fraction of the incomes of their seven-figure-billing commercial law counterparts, but their gross income will tip into the six figures. They, however, are the superstars. For us mortals, who have seen an average real-terms cut in legal aid of 37 per cent between 2007 and 2013, we hover around a median annual net income of £27,000.[10] Which is not to be sniffed at. It's more than the national average. But, to give a little perspective, it's less than the starting salary for a grad-uate manager at Aldi, who, the job spec indicates, will be working fewer than the 60 or 70 hours that goes into a barrister's week.[11]

At entry level, pay can be brutally low. You start pupil-lage having racked up debts of up to £75,000. You are dependent on doing magistrates' trials for £75 a day – including prep and travel – and the occasional glamorous trip into the Crown Court to cover somebody else's mention hearing. You will put in a minimum of 60-hour weeks for what works out at around £5 per hour. A friend of mine calculated that in her first full year of qualified practice, she would literally have been better off on benefits. For the first few years, you will gross between £10k and £20k a year. For your peer at a top commercial chambers or at a big City solicitors' firm, you can add a zero.

Again, it's a lament that appears calculated to generate sympathy, but that's not what I'm seeking. Working on publicly funded cases provides a genuine and lasting sense of reward, for the soul if not the purse. There is very little that tops the satisfaction of securing an acquittal for a defendant who, without legal aid, would not have been able to defend themselves. Knowing that you are part of a system that extends these protections to the most vulnerable, and often least sympathetic, people in society can reaffirm one's dwindling faith in our humanity, and society's fidelity to our first principles. That, I dare say, is the reason why, despite our constant raging against the machine, so many of us stick with legal aid work.

So I don't seek sympathy for my career choice, not a bit; rather, I raise the issue of our sometimes-humble incomes to reinforce this simple point: legal aid cuts were not necessary. We were not outspending every other country. Fistfuls of fifties were not being stuffed down the gullets of fat-cat lawyers. Legal aid was being spent on paying professionals a modest income to do a lot of very unpleasant work that the state kept generating. And, surprisingly, when the state stopped prosecuting as many people, the spend started to fall.

But such pleas had no effect on the MoJ. Indeed, they welcomed them. Because the louder we lawyers protested about legal aid myths, the greater was the tumult under cover of which the government could open up its second front. Whilst purring that 'generous legal aid' would still be available for those in need of it, the Ministry set about removing it entirely from certain classes of people.

Which brings us back to the Innocence Tax.

*

The Dawn of the Innocence Tax

If you had been charged with causing death by dangerous driving before 1 October 2012, you would have had two options. You could either have availed yourself of legal aid, which was available to all defendants in Crown Court cases. Or, if you didn't like the look of what public funds gets you (i.e. someone like me), you could have paid privately for a better class of representation.

Depending on your income, you might have had to pay 'contributions' towards your legal aid bill, but you would recoup that money if you were acquitted. Similarly, if you had paid privately and were acquitted, you were entitled to a 'Defendant's Costs Order' (DCO), by which the state would pay costs 'of such amount as the court considers reasonably sufficient to compensate [the defendant] for any expenses properly incurred by him in the proceedings'. In other words, your legal bill, or the vast bulk of it, would be taken care of by the state, paid out of what was referred to as 'Central Funds'. It was recognized that you hadn't chosen to be prosecuted, and as the winning party to the litigation, your reasonable costs would be reimbursed. Pounds and pence would usually be thrashed out between the solicitor and the Legal Services Commission (the predecessor to the Legal Aid Agency), but as a rule, an acquitted defendant would not be out of pocket for his suffering.

So what changed?

The public having been assured of the unsustainability and immorality of the legal aid budget, the terrain was primed for the enactment in May of that year of the Legal Aid, Sentencing and Punishment of Offenders Act (LASPO) 2012. The Act attracted attention at the time and afterwards for its wholesale uprooting of civil legal aid. Hooting the same false claims over the civil legal aid bill as per the criminal, the government removed legal aid from swathes of areas of law where vulnerable people were most desperately in need of access to justice, such as family law, welfare, housing, immigration, medical negligence and debt. It was described by Labour peer and shadow legal aid spokesman Lord Bach, himself an experienced former criminal barrister, as 'picking on people who can't defend themselves' and 'a bad day for British justice'.[12] His comments were by no means unique. Law centres across the country closed, legal aid firms went to the wall and ordinary people found themselves without any help in enforcing their basic rights. Abused women were forced to confront their violent ex-partners alone in family proceedings.[13] Vulnerable tenants were at the mercy of rogue, unimpeachable landlords. Children were expected to negotiate tortuous immigration proceedings by themselves. Little surprise that in 2016 Amnesty International published a panicked report warning that the cuts have 'decimated access to justice'.[14]

But what also slipped in, under Schedule 7 of the Act, was a change to Defendant's Costs Orders. As of 1 October 2012, private-paying defendants charged in criminal proceedings would no longer be able to recoup their costs. Defendant's Costs Orders in the Crown Court were abolished. The rationale was that, as legal aid is universally available, the taxpayer should not be required to meet the commercial-rate legal costs of those who choose to go private. It's like healthcare, the argument ran. You are not obliged to use the NHS, but if you snub it for BUPA, you foot the bill.

This argument was prefigured by a rash of conveniently positioned tabloid tales of celebrities, including footballer Steven Gerrard 'pocketing' over £300,000 on a Defendant's Costs Order following his acquittal of a charge of affray at Liverpool Crown Court.[15] And it had a certain superficial charm to it.

But tug at the theory and it unravels. Because, considering the health analogy, the state by and large does not intentionally hospitalize its citizens. If it did, and it started circumscribing the manner in which the people whose limbs it had snapped could seek treatment, the injured might feel slightly aggrieved. But perhaps more persuasively, there is an issue of equality of arms here. Legal aid may not afford you representation of the same calibre as the prosecution. Under legal aid, the presumption is that you will be represented by a single junior barrister. For particularly complex or serious cases, you can apply to a judge for a second junior barrister to share the workload, or in the most serious cases for legal aid to cover a QC. But there is no guarantee. The test for 'extending the legal aid certificate' is strict, and over the last few years has become increasingly restrictive, as judges have been repeatedly mithered by secondary legislation to reduce the number of applications they grant. The fact that the prosecution has instructed a QC, for example, does not mean that you as a defendant are automatically entitled to one.

It may be, therefore, that, as a falsely accused defendant being prosecuted by a vastly experienced silk, you would reasonably wish for someone similarly excellent to defend you. And if legal aid won't stretch to it, and with no 'top-up' system permitted, you may find yourself with no choice but to go private. And if you did, under this scheme, you would have been left to pay the costs, whatever the outcome at trial. This was the fate visited upon Conservative MP Nigel Evans in 2014, who, having chosen to pay privately to successfully defend himself of allegations of sexual assault, found himself £130,000 poorer due to the reforms poetically brought in by his own party.[16]

Whatever the principled objections one might throw at this arrangement, however, it at least had the advantage of ensuring that all those accused of serious offences in the Crown Court had access to legal aid. Even if you were rightly fearful that your quality of representation might be outmuscled by the prosecution's, you had the security of knowing that there was a lawyer available to you, and that if your innocence was not impeached, it would not cost you a thing.

Then, in January 2014, the government turned the screw. Determined to squeeze every drop of blood from the budget, it introduced a means test in the Crown Court. If you had a disposable household income – your partner's means were taken into account – of £37,500 or more, you were excluded from legal aid. As a 'balance', it relaxed the ban on Defendant's Costs Orders in the Crown Court for people who applied for but were refused legal aid and were subsequently acquitted. However, there was a kicker: a Defendant's Costs Order could only be claimed *up to legal aid rates*. This aligned Crown Court proceedings with the regime that had operated in the magistrates' courts since 2012, where a disposable household income of £22,325 shut you out of legal aid. So now, if you qualified for legal aid, you would get it. But if you were above the threshold, you were left at the mercy of the market, with the state making only a token contribution to your costs if you were acquitted.[17]

As we have already seen, legal aid rates are significantly lower than market rates, sometimes to the extent that the lawyers involved are operating at a loss. So paying on the open market, at the rate that you once would have claimed in full under a Defendant's Costs Order, will invariably cost you more than you can ever hope to recover. Private fees can be as much as ten times legal aid rates, leaving an acquitted defendant tens, even hundreds, of thousands of pounds out of pocket. And before claims of extortion are levelled at the lawyers, it is worth remembering what the fees payable from Central Funds under an old-school DCO actually represented. These were not blank cheques. They provided for fees proximate to market rates for legal professionals, but were still the subject of close scrutiny by costs assessors. The test that was applied by the Legal Services Commission and costs judges was whether the fees claimed under a DCO were 'reasonably sufficient' and 'properly incurred'. By cutting DCOs, by definition the government has deemed that 'reasonably sufficient' and 'properly incurred' legal expenses sustained by a formally not guilty citizen should not be paid.

At this point, it should also be pointed out that legal aid fees are officially considered to be not a 'proper professional fee' by the Bar Council. According to the Bar Code of Conduct, one of the limited occasions on which barristers can ignore the 'cab rank' rule and refuse a case is where there is no 'proper' fee. So low has the rate fallen through cuts and inflation, that criminal legal aid cases have, since 2003, been expressly identified by the Bar Council as ones where a barrister can refuse to act.[18]

Tying this together, we now have a situation where the government has abolished legal aid for those with a not-immodest joint disposable annual income of £37,500, and deemed that if you, the innocent, incur proper and reasonable private costs in securing your acquittal, the state will only contribute at a rate *which by definition* is not a 'proper professional fee'.

In June 2010, the High Court responded to the previous Labour government's attempt to introduce a similar cap to DCOs:

> . . . A defendant ought not to have to pay towards the cost of defending himself against what might in some cases be wholly false accusations, provided he incurs no greater expenditure than is reasonable and proper to secure his defence. Any change in that principle is one of some constitutional moment. It means that a defendant falsely accused by the state will have to pay from his own pocket to establish his innocence.[19]

Ruling the government's regulations unlawful, the High Court was highly critical of the attempt to achieve such a 'decisive departure from past principles' through unscrutinized secondary legislation. The coalition government in 2012 and 2014 learned from this and, by smuggling the Innocence Tax into an Act of Parliament, ensured that when a legal challenge inevitably came, parliamentary supremacy meant that the Innocence Tax could not be said to be unlawful.[20]

It may be lawful. But it is abhorrent. Retreating to my favoured health analogy, this is the government deliberately breaking your legs, and telling you that you must go private, but that they will only contribute NHS rates. Or, otherwise, you feel free to treat yourself. See how that works for you, pal.

For those who can afford the financial hit, the position is repellent enough; but the greater peril faces those who can't – the families who meet the government's threshold for cutting off legal aid, but who have no means to pay up-front for private solicitors, private barristers and private expert witnesses. For these innocents, the Innocence Tax inflicts a Sophie's Choice between their family's financial security and their liberty. Some will be compelled to gamble on the latter. I cast my mind back to the acquittals I secured on legal aid pre-2014 for defendants from middle-income families, and wonder for their fates in these new times. What on earth would they have done?

As a final, desultory boot in the genitals of justice, it is illuminating to consider private prosecution fees. Because the imperative to find 'efficiencies' in criminal justice has not extended to private prosecutors. While CPS prosecutions are funded from CPS coffers, private prosecutors have the right to apply to Central Funds for the costs of bringing a prosecution, *even where the prosecution loses*.[21] And the fees claimable are significantly higher than legal aid rates. The test, in fact, is evocative. The court may 'order the payment out of Central Funds of *such amount as the court considers reasonably sufficient* to compensate the prosecutor for any expenses *reasonably incurred* by him in the proceedings'. The Lord Chief Justice has gone so far as to suggest that there should be a presumption in favour of awarding these prosecution costs, unless there is 'good reason for not doing so, for example, where proceedings have been instituted or continued without good cause'.[22]

We thus have the theoretical pantomime of a private prosecutor falsely accusing an innocent person of a crime, bringing a case to trial, losing and walking away financially restituted, while the innocent, victorious defendant is forced to sell his home to pay the costs of his acquittal.

It is morally and philosophically indefensible that we have allowed our justice system to degrade such that this scenario is possible. We have a system which forces a wrongly accused person from a middle-class family to choose between financial destitution and the fool's gamble of self-representing in criminal proceedings. The Innocence Tax's philosophical underpinning can only be read one of two ways: either as an inversion of the presumption of innocence, a sly wink to our worse selves that an accused is always in some way responsible for his being corralled into the justice system. Or it is a concession that though accused people may well be genuinely innocent, so little does the average voter understand or care about the criminal courts that rampant butchery of the rule of law can be gotten away with unscrutinized.

The consequences of the Innocence Tax are exhaustively threefold: the cost of justice will fall; more innocent people will be financially ruined; more innocent people, forced to self-represent, will be convicted. There is nothing else. These reforms, like so many others, care nothing for quality. There is no pretence that this will improve the standard of justice;

to the contrary, its diminution is tacitly accepted as a price worth paying for knocking a few million off the legal aid bill.

We could – no, we should – have legal aid available to everyone accused of a criminal offence; repayable by the convicted who have the means; for those without, it should be written off as the baseline cost of a civilized society that prizes the value of justice done properly. But through our silence, we accept the government's lesser alternative, and the perverse, grotesque results that follow. The numbers of self-representing defendants are rising. I see it in the Crown Courts. The government has conducted research on the number of self-representing defendants, but has refused to publish the results, no doubt through shame of what they will show.[23] Although no official figures are kept in the magistrates' court, anecdotal evidence and common reason holds that unrepresented defendants are more common there too. Ordinary people are expected to do courtroom combat with seasoned legal professionals, without knowing the first thing about the law. People stepping onto the battlefield armed with a paper hat and a wooden spoon.

We see, on a daily basis, the appalling spectacle of

> . . . unrepresented defendants not understanding what they were charged with, pleading guilty when they would have been advised not to, and vice versa, messing up the cross-examination of witnesses, and getting tougher sentences because they did not know how to mitigate.[24]

As previously discussed, and as every lawyer will tell you, it is the falsest of economies. A litigant-in-person, unacquainted with the rules of evidence or procedure, is guaranteed to lengthen proceedings, add layers of confusion and complexity and run up far higher costs in added court time than would ever be expended on having a hack like me defend him on legal aid rates. But it *sounds* cheaper. So it ticks the ministry's box.

A grim report by charity Transform Justice included a case study in which a man wrongly accused of an offence of criminal damage ended up paying more to be acquitted than he would have paid by way of a fine had he simply pleaded guilty.[25] Again, such instances are not accidents, they are designs of our system. And they exist because no one gets elected promising a better justice system. Just a cheaper one. Other things matter more.

On 19 March 2014, two months after the Innocence Tax took its current form, the government in the Budget proudly announced a 1p cut to duty on a pint of beer, and a freeze to duty on cider and spirits. The cost to the taxpayer of this largesse was estimated at £300 million per year.[26] The figure that *had* to be cut from criminal legal aid, that could *not* be avoided, that meant it was *necessary* to punish the wrongly accused and increase the risk of innocent people going to prison, was £220 million per year.

As I say, it's a matter of priorities.

8. Trial on Trial: Part I
– The Case Against

'An advocate, by the sacred duty which he owes his clients, knows in the discharge of that office but one person in the world, that client and none other. To save that client by all expedient means, to protect that client at all hazards and costs, to all others, and among others to himself, it is the highest and most unquestioned of his duties; and he must not regard the alarm, the suffering, the torment, the destruction which he may bring upon any other.'

Henry Brougham, defence counsel at
the trial before parliament of Queen Caroline, 1820

There is a near-tangible buzz that descends upon the courtroom and reverberates off the walls as the panel of prospective jurors files into court. It fizzes as the final twelve are randomly selected, sworn and formally welcomed by a judge exuding something on the scale between grandfatherly bonhomie and bubbling misanthropy. And, as the prosecutor at the judge's invitation takes to their feet to deliver the opening speech, the buzz soars, whizzes furiously and then, as the first word falls, it drops and settles, but never disappears. It gently underscores everything that follows; a steady, incidental hum unobtrusively heightening the significance of each spoken word, each nervous pause and each fidgety physical tell. For it is from this, the oral presentation of evidence and its professional, adversarial deconstruction, that the jury will divine their verdict, and justice will be delivered.

And so we return to the illustration, first sketched with Mr Tuttle, which perhaps best depicts our conception of criminal justice. In reality, it displays only the tip of the iceberg, the less than 1 per cent of criminal prosecutions that are determined by Crown Court trial, but the image remains totemic. And its familiarity subtly reinforces our faith in its worth. There is an instinctive cultural trust in the adversarial trial process as a guarantor of justice; a true belief that the denouement of each trial will match the justice of the final act of *Twelve Angry Men*.

That, after all, is the premise on which I base the observations and criticisms in the preceding chapters. In the opening pages, I boldly proclaimed that 'our adversarial system, when it works, is the greatest guarantor of individual liberty there is.' The problem, as I characterize it, is the acts or omissions by others – normally the state – which by negligence, recklessness or specific intent impede the smooth running of an intrinsically good system. If the case has negotiated its way successfully through the pre-trial labyrinth to the swearing of a jury – if the evidence has been gathered and not lost, if the witnesses have attended, if the interpreter is present, if the defendant has been produced from custody, if the court can actually accommodate a trial – the hard part, surely, is over? The trial itself will by mere virtue of its internationally celebrated configuration – part evolution, part intelligent design – give the 'right' result. The prosecution will deliver a fair and balanced opening speech. Its witnesses will each give oral evidence of what they know; initially prompted by non-leading, open questioning from the prosecution advocate, before being tested by closed, leading questions in cross-examination from the defence.

Following the prosecution case, assuming the judge is satisfied that there is sufficient evidence for the matter to continue, the defence will have its turn, calling the defendant to give evidence (if he so chooses) and any defence witnesses. The advocates will then with equal aplomb each present their closing arguments to the jury, before the judge fairly sums up the evidence and directs the jury on the applicable law. When the jury returns, it will present us with a neatly wrapped verdict of no more than two words, which, whatever it may be, we can be satisfied represents Justice.

And it is that faith in process as justice that explains and justifies my role as an advocate. It is what permits me to bat away with ease *the* inevitable dinner party questions – *How do you defend someone you believe is guilty? Have you ever prosecuted someone you think is innocent?* – with a nonchalance that belies the gravity of the argument. I am just a cog in the machine. Impersonally carrying out my role is key to ensuring that the delicate justice ecosystem remains in symbiosis. Once the advocate allows personal sentiment to usurp cold professional judgment, the whole adversarial system is jolted out of whack. I would be trespassing on the role of the jury. I am not here to form views or share feelings. I am here to promote my client's cause, without fear or favour, to the best of my ability. That is my function; a footsoldier for justice, marching to the adversarial beat.

If in so doing, I help to secure the acquittal of someone who is in fact guilty, or the conviction of someone who may be innocent, that is frankly not my professional concern. The jury had the evidence, fairly and lawfully presented and scrutinized. It was for those twelve neutrals, not me, to decide whether the state had made them sure of guilt. I am but a vessel.

If, in order to secure that result for my client, it was necessary to persuade the judge, properly and lawfully, to hide some relevant evidence from the jury, for fear that it was unduly prejudicial, or because of its dubious probity, or the unfair circumstances in which the police obtained it, that would have been not only within the rules of the game, but my duty as his counsel.

If, as a consequence of my fierce cross-examination and scornful, blustering closing speech, a genuine victim of an unspeakable crime has – to channel Lord Brougham – their suffering, their torment, their destruction multiplied, that must regrettably be filed under 'collateral damage' in the noble battle to protect individual liberty, and to ensure that only where the state's evidence proves guilt beyond doubt will a man's freedom be curtailed. As I haughtily declared earlier when considering the clash between the rights of victims and the rights of defendants, the former just *have* to accept that they will ultimately be subjugated to the latter, because the proper functioning of adversarialism requires it.

But such glib, smug homilies, delivered with the self-assured and clinical complacency of someone who has had such lofty abstract ideals implanted since the first year of law school, allow me to avoid critical examination of the awkward, deeper assumptions that underlie not only our mode of justice, but my very (professional) existence. Such as whether adversarial criminal justice is all it is cracked up to be. Whether too much – truth, dignity – is sacrificed on its altar. Whether a system that does not have as its stated aim the pursuit of truth, but instead rewards the best game player in a winner-takes-all contest, can really be said to deliver 'justice' in a sense understood by anyone outside of legal circles. And whether, if we have abandoned – or never even prized – truth as a guiding principle of our trials, we are doing gross injury to Enlightenment principles, with the result that all of us – defendant, victim and society – are wronged.

I try to avoid those questions. Because more inevitably follow.

Am I a morally neutral officer of justice, faithfully playing my allocated role in the production line? Or am I, and thousands like me, complicit in a warped, harmful model of criminal inquiry, only semi-conscious of the real, irremediable devastation that we wreak? When I mount my high horse and decry government violence to fundamental pillars of justice, am I a first-class passenger complaining about the limited buffet options on the *Titanic*? Is the lesson that I should be taking from the things that I see in the courtroom not that our criminal justice system is broken for the trivial reasons upon which I and my colleagues fixate, but that its very premise is inherently, immorally flawed?

We need to talk about adversarialism.

Jay's case is one that will stay with me until I retire. Not because of the nature of the allegations against him; their horror is sadly matched by their ubiquity in the Crown Courts. Nor because he was the first acquitted client whose protestations of innocence I found, on that deeper, forbidden, personal level, difficult to accept. But rather because the circumstances of his case, and of my role in it, taken together probably summon up to a layperson a flesh-and-blood illustration of a system not working. Of adversarialism as an impediment, rather than a conduit, to justice.

Broken down to its bare essentials, on the basis of everything I saw in that case, and everything I heard at trial, I think Jay repeatedly raped his children from school age to adulthood. And my efforts helped secure his acquittal.

To restate some of the professional and ethical basics: I of course didn't *know* that Jay was guilty. He never admitted as such; indeed, his instructions remained a firm 'Not Guilty' from the moment he strolled into the conference room, reeking of stale cigarettes and Brut, and wedged his giant rolls of belly awkwardly into the chair at the opposite end of the table. Had he ever admitted to me, or to the senior barrister leading me, that his two daughters were truthful when, aged twenty-four and nineteen, they attended a quiet suburban police station to calmly report that their father had raped and sexually abused them from the age of five, I would not have been able to defend him in the same way.

My duties are strictly set out in the Bar Code of Conduct: if a client tells me that they did something, I cannot positively assert in court that they did not. Contrary to popular conception of defence lawyers as lying slyly in cahoots with their clients, privy to the details of their guilt but dishonestly presenting a picture of positive innocence to the trusting jury, professional ethics are clear. My overriding duty is to the court. While the client enjoys legal privilege – and so I won't reveal it to the court if he confesses his guilt to me – I cannot present a positive case that I know not to be true. Were I to do so, I could be hauled before a disciplinary hearing and disbarred.

Therefore, where a client confessed, the only way I could continue to act would be if he decided to plead guilty, or if he maintained his not guilty plea but instructed me to 'test the reliability of the evidence' without advancing a positive case that he was innocent. This would mean that I was in effect defending him with an arm tied behind my back. I could gently probe the evidence of the witnesses by drawing out inconsistencies and asking the jury, 'Are you sure of guilt?' But I couldn't suggest to a witness that they were lying, or submit to the jury in my speech that my client did not do the alleged act. If the client wished to nevertheless advance a positive defence, I would be, in the jargon, 'professionally embarrassed'. I would have to withdraw, and he would have to find a new barrister to whom he could give fresh instructions of innocence.

But where a client maintains his lack of guilt, in spite of

what may be overwhelming prosecution evidence, I am obliged, having robustly advised him on the likelihood of conviction, to present his unlikely defence in as persuasive and attractive a way as possible. This is in practice the day job. Defending not just the indefensible, but the patently ludicrous. Inviting a jury to consider that, maybe, black is not, as the prosecution so outlandishly claim, black, but might instead be, if you squint hard enough, a shade of something if not white, then at least not a million miles away from grey. Maybe, as I in one of my earliest trials had to sincerely put to three unimpressed magistrates, the six independent prosecution witnesses who saw my client merrily carrying a stolen television to his car, had suffered a collective onset of poor vision and faulty memory. And that the crystalline high-resolution CCTV footage supporting the witnesses' identical accounts was not crystalline enough to make the court *sure*.

And this is key to adversarialism. The prosecution will be presenting their case as persuasively as they can, whatever views the advocate might privately hold about the witnesses' credibility. Equality of arms requires that the defendant has his case, irrespective of whether his advocate believes it, put before the court with the same articulacy and force. That, after all, is the legacy of the eighteenth-century barristers elbowing their way into the trial process and incrementally enlarging their roles. The accusatorial system, which involved the state – usually a citizen prosecutor assisted by the investigating magistrates we met earlier – versus an unrepresented defendant singing for his supper, gave way to professionalized adversarial trials, with lawyers taking centre stage in their presentation of the competing cases.

In practice, this exercise involves not simply the presentation of an alternative case, but the demolition of your opponent's. That is the core of defence strategy. My pupil-master would often say that prosecuting is constructive and defending is destructive, and while not always true, the proposition is generally sound. A defendant will often have a positive case to advance (usually either 'it wasn't me' or 'it never happened'), and will usually wish to give his own evidence and call defence witnesses in support of his 'case', but there is no burden on him to prove anything. If his lawyers can do enough damage to the prosecution case, that may be enough to establish reasonable doubt in the jury's mind and secure the precious Not Guilty.

In Jay's case, the nature of the allegations meant that destruction was our primary strategy. Allegations of non-recent sexual offences make for extremely difficult cases for many reasons. For the defence, a particular hurdle is that, due to the passage of time, it is often impossible to recall specifics of what one might have been doing on a given day, and thus to meet the allegations head on. In some jurisdictions, there are statutes of limitations which prevent criminal proceedings being brought after a certain period of time, for this very reason. But in England and Wales, there is no such bar. It is increasingly common to see defendants prosecuted for alleged offences said to have occurred forty or even fifty years ago, even though it presents an immediate difficulty when trying to 'disprove' the prosecution allegations.

So when Jay's eldest daughter, Mysha, claimed that back in the late 1980s her dad took to coming into her bedroom on the nights that her mum was visiting relatives, removing Mysha's nightie and engaging her in progressively sinister 'secret games', all Jay could say was: that never happened. This is not the type of case where appeals could be made for defence witnesses, or even where Jay could point to a specific date and provide an alibi to disprove Mysha's account. When the younger daughter, Tamara, made near-identical allegations of acts committed against her, the problem only doubled. In such a case, attack is not just the best but the only form of defence.

Which is where I came in. Being at this stage not sufficiently senior to be doing cases of this gravity on my own, I was instructed as a 'junior' advocate to support the 'leading' barrister, George. The division of labour was neat and crisp – George handled 'the big picture', namely strategy and the advocacy, while I, apparently, was 'the details monkey'. The reason that the legal aid certificate was exceptionally extended to allow George the privilege of my companionship was due to the volume of unused material generated by the prosecution during the investigation, and which fell to be disclosed to the defence as potentially helpful to our cause. My role was to comb through the floor-to-ceiling boxes of mostly handwritten, yellowed 1980s/90s local authority records and dig out anything that might conceivably help us at trial.

In historic sex cases, disclosure of local authority records is a necessary but messy component. The sad reality of such cases is that the families have often, for various reasons, previously come to the attention of local authority social services or children's support services. Jay's wife, Farah, had a long history of alcoholism, and the girls had spent their childhoods bounced back and forth between the family's squalid, unkempt home and a sequence of foster carers. The history of Social Services' involvement with the family stretched over fifteen years, the official records of which lay in local authority archives. One of the first jobs for the CPS is to obtain such material and inspect it to see whether any of it either supports the prosecution case, or might reasonably assist the defence.

Why are these records so important? For the prosecution, it's because they might contain evidence of contemporaneous complaint. They might show, for example, that Mysha said something apparently innocuous to a social worker in 1996, which in the light of what is now alleged is highly significant. Or even, as is not uncommon, that she reported the allegations years ago but was ignored or disbelieved in accordance with the zeitgeist.

For the defence, Social Services' records can be helpful because they contain something that undermines the complainants' credibility. The records might show that, at the time that they were supposedly being abused, they not only made no complaint, but were recorded by eagle-eyed social workers as behaving in a way entirely at odds to what one might 'expect' from an abused child. Or the records might point to a possible defence witness. Or there might be reports of the complainants having been compulsive liars. Or, the silver bullet for the defence, there might be reports of the children having made similar, provably false complaints in the past.

Obtaining the material is not a straightforward process. Records might by now be incomplete or missing. If, as was the case with Jay, the family moved between a number of local authority areas, there will be paperwork buried in the administrative webs of several different public bodies. Local authorities may also have merged or restructured over time; children's homes may have closed, or private agencies may have provided some of the services. Invariably, it will emerge from the records obtained that there exists yet further relevant material, such as education, medical or counselling records. Or documentation generated in the course of family court proceedings, which has its own complex legal dimension. The practicalities of gathering all relevant material can be fiendish. Once the prosecution has unwrapped what they believe to be the last Russian doll in the sequence, they could be staring at tens of thousands of pages of records. If they are diligent in their duties, they will carefully examine the full extent of the records, and be properly selective in what they disclose, dutifully applying the disclosure test – i.e. whether the material is reasonably capable of undermining the prosecution case or assisting the defence. In practice, one finds that the prosecution tends to either disclose far too little, leading to repetitive requests from the defence for documents which one can infer are clearly relevant, or disclose far too much, lazily dumping all manner of records, some of which might help the defence, but many of which are neutral or irrelevant. In theory, with material of this type, the judge should act as second filter to scrutinize the disclosure process. Sometimes, the less motivated, or those lacking in time, will just reach for the rubber stamp.

Which was where we found ourselves with Jay. After a little early constipation in the disclosure process, we – or I – were now looking at a prosecution mega-dump. Every day, it seemed, a new box of unpaginated, barely legible documentation landed in chambers, to the evident dismay of the junior clerk who had to lug it up six flights of stairs to what George grandiosely referred to as 'the War Room'. It was in reality a cupboard with a tiny desk now walled by seven-foot-high turrets of precariously stacked boxes, where I would while away every moment that I was not in court for the three months between my instruction and trial.

The brief was simple: identify, mine and polish every atom that would help us show the jury that these two girls were lying fantasists. By painstakingly scrutinizing every recorded interaction between the children and the state over two decades, it was possible to piece together a chronology of individual incidents which, taken together, could be refracted in the courtroom as two lifetimes of dishonesty and unreliability.

Every time one of the girls had told a fib at school, or regaled a foster carer with a tall tale, or denied being the one who pinched a biscuit from the tin, or in any other way acted in a manner that could be spun as evidence of untruthfulness, it went in my schedule. When it emerged that Mysha was admitted to hospital at age seventeen with a severe psychiatric disorder, every recorded instance of hallucination, confusion or inconsistency was carefully tabbed and entered into the chronology. On another occasion, a thirteen-year-old Tamara had climbed out of the bedroom window at her foster carer's house to spend a night drinking with an older man. The missing child report containing the silly, false name she instinctively gave to the police when they found her, before quickly admitting all, was duly weaponized. No mis-step or human frailty was too small or too insignificant. And there was a lot. Not all of this would ultimately go before the jury – the judge has to be satisfied that 'bad character' evidence meets the statutory tests – but much of it did.

There was dynamite lurking within the records, too. Each girl had made previous allegations of sexual abuse against other men, some of which were provably false. Mysha had told a primary school teacher about a fictional neighbour who she said had touched her. Tamara had made repeated false complaints of violence against her foster carers. Aged thirteen, she told a school nurse that she was having sex with a nineteen-year-old, and then denied it, and then repeated it to other friends. She had faked a pregnancy, and then a miscarriage.

There are two interpretations, of course. One is that these were two untrustworthy fantasists, habitual liars from a young age who would lie to get their own way, or for attention, unable to see or care about the consequences for others, and who had carried their propensity for untruthfulness through childhood, adolescence and beyond. The second is that they were damaged, abused children. All children tell fibs about taking biscuits. And blame things on their siblings. And lie about going out when they're teenagers. If children are horrifically and gruesomely abused by their father from a young age, they can break. They can act out for attention, send out flares, lose their sense of self and their grip on the reality of their nightmare. Each and every instance of their deviant or disordered behaviour might be traced back to that original, unspeakable, ultimate breach of trust. Every disprovable claim made against other men becomes, under this light, a cipher for what was being done to that little girl by her dad.

But the first is the tapestry that you weave when defending. That is the essence of adversarialism. Each side has its 'case theory'. Ours was that Jay was a good dad doing his level best with a drunk wife and two demonical, lying, fucked-up kids. And every strand of evidence has to be twisted and threaded so as to fit in with that theory. You shine a fog light on each tiny imperfection in the opponent's case, and carefully deflect any weakness in your own. For evidence which contradicts your case theory, you have two options: destroy it in cross-examination, or try, lawfully, to hide it from the jury.

Cross-examination

The true purpose of cross-examination, it is suggested in *Archbold*, the leading criminal practitioner text, is 'to elicit answers to matters of fact'.[1] I would respectfully suggest that this is only half the story: the main purpose is to cause the witness to say what you, the advocate, want them to say. And, in so doing, to improve your client's case. Where your case is that this particular witness is a lying hound, cross-examination serves a further utility: to destroy that person's credibility.

The order of witness examination goes like so. The party calling the witness will conduct the examination-in-chief, asking open questions designed to elicit all the relevant information contained in the witness statement. No leading questions are allowed at this stage. No, 'It's correct that this defendant robbed you, *isn't it*? [WINK WINK]' is permitted. No one in an English court is going to actually say the word 'objection', but your opponent will stand up with a concerned, furrowed frown and calmly say, 'Your Honour . . .', prompting an immediate judicial reprimand for your breach of protocol.

Cross-examination, by contrast, is the art of the closed, leading question. While I do not hold myself up as an authority on the art, usually blustering my way through trials while gawping enviously at the skills of my opponent, I'm familiar with the theory. And the exercise is not about extracting truth, or assisting the jury in having as much information as possible before them. It is about leading the witness to the answer that you think you can manipulate them into giving.

The tactics are drilled into you at law school. Keep questions short and closed. Give the witness minimal room for manoeuvre or free-form speech. You want a yes or no answer. Don't ask a question if you don't already know what answer you're going to get. The theoretically perfect cross-examination is a series of short questions, the final of which forces the witness to give only one answer – the answer you, the advocate, desire.

Undermining the credibility of a witness is rarely difficult. Trials are held many months, sometimes years or decades, after the event. They will also take place at least several months after the witness has given their first account to the police in the form of their witness statement. The witness statement is a delightful tool for chipping away at a witness' credibility. It does not stand by itself as evidence, as we insist in criminal trials on oral evidence; a witness can refresh their memory from their statement, but all their evidence must be given live. If a witness gives an answer in evidence that differs in any way from something said in their witness statement, that right there is your first easy example of how defective this witness has proved herself to be. If the witness, confronted by the smirking advocate brandishing her contrary statement, immediately corrects her evidence to fit with the statement, she's making it up as she goes along. If she suggests that the police officer composing the statement must have made an error (as the police occasionally do), the witness is theatrically guided to their signature on each page of her statement, while the tutting advocate asks, wide-eyed and pious, what else in her signed witness statement the witness didn't bother to check for accuracy.

Multiple witnesses offer multiple opportunities for inconsistencies, for the simple reason that a group of honest witnesses giving an honest account of something that happened will all naturally diverge in their perceptions and recollections. There will always be something for the advocate to pluck out as 'proof' of unreliability. Mysha and Tamara both said that they had first discussed the abuse with each other two years ago, around six months before they decided to go to the police. When, inevitably, the evidence of these two poorly educated, psychologically vulnerable women diverged on the exact words used and precise dates, times and movements of that day, this, we crowed, shows that they're making it up. When they differed in their evidence, it was because they were tripping up in their own lies. When they were eerily similar in what they said, it was because they were in cahoots.

When you can add to your default armoury some concrete examples of unreliability and lies, as we had in our schedule, you've got a day's worth of brickbats you can throw in as well. Particularly if, as with Tamara, you get caught out lying in your evidence. She had told a counsellor, a few years ago, that she was going to 'get my own back big time' on Jay. The context was unclear, but it was established from the records, and the counsellor himself, that Tamara had used those words. The prosecution agreed that this was so. This fit neatly with our case theory of malicious complaint, although in deploying it we were taking the risk that the prosecution would spin it as the natural rage of a girl whose childhood was stolen by her predatory father. Tamara though, rather than offering this context when confronted with the comment in cross-examination, denied making it at all. She lied. And, George was able to put to her – and to the jury in his closing speech – this was the lie that gave the lie to everything else. It was but the tip of the iceberg. One proven lie – a lie *on oath, members of the jury* – that casts into question everything else she has told you. Remember, when you consider her tear-streaked video interview that she gave to the police (that being the way that evidence-in-chief is given in sex cases), and ponder the hysterics she 'convincingly' exhibited when challenged on her evidence, that this girl is a proven liar. And please, ladies and gentlemen, assess all of her evidence with that in mind.

By the end of the witness' evidence, if cross-examination has been successful, the jury should be questioning everything about the witness other than what you want them to accept. If enough damage has been done to the inherent credibility of the witness, the jury may be distracted from what, on its face, is an internally coherent and utterly compelling portrait of a real-life event.

Excluding Evidence

Of course, you can altogether avoid having to challenge or cast a favourable gloss over awkward prosecution evidence if that evidence doesn't get before the jury in the first place. One of the unique features distinguishing common-law adversarialism from the Continental inquisitorial procedure is how much energy goes into ensuring that the fact-finding tribunal is *not* in possession of all the facts.

Rules of evidence in criminal proceedings are horrendously complex. As with the adversarial format itself, rules of evidence emerged piecemeal from the eighteenth century as barristers, restricted to assisting the courts on 'matters of law', enlarged their roles by finding ever new and exotic ways to push the boundaries. At their heart, rules of evidence aim to confine what is put before the jury (or magistrates) to that which is relevant to the issues. Nothing is gained by taking up court time clouding the jury's task with irrelevant data. Further to that, though, the law has developed to act as a 'quality filter', and to excise evidence which may be relevant, but with which it is deemed juries ought not to be trusted.

Some of these are designed to eliminate evidence that by its nature is of lower quality, such as the rule against hearsay. Put simply, assertions made out of court are not admissible as evidence of their truth except in tightly defined circumstances. And so, if Joe tells a police officer that he saw Jim stab Fred, Joe would have to come to court and give that evidence on oath. Neither his witness statement, nor the evidence of the police officer as to what Joe said, would be admissible instead. The rationale is that the source of hearsay evidence cannot be directly challenged, and as 'second hand' evidence is inherently more likely to be unreliable. But it is not *always* so. And the exclusionary rule means that evidence which is potentially relevant, and which could be entirely reliable, might be withheld.

Other exclusionary rules are ostensibly aimed at avoiding undue prejudice to the parties. An obvious example is the law on bad character. The starting point is that evidence of a defendant's previous 'bad character' – which doesn't just include convictions, but any conduct of a 'reprehensible' nature – is inadmissible. The jury ordinarily will hear nothing about it. A fun part of a trial arrives immediately following a guilty verdict, when the prosecutor will rise to their feet and, in a theatrical display of 'Here's What We Didn't Tell You', read out to the agape jury the defendant's impressive list of previous convictions. Again, the reason for this appears sound: there is a risk that a jury may attach undue prominence to someone's previous roguery with the result that they fail to properly scrutinize the evidence for the present allegation. The same applies to the bad character of non-defendants. My schedule of Mysha and Tamara's historical misdeeds was not automatically admissible; much of my effort went unrewarded, as the judge properly applied the strict legal test for allowing the complainants to be cross-examined about their bad character, and many instances of the more minor or unverifiable instances of childhood misbehaviour were ruled out.

Other relevant evidence, which is neither hearsay nor bad character, may be excluded at the judge's discretion if it is deemed to 'have such an adverse effect on the fairness of proceedings' that the court ought not to allow it.[2] Such applications are often made where, for example, there has been a breach of the codes of practice that govern police investigations. If an identification procedure does not comply with the applicable code of practice, the positive identification of the suspect by an eyewitness may be excluded. Partly this is to prevent low-quality or contaminated evidence from polluting the purity of what the jury hear, partly public policy dictates that it is important that there are meaningful consequences for the prosecuting authorities breaking law and procedural codes.

And so, rather than placing all relevant evidence before the jury with appropriate warnings and directions as to the caution with which they might want to approach parts of it, we instead legally purify the evidence out of what can only be a fundamental mistrust in the ability of juries to consume the raw produce appropriately. This is a paradox at the heart of the jury system. It is not for those twelve to decide whether evidence is reliable, or whether it is fair to take it into account. We fear the jury's human weaknesses, while simultaneously lauding its innate and unimpeachable sense of fairness. Is this tenable? Or does this all add up to a picture of incomplete information being put before an admittedly irrational tribunal?

The filtration of evidence in adversarialism isn't limited to what is excluded. Because an application to exclude presumes that the relevant evidence has been obtained. Often it hasn't. The presentation of evidence is for the parties, rather than the court, and anything that is not supplied cannot be considered. The oath that jurors swear is to decide cases on the evidence. They must not conduct extra-curricular research online, or speculate about what other evidence might exist. Their tests must be conducted using only the tools handed to them in the courtroom laboratory. If the prosecution has missed or forgotten something, it remains forever buried. When ploughing through the unused material, I noticed a social worker's notes from 1993, recording Mysha as suggesting that her dad was doing things at home that made her uncomfortable. The prosecution had missed this helpful evidence of contemporaneous complaint. They had not spotted it, not pursued it, and not spoken to the social worker to get further detail. And, it being not in the least helpful to our case, this valuable comment, no doubt long-forgotten by Mysha, was never brought to the jury's attention.

Tactical manoeuvres by the parties further limit the jury's access to relevant information. A key question of an opposing witness may deliberately not be asked by a seasoned pro, aware that her case is stronger without Schrödinger's cat's welfare being confirmed. The evidence called by each side is selective and partial. Neither side is going to knowingly call a witness who will torpedo their own case. Sometimes, when defending, this means not calling someone who the jury may be very keen to hear from. Such as Jay's wife, Farah. She, standing by her man, was keen to give evidence in his defence, to say how she had seen no signs of abuse in the family home, and what awful, mendacious children she had

239

raised. But no way was George or I putting her in the witness box and gifting the prosecution the opportunity to demonstrate to the jury quite how ineffective a protector the girls' mother was. How easily she would have been manipulated by Jay. How plentiful were the opportunities for him to do to those children whatever he damn well pleased.

And sometimes tactics demand that the defendant himself exercise his right to silence and not give evidence. Counter-intuitive though it may sound, there are some trials – particularly where you fear a client may blunder his way to convicting himself in the witness box – where you advise that he remain silent and hope that enough damage has been done to the prosecution case in cross-examination for the jury not to be sure of guilt. Of course they'll think he's *possibly* or *probably* guilty. But if the prosecution witnesses have been poor, it is possible to persuade a jury that, even without the defendant's account on oath, they cannot be sure beyond reasonable doubt that he is guilty. The risk however is that the jurors, as they are entitled to do, draw an inference that is adverse against your client from his silence, and proceed to convict him. In such cases, it can be difficult, I have found, to shake the feeling that you as the advising advocate are in some way to blame. That, even if the advice you gave was spot on, your client is being punished for your gamble. The narrative that you fear – and to which they, if innocent, will forever cling – is of a blameless person unjustly deprived of their freedom because they were persuaded by their barrister to play the game and roll the dice, rather than simply tell the truth.

Inquisitorialism: A Search for Truth?

The word 'game' hangs in the air. Because that is often what adversarialism amounts to. It does not seek to take a cool, impartial look at all available evidence. It does not calmly invite differing interpretations of a comprehensive fact-gathering exercise. The police, conscious of the political imperative to achieve convictions, investigate alone, under their own steam. They pass what they find to the CPS, which selects the evidence that points towards guilt. The defence try to exclude parts of that evidence, throw in some of their own, equally partial, while lobbing smoke bombs into the arena in the hope that some may damage the prosecution witnesses, or at the very least distract the jury. Who, let us not forget, we cannot trust in possession of the full facts, lest they misapply them or otherwise disgrace themselves.

It is difficult to see how, in that framework, truth is ever supposed to emerge. Particularly in contrast to the alternative, European model – inquisitorialism. Which, whatever variant of system you alight upon, is premised on and marketed as a neutral search for objective truth.

There are many and varied inquisitorial systems, but it is worth a whistlestop tour of some of the main common features. The headline is that rather than equip two adversaries with the means to present their own partial evidence to an independent fact finder, all roles are vested in the state.

Typically, the criminal investigation is carried out by judicial police officers, under the supervision of the prosecutor, who decides whether to pursue the matter to a trial. Evidence is gathered both for and against the accused in a disinterested and objective manner, and the investigation and its findings are documented in a file, or dossier. The prosecutor's objective is not to obtain a conviction – unlike the CPS, under political pressure to deliver acceptable, although ever-undefined, conviction rates: – her public duty is to search for and uncover the truth. In some jurisdictions, the prosecutor is supplanted by an investigating magistrate who takes responsibility for the investigation. Witnesses will be examined and their testimony recorded in the investigative stage, with all evidence placed in the dossier.

The defence will be entitled to inspect the dossier before trial and offer representations on any further investigation that should be instigated. Once the prosecutor or investigating magistrate is satisfied that all necessary investigative measures have been exhausted, the completed dossier, containing all the evidence, is put before the trial court. This is usually a single judge, or a mixed panel of professional judges and laypersons.

Trial itself takes on a very different, almost anti-climactic feel. And there *will* be a trial. Guilty pleas and plea bargains do not exist, capable as they are of obscuring truth. While a defendant can admit his misdeeds in evidence, the court must still establish exactly what took place. The trial is judge-led. In most cases, the crucial decision is reached solely by reference to the hundreds of pages of witness statements, expert reports and photographs that comprise the dossier. While the witness evidence should theoretically be repeated orally, the judge may dispense with the requirement that witnesses attend. The role of the lawyers is therefore marginalized. There is no hostile cross-examination for the edification of a rapt jury; little cross-examination, in fact, at all. While there will be a defence lawyer, their role is usually limited to handing in written submissions on the law and evidence, and suggesting questions that the judge might wish to ask of a witness. In jurisdictions where oral questioning is allowed, it tends to be perfunctory and non-aggressive. No Garrows enlarging their role and demolishing terrified witnesses in a verbal frenzy. No Georges teasing out the inconsistencies in the evidence of first Mysha and then Tamara, clobbering them relentlessly with a club of bad-character evidence as they thrashed around on the video monitor, their eyes searching desperately, fruitlessly for help. In some inquisitorial jurisdictions, including Germany,

Austria, Norway and Sweden, complainants are permitted to assist the prosecutor as a 'subsidiary prosecutor'. Rather than being viewed as a powerless appendix to the prosecution case, served on a plate to a salivating defence lawyer, a victim can assume a meaningful role in their own right. Their dignity is preserved both by the manner of questioning and the significance accorded to their status.

Crucially, exclusionary rules of evidence are anathema. The only test for admissibility is relevance. Hearsay is a non-concept. The judge is trusted to weigh up the evidence, distinguish between primary and secondary accounts and attach appropriate significance to what appears in the dossier. Previous convictions of the defendant are not only admissible but considered important to the determination of guilt or innocence. If there is any evidence which the court considers ought to have been obtained, further inquiry can be ordered. Note the contrast to the jury, which, if it meekly approaches the judge and asks for more evidence, is told firmly that, 'You've had all the evidence there is,' and ordered to get on with reaching a verdict. In inquisitorialism, no relevant questions go tactically unasked. No reasonable avenues of inquiry lie uncharted due to the awkwardness they might portend to the parties. The finder of fact is not, as juries are here, prosecuted and gaoled for undertaking extra-curricular research into the case; it is encouraged to amass whatever information it feels it needs to get to the bottom of the case.

When the court retires to consider whether guilt is proved to the standard of *intime conviction* – roughly translated as 'deeply and thoroughly convinced'[3] – it must provide not only a one- or two-word verdict, but reasons for its conclusions.[4] Whereas the sanctity of the jury's verdict renders it a criminal offence in England and Wales to ask for or disclose details of a jury's deliberations, leaving the Court of Appeal to speculate as to what a jury *might* have been thinking, the truth, as the court finds it to be, is clearly and publicly set out and justified.

If the court found the witnesses credible, but in light of the lack of supporting evidence could not faithfully hold themselves out as sure to the requisite standard, that crumb of comfort could be offered to the devastated complainants as the not guilty verdict was returned. If the court was satisfied that a complaint was malicious, they could set out on public record the words that the acquitted defendant could forever embrace when faced with the inevitable, ugly, no-smoke-without-fire whispers that are invited by a blank, expressionless Not Guilty.

The adversarial model – or at least our version of it – eschews narrative verdicts. Instead of the verdict being the conclusive answer, it is often the catalyst for further questions that can never be resolved. Win or lose, that's your only certainty. And so, after George, with the aid of that damned schedule, tossed grenade after grenade after grenade into the evidence of the two girls – the word 'liar' bouncing around the courtroom on a loop as he softly and politely tore each complainant apart – and after Jay went into the witness box and gave a fumbling, evasive performance in his defence, and after the jury returned with their verdicts, the foreman repeating 'Not Guilty' seventeen times as we advocates maintained our poker faces, no one could say where the truth lay; or even where it began.

All we had – and all we, for Jay, needed – was that inscrutable, favourable answer to those seventeen binary questions. But that was far from the truth. And that verdict and its obnoxious unknowability, although satisfactory for our client, didn't get to the truth of what had taken place over the last twenty years.

*

Why do I say that I think Jay was guilty? Just a hunch. There was the material in the Social Services' records, none of it conclusive, but much of it painting a clearer, darker picture than that achieved by the prosecution at trial. There was the way Jay presented in his evidence; his lukewarm denials contrasted to the raw hysteria of the complainants when challenged. There was his demeanour in that very first conference. The way he said, as we shook hands at the end, 'Just get me off, yeah?', delivered with the same casual arrogance I'd seen a hundred times before in career burglars who know they're playing the game. There was the way he didn't seem burdened in the way that I imagine *I* would be burdened if my children – my flesh and blood – accused me of those unspeakable, monstrous things. There was his reaction on acquittal; not so much screaming blessed relief as shrugging pleasant surprise. All those little tells.

They could be wrong, of course, and possibly speak louder to my own prejudices than anything else. But something about the evidence, about him, about *them*, made the acquittal feel, if not wrong, at least not right. As we watched the victorious Jay drag a glazed Farah out through the front revolving door of the court precinct and back to their cursed normality, George turned to me.

'He did it, didn't he?'

I nodded. 'I think so.'

George grimaced.

'Those poor fucking girls.'

George's practice was these cases. He did little else. When he spoke of them normally in chambers, it was with the learned indifference and gallows humour that sex barristers adopt out of self-preservation. He, like so many of his call, was impervious to cloudy emotion. He was just a player of the game. But as we dragged our suitcases in tandem over the cobbles towards the station, he was oddly withdrawn.

His jolly, polished, public-school charm had slipped, replaced with a grimace of pursed reflection.

'Have you ever before . . . ?' I began.

He shook his head. And we walked on in silence. As we did, the questions that we rarely confront, whether through training or simply lack of time to give them proper thought, started percolating through my mind, melding together in a sticky ball of inseparable, unanswerable interrogations. Can we say that justice has been done in this case? What will happen to those vulnerable, broken girls, disbelieved by their family and now formally disbelieved by the state? What happens to the thousands like them? The many genuine victims of abuse, punished repeatedly in a vicious circle of institutional torture. Those children who are failed by the state, are abused and damaged, and who act like children who are abused and damaged, only to grow up and find that the justice system will use that damaged behaviour as reason to disbelieve them. The agony of their cross-examination, the final nails hammered into their remaining vestiges of dignity – is this the way to establish the truth? Is any of this, any of what we tacitly accept as Our Way of Justice, justifiable in the modern era, when other countries find ways to dispense criminal justice without so much overt public pain?

And today, as I look back over the arguments that speak for themselves, if I were to ask myself whether I agree with the caustic observations of one academic who scorns the notion of truth emerging through adversarialism – opining that:

> The adversary dynamic invited distortion and suppression of the evidence, by permitting abusive and misleading cross-examination, the coaching of witnesses, and the concealment of unfavourable evidence . . .[5]

– I would have to say yes. Professional ethics of course prohibit *abusive* cross-examination and witness coaching, and concealment of evidence is a bit value-laden for my taste, but the distortion and suppression of evidence is undeniable. It is integral to the process. And, to me, it is impossible to say, with a straight face, that our method is the best truth-seeker, or the best guarantor of the dignity of witnesses. It isn't. We prize a system that often deliberately frustrates primary enlightenment principles and accepts the obliteration of human dignity as its market price, with the consequence that people who are probably guilty get away with it.

But does it follow that I would entertain replacing it with something akin to inquisitorialism? Pulling down the scaffolding and starting construction anew, with a collective focus on neutral and objective state truth-seeking?

My answer to those latter questions is, on balance, no. And the next chapter sets out why.

9. Trial on Trial: Part II
– The Case for the Defence

'It is of more importance . . . that innocence should be protected, than it is, that guilt should be punished; for guilt and crimes are so frequent in the world, that all of them cannot be punished . . . But when innocence itself, is brought to the bar and condemned, especially to die, the subject will exclaim, "It is immaterial to me whether I behave well or ill, for virtue itself is no security." And if such a sentiment as this were to take hold in the mind of the subject, that would be the end of all security whatsoever.'

Defence counsel John Adams' closing address
to the jury in the murder trial of British soldiers
following the Boston Massacre, 1770[1]

The police officer's eyes switched from me, to the Crown Prosecution Service caseworker, and then back to me. He shot a glance to the door, possibly measuring whether he could avoid answering my question with a well-timed dart for freedom out of the police room, down the spiral staircase and through the court lobby to the exit. I repeated the question: 'You knew the defendant was mentally vulnerable, yet you interviewed her, with no solicitor or appropriate adult, with no caution, in her own living room, for three hours, before writing out a full confession, which you told her she had to sign?'

Still nothing. Shaz, my caseworker, coughed awkwardly.

'Well,' I nodded slowly, 'unless you tell me that I'm wrong in that assessment, I'm going to have to make a call to the CPS lawyer and we're binning this case today. And it's something that I expect will be raised higher up, as well.'

The officer stared back, and silently nodded. For a breach of PACE – shorthand for the Police and Criminal Evidence Act 1984, which, with its codes of practice, sets out strict rules for police investigations – this was almost impressive in its scope. My officer, it had become apparent when I picked up the brief for trial the night before and spoke to defence counsel on the phone, had breached almost every rule in the book. The sole evidence against Mary, a psychiatrically un-well young woman who was well known to the police, was a confession that she had given to our officer. Further enquiries revealed that the 'confession' amounted to Mary's signature at the bottom of a two-page monologue drafted by our officer, who had attended Mary's home and, instead of ar-resting her and taking her to the police station for a recorded interview, had harangued Mary until she agreed to sign the offending document. She was not cautioned, she was not told of her right to legal advice, there was no appropriate adult present (a requirement in all interviews with a mentally vulnerable defendant) and no record was made of what Mary had said during the three-hour 'interview'.

As the enormity of his conduct was repeated back to him for a final time, the officer looked ready to cry. He couldn't have been more than twenty-five. His first Crown Court trial, he'd proudly told me when I entered the police room. And it was a sure-fire winner. Before the trial was even due to be called on at 10.30 a.m., I had authorization to bring the prosecution to an abrupt end.

*

Any system of criminal justice which in the name of truth-seeking entrusts investigation, presentation of evidence, witness interrogation, adjudication and sentence exclusively to the state does so on two principal assumptions: that the state is competent to find the truth, and that its neutrality in seeking it is unimpeachable. These are the twin assumptions that underlie inquisitorialism. And both are dangerously untenable.

Mary stands as an example which was thankfully caught before serious harm was done. Warren Blackwell was not so lucky.[2] On 31 December 1998, he was seeing in the New Year at a social club in his local village in Northamptonshire, with his wife of six years. Over the course of the evening, he was introduced to a woman, Susan, and as alcohol flowed they played a game of pool. After the clock chimed midnight, Susan took a break from the revelry and wandered outside to catch some fresh air. As she stepped outside, she heard a familiar male voice behind her. 'Happy New Year,' the man said.

Susan recognized the voice, but before she could turn around, the man took hold of her. She felt the metallic sting of a knife pressed against her left thigh, and froze in fear as she was grabbed roughly by the arm and dragged down an alleyway, away from the club and towards a grassy area. Although dark, Susan could see in the amber glare of the streetlight that this was the man from the club; the man she had played pool with. It was Warren.

He grabbed her breast and tried to kiss her. When she didn't respond, he became angry and punched her in the face four times. He then pushed her to the ground, sat on her legs and placed something cold and metallic on her bare stomach. Looking down, Susan saw that it was a blunt object that looked a bit like a file, approximately nine inches long and an inch wide. The man tugged her trousers down to her knees. He took the metal object and pushed it between her legs, into her vagina, causing agonizing pain. When he had finished, he punched her once more to the face, hard enough to knock her unconscious.

When Susan awoke, she was surrounded by concerned locals, who had found her outside on the ground. The assault was reported to the police. There was no forensic scientific evidence – such as DNA – to link any specific individual to the attack, but when inspected by doctors, Susan was found to have bruising on her arm, scratches to her thigh and lacerations on her genitals, which appeared consistent with her account. She attended an identification procedure on 19 January 1999, and picked out Warren Blackwell as her attacker.

This was how the prosecution opened its case at Warren Blackwell's trial for indecent assault at Northampton Crown Court in October 1999. Warren Blackwell denied that he had done any such thing. He told police when arrested, and the jury at trial, that he had been at the club that night and had played pool with Susan, but knew nothing of what had happened to her outside. This, it was said on his behalf, was a terrible case of mistaken identity. She had seen him that night at the club and must have confused him for her attacker.

And that was how the judge summed up the case to the jury. It was never suggested for a moment, by anyone at trial, that the attack had not happened. Nothing had been disclosed to the defence by the prosecution to suggest that Susan might not be truthful.

The jury returned on 7 October 1999 with the majority verdict of guilty that precipitated the imposition of a three-year sentence of imprisonment, and the state entered on its official records the indisputable finding of fact that Susan had been violently and sexually assaulted, and that the man responsible was Warren Blackwell.

Except, it transpired, he wasn't. The entire story, the

Court of Appeal later heard, was a fiction. And what was more, the police had suspected as much the entire time.

The truth did not emerge, however, until after Warren Blackwell had served his prison sentence. And not just the three-year sentence imposed by the trial judge; the sentence was referred to the Court of Appeal by the Attorney General as 'unduly lenient' given the viciousness of the assault. The Court of Appeal agreed that three years was insufficient, and on 22 March 2001, the same day that it refused his renewed application for leave to appeal against his conviction, the Court increased his sentence to five years. He served two thirds of that sentence – three years and four months – before being released.

Innocent, wrongly convicted and then kicked one final time by the Court of Appeal, Warren Blackwell sought help in the last refuge available to him – the Criminal Cases Review Commission. The CCRC is a statutory body established in 1995 to investigate alleged miscarriages of justice. Once an appeal has been refused by the Court of Appeal, the only route to having a conviction reconsidered is if the CCRC investigates and concludes that, due to some new evidence or new legal argument, there is a real possibility that the Court of Appeal will quash the conviction. In that scenario, the CCRC will refer the case to the Court of Appeal, which will consider the new grounds of appeal and decide whether the conviction is unsafe.

Warren Blackwell applied to the CCRC on 14 October 2002. The Commission investigated, drawing in part on enquiries conducted by a private investigator hired by the Blackwell family while Warren was in prison. Due to the number of applications received and its limited resources, it can take some time for the CCRC to investigate. But by the time it had finished, its findings were astounding.

Susan was well known to the police. Not only did she have a record of previous convictions for offences of dishonesty, which were not disclosed to the defence at trial, but she had developed a reputation as something of a serial complainant. Between October 1998 and June 2001, Susan made a succession of allegations, some involving her being grabbed at night, from behind, by strange men who led her to secluded areas, forced her to lie down, pulled her trousers down to her knees and brutalized her. Many complaints were accompanied with apparently corroborative injuries. But medical and other evidence showed that the injuries had been self-inflicted, or pre-existed the alleged incident.

In each instance, the relevant police force investigated and concluded that Susan's allegations were fabrications, and the injuries self-inflicted. This interpretation was supported by psychiatric and medical records obtained by the CCRC, which were in the possession of the CPS during Warren Blackwell's trial but not disclosed to the defence.

The CCRC gathered evidence from numerous other witnesses who knew Susan well – including Susan's former husband, mother, daughter and former boyfriends (including her fiancé at the time of the New Year's Day incident) – all of whom confirmed that Susan was a prolific and convincing liar. Susan's daughter referred to a specific incident in 1999 in which she had witnessed her mother harming herself and then claiming that she had been attacked.

Putting this all together, the CCRC referred the case to the Court of Appeal: 'There is evidence that was not adduced at trial that, when considered as a whole, provides a strong case to support the conclusion that [the complainant] was NOT the victim of any assault and that her injuries were self-inflicted.'

The prosecution could not sensibly and did not oppose the appeal, conceding the above ground of appeal, and expressly invited the Court of Appeal to find that the conviction was unsafe. On 12 September 2006, nearly seven years after his trial, Warren Blackwell's conviction was quashed, with the Court of Appeal expressing its grave concerns over the prospect of further Warren Blackwells being snared by Susan and her lies.

The matter didn't end there though. There was a second ground of appeal, which in the end was not determined by the Court of Appeal (as the appeal was successful on the first ground). This related to averred disclosure failings by the prosecution during the trial. We've already considered disclosure – the prosecution's legal obligation to provide the defence with material that might reasonably assist the defence or undermine the prosecution case – earlier. Here, while some of the fresh evidence arose out of events postdating the 1999 trial, Susan's previous convictions and psychiatric and medical records were known to the prosecution but consciously not disclosed. Furthermore, there was a wealth of information that Northamptonshire Police were given about Susan before, during and shortly after the trial, which, had it been disclosed, may well have resulted in the wrongful conviction being overturned early enough for it to have spared the innocent appellant from serving his full prison sentence. Warren Blackwell therefore complained to the Independent Police Complaints Commission. The report concluded that this case had been riddled with serious disclosure failings throughout.

Publishing its investigative findings in June 2010, the IPCC announced:

> Warren Blackwell was subject to a terrible miscarriage of justice . . . On top of weaknesses in the original police investigation, a detective failed to disclose to senior officers, the CPS or the defence, crucial information about the credibility of the complainant, all factors which contributed to the wrongful conviction.[3]

The investigation found that an officer from another

force had expressed concerns to a Northamptonshire detective over Susan's reliability, both before and after Warren Blackwell was charged. This officer, who knew Susan from her participation as a witness in another trial, said that she 'appeared to enjoy police attention', and that there were concerns over her honesty. The Northamptonshire detective, agreeing that Susan appeared 'unreliable' and 'unstable', did not think to pass this vital information to his colleagues or to the CPS. The IPCC further found that there were numerous discrepancies in Susan's account that were not properly challenged during the police investigation. There were also two eyewitnesses who told police that they had walked past the scene of the alleged attack at the time that Susan claimed she was being assaulted, and had seen nothing of the sort; two eyewitnesses from whom *no witness statements were ever taken*. Post-conviction, while Warren Blackwell was locked in a prison cell, a Northamptonshire detective received information of the false complaints made by Susan in 2000 and 2001, which bore striking similarities to the 1999 case. The detective did not bring this information to the attention of senior officers or the CPS.

To top off its numerous findings of misconduct, the IPCC expressed its 'dismay' at the unexplained delay in Northamptonshire Police issuing a formal apology to Warren Blackwell; noted with disgust that a culpable detective constable whom the IPCC determined should have faced a full misconduct hearing had avoided it by swiftly retiring, and observed that, in a final jaw-dropping exhibition of institutional chutzpah, the Chief Constable of Northamptonshire had not withdrawn the commendation given to the detective constable for his fine work in the original investigation.

I make no apology for the level of detail, because this case demonstrates, in glorious, terrifying technicolour, the danger of assuming, as inquisitorialism does, that if you are falsely accused of a crime, the state is capable of pulling together all the relevant information that you will need to secure your acquittal. And while it may be argued that Warren Blackwell's is an extreme example, it only stands as such because its failings were ultimately exposed on the grandest stage of all.

The Myth of State Competence

The first thing to state clearly, for the avoidance of doubt, is that instances of malicious sexual allegations are rare. Exact figures are obviously unknowable, but at the last estimate, there were roughly only twenty prosecutions of malicious rape complaints per year,[4] while there are approximately 7,000 annual complaints of rape made to the police.[5] Under-reporting of sexual offences is widely accepted to be numerically far more prevalent than malicious complaints.[6] Popular misconceptions abound in this field, largely due to misunderstandings as to what the burden of proof, and an acquittal, actually means. Where there is no conviction after a defendant is charged, as occurs in 42.1 per cent of rape cases, it does not automatically follow that the complaint was false. Many sex cases come down to a grainy issue of consent, or reasonable belief in consent, or identification, where a *not guilty* means just that – the jury was not sure of guilt, rather than sure of innocence. An acquittal should not be mistaken for a finding that a complainant was untruthful. Susan is in the minority.

However, I use Warren Blackwell's case as a stark illustration of the serious consequences that can flow when the state machinery is assumed to be competent, particularly in the error-strewn field of disclosure.

For, like Warren Blackwell, hundreds of thousands of other defendants find themselves victims of prosecution disclosure failings every year. For many, especially the guilty, little will turn on these errors. But for the innocent, there may be an Aladdin's cave of disclosable material, relevant to your case, which the police and CPS have failed to obtain or reveal. Every morning of every trial I defend is spent chasing the prosecutor for disclosable material that my solicitors have repeatedly requested to no avail. Rarely is the Schedule of Unused Material – which should contain a list of *everything relevant to the investigation* generated by the police in the investigation, with each item reviewed and marked either 'disclosable' or 'not disclosable' – complete. Sometimes the overworked CPS lawyer who is supposed to have assessed the material will admit to not having seen it, but having rubber stamped the police's assessment.

Many failures are fortuitously caught in the act; but the margins are often so fine as to leave me with a lasting feeling of physical sickness.

A colleague in chambers once grabbed me and, pallid-faced, told me of his case that morning in which his client, who had been remanded for six months awaiting trial for a serious kidnapping, had been freed at beyond the eleventh hour after the prosecutor casually disclosed mobile phone and cell-site evidence that proved the alibi that the defendant had pleaded all along. After much pressure from the judge, the prosecution agreed to drop the case just as the jury were about to be empanelled.

A few years ago I defended a serious allegation of violence. A week into the trial itself, after my client, David, had been told something by a friend of a friend of a friend who had seen something on Facebook, we badgered the prosecution to investigate, and it was disclosed that the complainant had the previous month been convicted of an offence of violence. The complainant, who David maintained was a violent liar, had recently been tried at Crown Court, and had given evidence in his defence on oath, and a jury had been sure that he was both violent and lying. Compelling, relevant and admissible evidence which ultimately helped to secure David's acquittal. But for these six degrees of social media separation, it would never have emerged.

A 2017 joint report into disclosure by HM Crown Prosecution Service Inspectorate and HM Inspectorate of Constabulary made for terrifying reading. The police and CPS, whether due to poor training or lack of resources, were failing time and time again to comply with their obligations in run-of-the-mill ('volume') Crown Court cases. The Schedules of Unused Material that were supposed to be drawn up by the police were 'wholly inadequate' in 22 per cent of cases. The CPS was failing to pull the police up on these obvious failures, and 33 per cent of CPS files examined by the inspectors were marked 'poor'. In over half of cases, CPS lawyers provided no explanation for their decisions as to what should and should not be disclosed to the defence. Audit trails of the disclosure process were unsatisfactory in 87 per cent of cases. The Chief Inspector, Kevin McGinty, said with apparent weary familiarity:

> The findings of this inspection will surprise no one who works within the criminal justice system as there appears to be a culture of defeated acceptance that issues of disclosure will often only be dealt with at the last moment, if at all. If the police and CPS are ever going to comply with what the law requires of them by way of disclosure, then there needs to be a determined cultural change. This is too important to be allowed to continue to fail.[7]

Serious Crown Court cases offer hardly greater comfort. Although the CPS's dedicated Rape and Serious Sexual Offences (RASSO) units perform their disclosure obligations to a higher standard than we see in the CPS's general knockabout caseload, a 'good' rating of just over 51 per cent[8] is hardly cause for celebration. It means that in nearly half of serious sex cases – cases such as Warren Blackwell's – the CPS is struggling to carry out its statutory duties of disclosure. And this, bear in mind, only represents the known failings – the errors or delays that are spotted and recorded. Miscarriages of justice like Warren Blackwell do not show up in official reports. They lie dormant, until, or unless, discovered.

Disclosure failure is not new. It is a problem that has been identified in report after report after report. And such levels of inadequacy persist notwithstanding our adversarial system; the defence solicitors and barristers actively needling the prosecution to do its job, to investigate further and to reconsider its analysis of what material might be relevant. I shudder to think what an inquisitorial system, which envisages no meaningful role for the defence in the investigative procedure or in the compilation of the dossier for the judge, would miss. Can it really sensibly be suggested, given what is known about the performance of the prosecuting authorities, that the state would organize its affairs better *without* an adversarial counterweight correcting its omissions? Given how the CPS struggles to manage its existing functions, are we ready to surrender the role played by defence lawyers to the exclusive competence of the state? Or in so doing, would we simply be increasing the number of Warren Blackwells in our prisons?

A further relevant example worth mentioning at this stage is the state of forensic scientific evidence in the criminal courtrooms. Scientific evidence plays an increasingly central role in criminal trials. Experience teaches that it is particularly persuasive with juries, who are prone to falling spellbound to scientific claims of infallibility from the witness box. In some cases, it is literally the only evidence: a DNA profile match alone, with nothing further to link a suspect to the scene of a crime, is sufficient for a court to safely convict.[9]

The assumption of the infallibility of scientific evidence has led to some of the most appalling miscarriages of justice in history, including the rash of mothers wrongly convicted of killing their babies on the basis of evidence given by discredited paediatrician, and prosecution expert, Roy Meadow. 'Meadow's Law' – his hypothesis that *one sudden infant death is a tragedy, two is suspicious and three is murder* – was backed by fallacious statistical analysis and was relied upon in the 1990s to convict a series of women insisting that their children had died of natural causes. While the Court of Appeal quashed a number of these high-profile convictions in the 2000s, the damage done to some of these women was irreversible. Sally Clark, a solicitor convicted in 1999 of killing her two infant sons, succeeded in her appeal in 2003, but died in tragic circumstances four years later, having never recovered from the effects of this most awful miscarriage of justice.[10]

Given its power over prosecutors and juries, the importance of accuracy in scientific evidence is plain. But the quality of forensic scientific services is in severe decline. In a money-saving exercise in 2012, the government's Forensic Science Service was closed, and forensic scientific analysis and pathology have since been subcontracted to private firms or carried out at police laboratories. The Forensic Science Regulator exposed the predictable false economies in 2017 in a withering report. The tendering system had resulted in a high turnover of providers, with work constantly changing hands and a consequent 'increase in quality failures and a loss of skills'.[11] There was a lack of standardization in scientific approach, and the interpretation of results varied across providers. Few organizations in 2017 were on course to secure accreditation and meet basic standards of competence.

Terrifyingly, the regulator noted instances of contamination, where extraneous material was inadvertently introduced into analysis. These risks were notably prevalent in Sexual Assault Referral Centres (SARCs) and police custody, where 'a number of concerning contamination-related issues' were identified in the medical examination of complainants and suspects.[12] In one example, DNA recovered from one complainant examined at a SARC was detected on intimate swabs from another complainant in an entirely different case, who was examined in the same facility. In another, the same medical practitioner was asked to examine both the suspect and the complainant in *the same case*. Had the suspect's DNA been found on the complainant's intimate swabs, this would have presented *prima facie* compelling evidence that sexual activity took place, but the actions of the forensic medical examiner would have entirely compromised any such finding. There would have been no way of knowing whether the DNA was transferred by direct contact between the complainant and suspect, or indirectly by the examiner. If it was the latter, and the contamination hadn't been identified or disclosed, there would have been utterly compelling – but potentially utterly wrong – scientific evidence on which a jury could convict.

The Myth of State Impartiality

Competence is of course only half the story. The other assumption underpinning inquisitorialism is that the state's motives are pure beyond reproach.

And while Hanlon's Razor holds that one should never attribute to malice that which is adequately explained by neglect, the history of British criminal justice shows that bad faith on the part of the prosecuting authorities is more than just the fantasy of the green ink brigade.

Indeed, Warren Blackwell only received a second bite at the appellate cherry thanks to the Criminal Cases Review Commission, which was established in 1995 following perhaps the most famous miscarriages of justice in our legal history – the series of wrongful convictions in the 1970s arising out of bombing campaigns attributed to the Provisional Irish Republican Army (IRA).

The collective labels – Guildford Four, Birmingham Six, Maguire Seven – are marked in the history books as monuments to prosecutions gone rogue. A web of misconduct, including false confessions, non-disclosure and patently unreliable expert scientific evidence, was only exposed decades after innocent men and women had been imprisoned for offences including murder.

I have enormous respect for police officers, and see every day how they risk their lives to serve and protect the public with a dedication to duty that many of us take for granted. It is impossible to successfully prosecute criminal cases without the graft and ingenuity of police officers who I will not hesitate to say rarely get the public recognition or gratitude that their sacrifices richly merit.

But they are not all perfect. Some are very far from perfect. Some lie, cheat, dissemble and break the rules in the same ways as their quarry on the other side of the thin blue line. Often, the lies – or mistakes, as no doubt they would wish the errors to be characterized with a charity they would not for a moment extend to a defendant – appear minor. But that doesn't lessen their seriousness.

There's the CCTV that displays the smart, uniformed plod standing before the jury losing his temper in the custody suite and smashing the suspect's head gratuitously into the wall. Or you'll discover the search log that shows that the drugs allegedly found in the defendant's bedroom were in fact retrieved from the far less incriminating communal hallway. We might see several versions of police witness statements, which allow us to track the sequential amendments that have been made, in the days after the event, to ensure that the officers' evidence all tallies, and that any inconvenient inconsistencies are ironed out before the final versions are served on the defence. The solicitor might discover by happenchance a witness helpful to the defence whose existence was notably withheld by the constable the witness spoke to at the scene.

These do not happen in every case. But they happen. And usually it's because the police *know* they've got the right person. Like in the TV procedural shows, the difficult part is over once the mystery is solved, the bad guy has been identified and an arrest has been made. Proving it in a court of law is just red tape. An irritation. If rules need to be bent to get the right result, so be it. Like with Mary, at the chapter's beginning. The officer *knew* she'd done it. So that was OK.

Such cases demonstrate the fallacy of assuming the state is able to neutrally 'seek' truth, as opposed to alighting on its own theory and embarking on *ex post facto* buttressing of that narrative. And this is a criticism often levelled at inquisitorial systems by those who work within: notwithstanding their oxymoronic designation as 'neutral' prosecutors, the prosecutor and police may bow to natural inclinations to take a partisan position against the suspect and construct a case against him.

The flaw runs deeper than the motivations of individual investigators, however: inquisitorialism is compromised by the inherent susceptibility of the state machinery to political influence. Not at the level of high conspiracy, but the subtler pressures that governments bring to bear on the administration of criminal justice. The ubiquitous ministerial intuition that cost savings can be made without public outcry by shearing the justice budget, cutting a few corners here and there, has been demonstrated at length. You do not need to be modelling a tinfoil hat to recognize that politicians incrementally dispense with systemic safeguards, increasing the incidence of wrongful convictions, to bank transitory credit for being Tough On Crime; often as a reflex to media campaigns to 'improve' conviction rates for particular offences.

The vulnerability of impartial state investigators to political influence has been exposed in recent years by the ruinous way in which the authorities have treated complainants and defendants in cases involving child sexual exploitation.

So gruesomely ubiquitous have become reports of vulnerable children preyed upon by monstrous men, many known to but not pursued at the time by the authorities, that the single-word appellations have become common shorthand. Yewtree. Savile. Rochdale. Rotherham. Aylesbury. Oxford. Bristol. Newcastle. All cases where men abusing positions of power – whether achieved instantly by celebrity or incrementally by organized, gang-based grooming – evaded justice for years due in part to institutional attitudes that not only undermined but flew in the face of official investigative and prosecution policy.

In each instance, the criminal justice system only creaked into action many years after the offences were committed, despite the distress flares sent up by victims – and, famously, in the Rochdale grooming case, by social workers – at the time. The reasons for this gross betrayal are multifaceted and still not fully known, to be considered no doubt by the ongoing Independent Inquiry into Child Sexual Abuse (IICSA), but some trends have already been identified. The police had been told to focus instead on other offences to hit important government targets.[13] There was reportedly an irrational disinclination to intervene in some cases on grounds of cultural sensitivity due to the racial profile of some of the offenders.[14] A fear of investigating a name as big as Savile conferred immunity to offend.[15]

A correction was required. No more, it was rightly said,

would someone alleging serious sexual abuse against a person of influence find their accusations surreptitiously buried amidst institutionalized disbelief or backscratching in smoke-filled masonic lodges. But the pendulum, for so long jammed against the interests of victims, swung violently to the other extreme.

When, in 2014, a man known as 'Nick' approached the police with a chilling tale of 1970s murder and paedophilia that stretched to the highest echelons of the establishment, officers listened, captivated. Nick described how he and other young boys were ritually abused from the age of seven by a ring of Cabinet ministers, army generals, heads of MI5 and MI6 and a former prime minister. Nick was raped by one of the politicians, who was only stopped from dismembering Nick with a penknife due to the intervention of the prime minister. Nick was allowed to keep the penknife as a memento of this incident. Two other boys were murdered in front of Nick in a vile sex game, while another was run over by a car to instil terror into the other victims of abuse.[16]

If this sounds like a warped nightmare, that's because it was utter fantasy. There was no evidence at all to substantiate Nick's claims, and ultimately, in 2016, he was investigated for attempting to pervert the course of justice.

But faced with this ostensibly ludicrous story in 2014, what did the police do?

We should perhaps start with what they *should* have done. Notwithstanding our adversarial settlement, the police are required by law to investigate allegations of criminal offences fully and impartially. The rationale is obvious: the police have unrivalled resources and legal powers to effect criminal investigations; they have powers to enter premises, arrest people, search addresses, seize evidence, conduct scientific tests and so forth. However thoroughly defence legal representatives may conduct investigations on an accused's behalf, they cannot realistically compete.

A binding Code of Practice[17] sets out in detail the steps that the police must take when a crime is reported. Chief among these is the duty to establish whether a crime has in fact been committed.[18] If the investigation leads the police to suppose that a crime has or may have been committed, their duty to investigate is explicitly broad, and they are obligated to investigate all reasonable lines of inquiry, *including those that point away from the suspect's guilt.*[19] If the police, having investigated fully, consider that there is sufficient evidence to support a prosecution against a suspect, the matter will usually be referred to the CPS for advice and a decision on whether to charge. Even post-charge, the police are required to maintain an open, enquiring mind and exercise neutrality in the disclosure process, as described earlier, to ensure that the CPS and the defence are provided with anything that might help the suspect.

Behind this set-up lies the presumption of innocence. Whatever the evidence might suggest, the suspect is innocent until proven otherwise, and the impartiality of the police, even in adversarialism, is integral to that principle.

But in late 2014, faced with Nick's account, the police took a different approach. They instantly *believed* it. At the launching of Operation Midland in December 2014, Detective Sergeant Kenny McDonald told a press conference: '[My colleagues] and I believe what Nick is saying is credible and true.'

The police did not merely say, as they would have been right to say, that they were treating grave allegations seriously and investigating thoroughly. Instead they started from the position that the men accused, whose names were flung around the media and whose lives were publicly upended, their homes searched and their reputations obliterated, were guilty.

The fire took hold. Politicians boarded the bandwagon,

with MPs lining up to repeat the accusations against the wrongly accused, elderly men. Tom Watson, who would later become deputy leader of the Labour Party, met Nick in person and publicly denounced one of the innocent men as 'close to evil'. Zac Goldsmith made similar allegations against the same individual. John Mann jubilantly tweeted that the apprehension of one of the accused was 'the first of many'.[20]

Fortunately, no charges were ultimately brought, as Nick's credibility unwound beyond restoration, and sixteen months and £2.5 million later the investigation was closed. But the damage to the lives of the accused men and their families had been done. The post-mortem into Operation Midland, conducted by retired High Court Judge Sir Richard Henriques, was brutal.

Why had the police been so quick to believe Nick, and to find him 'credible and true'? The answer, it emerged, was because they had been told to. Since 2002, the College of Policing's strategy had been expressed thus: 'It is the policy of the [police] to accept allegations made by the victim in the first instance as being truthful. An allegation will only be considered as falling short of a substantiated allegation after a full and thorough investigation.'[21]

A 2014 report on police crime-reporting by HM Inspectorate of Constabulary went further, recommending that: 'The presumption that the victim should always be believed should be institutionalized.'[22]

The use of the word 'victim' as a substitute for the neutral, court-approved term 'complainant' was conscious. Under the strategy, any complainant immediately inherited the established status of 'victim'.[23] To do otherwise, the police claimed, would have a 'significant detrimental effect on the trust victims now have in authorities'.[24]

This overcorrection to the unforgivable failings of the past is politically entirely understandable. But in practical, legal and philosophical terms, it is unspeakably dangerous. That the policy passed under the radar at the time of its adoption without attracting greater attention is a failing that falls partly on us in the system. For it shamelessly inverts the burden of proof. Stage one of the investigative process – *has a crime been committed?* – is rendered redundant. Whereas for the children of Rochdale or Savile, the default conclusion of the police was always 'No', the equally unsatisfactory default under this model is 'Yes'. The box is already ticked, no questions asked. Only if the police are satisfied of the opposite will it ever be unticked.

I can do no better than directly quote Sir Richard: this policy 'perverts our system of justice and attempts to impose upon a thinking investigator an artificial and false state of mind'.[25] It 'has and will generate miscarriages of justice on a considerable scale'.[26]

The report on Operation Midland laid bare the toxic consequences of the Met's approach. In the culture of belief, nonsensical allegations are not properly challenged or tested until far too late. Conspiracy-laden ramblings are treated as immutable, protected from the same rigorous examination as the police apply to the denials of guilt by the falsely accused. Evidence tending to contradict the truth of a complaint gets underplayed, confirmation bias prioritizing that which might support what the police have been mandated to believe.

And, as sure as night follows day, the culture of belief led to the police in Operation Midland bending the rules. Sir Richard found an extraordinary forty-three separate failings in the investigation. Police officers misled a judge in order to secure the search warrants that permitted them to make highly publicized 'raids' on the addresses of elderly, frail suspects, despite there being 'no reasonable grounds to believe an indictable offence had been committed'. Officers helped Nick complete claims for compensation.[27] Partiality superseded logic and rationality, causing the investigation – and the pain to the accused – to be dragged out for far longer than was justified. As a result of the report's findings, four detectives and a deputy assistant commissioner were referred to the IPCC.

I repeat the earlier caveat: my reliance on Nick and Susan must not be misconstrued as suggesting that most, or a significant proportion, of sexual complaints are malicious. But *some* are. And the uncomfortable question follows: how many Nicks, or Susans, presented to the police in those fourteen years where the culture of belief prevailed and found themselves not respectfully challenged on the oddities of their stories, but immediately confirmed as survivors of atrocious abuse?

How narrowed was the scope of those investigations? How many leads were not chased up? How many concerns about a complainant's credibility were suppressed? How many disclosable documents went unscheduled, or undiscovered, due to their apparent irrelevance to the certainty invested in the complainant's word? And how many innocents are now locked up and branded, like Warren Blackwell, sexual predators of the foulest kind, due to the displacement of cool, legally imposed investigative neutrality with political doctrine?

And if there are – and we must concede the possibility – innocent people deprived of their liberty due to this culture of belief, this was a culture not of the law's making, but of politics'. And while adversarialism is of course no panacea to this problem, inquisitorialism's vulnerabilities to unchecked political influence are cast into stark relief. Loading the entirety of the evidence-gathering process onto a state agency so readily impregnable by dogma antithetical to fairness, truth-seeking and even the letter of the law, to my mind stores up more scope for injustice than can be tolerated. Under adversarialism, at least the fancies of false accusers, or the malfeasance of the police, are guaranteed the energetic challenge at trial, under cross-examination, that the politics of the investigator may lay asunder.

For me, the lesson of history is that the state alone cannot be trusted to find the truth. Whether it's incompetence or politics, stumbling blocks spring up. And if that concession is permitted, it strikes me that the only meaningful safe-guard is an independent, non-state actor to put forward the defence case, with the same force, skill and dedication as the prosecution, and to challenge the prosecution's assump-tions with equal vigour. And for the parties to invite an independent tribunal to consider whether the allegation is proved to the necessarily high criminal standard. Which brings us round to some form of adversarialism.

And from that, the rest falls into place. It follows, I think, that there should be quality controls on the evidence that goes before the independent finder of fact, whether it's a jury or professional judge. Relevance cannot be the sole litmus; a realistic and humane system must recognize inherent human weaknesses and cognitive biases, and shield the tri-bunal of fact from material which is likely to distract from, rather than assist, its assessment of the evidence. Knowing that the defendant accused of stealing a bike was once con-victed of flashing at schoolgirls may well be interesting, and may well say something about his general character; but does it really offend the object of justice to withhold this information from a jury? Or does it ensure fairness by making sure his guilt isn't determined by prejudicial, irrele-vant details unrelated to the evidence?

If a confession is obtained by oppression or in circum-stances where its reliability is compromised, surely it is right that the state not be rewarded for the abuse of its power, and that the prejudicial evidence be kept out of the evidential 'pot'? If Nick had been able to bolster his fantastical allegations by adducing evidence from someone to say, 'I heard tell of similar stories back in the day,' would striking that hearsay out of the evidential matrix be wrong, or in so doing would we be maximizing the calibre of evidence that the tribunal will take into account, avoiding unfairly boosting a weak prosecution case? Given what is known about the proven and inherent unreliability of identification evidence, and of the countless miscarriages of justice that have arisen due to honest, convincing and mistaken witness identifications, is it not only proper to ensure that, where such evidence is allowed, the tribunal is directed – as juries are – to examine it carefully and to be alert to the weaknesses?

The answers to those questions, for me, justify the principle of exclusionary rules of evidence, and the corollary rules that govern the use to which evidence can be put, and which set down guidance and warnings for fact-finders. How and where the boundaries of such rules are drawn are matters of debate for weightier, specialist texts, but the principle of filtering evidence to remove impurities, and to minimize the likelihood of wrongful convictions, is perhaps not as far from truth-seeking as might be asserted. It could even, tentatively, be suggested that by so doing we are increasing the chances of the fact-finder reaching a logical and reasoned decision.

Or, if I am overreaching in suggesting that exclusionary rules aid truth-seeking, perhaps I can swivel in this way: truth-seeking, in the way that advocates of inquisitorialism envision it, is not – and should not – be the purpose of criminal justice systems in any event. It is too much. In many cases, it cannot be done. This is not a lazy appeal to postmodernism; just practical reality. There are too many variables, too many unknowns lying outside the scope of reasonable and proportionate investigation, and too many competing truths – such as two men each truly believing the other to be the aggressor – for us to be able to assert with any confidence that we have uncovered the singular 'truth' of a scenario.

How on earth, for example, can any investigator, however well resourced, uncover the full truth of what happened twenty years ago, in the darkened bedrooms of a three-bed suburban terrace, when Jay's daughters got ready for bed? How is a jury, decades on, expected to resolve every question that would need to be resolved to arrive at a full exposition of that family's sad history? I don't think it reasonably can be. I think the best we can hope for is that the jury can determine enough from the evidence to answer the question, *on the evidence, are we sure that the defendant is guilty of this criminal offence?* To ask more than that of the criminal process, to suggest that by reconfiguring the system and restacking the deck in favour of the state we will more easily arrive at a neatly rounded, objective truth, is beyond ambitious. It is a pretence.

This is perhaps why, in the evolution of our legal system, we have never explicitly heralded truth as our guiding light. The progression from confrontation trial, where a citizen prosecutor helped by Marian magistrates was pitted against an unrepresented accused, to adversarial combat between two legally qualified proxies, was never premised on improving the likelihood of discovering the truth of a quarrel. Instead, each increment – from the right to be represented by defence counsel for arguments of law, to the right of counsel to examine witnesses and address the jury, to counsel-led exclusionary rules of evidence, to the right to legal aid – had as its aim the redressing of imbalance, tilting the scales away from the state and towards the individual.

And while seeking universal truths is, for me, an ambition too far, protecting individual liberty is something that I think our system, when it operates correctly, has done quite well. In impliedly acknowledging the limitations of criminal inquiry, and settling instead for a mechanical process designed to spit out a verdict which, due to the agreed fairness of the system, we are content to term justice, we display pragmatism, rather than defeatism.

I do not suggest for a moment that the system in its present form is beyond reproach. There is vast scope for improvement. The obsession with witnesses giving oral evidence-in-chief, for example, is for me an anachronism better suited to an age when a witness would not have to wait months, if not years, for a trial date. In civil proceedings, witnesses give a full witness statement, which stands as their evidence-in-chief, and attend trial solely to be cross-examined on its contents. This, to me, appears an uncontentious compromise, allowing the 'freshest' version of events to be their primary evidence. Complainants in sex trials will usually have their contemporaneous video interview with the police stand as their evidence-in-chief; extending similar measures to all witnesses may avoid unfairness arising from fading memories being exploited by either side.

Given a soapbox, I would also require juries to give reasons for their verdicts; to set out clearly their findings of fact, with reasons in support of those findings, and how the law applies to them. Magistrates and District Judges already give reasons for verdicts, as do juries in inquests. In Spain, juries deliver verdicts in five parts: a list of facts held to be established; a list of facts held to be not established; a declaration of guilty or not guilty; a succinct statement of reasons for the verdict, indicating the evidence on which it is based and the reasons supporting the establishment (or not) of relevant facts and a record of all events that took place during discussions, avoiding any identification that might infringe the secrecy of the deliberations.[28] Not every issue would have to be decided; I would not be insisting

273

upon an inquisitorially delivered narrative of truth. Rather, as currently directed, juries would continue to decide only the issues that they consider necessary and relevant to reaching a verdict. But it would offer a compromise; it would give all concerned – defendants, victims and public – an insight, and an ability to pinpoint any flaws or errors in the jury's reasoning; rather than relying on the Court of Appeal to somehow divine what the jurors were thinking.

And there are many other areas where I could, and would, propose technical reform to the operation of the adversarial jury system. However, remodelling it in the image of a doomed pursuit of an elusive, undefined 'truth' would not be in my manifesto.

So if I am content to abandon truth as a necessary component of justice, then what of human dignity? What about the impact of adversarial trial combat on witnesses? On complainants? On genuine victims? Those who are victimized not once but repeatedly by the brutality of cross-examination?

Again, after much consideration, I don't think I can offer a solution. Some of the misery can be mitigated; cross-examination can, and usually is, delivered calmly and sensitively, with most advocates aware that it is often easier to draw out inconsistencies and undermine credibility behind a facade of softness. The image of an overbearing wigged professional hounding a weeping witness is rarely attractive, and for tactical reasons I try to avoid it. Judges are increasingly quick to stop advocates verbally pummelling a witness once the point has been made. And the protections in place for vulnerable categories of witness are being ever-expanded and reformulated, as we considered earlier.

But there will be cases where there is simply no other approach than to firmly and clearly put to a witness: *you are lying*. And to make them relive every second of the events they describe so that you can clinically and decisively shred every sentence they deliver, building to a closing speech where you publicly implore a jury to reject the complainant as a liar. Because where a defendant gives those instructions – *this is a malicious fantasy* – it is not for the system, less still for the advocate, to proceed on the assumption that the witness is telling the truth. To do so, to embrace the philosophy of Operation Midland is to protect the Nicks and condemn the Warren Blackwells. Had the defence advocate in Warren Blackwell's trial been given a sniff of the disclosure that demonstrated the complainant's proclivity for fantasy, no doubt that trial would have exhibited the robust cross-examination of an ostensibly distraught 'victim'. And that would, we know in retrospect, have been only right and proper.

The problem, of course, is that it is impossible to predetermine the genuine complaints from the Susans. Which leaves us with only two options – err in favour of the defendant, and risk a guilty defendant evading justice. Or err in favour of the complainant, and risk imprisoning an innocent.

To the victim swallowing a not guilty verdict and watching their tormentor walk free from court, the formulation of William Blackstone – *It is better that ten guilty persons escape than one innocent suffer* – must ring as the kind of vapid philosophical cliché that is easy to embrace when you've never been the casualty of one of those ten. When I speak to sobbing complainants and their families at court after an unsuccessful prosecution trial, the idea that they would find comfort in me reminding them that their pain is worth only one tenth of the wrongfully convicted is unthinkable. How do you begin to quantify injustice?

But it perhaps, possibly, becomes clearer with distance. When we ask what sort of society we want, can we tolerate imposing the ultimate coercive sanction – permanent deprivation of liberty – upon people who we agree may reasonably be entirely blameless? How much scope for abuse would it give the state to create criminal offences carrying terms of life imprisonment, knowing that any citizen can be convicted on the basis of 'might have done it' rather than 'sure he done it'?

Criminal law, we must remember, is the ultimate sanction for alleged wrongs; not the only. For victims denied justice in the criminal courts, other – admittedly lesser – routes exist. Civil claims for unlawful harm caused, where the standard of proof is lower and the remedy financial, may feel like a lesser justice, but are nonetheless available. There is no alternative remedy for the wrongly convicted.

The impact for humanity of not doing all that is reasonable to avoid the conviction of the innocent and its direct, irreversible consequences is, for me, captured by the sentiment of John Adams at the chapter's outset. This is why we venerate the presumption of innocence, and why, where there is an irreconcilable clash of interests, the system must operate in the defendant's favour.

Which swings us, finally, back round to Jay. And why, in spite of whatever personal views I might have held, and notwithstanding the impact of the proceedings on his family, I believe justice was done. The process, and the verdict, were right. Even if I had the right to judge him – and as his counsel, I do not and should not – would I declare myself *sure* of his guilt beyond reasonable doubt? I don't think I would. Whatever standard of certainty I am able to move myself to, it is not enough. And if it were me, accused of the most heinous crimes, it would not help me sleep, as I slipped into the top bunk of my cell, to know that twelve strangers, who knew nothing about me beyond what they were told in a court of law, thought I *might* have done, or *probably* did, what I was accused of doing. If there was any doubt in their minds, I would want the benefit of it.

Yes, I found Jay's daughters convincing. But I may well

have found Susan convincing, staring into the whites of her eyes across a courtroom as she sobbed through her evidence. And the whole point of juries, their essential function, their joy, is that we take decisions away from the tired eyes of jaded legal professionals and entrust them to the collective wisdom and life experience of twelve everymen and -women. Jay's jury saw and heard everything that the parties found and considered relevant, and were not sure of his guilt. They didn't – couldn't – declare him innocent; but where there was doubt, as I have to recognize there was, they properly exercised it in his favour.

And whenever I vacillate in my view on whether, in essence, we are doing things right in our system, one question springs back, boomerang-style, and smashes against my synapses: what system would *I* want as the falsely accused? Knowing what I already know after only a few years exposed to the grimy coalface of the criminal justice system, would I have faith in an inquisitorial jurisdiction where the state, with its variable competence and political vulnerability, controlled my fate throughout? Or would I trust the presentation of my case to an independent solicitor and advocate, and hope that twelve ordinary people, shown evidence that is relevant, reliable and fairly adduced, would find the prosecution insufficient to convict me?

Every time the answer is the same.

10. The Big Sentencing Con

'Nearly 80 per cent of Brits believe the country is soft on crime, a shock new survey has found. The ComRes poll for the *Mirror* revealed there is a widespread view that criminals get off too lightly and sentences are not tough enough. More than three-quarters of all those quizzed said punishments did not match the crime. And four in five are not happy with the justice system and believe offenders are treated much more leniently than in the past. The findings come as the government promises to crack down on offenders.'

The *Mirror*, 21 June 2014[1]

As the word 'guilty' tumbles from the foreman's mouth and casts the ashen defendant into a silent stasis, the question burning through the hearts of the courtroom immediately self-extinguishes and reignites. 'Did he do it?' suddenly becomes 'What's he going to get?' The twelve judges of fact in the jury box enjoy the formality of the prosecutor reading out the defendant's previous convictions, and are then thanked for their civic duty as their function ends and the defendant's fate is formally transferred into the hands of the judge of law.

The newly minted convict will have been advised by his lawyers of the sentence he should expect upon conviction, but we always couch and qualify and (in my case at least) try to avoid specific figures that can be thrown angrily back in our faces in the cells with a globule of spit. Court of Appeal sentencing case law, nowadays largely supplanted by formal Sentencing Guidelines, allow both the prosecution and defence advocates to make targeted submissions to the Crown Court as to roughly what the correct sentence *should* be. But there are no guarantees.

Curiously, the reaction in court is usually the same, whatever the sentence. If the judge delivers good news – anything other than immediate imprisonment generally qualifies – the defendant will take it with poker-faced stoicism. Sometimes family members in the public gallery will coo or cheer, or the defendant might squawk a 'thank you, Your Honour' as the dock is unlocked, but mostly proceedings conclude with a striking absence of emotion.

Likewise, if the judge hands down bad news – and the judicial remark, 'Your barrister has said everything that could be said,' is the giveaway that immediate prison is coming – it is normally greeted with a stiff upper lip in the dock. Outbursts of emotion, even from first-time defendants facing a lengthy prison sentence, are rare. On that front, special mention must go to a defendant at Chelmsford Crown Court in August 2016, who, upon receiving his eighteen-month sentence for racist abuse, told Judge Patricia Lynch QC that she was 'a bit of a cunt'. Her Honour's reply – 'You are a bit of a cunt yourself' – was a little naughty, but also, in many ways, everything that could be said.[2]

Outside the courtroom – in the lobby or down in the court cells – the emotional strictures are loosened, and tears of joy or sorrow flow more easily. When I'm trooping downstairs to the cells, the natural inclination is to try to find a positive to draw the sting of the immediate shock; although, unless the sentence is so high as to potentially justify an appeal, my soothing words often amount to little more than the impotent observation that the sentence 'could have been worse'. Aside from giving as much inside information as I, someone who has never served a prison sentence, can, and assuring the defendant, from a similar position of ignorance, that the sentence will go quicker than he expects, there's often nothing constructive that I can say. He'll go, stony-faced and perhaps red-eyed, handcuffed to the white-shirted cell staff to wait for the van to take him to an available prison, while I retreat back upstairs to normality.

The impact of sentence of course doesn't end there. The aftershock is felt outside the court walls. How the defendant is treated, and what sentence he gets, is important also to the victim, sitting nervously in the public gallery as justice is meted out to her abuser. And it matters to the public, who must after all have confidence in the outcomes of our criminal justice system if it is to maintain its legitimacy. This, it seems, is where we have a problem. Because the tone of public debate over the way we sentence those who break the law would suggest that we are getting things seriously wrong.

The old faithful that is revisited in the tabloids most weeks is the Out of Touch Judge 'letting off' some foul, acne-scarred, daemonic hoodie with a 'slap on the wrist' for a capital offence. Presumably there's an industry template for such stories, as the formatting never wavers: there'll be a photo of the yobbo, fag in mouth, leaving court (ideally giving a middle-finger salute to the goading cameras), juxtaposed with a portrait photograph of the humourless-looking judge. The photo will usually show the judge in their ceremonial, full-bottomed wig, which is never worn in court – judges on the bench have since the 1840s worn a short frizzy horsehair wig, like a barrister's but with tighter, bubble-permed sides – but which successfully emphasizes to the readership how old-worldy and disconnected this crusty enemy of the people is.

And the angle is always the same. The lip will quiver but the outrage will not quaver. We Are Going to Hell in a

Handcart. Dangerous, remorseless ASBO-fiends who would slaughter us in our beds are having their anarchic urges indulged, worse encouraged, by lefty liberal elitist judges who defy the public will and bend the rules to keep fiends out of prison. Those who are sent to prison are sent to rudderless holiday camps where they get free Sky TV and reacharounds paid for by YOU the taxpayer, and in any event are not sent there for long enough. Considered conclusion: sentencing of criminals is a con.

And, for what it's worth, I agree. With the conclusion at least, if not the diagnosis.

Sentencing of offenders often amounts to a giant confidence trick on the general public. The law – decades of on-the-hoof populist legislating – is impossible to understand. Sentences passed are often entirely out of kilter with public expectations, and the same criminal behaviour can be dealt with entirely differently in alike cases. Worst of all, there is an inherent dishonesty in the presentation of criminal sentencing, arising out of a lack of clarity as to what those setting policy want to achieve. Each new dawn heralds a fresh ministerial vacillation over the purpose of sentencing; contorting in the political winds. The public is treated to schizophrenic episodes where a pledge to reduce prison numbers (achieved through rehabilitation, investment in prisons and a sparing use of custodial sentences) is entertained concurrently to vows of longer sentences, spartan prison regimes[3] and bans on prisoners receiving books.[4] Meanwhile, the only consistent narrative on which the public can depend is that 1990s counsel of despair – 'Prison Works' – which is kept on life support in tabloid editorials, their fatuous commentary generally left uncorrected by pusillanimous politicians.

Sentencing, it seems clear to me, does not appear to achieve what the public are led to believe it should. And it will remain a con as long as we fail to be honest about what sentences mean, what we want from our sentencing policy and how that might best be achieved.

Is It the Judges?

If you believe what you read, the problem is the judges; politicized and activist, imposing their own political ideals on sentencing decisions. Thus we end up with sentences that lack consistency and haemorrhage public support.

And it would be foolish to deny the influence of personal factors in judicial decisions, least of all sentencing. While the judicial oath binds judges *to do right to all manner of people after the laws and usages of this realm, without fear or favour, affection or ill will*, they remain susceptible to the same human frailties and cognitive biases as the rest of us. No two judges are the same, and two similar defendants might be sentenced entirely differently depending on their tribunals. Who you get is often determinative of what you get.

If there has been a trial, the same judge will usually pass sentence, but where a defendant has pleaded guilty, it is normal for a judge to be randomly allocated for the sentence hearing. Frequent flyers become well acquainted with the judicial personalities in their local courts, and the seasoned crim sitting opposite you can either break down in tears or dance on the table with jubilation (I've seen both) when you tell them the identity of their sentencing judge.

Given what is known about the social, educational and professional backgrounds of judges, it's difficult to entertain the tabloid conspiracy that any criminal judges congregate on the far left of the anarcho-communist spectrum, but it's undeniable that some are more lenient than others. There can sometimes be a rather unedifying scrabble when the barristers in a court list get wind that another courtroom with a gentler judge has finished early and is looking to take work, as a succession of pleading wigs jostle *sotto voce* with the court clerk to be reserved a seat on the chopper out of Saigon.

Avoiding irritating the judge is also key to any hope of a lenient sentence. And this applies just as much to your advocate. If the judge likes the barrister or solicitor, they will be more disposed to taking a chance on a borderline defendant. Being junior, particularly at the very beginning, I found that pity was a strong card to inadvertently play. I have no doubt that in several of my cases, the judge took one look at the baby gopher-on-ice defending and passed a much more merciful sentence than was warranted. On the other hand, I have watched as judges struggle to disguise their contempt for the defence barrister, or the terrible points they are making in ostensible mitigation, and where you can almost see the judge mentally adding months onto the sentence the longer the plea in mitigation goes on.

A local legend concerned a (now-retired) judge who was once sentencing a nasty domestic assault. At the hearing, the defendant's wheelchair-bound mother, for whom the defendant was said to have caring responsibilities and whose tragic plight formed a central plank of his barrister's mitigation, was strategically seated on the front row of the public gallery, quietly sobbing throughout. The judge handed down three years. He then called the barristers into his chambers, took off his wig and said, 'What do you reckon, chaps? Bit harsh? I was going to give him two, but then he wheeled his sympathy act in.'

It is not just personality. Environmental factors play their part. I can assure you from anecdotal experience that if your sentence is moved over lunch to a judge who had geared himself up for an afternoon off, it will not end well, and disappointment as a driver of long sentences has some basis in academic research. A working paper by two economists studying juvenile court sentences in Louisiana between 1996 and 2012 reported robust findings that longer sentences were imposed by alumni of Louisiana State University following unexpected defeats for the Tigers, the LSU football team.[5] Other factors were controlled – the only explanation for the disparity was that judges were carrying their disappointment into the courtroom and visiting it upon the unlucky defendants.

Tiredness and hunger have also been shown to be relevant. An American study published in *Psychological Science* in December 2016 suggested that on 'sleepy Monday' – the day after the switch to daylight saving time – sentences imposed by judges were 5 per cent higher than on any other day of the year.[6] An Israeli study of parole board decisions in 2011 showed that a prisoner's chances of release receded to near zero as the clock ticked towards lunchtime, immediately after which the likelihood soared.[7] Again, this is borne out in practice, as any barrister who has shoehorned their sentence hearing into the morning list at 12.58 and keeps the judge's stomach rumbling beyond 13.30 will attest. Quite literally, what the judge had for breakfast may influence your sentence.

On a more sinister note, Ministry of Justice research published in 2016 purported to demonstrate an association between ethnicity and the likelihood of a prison sentence in the Crown Court. Under 'similar criminal circumstances', the odds of imprisonment for offenders self-reporting as black, Asian and Chinese or other were higher than for offenders from self-reported white backgrounds (53 per cent, 55 per cent and 81 per cent higher respectively).[8] These statistics should be treated with caution, as the analysis suffered from significant limitations (particularly in its definition of 'similar criminal circumstances');[9] however I would not suggest that such trends do not exist. There is a vast body of psychological research demonstrating the prevalence and power of unconscious bias in human decision-making, and how we are hard-wired to respond positively to those we perceive as similar to us, and to react against those we perceive as different.[10] It would appear arguable as a matter of common sense that the composition of a judiciary in which only 6 per cent identify as Black, Asian or Minority Ethnic (BAME)[11] might lead to overall sentencing outcomes which reflect an unconscious preferential treatment of white defendants compared to BAME defendants convicted of similar offences.

But while inconsistency in sentencing might be accounted for in part by idiosyncratic judicial behaviour and cognitive bias, it is only a tiny piece of the jigsaw. The main reason for incoherent sentencing outcomes and policy isn't capricious judges; it's that incoherence is embedded in the sentencing framework.

'Hell is a Fair Description of These Sentencing Laws'

A sentencing hearing broadly takes three parts: one, the prosecutor outlines the facts of what the defendant has done, and draws the court's attention to relevant law and guidelines – note, unlike in America, the prosecutor does not actively call for the highest sentence possible, nor are neatly wrapped 'plea bargains' presented for a judge to green-light a sentence agreed between the parties. Two, the defence advocate advances a 'plea in mitigation', presenting the mitigating features of the offender and offence, and persuading the judge to take the most lenient course. Three, the judge passes sentence.

The third part sounds easy. It's not. Sentencing a defendant is not simply an exercise of a judge plucking a figure out of the air, whacking a non-existent gavel and barking, 'Take him down.' The law and procedure is hideously, unnecessarily complex.

To try to make sense of sentencing is to roam directionless in the expansive dumping ground of the criminal law. Statutes are piled atop statutes. Secondary legislation bearing titles unrelated to the amendments they make to primary legislation and the half-baked, half-enacted and half-revoked brainchildren of some of our dimmest politicians lie strewn across the landscape, stretching out farther than the eye can see. The many hundreds of legislative provisions exceed, at a conservative estimate, 1,300 pages.[12] If one were seeking a totem to the despair caused by the work of licentious, headline-chasing governments revelling in the ruin they wreak, sentencing law would be it.

And this is only the structure; that page count does not include the hundreds of sheets of Sentencing Guidelines and thousands of Court of Appeal judgments that steer judges on the detail.

The burden of the sentencing exercise is therefore huge. There are a range of sentences each with their own qualifying criteria, from discharges and fines through community orders to custodial sentences, both immediate and suspended. There are mandatory life sentences, automatic life sentences (not the same thing), discretionary life sentences, extended sentences of imprisonment (various iterations of which each carry their own special complex provisions about prisoner release dates), special sentences for 'offenders of particular concern', hospital orders (with or without restrictions) and mandatory minimum custodial sentences, to name a few. And that's before one considers the ancillary orders – some discretionary, some mandatory – that attach to certain offences: driving disqualifications, penalty points, endorsement of driving licence, extended driving retests, restraining orders, Sexual Harm Prevention Orders, Serious Crime Prevention Orders, compensation orders, ancillary financial orders, confiscation orders (under no fewer than three different statutory regimes), deprivation orders, forfeiture orders, dog destruction orders, criminal behaviour orders, company director disqualification orders, recommendations for deportation, credit for time spent on bail on a qualifying curfew, mandatory statutory surcharges (of a dizzying array of ever-changing figures depending on the sentence and the date of the offence) and costs.[13] And this is just adult offenders – youth sentencing boasts its own panoply of (arguably even more confusing) overlapping provisions.

The Law Commission, the independent statutory body charged with researching and publishing recommendations for potential law reforms, put it succinctly in 2015: 'For a lay person to discover the law would be practically impossible.'[14]

More times than I can recall have I watched a client's eyes glaze over as I try to explain, in as clear terms as I can, the possible sentence that he faces. Given how much rides on sentence – the likelihood of getting a certain type of sentence will often inform whether a defendant pleads guilty or not – it is outrageous that the law appears deliberately incomprehensible to those who need to understand it most.

And it's not just the public. Lawyers and judges are often flummoxed. In 2012, the sentencing expert Robert Banks examined 262 randomly selected Court of Appeal cases and found that in ninety-five – that is 36 per cent – unlawful sentences had been passed by the Crown Court. That's not simply that the Court of Appeal thought that the sentences were too long; rather the Crown Court judge had done something that they did not have the power to do, or had not done something they were legally required to. These were not all points advanced by the barristers drafting the grounds of appeal either; many were missed and only spotted by the Court of Appeal's own lawyers.[15]

In a High Court case in 2010 concerning the release dates of a prisoner in custody, Mr Justice Mitting was moved to observe:

> [Explaining the effect of the sentence and the release date] is impossible. Indeed, so impossible is it that it has taken from twelve noon until twelve minutes to five . . . to explain the relevant statutory provisions to me, a professional judge. The position at which I have arrived . . . is one of which I despair. It is simply unacceptable in a society governed by the rule of law for it to be well-nigh impossible to discern from statutory provisions what a sentence means in practice.[16]

Lord Phillips in the Supreme Court went one further, stating: 'Hell is a fair description of the problem of statutory interpretation caused by [these provisions].'[17]

It's all very well requiring judges to give reasons for and to explain the effect of sentences 'in ordinary language,'[18] but this is hampered if the court itself is struggling to work out what is going on. And the confusion defeats the founding precept of open justice. There is no point whatsoever in throwing open the courtroom doors to the public if the law being discussed is not even understood by the lawyers. Little surprise that, whenever I ask a defendant or a victim after a sentence hearing whether they were able to follow what was happening, the answer is, without fail, a wide-eyed 'No'.

Release dates of prisoners is a particularly egregious example of courts failing to explain the effect of sentences, with serious consequences for public confidence. Criminals not serving the sentence that is handed down in court is a red flag to Middle England, and largely the anger arises because the explanation behind early release, and the earliest date on which a prisoner might be released, are never specified in court.

All defendants serving a standard determinate prison

sentence are automatically released on licence after serving half of their sentence. The reasons are that this (a) helps to reintegrate the offender back into the community while retaining a power to recall him to prison if he fouls up; and (b) reduces prison numbers (about which more later). You may or may not agree with those justifications, but there they are. That part is easy to understand, if not accept. But that's only half the story; for a variety of reasons, 'half way' is rarely the actual point of release.

Some defendants will be released well in advance of half way, under Home Detention Curfew (HDC)[19] or Release on Temporary Licence (ROTL), which includes Resettlement Day Release, Resettlement Overnight Release, Childcare Resettlement Leave and Special Purpose Licence. Days spent on remand in custody are automatically, and rightly, counted as days already served. If a defendant has had a condition of an onerous curfew (nine hours a day or more) whilst on bail, every two days so spent count as a day towards sentence.

The problem is that the calculation of these dates and a defendant's eligibility is, as the High Court comments above demonstrate, often impossible for a sentencing judge to work out and pronounce on the spot. The calculation is usually made by the prison once the offender is processed (and is usually subject to a further risk assessment closer to the release date). So in court the date of release is left deliberately vague. The public hear, 'Three years in prison, of which you will serve up to half, minus days spent on remand/subject to a qualifying curfew,' and are then aghast when they learn that the defendant has been released after only a few months of that sentence. This, they fairly complain, is not what it said in the brochure. No one tells us, the public – or the victim – that the headline numbers rattled out in court bear little resemblance to time thenceforth served.

The fault for this confusion lies solely with the legislators who have given us this system. When it comes to failing to explain *reasons for* sentences, however, the legal profession must admit its culpability. Most judges do a good job, but there are common traps. 'Ordinary language' to a judge or barrister does not always accord with 'ordinary language' to ordinary people. We legal professionals all slip too easily into the native lingo of the criminal courts that carries little meaning to outsiders. 'Totality' is one example. This sentencing principle holds that where someone is being sentenced for multiple offences, we do not adopt a US-style approach of cumulating multiple consecutive terms resulting in whacking great sentences of up to several hundred years; instead the court must consider the offending in the round and pass an overall sentence that is just and proportionate. So, for example, if John sells a small bag of cannabis to four people and is sentenced for four counts of supplying a controlled drug of Class B, the judge does not take the sentence that would be passed for one such offence (roughly twelve months' imprisonment) and multiply it by four. She would instead pass an increased sentence, say eighteen months, concurrent on each count. Sometimes consecutive sentences are appropriate, such as when someone is being sentenced for two unrelated offences, or where there are separate offences against separate victims; but again, the judge will have regard to totality and will rarely pass for each offence the sentence that would have been passed in isolation.

Again, you may not agree with that approach; your personal view may be that we *should* have consecutive American-style sentences. Four offences of selling cannabis are, you might argue, four times as serious as one, and the equivalent of 4 four-and-half months for a single offence is insufficient. But totality is the principle that judges are required by law to apply, and is usually the reason why someone might be convicted of multiple offences and receive a sentence that appears, in isolation, unexpectedly low.

Frequently though, rather than explaining this, the judge will simply say, 'I have had regard to totality,' a shorthand understood by the legal professionals, but virtually meaningless to anyone else. Anyone overhearing and wanting to look up 'totality' would not know in which of the 1,300 pages of fragmentary sentencing legislation to start.[20]

The Law Commission is presently developing a new comprehensive Sentencing Code for 2018, with the overdue aim of drawing all existing sentencing law and procedure into a single streamlined document. However, while a noble and vital endeavour, it would be naive to think that this alone will mend the disconnect between the public and the law. Because complexity aside, the rationale of sentencing policy can be difficult to understand.

Guidelines and Statutory Maxima

It is hard to explain, for example, the sentencing ranges and starting points prescribed by the Sentencing Guidelines, which are published by the Sentencing Council (an independent non-departmental body of the Ministry of Justice) and which judges are required by law to follow.[21]

Guidelines exist for a wide range of, although not all, offences, and operate by way of convoluted flow charts and grids designed to assess seriousness by reference to concepts of 'harm' and 'culpability'. By feeding the facts of a case into the guidelines, you should arrive at a 'category', which provides for a sentence 'starting point' and a range. By then considering a further list of potential aggravating and mitigating factors (such as previous convictions), the judge can move the sentence up or down the category range as appropriate, to arrive at the sentence (before any deductions for guilty pleas).

The guidelines themselves are drafted by the Sentencing Council following public consultation, but in some ways run counter to public intuition. For a start, none of the sentencing ranges go up to the statutory maximum sentence. In some cases, it is not even close. The guideline for inflicting grievous bodily harm with intent, the most serious offence of violence short of homicide carrying a maximum of life imprisonment, provides for an offence range (i.e. from the bottom of the lowest category to the top of the highest) of three to sixteen years' imprisonment. Although the court can sentence outside the offence range if it would be 'contrary to the interests of justice' to sentence within it, what this means in practice is that most offences carry an artificially low ceiling, well below the maximum sentence set by Parliament.

So when I was defending a man, Michael, who on a night out had got very drunk and, in a petty argument with a girl he was chatting to in a club, had bitten a chunk out of her cheek leaving life-altering scars, even though on paper he had been charged with an offence carrying a maximum of life imprisonment, he, I and the courts knew that it was extremely unlikely that he would be looking at a sentence beyond sixteen years.

For the victim this is often hard to understand. I've sat opposite complainants in court witness rooms, who have been told by the police that their violent ex-boyfriends have been charged with assault occasioning actual bodily harm, an offence carrying up to five years' imprisonment, and have had to break it to them that, actually, the highest category on the Sentencing Guidelines envisages a starting point of only eighteen months, with a range not going beyond three years. When they shout and scream and cry in frustration, I can't help. I can't explain why. I just sit there nodding dumbly, another officious bearer of bad, irrational tidings.

The absence of a holistic or consistent philosophy under-pinning sentencing policy is laid bare when you compare guidelines for different offences:

— Debbie, a thirty-eight-year-old prostitute, sells a wrap of cocaine to feed her addiction. The starting point for sentence is four and a half years' imprisonment.
— Charlie rapes a nineteen-year-old girl in her flat after being invited home. The starting point on the Sexual Offences Guideline is five years' imprisonment.
— Harris runs a nifty scam from his second-hand car business and cheats Her Majesty's Revenue and Customs of £2 million in VAT. He's looking at an eight-year starting point.[22]

Accepting the ruinous social and individual impact of supplying Class A drugs, and even ignoring the plain reality that its true devastation is rooted in the implausibility of prohibition, it would take a bold anti-drugs campaigner to submit that selling a wrap of coke is, on any assessment of harm or culpability, broadly equivalent to a rape. And I doubt you'd find anyone to agree that depriving the taxman of 0.0006 per cent of its revenue is even worse.

The fault does not lie solely with the guidelines – their starting points and ranges are anchored to (sometimes age-old) Court of Appeal cases, and subject to statutory maxima set by Parliament. And some of these maxima make no sense. A classic example is assault. If I punch you and chip your tooth – assault occasioning actual bodily harm – the statutory maximum is five years' imprisonment. If I punch you and you fall, bang your head and suffer irreversible paralysis – inflicting grievous bodily harm (without intent) – the statutory max is the same. The guidelines provide for marginally inflated starting points and ranges for the latter, but they are dancing on the head of a pin.

These stand as but a handful of examples of the often-perverse operation of the law and guidelines, many of which tie the judge's hands in irrational binds, and none of which are easily explicable to the watching public. But they, like the unjustified complexity of the legislation and procedure, are merely symptoms of a deeper malaise. The broader problem is that our lawmakers in Parliament and government refuse to be honest, with the public or with themselves, about what we are trying to achieve with sentencing policy.

What Are We Trying to Achieve?

For me, this is the question that I avoid. Because, day to day, the criminal justice system can feel like a numbers game. Get 'em charged, process them as swiftly as possible through the courts, impose a sentence and wait and see what happens. If they come back, hit reset and try the same damned formula. As long as people are being convicted and sentenced, the system must be working. Complicity in the aphorism defining insanity as repeating the same thing and expecting different results can be difficult for us to admit.

The official purposes of sentencing – and, by logical extension, the criminal justice system – are set out in legislation:[23]

(a) The punishment of offenders
(b) The reduction of crime (including its reduction by deterrence)
(c) The reform and rehabilitation of offenders
(d) The protection of the public
(e) The making of reparation by offenders to persons affected by their offence

But balancing and reconciling these often-conflicting aims in practice is not easy. Particularly given the demographic of the people most frequently before the courts.

When I prosecute a twenty-three-year-old man with

severe autism and ADHD, who has the learning age of a thirteen-year-old and acts out his frustrations through spontaneous bursts of increasingly serious violence against his sixty-two-year-old mum, what should the court do? When Darius, our mentally unwell youngster from earlier, inevitably comes before the courts again for his inability to follow the rules of civilized society, which of (a) to (e) do we prioritize?

When we see the victims of yesterday's crimes – the abused daughters of the guilty Jays, for example – descending into spirals of theft, drug abuse and drug supply, bounced for years between prison and the streets, how do the abstract principles above take practical effect? Some such delinquents can be glued back together by the tireless efforts of the Probation Service and substance abuse workers, but many can't. Community orders or suspended sentences with drug rehabilitation requirements have been tried a dozen times, and a dozen times have failed. What next?

When I defend a young kid carrying knives for his gang leaders, the only role models in his uneducated, unsupported shit bucket of a childhood, how does anyone in the system persuade him to give up the only security he knows, when his mates have all been shot or stabbed? How do you persuade him to put down his arms, cut his associations and gamble his life on a rigged roulette wheel for the prize of a law-abiding suburban existence that he thinks people like him can never win?

While the courts do their best to wrestle sensitively with these imponderables, the mood music outside the court buildings spun by media and political DJs is one-note: prison. Prison for all.

That last example is a case in point. When statistics in 2015 indicated a troubling rise in youths carrying knives, the analysis was blunt. Parliament had no truck with the proposition that focusing on intensive community rehabilitation and addressing the social attitudes that normalize knife-carrying in certain subcultures might reduce crime and protect the public, and could be combined with a non-custodial punishment that satisfied our need for vengeance. Instead, they looked at the list, turned (a) up to eleven and to tabloid joy introduced mandatory minimum sentences of six months' imprisonment for repeat knife carriers.[24]

It didn't matter that statistics demonstrate that short prison sentences under six months are ineffective in preventing reoffending;[25] it didn't matter that we would be introducing young people, who may not be otherwise criminally sophisticated, into an environment with hardened criminals who habitually carry weapons far more dangerous than knives. It didn't matter that the experienced judge hearing the case, who knows the individual facts and is best placed to assess how to balance the competing purposes of sentence, may have considered that a non-custodial sentence best protected the public. Prison works. Repeat after me, children. Prison works.

And I've seen these young people sucked in. We all have. The first custodial sentence is rarely the last. And in their cases, as with so many others, it can often feel as if the needle is stuck on retribution, at the cost of all else.

Prison has become our cultural default; a synonym for justice. If someone commits a crime, we expect them to be 'locked up'. Those, such as bankers, whose despised behaviour society wishes were criminal, should be 'behind bars'. A criminal conviction, that permanent, life-altering stigma of one of society's fallen angels, is never enough. Nor is it sufficient to pass a sentence designed to promote reparation, such as a compensation order or a community order comprising a form of restorative justice. Nor for a prison sentence to be suspended, to hang the Damoclean sword over the offender's head as a bond of good behaviour.

Restrictions on liberty other than prison – such as curfews or several hundred hours of unpaid work in the community – don't count as punishment. They are 'soft'. Never mind that any practitioner can give you a list of clients who have literally begged the judge to send them to prison rather than do unpaid work – as with Kyle, the young man we met earlier in the magistrates' court. If it's not custody, the defendant will 'walk free from court'. The judge will be a 'woolly liberal'. The criminal will have been given a 'slap on the wrist'.

A depressing example did the rounds in late 2016, as a Conservative MP's Private Member's Bill – the Awards for Valour (Protection) Bill – gained the approval of the House of Commons Defence Select Committee and took one step closer to the statute book. This Bill sought to criminalize 'Walter Mitty' characters who wore unearned medals or insignia awarded for valour 'with intent to deceive'. Note that this Bill was not aimed at those who falsely wear honours to gain financial advantage, such as collecting for a fake charity; fraud laws already cater for those. Rather the explicit target of the Bill was people – usually tragic, deluded and mentally unwell old men – who caused no harm other than the insult felt by the military. And, of course, a conviction and the payment of a fine, or compensation order, was not a sufficient maximum penalty; the Bill called for prison sentences of up to six months.

I am guilty too. In this chapter I have embraced the same ingrained assumptions. When I condemn Sentencing Guidelines and statutory maxima for violent and sexual offences, I do so in broad, abstract, quantitative terms. I ask whether the prison sentence in a hypothetical scenario is 'enough' or 'too much', as if the inquiry ends once our vengeance is sated by the quotient of punishment. Those are the terms of our public debate.

And I should know better. I've been in the court prison

cell when mentally ill clients, who have just been imprisoned for serious, nasty offences, have been smashing their heads against the cell walls, howling as hordes of G4S officers rush in to tackle them to the ground 'For Their Own Safety'. It is clear that the only thing that their incarceration will do is satisfy our need for punishment, when so much more is required.

Our national fetish has seen the England and Wales prison population soar by 90 per cent since 1990, standing at 85,500.[26] We imprison people at a higher rate (146 per 100,000) than anywhere in Western Europe. Northern Ireland, by comparison, has an imprisonment rate of 76 per 100,000. Sweden's figure is 57. Iceland's is 38.[27] Nearly 68,000 people were sent to prison in 2016. 71 per cent had committed a non-violent offence. And our sentences are getting longer. The average prison sentence for indictable offences has increased by over 25 per cent in the last decade.[28] We have more prisoners sentenced to an indeterminate term of imprisonment than in the other forty-six countries in the Council of Europe combined.[29]

I don't for a moment suggest that prison isn't ever the right sentence; some offences are plainly so serious that justice can only be met by prioritizing punishment and immediate public protection through a lengthy custodial sentence. Often people who receive prison sentences have done awful things. Something that never fails to surprise me in this job is the capacity of human beings to hurt each other, in particular those they either claim to love or barely know. Some days you have to self-numb to get through some of the Victim Impact Statements given by those affected. A young teacher describing how, following an unprovoked attack on her and her husband outside a restaurant by two passing thugs, she had miscarried their first child and, a year later, was still unable to leave the house and was regularly self-harming, will never leave me.

Sympathy for those who inflict such wanton destruction is difficult to come by.

But many people in prison are not monsters. And even for those who are, the limitations of prison as we currently do it are known and trite. Yes, it punishes and temporarily incarcerates, but its utility beyond that is negligible. Counter-intuitive though it may sound, there is no proven causative link between higher prison numbers and lower crime rates; while crime as measured by the British Crime Survey fell over the 1990s as incarceration levels soared, they also fell in Western countries with significantly lower imprisonment rates.[30] A leaked memo from the government's strategy unit in 2006 suggested that 80 per cent of the decrease in crime was attributable to economic factors, not the swollen prison population.[31] But even if that is wrong, and high rates of incarceration can be shown to keep numbers down, it is plain that our model has little to offer by way of rehabilitating or 'improving' the people that we're releasing onto the streets. 46 per cent of all prisoners re-offend within a year of leaving prison. For those serving short sentences of less than twelve months, this increases to 60 per cent.[32] Prison as we presently do it is an expensive way of making bad people worse. This is largely because while our politicians and media talk tough about longer prison sentences, they do not want to pay for them. Few votes and fewer clickbaits are found in a More Money for Prisoners campaign. But, with a few notable exceptions – such as Ken Clarke MP as Justice Secretary and former Deputy Prime Minister Nick Clegg – there is a conspiracy of cowardice that prevents politicians from treating the public like adults. The binary choice that should be presented is simple: *We can either keep rising numbers of prisoners in humane prisons that serve a purpose beyond warehousing, for which the Exchequer – ultimately you, the taxpayer – must pay through higher taxation; or we can shift paradigms and explore evidence-based policy from abroad that would see the use of prison radically reduced, and non-custodial, restorative and rehabilitative alternatives envisaged not as a 'get-out' but as meaningful components of a working justice system.*

Instead, recent administrations have opted to keep rattling the custodial sabre, but not only have they not provided the additional funds that a rising prison population requires, they have on the altar of austerity slashed the prison budget by a quarter. Between 2010 and 2015, the National Offender Management Service (NOMS), which, until 2017 (when it was reimagined as HM Prison and Probation Service), was responsible for prisons in England and Wales, had its budget cut by £900 million.[33] In order to make nearly £1 billion of savings, prison staffing levels were reduced by 30 per cent. As of 2016, there were 13,720 fewer staff in the public prison estate looking after 450 more people.[34]

In a drag race to the bottom, 'benchmarking' was introduced, in which publicly run jails were required to peg their costs to the same level as the 'most efficient' – read 'cheapest' – in the private sector. One of the reasons that private sector prisons were so 'efficient' is that for seventeen years they have had higher rates of overcrowding than public sector prisons – shoving more prisoners into tinier spaces.[35] A quarter of the prison population is overcrowded, with prisoners doubling up in cells designed for one person,[36] in order to secure an arbitrary 20 per cent reduction in the cost of prison places (now at £35,000 per year).[37] Around the same time, Chris Grayling MP, Secretary of State for Justice between 2012 and 2015, announced his populist plans to make prisons, already hideous tombs of violence, death and terror, 'less lax' and more 'spartan', introducing severe restrictions on prisoners' 'privileges' – which famously included an unlawful ban on prisoners being sent books[38] – and displaying a bizarrely prurient obsession with stopping inmates having sex.[39] It was not enough to deprive people of their liberty; their lives had to be made extra intolerable to satisfy the public's perceived lust for blood.

The human cost has been horrific.

Stepping inside a prison will immediately quell any agreement you may have with red-top caricatures of holiday camps. Prisoners are locked up for up to twenty-three hours a day in filthy, dilapidated cells in which they eat all their meals and use an unscreened lavatory in front of their cellmate.[40] Cockroaches crunch underfoot, surrounded by broken glass, peeling ceilings, broken fittings, graffiti and damaged floors.[41] Giant rats' nests add infestation to the population.[42] Drugs have flooded in as prison staff struggle to maintain order.[43]

The vast majority of prisons – 76 out of 117 as of May 2017 – are overcrowded.[44] Violence is off the scale. In the year to June 2017, there was a record high of 41,103 incidents of self-harm and 27,193 assaults. The violence is not just between prisoners; there were 7,437 assaults on prison staff, a rise of 100 per cent in one year. Sexual assaults more than doubled between 2011 and 2016.[45] In February 2017, inspectors concluded that 'there was not a single establishment that we inspected in England and Wales in which it was safe to hold children and young people'.[46] Prison deaths are at record levels: 354 prisoners died in custody in 2016. Of these, 119 were suicides.[47] And not surprising given what is known about prison demographics.

Prisoners are largely drawn from the most damaged and dysfunctional nooks of society. The majority have the literacy skills of an eleven-year-old.[48] An estimated 20–30 per cent have learning difficulties, although the vague figure is a reflection of the damning failure of the prison system to identify and support them.[49] Over half of women prisoners and over a quarter of men report being abused as children. Mental health problems exhibiting symptoms of psychosis are reported by 26 per cent of female prisoners and 16 per cent of men, compared to 4 per cent of the general population.[50] Drug and alcohol abuse feature for the majority[51] and 15 per cent are homeless.[52]

And how are these complex factors addressed? How do prisons begin the sensitive, vital exercise of trying to delicately unstitch and repurpose the damaged fabric of these lives? They don't. They can't. 'Purposeful activity', which comprises education, work and other rehabilitative programmes, is at record lows, with only a quarter of prisons marked as 'good' or 'reasonably good', an inevitable consequence of staffing levels that mean prisoners are unable to leave their cells.[53] Three-quarters of educational facilities inspected by Ofsted were 'inadequate' or 'requiring improvement'.[54] The overall performance of a quarter of prisons was marked 'of concern' or 'of serious concern'.[55]

In late 2016, as the violence swelled, and caged, mentally ill and unsupported men killed themselves and each other, and prison staff threatened industrial action,[56] and prisoners rioted to an extent unknown since the early 1990s, the government pledged to invest £1.3 billion over four years to fund 10,000 new prison places, and to recruit 2,500 officers. But even assuming that quality recruits will be attracted by the £9 per hour rate and sufficiently equipped by a ten-week training scheme – which is the shortest in any jurisdiction in the world[57] – this will still not even restore prisons to the under-resourced levels of 2010.[58] And the government, with an eye on the tabloid press, has publicly ruled out anything as sensible as reducing the number of people our courts are imprisoning.[59] Grown-up debate and evidence-based policy-making remains as elusive in prison policy as it does in our country's infantile attitude to drug prohibition; a revisitation of which would be one practical way of getting a lot of people who pose no threat to society out of prison.

So we can look forward to the Big Sentencing Con

continuing, with more and more damaged people ware-housed in fatally dangerous, squalid conditions on the general happy agreement that this is what a successful justice system looks like. The only concession to lowering numbers remains the minor reductions carried out by sleight of hand post-sentence, in the guise of those little-known, complex early release provisions understood by no one. This valve may be opened to effect temporary pressure relief, but is neither a sustainable solution to overcrowding, nor does its use for that purpose command public confidence. Watching politicians surfing the airwaves to boast about tougher sentences for the fiends *du jour*, only to discover that said fiends are serving a fraction of that sentence because we don't have the resources to keep them imprisoned, starts to look like one of the biggest public cons of all.

A final word should be said about honesty. Rail as I might against the political bent of tabloid commentary, editors are of course free to pursue whatever pro-prison agenda sells copy. I may not like it, I may think that it perpetuates our regressive prison fetish, but a free press can and should make whatever arguments it likes. Where I draw the line, however, is where argument is supported by half-truth and misrepresentation. For while, as I have accepted, some inaccurate reporting is a product of the complexity of the law, quite often it is not. It is attributable to what is at best a reckless disregard for the truth; at worst, bad faith.

In most cases, judges do explain, in accordance with their legal duty, the effect of the sentence passed and the reasons for it. And usually there is a cogent explanation for what might appear to be a light sentence. Reporters present in court will know that the judge has read three psychiatric reports, a probation Pre-Sentence Report and a catalogue of further medical references, and has after much consideration concluded that, exceptionally, this repeat burglar would be better off treated in the community, under a suspended sentence with stringent punitive and rehabilitative requirements. Sometimes the judge will explain that she is acting pragmatically. She may see that, because of the time spent on remand by the defendant, the custodial sentence she is required to pass on the guidelines would mean the defendant has already served his sentence, and may therefore impose a community order to ensure that the court retains a measure of control over the defendant for the next few years. Or, on the other end of the scale, the judge might loudly complain that she cannot, because of the guidelines or maximum sentence available, impose a lengthier spell in prison, perhaps following a prosecution decision to accept guilty pleas to less serious offences that dramatically clip the judge's sentencing wings.

But such context is frequently absent in the news reports. And it is wholly dishonest. One case that I appeared in saw the judge open his sentencing remarks with a lengthy diatribe against the inadequacy of his sentencing powers as set by Parliament. 'If I could give you more, I would,' he told my smirking client as he handed him the maximum available. When the sentence was reported by a national tabloid, the judge's 'lenient' sentence was 'outrageous'. 'Something needs to be done about that judge,' the pull quote read. The judge's remarks were not reported.

The list of deadly sins continues. 'Walk free' is used to describe a suspended sentence of imprisonment, with no explanation either of the requirements – unpaid work, curfew, drug treatment – that the judge attached, nor of the way in which suspended sentences work: namely, if you re-offend or don't do your requirements, you're going inside. The judge will have explained for the record why the sentence is suspended; this should be reported.

We see a constant failure to explain that defendants who

plead guilty – thereby sparing the witnesses and public the ordeal and expense of a trial – are entitled by law to a reduction in their sentence of up to a third. If this concept offends you, you can view it another way: someone having a trial gets a stiffer sentence. But failing to provide a reader with this vital context renders whispers of *soft sentence, soft sentence* entirely mendacious.

The point is perhaps best made by the opening quotation from the *Mirror*. As set out earlier, the figures show incontrovertibly that courts are imprisoning more people and giving them longer sentences than ever before. If 80 per cent of the public genuinely believe that offenders are treated 'more leniently than in the past', they are certainly being conned. But not by the system; rather by those from whose reporting the public are deriving these distorted, unevidenced views.

11. The Courage of
Our Convictions: Appeal

'It is to the glory and happiness of our excellent constitution, that to prevent injustice no man is concluded by
the first judgment; but that if he apprehends himself to
be aggrieved, he has another Court to which he can
resort for relief; for this purpose the law furnishes him
with appeals, with writs of error and false judgment.'

Lord Pratt CJ, *R v Cambridge University,*
ex parte Bentley (1723) 1 Str 557[1]

The impact of being imprisoned is difficult to estimate. The
entire edifice of a life crumbles. It's not simply the immediate, day-to-day horror of prison life; the squalor, the
boredom, the omnipresent threat of bloody violence, the
nervously watching your schizophrenic cellmate crouching
over a radiator forging a shiv from a melted toothbrush and
razor blades and wondering into whose neck it will ultimately be plunged. That part, I have been told, you learn to
normalize. Or at least to self-inure. The killer is what is
happening outside the prison walls.

Your family and friends tell you on visits how they miss
you, but while you are sitting caged in stasis for twenty-three
hours a day, their lives carry on. And the absence of the daily
minutiae of a free existence which we all take for granted
creates the spaces of darkest loneliness. Your children are

growing up and hitting their milestones, which you will enjoy second-hand through teary retellings over a screwed-down table in a raucous visiting hall flanked by guards. Your partner is going to work, and doing the weekly shop, and going for drinks, and seeing friends, and attending parents' evenings, and imbuing rich new experiences, and cultivating new friendships, and maybe falling in love with someone able to offer more than a weekly bulletin on prison non-living. And day by day, they, your children and your friends are adjusting to a life in which you are incrementally shunted from centre stage to noises off. Some will wait for you; if your sentence is short, the bonds may withstand the strain. But many won't. People move on. They had lives before you. They've survived life without you. Even if they believe in your innocence and can withstand the stares, the gossiping, the incredulous looks – *she's standing by him?!* – and the vicarious loss of reputation, the trauma of separation will ebb away at resolve.

What I want to talk about in this chapter is what happens when the state admits that it was wrong to wreak this devastation in the lives of one of its citizens. Where a miscarriage of justice is identified by the Court of Appeal, an unsafe conviction is quashed and a wrongly imprisoned parent, sibling, spouse, child or friend walks out of the prison gate, what amends does our society make? How do we begin to put things right for one among us who has been so grievously wronged?

If Dostoevsky was right, and the degree of civilization in a society can by judged by how it treats its prisoners – those who have been justly convicted – an equally valid test is surely how it treats those who are wrongly convicted, and have suffered manifest injustice at the hands of the state.

On this count, I fear, we do not acquit ourselves well.

*

On 13 December 2013, seventeen years after his prison cell door slammed shut for the first time, Victor Nealon watched over a video link from HMP Wakefield as the Court of Appeal considered his appeal against his conviction.

This was not his first appeal. Having been convicted on 22 January 1997, he had unsuccessfully appeared at the Court of Appeal in 1998. His conviction was on that occasion deemed safe and upheld, as was the life sentence imposed for the offence of attempted rape. He had now spent 6,169 nights sleeping in Wakefield prison, serving far longer than his seven-year minimum term, his refusal to admit the offence scuppering any chance of parole. Today, after his case had been picked up and referred by the Criminal Cases Review Commission, was his very last chance.

The offence itself took place in August 1996. There was no doubt that an offence was committed; the victim, Miss E, was attacked outside a nightclub by a stranger, who had knocked her unconscious, unbuttoned her blouse and groped her bra, and tugged at her knickers and tights, before she fortuitously regained consciousness and fought him off. She had recognized the attacker as a man she had noticed staring at her earlier in the night. She recalled that he had a lump on his forehead and was wearing a distinctive paisley shirt. Other witnesses had also seen this suspicious male. An e-fit was created by the police based on Miss E's description, and Mr Nealon was arrested.

He told police that he had never been to the nightclub, and immediately offered to undergo a DNA test. No test was carried out by the police. Instead, the prosecution case at his trial relied largely upon the purported identifications of those other eyewitnesses. Only one among many picked out Mr Nealon during the identification procedure. Others were only able to give descriptions of the man with a lump on his forehead and the paisley shirt. Another was sure that the attacker had a strong Scottish accent. At trial, there was no evidence that Mr Nealon had a lump on his forehead. Neither, his partner confirmed, did he own a paisley shirt.[2] And, it was clear to the listening jurors, Mr Nealon was unmistakably Irish.

The jury nevertheless had accepted the somewhat vague and inconsistent identification evidence, and found Victor Nealon guilty. The dismissal of his first appeal in 1998 looked to have shut the door on any prospect of challenge.

Then, in 2010, following a development in the law, Mr Nealon's solicitors were able to apply for scientific tests to be carried out on the victim's clothing. And the findings were significant. DNA testing indicated the presence of saliva on her blouse and bra cups, where her attacker had groped her. Critically, this saliva was not Mr Nealon's. The clothes that the victim had worn that night were new, and the DNA testing excluded the possibility that the saliva had been deposited by her boyfriend, any of the eight police officers involved in the investigation, any of the four men who came to her aid at the scene of the attack and the scientists. In other words, 'Every sensible inquiry that could be made to identify an innocent source of the DNA [had] been made.' The only reasonable explanation was that it had been left by the attacker.[3] Who could not have been Victor Nealon.

The three judges of the Court of Appeal, having heard this evidence, did not take long to hand down their decision. The effect of this fresh evidence upon the safety of the conviction was, they said, 'substantial'. The conviction was quashed. Later that day, Victor Nealon was released, a free man. Seventeen years behind bars, wrongly branded a violent, dangerous sex offender, were over.

The esoteric workings of the Court of Appeal (Criminal Division) rarely flicker onto the public radar. To the media, appellate proceedings are a confusing, befuddling addendum to Crown Court trials – even more impenetrable and with even more loquacious judgments – and newsworthy only in a minority of high-profile cases. For junior practitioners like me, trips to the CACD are an exercise in regressing to the terror of a year seven pupil on their first day at big school, desperate to simply make it out alive and without anyone's head being shoved down a U-bend. Even seasoned hacks, such as my pupilmaster who prowled the Crown Courts for years with a fearless territorialism that fell just short of marking the perimeters of his favourite courtroom, admit that when they are beckoned through the archway of the Royal Courts of Justice and into the lair of the Lord and Lady Justices of Appeal, they're not *entirely* sure what they're doing.

But to the Victor Nealons stuck in our prisons, the Court of Appeal is everything. It is the last vestige of hope. When the jury verdict has been returned and the judge has sentenced, the only people who can unlock your cell door and quash a wrongful conviction or reduce an excessive sentence are the three[4] monochrome figures towering over the benches in the first-floor courtrooms at the Royal Courts of Justice on London's Strand.

Between October 2015 and September 2016, ninety-four appellants successfully appealed their convictions as 'unsafe', and 924 successfully appealed their sentence as 'manifestly excessive' or 'wrong in law or principle', the respective tests that apply. They are the fortunate few. You can only appeal to the Court of Appeal with permission (or leave), either of the Crown Court judge (which is, unsurprisingly, rare) or of the Court of Appeal itself. If permission to appeal is refused, or if permission is granted but your substantive appeal is dismissed, that is the end of the line (save for the exceptional circumstances, such as with Warren Blackwell and Victor Nealon, where something new emerges and the Criminal Cases Review Commission agrees to refer a conviction back to the Court of Appeal).[5]

The statistics are not in your corner. Putting the numbers above into perspective is a sobering exercise. Those ninety-four successful conviction appeals in 2016 were drawn from a pool of 1,417 applications, giving a success rate of 6.6 per cent. And that's only applications lodged. Most defendants do not even try to appeal their convictions, and if you consider that roughly 70,000 Crown Court convictions were recorded over a similar period,[6] you can arrive at a (very unscientific) overall 'quashing rate' of 0.13 per cent.[7] Put another way, 99.87 per cent of all convictions are upheld. Which looks a little insurmountable.

Of course, in reality the raw data tells you very little. An 'ideal' appeal rate is about as easily identifiable as an 'ideal' conviction rate. Short of the facile observation that an appeal success rate of either zero per cent or 100 per cent suggests that something is seriously amiss, it is very difficult to draw meaningful conclusions on whether our first instance or appellate systems are working. 99.87 per cent of convictions remaining undisturbed may be a sign of many things. It could be a reflection of a trial method that reliably returns safe convictions in the overwhelming majority of cases. Or it could be that there is a wave of miscarriages of justice being excluded by unduly strict principles of appeal. Likewise, that only 6.6 per cent of applications for leave to appeal result in successful appeals may appear startlingly low, but there are possible explanations. Roughly 10 per cent of applications will be lodged by unrepresented applicants who have been advised by their trial lawyers that there is no merit in an appeal, and have decided to chance their arm with a speculative appeal.[8] Some counsel may positively advise over-optimistically, with an eye on placating a difficult client or generating further work. Frequently, errors in the trial process will have been correctly identified by the lawyers, or fresh, relevant evidence will have been found, but the Court will disagree that these are so serious as to justify interfering with the conviction.

Academic criticism abounds over the operation of the Court of Appeal, and the extent to which the Lord and Lady Justices of Appeal contrive to justify upholding convictions in the face of what is said to be plain error and injustice. In too many cases, the argument goes, do the Justices and Lord and Lady Justices of Appeal find a way to minimize failings in the trial process or explain away obvious flaws in the conviction with a judicial, 'Yes, but . . .'. And certainly there are instances from history which rather embarrass the Court of Appeal in this respect. Criminal law commentators McConville and Marsh offer this unappealing summary:

> There has been an official determination to uphold convictions in the face of abundant contrary evidence . . . For example, in the Bridgewater case, three of the defendants (the fourth had died in prison) wrongfully convicted in 1979 were not exonerated until 1997 after six separate police inquiries and two earlier failed appeals; the Guildford Four, convicted in 1975, were not exonerated until 1989, one of their number (Giuseppe Conlon) having died in prison; in the related case of the Maguire Seven, their appeals did not finally succeed until 1991; Stefan Kiszco, convicted in 1976 of a murder he could not have committed, had his appeal dismissed in 1978, with Bridge (the trial judge at the Birmingham Six) stating that there were 'no grounds whatever' to allow the appeal with the result that Kiszco was not cleared until 1992 . . . and the Cardiff Three convictions for murder in 1988 were not overturned until 1992 and the defendants not exonerated until the real killer was convicted in 2003.[9]

However, not knowing personally the senior judiciary Class of 2018, I am not going to assume their politics, least of all pin upon them the sins of their predecessors, nor enter the debate over whether the Court of Appeal is or is not inherently small-c conservative. Others have the space and intellectual ability to do that issue far greater justice than I could hope to. Instead, I want to focus on what takes place once an innocent victim of a miscarriage of justice finally succeeds in persuading the Court of Appeal to quash his conviction. After that judgment is handed down, how does the state begin to make amends?

The tone is set by the conspicuous absence of fanfare that accompanies the correction of state error. Save for the exceptional cases that catch the eye of the press, the public hears nothing about unsafe convictions. Of the 625 unsafe convictions quashed by the Court of Appeal between October 2011 and September 2016,[10] you can probably count on one hand the number that received attention outside the law reports.

Of course, not every quashed conviction represents a finding of innocence. Some of those successful appellants will have had retrials ordered and gone on to be reconvicted. Some will be cases in which prosecutorial or police misconduct, rather than insufficiency of evidence, lie behind the quashing. But nevertheless, those 625 wrongful convictions – roughly 100 a year – are remedied in the dark. While the Crown Prosecution Service calls a press conference upon merely *charging* a defendant in a high-profile case, no corresponding public acknowledgement of failure comes forth from the system when it fouls up. No apology escapes official mouths.

When in August 2016, the Attorney General's office proudly boasted that 'more than 100 offenders had their prison sentences lengthened' by the Court of Appeal under the Unduly Lenient Sentence scheme in 2015,[11] the government found no space to mention, for balance, that over roughly the same period nearly ten times as many sentences (997) were reduced by the Court of Appeal as manifestly excessive or unlawful.[12]

Perhaps this issue of presentation is a reflection of public attitudes. No one wants to think that the system fails. We trust that the man behind bars deserves to be there. It is far more comforting to focus on celebrating the police rounding up the bad guys than to dwell on the occasions where the wrong person suffers.

But the problem goes deeper than PR. How we substantively treat those people – ordinary men and women – who have been fed into the justice machine, mangled, battered, confined and, years later, spat back out onto the streets, is inexcusable.

When justice is eventually restored, and the Court of Appeal clerk faxes the order to the prison to confirm your release, you stand in the prison car park, with the prison-standard £46 travel money in your pocket, a free man, but one frozen in time. Ready to pick up where you left off, only to find that your life has fast-forwarded without you in it. If years have passed, joblessness, friendlessness and mental trauma may be the least of your worries; finding somewhere to sleep on that first night of freedom is the immediate battle.

In many respects, the released innocent is worse off than the released convict, the latter of whom will at least have a measure of institutional assistance with their reintegration. A probation officer will help those on licence to access services for accommodation, or mental health support. Not so for the wrongly imprisoned, awkwardly shuffled out of the building with the minimum of fuss. *Good luck rebuilding your life from scratch.*

Victor Nealon knows the feeling. Upon his conviction being quashed, he was taken from HMP Wakefield and dumped at a railway station with £46 in his pocket. He relied on the kindness of strangers, including a journalist and his MP, to put him up while he tried to piece together his life.[13]

The final insult came when he tried to apply for compensation. Money cannot possibly restitute seventeen years lost from a human life nor the perennial mark of the wrongly convicted sex offender, but it would be something. A gesture of goodwill by the state, to apologize for a plain miscarriage of justice, is the least that should be offered. Unfortunately for Mr Nealon, he became one of many victims of the government's crushingly tight grip on the reins of compensation for the wrongly convicted.

We are required by international law – article 14(6) of the International Covenant on Civil and Political Rights 1966 – to provide a compensation scheme for victims of miscarriages of justice. From 1976, when the ICCPR entered into force, the UK operated a discretionary compensation system for this purpose. In 1988, following pressure exerted on the UK to put the compensation scheme on a statutory footing, Parliament enacted section 133 of the Criminal Justice Act 1988, which provided for payment of compensation where a person's 'conviction has been reversed or he has been pardoned on the ground that a new or newly discovered fact shows beyond reasonable doubt that there has been a miscarriage of justice.'

The term 'miscarriage of justice' was not initially defined. Therefore the courts, in a series of cases, were forced to step into the breach and offer some guidance. After all, not all quashings of convictions necessarily represent miscarriages of justice. But many will. To cut a long common law story short, the position as of 2011 was that the courts had identified four possible categories of quashed conviction:

(1) Where the fresh evidence shows clearly that the defendant is innocent of the crime of which he has been convicted

(2) Where the fresh evidence so undermines the evidence against the defendant that no conviction could possibly be based upon it

(3) Where the fresh evidence renders the conviction unsafe in that, had it been available at the time of the trial, a reasonable jury might or might not have convicted the defendant

(4) Where something has gone seriously wrong in the investigation of the offence or the conduct of the trial, resulting in the conviction of someone who should not have been convicted

The statutory scheme, the Supreme Court ruled by a majority in 2011, should cover (1) and (2), but not (3) or (4).[14] A narrow interpretation, one might feel, but one which would offer compensation to those such as Victor Nealon.

Not narrow enough though, for the Ministry of Justice presided over by Chris Grayling. Despite the fact that payments under the compensation scheme were already scant – out of forty to fifty applications each year, around two or three are deemed eligible for compensation, and the maximum payments have been restricted (no more than £500,000 for up to ten years in prison, and no more than £1 million where over ten years) – it was decided to make it tougher.[15]

'Miscarriage of justice' was redefined. A new subsection (1ZA) was inserted into the legislation, which provided: '. . . there has been a miscarriage of justice . . . if and only if the new or newly discovered fact *shows beyond reasonable doubt* that the person *did not commit the offence.*'

Going back to our list of four, this restricts eligibility to Category 1. Unless the 'newly discovered fact' proves beyond reasonable doubt that you did not commit the offence, you will be excluded from the scheme. Which is a frankly impossible standard to meet. You are asking people to prove a negative. The DNA evidence in Mr Nealon's case cannot prove conclusively that he is innocent; *theoretically* he could have committed the offence without depositing any DNA, and the unknown male's DNA could have been innocently deposited in highly suspicious places by some convoluted method of third-party transfer. The DNA finding alone cannot positively exclude anyone. It can't exclude me. Or you. Either of us could have attacked Miss E and been fortunate enough not to have left traceable DNA. We didn't, of course; but in the absence of an alibi we couldn't *prove* that. So if we were mistakenly identified, tried and convicted, and wanted compensation for seventeen years of our lives wrongly spent in prison, we would be left swinging in the breeze. Just like Victor Nealon was when the MoJ refused to pay him a penny. And when, in 2016, the Court of Appeal refused his challenge to the lawfulness of this nasty, spiteful non-compensation scheme.[16]

In his legal challenge, Victor Nealon argued that the operation of the scheme amounted to a perversion of the presumption of innocence guaranteed by Article 6(2) of the European Convention on Human Rights. The Court of Appeal disagreed, using (in my view) highly tenuous reasoning, and Mr Nealon has since been granted permission to appeal to the Supreme Court; but whether lawful or not, this state of affairs is morally repugnant.

Our system operates so that unless you can prove to the highest legal standard that you are innocent, no miscarriage of justice will be acknowledged. It creates a legal fiction as to what constitutes a 'miscarriage of justice', entirely at odds with our common understanding of the term. This much was recognized as long ago as 1994, before the scheme was further tightened, when Master of the Rolls Lord Bingham said of an applicant:

He is entitled to be treated, for all purposes, as if he had never been convicted. Nor do I wish to suggest Mr.

Bateman is not the victim of what the man in the street would regard as a miscarriage of justice. He has been imprisoned for three and a half years when he should not have been convicted or imprisoned at all . . . But that is not, in my judgment, the question. The question is whether the miscarriage of justice from which Mr. Bateman has suffered is one that has the characteristics which the Act lays down as a pre-condition of the statutory right to demand compensation.[17]

As a consequence, we now have a stratum of purgatory populated by the dispossessed 'nearly innocent', whom we agree are victims of miscarriages of justice as 'the man on the street' understands the term, but who are expected to lump the consequences of their wrongful convictions as the price to pay for membership of our enlightened democratic society. It is difficult not to see this as an admission that, notwithstanding the traditions by which we set so much stock, we still bend to the no-smoke-without-fire whispers of our worse natures. Rather than accept and admit official wrongdoing, we set unattainable standards for victims of miscarriages to meet, and, when they inevitably fail, can reassure ourselves deep, deep down that this person didn't *really* suffer. There's a shade of grey. The system got the right person, we just couldn't *prove* it in court. The state did not fail. No injustice was caused. Move along please.

And this attitude, to me, strikes at the heart of the entire purpose of our criminal justice system. It uproots what we all understand by innocence and guilt, and erects artificial reconstructions of those terms for the sole purpose of saving the government money. The state is told that, where the conviction it has secured against one of us is *so undermined that no conviction could possibly be based upon it*, it need not say sorry. The deliberate ruination of entire lives, where the burden and standard of proof that we cherish so noisily has been fatally compromised, can be shrugged off as not even worthy of apology. And again, it is something the state has given itself the power to do without anyone in the general public, save for the unfortunate Victor Nealons of our society, becoming aware; the casual cheapening and silent degradation of our most basic dignities.

In October 2016, reborn as Secretary of State for Transport, Chris Grayling announced that he was introducing a new, more generous compensation scheme for passengers whose trains were delayed by fifteen minutes. It was only fair, he said, to 'put passengers first' and to 'make sure that they receive due compensation' for inconvenient events outside their control.[18]

12. My Closing Speech

'Justice? – you get justice in the next world, in this world you have the law.'

William Gaddis, *A Frolic of His Own* (1994)

James had it all. He was a junior doctor, recently turned thirty-three and well on the way to exceeding the predictions of professional greatness that had hovered over him since medical school. He was married to Nikki, a thirty-two-year-old teacher, and having recently bought their first home in a green-flecked suburb outside the big city, the two were making imminent plans to fill its small rooms with a much yearned-for family.

For James' thirty-third birthday, Nikki booked a spot at an achingly hipster cocktail bar, where they could enjoy some ostentatiously expensive gin concoctions before dinner. As Nikki nestled into their booth, James, clean-shaven and wearing his red-chequered birthday shirt, wandered towards the bar. Jostled by the throng of noisy bodies either side of him as he waited, he eventually washed up at the counter. The multi-pierced barman took James' order, and set about mixing two sloe gin fizzes. Feeling a sharp nudge to his right, James noticed that a worse-for-wear customer had elbowed his way to the front, and had barged his hulking frame in front of two women patiently queueing next to James. As he paid for his drinks and thanked the barman, James pointed to the women to indicate that they were next in line to be served.

What followed, James could not properly describe even by the time of his trial. He knew that something was shouted as he walked away. He knew that he felt a shove from behind, and that as he dropped to his knees, cutting his hands on the glasses as they smashed, punches rained above him. As the brawl took hold and spread like wildfire, James tried to crawl away from the bar, intent on getting to Nikki to get her away to safety. Trampled by the stampede and assuming that she must have made it safely outside, he dragged himself to the exit.

As he stumbled into the rain, he saw Nikki standing by a lamp post and breathed a sigh of relief. He walked over through the flashing sirens, pressing his hands together to stem the bleeding, but before he could reach her, a voice rang out. 'That's him – the one in the red shirt.'

Those words formed the strapline for the prosecution case. A baffled James was arrested, handcuffed and taken away, only learning at the police station the reason for his detention: the pushy man at the bar – Richard – had been struck to the face repeatedly with a broken glass, and viciously attacked while on the floor. The injuries, it would later transpire, were horrific – loss of an eye, multiple facial fractures and bleeding to the brain resulting in permanent damage. And what was agreed by the prosecution witnesses was that the man responsible was wearing a distinctive red shirt. Low-quality CCTV from above the bar showed an unidentifiable male in a red shirt forcing a glass powerfully into Richard's face, and kicking and stamping on his head repeatedly as he fell to the floor. James was positively identified by one patron as being 'the guy in red', although not by Richard, who was unable to recall the face of his attacker.

The prosecution case relied upon the fact that the CCTV

from above the bar showed only one male in a red shirt at the bar at the time that it was agreed James was there. The cuts to James' hands were further evidence, they said, that he had held the glass as it smashed into Richard's face. James' insistence of non-involvement, of crawling away as the violence unfurled, was dismissed as a desperate lie.

Notwithstanding the rather patchy evidence of identification, an inexperienced CPS prosecutor, struggling to apply the Full Code Test and conscious that Richard's case was being championed by a local and vocal MP angry about the scourge of alcohol-fuelled violence, decided that there was a realistic prospect of conviction, and James was charged with inflicting grievous bodily harm with intent. His disposable household income being over the £37,500 threshold for Crown Court representation, he did not qualify for legal aid and was forced to seek private legal assistance. Private rates of hundreds of pounds per hour were beyond him – he and Nikki were far from wealthy in any meaningful sense – and so he was forced to shop around for a deal, eventually settling on one of the few local solicitors' firms not forced to close by the crippling legal aid cuts. He stumbled across the glass-fronted offices of Keres & Co., whose private rates, although steep, were comparably affordable. 'The work starts here,' the pin-striped, lime-tied Mr Keres beamed at James as he signed the five-figure cheque for payment on account. But in truth the work stopped there. Minimal preparation was done by Keres, or by the ethanol-scented barrister instructed from a local chambers, favoured as he would tip Keres a tasty portion of his legal aid advocacy fees in exchange for briefs beyond his competence.

On the day of James' first appearance at the magistrates' court, he and Nikki got up at 6 a.m. to embark on the two-hour drive to his nearest combined court centre, the local magistrates' courts all having been closed and sold off as part of Her Majesty's Courts and Tribunals Service's 'estate optimization agenda'. They waited from 9.30 a.m. until 6 p.m. for James' case to be called on and sent to the Crown Court.

By his first appearance at the Crown Court the next month – another all-day wait at court – the CPS had served no papers, but with a resigned sigh the judge fixed a date for trial and gave various directions that all present knew were likely to be missed.

The evidence eventually landed, six weeks late, but disclosure was something else altogether. Keres and the booze-hound barrister made little effort to chase the prosecution; meanwhile, at the undermanned CPS offices, the Schedule of Unused Material was left woefully incomplete and only a fraction of the disclosable material was given to the defence. In the absence of a defence team pressing the CPS, it somehow became accepted that the exercise must have been completed and that nothing relevant fell to be disclosed.

Had all relevant material been scheduled, reviewed and disclosed, the defence would have been alerted to several key items. CCTV seized from the other end of the bar showed, from a wider angle, the outline of a second male in a red shirt, crawling on the floor away from the fracas at the moment that the first red-shirted man was glassing Richard. A completed schedule would also have alerted the defence to the existence of two independent witnesses at the bar, each of whom described the culprit as having heavy designer stubble. These accounts were recorded by two attending police officers who never gave statements, and whose pocket notebooks were never scheduled as unused material. Analysis of the glass fragments found on Richard's clothing, conducted but again not disclosed, demonstrated that the type of glass was consistent with one of the bar's pint glasses; a different glass type to that used in the highball gin glasses that James was carrying. None of this emerged.

When the trial date rolled around, the family attended in their Sunday best and waited nervously on the wooden benches in the court lobby. The trial was floating, and, as predicted by the barrister at 9.30 a.m., it floated into the afternoon and into an adjournment eight months hence. Eight months came; the adjournment this time was because a witness was in Spain, having been given the wrong dates by the Witness Care Unit. At the third time of asking, two years after James' initial arrest, the trial went ahead.

It would be easy to blame the lack of preparation by the half-cut defence barrister for the result, but the CCTV played well with the jury. 'The guy in red' could only be James, the prosecutor crowed, and based on the evidence before the court, it was difficult to disagree. The guilty verdict was met by a stunned silence, broken only by a shriek of despair from Nikki as she fled the courtroom.

James bowed his head while sentence was passed. With his family and friends listening, the judge told James, in words to be printed in every national newspaper: 'This was an unprovoked, sustained and wicked attack with a weapon, which left an innocent member of the public with life-changing disabilities. Notwithstanding your character references, this is an appalling act of drunken violence which requires a deterrent sentence.' Thirteen years' imprisonment was severe but not appealable, the barrister told James in the cells afterwards. An application for leave to appeal against the conviction and sentence was lodged half-heartedly, knocked back by the Court of Appeal, renewed and dismissed.

The private legal fees were substantial. Sniffing blood, the CPS had also applied for their own five-figure costs, a sizeable chunk of which were awarded. Their would-be-family home had to be sold. Nikki, forced to move in with her parents, visited James as he was bounced from prison to prison around the country, but time was cruel. The family they had put on hold started to feel like it might never materialize. Some marriages survive prison. James and Nikki's, after four years of trying, did not.

Five years into his sentence, James in desperation approached the Criminal Cases Review Commission. The curiosity of this mild-mannered doctor having allegedly committed such wanton violence piqued interest, and an investigation kicked into gear. After nine months, the full extent of the disclosure failings at trial were finally uncovered. It was clear: it could no longer be said with any certainty at all that James was the attacker. If anything, the fresh evidence suggested strongly that he was not.

The prosecution had to admit that the conviction was unsafe when the case was referred back to the Court of Appeal, and the Court agreed. The conviction was quashed.

Aged forty-two, James' liberty and reputation were finally restored, six years after his conviction. The financial punishment, however, was ongoing. Dismissed – fairly, in law – for gross misconduct upon his imprisonment and struck off by the General Medical Council, he was forced to seek private legal help to restart his career. While he could claim back some of his legal fees, the Innocence Tax prevented full recovery of his six-figure bill. As for the notion of compensation for the six lost years spent wrongly locked in a cell, James' application was rejected out of hand. The fresh evidence did not prove beyond reasonable doubt that you are innocent, the officious response informed James in terms. While your conviction may be unsafe, and while you may have suffered a miscarriage of justice as the man on the street would understand the term, the legal test is not satisfied.

You, James was told, are not guilty, but not quite innocent enough.

*

James' story, unlike the cases in the preceding chapters, is not real. But it could be. James could be your parent, your grandparent, your spouse, your sibling, your best friend, your child. He could be you. Every twist of systemic injustice is one that we see played out in the lives of ordinary people every single day.

In isolation, or even paired, the failings might be overcome or disguised on the road to a just outcome, but when they are not, or where multiple flaws are compounded, and a miscarriage of justice occurs, the devastation is quantified in human lives. This is the risk posed to the cast list in each of the half-million criminal cases churned every year, and the loved ones of those involved, and their loved ones, and theirs; all in some way affected. Each of us is as reliant on a functioning system as the other. Each of us is vulnerable to the flaws.

Equally plainly, each of these flaws is consciously enabled. Each is either deliberately designed – such as the Innocence Tax, or the restriction of compensation for miscarriages of justice – or is the product of populist, tough-on-crime, anti-defendant posturing, or betrays warped spending priorities whereby politicians persuade voters that 1p off a pint of lager is a better investment than a working justice system.

And this book offers only a severely cropped snapshot. Problems in criminal justice spill all over the margins. There has not been space to consider the scandal of youth justice, viewed and funded as an afterthought to the adult criminal courts, wherein vulnerable children accused of the most serious violent and sexual offences are tried on the cheap by magistrates, and prosecuted and defended even more inexpensively by often inexperienced advocates treating the Youth Courts as a training ground for the Big League.[1]

The list goes on. The tearing up of local probation service trusts in 2014 has been the disaster that was predicted.

The supervision of low- and medium-risk offenders in the community – those carrying out a court-mandated community order and those released from prison on licence – was contracted out to private 'Community Rehabilitation Companies' (CRCs) who were paid by results, leaving a financially depleted public rump (National Probation Service) to deal with the high-risk crims. There has followed a stream of reports criticizing the woeful performance of many CRCs, repeating recurring complaints from demoralized staff. Two thirds of released prisoners did not receive sufficient help from their CRC in relation to accommodation, employment or finances.[2] Probation services at a CRC in north London were condemned for having 'unmanageable caseloads, inexperienced officers, extremely poor oversight and a lack of senior management focus and control', which rendered the public 'exposed unduly to the risk of harm'.[3] The Inspectorate of Probation even found that some CRCs were instructing staff not to take any action against offenders who breached their community orders, as under the 'payment by results' contract a proven breach would incur a financial penalty.[4]

Meanwhile at the National Probation Service, inexperienced, inadequately trained staff are monitoring ever-increasing caseloads of high-risk offenders in the community. One employee reported that the target culture had reduced him from seeing his offenders weekly for an hour to holding appointments once a month for an average twenty minutes.[5] These are the institutions we entrust to supervise and rehabilitate the most damaged and dangerous among us. At twenty fucking minutes once a month.

Finally, it would be remiss not to spare a brief mention for the plight of my own unloved species. The criminal Bar, loath though we may be to publicly trumpet it and indecorous a boast as it may sound, is an irreplaceable public resource. Put aside the pantomime dress and the hangover Latin; distilled to its core principles, a cadre of independent, self-employed, expert legal consultants and specialist advocates, available for instruction to either prosecute or defend, without fear or favour, is a national asset. But it is one which all signs indicate will not survive. Judges have perceived a plunge in the quality of criminal advocacy in recent years, and the criminal Bar is an ageing profession, with fewer young members than in the past.[6] The reduction of legal aid fees is pointedly cited as a factor deterring the brightest graduates from entering publicly funded crime, and there is no doubt that, once a tenant, the miserly starting pay – £12,000 gross per year – forces many out of the job in the first five years. I have seen it. I recognize that this may look like the most unattractive special pleading in pinstripes, but the simple fact is that the same factors that squeeze good solicitors out of publicly funded crime pertain to barristers of today and of tomorrow. The old guard, who fattened themselves on overly generous pre-1990s legal aid, scorching the earth and public perceptions for those of us who followed, will die out in the next decade or two. Those who will emerge from Bar school to fill their places are likely to be mostly those with independent financial means to supplement the gruel, unhelpfully reinforcing class stereotypes at the Bar, or those unable to cut it in a more lucrative specialty. And I'll repeat – if you are wrongly accused of a crime, you want a good barrister to defend you. If you are the victim of crime, you want a good barrister to prosecute it.

And of course, you want your case in front of a good judge. If the quality of criminal advocates and solicitors diminishes, the pool from which Crown Court Circuit Judges are plucked dwindles. And so too the pool of Circuit Judges from which High Court justices are picked, and Lord Justices of Appeal and eventually Supreme Court Justices. We are already feeling the pre-tremors as Crown Court and High Court vacancies lie unfilled due to, in the words of the chair of the Judicial Appointments Commission, 'a serious shortfall of suitably qualified applicants'.[7] The dip in competence won't be immediate. It may not even be perceptible. But the effects will be felt. The senior judiciary are the people whose wisdom underpins our democracy. Their judgments, in the High Court, Court of Appeal and Supreme Court, have immediate, real-life effects, not only to the applicant or appellant in front of them but to the defendants, victims and public in millions of criminal cases in which precedent is applied. Our constitution relies upon the judges to ensure that government acts in accordance with laws passed by Parliament, and to intervene when the state overreaches to infringe our freedoms. A diminution in quality among the judiciary ultimately diminishes us all.

The race-to-the-bottom in criminal justice thus stretches all the way to the top. Every component of the system is infiltrated to some degree by negligent, reckless or malicious maladministration. Of itself, this is hardly unique; professionals in every other area of public life could no doubt regale at similar length legitimate complaints of underfunding and managerial or ministerial incompetence. But where I fear law differs, to return to my opening theme, is in how seldom the failings are echoed outside our tiny professional bubble; and, on the rare occasions that a scandal in justice is dragged into the spotlight, in how fleetingly and superficially the scrutiny endures.

When photographs are released of patients lying on trolleys in hospital corridors, the parlous finances of the NHS fill the front pages, double-spreads, op-eds and vox pops, as commissioning editors scramble to amplify the horror stories of real-life victims of our distorted political priorities, seeking the counsel of professionals stuck in the system. Working our way down the hierarchy of needs, near-comparable excitement is whipped up by crowded classrooms, overworked teachers, social care crises, immigration, transport strikes, welfare reform, pensions, low pay, the merits or demerits of Brexit and footballers' exploits.

Twenty thousand leagues under that we see the justice system. Occasionally we might all swoon on the temporary intoxication of just and righteous anger at a judge's (usually misreported) comments when imposing an insufficiently heavy sentence on some unlovely villain, or by the decontextualized figures of legal aid expenditure, or, as in late 2017 and early 2018, when disclosure errors are unmasked in rape cases involving young, photogenic, middle-class defendants, but little else registers. Coverage of high-profile criminal trials will come and go without anyone pausing to notice the bodies of adjourned cases piling up in the court corridors, or the regular denial of justice to victims of domestic violence, or the indignities doled out to all – witnesses, defendants, jurors – who involuntarily encounter the system and are expected to bend to its vicious incompetence and caprice.

In an age where repetitive bursts of spontaneous public outrage are key to feeding the twenty-four-hour news cycle, it feels like too much to ask that a few more drops be squeezed out for our pet cause. But it shouldn't be. The public *should* be outraged. In every crumbling, decaying magistrates' court and leaking Crown Court in the land, we see every day the law's equivalent of untreated, neglected patients on hospital trolleys. And every day it is met by a wall of silence.

It follows, inevitably, that if people are not aware of the problems, they cannot be expected to meaningfully contribute to proposed solutions. And herein greater dangers lie, for it is against this backdrop of apathy that far-reaching reforms, such as the Innocence Tax, can be presented as the answer to a misunderstood question and swiftly imposed to little opposition, their true intended effects only becoming apparent after the event.

I don't fool myself that universal engagement is possible, or even desirable – complex justice reform is not the stuff of prime-time TV or viral web sensations. But we must be able to do better than we presently are. It must be possible, given the human interest lying at the core of the system and flowing through the capillaries of every criminal case, to inspire a *little* more interest in what's going wrong, and what is being proposed to solve it.

So what is the blockage? Why is justice, its destruction and its purported patching-up of so little consequence to so many of us?

For what it's worth, I think the answer is threefold and interlinked.

Public Legal Education

Firstly, public legal education in our country has historically been appalling. Upon arriving at university as a law undergraduate in the early 2000s, I knew nothing about the justice system other than what I had erroneously gleaned from American TV. Everyday social interactions reveal that I am far from alone. A distressing number of my educated, professional friends genuinely understand my day to involve strutting around a courtroom barking 'objection' while spinning deliberate lies to a jury as a judge in a full-bottomed wig twirls his gavel. Despite having the phrase 'guilty beyond reasonable doubt' ingrained in our vocabularies from an early stage, the notion that I might be defending someone who is genuinely innocent rarely seems to be entertained in my conversations with non-lawyers. That there may be serious faults with criminal justice is not even countenanced, unless and until, of course, someone attends jury service, after which their reforming zeal exceeds even my own.

The starting point is school education, and on this front,

after many years of justice campaigners thwacking their drum, progress is finally being made. Citizenship classes on the national curriculum aim to teach young people about the fundamentals of the law and operation of the justice system. Legal representative bodies and charitable organizations work with many schools to bring practitioners directly into classrooms, encouraging participation in and developing critical thinking about the law. There is a visible emphasis on justice education that was entirely absent from my comprehensive education two decades ago.

However, school-level education is only the first, and probably easiest, step. How to reach the wider public is the grander conundrum. While charities and the legal profession run a series of community outreach programmes, these will realistically touch only a tiny percentage of the population. Institutional and cultural change is needed.

We could start with the law itself. Given that it is a fundamental requisite of the rule of law that a citizen be able to know their legal rights and obligations – ignorance of the law providing no defence to criminal liability – it is correspondingly a fundamental defect that our law is incomprehensible and inaccessible to swathes of the populace. Criminal law statutes, many of which hark back to the Victorian age, are often linguistically impenetrable. Non-stop political tinkering has left the general criminal law piecemeal and incoherent, dotted throughout thousands of statutes and statutory instruments. These are interpreted and refined by many more thousands of common law court precedents, in the judgments of which judges spool their unique form of English over scores of pages, never failing to use a hundred words where one would suffice. How a person charged with a simple criminal offence, such as theft, is expected to begin to negotiate their way around the laws of evidence and procedure that will govern their fate is a mystery.

In 1998, Lord Bingham, then Lord Chief Justice, echoed

nineteenth-century calls for a unified criminal code, drawing all criminal law and rules of procedure together in a single document, as exists in Canada. Twenty years later, there is no code; just even more mass-produced, disparate criminal legislation. Even if a unified criminal code is too much to ask – and it shouldn't be – Parliament could at least help by decelerating the rate of legislating and by ensuring that all future statutes and instruments comply with the Office of Parliamentary Counsel's 'Good Law' initiative, which strives to keep new legislation as straightforward and plainly expressed as possible, with a similar edict handed to judges when writing their judgments.

And as a bare minimum, Parliament should ensure that the entirety of the updated law of the land is freely and immediately available to its constituents. The government's free website www.legislation.gov.uk is hopelessly, dangerously out of date. Resources are simply not made available to update its contents as quickly as Parliament bashes out new law and amends existing statutes – so many pages are marked with a disclaimer that there are 'outstanding changes not yet made by the editorial team'. At the time of writing, basic criminal statutes were years out of date, including those relating to matters as essential as the use of reasonable force in self-defence[8] and driving disqualifications.[9]

This has been an endemic problem not just for the public but for practitioners and the courts. In a Court of Appeal case in 2008, barristers had relied upon legislation downloaded from the official government website, only for it to be spotted as the court was ready to give judgment that the legislation was out of date and no longer applied. The court condemned as 'lamentable' the position that 'there is no comprehensive statute law database with hyperlinks which would enable an intelligent person, by using a search engine, to find out all the legislation on a particular topic.'[10] Over a decade on, up-to-date legislation remains out of reach of the public, including those tossed outside the scope of legal aid and forced to teach themselves.

When it comes to case law, the position is no better. Traditionally, the state has made next to no effort at all to publicize judgments of the High Court or Court of Appeal. If, representing yourself on a fraud charge, you want to check what the Court of Appeal has said about the interpretation of 'dishonesty', for example, you are reliant either on expensive commercial providers, hard copies of the law reports in select libraries, or the charity of the British and Irish Legal Information Institute (BAILII). While BAILII does a wonderful job in bringing the online transcripts of many judgments to the public, its limited means prevent it from providing a comprehensive database of all judgments, and there is neither the search functionality of commercial legal databases, nor the commentary that appears in commercial law reports to assist the reader in quickly identifying the significance (or not) of the court decision. While the MoJ has now contracted BAILII to publish new judgments, BAILII is still dependent on charitable donations to meet its modest £160,000 per annum running costs, and there is no indication that the MoJ will furnish funds to ensure that all judgments, present and historic, are uploaded and made available to search with comparable ease to commercial providers. The MoJ is content to throw crumbs at a charity in lieu of funding meaningful public access to the law, an utterly embarrassing spectacle for a self-styled exporter of democracy and the rule of law.

Political and Media Accuracy

In 2016, an overdue All Party Parliamentary Group (APPG) on Public Legal Education was founded. One would hope that it identifies making the law available its top priority.

This APPG might also wish to consider whether its colleagues in the House ought to be a little better-informed and more honest in their public pronouncements. Pontificating on criminal law presents an easy and often irresistible opportunity for lawmakers to register political credit, and many views expressed often appear tailored to tickling party political G-spots, rather than achieving any nobler aim.

There will always be a backbencher ready to denounce the 'outrageous' headline legal aid expenditure on a grisly case, implying to constituents that the civic safeguard of determining guilt through a fair trial is just an unnecessary inconvenience dreamed up to fill the boots of lawyers. When a judge is crucified for passing a sentence, rarely does a politician have the courage to step into the firing line and point out that the full facts are unknown, and that most sentencing decisions are constrained by factors outside a judge's control. Far better for the constituency newsletter to pick up its pitchfork and join the villagers on talk radio calling for judicial heads to roll. Strengthening the hand of the prosecution in the name of victims' rights is a cause to which most will happily sign their name. Publicly campaigning for the rights of the accused is left to us, the legal aid leeches pushing to put more paedophiles on the beat.

Dissembling about the law to gain support for amending it is a particularly prevalent, if hardly new, sin. We looked earlier at Harriet Harman MP's proposal to outlaw all questioning and evidence of a complainant's sexual history. To push this agenda, Ms Harman gave quotes to the press alleging that the present legal test for allowing sexual history evidence to be admitted[11] was 'based on the notion that there are two sorts of woman – a woman who is to be believed, who is virtuous, and a fallen woman who has had previous sexual activity and is not to be believed.' Furthermore, she suggested that the law allowed such evidence to be admitted where 'it is of no evidential value.'[12]

Now if true, Ms Harman's campaign would be entirely proper. But it wasn't true. Not even a bit. Firstly, no evidence, sexual or otherwise, is ever admissible in a courtroom unless it is relevant and of 'evidential value', and sexual history evidence is *only* admissible where not admitting it might lead to the jury reaching an unsafe conclusion. Secondly, more egregiously, the entire purpose of the legislation Ms Harman was trying to change was to eliminate from courts the very 'notion' that she attacks. If it appears to a judge that the defence are applying to rely on sexual history evidence to attack a complainant's credibility – for example to evoke the myth that 'unchaste women' are less worthy of belief – the statute *expressly disallows it*. If such things were indeed happening in criminal trials, the problem would have been that the existing law was not being applied properly by the courts. It was entirely fallacious to claim that the legislation permits such things, and therefore *had* to be changed. Harman's Law was a straw man argument of jaw-dropping audacity, the known effect of which, as we saw earlier, would have been serious miscarriages of justice.

Sometimes, our elected representatives will not even bother to lay the groundwork; they will simply run straight to the Commons with a private member's bill drafted on a crisp packet seeking to vanquish whatever chimera excites them today. In March 2016, the 'Send Them All Back Bill' – yes, really – proposed by Philip Hollobone MP[13] aimed to provide for automatic deportation for any foreign national convicted of a criminal offence for which a prison sentence was *theoretically* available. This includes, as one might imagine, a lot of criminal offences, most of which never see anyone imprisoned. The upshot was that the Bill, which fortunately foundered, would have automatically deported a foreign national who had been living blamelessly in the UK for twenty years and took their daughter out of school to go on holiday.[14] Or someone who kissed their partner in a public toilet.[15] Or took a can of beer onto a coach headed to a football match.[16] Or tweeted an MP to tell him he was a flipping ninny for devising probably the world's stupidest law.[17]

How, we might reasonably ask, can the public be expected to have an accurate understanding of criminal law when their MPs go to such lengths to misunderstand, misrepresent and abuse it? Why would someone take the time to acquaint themselves with the principles of a legal system which, their representative assures them in the newspapers, is so plainly an ass?

And the subject cannot pass without a brief mention of those newspapers, whose grasp of the law – from the nuance through to the basic facts – appears looser each day. The financial strangulation of local journalism and dedicated court reporters means that national news outlets frequently rely on incomplete press releases from the police, or partial accounts from the victims, or the mis-transcribed, unverified shorthand of a rushed cub reporter. Throw in a choice quote from a conveniently outraged MP, and you have a Twitter storm brewing before anyone has paused to double-check the premise of the controversy.

Basic concepts – such as the distinction between 'not guilty' and 'innocent' – are misunderstood or wrongly parsed. No sub-editor will intrude on their star columnist's copy approval when she reacts to an acquittal in a sex case by illogically calling for the prosecution of the complainant as 'a liar'. Sentencing remarks are rarely obtained in full before an out-of-context quotation is used to whack a judge. Occam's razor is tossed out of the window, it being far easier to sensationally condemn on limited information than to find a legal expert to offer a calmer, more mundane explanation. 'How was this person convicted/acquitted?' readers will be urged to scream, without the outlet having meaningfully reported the evidence on which the jury based their decision.

Against this backdrop, the decline of public understanding becomes clearer: if the law is inaccessible, and you depend for your information on unreliable sources, confusion and disengagement are unavoidable.

It Will Never Be Me

But thirdly, and finally, I fear that we struggle to inspire passion for criminal justice because of complacency. People do not feel invested because they don't think the system directly affects them. Try as I might to elevate criminal justice alongside health and education, it's a doomed mission. We know our GPs, and visit our hospitals, and see teaching standards reflected in our children's school reports. With criminal justice, for most people most of the time, we're talking in the abstract. We may feel empathy for battered victims on the news, tut loudly at the news that the Metropolitan Police are only solving 6 in 100 burglaries,[18] and gobble Netflix documentaries on miscarriages of justice, but unless crime comes for you, kicks down your door and howls in your face, there will always be that thin layer of protective film between you and the system.

It is only ripped off, and the weeping sores exposed, at moments we dare not dream of. We don't want to think about being a witness to our husband's stabbing. Or supporting our wife through her rapist's trial. Or receiving the phone call reporting that our straight-A son's exam celebrations got a bit lairy and ended in him taking his mate's dad's Jag out for a spin, wrapping it round a lamp post and killing his three passengers. Or our grandfather being accused of sexually abusing young boys as a Scout leader in the 1950s. Such things don't happen to *people like us*. The criminal courts are not the place for people like us. Legal aid isn't something that is ever going to affect people like us.

But such things do. The criminal courts are. Legal aid is. There is comfort in the popular tableau of criminal courts as a revolving door of society's most unlovely, and the statistics do not lie; most offences are committed by established criminals. Much of my professional life is spent flipping through conviction records of defendants with a lengthier acquaintanceship with the courts than I will probably ever accrue. And some of these will be nasty lags trying to game the system, and the thought of public money that could be diverted towards schools or hospitals being spent on proving their obvious guilt is instinctively galling.

To focus on this, though, is to fall twice over into the rhetorical trap of those who have brought the criminal justice system to its knees. Firstly, the fallacy demands that we ignore the many people – around 137,000 in 2016 – who each year enter the criminal justice system having never been in trouble before.[19] Some of these will be rum coves for whom this marks the first rung on a career ladder leading to exponentially more serious criminality and correspondingly longer prison sentences. Many, however, will be good, imperfect people – our family, friends, neighbours and workmates – who have made a mistake. People like us. Forgetting this is to forget our roots; our common human interest in a system designed not as a production line for damning the irretrievable, but as a means by which we all deal with each other, fairly, justly and humanely, when one of us is accused of falling short.

Secondly, it is that word – 'accused' – that we are also encouraged to overlook. Many first-time entrants to the system will be innocent and will emerge from the other side with their reputation intact. Also blameless will be some of those aforementioned Obviously Guilty Lags, who have been wrongly identified, assumed guilty by association or, in the worst cases, fitted up by police officers taking a shortcut by pinning it on the usual suspects. And their wrongful conviction matters not just as a point of principle, but, if the case has to be made in less woolly terms, of practicality. You do not want the police nabbing just *a* burglar when your home is ransacked. The common play of burgling a house, waiting for the contents to be replaced and then going back for seconds, means you want the police to get the right one.

That we are all equally dependent on working justice, even if we do not envisage ever having to directly engage it, is the message that I fear we have lost somewhere along the way. We have allowed the dehumanization and othering of 'criminals' to psychologically divorce us from something we in fact own. We don't grudgingly fixate on the cost to the NHS of disease or injury sustained through lifestyle choice; we instead apply an empathetic, or at least pragmatic, *There But for the Grace of God*. We want *better* treatment and more resources for people we don't know, however unpleasant or undeserving they may be, for that very reason. Any health secretary venturing that having 'one of the most generous health systems in the world' was a self-evident justification for slashing the budget year-on-year, closing hospitals and removing certain types of people from free healthcare altogether, would not survive the day. The pain of others, we would instinctively recognize, is our own.

My naive, hopeless hope is that we might one day reimagine functioning, accessible criminal justice as a comparably vital policy of universal insurance. That somehow, from somewhere, we will enjoy a collective cognitive shift, in which we start viewing criminal justice, the courts and legal aid as not just for bad people rightly accused, but good people wrongly accused, bad people wrongly accused, good people rightly accused, and everyone in between. Dreaming the improbable, it might be that in such a utopia we contemplate diverting political attention and public funds *towards* the criminal justice system, with the unabashed intention of improving something the first principles of which we claim to proudly hold central to our national identity. Maybe we could find ourselves even growing to love it.

We should. For all that the preceding pages might reasonably be interpreted as a counsel of despair, there is much that is fundamentally good about our justice system. The underlying principles, accidental and incoherent though their evolution may have been, have been exported around the globe for good reason: the presumption of innocence and burden of proof, the right to a fair trial, the right to independent legal representation, equality of arms, an independent judiciary, non-partisan tribunals of fact and the other fiercely debated, non-exhaustive aspects of the rule of law on which our present settlement is premised, all stand as self-evidently necessary to our instinctual conceptions of justice. And our loyalty to those principles is often absolute, in theory if not in execution.

And there are the people. The brilliant, magnificent people. The police officers risking their lives to protect those of us who snipe light years from the front line; the CPS prosecutors and caseworkers persevering in the face of critical under-resourcing and valiantly pushing those rocks up those hills; the defence solicitors trekking to police stations at 11 p.m., and then again at 4 a.m., and then to court at 9 a.m., and then the office at 5 p.m., and home at 10 p.m. to start the cycle again in the thankless service of society's voiceless; the judges and magistrates, each day carrying the burden of taking instantaneous life-changing decisions in the full glare of the public; the forgotten, vital court staff chaperoning the wobbling mine train along the rickety rails; the probation staff and prison officers doing their best to save the unsaveable and in so doing keeping us all safer as we slumber; I dare say even some of the barristers deserve a mention. All of these people, and many more I have omitted to list, each morning step through the crumbling portico and onto the wastelands to toil, under intolerable restrictions to no clamour or acclaim, usually far beyond their obligated hours, to preserve an edifice of a justice system. They do so with an indefatigability, gallows humour and unremitting commitment to public service that makes my job, for all its many frustrations, a privilege.

The building blocks are all there for something truly exceptional. And perhaps, it occurs to me, this is why it is so difficult to raise excitement. The superiority of the way we do criminal justice – *not like those crazy Americans* – is culturally ingrained. If people learn one thing about our justice system, it's that it's the Best in the World. Pushed to substantiate they may well falter and gabble something about Magna Carta, but the narrative at least is drummed home. Maybe these unexamined narratives lead to false assumptions, and a failure to contemplate the disconnect between what we tell ourselves about our legal system and our understanding of how it operates in practice.

Ultimately this takes us back to the distinction, drawn by William Gaddis at the chapter's dawn, between law and justice. We have a legal system. Properly tended, cherished and resourced, faithful to our celebrated core principles, it is also a justice system. But the synchronicity is not guaranteed. If principles of justice are neglected, you are left muttering Gaddis' opening line. *A Frolic of His Own* drew a bleak distinction between a self-obsessed, avaricious legal profession out for itself, and shared, neglected notions of justice. I have no standing to disagree with his taking fire at 1990s US litigation culture; I would in fact agree that the law, both in the US and in our country, has historically often found itself out of step with justice, the fault lying as frequently with those within the system – the lawyers and judges – as with the framework. But in 2018 England and

Wales, I would suggest that the disconnect between criminal law and justice lies elsewhere. It is not the enemy within, betraying our ideals of justice; instead we should beware the enemy outside. Today's danger is not the actors but the director; the state moving the pieces and pulling the strings, in the haphazard choreography explored over these pages.

The end result, nevertheless, is the same. When we lose sight of justice, it unfastens and floats away, leaving us with a nominal legal system; but not a justice system.

Until we recognize and embrace this, it is hard to see how and from where the impetus will arise for anything to improve. The record will be stuck on repeat. The wrongful convictions, collapsing prosecutions, investigative failings, underfunded defences, abiding delays, repetitive adjournments, errors in disclosure and institutional insouciance will continue to be bemoaned in robing rooms; analysed in legal and academic echo chambers; ignored by those for whom the vagaries of fate have not yet led to the courtroom door; and suffered in silent darkness by those the system exists to protect.

In its own modest way, I hope that this book drags us a little further as we bend and stretch towards the light.

Notes

Introduction: My Opening Speech

1. For those uninitiated with this 1990s BBC treat, contestants, including an aggrieved Lionel Blair, would air their grievances in a mock courtroom chaired by 'Judge' Julian Clary. The 'clerk' was Captain Peacock from *Are You Being Served?* It was quite something.
2. Sarah F Brosnan, 'Justice-and-fairness-related behaviours in nonhuman primates', *Proc Natl Acad Sci USA*, 18 June 2013; 110 (Suppl 2): 10416–10423, https://www.ncbi.nlm.nih.gov/pmc/articles/PMC3690609/
3. House of Commons Public Accounts Committee, 'Efficiency in the Criminal Justice System', 23 May 2016, http://www.publications.parliament.uk/pa/cm201617/cmselect/cmpubacc/72/7202.htm
4. House of Commons Hansard, 'Crown Prosecution Service: Funding', 11 January 2017, vol 619, col 147 WH https://hansard.parliament.uk/Commons/2017-01-11/debates/3CCEE460-C6B8-44B5-A7C3-677947ECEA19/CrownProsecutionServiceFunding
5. *R (Henderson) v Secretary of State for Justice* [2015] EWHC 130 (Admin), http://www.bailii.org/ew/cases/EWHC/Admin/2015/130.html

1. Welcome to the Criminal Courtroom

1. *United States v Rabinowitz*, 339 US 56 (1950) at US 69.
2. Most of us spend our entire time at parties saying 'that's

only in the American system actually' because their crime dramas have been so culturally pervasive.

3. European Justice, 'Rights of Defendants in Criminal Proceedings in Belgium', https://e-justice.europa.eu/content_rights_of_defendants_in_criminal_proceedings_-169-be-en.do?member=1 [accessed 6 June 2017]

4. Human Rights Watch, 'Saudi Arabia: Court orders eye to be gouged out', 9 December 2005, https://www.hrw.org/news/2005/12/09/saudi-arabia-court-orders-eye-be-gouged-out

5. John Hostettler, *A History of Criminal Justice in England and Wales*, Waterside Press, 2009.

6. Although the introduction of the common law by Henry II introduced greater consistency, it was only in the nineteenth century that court precedents hardened into binding authorities in the sense understood by modern lawyers.

7. Geoffrey Rivlin, *Understanding the Law*, Oxford, 2000; Theodore FT Plucknett, *A Concise History of the Common Law*, Butterworth, 1956; Judy Hodgson (ed), *The English Legal Heritage*, Oyez Publishing, 1979, cited at https://www.judiciary.gov.uk/about-the-judiciary/history-of-the-judiciary/

8. With the very rare exception of cases involving either exceedingly complex fraud or where a jury has been tampered with, in which instances the law provides for a judge alone to try the allegations.

9. People who have a defined 'mental disorder'; people on bail for a criminal offence; people who have received a prison sentence in excess of five years; and people who, in the last ten years, have completed a prison sentence or a community order are not eligible. Judges can also discharge anyone deemed 'not capable' of acting as a juror; for example a person not able to speak English.

10. Administration of Justice (Miscellaneous Provisions) Act 1933.

11. 'The Trial of William Penn and William Mead, at the Old Bailey, for a Tumultuous Assembly' (1670) 6, *Cobbett's State Trials* (1661–78: Charles II), col 951, at col 963.

12. Geoffrey Rivlin, *Understanding the Law*, Oxford, 2000; Theodore FT Plucknett, *A Concise History of the Common Law*, Butterworth, 1956; Judy Hodgson (ed), *The English Legal Heritage*, Oyez Publishing, 1979, cited at https://www.judiciary.gov.uk/about-the-judiciary/history-of-the-judiciary

13. Hostettler, op. cit., p.127.

14. Quoted in *R v Connor & Others* [2004] UKHL 2, per Lord Steyn at [7].

15. *R v Ghosh* [1982] QB 1053. With exquisite timing, as this book was going to print the Supreme Court gave a ruling in a non-criminal case which appeared to overrule Ghosh and redefine dishonesty. Academics are split on whether this has an immediate impact on the criminal law, but it is likely that this will be addressed by the Court of Appeal (Criminal Division) soon. (*Ivey v Genting Casinos* (UK) [2017] UKSC 67.)

16. It was not ever thus, however; prior to 1898, the accused was only allowed to give an unsworn statement in his defence, putting him at something of a disadvantage.

17. 'The History of the CPS', http://webarchive.nationalarchives.gov.uk/20070205205701/http:/www.cps.gov.uk/about/history.html

18. See the Royal Commission on Criminal Procedure (Philips Commission) 1978, http://discovery.nationalarchives.gov.uk/details/r/C3028

19. Some barristers are qualified to undertake 'public access' work, where members of the public can directly instruct a barrister without going through a solicitor, but this is very rare in the criminal context.

20. See John H Langbein, *The Origins of Adversary Criminal Trial*, Oxford University Press, 2005.

21. The Statute of Westminster I, 1275.

22. *Woolmington v DPP* [1935] AC 462.

23. Natwest Professional Trainee Loan Scheme, Illustrative Example for loan of £20,000 at fixed rate APR 8.90 per cent, http://www.natwest.com/content/personal/loans/

professional/downloads/AppForm_college_of_law.pdf
[accessed 17 June 2017]

24. In practice, some of these twelve 'qualifying sessions' can be met by attending courses, lectures and residential weekends at the Inns of Court. And the era of compulsory dining is under threat from proposed reforms. See 'BSB training plans could curb role of Inns – including compulsory dinners – and end 12-month term for pupillages', *Legal Futures*, 4 October 2017, https://www.legalfutures.co.uk/latest-news/bsb-training-plans-curb-role-inns-including-compulsory-dinners-end-12-month-term-pupillages

25. For greater discussion of the scope of the Rule of Law than space here allows, see AV Dicey, *Introduction to the Study of the Law of the Constitution*, 8th ed, Macmillan, 1915; Thomas Bingham, *The Rule of Law*, Penguin, 2010.

26. 'A History of the Judiciary', https://www.judiciary.gov.uk/about-the-judiciary/history-of-the-judiciary/

2. The Wild West: The Magistrates' Court

1. Cited in A Gifford, *Where's the justice? A Manifesto of Law Reform*, Penguin, 1985.

2. Save for the very rare occasions where a 'voluntary bill of indictment' is granted by the High Court, which allows proceedings to begin in the Crown Court. This is exceedingly rare, but I include it in the endnotes to stave off pedants.

3. In 2016, 1,456,177 defendants were proceeded against at magistrates' courts. 99,952 were ultimately convicted, acquitted or sentenced at a Crown Court. Ministry of Justice, 'Criminal Justice System Statistics Quarterly, England and Wales, 2016' (final), figure 1.1, 18 May 2017, https://www.gov.uk/government/uploads/system/uploads/attachment_data/file/614414/criminal-justice-statistics-quarterly-december-2016.pdf

4. As of April 2016. See House of Commons Justice Committee, 'The role of the magistracy', 17 October 2016,

https://www.publications.parliament.uk/pa/cm201617/
cmselect/cmjust/165/16502.htm §1.1.

5. Again, there are certain exceptions where there are related
   and more serious offences which are to be tried in the
   Crown Court, and some summary offences can be tried in
   front of a jury alongside those. Section 40 of the Criminal
   Justice Act 1988.

6. For adults, at least. The Youth Court has the power to hear
   'indicatable only' cases involving under-eighteens.

7. Roughly 94 per cent remain in the magistrates' courts,
   around 5 per cent plead guilty or have their case dropped
   at the Crown Court and the remaining 1 per cent maintain
   their not guilty plea and have a jury trial.

8. Except in the case of magistrates sitting at the City of
   London Magistrates' Court, who wear fur-trimmed gowns.

9. National Audit Office, 'Efficiency in the criminal justice
   system', March 2016, p.10, https://www.nao.org.uk/
   wp-content/uploads/2016/03/Efficiency-in-the-criminal-
   justice-system.pdf

10. Including formal Criminal Procedure Rules and initiatives
    such as 'Stop Delaying Justice' and 'Transforming Summary
    Justice'.

11. Bartle, 'Historical origins of the stipendiary magistrate'
    (1995), 159 JPN 126.

12. Cited in P Derbyshire, 'For the new Lord Chancellor – some
    causes for concern about magistrates', *Criminal Law Review*
    (1997), Dec, pp.861–74.

13. Home Affairs Committee Third Report, Session 1996–1997,
    'Freemasonry in the Police and the Judiciary', vol II (1997).

14. See e.g. Lord Justice Auld's 'Review of the Criminal Courts
    in England and Wales (2001)'; 'Criminal Justice: the Way
    Ahead', Home Office, February 2001.

15. HC Justice Committee, 'The role of the magistracy', op. cit.,
    ch 3; P Gibbs, 'Magistrates: Representatives of the People?'
    (2014), http://transformjustice.org.uk/main/wp-content/
    uploads/2014/01/Transform-Justice_magistrates-Jan-
    2014.pdf

16. Crown Prosecution Service, *Annual Report 2016–17*, tables 3 and 7, https://www.gov.uk/government/uploads/ system/uploads/attachment_data/file/628968/CPS_annual_ report_2016_17.pdf These totals include cases 'proved in absence', where a defendant does not attend their trial and the court decides to proceed anyway. These are more common in the magistrates' court than the Crown Court, but even adjusting the figures by removing these leaves a magistrates' conviction rate of 60.2 per cent (28,424 convictions out of 47,193 trials).

17. Under the Marian Committal Statute of 1555.

18. John H Langbein, *The Origins of Adversary Criminal Trial*, Oxford University Press, 2005, p.40.

19. *R v Bingham Justices (Jowitt)*, quoted in *The Times*, 3 July 1974.

20. Transform Justice, P Gibbs, 'The role of the magistrate?', January 2016, http://www.transformjustice.org.uk/ wp-content/uploads/2016/03/TJ-JAN_JUSTICE-COMMITEE-ENQUIRY_FOR-PRINT.pdf

21. HC Justice Commitee, op. cit., §79–83.

22. P Gibbs, 'The role of the magistrate?', op. cit.

23. Transform Justice, P Gibbs, 'Fit for purpose: do magistrates get the training and development they need?', December 2014, http://transformjustice.org.uk/main/wp-content/ uploads/2013/05/TJ_MAGISTRATES-TRAINING.pdf

24. The Bach Commission on Access to Justice, *Interim Report*, November 2016, p.7, http://www.fabians.org.uk/wp-content/ uploads/2016/11/Access-to-Justice_final_web.pdf

25. Ministry of Justice, *Decision Impact Assessment on Her Majesty's Courts and Tribunals Service proposals on the provision of courts services in England and Wales*, IA MoJ003/2016, https://consult.justice.gov.uk/ digital-communications/proposal-on-the-provision-of-court-and-tribunal-es/results/impact-assessment.pdf; Justice Committee, 'The role of the magistracy', §84.

26. 'The strengths and skills of the Judiciary in the Magistrates' Courts', Ipsos Mori, November 2011, http://www.justice.

gov.uk/downloads/publications/research-and-analysis/moj-research/strengths-skills-judiciary.pdf

27. 'DPP under fire at justice committee', *The Law Society Gazette*, 15 December 2015, https://www.lawgazette.co.uk/law/dpp-under-fire-at-justice-committee/5052738.article

28. 8,304 staff were employed by the CPS in 2010 (CPS *Annual Report, 2010, Our People*, http://www.cps.gov.uk/publications/reports/2010/our_people.html). In 2016/17, the number employed was 5,639 (CPS *Annual Report, 2016/17*, p.29, https://www.cps.gov.uk/publications/docs/annual_report_2016_17.pdf)

29. *R (DPP) v Birmingham Magistrates' Court* [2017] EWHC 3444 (Admin). Fortunately, the prosecution appealed and the High Court quashed the DJ's refusal to adjourn and directed that the trial go ahead on a new date.

30. Sentencing Council, 'Allocation Definitive Guideline' (2015), https://www.sentencingcouncil.org.uk/wp-content/uploads/Allocation_Guideline_2015.pdf

31. Ministry of Justice, 'Transforming Our Justice System', (2016), https://www.gov.uk/government/uploads/system/uploads/attachment_data/file/553261/joint-vision-statement.pdf

32. Section 154 of the Criminal Justice Act 2003.

3. Imprisoning the Innocent: Remand and Bail

1. D Blunkett, 'Radical reform to prison can rehabilitate', *Observer*, 3 February 2002, https://www.theguardian.com/politics/2002/feb/03/labour2001to2005.prisonsandprobation

2. Howard League, 'Revealed: The wasted millions spent on needless remand', August 2014, http://www.howardleague.org/needless-remand/, cited in E Cape and T Smith, 'The practice of pre-trial detention in England and Wales: Research report' (2016), University of the West of England, Bristol, pp.31–33, https://www.fairtrials.org/wp-content/uploads/Country-Report-England-and-Wales-MASTER-

Final-PRINT.pdf. Figures for the year up to 2016 were broadly similar – a total of approximately 67,200 persons remanded by the magistrates' or Crown Court. Ministry of Justice, *Criminal Justice Statistics Quarterly*, December 2016, 'Remands – Crown Court' and 'Remands – Magistrates' Court', https://www.gov.uk/government/statistics/criminal-justice-system-statistics-quarterly-december-2016

3. Section 81 of the Senior Courts Act 1981. If the case is staying in the magistrates' court, a second application can be made, advancing the same argument, on the occasion subsequent to the first appearance (but no other – Sched I, Part IIA of the 1976 Act). So technically you could get three bites at the cherry – first appearance, second appearance and appeal to Crown Court judge. The court thereafter remains under a technical duty to consider bail at each subsequent hearing, without hearing submissions, but absent new information the remanded defendant is going nowhere.

4. The custody time limit for trial of a summary only offence is fifty-six days; for an either-way offence tried summarily, it is seventy days.

5. Section 240A of the Criminal Justice Act 2003.

6. *R v Defreitas* [2011] EWCA Crim 1254.

7. In 2016, 67,214 persons were remanded by the magistrates' and Crown Courts. Of these, 9,954 were acquitted or had the charges discontinued or dismissed. Crown Court: Ministry of Justice, *Criminal Justice Statistics Quarterly*, December 2016, 'Remands – Crown Court' and 'Remands – Magistrates' Court', https://www.gov.uk/government/statistics/criminal-justice-system-statistics-quarterly-december-2016

8. C Foote, 'The Coming Constitutional Crisis in Bail: I and II', (1965) 113 Univ. Pa. L. Rev 959, cited in T Schnacke, 'The History of Bail and Pretrial Release' (2010), https://www.pretrial.org/download/pji-reports/PJI-History per cent20of per cent20Bail per cent20Revised.pdf

9. Section 4 of the Bail Act 1976.

10. Section 5 of the Bail Act 1976.

11. Criminal Procedure Rule 8.3 – Where a defendant is

produced before the magistrates from police custody, this is the bare minimum. Where a defendant is not produced from police custody, the defence are entitled to a summary of the defendant's police interview and any witness statement or exhibit that the prosecutor considers material.

12. Cape and Smith, op. cit., p.54.
13. Ibid., p.53.
14. Ibid., p.117.
15. Section 22 of the Prosecution of Offences Act 1985.

4. Watching the Guilty Walk Free: Prosecuting on the Cheap

1. 'Is the CPS on "brink of collapse"?', BBC News (Danny Shaw), 15 September 2015, http://www.bbc.co.uk/news/uk-34246664.
2. See for further examples *The Prosecutors 'Conventions' 2009* http://www.cps.gov.uk/legal/p_to_r/prosecutors__convention/
3. Section 6(1) of the Prosecution of Offences Act 1985.
4. Crown Prosecution Service, *Annual Report 2016–17*, https://www.cps.gov.uk/publications/docs/annual_report_2016_17.pdf
5. *The Code for Crown Prosecutors* (2013), https://www.cps.gov.uk/publications/docs/code_2013_accessible_english.pdf
6. There are restricted circumstances in which a lesser test (the 'Threshold Test') can be applied, but we need not worry about that for now.
7. See *The Director's Guidance on Charging*, 5th ed (2013), http://www.cps.gov.uk/Publications/directors_guidance/dpp_guidance_5.html#a11
8. Section 39 of the Offences Against the Person Act 1861, seeing as you ask.
9. Her Majesty's Crown Prosecution Service Inspectorate and Her Majesty's Inspectorate of Constabulary, 'Joint Inspecting of the provision of charging decisions', May 2015.
10. HM Crown Prosecution Service Inspectorate, 'Business as usual? A follow-up review of the effectiveness of the

Crown Prosecution Service contribution to the Transforming Summary Justice Initiative', June 2017 at §4.21, https://www.justiceinspectorates.gov.uk/hmcpsi/wp-content/uploads/sites/3/2017/06/TSJ_FU_thm_June17_rpt.pdf

11. HM Crown Prosecution Service Inspectorate, 'Better Case Management: A Snapshot', November 2016, at p.7, https://www.justiceinspectorates.gov.uk/hmcpsi/wp-content/uploads/sites/3/2016/09/BCM_thm_Nov16_rpt.pdf

12. A joint inspection of prosecution disclosure by HM CPS Inspectorate and HM Inspector of Constabulary in 2017 found 'significant failure' across the police and CPS (§1.4). Out of the cases reviewed, in 78 per cent the police compliance with disclosure was 'poor' or 'fair', with the figure for the CPS 77 per cent. 'Making It Fair: A joint inspection of the disclosure of unused material in volume Crown Court cases', July 2017, http://www.justiceinspectorates.gov.uk/cjji/wp-content/uploads/sites/2/2017/07/CJJI_DSC_thm_July17_rpt.pdf

13. 8,304 staff were employed by the CPS in 2010 (CPS *Annual Report, 2010, Our People*, http://www.cps.gov.uk/publications/reports/2010/our_people.html). In 2016–17, the number employed was 5,639 (2016–17 report, ibid., p.29); Crown Prosecution Service *Annual Report 2014–15*, https://www.cps.gov.uk/publications/docs/annual_report_2014_15.pdf

14. *Daily Express*, '£50m chaos of lawyers fleeing the CPS', 8 September 2013, http://www.express.co.uk/news/uk/427738/50m-chaos-of-lawyers-fleeing-CPS

15. CPS *Annual Report 2016–17*, op. cit., p.14.

16. Royal Commission on Criminal Justice (1993), §17.

17. The 'Peter Principle', for the uninitiated, is the concept in management theory that postulates that in hierarchical organizations, 'managers rise to the level of their incompetence'. Laurence J Peter and Raymond Hull, *The Peter Principle: Why Things Always Go Wrong*, New York: William Morrow and Company, 1969, p.8. It was

also, you may recall, a mid-1990s sitcom starring Jim Broadbent.

18. CPS expenditure in 2016–17 was £491m, see *Annual Report*, op. cit., p.14. The cost of the subsidy for TV licences for over-75s is an estimated £750m. 'BBC to take on £750m cost of subsidy for over-75s in licence fee deal', *Guardian*, 6 July 2015, http://www.theguardian.com/media/2015/jul/06/bbc-pay-cost-free-tv-licences-over-75s-fee-deal

19. Schedule 3 para 2(2) of the Crime and Disorder Act 1988.

20. Between September 2010 and September 2016, the number of police officers fell by 18,991, or 13 per cent. Overall police budget, excluding counter-terrorism grants, fell by 20 per cent between 2010 and 2015. 'Reality Check: What has happened to police numbers?', BBC News, 26 May 2017, http://www.bbc.co.uk/news/election-2017-40060677

21. CPS expenditure in 2016–17 was £491 million, ibid. Divided by 66 million (estimated population of United Kingdom mid-2016, according to Office of National Statistics https://www.ons.gov.uk/aboutus/transparencyandgovernance/freedomofinformationfoi/ukpopulation2017, accessed on 3 December 2017) gives a per capita cost of 2.04 pence per day.

22. HM Chief Inspector of the CPS: Five Year review and annual report 2014–15, Executive Summary, https://www.justiceinspectorates.gov.uk/hmcpsi/wp-content/uploads/sites/3/2015/03/HMCPSI_CIAR_2010-15_ExecSum.pdf

23. BBC News, 'Is the CPS on "brink of collapse"?' (Danny Shaw), 15 September 2015, http://www.bbc.co.uk/news/uk-34246664

24. HMCPSI, 'Thematic Review of the CPS Rape and Serious Sexual Offences Units', February 2016, https://www.justiceinspectorates.gov.uk/hmcpsi/wp-content/uploads/sites/3/2016/02/RASSO_thm_Feb16_rpt.pdf

25. R Jory QC and S Jones, 'The aged accused', *Counsel Magazine*, November 2016, https://www.counselmagazine.co.uk/articles/the-aged-accused

26. *The Times*, 'Justice system under threat from "tsunami of

sex cases"', 13 May 2017, https://www.thetimes.co.uk/
article/justice-system-under-threat-from-tsunami-of-sex-cases-
snmzjlbjq

5. The Devil's Greatest Trick: Putting the Victim First

1. 'Guaranteed support for victims of crime', 29 March 2013,
   https://www.gov.uk/government/news/guaranteed-support-for-
   victims-of-crime
2. House of Commons Public Accounts Committee, 'Efficiency
   in the Criminal Justice System', 23 May 2016, p.11, http://
   www.publications.parliament.uk/pa/cm201617/cmselect/
   cmpubacc/72/7202.htm
3. Ibid., p.1.
4. Ibid., pp.9–11.
5. Ibid., p.5.
6. Ibid., p.15.
7. Ibid., p.6.
8. Total of outstanding cases at the Crown Court was 39,600
   as of June 2017. Ministry of Justice, *Criminal Justice
   Statistics Quarterly*, England & Wales, April to June 2017,
   (28 September 2017), https://www.gov.uk/government/
   uploads/system/uploads/attachment_data/file/647587/ccsq-
   bulletin-apr-jun-2017.pdf
9. National Audit Office, 'Efficiency in the Criminal Justice
   System', 1 March 2016, pp.12–16; Ministry of Justice,
   Criminal Justice Statistics Quarterly, June 2017, 28
   September 2017, table T4, https://www.gov.uk/government/
   statistics/criminal-court-statistics-quarterly-april-to-june-2017
10. National Audit Office, 'Efficiency in the Criminal Justice
    System', 1 March 2016, p.17.
11. HL Deb, vol 774, 14 July 2016, https://hansard.
    parliament.uk/lords/2016-07-14/debates/16071439000431/
    CourtsResourcingAndStaffing
12. 'Foleshill rape trial: Judge orders re-trial after interpreter
    mistranslates evidence', *Coventry Telegraph*, 2 August 2016,

http://www.coventrytelegraph.net/news/coventry-news/
foleshill-rape-trial-judge-orders-11695908

13. 'Nepalese officer Kumar Lama torture trial adjourned',
BBC News, 18 March 2015, http://www.bbc.co.uk/news/
uk-england-sussex-31932371

14. Independent Review of Quality Arrangements under the MoJ
Language Services Framework Agreement 2014, https://www.
gov.uk/government/uploads/system/uploads/attachment_data/
file/388333/matrix-report.pdf

15. 'Thousands of court cases adjourned due to failures
in interpreting services', *Guardian*, 4 May 2016,
https://www.theguardian.com/law/2016/may/04/
thousands-of-court-cases-adjourned-due-to-failures-in-
interpreting-services?platform=hootsuite

16. Her Majesty's Crown Prosecution Service Inspectorate,
*Thematic Review of the CPS Rape and Serious Sexual
Offences Units*, February 2016, p.4, https://www.
justiceinspectorates.gov.uk/hmcpsi/wp-content/uploads/
sites/3/2016/02/RASSO_thm_Feb16_rpt.pdf

17. Ibid., p.31.

18. Ibid., p.34.

19. 'Closures of courts and tribunals in England and Wales
Announced', BBC News, 11 February 2016, http://www.bbc.
co.uk/news/uk-35552199

20. RASSO Thematic Review, op. cit., §4.19–21

21. 'An independent inquiry into allegations made against Lord
Greville Janner', 19 January 2016, http://www.cps.gov.uk/
publications/reports/henriques_report_190116.pdf

22. Crown Prosecution Service, 'The decision not to prosecute
Lord Janner – statement from the DPP', 16 April 2015,
http://www.cps.gov.uk/news/latest_news/lord_janner/

23. Section 41 of the Youth Justice and Criminal Evidence Act
1999.

24. Prisons and Court Bill 2017, Notices of Amendments: 23
March 2017, https://publications.parliament.uk/pa/bills/
cbill/2016-2017/0145/amend/prisons_rm_pbc_0323.1-2.html

6. Defenceless and Indefensible

1. This quotation is widely and frequently attributed to Clarence Darrow, memorializing beautifully his legacy as 'Attorney of the Damned', but as with so many legendary citations, verifying when, where and even if Darrow actually said it has proved beyond my wit.

2. The Sentencing Guidelines for Reduction in Sentence for a Guilty Plea do provide for an exception to the general rule where 'further information, assistance or advice is necessary before indicating plea', which should cover the scenario outlined. However, once the plea is entered, it is at the discretion of the sentencing court whether they accept your argument to fall within this exception. There are no guarantees. 'Reduction in Sentence for a Guilty Plea Definitive Guideline' (2017), Sentencing Council, p.7.

3. *R v Lawrence* [2013] EWCA Crim 1054; 2 Cr App R 24.

4. See for example Criminal Law Solicitors' Association statement on prosecution inadequate or late disclosure, 6 June 2016, https://www.clsa.co.uk/index.php?q=clsa-statement-on-prosecution-inadequate-or-late-disclosure

5. CrimPR 1.1, cited in *Director of Public Prosecutions v Chorley Justices* [2006] EWHC 1795 (Admin).

6. *Malcolm v Director of Public Prosecutions* [2007] EWHC 363 (Admin).

7. As given in evidence (at 290) to House of Commons Constitutional Affairs Committee, 'Implementation of the Carter Review of Legal Aid', 3rd Report 2006–7, vol. I, §67.

8. Average hourly rate of an electrician quoted at £90 per hour, http://www.my-plumber.co.uk/prices/

9. Ministry of Justice, 'Transforming Legal Aid: Delivering a more credible and efficient system', April 2013, https://www.gov.uk/government/consultations/transforming-legal-aid-delivering-a-more-credible-and-efficient-system. 46 per cent between 1998 and 2005, as compared to 37 per cent over the same period

10. Otterburn Legal Consulting, 'Transforming Legal Aid:

Next Steps. A Report for the Law Society of England and Wales and the Ministry of Justice' February 2014. https://consult.justice.gov.uk/digital-communications/ transforming-legal-aid-next-steps/results/otterburn-legal-consulting-a-report-for-the-law-society-and-moj.pdf

11. The Report stated: 'The supplier based is not financially robust and is very vulnerable to any destabilizing events . . . There are very few firms which can sustain the overall reduction in fees . . . which would be very much greater than 17.5 per cent in some parts of the country', ibid., pp.5–8.

12. See, for example, then Justice Secretary Michael Gove MP's speech to the Legatum Institute on 23 June 2015, https://www.gov.uk/government/speeches/what-does-a-one-nation-justice-policy-look-like

13. See, for example, 'Touting situation is deteriorating', *The Law Gazette*, 10 August 2016, https://www.lawgazette.co.uk/analysis/comment-and-opinion/touting-situation-is-deteriorating/5057070. article?utm_source=dispatch&utm_medium=email&utm_campaign=GAZ10082016

7. Legal Aid Myths and the Innocence Tax

1. http://www.jonathandjanogly.com/content/jonathan-djanogly-speaks-cambridge-union-debate

2. I am indebted for my understanding of the history of legal aid to the research of the late Court of Appeal Judge Sir Henry Brooke, whose invaluable personal website (www.sirhenrybrooke.me) is indispensable reading for anyone interested in justice. Any errors or misinterpretations of his endeavours in my efforts to extract a skeletal outline from his in-depth study are entirely my errors, and the credit for the intellectual toil and time-consuming research is entirely his.

3. Roger Bowles and Amanda Perry, 'International comparison of publicly funded legal services and justice systems',

University of York, Ministry of Justice Research Series 14/09, October 2009, http://217.35.77.12/CB/england/research/pdfs/2009/comparison-public-fund-legal-services-justice-systems.pdf

4. National Audit Office, Ministry of Justice, 'Comparing International Criminal Justice Systems', March 2012, https://www.nao.org.uk/wp-content/uploads/2012/03/NAO_Briefing_Comparing_International_Criminal_Justice.pdf

5. Ministry of Justice, *Legal Aid Statistics in England and Wales, January to March 2017* (29 June 2017), https://www.gov.uk/government/uploads/system/uploads/attachment_data/file/631334/legal-aid-statistics-bulletin-jan-mar-2017.pdf

6. Bar Council Response to Transforming Legal Aid Next Steps (2014), http://www.barcouncil.org.uk/media/235755/bar_council_response_to_the_transforming_legal_aid__next_steps__final.pdf

7. 'Labour has created 3,600 new offences since 1997', *Telegraph*, 4 September 2008, http://www.telegraph.co.uk/news/uknews/2679148/Labour-has-created-3600-new-offences-since-1997.html

8. Sir Henry Brooke, 'The history of legal aid, 1945–2010', https://sirhenrybrooke.me/2016/07/16/the-history-of-legal-aid-1945-to-2010/

9. House of Commons Constitutional Affairs Committee, 'Implementation of the Carter Review of Legal Aid', 3rd Report of Session 2006–7 at [27], http://www.publications.parliament.uk/pa/cm200607/cmselect/cmconst/223/223i.pdf

10. Channel 4 News Fact Check, 'Should barristers keep their wigs on?', 6 January 2014, https://www.channel4.com/news/factcheck/factcheck-violins-barristers

11. The Aldi Area Manager Graduate Scheme offers a starting salary of £44,000, rising to £73,450 after four years, with a fully-expensed Audi A4 thrown in. https://www.aldirecruitment.co.uk/graduate [accessed 16 August 2017]

12. 'Labour Peer condemns legal aid cuts', *Guardian*, 2 May 2012, https://www.theguardian.com/law/2012/may/02/labour-peer-legal-aid-cuts

13. 'Domestic violence victims forced to face abusers in court due to legal aid cuts', *Guardian*, 28 January 2016, https://www.theguardian.com/law/2016/jan/28/domestic-violence-victims-forced-to-face-abusers-in-court-due-to-legal-aid-cuts

14. 'Cuts to legal aid have "decimated access to justice" for thousands of the most vulnerable', Amnesty International UK Press Release, 10 October 2016, https://www.amnesty.org.uk/press-releases/cuts-legal-aid-have-decimated-access-justice-thousands-most-vulnerable

15. 'Public handed bill for celebrity legal aid as acquitted stars claim massive fees', *Mirror*, 27 June 2011, http://www.mirror.co.uk/news/uk-news/public-handed-bill-for-celebrity-legal-137655

16. 'MP Nigel Evans: Trial made me realize impact of legal aid cuts', *ITV News*, 14 April 2014, http://www.itv.com/news/story/2014-04-13/nigel-evans-wants-cps-to-pay-130k-legal-bills/

17. Section 16A of the Prosecution of Offences Act 1985.

18. Bar Code of Conduct, Rule C29, https://www.barstandardsboard.org.uk/media/1731225/bsb_handbook_sept_2015.pdf

19. *R (The Law Society of England and Wales) v The Lord Chancellor* [2010] EWHC 1406 (Admin), http://www.bailii.org/ew/cases/EWHC/Admin/2010/1406.html

20. *R (Henderson) v Secretary of State for Justice* [2015] EWHC 130 (Admin), http://www.bailii.org/ew/cases/EWHC/Admin/2015/130.html

21. Section 17 of the Prosecution of Offences Act 1985.

22. Practice Direction (Costs in Criminal Proceedings) [2013] EWCA Crim 1632, §2.6.

23. 'MoJ refuses to publish research on unrepresented defendants', *Law Society Gazette*, 31 March 2017, https://www.lawgazette.co.uk/law/moj-refuses-to-publish-research-on-unrepresented-defendants/5060489.article

24. Transform Justice, 'Justice Denied? The experience of unrepresented defendants in the criminal courts', April

2016, http://www.transformjustice.org.uk/wp-content/
uploads/2016/04/TJ-APRIL_Singles.pdf

25. Transform Justice, 'Innocent but broke – rough justice?',
October 2015, http://www.transformjustice.org.uk/
wp-content/uploads/2015/10/TRANSFORM-JUSTICE-
INNOCENT-BUT-BROKE.pdf

26. 'Budget 2014: Beer duty cut by 1p', BBC News, 19 March
2014, http://www.bbc.co.uk/news/business-26644768

8. Trial on Trial: Part I – The Case Against

1. *Archbold: Criminal Pleading, Evidence and Practice 2017*,
Sweet & Maxwell, 2016, §8–217.

2. Section 78 of the Police and Criminal Evidence Act 1984.

3. R L Lerner, 'The Intersection of Two Systems: An American
on trial for an American Murder in the French Court
d'Assisses' (2001) 19, *University of Illinois Law Review* 791
at 796.

4. J Doak, C McGourlay and M Thomas, *Evidence in Context*,
3rd ed, Routledge, 2012, pp.34–42.

5. J H Langbein, *The Origins of Adversary Criminal Trial*,
Oxford University Press, 2005.

9. Trial on Trial: Part II – The Case for the Defence

1. W Wemms, J Hodgson, *The Trial of the British Soldiers, of
the 29th Regiment of Foot*, Boston, 1770.

2. The details of Warren Blackwell's case are taken from the
Court of Appeal judgment in his successful appeal on 12
September 2006 (*R v Blackwell* [2006] EWCA Crim 2185)
and the Independent Police Complaints Commission Report
concerning complaints made by Mr Warren Blackwell
against officers from Northamptonshire Police, published
18 June 2010, https://www.ipcc.gov.uk/sites/default/files/

Documents/investigation_commissioner_reports/redacted_
blackwell_report.pdf

3. 'IPCC publishes findings from investigation into Warren
Blackwell's complaints against Northamptonshire Police', 18
June 2010, https://www.ipcc.gov.uk/cy/node/19345

4. '109 women prosecuted for false rape claims in five years,
say campaigners', *Guardian*, 1 December 2014, https://www.
theguardian.com/law/2014/dec/01/109-women-prosecuted-
false-rape-allegations

5. 'Violence Against Women and Girls Crime Report 2015–16',
Crown Prosecution Service, September 2016, p.6, http://
www.cps.gov.uk/publications/docs/cps_vawg_report_2016.
pdf

6. See HM Inspectorate of Constabulary, 'Crime-recording:
making the victim count', November 2014, http://www.
justiceinspectorates.gov.uk/hmicfrs/wp-content/uploads/crime-
recording-making-the-victim-count.pdf

7. Figures and quotes taken from HMCPSI and HMIC,
'Making it fair: The disclosure of unused material
in volume Crown Court cases', 18 July 2017, http://
www.justiceinspectorates.gov.uk/hmcpsi/inspections/
making-it-fair-the-disclosure-of-unused-material-in-volume-
crown-court-cases/

8. https://www.justiceinspectorates.gov.uk/hmcpsi/wp-content/
uploads/sites/3/2016/02/RASSO_thm_Feb16_rpt.pdf

9. *R v Tsekiri* [2017] EWCA Crim 40.

10. See, for further information, the website maintained by Sally
Clark's family at: www.sallyclark.org.uk

11. Forensic Science Regulator, *Annual Report 2016*, 6 January
2017, p.7 https://www.gov.uk/government/publications/
forensic-science-regulator-annual-report-2016

12. Ibid., p.17.

13. 'Police "sorry" over Rochdale child abuse failures',
BBC News, 13 March 2015, http://www.bbc.co.uk/news/
uk-england-manchester-31857066

14. 'Revealed: conspiracy of silence on UK sex gangs', *The
Times*, 5 January 2011, https://www.thetimes.co.uk/

article/revealed-conspiracy-of-silence-on-uk-sex-gangs-gpg5vqsqz9h

15. Her Majesty's Inspectorate of Constabulary, 'Mistakes were made: HMIC's Review into allegations and intelligence material concerning Jimmy Savile between 1964 and 2012', 12 March 2013, http://www.justiceinspectorates.gov.uk/hmicfrs/publications/mistakes-were-made/

16. 'Operation Midland: how the Met lost its way', *Guardian*, 21 March 2016, https://www.theguardian.com/uk-news/2016/mar/21/operation-midland-met-police-paedophile-ring/

17. Code of Practice under Part II of Criminal Procedure and Investigations Act 1996.

18. Ibid., §2.1.

19. Ibid., §3.5.

20. 'Operation Midland: how the Met lost its way', op. cit.

21. Sir Richard Henriques, 'An Independent Review of the Metropolitan Police Service's handling of non-recent sexual offence investigations alleged against persons of public prominence', 31 October 2016, http://news.met.police.uk/documents/report-independent-review-of-metropolitan-police-services-handling-of-non-recent-sexual-offence-investigations-61510 , §1.21

22. Cited in Henriques, ibid., at §1.21.

23. Ibid., §1.13.

24. Ibid., §1.16.

25. Ibid., §1.32.

26. 'Operation Midland police fell for "false claims" of VIP abuse, report says', *Guardian*, 8 November 2016, https://www.theguardian.com/uk-news/2016/nov/08/operation-midland-riddled-with-met-police-errors-report-finds?CMP=share_btn_tw

27. 'Operation Midland: Police helped Nick claim compensation for false allegations', *Daily Telegraph*, 9 November 2016, http://www.telegraph.co.uk/news/2016/11/09/operation-midland-police-helped-nick-claim-compensation-for-fals/

28. *Taxquet v Belgium* (2012) 54 EHRR 26 at [57].

10. The Big Sentencing Con

1. 'Britain too soft on crime say 80 per cent of public, shock new survey reveals', *Mirror*, 21 June 2014, http://www.mirror.co.uk/news/uk-news/britain-soft-crime-say-80-3735581
2. 'Judge and defendant exchange insults in court', *Guardian*, 10 August 2016, https://www.theguardian.com/uk-news/2016/aug/10/judge-defendant-john-hennigan-exchange-insults-chelmsford-court
3. Chris Grayling MP, 'No more Sky subscriptions. No more 18 certificate DVDs. Why I'm launching today's tougher prison regime', 30 April 2013, http://www.conservativehome.com/platform/2013/04/chris-grayling-mp-embargoed-until-0001-tuesday-30th.html
4. 'Prison book ban is unlawful, court rules', *Guardian*, 5 December 2014, https://www.theguardian.com/society/2014/dec/05/prison-book-ban-unlawful-court-chris-grayling
5. O Eren and N Mocan, 'Emotional Judges and Unlucky Juveniles', September 2016, http://www.nber.org/papers/w22611, reported in *The Atlantic*, 'Judge's Football Team Loses, Juvenile Sentences Go Up', 7 September 2016, https://www.theatlantic.com/education/archive/2016/09/judges-issue-longer-sentences-when-their-college-football-team-loses/498980/)
6. 'Switching to Daylight Saving Time May Lead to Harsher Legal Sentences', *Psychological Science*, 14 December 2016, https://www.psychologicalscience.org/news/releases/switching-to-daylight-saving-time-may-lead-to-harsher-legal-sentences.html#.WJCNKWVIhEI
7. S Danziger, J Levav and L Avanaim-Pesso, 'Extraneous factors in judicial decisions', published in *Proceedings of the National Academy of Sciences of the United States of America*, 25 February 2011, http://www.pnas.org/content/108/17/6889
8. K Hopkins, N Uhrig and M Colahan, 'Associations between ethnic background and being sentenced to prison in the

Crown Court in England and Wales in 2015', 16 November 2016, https://www.gov.uk/government/statistics/associations-between-ethnic-background-and-being-sentenced-to-prison-in-the-crown-court-in-england-and-wales-in-2015

9. The analysis used seventeen broad 'offence groups', and compared defendants from different ethnic backgrounds within these groups. The groups each comprised a wide range of offences; for example 'violence against the person' included crimes ranging from common assault to murder, and drug offence categories did not distinguish between Class A and Class B offences, or between possession and supply. Furthermore, the statistical modelling did not take into account aggravating and mitigating features of the offences. Further analysis is therefore required into sentencing of specific offences, including aggravating and mitigating factors, before any meaningful comparisons might be drawn.

10. See, for example, M R Banaji and A G Greenwald, *Blind Spot: Hidden Biases of Good People*, Delacorte Press, 2013. The authors developed the famous Harvard Implicit Association Test, which has been widely employed to demonstrate hidden attitudes and beliefs that determine our preferences for certain groups over others.

11. Her Majesty's Courts and Tribunals Service, *Judicial Diversity Statistics 2016*, https://www.judiciary.gov.uk/publications/judicial-statistics-2016/

12. Law Commission, 'Sentencing law in England and Wales: Legislation currently in force', 9 October 2015, http://www.lawcom.gov.uk/wp-content/uploads/2015/10/Sentencing_law_in_England_and_Wales_Issues.pdf

13. At present, there is also a duty on the court to impose a Criminal Courts Charge (CCC) in each case. Due to the way in which Parliament repealed this ridiculous law, which required courts to charge penniless defendants hundreds of pounds that they could never pay, there now technically exists a duty on courts to impose a CCC in the sum of £0 in each case.

14. Law Commission, 'Sentencing law in England and Wales: Legislation currently in force', op. cit., p.iii.

15. R Banks, *Banks on Sentence* (8th ed), 2013, vol. 1, p.xii, as cited in Law Commission, 'Sentencing Procedure Issues Paper 1: Transition', 2015, http://www.lawcom.gov.uk/ wp-content/uploads/2015/06/Sentencing-Procedure-Issues- Paper-Transition-online.pdf

16. *R (Noone) v Governor of Drake Hall Prison & another* [2008] EWHC 207 (Admin); [2008] ACD 43 at [1], as cited in 'Sentencing Procedure Issues Paper 1', op. cit., p.7.

17. Ibid., [2010] UKSC 30 at [1].

18. Section 174 of the Criminal Justice Act 2003.

19. Those serving a sentence of between three months and four years are eligible (subject to a risk assessment) for release between two weeks and four and a half months before the halfway stage, depending on the length of sentence.

20. In fact, the only mention in legislation is at s.166 of the Criminal Justice Act 2003, which confirms that the common law principle of totality continues to apply.

21. Section 125(1) of the Coroners and Justice Act 2009.

22. Drug Offences Definitive Guideline, Category 3 Significant Role (Supply of Class A); Sexual Offences Definitive Guideline, Category 3B (Rape); Fraud Definitive Guideline (Cheat the Revenue), Category 3A.

23. Section 142(1) of the Criminal Justice Act 2003.

24. Or a four-month Detention and Training Order for defendants aged sixteen or seventeen.

25. Ministry of Justice (2016), *Proven reoffending statistics quarterly: July 2013 to June 2014*, London: Ministry of Justice, Tables C1a and C2a.

26. House of Commons Briefing Paper, 'UK Prison Population Statistics', SN/SG/04334, 20 April 2017; Ministry of Justice (2017), 'Population and capacity briefing for 16 June 2017', London: Ministry of Justice; Ministry of Justice (2017) 'Offender management statistics quarterly: October to December 2016', London: Ministry of Justice. Cited in Prison Reform Trust, 'Prison: the facts' (2017), http://www.

prisonreformtrust.org.uk/Portals/0/Documents/Bromley%20
Briefings/Summer%202017%20factfile.pdf
27. International Centre for Prison Studies website, http://www.
prisonstudies.org/highest-to-lowest/prison_population_
rate?field_region_taxonomy_tid=14, accessed on 15
November 2017
28. The average custodial sentence length for indictable offences
in March 2007 was 15.3 months. In March 2017 the
average sentence length for such offences was 19.5 months.
Ministry of Justice, *Criminal Justice Statistics Quarterly*,
March 2017, https://www.gov.uk/government/uploads/
system/uploads/attachment_data/file/638225/cjs-statistics-
march-2017.pdf
29. The Howard League for Penal Reform, 'Faint Hope: What to
do about long sentences?' (2016), http://howardleague.org/
wp-content/uploads/2016/03/Faint-Hope-What-to-do-about-
long-sentences.pdf
30. Full Fact, 'Has crime fallen regardless of changes to prison
numbers?', 24 October 2012, https://fullfact.org/crime/has-
crime-fallen-regardless-changes-prison-numbers/
31. 'Secret memo warns Blair of crime wave', *Sunday Times*, 24
December 2006.
32. Ministry of Justice (2016), 'Proven reoffending statistics
quarterly: July 2013 to June 2014', London: Ministry of
Justice, Tables C1a and C2a. Cited in Prison Reform Trust,
op. cit.
33. National Offender Management Service (2015), *Annual
Report and Accounts 2014/15*, London: The Stationery
Office. Cited in Prison Reform Trust, op. cit.
34. Ministry of Justice (2016), 'National Offender Management
Service workforce statistics: March 2016', London: Ministry
of Justice, Table 2, Ministry of Justice (2016), 'Offender
management statistics quarterly: October to December
2015', London: Ministry of Justice Table A1.1. and 1.1.
Cited in Prison Reform Trust, op. cit.
35. Ministry of Justice (2015), *Prison and probation
performance statistics 2014 to 2015*.

36. Ibid.
37. Ministry of Justice (2016), 'Costs per place and costs per prisoner', NOMS *Annual Report and Accounts 2015–16*; National Offender Management Service Annual Report 2009/10, Table 1. Cited in Prison Reform Trust, op. cit.
38. 'Prison book ban is unlawful, court rules', *Guardian*, 5 December 2014, https://www.theguardian.com/society/2014/dec/05/prison-book-ban-unlawful-court-chris-grayling
39. In 2014, Chris Grayling refused to allow prisoners to cooperate with the Commission on Sex in Prison, set up in 2012 by the Howard League for Penal Reform with then Justice Secretary Ken Clarke's approval. Grayling was reported to have said, 'Prisoners aren't going to have sex on my watch.' 'Chris Grayling blocks inquiry into sexual assaults inside jails', *Independent*, 3 May 2014, http://www.independent.co.uk/news/uk/crime/chris-grayling-blocks-inquiry-into-sexual-assaults-inside-jails-9321406.html
40. '"Staggering" rise in prison violence means youth jails are no longer safe, prison watchdog warns', *Independent*, 18 July 2017, http://www.independent.co.uk/news/uk/home-news/rise-in-prison-violence-youth-jails-young-offenders-no-longer-safe-watchdog-warns-government-a7846886.html
41. 'Men's prison conditions so "degrading" inmates "crunch cockroaches underfoot", warns watchdog', *Independent*, 25 July 2017, http://www.independent.co.uk/news/uk/home-news/uk-prison-conditions-men-degrading-poor-cockroaches-watchdog-home-office-bristol-inspectorate-howard-a7858626.html?amp
42. HM Chief Inspector of Prisons for England and Wales, *Annual Report 2016–17*, https://www.gov.uk/government/publications/hm-chief-inspector-of-prisons-annual-report-2016-to-2017
43. HM Inspectorate of Prisons (2015), 'Changing patterns of substance misuse in adult prisons and service responses', London: HMIP.
44. Ministry of Justice (2017) *Monthly Population Bulletin*, May 2017

45. Ministry of Justice (2017), *Safety in Custody Statistics Quarterly,* update to June 2017.
46. '"Staggering rise"', op. cit.
47. Ministry of Justice (2016), 'Safety in custody statistics quarterly update to December 2015', London: Ministry of Justice, cited in Prison Reform Trust, op. cit.
48. Skills Funding Agency (2015), 'OLASS English and maths assessments: participation 2014/15', London, cited in ibid.
49. Criminal Justice Joint Inspection (2015), 'A joint inspection of the treatment of offenders with learning disabilities within the criminal justice system – phase two in custody and the community', London: HM Inspectorate of Prisons, cited in ibid.
50. Ministry of Justice (2013), 'Gender differences in substance misuse and mental health amongst prisoners, Results from the Surveying Prisoner Crime Reduction (SPCR)', cited in ibid.
51. Ibid.
52. Ministry of Justice (2012), 'Research Summary 3/12, Accommodation, homelessness and reoffending of prisoners', London: Ministry of Justice, cited in ibid.
53. HM Chief Inspector of Prisons (2015), *Annual Report 2014–15*, London: The Stationery Office, cited in ibid.
54. Ofsted (2015), *The Annual Report of Her Majesty's Chief Inspector of Education, Children's Services and Skills 2014/15*, Manchester, Ofsted, cited in ibid.
55. Ministry of Justice (2015), *Prison Annual Performance Ratings 2014/15*, London: Ministry of Justice and *Prison performance digest 2012–13*, cited in ibid.
56. 'Prison officers stage unofficial walkouts in England and Wales', BBC News, 8 July 2016, http://www.bbc.co.uk/news/uk-36737016
57. 'Liz Truss's £9-per-hour prison officers won't produce safe, human prisons', *Guardian*, 3 November 2016, https://www.theguardian.com/commentisfree/2016/nov/03/liz-truss-prison-officers-prisons-staff-prisoner

58. 'What is going wrong with the prison system?' 26 January 2017, BBC News, http://www.bbc.co.uk/news/uk-38596034
59. 'Prisoner numbers will not be cut to achieve a political "quick fix", Liz Truss to warn', *Telegraph*, 13 February 2017, http://www.telegraph.co.uk/news/2017/02/13/prisoner-numbers-will-not-cut-achieve-political-quick-fix-liz/

11. The Courage of Our Convictions: Appeal

1. At 564–5.
2. *R v Nealon* [2014] EWCA Crim 574, http://www.bailii.org/ew/cases/EWCA/Crim/2014/574.html
3. *R (Hallam and Nealon) v Secretary of State for Justice* [2016] EWCA Civ 355, Annex at [8].
4. Or, if you are particularly important, you might have the privilege of a five-strong Court.
5. Of 21,514 applications received between the CCRC's inception in April 1997 and 31 October 2016, only 2.9 per cent have been referred to the Court of Appeal as convictions carrying a 'real possibility' of being quashed, and only 1.9 per cent of that total resulted in successful appeals. CCRC case statistics, http://www.ccrc.gov.uk/case-statistics/
6. Ministry of Justice, *Criminal Justice Statistics Quarterly, June 2016*, https://www.gov.uk/government/uploads/system/uploads/attachment_data/file/570022/criminal-justice-statistics-quarterly-update-to-june-2016.pdf
7. Comparing the appeals figures from 2016 with Crown Court statistics from the same period is an obviously imperfect exercise, as the appeals dealt with in 2016 will not all relate to Crown Court proceedings that concluded in the same period. But in the absence of better data, it gives a rough perspective of the odds of successfully appealing.
8. Court of Appeal (Criminal Division), *Annual Report 2015/16*, https://www.judiciary.gov.uk/wp-content/uploads/2017/02/cacd-lcj-report-2016-final.pdf
9. M McConville and L Marsh, *Criminal Judges: Legitimacy,*

      Courts and State-Induced Guilty Pleas in Britain, Edward
      Elgar, 2014.
10. Court of Appeal (Criminal Division), *Annual Report
     2015/16*, Annex F.
11. 'Unduly Lenient Sentence scheme ensuring justice for victims
    of crime and their families', https://www.gov.uk/government/
    news/unduly-lenient-sentence-scheme-ensuring-justice-for-
    victims-of-crime-and-their-families--2
12. Court of Appeal (Criminal Division), *Annual Report
    2015/16*, Annex F.
13. The Justice Gap, 'Our lack of care for victims of miscarriages
    of justice is nothing short of a scandal', Mark Newby, June
    2016, http://thejusticegap.com/2016/06/lack-compensation-
    victims-miscarriages-justice-nothing-short-scandal/
14. *R (Adams) v Secretary of State for Justice* [2011] UKSC 18,
    [2012] 1 AC 48.
15. Explanatory notes to Anti-Social Behaviour, Crime and
    Policing Act 2014, Part 13, Compensation for miscarriages
    of justice, §89, http://www.legislation.gov.uk/ukpga/2014/12/
    notes/division/3/8/1
16. *R (Hallam and Nealon) v Secretary of State for Justice*
    [2016] EWCA Civ 355.
17. *R v Secretary of State for the Home Department, ex parte
    Bateman* [1994] 7 Admin LR 175.
18. 'Rail delays: New plans to compensate passengers', BBC
    News, 13 October 2016, http://www.bbc.co.uk/news/
    uk-37638802

12. My Closing Speech

1. See 'Youth Proceedings Advocacy Review: Final Report',
   October 2015, https://www.barstandardsboard.org.uk/
   media/1712097/yparfinalreportfinal.pdf; Bar Standards Board
   Response, May 2016, https://www.barstandardsboard.org.uk/
   media/1761020/youth_advocacy_review_report_may_2016.pdf
2. HM Inspectorate of Probation, *Transforming*

Rehabilitation: Early Implementation 5, p.20, http://www. justiceinspectorates.gov.uk/hmiprobation/wp-content/uploads/ sites/5/2016/05/Transforming-Rehabilitation-5.pdf

3. HM Inspectorate of Probation, *Quality & Impact inspection: The effectiveness of probation work in the north of London*, p.4, https://www.justiceinspectorates.gov.uk/hmiprobation/ wp-content/uploads/sites/5/2016/12/North-of-London-QI-Report.pdf

4. HM Inspectorate of Probation, ibid., p.20.

5. '"The job used to have integrity": readers on Britain's probation services', *Guardian*, 9 December 2016, https://www.theguardian.com/society/2016/dec/09/ the-job-used-to-have-integrity-readers-on-britains-probation-services?CMP=twt_gu

6. 'Independent criminal advocacy in England and Wales: A Review by Sir Bill Jeffrey', May 2014, p.5, https://www.gov. uk/government/uploads/system/uploads/attachment_data/ file/310712/jeffrey-review-criminal-advocacy.pdf

7. 'Courts are running out of qualified judges, peers are told', *Guardian*, 1 March 2017, https://www.theguardian.com/ law/2017/mar/01/courts-are-running-out-of-qualified-judges-peers-are-told

8. Section 76 of the Criminal Justice and Immigration Act 2008.

9. Section 35A of the Road Traffic Offenders Act 1988.

10. *R v Chambers* [2008] EWCA Crim 2467 at [70].

11. Section 41 of the Youth Justice and Criminal Evidence Act 1999.

12. 'Harriet Harman calls for ban on lawyers asking rape victims about their sexual history after Ched Evans', *Evening Standard*, 24 March 2017, http://www.standard.co.uk/news/ politics/harriet-harman-calls-for-ban-on-lawyers-asking-rape-victims-about-sexual-history-after-ched-evans-a3498921.html

13. Foreign National Offenders (Exclusion from the UK) Bill, https://publications.parliament.uk/pa/bills/cbill/2015-2016/0034/150034.pdf. Hollobone told the House, 'I had wanted to call the Bill the "Foreign National Offenders

(Send Them All Back) Bill", but that was not allowed by the parliamentary authorities.' Hansard, 11 March 2016, col 545, https://publications.parliament.uk/pa/cm201516/cmhansrd/cm160311/debtext/160311-0001.htm

14. Section 444(1A) of the Education Act 1996.
15. Section 71 of the Sexual Offences Act 2003.
16. Section 1(3) of the Sporting Events (Control of Alcohol etc) Act 1985.
17. Section 127(1) of the Communications Act 2003.
18. 'Metropolitan police solved just 6% of burglaries last year', *Guardian*, 21 August 2015, https://www.theguardian.com/uk-news/2015/aug/21/metropolitan- police-burglaries-labour-budget- cuts-conservatives
19. Ministry of Justice, Offending history tables, Table Q6.3 (September 2016).

Acknowledgements

I don't profess to know much about such things, but a series of acknowledgements by an anonymous author to people whom they do not know and have never met strikes me as inherently odd. Nevertheless, if I might be indulged in my strangeness, I would like to put on record my eternal gratitude to those from whose wisdom and generosity I have benefitted more than I can express on paper.

Thank you to my wonderful agent Chris Wellbelove, who dragged me out of the blogosphere and into ink, and to my brilliant editor, Jamie Coleman, for their trust, guidance, ingenuity and infinite patience in herding an obstinate barrister through the contours of the literary world, an exercise akin to shepherding kittens up the Travelator on *Gladiators*. I am further indebted to the expertise of Chloe May and Laura Carr in Editorial Services, who actually made this into a book, to Liz Marvin for her eagle eyes in the copy-editing process, and to Hannah Corbett and Dusty Miller for drumming up more publicity than is good for my ego.

This book would not have come into being but for my blog and the attention generously lavished on it by a number of 'Twitter friends'. To name individuals would risk inevitably leaving out many, without whose support, advice and criticism my online presence would have amounted to screaming into a void. However, I would like to give special thanks to Matthew Scott and David Allen Green, the big beasts of the legal blogosphere, whose support at the beginning (and thereafter) exposed my writing to a much larger audience than was probably deserved. I hope that the many others to whom sincere gratitude is due know who they are.

Further thanks are owed to the commissioning editors who have entrusted column inches to an anonymous legal loudmouth, especially Laura Clenshaw, Barbara Speed, Felicity Morse, Serena Kutchinsky, Katie King and Jasper Jackson.

A number of people have been incredibly kind in agreeing to read parts of the manuscript and contribute feedback and ideas which have been utterly invaluable. In particular, I would like to thank Dr Hannah Quirk and Dr Philip Handler from the University of Manchester; Zoe Gascoyne of Quinn Melville Solicitors; Penelope Gibbs of Transform Justice; Matt Stanbury of Garden Court North chambers; Lyndon Harris, the Final Word on all matters criminal sentencing; Andrew Keogh of *Crimeline*, the font of all criminal law knowledge; and last, but certainly not least, Mary Aspinall-Miles, for help and advice of a volume and quality that should really attract a fee (legal aid rates only, I'm afraid). Sir Henry Brooke, the Court of Appeal judge and tireless campaigner for access to justice, whose energy, commitment and compassion were universally acknowledged by all in the justice system, sadly passed away in January 2018. He had generously granted me permission to fill the gaps in my own legal and historical knowledge from his peerless blog, a mark of the kindness for which he was known and will be remembered. On the shoulders of such giants I hope to tentatively perch.

Any parts of this book that are well-received are almost certainly down to the efforts of the above. All misconceived opinions, errors and omissions are my own.

To those working in criminal justice – the lawyers; the judiciary (professional and lay); the police; the tireless and under-appreciated administrators, caseworkers and lawyers of the Crown Prosecution Service; the staff of Her Majesty's Courts and Tribunals Service; and to all of those who rely on the system – the defendants, victims and witnesses of today and tomorrow – I offer my sincere and unending admiration for your fortitude, and all the good that you do. I hope that it is clear that, when I criticize the inadequacies of our system, I do so not intending to bury those who toil within, but to praise them. They all, each and every one, deserve better.

And finally, some form of thanks is probably warranted for the person who inspired this entire reckless enterprise; who compelled me, out of a heady cocktail of love and frustration, to start a blog, imperil my professional reputation and inflict my misanthropic lawsplaining on the digital world. I owe you more than I let you know. — *SB*

A Selection of Titles from Paul Doherty

The Brother Athelstan Mysteries

THE NIGHTINGALE GALLERY
THE HOUSE OF THE RED SLAYER
MURDER MOST HOLY
THE ANGER OF GOD
BY MURDER'S BRIGHT LIGHT
THE HOUSE OF CROWS
THE ASSASSIN'S RIDDLE
THE DEVIL'S DOMAIN
THE FIELD OF BLOOD
THE HOUSE OF SHADOWS
BLOODSTONE *
THE STRAW MEN *
CANDLE FLAME *
THE BOOK OF FIRES *
THE HERALD OF HELL *
THE GREAT REVOLT *
A PILGRIMAGE TO MURDER *
THE MANSIONS OF MURDER *

The Canterbury Tales Mysteries

AN ANCIENT EVIL
A TAPESTRY OF MURDERS
A TOURNAMENT OF MURDERS
GHOSTLY MURDERS
THE HANGMAN'S HYMN
A HAUNT OF MURDER
THE MIDNIGHT MAN *

* *available from Severn House*

THE MANSIONS OF MURDER

THE MANSIONS
OF MURDER

Paul Doherty

CRÈME de la CRIME

This first world edition published 2017
in Great Britain and the USA by
Crème de la Crime, an imprint of
SEVERN HOUSE PUBLISHERS LTD of
19 Cedar Road, Sutton, Surrey, England, SM2 5DA.
Trade paperback edition first published
in Great Britain and the USA 2018 by
SEVERN HOUSE PUBLISHERS LTD

British Library Cataloguing in Publication Data
A CIP catalogue record for this title is available from the British Library.

ISBN-13: 978-1-78029-100-0 (cased)
ISBN-13: 978-1-78029-582-4 (trade paper)
ISBN-13: 978-1-78010-914-5 (e-book)

All Severn House titles are printed on acid-free paper.

Severn House Publishers support the Forest Stewardship Council™ [FSC™],
the leading international forest certification organisation.
All our titles that are printed on FSC certified paper carry the FSC logo.

Typeset by Palimpsest Book Production Ltd.,
Falkirk, Stirlingshire, Scotland.
Printed and bound in Great Britain by
TJ International, Padstow, Cornwall.

HISTORICAL NOTE

By the late autumn of 1381 the Great Revolt in England had been successfully crushed. Young King Richard II was eager to make his authority felt, even though he continued to act under the brooding shadow of his uncle, John of Gaunt. London had been purged of all rebels and the city soon recovered from its occupation by the peasant armies. The courts reopened, a Parliament was summoned to sit at Westminster and the great lords began to gather, ready to flex their muscles as the murderous rivalries which divided them surfaced yet again. The nobles knew that whoever controlled London would also control Westminster, the Crown and the great offices of state. The lords played out their bitter enmities by using and exploiting the violent gangs of the city, the 'rifflers', who swarmed through the slums either side of the Thames. The lords regarded these as a huntsman would his pack of dogs so, when they whistled, the packs would gather to bay for blood . . .

To Alan Mair
"Keep running the good race to take the prize"
(I Cor. 9:24)

PART ONE

Scrippet (**Old English**): he who sets the watch

'**B**lood stains the face of the moon, dark shadows mist the sun' – or so the Benedictine chronicler in the majestic Abbey of Westminster defined the times, the year of Our Lord 1381. A season for portents, auguries, dreams and prophesies. Strange lights seared the night sky above the King's own city of London. People stared and wondered. The Great Revolt had been cruelly crushed. The bloody wine-press of the noble lords had ground it to nothing. The Masters of the Soil such as the likes of Norfolk, Beaumont, Fitzalan of Arundel and, above all, John of Gaunt, uncle of the young King Richard II and self-proclaimed regent of the realm, made their power known. The war in the shires was drawing to a bloody end. The peasant rebels, with all their high-sounding titles and claims to power; the Great Community of the Realm, the Upright Men, and their street warriors the Earthworms, were nothing more than a fading memory. Those rebels who had survived the great hunt and savage persecution by the lords could only quietly pray for hundreds of their comrades whose corpses still rotted on gallows and gibbets as far north as Alnwick and as far south as Dover. The Great Cause was finished. The dream was dead. No new Zion would come down from heaven and sink its foundations into the muddy banks of the Thames.

However, as the Westminster chronicler was quick to point out, the Great Revolt might be finished, but human wickedness, especially in London – the new Babylon – flourished richly and swiftly as cockle amongst the wheat. Peace reigned, but it was a peace which allowed every form of sin to crawl out of its hiding place. London had been brought back under the authority of the Crown. Parliament sat at Westminster. The Commons exercised their authority from St Stephen's Chapel

or the great chapterhouse of the abbey. However, Crown, Lords
and Commons, not to forget the masters of the city who
sheltered in the Guildhall, were fearful of a new danger. A
great scourge was now raising its head as peace and harmony
allegedly returned. The great gangs of London, the rifflers and
the roaring boys, were also making their presence felt. These
legions of the damned, as the chronicler described them, were
not supposed to exist. People could reject them and their
wicked doings as the work of those who gossip and chatter,
claim that the danger they posed was all shadow and no
substance. Nevertheless, the gangs were there, like the great
rats which plagued the sewers. They did not like to be caught
out in the open, but their brutal acts were clear enough for all
to see. The chronicler emphasised this important fact. Hadn't
his own abbot expressed this riddle, a paradox for all the good
brothers to ponder on? How the great London gangs did exist,
but they only moved or acted by courtesy and favour of the
lords: Gaunt, Arundel and the rest, who could whistle up their
packs of wild dogs whenever they wished.

Of all the gangs and covens of rifflers, none was more feared
than the Sycamores under their leader, Simon Makepeace, also
known as 'The Flesher'; a brutal soul, tavern master, mine
host, and owner of the Devil's Oak, close to the Thames in
Queenhithe ward.

The tavern squatted like a great, fat, bloated toad with dirty,
leprous warts, at the heart of a maze of alleys and runnels
which reeked to high heaven of dirt and filth. The tenements
lining these needle-thin paths were propped up by makeshift
struts and rotten beams, their windows sealed with iron-bound
shutters. Nevertheless, people lived here, the midnight folk,
crammed as fast and as thick as lice on a slab of putrid beef.
The denizens of these hellish dwellings clustered around makeshift braziers full of smoking, dusty charcoal. The stench of
singeing clothes and unwashed flesh curled everywhere. The
braziers provided a little light, some warmth, as well as being
a source of putrid food. The tenements were places of perpetual
twilight, where figures crawled – dark, crouching shapes
against the poor light – so it looked as if Judgement Day had
dawned and every obscure grave was giving up its dead.

Once night fell, men, women and children slunk out to hunt for whatever they could, along with the great, grey rats, though even these rodents sensed that the staircases and stairwells in these mouldering mansions were most dangerous, teetering on the verge of collapse. Instead both dwellers and vermin used the Jacob's ladders, rickety staircases built on the outside of the tenements.

Hell's buttery, as this part of Queenhithe adjoining the Thames was so aptly known, was a shadowy, dismal place full of steaming filth. Everything loathsome and decaying could be found here. Dens of depravity where murder had taken up residence under smoke-stained ceilings. Thieves and prostitutes, pimps and cunning men crawled amongst the cockroaches, which scampered in vast hordes across the rotting floors, where dirt swilled ankle-deep. Along the narrow runnels stood decaying alehouses, their taprooms nothing more than amphitheatres where a wooden circular fence about five feet high ringed a sand-filled arena. Here the huge grey rats from the nearby wharves were pitted against ferocious terriers and, when the rats had been specially starved, against each other.

All of London's grotesques gathered to watch: the likes of Daniel the Damned with his huge dead eyes in a coarse, bloated face, who offered to bite off the head of a rat for a penny and that of a mouse for a farthing. Daniel had clashed with some of the Fleshers' followers and had promptly disappeared, never to be seen again. Killings were commonplace. Murder in all its gruesome forms a daily occurrence. Just before the Great Revolt, one of the rotting tenements in Hell's buttery had abruptly collapsed. Officials of the ward decided to clear the site and they filled sack after sack with human bones found beneath shattered floorboards, above crumbling ceilings and between plastered walls.

One place amidst all this squalor was owned and controlled by the Flesher. Gossiping locals called it the 'Mansion of Murder', a three-storey building set in its own square of overgrown garden, fenced off by palings at least two yards high; each post was surmounted by razor-sharp spikes to deter anyone foolish enough to try and force entry. The only gate into the garden was iron-bound and studded: bolts at top and bottom held it fast whilst the main lock, although dirty and chipped, had been fashioned by the most skilled locksmith.

The Mansion of Murder had once belonged to the Guild at St Dismas, a group of men and women who tried to work amongst the dispossessed in Hell's buttery. The Guild had been forced to withdraw after three of its members had been found floating naked in the Thames, hands tied behind their backs, their throats slashed from ear to ear. Once the Guild had left, the mansion had immediately been seized by the Flesher, owner of the nearby Devil's Oak tavern. He had cleaned and swept it, raised the high paling fence, and had the great gate rehung and secured. No longer a House of Mercy, the mansion was a blasphemous mockery of what it had once been. According to those paid to glean news and information along the quaysides, this house of murder had been stripped of furniture, hangings and any ornamentation. Just three galleries of dusty wooden floors, plastered ceilings and flaking walls. At either end of this sinister dwelling stood a winding staircase. A kitchen, buttery and chancery chamber ranged along the ground floor, with more chambers on the galleries above.

The mansion also had cellars, which stretched the entire length of the building: dark, grim rooms once used for storage. The street sparrows who collect rumour, God knows how, claimed these cellars housed two war mastiffs, hell-hounds, long, sleek and short-furred, with bulbous heads and huge jaws. The Flesher kept these within and so transformed the House of Mercy into a place of terror. Those who crossed the Flesher, or failed this ugly-souled captain of the night, were taken to the Mansion of Murder, thrust through its one and only door, every other entrance being bricked up, whilst the windows on all three floors were mere lancets. The Mansion of Murder became a prison, though the captive did not survive long. Once the door was locked and bolted, the hounds soon learnt that new prey was available. Starved and ferocious, they'd slope up the cellar steps, eager for the hunt. People sometimes heard their growling, their horrid howling at some unearthly hour. Others claimed to have heard the screams and death cries of those the Flesher had imprisoned there.

However, what could be done during a season when there was blood on the face of the moon and a dark mist across the sun? A time when the King's writ did not run along the warren of filthy runnels next to the riverside in the ward of Queenhithe. What objection could be raised? The Flesher, if anyone had the temerity to question him, could cite the law. He would argue that the former House of Mercy was now his property. Consequently, he had the right to protect it and to use guard dogs to ensure it remained safe and secure, especially in this time of troubles when the law was, perhaps, not as strong as it should be. Moreover, he – or rather his lawyer Master Copping – would argue that it was hardly his fault that intruders, housebreakers, murderers and trespassers who broke into his valuable property paid the price.

On the eve of the Feast of All the Angels, the year of Our Lord 1381, Eudo Ingersol, mailed clerk in the secret employ of the city council, leaned against the door of the Mansion of Murder now firmly locked behind him. He tried to calm the terrors seething within him; his throat was dry as sand, his heart pounding so hard he found it difficult to breathe. The Flesher had tried him and found him guilty. Ingersol had been brought here to die.

The clerk peered through the darkness, eyes and ears straining. Then he heard it: the low rumble of a bark, the snarling and growling of the great war dogs in the cellar below, now alert to a new victim, of the fresh meat that he would supply for the hunt. Eudo wiped sweat-soaked palms on his leather jerkin. He did not have his dagger with him, he had left that at St Benet's, whilst Raquin, the Flesher's other henchman, had made sure he carried no weapons. A heart-chilling, blood-freezing howl echoed through the house. Ingersol crouched down. He fought to control his breath as he crossed himself. The ominous patter of clawed feet and that harsh breathing of the mastiffs echoing as they sloped up the cellar steps to hunt him.

Early in the morning of the feast of St Luke, the year of Our Lord 1381, Martha Ashby prepared herself for the day. Martha was housekeeper and confidante of Reynaud Filleby, parson and parish priest of St Benet's, an ancient church, its great sprawling graveyard almost stretching down to the Queenhithe wharves along the Thames. Martha had waited patiently for the first glow of sunrise when the bells of St Benet must begin their pealing, their clanging summons to attend the Jesus Mass and so greet the dawn. Parson Reynaud was strict in this, even if he ignored or flouted the more serious mandates of both Christ and Holy Mother Church. Martha would have to follow her usual routine. She climbed the steps up to the first gallery of the priest's house. She walked quietly down the passageway to the left, knocked on the door of Curate Cotes' chamber and, receiving no answer, opened it: the room was empty. The window shutters were pulled back, the small four-poster bed undisturbed, the curate's gown slung over the coverlet, his chamois slippers still pushed under the bedside table.

Satisfied that all was as it should be, Martha hurried to Parson Reynaud's chamber to the right of the staircase. She knocked and, without waiting, opened the door. Again the chamber lay silent, the shutters undisturbed, as well as the sheets and coverlet on the great four-poster bed. No candles glowed on their spigots and the capped taper on the bedside stall had not been lit. Mistress Martha tried to control her curdling anxiety and apprehension as she hastened down the stairs. All seemed to be going well, but Martha had certainly learnt how life was fickle and cruel.

She went into Parson Reynaud's chancery chamber and picked up the key to the devil's door, the postern on the west side of the church. She slipped this into the pocket of her gown, which she carefully patted, and hurried out of the house. Martha locked the door behind her and hastened down the coffin path which wound through the ancient graveyard. On either side lay the thousands of dead buried there since the church had been built at least two centuries ago, or so Parson Reynaud had informed her, a veritable forest of tomb crosses, memorial stones, funeral plinths, and all the other insignia of the houses of the dead which ringed St Benet's. All of these were to be removed as Parson Reynaud carried through his own proposed harrowing of this ancient cemetery.

The graveyard was a truly haunted place, with the darkness

now thinning and a stiff morning breeze bending the long, coarse grass, bramble and gorse which grew so vigorously across the cemetery, as if to hide and smother all signs of death and decay. A ghostly place, so Parson Reynaud had declared, where the shades of the dead could often be seen trailing around the tombs and grave plots. Mistress Martha, however, was of a more practical disposition. She believed such wraiths were just the wisps and shapes created by the thick river mists which crept in from the Thames to smother this sombre place in its chilling embrace. Such a mist was now seeping in as dawn broke and the birds in the ancient yew trees began their own morning matins.

Mistress Martha paused halfway down the path: she glanced quickly around and shivered. This was God's Acre, the last resting place of Christ's faithful departed: it should be a sacred and consecrated sanctuary, yet Martha knew different. The housekeeper stared out over the sea of shifting gorse. In the poor light, the cemetery looked more like the place it truly was: a whitewashed sepulchre, all seemingly proper without but, in truth, full of all kinds of dark filth and rottenness within. Martha opened her eyes, drew a sharp breath to calm herself and hurried on. She reached the devil's door as planned and tried the key, but could not make it grip as it was locked on the other side. She leaned against the hard wood, then straightened up as she heard approaching footsteps. Glancing to her right she saw the bobbing lantern light and shadowy shapes hurrying through the murk.

'Good morrow!' she called.

'Good morrow, Mistress Martha. God's blessings on you.'

Sexton Spurnel, a small, thickset, fussy man hurried up, all breathless, in one hand a lanternhorn, in the other a key ring.

'I've been to the postern door at the front.' He leaned closer, his bearded lined face anxious under a mop of dirty-grey hair which, Martha believed, hadn't been washed since the bathing days at the end of Lent. The sexton stared pleadingly at the housekeeper, the cast in his right eye even more pronounced.

'All the doors,' he hissed, 'are locked. I've tried the main entrance, the postern door to the side, the corpse door and now this.' He almost pushed Martha aside as he tried a key.

'It won't go in,' Martha declared.

'Like the other three.' The sexton rattled the key in the devil's door. He took it out and pushed it back in.

'I've tried it,' Martha offered.

'This is no different,' the sexton wailed.

'From what?'

Both housekeeper and sexton turned to greet Curate Cotes, who came hurrying through the half-light with Nathaniel Cripplegate, leader of the parish council, close behind him. Martha considered both men to be a startling contrast to each other. Despite the poor light, how Curate Cotes had spent the previous evening was more than obvious: his scrawny black hair, thick with grease, was a tangle; his pasty face even paler; his bloodshot eyes and stubbled chin eloquent testimony to heavy drinking and hours of carousing. Ale and food stained the curate's shabby black cassock, whilst his breath stank like a brewer's yard. Cotes seemed all a-flutter, muttering questions about the whereabouts of Parson Reynaud.

'He is not in his bed,' Martha declared.

'And he doesn't seem to be in the church either.' The sexton added: 'If he was, he would certainly hear the clattering of these keys. I mean, I have now tried all four doors.'

'Something must be very wrong.' Nathaniel Cripplegate slipped through the pool of light thrown by the lanternhorn. 'Oh yes,' he repeated, 'something must be very, very wrong.'

Martha scrutinised the council leader carefully and quietly wondered if he would appreciate it if she bestowed a blessing on him. Cripplegate was a widower, and Martha often wondered who looked after him, as he was always so neat and precise in both his dress and appearance. Despite the early hour, Cripplegate's grey hair, moustache and goatee beard were neatly clipped, his sallow face oiled; his deep blue cotehardie, with matching hose and ankle-high leather boots, was of the finest quality and spotlessly clean.

'Can't you do something?' Curate Cotes pleaded with Cripplegate. 'After all, you are a locksmith – a very skilled one, too, much respected by the guild.'

'I am not a miracle worker,' Cripplegate murmured.

'So what do you suggest?' the sexton demanded.

'We should force a door,' Martha spoke up quickly. 'And it should be this one. The others, like the main entrance to the church, are of solid oak. Parson Reynaud always said they turned the church into a fortress. Oak is hard to shatter and very slow burning, but this one,' Martha tapped the door, 'is made of wooden slats. All we have to do is break two of these free and we will be able to reach the lock and the bolts inside.'

The rest quickly agreed. Sexton Spurnel hurried across to the small death house deep in the cemetery and returned with a hammer, axe and crowbar. Martha heaved a sigh of relief as the rest hastened to help the sexton. Using axe, hammer and crowbar, they hacked at the stout wooden slats near the lock. Eventually these were wrenched free so the sexton, at Cripplegate's bidding, could slip his hand through the gap and turn the key in its lock. He stretched his arm to loosen the bolts at both top and bottom. The sexton then kicked the battered door open and, lifting the lanternhorn, led the rest into the cold, inky darkness of the nave. No candle burned or cresset torch flared. Curate Cotes was so nervous his teeth chattered as he whispered the same prayer time and time again. The sexton moved to the candle-chest just inside the entrance, beneath the now blocked-up leper squint. He crouched down, unlocked the box and took out four tallow candles, which he lit from the lanternhorn, giving one to each of his companions. Curate Cotes took his and cautiously walked towards the coffin, which had been churched the previous evening. He lifted the candle to get a clearer view and screamed.

'It's gone!' He screeched. 'Look, it's gone!'

The others gathered around and stared in horror at the coffin. The purple-gold pall cloth had been pulled to the floor. The casket lid had been unscrewed and thrown some distance away but, most surprisingly, the linen-wrapped cadaver had disappeared. Nothing inside but the casket's white-cushioned interior, peppered with the scraps of herbs sprinkled on the now vanished corpse. Cripplegate glimpsed the scrap of dirty parchment pinned to the discarded lid. He prised this loose and held it up.

'For its return,' he read, 'at a time and place of my choosing, with no trickery and deceits, fifty gold crowns.'

'In God's own name!' Cripplegate breathed. 'A king's fortune. But why all this? Who is responsible? What—'

He was cut short by Martha's piercing scream. She had wandered across to the corpse door before going into one of the chantry chapels along the north transept. Like the other chantries, this was a small, carpeted chamber with all the furniture such a chapel needed, a place of prayer dedicated to a local saint. Martha now stood, one hand over her mouth and nose as she pointed to Parson Reynaud, sitting in the celebrant's chair just within the doorway. The old priest lay slumped in the seat, his pasty-white face twisted in the shock of death caused by the death wound, a cruel slit deep in the left side of his chest. The stench from the corpse was offensive. The sheer horror of the old priest's life being cut short so brutally in such a consecrated place created a deep sense of creeping evil. Curate Cotes crouched down to half sit on the prie-dieu just outside the chantry chapel, where a penitent would kneel to be shriven by the priest sitting on the other side of the trellised screen.

'I'd best open the postern door,' Sexton Spurnel whispered, desperate to escape the horrid scene. He hurried down the nave, into the deep shadows which cloaked the main entrance, his hurried footsteps rapping through the silence.

Martha was about to crouch down to study Parson Reynaud, this old man whom she had tried to serve, when Sexton Spurnel's scream heralded further horrors. They hastened towards the bobbing light of the lanternhorn. The sexton had placed this down on the ancient cracked paving stones; he now knelt before the corpse of a man slouched in the sexton's chair just within the doorway. The victim sat rather crookedly, his unshaven face caught in the sharp rictus of death, one hand lolling over the armrest, as if reaching for his warbelt on the floor, the other almost touching the deep wound on the left side of his chest.

'Daventry,' Martha murmured. 'Daventry, Arundel's man. He visited Parson Reynaud yesterday.' Her fingers flew to her lips. 'Murder, sacrilege and blasphemy, oh sweetness!'

'What!'

'Master Cripplegate, Curate Cotes. The arca in the sacristy!'

All three hurried back down the nave and into the long, cavernous sacristy. The door to this hung open and, even before they placed their candles on the table, they could see that the trap door hidden in the far corner had been thrown back.

'I am now in charge,' the curate screeched.

'No you are not!' Cripplegate pushed by him and went down the cellar stairs. 'In heaven's name!' Cripplegate's voice echoed up. 'The arca has been opened, not a farthing remains. We have seen enough. We can do no more. Sexton Spurnel, fetch the sheriff's men . . .'

'Go forth Christian soul, may the angels of God greet you so you do not fall into the hands of the enemy, the Evil One, the Son of Perdition.'

Athelstan, Dominican friar and parish priest of St Erconwald's in Southwark, blessed for the last time the freshly turned burial mound which now housed the mortal remains of 'Fat Margo', as she was popularly known in the parish, though in the Book of the Dead, the Record of Remembrance, she was recorded as 'Margaret Grenel, widow, seamstress and embalmer of corpses.'

'Now you have gone to your eternal reward,' Athelstan murmured, staring down at the heavy wooden cross on which Crispin the carpenter would carve the dead woman's name and the date of her death, 'The Feast of St Michael, 29 September, the Year of Our Lord 1381.' Athelstan handed the asperger's rod and bucket back to Crim the altar boy and stared round at the parish council grouped behind its leaders, Watkin the dung-collector and Pike the ditcher. He nodded at Ranulf the rat-catcher and others of the parish now eager to return to the church before flocking to the Piebald tavern and the tender ministrations of its owner Mine host Jocelyn, the one-armed former river pirate. Fat Margo in her will, a scrap of parchment written some three years earlier, sealed, tied with ribbon and deposited in the parish chest, had left her small house and all its moveables 'for the parish community to be merry at table and faithful in their devotion to St Erconwald.' She had specifically added, to Athelstan's great amusement, 'that the parishioners toast her memory, to wish her God speed in her journey to paradise on the very day of her burial.' She also added that they 'do not think or say any ill of her on account of what might be revealed.'

'God knows what Margo meant by that,' Athelstan murmured.

'Pardon Father?'

Athelstan broke from his reverie and stared at the lined, close face of Mauger the parish clerk, who stood, church ledgers in one hand, his bell of office in the other. Athelstan glanced quickly at all the parishioners gathered around the freshly turned grave mound. He glimpsed Ranulf the rat-catcher who, the previous evening, when Margo's corpse was churched, had told the parishioners gathered for a church ale in the nave of St Erconwald's a ghost story about a rat-catcher. Apparently Ranulf's associate was visited by the devil and given the gift of being able to know what every rat was saying. He also knew what the rodents were doing, nibbling at larders, sniffing at babies or gnawing on corpses in the graveyard. Athelstan's parishioners had expressed their horror and delight, and the conversation soon turned to how Fat Margo hated rats and kept her house spotlessly clean, so much so that she was reluctant to allow anyone, including Athelstan, into her neatly scrubbed kitchen. In all, Ranulf had thoroughly enjoyed himself, though he now looked much the worse for wear. The rat-catcher's two champion ferrets, Audax and Ferox, were scrabbling, eager to be released, desperate to be despatched down some crack or crevice in their constant, bloody war against the horde of rats which plagued Southwark and beyond.

'Father, is it finished?' Athelstan caught Watkin's pleading tone.

The dung-collector and his henchmen had schooled their rugged, wind-whipped faces into masks of seeming piety, but they were impatient to be gone. Matters spiritual did not have much of a hold on Watkin and Pike, these two stalwarts of the parish council. They were not avid Gospel-greeters, and would soon show their disapproval if parish services became prolonged for more than necessary.

'You are impatient to say farewell to Margo as you are to greet her,' Athelstan teased. Both parishioners stared open-mouthed at the riddle Athelstan had posed.

'We are thirsty,' Moleskin the boatman called out. 'Father, it will soon be time for the Angelus bell.'

'So it will be,' Athelstan agreed. '*Procedamus in Christo* – let us proceed in Christ. Back to the church it is.'

The funeral procession lined up. Crim led the way, his capped candle, on its stick under a metal shield, fluttering bravely in the autumn breeze. Behind Crim, Mauger ponderously rang his bell, alerting the faithful to the funeral cortège. Athelstan glanced around as he gripped his psalter more tightly. Autumn was certainly making itself felt. The glossy green of summer was fading. The wild flowers were past their full glory and the ground was littered with growing mounds of discarded brown leaves. The breeze was not so warm. The sweet fragrances of the fresh grass which had sprouted so lovely and lush were tinged with corruption. Michaelmas had come and gone. Soon they would celebrate the October feasts and the rhythms and cycles of the seasons would continue. Parish life settling down for the long approach to Advent and the preparations for Christmas.

'And so life in all its riches will run its course,' Athelstan murmured as he glimpsed Cecily the courtesan and Clarissa her sister slipping away from the line of parishioners with Simon the skinner and William the weaver.

The funeral procession passed the old death house, now the home of the madcap beggar man Godbless and his omnivorous, filthy goat Thaddeus. Godbless constantly talked to the goat, as he was doing now, oblivious to the mourners passing his makeshift cottage and well-tended vegetable patch. The cortège left through the lychgate on to the great concourse stretching before the church. Athelstan caught sight of his close friend and constant dining companion the great, one-eyed tomcat Bonaventure on the prowl to the right of the church, where an old water duct was used by different vermin scurrying in and out of the building. Bladdersmith the beadle had opened the main door and stood on the steps with Judith the mummer next to him. She gazed expectantly at Athelstan, who smiled falsely to hide his exasperation. Judith was zealous in the extreme and pestered Athelstan constantly about staging a mummer's play based on the legend of Bigorne and Fillegut, the mythical beasts who devoured lecherous husbands. The story of the play centred on a meeting between these and their counterparts, Chice-fache and Pinchbelly, who gobbled down sharp-tongued wives. Judith had shared her ideas with the parish, who were equally enthusiastic about staging the play. They were already settling scores by choosing who would be best for what part, Watkin and Pike being foremost in the brewing mischief. Athelstan had decided to keep both these worthies under scrutiny. They were up to some devilment, though Athelstan couldn't detect what, except that Watkin had bought a magnificent new dung cart, specially constructed by Crispin the carpenter. Apparently Watkin had, God knows how, sealed an indenture with the good burgesses of Queenhithe to assist in the clearing and cleaning of their sewers, midden heaps and lay stalls.

'Father?'

Athelstan blinked and glanced round. He was so lost in his own thoughts he had abruptly paused just within the doorway of St Erconwald's whilst the rest of the procession had streamed ahead, threading its way through the door of the rood screen. Athelstan walked quickly down the nave. Benedicta the widow woman hurried beside him, her lovely olive-skin face full of concern, her eyes bright with agitation. Athelstan stopped at the foot of the sanctuary steps.

'Benedicta, what is the matter?'

'Father,' she grasped his wrist. 'You must come with me.' She leaned closer. 'You must see this.'

'You've been in Margo's house? You were—'

'Father, never mind that. You must come, please!'

A short while later, Benedicta led her parish priest down Spindle Avenue and into Margo's comfortable red-brick cottage which stood in its own garden plot. Benedicta hastily unlocked the door and, plucking at Athelstan's sleeve, took him across the solar, through the kitchen and buttery, and into a small scullery which housed the back door and stairs leading down into the cellar. Athelstan noticed how the trap door had been reinforced with strips of iron whilst locks and bolts ranged along all three sides.

He followed Benedicta down into the square, box-like

chamber, which glowed with lights from the wall cressets and candle spigots on the table, where two men sat with goblets and platters before them. Athelstan walked towards this and froze. He had seen embalmed corpses before and realised the grey-haired, stout man and his younger colleague – possibly his son, were cadavers: cleared, cleansed and skilfully embalmed. The bodies had been prepared, then dressed again and placed on these two chairs. Athelstan sniffed; putrefaction had not set in, although the faces and hands looked as if they had been fashioned out of wax, whilst the eyes of both corpses had receded deep into their sockets. Again Athelstan checked but there was no stench of corruption. Indeed, a grille high in the wall allowed in fresh air, whilst herb pots placed around the chamber and in wall crevices exuded a sharp sweetness.

Athelstan stared in amazement at these two figures. The sheer ordinariness of the situation chilled him. The men were dead, probably for some time, yet they sat as if expecting their souls to return at any moment. He also noticed how the platters before them contained stale crumbs, whilst wine dregs could be detected in the two goblets. The corpses sat slightly towards each other, as if deep in conversation, one hand close to the knife beside the platter, the other leaning against the table edge: the elder man wore a distinctive mail-studded wrist guard, though the younger corpse only bore the mark left by one on his right wrist.

'This is what Margo was referring to in her will,' Athelstan whispered. 'Something about not thinking ill of her when we made the discovery.' He gestured at the gruesome scene. 'This is it.'

Benedicta just stood petrified, fingers to her lips. 'I came in here.' She whispered. 'Everything was so tidy. I was listing what she had left. I went into the buttery and saw the trap door. It's just so ordinary,' she breathed out, 'that's what I thought. Two dead men sitting at a table, yet they seem alive. I did hear rumours . . .'

'About what?'

'Brother Athelstan . . .'

The friar and Benedicta turned as Mauger came clattering down the steps. 'Brother . . .'

The bell clerk stopped in amazement, then fell to his knees as he realised the full truth about the two grotesques sitting at the table.

'Saints and sinners,' Mauger gasped. 'Lord have mercy! Christ have mercy! Lord have mercy on us all.' Mauger sat back on his heels, staring at the macabre sight. 'I wonder, yes they must be.' The bell clerk got to his feet and nervously approached the table, staring at the faces of the embalmed corpses.

'What?' Athelstan asked.

'About eighteen years ago, I think it was that, Father. Yes, eighteen years ago, John of Gaunt organised a great chevauchée into Normandy. The commissioners of array were sent out searching for all able-bodied men, especially archers.' Mauger pointed to the far corner where two yew bows rested next to bulging quivers of yard-long shafts. 'All able-bodied men were summoned to the standards in Moorfields,' Mauger continued. 'If I recall parish gossip, Margo's husband Henry, and Walter their son went with them, marching down to Dover before being shipped across to Calais. According to Margo, both husband and son were killed in France leaving her a widow . . . but they didn't go. She must have murdered them . . .' Mauger's voice faltered.

'She was most skilled,' Benedicta declared. 'For years Margo prepared corpses for burial for our parish and neighbouring ones. She was loved, respected. I never dreamt she harboured such a secret.'

Athelstan went and sat on an overturned barrel, staring at the gruesome scene that was at once so ordinary and yet so chilling. He tried to recall what he knew about the merry soul who had lived in this cottage along with these ghosts. Margaret Grenel, to give her full and proper name, attended Mass on Sundays and feast days. She involved herself in parish festivities, though he could never recall her coming to be shrived. Athelstan shivered as he murmured a prayer for her soul.

'Poor woman,' he whispered. 'Her husband and son being commissioned for war – as in so many families; yes, even mine,' he added bitterly. Athelstan wondered what had truly happened here. The King's wars would often provide a path to freedom for many men. They were delighted to receive the royal writ and flock to the standards for a life allegedly made more exciting with the prospect of plunder and ransoms as well as escape from the crushing boredom of ordinary life. After all, Athelstan ruefully reflected, hadn't he, what seemed like an eternity ago, inveigled his own brother to join him in the King's array across the Narrow Seas? He and Francis/ Stephen had been fascinated at the prospect of glory, the riches to be won, of being knighted on the battlefield, a fitting thanks for some act of bravery. Instead they had descended into Hell's own nightmare. Athelstan's beloved brother had been killed, his corpse brought back for burial at a Carthusian house close by the pilgrim's route to Canterbury. Athelstan's life had been shattered, not only at the loss of his brother, but his parents, broken hearted, falling ill and dying out of sheer grief.

'She must have objected, tried to stop them.' Athelstan hastily blessed the gruesome scene. 'They must have been obdurate,' he continued, 'both father and son, so she decided to kill them, probably with poison. Once they were dead she would remove their heart, stomach and entrails. Drain the fluids, packing the corpses with aromatics, herbs and spices, similar treatment being given to the skin, especially the face.'

'Can this be done?' Benedicta exclaimed.

'Yes, believe me, I have seen it done. Go into the city, Benedicta. Visit some of the churches. You'll hear about knights killed fighting alongside the Teutonic Knights in Lithuania, and even further east. Their corpses were embalmed, carefully preserved and shipped back for burial in some of our London churches. I understand it is not as difficult as people think. In Italy they have even found corpses perfectly preserved, through no artifice but simply the composition of the ground they were buried in. I suggest Margo was very skilled and had considerable experience in the management and preparation of cadavers.'

'Oh Lord, what shall we do?' Mauger moaned.

'Yes, what shall we do?' Athelstan echoed. He went and sat down on the third high-backed chair close to the table. Using his finger, he traced the stains left by the wine cup. 'These are fairly recent,' he murmured. 'Margo must have come here to dine, to talk as if her husband and son were still alive. God have mercy on them all.' He sketched a cross in the air. 'The human heart is a veritable maze within a maze of emotions, dreams, nightmares – and whatever else flits through this vale of tears.' Athelstan peered closer at the two grey-faced corpses, noticing the half-open eyes, the texture of hair, moustache and beard. He repressed an abrupt shiver of fear and a gnawing unease, a deepening uncertainty about what he was actually seeing. Despite the obvious horror, there was something else hidden away in this dreadful cellar.

'I suggested that she murdered them. On immediate reflection, I am not too sure.'

'What do you mean, Father?'

'Well, Benedicta, I was too hasty. First, Margo may have been many things, but she wasn't an assassin. I don't think she had a murderous heart. In fact, I don't believe she had a wicked bone in her body. So why would she kill her husband and son? That would be the work of some monster from Hell. Secondly, why embalm and keep them here? Was there something else she was trying to hide? Were these two men killed and she was unable to explain their deaths – hence this? Thirdly, Margo made no attempt to hide this from us once she had died. In fact, she actually warned us in her will that we would come across something unexpected, and not to think ill of her, which means she regarded herself as innocent.' He shook his head. 'But that doesn't explain the death of these two men or why their corpses are here.'

'What shall we do?' Mauger moaned.

'You have already asked that,' Benedicta snapped.

Athelstan glanced quickly at the widow woman, his sole comrade and keen-witted confidante. Benedicta seemed deeply preoccupied, as if she too was uncertain about what had happened.

'I do wonder if there is more to this than meets the eye,' she murmured.

'I agree,' Athelstan replied, getting briskly to his feet. 'Oh Mauger, why are you here, how did you know?'

'I overheard Benedicta insisting that you leave the church. I sensed you were coming here. Since Margo's funeral was over . . .' The bell clerk's voice trailed away as if he was totally distracted.

Athelstan stared at Mauger: a fairly youngish man with black hair parted down the middle which fell to his shoulders. He was dressed in jerkin and hose, a pair of gloves pushed into his belt. He wore mud-caked boots, his lined face all puckered in concern.

'Do you know something, Father?'

'What, Benedicta?'

'Margo crossed the river to receive treatment at St Bartholomew's hospital. She left the keys to her cottage with the parish, yes?'

'Agreed,' Mauger spoke up. 'She left her will and keys in the parish chest.'

'When I came here,' Benedicta continued, 'I had a feeling that someone had visited this house.'

'A thief?' Mauger asked quickly.

'I don't know.' The widow woman shook her head. 'I had the feeling that the house had been searched. Just a suspicion.' She half smiled. 'We women are much neater and more precise in what we do.'

'Explain,' Athelstan insisted.

'Well, go back upstairs in the buttery, kitchen and solar. You'll find small objects have been moved. You can see where they once stood for some time, but then they have been shifted. Go on, Father, have a look.'

Smiling to himself, Athelstan went back up the steps into the buttery and kitchen. Looking around, he agreed with Benedicta. Margo had been very precise and neat. He suspected that when she embalmed a corpse she did so in the solar, then cleared up afterwards, although most of the work was usually completed in the parish death house. It was as if Margo, because of the grisly work she did, made sure everything else in her life was neat, orderly, even fragrant. Small flower vases stood on sills and ledges, whilst pots of herbs had been placed in wall crevices. The fireplace was neatly swept and the irons carefully hung. Athelstan walked around and realised Benedicta was correct. It would be logical to have the occasional pot or vase moved a little to the right or left, but he noticed all of them were out of line, as if somebody had been looking for something. He recalled the trap door and went over and studied it carefully. He noticed the padlocks and bolts, as well as the large chest which had once covered the sealed entrance. Murmuring to himself, Athelstan returned to the cellar. Mauger still crouched there, looking anxious and furtive. Benedicta was staring at the two corpses, as if fascinated by them.

'Benedicta, did you pull away the chest, and where did you find the keys to the locks on the trap door? Surely they were not with the key to the house? Margo only deposited her will and one key in the parish chest.'

'I follow my parish priest,' Benedicta grinned, 'and try to be thorough in everything. I looked at the chest and thought, what was that doing in a buttery? I opened the lid and it contains, as you can see, nothing but blankets.'

'Of course,' Mauger whispered, 'such a chest is usually kept in the solar.'

'I thought the same. I pulled it away and saw the trap door. I then thought that Margo would not keep its keys too far away. If you feel beneath the chest, there is a nail. I found the keys to the locks tied to that. In fact, as I pulled the chest away, I heard a chink, though there is nothing in the chest to make such a noise.' She opened her purse on her belt and took out two small keys on a ring. 'You'd best keep these, Father. Now, Mauger,' she turned back to the bell clerk, 'why are you here? You never did answer Father?'

'Tiptoft,' he replied, still distracted. 'Sir John Cranston's courier.' The bell clerk shook himself from his reverie and sprang to his feet. 'Oh Lord, I forgot in all the hustle-bustle. Brother Athelstan, Tiptoft is waiting for you at the church. Sir Jack needs you urgently at St Benet's Woodwharf in Queenhithe.'

'A den of iniquity,' Benedicta breathed.

'So there must be mischief brewing there,' Athelstan declared. 'Look – Benedicta, Mauger, not a word to anyone about this. Lock and seal both this cellar and the house. I am going to meet Sir John, but I will ask Tiptoft to take an urgent message to Brother Philippe, who has now returned to the mastership of St Bartholomew's. I need him to study these corpses.' The friar blessed the chamber. 'Now I must go.'

Athelstan headed off to collect Tiptoft; he was ensconced with the parish council in the Piebald tavern. Cranston's messenger, dressed in the usual light green livery of a royal verderer, was all a-quiver with the 'horrid news'; he was regaling Athelstan's parishioners, who were always agog for any scandal, with it. How the church of St Benet's Woodwharf was now a house of corpses: men cruelly stabbed to death whilst something equally evil had been discovered in the crypt . . .

'But worst of all,' Tiptoft proclaimed, as Athelstan paused to listen just within the doorway, 'the arca has been broken into and the Flesher's money stolen!' Athelstan could almost feel the pall of deep fear descending on this usually merry taproom. Athelstan beckoned Jocelyn over.

'The Flesher?' he queried.

'Brother, the Flesher was baptised, though he is such a demon I doubt if he ever was! He was raised from the font as Simon Makepeace. He is called the Flesher because of his previous life.' Jocelyn stared quickly around. 'I think he's slaughtered everything that crawls under God's sun, both man and beast. He captains the most violent gang of rifflers in the city. He is the bane of Queenhithe—'

Jocelyn's description was cut short by Tiptoft's cry of recognition as he glimpsed Athelstan. The courier drained his tankard and pushed his way through the throng, his ghostly-white face beneath his fiery red, nard-streaked hair wreathed in a grimace.

'Brother Athelstan, Sir Jack awaits you with a veritable litany of murders.'

The courier almost pushed Athelstan out of the tavern, with Moleskin the boatman close behind, offering to take them for free across the Thames, an offer neither Athelstan or Tiptoft could refuse. Moleskin was eager to know more about these gruesome murders and all the mayhem and mystery at St Benet's.

The boatman summoned up others from his Guild of Watermen and Oarsmen and swiftly recruited a crew to row his great, six-oared barge from the Southwark side to St Paul's wharf. Athelstan and Tiptoft clambered in, made themselves as comfortable as possible, and Moleskin cast off. A choppy, cold journey. The bargemen seemed more interested in questioning Tiptoft about the gory details he'd glimpsed in St Benet's than concentrating on the sullen, swollen waters of the Thames. Athelstan found it difficult to remain calm: the barge pitched and fell as it battled the power of the river. He tried to distract himself by glancing to either side at the myriad of small vessels which darted here and there like water beetles. Occasionally a magnificent cog would break through the thinning mist, some great merchant ship of the Hanse, with sails bulging and flags fluttering. War barges, crammed with hobelars and mailed archers, made their way to the different quaysides, the captains on the prow blowing horns as a warning to the smaller craft – the herring boats and purveyance skiffs – to pull away. Athelstan wiped the spray from his face and stared up at the sky. It was a fairly cloudy day; autumn was sweeping in with all its fading glory.

'Jesus mercy,' Moleskin muttered.

Athelstan, sitting in the canopied stern, looked round the leather-stretched hood. They were now approaching the Woodwharf, pulling past a barge making its way from the quayside, a massive, high-prowed craft painted blood-red from stern to poop, six oarsmen on either side, all hooded in deep cowls and dressed completely in inky garb. On the high stern of the barge stood its master, the Fisher of Men, clothed in the robes of a Benedictine monk. He wore a mask over his face, and mailed gauntlets on his hands. No one knew who he really was. Some maintained he was a hospitaller who had been to Outremer and come back with the dreadful disease of leprosy. Others whispered that this was true, but that he had been cured by a miracle. This eerie, midnight figure, aware of Athelstan's stare, turned and raised his hand in greeting before turning back to his henchman, Icthus, who stood just behind the Fisher. An equally eerie sight, Icthus, despite the river cold, was dressed only in a linen tunic. He took his name from the Greek word for fish, because that is what he looked like, with his webbed hands and feet, his completely hairless face, sloping brow and cod-shaped mouth. He was a born swimmer, as fast as the great silver-skinned salmon or twisting porpoise. As now, he always stood ready, at his master's bidding, to slide overboard to bring in some corpse bobbing in the waters, the victim of an accident, suicide or murder. They would take what they culled from the river, the slime-covered corpses, back to their Chapel of the Drowned Men on its deserted quayside just past La Reole. Once the cadavers were cleaned and purified, they would be publicly exhibited, their descriptions proclaimed so grieving relatives, if there were any, could come and claim the corpse and pay the appropriate fee.

The rowers of this funeral barge were all grotesques and misfits, who hid their twisted bodies and malformed faces behind masks and visors. Moleskin believed they were the best rowers on the river, and Athelstan watched as they bent over the oars, chanting a death song as their craft cut through the water. The friar wondered if they were involved in the mysterious business at St Benet's, the spire of which Athelstan could now glimpse as Moleskin's barge aimed like a lance towards the quayside. Once they had come alongside, the friar, Tiptoft, Moleskin and his merry crew promptly disembarked. Athelstan would have immediately despatched the courier with urgent messages for Brother Philippe at St Bartholomew's, but Tiptoft gripped the friar's arm and squeezed.

'Brother, we are about to enter the kingdom of the damned, the realm of chaos, and so thread the devil's valley. I must accompany you.' Tiptoft tapped the hilt of his short sword in its deerskin sheath. 'Brother Athelstan, Sir John would have my head if anything happened to you.' The courier was determined, so Athelstan shrugged and let him have his way. They entered the devil's warren, the alleyways of Hell, narrow strips of dirt-caked ground which twisted like snakes between the overhanging rotting houses and decaying walls. They entered a stygian darkness where the sunlight was never glimpsed and the air reeked of every putrid stench. The lanes were deserted and lonely, though occasionally some figure flittered through the murk, a dark, darting shadow in the gloom. A place of dread where the very silence was fraught with danger.

Occasionally a dog would howl, whilst behind mouldering fences Athelstan heard the snuffle and grunt of half-wild pigs. Rats swarmed across the streets as if they owned this man-made

Hades. A door was swiftly flung open and then crashed shut. A wooden shutter rattled on the building opposite and a strident voice shouted, 'King's men; Cranston's courier with Athelstan who cherishes the poor.'

At last they cleared the maze and entered the great, cobbled concourse in front of St Benet's – an ancient church in many styles with towers, transepts and side chapels added on to the great soaring nave built centuries earlier. A grim and forbidding house of prayer, broad, sweeping steps led up to the main entrance, with a narrow postern door to its left. On either side of this ancient church stretched the parish cemetery, a sea of tumbled crosses, headstones and tomb markers. The cemetery, however, looked as if it was being cleared. The postern door abruptly opened and Sir John Cranston, Lord High Coroner of London, strode out in all his velveteen glory. 'Sir Jack,' as he liked to announce himself, was dressed in a dark blue cotehardie over a high-collared linen shirt; the silver buttons down the middle gleamed in the sunlight. He wore hose of the same colour and texture, pushed into stout leather riding boots, with spurs which jingled like a host of elfin bells. The coroner had his broad warbelt displaying sword and dagger strapped around his generously endowed waist. On his head a beaver hat, his white-whiskered face oiled and trimmed, beaming with the joy of a man who loved the comforts of both table and the bedchamber. The coroner stood stretching himself, cloak thrown back, hands on his hips. Athelstan called out from the entrance of the alleyway and raised a hand in greeting. Cranston, grinning from ear to ear, trotted nimbly down the steps, strode across, nodded at Tiptoft and embraced Athelstan in tight hug. He kissed the friar on each cheek then stepped back.

'Welcome little monk.'

'Friar, Sir John.'

'As I said, welcome.' Cranston beamed.

'And the Lady Maude? All is well? The two poppets, your household?' Athelstan gently poked Cranston in the stomach. 'Nor must I forget the Irish wolfhounds, Gog and Magog?'

'All are well. Lady Maude is truly a cypress under which I shelter, whilst the twins grow strong and straight like the cedars of Lebanon. They still believe,' he added wearily, 'that Gog and Magog are there to be ridden. It's so good to have them back.' Cranston narrowed his eyes. 'It was so blessed,' he repeated, 'to meet them in Canterbury.'

Athelstan smiled and glanced away. He, Sir John and most of the parish of St Erconwald's had made a most singular pilgrimage to St Thomas a Becket's shrine in Canterbury. Here, Cranston had met his family again after their long stay in the countryside during the turbulent bloody days of the Great Revolt. Cranston and the entire parish had returned refreshed and renewed, and it was just as well, as more murderous mysteries emerged from the seething life of the city. Cranston brought one hand down on the friar's shoulder.

'My friend,' he murmured, peering down, 'how are you?'

'In a while, Sir John, but what is happening here?'

'A bubbling broth of murder, theft, blasphemy and sacrilege.'

'Sir John?'

'Let us walk very warily into this.' Cranston jabbed a thumb, pointing back at St Benet's. 'There is an inscription carved above the doorway there. I believe its translation runs, "This is a terrible place, the House of God and the Gate of Heaven." Believe me, Brother, the first half of that proclamation is true. The second half beggars belief. So come, my little ferret of a friar, watch and listen.'

Athelstan pulled a face, crossed himself and asked Cranston to despatch Tiptoft to Brother Philippe at St Bartholomew's. Once the courier learnt the message by rote and left, Athelstan followed the coroner up the steps and through the door, into the vestibule of St Benet's. A place of shifting light and moving shadows, Athelstan immediately sensed the sinister gloom which pervaded this place, cold and dank, whilst the poor light made it even more threatening. Flaxwith, Cranston's principal bailiff, stood on guard just inside the door with his cohort of stalwarts. Samson, Flaxwith's mastiff, which Athelstan regarded as the ugliest dog north of the Thames, yipped in delight at Cranston's appearance, and would have leapt on the coroner but for the leather leash around his thick, muscular neck which kept him close to Flaxwith's boots. The chief bailiff indicated with his head toward a cluster of shadowy figures gathered around the baptismal font.

'Leading parishioners,' he whispered.

'Take them into one of the chantry chapels,' Cranston growled. 'They are not to leave until I have questioned them.'

Athelstan waited for these to go, then walked over to study the painting on the wall where the parishioners had been gathered. Athelstan loved the different frescoes that decorated the London churches. Indeed, thanks to his own parish artist, the Hangman of Rochester, Athelstan was becoming quite a peritus, an expert on the different styles. He could see that the painting close to the baptismal font was very old and clumsily illuminated, the scene almost scrawled, its colour fast fading. Nevertheless, this ancient fresco vividly depicted a world turned upside down. A jester sat enthroned, crowned with a cap sporting pointed ears and bells; his monkey-face was a mask of mockery as he presided over a topsy-turvy world where all reality was cleverly twisted. A cohort of mice hanged a cat. Hares with human faces rode to the hound. Chickens terrorised a fox whilst a weasel kissed a falcon. Athelstan wondered if this was the world he was now entering? A church where bloody murder had been committed, a holy place which housed horrid blasphemy, because so-called Christian souls had committed the most appalling acts.

Cranston tapped him on the shoulder and led Athelstan across the vestibule to a figure slumped on the sexton's chair to one side of the main door. At first Athelstan thought the man was asleep. Cranston pushed the lanternhorn closer so Athelstan could inspect the corpse in all its gruesome horror. The friar hurriedly sketched a cross in the air as he crouched to study the cadaver.

'Giles Daventry,' Cranston murmured. 'One of my Lord of Arundel's henchmen. More of that later. Just look and learn, Brother.'

Athelstan, murmuring a prayer, did so. Daventry was a fairly young man, his black, greasy hair untended, his harsh face and chin unshaven. He sat, or rather slouched in the chair, one hand over its armrest, the other pointing towards the deep death wound in the left side of his chest. Daventry was dressed in a leather jerkin, woollen hose and scuffed leather boots; his warbelt lay on the floor beside him. Daventry's face was frozen in the rictus of violent death, startled by its suddenness as he sat in that chair, legs apart. The dead man's flesh was cold, hardening, whilst the blood which had spurted from the wound as well as through his nose and mouth had congealed as it dried.

'Here is a fighting man, yes, Sir John?'

'I agree.'

'He has been dead some time, so he probably came into the church yesterday evening. We don't know why, nor the reason for him sitting in the sexton's chair, but he does so after taking off his warbelt, which he placed on the floor beside him. Now, from the very little I know, the henchmen of great lords are soldiers, men steeped in violence; consequently – like the mastiffs they are – alert to any danger. But this is not the case here. Daventry is relaxed. His killer approaches and he still remains relaxed. Daventry senses no danger. The killer leans down, his knife concealed, then he strikes. But who, why and whatever are the mystery.'

Athelstan scrutinised the cracked paving stones around the sexton's chair, but he could detect nothing amiss, no scuff marks or sign of the chair being pushed backwards and forwards. Athelstan shook his head and blessed the corpse.

'There's more?' he murmured.

'Of course.'

Athelstan sighed, got to his feet and followed the coroner down the long, gloomy nave. It reminded Athelstan of a tithe barn used by his father: a dark, high shed lit by cresset torches fixed to a row of pillars either side, as well as by the lancet windows high in the wall. Transepts had been built on to the north and south side of the church. Each of these contained small chantry chapels behind dark, oaken trellised fencing. At the far end of the church rose a sombre rood screen, which divided the sanctuary from the nave. To the left of this stood the lady altar and to the right the Chapel of St Benet, the patron saint of the parish. Cranston first took Athelstan over to the coffin, which stood on trestles before the rood screen entrance. Athelstan gazed in astonishment at the empty casket, its lid unscrewed and thrown to one side along with the purple-gold burial pall, the white-cushioned interior gleaming in the light. Athelstan leaned closer and smelt the herbs that had been crammed around the cadaver.

'Look on that and weep,' Cranston intoned. 'Notice the coffin, Brother, made of the finest elm wood. The bronze bolts, handles and screws are the work of a craftsman. Believe me, Brother, this empty coffin could spark bloodshed and the most murderous affray across London.' Cranston dug into his pouch and took out a soiled scrap of parchment. Athelstan read the message. How the corpse would be returned at a certain time and in a certain place of the writer's choosing in return for a ransom of fifty gold crowns.

'The devil's ransom,' Athelstan murmured.

'And the devil to pay,' Cranston agreed. 'That casket once housed the mortal remains of Isabella Makepeace. What a name! She was the mother of London's most vicious and notorious riffler, known to all and sundry as the Flesher. A man who fears neither God nor man. A great thief, Simon's problem, and it always has been, is that he cannot distinguish between his property and everybody else's. He takes what he wants and he will not be checked, be it the property of the Crown or Holy Mother Church. A soul conceived in sin, he was born to sin most vigorously. The Flesher will regard this empty coffin as an act of war.'

'Yes, yes,' Athelstan intervened, 'I have heard about the Flesher.'

'And you will be told more later – but come, the deceased Parson Reynaud awaits us.'

Cranston took Athelstan across to the chantry chapel close to the lady altar. Its curtain had been pulled back. Parson Reynaud sat crookedly in the celebrant's chair on the inside of the trellised screen, a prie-dieu on the other side; anyone wishing to be shrived would kneel there and await absolution. Athelstan studied this arrangement, a common one in many churches, including his own. He pinched his nostrils at the fetid smell. He then knelt down and swiftly blessed the corpse, murmuring the requiem as he studied the old priest's wiry grey hair, the lined face with the toper's nose and thick, blood-encrusted lips. Like Daventry, Parson Reynaud squatted legs apart, one hand lolling down, the other close to the heart-wound deep in the left side of his chest. The dead priest was dressed in a thick green woollen cloak thrown around his shoulders, a jerkin and hose of the same colour with the softest slippers on his feet. The fingers of both hands were decorated with jewelled rings and an intricately carved bracelet circled his left wrist. Athelstan also noticed the gold filigree chain around the parson's neck; from it hung a silver heart with the inscription, 'Love conquers everything' etched on to it.

'A man of the world,' Athelstan murmured. He peered closer at a second chain with a coffer key hanging on it.

'Remember that, Brother.'

Athelstan glanced up at the coroner.

'Why?'

'In a while, what do you think?'

'Well, he wasn't killed to be robbed,' Athelstan gestured at the jewellery. 'So we must look for some other motive. This priest intended to shrive penitents or meet someone. He must have come in just before dark yesterday evening. The killer was either waiting or followed him in. He approached and, as swift as a pouncing cat, drove a dagger into the old priest's chest. God rest him. Someone should administer the last rites.'

'Let the curate do that,' Cranston retorted. 'We are busy enough and I have more to show you.' Athelstan leaned on the screen to get up, once again noticing the sober yet very costly raiment on the old priest, as well as the expensive jewellery. Athelstan immediately recalled that gruesome scene in the cellar of Margo's cottage.

'That's it,' Athelstan snapped his fingers. 'That's it, that's it!'

'What, little friar?'

'Their clothes, the Grenels' clothes. They were clean, they were new.'

'Grenel?' The coroner shook his head. 'That name echoes down the years. What, oh my goodness, yes . . .'

'Sir John, not now.' Athelstan shook his head. 'Let us concentrate. It would seem an assassin swept through here late last evening.'

'And one who loves gold.' Cranston plucked at Athelstan's sleeve and led him up across the sanctuary into the sacristy; a long chamber with a table, chairs, stools, aumbries and a stack of shelves screwed to the wall. Athelstan immediately glimpsed the trap door thrown back and the heavy, iron-bound coffer with its weighted base standing to the right of this. The concave lid of the arca had been tipped back and, as he knelt beside it, Athelstan noticed the two intricate but quite distinctive locks.

'This must have held a treasure,' Athelstan murmured. 'That's why it was fashioned like this, with special locks fitted. One of the keys to open it still hangs around that dead priest's neck, yes? And the other?'

'Around the fat, thick-skinned throat of the Flesher, Simon Makepeace. I believe he is now in council with Fitzalan at my Lord of Arundel's Thameside mansion. He will arrive here in a truly murderous rage. I will explain that later, but finally . . .'

Corbett led Athelstan back down the nave through the shattered devil's door and out into the cemetery. They followed the path round to the back of the church and the cracked, worn steps leading down into the crypt, its heavy double doors flung back. Two of Flaxwith's bailiffs stood guard over four pathetic bundles of bones, each partially covered with a shabby canvas corpse cloth. Cranston and Athelstan went gingerly down the chipped, moss-strewn steps. At Cranston's insistence, the corpse sheets were removed to reveal four skeletons; shards of dry skin still clung to the bones, tufts of hair to the skull. Cranston knelt down and turned all four over so Athelstan could see the horrid blow to the back of each head.

'From the little I know,' Cranston squinted up at Athelstan, 'these humble bones belong, in God's eyes, to four young women. Each of them was killed by a hatchet blow to the back of the head.' He pulled a face. 'Now that's the mark of the Flesher. He loves to kill with a cleaver to the face, which splits the head from brow to chin or,' he waved a hand, 'a clean cut to the back of the head, hence his name.'

'And you think this is the Flesher's handiwork?'

'Probably.'

'And these remains are whores, prostitutes, street workers?'

'Yes, Brother, happy girls from the stews and brothels along the Thames.'

'And how were they discovered?'

Cranston pointed towards the dark, yawning crypt. From where he stood, the friar could glimpse the high fence or palisade, and one mound after another of skulls and bones lying beyond it.

'Flaxwith came down here more out of curiosity than anything else. Of course Samson followed. Now that dog may have the ugliest face, but he also has the most tender nose. Flaxwith's dog can sniff out dead human flesh better than anything which crawls or flies beneath God's blue sky. Samson trotted round the outside of that palisade till he reached the gate, where he paused, barking and pawing at the wood. Flaxwith let him in and Samson began to nose amongst the remains just inside. Flaxwith brought a lantern and glimpsed these four skeletons piled close together.' Cranston sighed, blowing his cheeks out. 'I suspect there are more remains like this in both the crypt and that God-forsaken cemetery. From the little I know, apart from his mother, the Flesher truly hated women, and loved nothing better than to become violent with them.'

Athelstan murmured a prayer and sketched a blessing above the skeletons. 'And there is no other indication of who they were or where they came from? Nothing else was found?'

'Brother, you see what Flaxwith did and, before you ask, if our priest or his sexton knew about this?' Cranston shrugged. 'Flaxwith received a very vague answer; apparently this crypt is never locked or bolted. There is only one entrance to it through the cemetery. Let's face it, Brother, there are no pockets in a shroud; nothing of value on a corpse, certainly not in St Benet's. So why should anyone enter a crypt? Most people would avoid such places as they would a leper house.'

'Unless they want to hide the effects of their heinous sin of murder.'

Athelstan gazed down at the skeletons. 'None of these have been in the soil for long. There's no mark or tinge of the grave, the mud and clay which become part of the bone. To a certain extent they are still white and gleaming. Sir John, I suspect these four have not been buried for long. They may have been dumped in some pit and, once the flesh was corrupted, dragged out and thrown in here . . .'

PART TWO

Hemp office (**Old English**): the condemned cell

B rother Philippe, keeper and master of the King's own hospital of St Bartholomew's, stood on the execution platform beneath the soaring gibbets known as 'The Elms' overlooking the great, open meadow of what was once known as 'Smooth Field', the great meeting place of the city. Above him, the nooses of the gallows hung like deadly black necklaces against the sky. Brother Philippe had seen so many die here; as today, he had been called as a witness, as well as to offer the Sacrament, before the condemned man was turned off.

Brother Philippe hated execution day. He stared out over the crowd, most of whom had come to watch another human being die. All the weird and the wonderful from London's underworld, be it Whitefriars, Hell's buttery, the Devil's Kitchen, or any of the other dens of despair which housed the lawless tribes of London's Hades. Brother Philippe's eyesight was not as good as he might wish, but he glimpsed the shifting sea of colour and pinched his nostrils at the myriad of smells wafting around him: smoke, fire, burning meat, cheap perfume, heavy sweat and the foul smells of the midden heaps. The Benedictine gripped his psalter more tightly as the sheriff's men abruptly shouted, 'Turn. Turn the ladder.' The executioner, the Hangman of Rochester, a member of Athelstan's parish at St Erconwald's, gripped the gibbet ladder but then paused. The hangman stared up at Roslin, the notorious robber indicted for numerous felonies and crimes perpetrated the length and breadth of the city. Brother Philippe followed the hangman's gaze.

Poor Roslin, a housebreaker who, by his own admission, had chosen to burgle – or at least try to – a merchant friendly to the Flesher. Roslin had been captured as he came out of the window of Goldsmith Blundel's house, and his booty seized which, for a fee, was returned to its owner. The Flesher's men had handed Roslin over to the sheriffs in order to claim the reward, as well as teach Roslin and everyone else that no robberies took place without the express permission of Master Makepeace. Brother Philippe chewed on his lip. He really must have words with Blundel about this matter; after all, Brother Philippe had recently done business with that powerful London merchant.

A thunderous roar from the crowd startled the physician from his reverie. The condemned man had now reached the top of the ladder, where he had been bound hand and foot, the noose fitted expertly around his neck. However, Roslin seemed determined to postpone his death for as long as possible, by delivering a homily on his nefarious career as one of the city's most notorious housebreakers. Once again, Brother Philippe stared out over the crowd. He was certain he glimpsed the fiery red hair of Tiptoft, Cranston's courier. The crowd shifted and surged slightly forward. Crucifixes were held up high in the air by the different guilds of those who flocked to The Elms on execution day to offer consolation to the condemned, their family and friends. Roslin had cheekily confessed he had neither friends nor family, but the Guild of the Hanged and the Society of the Good Thief still gathered at the foot of the scaffold to sing songs of mourning and the psalms for the dead. Ale carriers, water-bearers and beer boys pushed their handcarts and shouted for business. Itinerant cooks carted their moveable stoves, grills and braziers, which gave off a pungent smoke, turning the air sickly with the rancid stench of the ancient meats being cooked. Hot-pot girls pushed their way through, with platters of steaming food from the many cook shops which fringed the open expanse of Smithfield. Pleasant faced and smiling, they tried to outbid the itinerant cooks, both with the freshness of their own appearance and the food they were serving. Pimps, sharp-eyed for any profit, led their string of whores for any buyer desperate enough to purchase the raddled bodies of these scarlet-clad prostitutes. Naps, foists, pick-purses and cunning men swarmed through the crowd, eager for any mischief and easy profit. Knights on their way to the tournament ground on the far side of Smithfield passed by in a blaze of heraldic colour and clash of armour, their great destriers snorting noisily as they pawed the ground.

'That's it, that's it. Turn him off!' the sheriff's man bawled. The Hangman of Rochester, eyes fixed on the prisoner, listened to the quickening beat of the tambour players on the steps of the execution platform. A hunting horn brayed and the hangman swiftly turned the ladder. Roslin fell like a stone until the noose abruptly tightened and a loud crack heralded the felon's neck had been broken. Immediately the mob which had come to witness the hanging broke up: some streaming back towards the stalls, piggeries or cattle pens; others eager to shelter and drink in the many ale booths, taverns and hostelries around the great field. A few of those who regarded the effects of a hanged man, be it his clothes or his flesh, as containing powerful properties, tried to climb on to the scaffold. They had drawn knives, blades and razors, and held these at the ready to slice a finger, cut some hair, shred a piece of clothing or peel a portion of the dead man's skin. The sheriff's men fought these off but they still persisted. The sorcerers, warlocks and wizards in their shabby black robes, dusty wigs framing faces ghastly-white with black kohl rings around their eyes, were determined to secure their macabre spoils. They fought and jostled the sheriff's men.

Brother Philippe decided he'd done enough. After all, he was not supposed to be chaplain at this execution. The nominated priest was Parson Reynaud of St Benet's Woodwharf, but he had died in the most mysterious circumstances, so Brother Philippe had been summoned to assist. The affray on the execution platform was growing worse, so Brother Philippe hurriedly blessed the hanging corpse now twisting and creaking at the end of the rope. He felt his elbow grasped, turned and smiled at the Hangman of Rochester.

'Come on, Brother,' the hangman urged. 'The sheriff's men are determined not to lose this fight. They are under strict instructions to gibbet Roslin's corpse on the approaches to London Bridge. The dead man incurred the wrath of the great ones of this city. I understand Parson Reynaud was to deliver Roslin the harshest of homilies.'

Brother Philippe nodded understandingly. The hangman gently insisted on escorting him off the scaffold; as he did so, the executioner explained how the physician must not be worried about Roslin, who was now past all caring, whilst the felon's death had been mercifully swift. The hangman added how he always arranged the rope and ladder so the condemned had their necks snapped in a few breaths rather than be slowly strangled. Brother Philippe, of course, had heard all of this before. The executioner's expertise at quickly despatching London's criminals to God's high court was now legendary. Indeed, the same could be said for the hangman's skill as a painter; his frescoes and wall paintings decorated St Erconwald's, as well as other churches in Southwark and beyond.

Out of the corner of his eye, Brother Philippe closely studied this eerie-looking individual, who had once been a parish anchorite. The hangman was garbed completely in black, which only emphasised his snow-white face, deep-set eyes and the long, corn-coloured hair falling down to his shoulders. Lost in thought about the sheer strangeness of his fellow men, Brother Philippe followed the hangman from the gallows site. They clasped hands and the physician watched the executioner stride back to claim Roslin's corpse. The Benedictine then turned towards the cavernous entrance of St Bartholomew's, only to find his way blocked by four men. Three of these were rifflers dressed in leather jerkins, woollen hose and stout marching boots. They looked unkempt, with long, tangled hair, bushy beards and moustaches. They sported an escutcheon on their right shoulder, which displayed a tree in full bloom; the branches were a deep brown, the leaves a bright, glossy green. They stood aggressively, thumbs thrust into the shabby warbelts fastened around their waists. Brother Philippe, refusing to be cowed, peered more closely at the insignia.

'Is that an elm tree?' he questioned. 'They once used the elms here in Smithfield to hang felons.'

'It's an oak tree.' The fourth person, dressed in the costly robes of a lawyer, stepped in between the physician and the rifflers.

'And you must be these gentlemen's legal representative?' Brother Philippe murmured.

'In a sense, yes. These are the Sycamores – retainers, household servants and henchmen of my master Simon Makepeace, owner of the Devil's Oak, a magnificent hostelry in Queenhithe ward with a splendid view over the river.'

'You can also get a splendid view of Smithfield from the top of the execution ladder.'

'Ah yes, Master Roslin.'

'And you are?'

'Josiah Copping. Lawyer, attorney and legal adviser to Master Makepeace.'

Brother Philippe stared at this little mouse of a man with his scrawny hair, worried black eyes, snub nose and thin, disapproving mouth. The lawyer beat his fingers impatiently against his stomach, whilst his companions showed their impatience by tugging at warbelts and shuffling their boots, looking about, as if fascinated by the colourful stream of people hurrying across Smithfield.

'I can see you are a busy man, Master Copping. I certainly am. What do you want from me, a physician? I must say you all look fairly healthy, although you three sirs,' Brother Philippe pointed at the rifflers, 'drink too much. You are red in the face and your noses are swollen—'

'Jewels,' Copping broke in. He now lost some of his simpering pleasantry.

'Jewels?' Brother Philippe questioned.

'You took an amethyst which gleamed a deep imperial purple to Goldsmith Blundel. You exchanged it for a sum of pounds sterling—?'

'Who told you that?'

'Master Blundel.'

'He really should be more discreet, I mean as a banker.'

'Master Blundel was grateful to my master, who helped capture Roslin and found the amethyst on his person,' Copping shrugged, 'along with other precious items. Apparently Master Blundel had been closing for the day. He was distracted for a short while and Roslin, like the shadow he was, seized what was on display at the back of the shop. He tried to escape but the hue and cry were raised. Apparently my master's men had a hand in his arrest. Roslin was caught, handed over to the sheriff's comitatus, and the stolen goods, including that amethyst, were returned to their rightful owner. My master admired it and asked Goldsmith Blundel where he had obtained the amethyst. The good merchant named you.'

'Most indiscreet. I shall certainly have words with Master Blundel.'

'So you did sell it to him?'

'I best go now – and tell your dogs,' Brother Philippe pointed at the rifflers, 'that I am a Benedictine monk, a royal physician on personal terms with my Lord of Gaunt, as well as His Grace the King. Just as importantly, I am also a personal friend of Brother Athelstan and Sir John Cranston, Lord High Coroner of London.'

Copping raised a hand and snapped his fingers. The rifflers stepped aside and Brother Philippe swept on.

'Oh, Brother?'

The physician turned.

'Grenel, did Margo Grenel give the amethyst to you?'

'Why not ask her yourself?' Brother Philippe snapped and walked on.

'Tell me,' Athelstan caught Cranston by the wrist as they walked back up the sanctuary steps towards the sacristy where Flaxwith had summoned all those Cranston wished to question. 'Tell me,' Athelstan repeated, 'why I saw the Fisher of Men on his great barque making his way across the river?'

'A new craft,' Cranston half chuckled. 'The Fisher has christened it *The Leviathan*. Yes, he came to see me to report on what he hadn't found more than what he had. But more of that later.'

Cranston led Athelstan into the sacristy, where Parson Reynaud's household had gathered. Martha Ashby, the housekeeper, had brought across a jug of light ale and a platter of croutons toasted lightly and smeared with herb cream cheese. The introductions were made and Cranston sat down at the head of the table, Athelstan to his right, whilst Flaxwith closed and guarded the door. Both coroner and friar gratefully accepted the refreshments. Cranston immediately began to eat. He ignored the ale, but now and then took a generous mouthful from the miraculous wineskin hidden so expertly beneath his cloak. Athelstan half smiled as he sipped and nibbled at what had been set before him. Cranston was playing his usual game: creating a silence which would both deepen and sharpen to test the keenest wits, whilst allowing both himself and Athelstan to study those gathered to answer their questions. Athelstan nodded at Martha as she took her seat at the far end of the table. A pretty, homely woman of no more than thirty-five summers, the housekeeper was garbed in a dark brown dress clasped high at the neck. Its sleeves were unbuttoned and unrolled slightly back to reveal elegant wrists and long, fluted fingers, the nails slightly painted. Martha's thick, rich auburn hair was neatly clipped under a short, white linen veil. She wore little jewellery, apart from a ring on her right hand. An astute, highly intelligent woman, Athelstan reflected, very much like Benedicta: good looking and good natured, kindly and welcoming, but with a steely will and a keen wit.

Curate Cotes, slurping at his tankard, was neither of these. The priest looked as if he had gone to bed drunk and unwashed, only to be dragged unceremoniously from it. Sexton Spurnel, a small, thickset man, sat nervously, one hand grasping his tankard, the other combing his thick moustache and beard. A worrier, Athelstan reasoned, very unlike Cripplegate, the leader of the parish council, who exuded a quiet confidence. A prominent member of the locksmith's guild, Cripplegate sat all neat and poised, his sallow, grey-moustached face carefully composed. He ate slowly, lost in his own thoughts, though now and then he would join the desultory conversation going on around the table.

Cranston coughed as Athelstan opened his chancery satchel and laid out his writing implements.

'We should begin,' the coroner declared.

'Sir John, first,' Athelstan pointed at the curate. 'Master Cotes, you will see to the anointing and blessing of the two corpses?'

The priest, his mouth bulging with food, nodded.

'Can I remind you,' Athelstan continued, 'that no Mass, or indeed any of the sacraments can be celebrated in St Benet's until the Bishop of London has purified and re-consecrated your church?'

'It's not my church,' the curate slurred. 'It's a den of thieves.'

'Enough of that,' Cripplegate declared. 'Brother Athelstan, I've already sent a messenger to Archdeacon Tuddenham. We will cooperate fully with the bishop and all the requirements of canon law.'

'Good, good,' Cranston declared, 'and you, sir,' he pointed at the curate, 'will show me and mine every respect. This is in fact a court, and I am the King's coroner.'

'And I am a cleric, you have no right—'

'I have every right!' Cranston bellowed, bringing his ham-like fists down on to the table. 'I couldn't care if you are related to the Holy Father in Rome. Murder has been committed in your church and you will be questioned.' Cranston glowered down at the curate, who sat slumped, suitably cowed, or appearing so, at the coroner's outburst.

'You haven't changed,' Cotes whispered, 'has he, my friends?'

The silence that ensued was abrupt and deep. Athelstan straightened up and cursed his own tiredness. He wasn't truly concentrating on what was happening. He sensed there was more to these people meeting around this table, not just the murderous mystery of St Benet's, but something else. Cotes's remark was meant to provoke memories of the past. Athelstan stared around. Was there a bond between these parishioners, or some of them, and the King's coroner? Had their lives brushed before and, if so, how and when?

'Let's begin,' Cripplegate demanded.

'Good, good,' Athelstan soothed, 'let us start with the empty coffin. It once housed Mistress Isabella Makepeace, yes?'

'Mother of Simon Makepeace,' Cripplegate declared. 'A venerable lady, past her eighty-fifth summer. She resided in her own chambers at the Devil's Oak.'

'The tavern owned by her son, Simon?'

'Yes, Sir John.'

'Known to others as the Flesher?'

'I cannot speak for others.'

'So, Mistress Makepeace dies,' Athelstan pressed on, 'and she's brought here?'

'Yes,' Martha replied. 'The corpse was brought in on

Monday. I dressed it for burial in the parish death house, a bleak enough place. Parson Reynaud churched it yesterday evening.'

'And you screwed on the lid, sealing the casket?' Athelstan asked.

'Yes,' she answered, 'and Master Makepeace came to pay his last respects to his mother. He placed red roses in her coffin. He ordered me to seal it. I did so in his presence. He stood and watched me close the coffin for burial.'

'And then?'

'I took it over,' the sexton declared. 'Mistress Martha, myself, Curate Cotes and Master Cripplegate also attended the churching. We placed the coffin on a wheeled sled and pushed it across to the church to where Parson Reynaud was waiting just before the rood screen.' The sexton drew a deep breath. 'The ceremony took place. The corpse was churched and left to the angels before the high altar. We never guessed what was going to happen.'

Athelstan nodded understandingly, even as he recalled one of Cranston's sayings: 'People's lives are like onions. You peel the top layer and realise the thickness and multitude of the skins beneath.' Athelstan was intent on peeling this particular onion to its very core. He stared at Martha, her pretty, slightly rosy face, the full parted lips and the merry, dancing eyes. Yes, Athelstan thought, it was time to peel this onion a little further.

'Mistress Martha?'

'Brother?' Her smile widened.

'You live in the priest's house?'

'Yes.' Her smile faded. 'My own room, a bedchamber. Seventeen years ago, Parson Reynaud hired me. We sealed an indenture kept in the parish archives. I looked after him and his house. I also, when I could, helped out in the parish; that's what I did.' She added meaningfully, 'Nothing else.'

'Though the good parson did his best to widen your duties,' the curate jibed. 'You were most sought after.'

'By you and him,' she replied coolly. 'But I put him in his place – and remember, Sir Priest, I have had to do the same with you, Curate Cotes. But, there again, you were so deep in your cups, you probably cannot remember such occasions . . .'

Cotes coloured and stared down at the tabletop. Athelstan glanced quickly at the others, but they all hid behind a mask of studious indifference.

'Mistress,' Cranston smiled at this very pretty but strong-willed woman, 'we thank you for your honesty and directness. What are your antecedents? How did you—'

'I can answer that,' Cripplegate declared.

'As can I.'

Athelstan whirled round and stared at the figure who had quietly opened the sacristy door. Flaxwith had been standing to one side and now blocked the visitor on the threshold. Athelstan rose and glimpsed the shadowy shapes behind their visitor.

'I am sure you can.' Cranston heaved himself up and, accompanied by Athelstan, gestured at Flaxwith to stand aside as he confronted these new arrivals.

'You should announce yourselves,' Cranston smiled. 'After all, you are the bell clerk, aren't you?' He jabbed a finger at the intruder. 'I know who you are. I certainly recognise the mouse-like features of Josiah Copping, bell clerk of this parish, clerk and legal advisor to Master Simon Makepeace, owner of the Devil's Oak. A true wolf in sheep's clothing, aren't you, Josiah, and where were you yesterday evening?' Copping, standing on tiptoe, peered over Cranston's shoulder at the others gathered around the sacristy table.

'I asked you a question.' Cranston advanced threateningly.

'I was in my house in Tumbleweed Lane,' Copping answered hastily. 'I . . . we have heard the dreadful news. My master is busy at Lord Arundel's mansion which lies—'

'I know London,' Cranston barked.

'I represent Mater Simon's interests. I need to be present at this meeting. After all, my lord, the Earl of Arundel, has the right—'

'Of advowson.' Athelstan spoke up. 'The right to appoint the priest and curate to this church?'

Copping looked Athelstan up and down. 'Ah, you must be the Dominican?'

'Yes, I must be.'

'You can join the meeting.' Cranston grabbed Copping by the front of his expensive robe and almost pulled him into the sacristy. 'You, gentlemen,' Cranston bellowed at the rifflers, their hands falling to their warbelts, 'can take your hands away from your swords. You can stay outside in the nave and say some prayers – it will do you all the world of good. And don't steal anything, or I will report you to the Flesher, as well as hang you on the gates to London Bridge.' Cranston slammed the door in their faces and pushed Copping towards the table. The lawyer hurriedly squeezed on to the bench beside the sexton.

'You were saying,' Cranston declared, 'or both of you were, about Mistress Martha's appointment here?'

'Oh, for the love of God,' the housekeeper exclaimed, 'I am a widow! My husband died when I was very young. He was a member of Nathaniel Cripplegate's Guild. He was a locksmith as well as a very distant relative to Parson Reynaud.' She added warningly, 'I kept house for the priest and that was all.'

'And last night,' Athelstan demanded, 'what exactly happened?'

'Mistress Makepeace's corpse was churched,' Curate Cotes declared, trying to assert himself. 'Compline was sung by myself and Parson Reynaud.'

'You gabbled through it,' Martha retorted, 'as you always do.'

'I believe the friar was talking to me.'

'I am eager to talk to anyone who will tell us the truth,' Athelstan smiled. 'But Martha, you tell us.'

'Compline was sung, Parson Reynaud returned to the house where Daventry was waiting. They were closeted in Parson's chancery chamber. Parson Reynaud then returned to the church and the chantry chapel of St John to hear the confessions of any parishioners who wanted to be shrived.'

'And you?'

'Brother, I retired to my bed.'

'And Curate Cotes?' Athelstan turned to the priest, who sat slumped against the table.

'I decided to visit certain parishioners.' The curate ignored the muffled laughter from the sexton as well as Cripplegate's sly smile. 'Afterwards I retired to the Devil's Oak to have something to eat and drink. I became tired, so I slept there,' he shrugged, 'until this morning.'

Athelstan was about to glance away when he caught the curate's change of expression, flitting and swift as a heartbeat, a knowing, clever look at Sir John. But then, as if the mask had slipped, the curate assumed the look of a born toper, still mawmsey with drink. Cranston now sat head down, slouched as if on the verge of one his brief naps, when he abruptly glanced up. 'The coffin, the old woman's coffin – it definitely held a corpse?'

'Of course,' Spurnel scoffed. 'I personally witnessed the casket lid being secured. I and the others lifted the coffin and pushed it on a sled from the death house to the church.' Others murmured their agreement to this.

Cranston got to his feet. He took a slurp from his miraculous wineskin and began to pace up and down the sacristy, forcing his audience to turn and watch him.

'So, you were all in your beds last night?' A chorus of agreement answered his question. 'Very good,' Cranston paused, 'and that includes you, Master Copping?'

'Yes, as I have said, I was indoors and remained there.'

'Mistress Martha, you had retired to your bed. You knew Parson Reynaud and Daventry had gone down to the church?'

'Only that the parson had. I really had no idea where Daventry was and, to be perfectly honest, I didn't really care.'

'Quite so, quite so,' Cranston agreed. 'But this morning, Mistress, you rose and found Parson Reynaud not in the house?'

'Not an exceptional situation,' she retorted. 'Sometimes Parson Reynaud went visiting. Sometimes,' she waved a hand airily, 'he drank and slept in the church.'

'What was exceptional,' the sexton interposed, 'was what happened this morning – usually a door was left open and people inside will respond to knocking and shouting. Today was different. I, Master Cripplegate and Martha found all four doors locked and bolted.'

'Explain,' Athelstan demanded.

'I tried the postern door at the front, not to mention the main door, then the corpse door. I met Martha at the devil's door. I could see that all four had their keys in the locks when I tried to insert mine. All four were also bolted, which is exactly the situation I found when we broke in this morning.'

'Broke in?'

'Three of the doors are solid oak. The devil's door is more recent and made of panelling – that's the door Martha had tried. She has a key to it.'

'Parson Reynaud,' Martha declared, 'insisted I have a copy of a key to one of the church doors. I use it occasionally. This morning was different. I could not insert the key whilst the door seemed tightly bolted from within.'

'We eventually decided to break the panelling,' the sexton continued, 'smash our way through so we could turn the lock as well as draw the bolts at top and bottom.' Spurnel coughed to clear his throat. 'Once we were in the church, we were confronted with one abomination after the other. The Parson and Daventry murdered. The coffin violated. The corpse gone and the arca robbed.' Spurnel gestured at the empty chest, still standing forlornly close to small barrels of altar wine.

'But you checked all the doors, once you were in?'

'Each and every one, including the devil's door, which we forced. Brother, I swear, every single door was bolted both top and bottom, the key turned fully in the lock.'

'So you would have us believe,' Athelstan declared.

'Brother,' Master Copping retorted, 'we are not here to make you believe anything. We are,' he held a hand up, 'as mystified as you are.'

'So,' Cranston intervened, retaking his seat, 'each door has two keys, no more?'

'Yes,' the sexton replied. 'Parson Reynaud held one set, I the other. Parson Reynaud always locked the church at night; you will find the keys on him.'

Cranston nodded at Flaxwith, who hurried out. He returned with a ring of keys, which he handed to the coroner, who dangled it in front of the sexton.

'Are they all in order?'

Spurnel took the ring, studied it closely, then passed it to Cripplegate for examination.

'Everything is in order,' the leader of the parish council murmured.

'Hand them to me,' the curate murmured. 'Can I keep them?'

'No, you can't,' Cranston snapped, and grabbed them back. He turned to Flaxwith. 'Where were they?'

'Deep in the pocket of Parson Reynaud's robe, Sir John.'

'Continue!' the coroner ordered.

'Whoever,' the sexton declared crossly, 'locked all four doors in the evening, I, as sexton, would open the church the next morning. Today, however, proved to be a real mystery.'

'Then let's define this mystery,' Athelstan retorted. 'We have an ancient church, its windows are high and narrow, and it has no other entrance or secret passageway, yes?'

'Brother,' the sexton shook his head, 'I would go on oath, no such secret tunnel or passageway runs in or out of our church.' The others agreed, shaking their heads in denial at such a possibility.

'And so this mystery becomes even more tangled. We have Parson Reynaud, an old priest, but wiry and strong.'

'Brother Athelstan, I agree,' Curate Cotes declared, smirking behind his hand. 'He was certainly active enough, as a number of the young ladies will attest.'

'He was an old soldier,' Cripplegate added. 'He served in the King's array.'

'And he wasn't alone in this church?' Athelstan declared. 'Daventry was an associate; either he came in with him or was close by. Both the parson and Daventry were stabbed cruelly to the heart. It must have been a swift cut, a sudden slash, the work of a professional assassin. What makes it more curious is there isn't any sign of any resistance or trace of a struggle? You would all agree with that? Good.' Athelstan nodded at their assent. 'Their killer, and I assume it is the same person, then opens the arca, the great money chest, and removes . . .' Athelstan paused and gestured at the chest. 'How much was in that arca?'

Silence greeted his question. Cripplegate and his companions stared stonily down the table.

'We asked a question,' Cranston declared quietly.

'My master,' Copping coughed, 'Master Simon kept his – or some of his – treasure here. He thought it would be safe in the arca of a sacred place, especially where the chest had two distinctive locks, he holding one key, Parson Reynaud the other. You must have seen it. The key is still on a chain around his neck—'

'How much?' Cranston barked. 'In God's name, how much to the nearest penny?'

'In gold and silver coin,' Copping whispered, 'about five thousand pounds sterling, perhaps even more.'

'A king's ransom!' Cranston exclaimed, whistling beneath his breath.

'And Master Simon now knows this has been stolen?' Athelstan asked.

'As he does about the death of the parson and Daventry,' Copping declared. 'You can imagine how angry he is. At the moment, he does business with Lord Arundel, but he and his henchmen will be here soon enough.'

'So,' Cranston pressed on taking a generous gulp from the miraculous wineskin, 'it would look as if the same person killed two able-bodied men without any trace of resistance or mark of violence. One of these certainly, Daventry being a man of war, skilled in arms. Both men would be alert; there is no trace of either being the victim of some sleeping potion or too much wine?'

'That's true,' Spurnel spoke up. 'As I left the church last evening, I passed both going in there. They seemed to be in good spirits.'

'They went in together?'

'Yes, Brother, nothing significant. Daventry was as we found him. I thought he would check on the arca then leave, whilst Parson Reynaud sat in the mercy chair to hear and shrive some penitent.'

'And did anyone come?'

'I saw no one,' Martha replied, 'but there again, I didn't see the parson or Daventry walk in together. I retired early to bed, as I believe everyone else did.' She glanced mischievously at the curate. 'Wherever that bed might be.'

'Very well.' Athelstan folded back the sleeves of his gown, a gesture to cover his complete confusion about what he was being told. He could detect nothing wrong, no loose thread to pull.

'All of you went your separate ways,' Athelstan murmured, 'and darkness descended. I cannot prove this, but I suspect Parson Reynaud and Daventry were murdered swiftly, one after the other. Once both had been killed, the assassin turned on the arca, robbed it, opened the coffin and plucked out that poor woman's corpse. But how he moved both plunder and cadaver is a mystery.' Athelstan pushed away his writing tray on the table before him. 'That must have been difficult. Two ungainly weights. A corpse and heavy sacks of coin. You would agree?'

'Of course,' Copping declared, 'it must have happened like that.'

'Heavy sacks of coin,' Athelstan repeated. 'Queenhithe at the dead of night is not the place to be carrying clinking bags which would have echoed like bells to the wolfsheads who swarm here. And, of course,' Athelstan continued, 'there is always the danger of being seen or being stopped. Oh yes, a true mystery.' He got up and, with Cranston's help, lifted the arca on to the table. Athelstan sketched a quick blessing in the air. 'My apologies please, but I shall return.'

Athelstan left the sacristy and hastened to where Parson Reynaud's corpse lay slumped in the mercy seat. He hurriedly found the silver chain around the dead man's cold, fat-creased neck and undid the clasp to pull off the key. Once back in the sacristy, Athelstan tried the key on one lock but it did not fit, though it slid easily enough into the second. Athelstan turned it and watched the lock spring up, the heavy, sharpened steel bolt, which would fasten deep into the tight groove carved into the edge of the coffer lid. Athelstan examined both locks carefully. 'The work of a true craftsman,' he murmured. 'Fashioned out of the finest steel with a strong spring, the bolt wedges into the groove to keep the heavy lid securely fastened to the body of the coffer. The wood is of the sturdiest oak and the entire arca is bound by bands of steel.' He smiled and pointed at Cripplegate. 'Your work, sir?'

'No, but I wish it was.' The locksmith rose, leaned over and stroked the polished lid. 'Believe me, Brother, this arca was specially fashioned. The locks are definitely the work of a master craftsman and, of course, there are those in London.' Cripplegate smiled thinly. 'To be honest, I envy such skill.'

'Do you recognise the work?'

'No, Brother, I don't, but skilled craftsmen can be found in other cities both here and across the Narrow Seas. Indeed,' Cripplegate tapped the arca with his fingers, 'I would wager, though I cannot prove it, this arca might be the work of some Hanseatic craftsman.'

'How long has the arca been here?' Cranston asked, pointing at Martha.

'Sir John, I don't know. Certainly as long as I have been.'

'I would agree,' Spurnel added. 'The arca has been here for years. I would regard it as part of the church.'

Athelstan chewed the corner of his lip as he stared at the treasure chest. He had heard of similar practices, where the powerful merchants preferred to deposit their monies away from prying eyes, yet still keep it immediately available. Goldsmiths could be over-inquisitive about the source of monies, as well as dishonest, whilst foreign bankers such as the Bardi faced the ever-present danger of their goods being seized by the Crown.

'Mystery within mystery within mystery,' he whispered.

'Pardon Brother?'

'Well, it's obvious, Master Copping. Murder, theft, the opening of the arca without using the keys specially fashioned for its lock. One key was found on the person of the dead Reynaud, but the other is in the firm grasp of Master Makepeace, yes?'

'It certainly is.'

'Yet that arca was robbed, that coffin pillaged, but the felon responsible left this church with all its doors bolted and locked from the inside, as if he could walk through solid stone carrying his gruesome trophy and ill-gotten gains. Sir John, we need to search even further as well as ask more questions.'

The coroner rose and pointed at the sexton. 'Why are there skeletons in the crypt; fresh bones with blows, clefts to the back of their skulls?'

Cranston's words immediately created a watchful silence.

'My Lord High Coroner is correct.' Athelstan brushed his robe. 'I accept there are cemeteries all over London, charnel houses and crypts full of bones. Nevertheless, the remains we found here are grouped together. I believe they were first buried in the cemetery for a short while, then tossed into the crypt without a by-your-leave?'

'Sir John, Brother Athelstan,' Spurnel gabbled springing to his feet, 'as my colleagues here will attest, the cemetery of St Benet's is a sprawling wastelend . . .'

'Look,' Cripplegate spread his hands, 'our cemetery is unbounded and stretches around the church like a great meadow.'

'It's a wild place,' the sexton blurted out, 'more of a wasteland than anything else.' Athelstan could see the sexton was deeply agitated. Cranston had certainly touched a rawness in the man's soul. 'Anyone can bring a corpse here,' the sexton continued. 'The crypt lies open; you could hide a dead body there, though of course the stink might alert you. However, Sir John, Brother Athelstan, I cannot mount a constant guard over our cemetery. Can you?' He pointed dramatically at the friar. 'Do you know, Brother, who lies buried in your cemetery?'

Cranston glanced at Athelstan, who winked back. The sexton was correct; even St Erconwald's was not free from what happened in the graveyards of many London churches – rambling, desolate places used by every kind of mischief-maker. Wizards, warlocks and witches would gather to dance beneath the midnight moon. They would light their fires and even plunder graves for human remains to use in their filthy rituals. Thieves would conceal stolen goods, and assassins the occasional corpse – the victim of a hapless accident, suicide, or murder. There were also those who simply wanted to get rid of their dead without paying their dues to God, man or the city. Yet this was different. Athelstan was building a picture of a truly wicked Parson Reynaud, a man who used religion as a cover for his own iniquity; a villain hand in glove with a leading wolfshead and riffler.

Athelstan glanced quickly around, but what role did these

people play? Were they Parson Reynaud's accomplices or his victims? Had one of them, or all, turned on their wicked parish priest and carried out justice, or at least what they regarded as justice?

Benedicta stood in the musty cellar beneath Margo's cottage and stared around the now empty chamber. Both corpses had been secretly removed, under Mauger's strict supervision, to the parish death house. Few as possible would know of the macabre scene they had stumbled upon here.

'Only God knows the secret ways of the human heart.' Benedicta repeated one of Athelstan's favourite aphorisms. She sat down on one of the chairs Margo had so carefully placed around the battered table. Benedicta smoothed this with her hand. According to Margo's will, this table and all the remaining moveables would be left to the parish. Benedicta wondered what truly happened here, still surprised at how this quiet, reserved, lonely parishioner had harboured such a secret. Margo had kept to herself, taking on the duty of corpse dresser, preparing cadavers to be churched and blessed in St Erconwald's and other parishes. In return Margo had received the coffin fees. She also worked as a seamstress but, apart from that, little else. People had mentioned how her husband and son had been excellent archers, master bowmen, but very little was known about them. The widow woman stared around. Margo seemed to have given most of her possessions away before moving across to St Bartholomew's Hospital about eight weeks ago.

'Yes, that's it,' Benedicta murmured to herself. She recalled Margo just before she left for the city; she was undoubtedly very ill: thin, even emaciated. Margo had confided to Benedicta how the humours in her belly had turned malignant and she could not stop the flow of blood or escape the constant pain. Brother Athelstan had furnished her with letters to Philippe, keeper of the hospital. On one occasion the friar had crossed to visit his ailing parishioner, but returned saying that Margo had been put into a deep sleep with the assistance of a powerful opiate. A week later, Benedicta had gone across to visit the sick woman. She found Margo sitting up in bed but very weak and delirious, babbling about the tales of Arthur and the magic of the Round Table and the treasures to be found there. Brother Philippe had confided to Benedicta that Margo would die within a week and, when she did, Watkin and Pike crossed the Thames to collect her corpse. Margo was brought back to St Erconwald's to be churched and blessed. The requiem had been celebrated, followed by swift burial in God's Acre. The poor woman's will, lodged in the parish chest, had left little of monetary value but, as Athelstan had said, 'We are all born without pockets and we go to God without pockets.' He added that for people like Margo, that was not difficult. She had lived without any real wealth. Nevertheless, Benedicta recalled Athelstan's surprise when he discovered how Margo had been able to afford costly care, physic and sustenance at St Bartholomew's.

Benedicta heard a sound from upstairs. 'Mauger!' she murmured, getting to her feet. She climbed the cellar steps, then stopped, heart in mouth, and stared at the three masked strangers standing between her and the cottage door. They wore hoods that masked their entire heads and faces, with slits for eyes, nose and mouth. They were garbed in dirty leather jerkins, patched hose and worn boots, but their warbelts were well furnished with sword, throwing knife and dirk. One of them carried an arbalest, primed and ready, whilst his two comrades wielded nail-studded maces.

'What do you want?' Benedicta gasped.

'Apparently the same as you. You are here to search, aren't you?' The man's voice was low and guttural. The crossbow came up, its jagged, pointed barb close to Benedicta's face.

'I am a friend of the deceased,' Benedicta replied sharply. 'I am looking after the few paltry items she has bequeathed to our parish, not to mention the sale of this cottage which, standing as close as it does to the Southwark bath-houses and stews, will not amount to much.' Benedicta's clipped, sharp tone made the riffler lower his crossbow.

'Who are you?' he demanded.

'More to the point,' Benedicta retorted, 'who are you? What right do you have to be here visored and hooded? What are you looking for?' Benedicta wiped clammy hands on her gown and deliberately stepped forward to confront these mysterious, sinister visitors. 'Who are you?' she repeated. 'This is my friend's cottage, now recently dead.'

'The jewels. The jewels, the precious stones,' the man rasped.

'What on earth . . .?'

'Toothsome, she is.' One of the rifflers stepped forward and put a hand out to claw Benedicta's breast. 'She'd fetch a good price amongst the ships.' The man's hand fell away as a crossbow bolt whirred through the air and smacked into the wall behind Benedicta. The wolfsheads turned. Mauger, Watkin and Pike pushed themselves into the room; each was armed with a crossbow. Watkin and Pike held theirs up as Mauger primed his with a fresh bolt.

'You should leave,' Mauger threatened.

'You shall leave,' Watkin echoed. 'And you shall stay away from our cemetery and our priest's house.' He loosed the lever on his crossbow and another barbed bolt whirled dangerously close to the intruders' heads.

'We'll leave,' the leading riffler rasped. 'But no more bolts or threats.'

'Agreed.' Mauger and his companions stood aside as the intruders swept by them in a swirl of sweaty cloaks and rasping, harsh breath.

'In God's name!' Benedicta leaned against a wall and dabbed a perfumed rag at her face and neck. 'By the Mass,' she breathed, 'what was all that about?'

'You'd best come.' Mauger grasped her gently by the arm. 'Mistress, I am sorry for your distress, but there is more. You must come.'

Mauger and his companions would say nothing more, so Benedicta followed them out into the street along the narrow, twisting coffin paths towards St Erconwald's. Benedicta, still not recovered from the shock of being threatened and abused, felt as if she was in a dream. Her mood deepened as she caught glimpses of the dark people who lurked deep in the shadows of the God-forsaken rotting houses she passed. A young girl, wearing a jester's mask, pulled a baby in its cot on a makeshift sledge. She did this with one hand whilst holding the leash of a three-legged dog that hopped along beside her. Beggars, faces round and white as the moon, screeched for alms, skeletal arms pushed out like the claws of a bird. Whores and their pimps touted for business. A gust of wind carried all the filthy stenches, even as the foul air was riven with screams, yells and curses and the strident crying of children.

Benedicta and her companions kept close, crossbows primed. They only relaxed once they broke free of the warren and entered the broader lanes leading down to the high-towered parish church. They reached the cemetery wall and went through the carved lychgate into the graveyard. Godbless was there, with Thaddeus standing patiently beside him. The beggar man had left his makeshift cottage and decided to cook a meal amongst the wild, high grass, warming a pannikin of goat's cheese.

'They have been here,' Godbless wailed. 'Demons from Hell. Three of them. Lucifer's captains. All masked and hooded, each living in one of Hell's blazing flames. They have dug the earth and harrowed the dead. They've crept across God's Acre,' he moaned, 'they were most violent. They were followed by the bagpipers of Hell, the fiddlers of the Underworld and Satan's own contortionists.'

'Mad as a March hare,' Mauger murmured. 'Come on, ignore him.'

Benedicta pressed the beggar man's hand and left him wailing. They hurried along the winding coffin path which cut across God's Acre to where Margo had been buried: her grave had been truly desecrated, the fresh soil clawed out as if dug by some beast, which had also plucked the coffin from its resting place. The lid had been wrenched off. Margo's thin corpse sprawled indecently, its linen shroud ripped to shreds.

'The same wolfsheads who attacked me,' Benedicta whispered, trying to curb the clammy fear which, despite the late autumn sunshine, chilled her body in a damp sweat. 'Who?' She turned to Mauger. 'Who would desecrate a poor woman's grave, abuse her corpse and ransack her pathetic belongings?'

'And if that's not bad enough.' The bell clerk plucked at Benedicta's sleeve, then told Pike and Watkin to gather Margo's corpse for reburial before leading the widow woman up out of the cemetery to the priest's house. Benedicta glimpsed Crispin the carpenter, busy repairing the door which Benedicta had closed and locked earlier that day. The door had been wrenched off its thick leather hinges. Inside, everything had been overturned and emptied: coffers, caskets and panniers ripped open, the bedloft violently ransacked, Athelstan's thin straw mattress slit and emptied. Benedicta's anger welled up so swiftly and strongly it forced tears to her eyes, as she gazed around this usually serene place that housed a man she deeply loved.

'I'll see those villains hang,' Benedicta exclaimed. 'But that will have to wait. Mauger, summon the entire parish council. Everything must be put right before our little friar returns . . .'

Athelstan was busy along the nave of St Benet's Woodwharf. The Dominican had seized a moment to inform the coroner about what he had discovered in Margo's cottage. Strangely enough, Sir John just looked surprised and whispered as if to himself, 'So that's what happened to both of them.' He refused to elaborate, saying the very walls had ears, whilst the Grenels were part of a greater tale he had to share with Athelstan. For the moment, the coroner insisted, they should concentrate on the mysteries before them. Athelstan agreed, and insisted on examining both corpses again, the friar making precise notes on the posture, dress and death wound of each of the victims. They then moved to the empty coffin, noticing that this had not been too damaged during the sacrilegious theft. Athelstan was more puzzled by how the corpse had been removed and taken out of the church. They eventually finished their examination, and had returned to the sacristy to scrutinise the arca when they heard doors opening followed by shouts and cries and the echo of booted feet along the nave. Cranston and Athelstan hastened out to meet a group of men who had gathered around the empty coffin.

'Who, Cranston?' One of the group stepped out of the shadows, raising a mailed fist at the coroner. 'Who did this? They will regret it as they die, and that will take them days. I—'

'Master Makepeace!' Cranston took a generous slurp from the miraculous wineskin and dramatically thrust the stopper back. He then moved his cloak so that Makepeace could see his warbelt. 'No threats!' Cranston warned. 'No threats from you at all. You may be the Flesher. You can call yourself London's own champion, but to me you are just a sly wolfshead who, so far, has managed to escape the hanging he so richly deserves.'

Cranston snapped his fingers. 'You and one of your companions may approach me and my noble secretarius Brother Athelstan, Dominican friar and parish priest of—'

'Of St Erconwald's in Southwark.' The Flesher finished the sentence as he lumbered forward to confront the coroner. He stood there, swaying on the balls of his booted feet, thumbs pushed into the broad black swordbelt clasped around his bulging waist. Athelstan stared in fascination at London's most notorious gang leader. The Flesher, he thought, looked the part: he was garbed in tawdry finery, a magnificent gold and blue houppelande with a high-collared edge fringed with ivory silver thread. The Flesher's boots were of the finest Moroccan, as was the warbelt with its sheathed sword and the dagger pouches. He sported gilt-edged spurs which jingled noisily, yet there was nothing pretty or soft about the Flesher. If a man's soul showed in his face, Athelstan quietly conceded, then this gang leader was twice as fit for Hell as any sinner could be. Simon Makepeace was an ugly man, with his egg-shaped head, broken nose and protuberant ears, which looked as if they had been chewed by a pig. He had heavily veined, hanging jowls, and his short bull neck was scarred with knife cuts, as was his unshaven face beneath a thinning mop of greasy black hair. He stood, his deep-set crafty eyes studying Cranston closely. Now and then his gaze would shift to Athelstan and his face bulged in what looked like a mocking smirk.

'Just one,' Cranston declared. 'I will meet you and one of your companions. Any more and I will have you all arrested.'

The Flesher leaned closer. 'On what charge?'

'On wasting the Lord High Coroner's time. One!' The Flesher took off a mailed gauntlet and snapped his fingers at the dark shadows who had followed him across from the coffin. A man stepped into the light and Athelstan heard Cranston's sharp intake of breath. The Flesher's companion looked truly sinister: he was garbed completely in black leather, jerkin, hose and boots, which only emphasised the man's corpse-like appearance; his face was as white as snow, with sunken cheeks; his thick eyebrows and lank, long hair were as inky as soot. He had large eyes which glittered balefully at them. A fighting man, Athelstan concluded, and one ready to take on the world. He came and stood close to the Flesher, turning slightly so he glanced at Cranston out of the corner of one eye.

'Raquin!' Cranston exclaimed. 'Gideon Raquin. Origin unknown, parentage unknown, country unknown, and yet a villain I know only too well.' Cranston gestured at both the Flesher and his henchman. 'Two cheeks of the same filthy arse. How long have you been in London, Raquin?'

'Since midsummer.' Raquin's voice was harsh, sharp and guttural. The only reaction to Cranston's studied insult by both men was a shuffling of booted feet, fingers brushing the hilt of sword and dagger. They let their hands fall away as Athelstan stepped forward and sketched a blessing in the air.

'Master Makepeace,' he declared, 'for what it is worth, I am truly sorry that your mother has died. I am distraught that she has not been allowed to rest in peace. You must have learnt about the horrors which have occurred here?'

'Yes, yes I have.' The Flesher's shoulders sagged as the tension lessened. Raquin stepped back out of the light. Cranston pointed at the retainers still standing close to the coffin.

'Tell your bullyboys to stay where they are. You, sir,' he nodded at the Flesher, 'along with your shadow, may join me and my secretarius in the sacristy.'

'And how is my Lord of Arundel?' Cranston asked as he closed the door and sat down at the top of the sacristy table.

'Very well,' Raquin retorted. 'And looking forward to the next Parliament being assembled at Westminster. He has certain questions to ask my Lord of Gaunt as well as other ministers of the Crown . . .'

He broke off as the sacristy door was thrown open and

Copping came in, hurrying to sit like a lapdog beside his master, whilst Martha brought in a tray of tankards.

'Fresh ale,' she murmured. 'I thought you could slake your throats.'

'There was a time,' the Flesher retorted, 'when you'd slake your own throat, Mistress Martha.' The Flesher was all vanity, eager to show off. Athelstan glanced at the housekeeper. Beneath the bustle, the work-day wimple and head veil, Martha was a very good-looking woman. In her youth she must have plucked the strings of many a man's heart. She did not even bother to acknowledge the Flesher's salacious comment, but placed the tray on the table, filled the tankards, served them and swept out of the sacristy. She was no sooner gone than there was a rap at the door, and Cripplegate along with Curate Cotes and Sexton Spurnel crept into the sacristy.

'None of you is needed,' Cranston growled. 'And I don't remember inviting you, Master Copping, but –' he flicked a hand at a tray – 'it accounts for why Mistress Martha brought in the extra tankards.'

Athelstan nodded, and whispered to the coroner how it would be best for all concerned if they stayed, and that included Mistress Martha. Cranston agreed and despatched Spurnel to bring the housekeeper back.

Martha returned, murmuring how she was busy, pointing to the barrels of altar wine still stacked against the wall of the sacristy.

'We won't need them for a while,' she declared. 'Parson Reynaud always liked to keep them close, so it's best if they are moved to the priest's house. Strange . . .' she added, taking her seat.

'What is, Mistress?'

'Well, Brother, the thieves who broke into the arca never tried to steal anything else, be it the wine, the chalices, the cruets. Even the altar cloths would have fetched a good price.' She sighed prettily, fanning her flushed face with her hand. 'What can be done?'

'Discover who these thieves were,' Cranston retorted, before taking a generous gulp from his wineskin. He pushed the stopper back, rubbed his hands, and began a pithy description of what they had discovered at St Benet's: Parson Reynaud stabbed in the heart at the mercy pew; Daventry, Arundel's man, murdered in a similar fashion on a chair close to the main door; the corpse of Isabella cruelly filched from its coffin; the arca chest opened and all the money stolen. There was also the question of the skeletons, at least four in number, with axe blows to the backs of their skulls.

Cranston paused, hands clasped as he stared at the Flesher, but the riffler's ugly face betrayed nothing, though his vein-streaked neck seemed to bulge in fury. He reminded Athelstan of a venomous toad getting ready to spit. Raquin lifted a hand to hide the smirk on his cadaverous face, whilst Sexton Spurnel, responsible for both the charnel house and God's Acre, reddened, shuffling his boots noisily as he stared down at the table.

'It's a mystery,' he mumbled.

'What is, Master Spurnel?' Cranston smacked the flat of his hand against the table top.

'Well, it's a mystery.' The sexton lifted his head. 'I mean, Parson Reynaud wanted the cemetery cleared.'

'Why?'

'I don't know, Sir John, but you've seen God's Acre around St Benet's?'

'Yes, it must be one of the largest cemeteries in London, but you don't know why Parson Reynaud wanted to clear it?'

'No, as I've said, I tried to have words with the parson,' the sexton continued. 'Our cemetery is large and open. It's easy for people to hide a corpse there, either in the undergrowth or simply by digging a shallow grave . . .' The sexton's words petered out.

'And can you throw any light on this?' Cranston pointed at the Flesher and Raquin. The riffler leader just shrugged. 'I asked you a question,' Cranston demanded.

'We left such matters to the parson,' the Flesher growled. 'Both the cemetery and the crypt lie open. Corpses could be left there. It's nothing to do with me.'

Cranston sat back on his chair, staring at the Flesher. Athelstan was more fascinated by Raquin, who slouched, one bony hand over his mouth. He continued to stare unblinkingly

at the coroner, with a deeply hostile, hate-filled glare. Athelstan
had never met such a sinister soul and felt a great malice
emanate from the Flesher's henchman. He reminded the friar
of a sorcerer in his black garb, with his hollow cheeks and
sunken, deep eyes, glittering with a malicious glee, his
grizzled hair hanging down like a tangle either side of his
snow-white face. Raquin moved his skeletal fingers, a slow,
rippling movement, as if that long hand contained a hidden
dagger. Athelstan's unease deepened. He felt a real flare of
fear. He and Cranston were in the presence of a most malevolent and malicious enemy. Athelstan could also sense that
Cranston was disturbed by Raquin, too; indeed there seemed
to be some bond between the two men – a curdling, unresolved
enmity from the past.

'So,' Cranston tapped his fingers against the table, 'none of
us knows anything about Parson Reynaud clearing the
cemetery, or why he kept it so open, and the same is true of
the crypt?'

'It would seem so,' Raquin sneered.

'And Daventry, why was he here?' Cranston demanded.
Silence greeted his question. 'Why?' Cranston repeated
menacingly.

'We don't know,' the Flesher retorted. 'My Lord of Arundel
has the advowson to this church. Daventry was a member of
his household. My Lord of Arundel probably sent him here
on some errand or other, so you'd best ask him.' He smirked.
'I am sure he will give you a worthy answer.'

'And who might kill my Lord of Arundel's messenger?'
Athelstan demanded. 'And why?' Again, silence.

'Or steal the corpse of Isabella Makepeace?'

Apart from the Flesher's whispered curses, the assembled
company didn't even stir, except for Martha who slowly rose,
pushing the chair back, smoothing out the creases on her gown.

'Brother Athelstan,' she declared quietly, 'before God, and
I am sure I speak for my companions here at St Benet's, we
know nothing about these horrid events.' A murmur of agreement echoed her words, though the Flesher, Raquin and
Copping remained sullenly silent.

'So all is well here, yes?' Athelstan declared sarcastically.

'Outside at night the dead sleep beneath a silver, silent moon, whilst here in this so-called sacred place, nothing can explain the mysterious blasphemies confronting us?' He glared at the riffler leader, who sat so repellent and repulsive.

'And no one can resolve,' Cranston thundered, 'how the arca in this church was opened? Two keys are needed for that.' Cranston held up the one taken from Parson Reynaud's corpse. 'We have this; the other, sir,' Cranston pointed at the Flesher, 'is still in your possession, yes?' The Flesher undid the clasp of his tunic, loosened the chain around his neck and slid both chain and key down the table.

'Little use it has now,' he growled.

'Who fashioned the arca locks?' Athelstan asked.

'A craftsman amongst the Hanseatics, he is now dead. Both keys were unique, as were the locks they fitted.'

'And that key never left you?'

'Up until now, friar, never.' The Flesher rubbed the side of his face. 'I treasured it and always kept it close.'

'Not even Ingersol could get hold of that,' Raquin spoke up, grinning at Cranston. 'Whatever his name, he liked to call himself the dagger man, the Sicarius. Some dagger man!'

Athelstan was surprised at Cranston's reaction. The coroner lurched from his seat, breathing heavily, one hand on the table, the other scrabbling for his knife sheath on the warbelt hung over the back of the coroner's chair.

'Sir John?' Athelstan, worried that his friend was suffering a seizure, sprang to his feet, even as the Flesher and Raquin got to theirs, cloaks going back to reveal their warbelts. Mistress Martha screamed. Cripplegate went to comfort her. Sexton Spurnel cursed beneath his breath, Curate Cotes sat still, narrow-eyed, watching everything, whilst Copping hurried to stand behind his master and Raquin. Cranston took a deep breath, calming himself before grasping his warbelt and strapping it on. Raquin still grinned, though the Flesher was more wary, as if he sensed his henchman had provoked the coroner too far. Athelstan was truly mystified at what lay behind all this.

'You,' Cranston pointed at Raquin, 'you tallow-faced, blistered tongue rogue . . .'

'I hear you, Sir John,' Raquin lisped.

'You and your master can leave,' Cranston continued. 'I am finished for the while, but I may follow you. Makepeace, I have the authority. Perhaps I will visit the Devil's Oak before long and search that house of sin from cellar to attic. I know why you let both the graveyard and crypt lie open here at St Benet's. You kept both as your sewer to throw in and hide the victims of your wickedness. Now, I swear, one day I will see you hang. I am the King's own coroner in London and never forget that.'

The Flesher made to object; Raquin's smirk had now disappeared.

'Shut up!' Cranston shouted. 'Shut up and sit down.' Both men did so. 'For the rest,' Cranston gestured around, 'take care of the corpses.' Cranston turned, nodded at Athelstan to follow, and swept out of the sacristy into the ghostly nave with its looted coffin and stiffening corpses.

Once outside, Cranston stood on the top step, breathing in deeply and shaking his head. 'Believe me, Athelstan, when I was a boy I had a nurse, Tabitha the Terrible, or so I called her. Tabitha liked nothing better than to frighten me to the very marrow of my soul with one macabre tale after another, especially at bedtime. Never mind prayers or psalms! Tabitha was the nearest woman I have met who was a witch in the true sense of the word. Anyway, she told me a story about twin cats, all spotty with black-blue skin and weird, glaring eyes. According to Tabitha, these cats prowled the world by night, sucking the breath of infants until they were husks of bone and skin, and how both cats had a special thirst for my breath. Well, when I think of Raquin, let alone meet him, that deep, childhood fear returns. God knows why; it's just a feeling in the heart of my soul that either he will be the death of me, or I of him.'

'Pray God it's the latter,' Athelstan whispered, staring anxiously at this closest of friends, now steeped in a dark mood he had rarely witnessed before.

'Leave me for a while,' Cranston smiled thinly. 'Let me calm my thoughts.'

Athelstan sketched a blessing and walked down the nave.

He turned right out of the church into God's Acre, stretching like a great common around St Benet's. Even in the full light of day, this field of the dead did not seem like a sacred place, but a dark, dank forbidding meadow with its forlorn, crumbling monuments. The ground was broken and littered by tough brambles, sturdy weed patches and bristling patches of bush and briar. Most of the crosses and headstones were much decayed; here and there a more recent burial was marked with a cleanly cut memorial stone but, in the main, the rest stretched in long lines of soil-packed mounds. At the far end of the cemetery, a trellised fence separated that part of the burial ground from the stately, three-storeyed, black-tiled priest house, built of grey ragstone. Picking his way carefully, Athelstan went deeper into the cemetery, towards what he thought must be the mortuary, a long, red-bricked chamber with a slated roof and three lancet windows either side of the garishly painted double door. Athelstan noticed the paths wending down from the priest's residence and the death house, the coffin paths which would be difficult to thread in the dead of night; any intruder would soon find themselves in difficulties. The place had a sinister, sad atmosphere, and when night fell it must become a place of nightmares.

Athelstan walked on past the now shattered devil's door. The friar noticed how a long row of empty burial pits lined that side of the church. Nothing more than deep holes in the ground, some half-filled, the others with heaps of crumbling soil beside them. Wheelbarrows, sleds and carts stood forlornly about. Eventually Athelstan reached the steps leading down to the charnel house. The doors to the ancient crypt hung open, the skeletons Flaxwith had brought out still lying in their pathetic horror. Athelstan studied these, then glanced around. Sexton Spurnel was correct. God's Acre at St Benet's was a wasteland, its crypt and open charnel house piled high with white, crumbling skeletons, skulls, shards of bone and other relics of the mouldering dead.

'You could murder my entire parish,' Athelstan whispered to himself, 'and bury them here without trace. God knows what this hideous place secretly hides, what blasphemies it shrouds?' Athelstan returned to the front of the church, where

Cranston stood threading his ave beads through stubby fingers. He glanced at Athelstan and winked.

'Well met, monk.'

'Friar, Sir John.'

'Let us adjourn to my personal chantry chapel.'

'You mean the solar at the Lamb of God in Cheapside?'

'Of course.' Cranston tripped merrily down the steps. 'Come, my little friar, let me educate you about the Flesher and his villainous coven.'

PART THREE

Dilp (**Old English**): a trollop

They hurried through the tangle of streets leading up into the heart of the city. Cranston walked purposefully, Athelstan trailing behind, distracted by what they passed. Now and again the friar caught sight of faces, pale and haggard, peering out from doorways or windows, only swiftly to disappear in a clatter of wood or chains. Cranston deliberately took Athelstan into what he called 'a maze of utter misery', which cut through the city, separating the rank corruption of the riverside from the warm, enveloping wealth of Cheapside, Poultry and the Inns of Court. They crossed sluggish ditches choked by coarse grass and rank weeds. They passed under the shadow of rotting houses, along alleyways which reeked of the most rancorous filth, where grey-furred rats fought each other for the rancid spoils of the midden heaps and lay stalls. They entered the 'black dens', the 'labyrinth of lamentations'; here nightmares gathered and fearsome apparitions could erupt in the dark. 'Mazes of murder', as Cranston called them. 'This,' he hissed at Athelstan, 'is what the Flesher controls. Look around, friar. The surging London mob crouches hidden here with its raging bloodlust, which can swell and spill out whenever Master Makepeace wishes. If he wanted, he could unlock this labyrinth and summon out all its monsters.'

They hurried along through the runnels and alleyways on to the streets, which broadened out as they reached the wealthy heart of the city. Here stalls and booths displayed the resplendent wealth of the Middle Sea and beyond: clothes, jewellery, household goods; all manufactured by skilled craftsmen, be it leather from North Africa, cloth woven in Liège, Arras and Hainault, or a finely turned cup from Cologne. London's great commercial thoroughfare was a most frenetic place: the perfumed air was riven by shouts and cries, whilst the eye was constantly distracted by the different sights and sounds.

Near the Tun, close to the great Conduit, Guildhall bailiffs had caught two housebreakers red-handed. The malefactors had been stripped naked and their clothes burned. Blackened ash, light cinder flame and fetid smoke were whirled up by the breeze. The two felons, forced to their knees, faced summary execution. Cranston and Athelstan could not pass. They had to stop and watch as a bailiff whirled his broad-blade cleaver and expertly severed both heads. The onlookers scattered, fearful of being splattered by the blood which squirted out of the severed necks, the heads bouncing away even as the torsos toppled over. The heads were collected and set on poles, the flies immediately swarming around them, the dead eyes glaring up as if watching them approach. Only then did Cranston grasp Athelstan by the arm and almost pulled him away.

'Sorry about that, Brother,' he murmured, 'but it's an ordinance of the city. All officials, especially the Lord High Coroner, must witness justice being carried out, bloody as it may be if you are in the vicinity. Right, my little monk.'

'Friar, Sir John.'

'All the same, there you go.'

And before Athelstan could protest, Cranston almost lifted his companion on to a stone plinth, then climbed up beside him. 'Now, my little ferret of a friar, what do you see?'

Athelstan stared out over the sea of drifting colour. 'Sir John, it's like watching different strands in a woven tapestry.'

'Precisely, my little friar. Now,' Cranston stared around, 'look, do you see that funeral procession, the coffin bobbing on the shoulders of those cowled mourners? Now it could be a genuine funeral, or the coffin might contain a victim of the Flesher's murderous rage being taken to some cemetery or charnel like that at St Benet's. I would wager a gold coin that our notorious Flesher patronises more than one church. Or,' Cranston was now warming to his subject, 'perhaps the coffin contains stolen goods being carried to this ship or that warehouse. Turn a little to the right. Do you see the travelling relic seller standing on an overturned cask, preaching about the wonders he's seen; dragons in the mountains of Syria or giants who prowl the forests of the ice kingdoms? Now, Brother, look at the number of urchins who gather to hear the relic seller's words of wisdom. In truth they are foists, sharp-fingered pick-pockets hungry for the unwary, ready to lift a purse. The relic seller is their master; he draws the crowd in and his scholars ply their skills. Close by, do you see the argument which has broken out between the minstrel in his multi-coloured jerkin and that itinerant cook with his smoking grill in the wheel-barrow? They are in fact brothers-in-arms who argue merrily to the enjoyment of passers-by who stop to listen in. However, they should keep their hands on their wallets. It's the same trick, Brother: create a disturbance, draw in a crowd and give your accomplices free rein. Nearby are old friends, the Cheapside whores resplendent in their orange and red wigs; not far away lurk their pimps, sharp-eyed with even sharper knives. All of these, Brother, pay allegiance and dues to Master Makepeace the Flesher. Woe betide anyone who does not pay the devil's tax or refuses that prince amongst rifflers his due. So,' the coroner helped Athelstan down, 'we continue to my chantry chapel.'

Cranston's 'chantry chapel' was the serene private solar in the Lamb of God, Cheapside's most magnificent tavern. Mine hostess ushered Sir John and Athelstan to the coroner's favourite window seat, overlooking a splendid garden with its flowerbeds, herb pots, shady arbours and reed-fringed stew ponds, where golden carp, one of the great delicacies of the tavern, swirled in the light green water.

The solar was a delightful chamber. The windows in the outside wall were filled with painted glass, richly hued tapes-tries decorated the pink-washed walls; all of these proclaimed stories from scripture which extolled the virtues of wine, although, as Athelstan conceded to himself, Sir John needed little encouragement to drink the blood-red Bordeaux. Cranston undid his warbelt and cloak, eased off his high-heeled spurred boots and sank back gratefully into the settle of the window seat. He snatched his beaver hat off, threw it on his cloak, then wiped his solemn white-bewhiskered face and hands with the perfumed towel that Mine hostess had supplied.

'Sir John, you are well?'

'Little friar, I need to tell you a tale – but first,' Cranston sat up, 'let us feed the hungry demon within.'

Mine hostess returned, hustling back with a jug of Bordeaux, goblets, and a bowl of minced venison cooked in a savoury sauce, along with fingers of the softest white bread and a dish of cooked vegetables. Cranston ate and drank as if starved. Athelstan blessed his food and picked at the dishes, he was not so much hungry as curious about what Cranston was about to tell him.

'In the beginning,' the coroner began, wiping both his fingers and mouth on the napkin, he took a generous gulp from the goblet and glared across the deserted solar, 'yes, in the beginning,' he murmured, 'I was a young knight, a King's man. On the feast of the Annunciation, the Year of our Lord 1363, I and a war barge of Tower archers received my final orders to meet a Hanseatic ship, *The Glory of Bremen*, at Queenhithe quayside. The German merchants were acting as intermediaries. The old King and his elder son, the great warrior who styled himself the Black Prince, father of our present King Richard, God bless him, had waged war sharp and cruel in pursuit of the French crown. Both the King and his heir were killers to the bone. They loved war. They would stir up strife in heaven. Anyway, you know the story. We English inflicted defeat after defeat upon the French and forced them to sign peace treaties in which France promised to pay the English Crown vast war damages.' Cranston took a sip of the wine. 'Edward and his son drained the Valois like a thirsty man shakes the very dregs from his goblet. Certain monies were outstanding, so the French agreed to hand over the Rose Casket containing the Twelve Apostles. No, no,' Cranston lifted a hand at Athelstan's interruption, 'let me explain. The Rose Casket had once been the property of the doomed Templars. It had been discovered in the Temple Mount of Jerusalem by Hugh Payens, who founded the order. The Rose Casket was an exquisitely crafted coffer with a beautiful concave lid, fashioned out of sandalwood and smelling as sweet as any heavenly fragrance. The casket was covered with intricately carved trailing roses, with petals of the purest gold and stems of the finest silver. Inside, resting on a purple samite cushion, were twelve precious stones: a diamond, an amethyst, a ruby, and so on. Stones so extraordinarily magnificent, each was worth a king's ransom. These were the Twelve Apostles, held in the Rose Casket by the French Crown in a special tabernacle at the royal chapel of St Denis. The English demanded these as payment. The French were forced to agree. The Hanse merchants would act as go-betweens, so *The Glory of Bremen* brought the Twelve Apostles to Queenhithe. I was to collect the treasure and transport it to the Tower.' Cranston picked up the goblet and cradled it in his hands. 'A fog-bound night, Brother, cold as cold can be. A river mist swirled like a host of ghosts. No one knew of our assignment.' He sighed. 'Or so they told us. We left *The Glory of Bremen*; our barge was a high-prowed war-craft called *The Song of the Sword*. We made good progress, moving out into mid-river, lanterns glowing; every so often a horn would bray to warn other boats to pull aside.' Cranston paused, the goblet halfway to his lips. Athelstan was surprised to see tears in the coroner's light blue eyes. 'Good men, Brother. Perhaps one or two of them may have been bastards, as I will explain, but our company were archers – skilled, able men, loyal to the Crown and each other. Veterans such as Henry Grenel and his son Walter. Oh yes,' Cranston smiled bleakly, 'those two were there. They vanished that night, not seen again till what you saw earlier today. There were others. A few of these you also met this morning; they too served on that war barge.'

Cranston drank noisily, staring into the middle distance as he became immersed in the past. 'Satan's tits, Brother, they were all there, each and every one a Tower archer: Sexton Spurnel, Nathaniel Cripplegate and Curate Cotes. Archers, Athelstan. Men of the royal war band. Well, until that evening anyway. Afterwards the cohort was dissolved . . .'

'Sir John,' Athelstan intervened, 'what happened? You mention the men we met this morning. All three were once under your command?'

'Tower archers, Brother. Royal bowmen. Sworn members of a select garrison. An honourable post, a token of great trust, or so I thought at the time. Anyway,' Cranston cleared his throat, 'we were mid-river. The Rose Casket with the Twelve Apostles lay in a sealed royal chancery bag. We thought all was safe. Men strained over the oars. I was standing in the stern, the captain of archers on the prow, two bowmen with him, one holding the beacon lantern, the other blowing on the hunting horn. All was quiet, when suddenly two other barges appeared on port and starboard. They surged in, swift as arrows finding their mark. They rammed us on both sides, even as their crews, hooded and masked, all garbed like the night, swarmed aboard *The Song of the Sword*. I drew my weapons and hurried to confront a stream of assailants, when I suffered the most cruel blow to the back of my head. I found myself falling and that was it. When I awoke, two days later, I lay in a bed in a whitewashed chamber at St Bartholomew's Hospital, with the most lovely woman bending over me.' Cranston smiled faintly. 'That was how I first met the Lady Maude. She was a member of the Guild of St Veronica and, along with other young ladies of good families, did charitable work amongst the poor and sick committed to the hospital. Now the effect of the Lady Maude's tender care is quite obvious to see. At the time, however, I was more concerned by what had happened than any wound and who was tending it.'

'And?'

'Little friar, a true disaster! *The Song of the Sword* had capsized. The Rose Casket and the Twelve Apostles had disappeared. Most of those in the royal barge were dead or missing, and that included the Grenels, both father and son. Some of the crew survived, including myself, Cotes, Spurnel, Cripplegate, and a few others. The old King and his eldest son were furious. Of course, somebody had betrayed us. As regards our attackers, it was a question of much suspected, little proved. However, the finger of suspicion was pointed strongly at Simon Makepeace the Flesher, along with his evil henchman, Raquin. Apparently both barges vanished as swiftly as they'd appeared out of the river mist. No one along the Thames claimed to have seen or heard anything about them.'

'Too frightened?'

'Possibly. The Flesher had just emerged as the foremost leader of London's rifflers. More precisely, if you study a map of the Thames and where we were attacked, it was not far from the water-gate of the Flesher's tavern, the Devil's Oak, which had opened the previous year.' Cranston shook his head. 'As for evidence, you are right, people are terrified of the Flesher and no one dare talk, even now. Athelstan, if someone was convicted of being part of that attempted robbery, then they are guilty of high treason and would suffer the most excruciating death.' Cranston sipped at his wine. 'Looking back, it was like a nightmare. One minute, I am standing in the stern of a barge and all is well, the next I am facing the fury of Hell.'

'And you still suspect the Flesher?'

Cranston leaned closer. 'Little friar, I don't suspect.' He patted his chest. 'I know the Flesher and Raquin were involved. Both men should hang.'

'But who informed the Flesher, provided him with all the details about the royal barge, its armaments, cargo, time and place? And, whoever did, should be very careful.'

'What do you mean?'

'Well, Sir John, if a member of your crew betrayed you, they were running a terrible risk. After all, they were on that barge on a freezing, misty night, where sword and dagger play would be brutal and swift. If there was a Judas amongst you, he too would face the same danger as you did. So none of your crew fell suddenly sick beforehand?'

'None.'

'But as you have said, somebody must have betrayed you?'

'Little friar, for eighteen years I have asked myself and others the same question, without a scrap of success.' He paused. 'I hear what you say about the danger our Judas faced; however, I still suspect one of those, or all of those we met this morning: Cotes, Spurnel and Cripplegate.'

'Strange that they are now members and officers of the same parish church.'

'Not really. They were all born and raised in Queenhithe. They joined the King's array together and served shoulder to shoulder beyond the Narrow Seas. Anyway,' Cranston sighed, 'we have no real idea who betrayed us.'

'But you suspect the Flesher, you virtually claim that he

was responsible. I've asked this before – surely you have some evidence?'

'Nothing, just a feeling about something I may have glimpsed but, apart from that, not a scrap of real proof. Just riverside tittle-tattle, chatter amongst the dark-dwellers and night-walkers about how the Flesher lusted after the Rose Casket and its contents. You see, Athelstan, at the time there was a great deal of gossip about the French having to pay war damages and the old King's demands for the Twelve Apostles. The Flesher does have friends and allies at Court . . .'

'Were any of the attackers wounded, captured or killed?'

'According to witnesses, and they could add very little to what I already knew, our attackers were highly organised and, if they had any casualties, they took their dead and wounded with them. And that's the Flesher, a villain with fingers and toes in every pie but impossible to pin down. Oh, we could bring a host of indictments against him, but his lawyer Copping would demand proof, whilst any witness who opened his mouth on Monday would have his throat slit by Tuesday. The Flesher sits in the darkest of corners and spins his sinister web. He did the same on the night of the great river battle. He and Raquin were responsible: they haven't forgotten, and they realise I certainly haven't.'

'Could someone else be responsible for the attack?'

'Possibly. Some curious tales did begin to surface. At one time even the French were suspected of trying to get their treasure back by stealth. I dismiss that as arrant nonsense; the source of such a story could well be the Flesher trying to protect himself. You see, Brother, the Rose Casket and the Twelve Apostles disappeared completely. Nothing has been seen or heard of them since that night, which probably means no one had them, either here or abroad.'

'And the Grenels?'

'They too fell under suspicion. Their corpses were never found – well, not until this morning. So yes, they were suspect, and yet matters grow even more mysterious. Something I have already referred to.' Cranston leaned closer, his voice barely above a whisper. 'The English Crown let it be known what had happened. It alerted all its officers and agents, not to mention our merchant community throughout the kingdom and beyond. The Crown charged every loyal subject with the solemn duty of reporting anything they learnt about the Rose Casket and the Twelve Apostles. If both were offered on the open market, or glimpsed in a private house, the Crown was to be informed. The proclamation was hedged with the most hideous punishment for anyone who failed in this matter, whilst offering the most generous rewards to those who could supply valuable information.' Cranston drummed his fingers on the top of the table. 'Nothing, Athelstan. The Twelve Apostles and their casket disappeared completely. And there's the mystery: why steal such a treasure but never offer it for sale? If the Flesher or anyone else had stolen it, eventually, one way or the other, we would have learnt that the Rose Casket and the Twelve Apostles were on the open market.'

'The treasure could have sunk with the barge?'

'Possible, but the river was truly scoured. You see, the barge didn't sink completely. It was badly damaged and listed heavily. Expert swimmers, men like Icthus, were sent in to search it from prow to stern. All they discovered were that the ropes which bound the royal chancery pouch had been cleanly sliced by a knife.'

Cranston fell silent, staring moodily at his empty platter. Athelstan was about to press him further on the Flesher, when the door to the solar swung open and the two beggars who haunted Cranston whenever he appeared in Cheapside slipped into the chamber; Leif, the one-legged mendicant, as he styled himself, and Rawbum, his constant companion, a former cook dismissed from his employment for being drunk and sitting down on a pan of boiling oil. These two miscreants edged their way forward. Leif half crouching, staring at Cranston's face. Rawbum, rubbing his backside with one hand, the other stretched out like a claw, eager for a coin.

'There is a monster appeared in Moorfields, north of the city,' Leif hissed. 'We need to inform you, Sir John . . .' Leif hopped back, Rawbum following, as Cranston rose threateningly to his feet.

'Although a dwarf,' Leif gabbled, 'the monster's head and

face are large enough for a giant. He has black eyes, flared nostrils, heavy stubble and fangs for teeth—'

'Yes, yes,' Athelstan interrupted, ushering them towards the door, 'but you can see Sir John is preoccupied.'

'The monster has fingernails, crooked and yellow.' Rawbum blithely took up the tale. 'He has the appearance of a prowling dog and he can devour a man in a single gulp.'

'Go,' Athelstan whispered hoarsely. He dug into the tattered wallet on the cord around his waist, drew out two of his precious pennies, and thrust these into the hands of the unfortunate beggars. They both stopped their lurid tale, turned, and promptly disappeared back into the taproom beyond.

'Thank you.' Cranston sat down as Athelstan came back to the table. 'I could not tolerate those two. My good humour is all but drained, Athelstan, whenever I recall the good men killed that night, not to mention the humiliation and disgrace at losing such a precious cargo.'

'But you were not blamed?'

'No I wasn't, Brother. As I have said, I received a crack on the head and disappeared beneath the fast-flowing river. I then surfaced and a fishing boat almost knocked me under again. I was dragged aboard and taken to Queenhithe. The old King, the Prince of Wales, declared they were convinced that I did all that I could . . .' Cranston paused, as if listening to a bell-like voice bellowing from the taproom that 'conserves of violets, roses and borage, along with a few drops of camphor, are good for those of a moist humour.'

'Lady Maude,' Cranston murmured, 'used such remedies on my bruised head, as well as feeding me delicious dishes such as tender chicken poached in wine, carp grilled over charcoal, along with soup of almonds.' The coroner smacked his lips, a dreamy look in his eyes. On any other occasion Athelstan would have laughed at Cranston's constant absorption with good food, yet the coroner remained oddly deflated, as if the defeat he had suffered some eighteen years earlier had returned in all its hideous strength. Abruptly, the coroner's mood changed; a puckering of the lips, a half-smile as if to himself, his right hand going out to caress the pommel of his sheathed sword, as if he was going to use that to swear some solemn oath.

'Sir John?'

'Before God, Athelstan, I tell you I do not know for sure who actually attacked us, or the Judas who betrayed us, nor can I prove that the Flesher and all his wickedness was responsible. However, and I am only telling you this as a penitent to his father confessor, wanting to be shriven,' the coroner drew a deep breath, 'the attack was swift and brutal. I saw a man race along the edge of the enemy barge and jump on to ours. He had a helmet on with a visor that closed over the mouth, but it hung open. I am sure the face I glimpsed was Raquin's, but I dare not mention that in public. The lawyers would regard it as an attempt to pass the blame on to an enemy without a shred of evidence to prove my allegation.' Cranston wove his fingers together, 'Raquin was hungry for my death that night. I still regard him as the greatest threat. God have mercy on me, but I believe I must kill him or he will undoubtedly kill me.'

Athelstan shivered as he clutched his goblet, eager to sip the thick, red wine.

'And now, as for the rest . . .' Cranston pushed away the platter in front of him. 'First, my little friar,' Cranston deliberately tried to lighten the mood. He quietly cursed himself for allowing his own morbid fears to surface: he could tell Athelstan was becoming deeply anxious. 'Parson Reynaud! Trust me, Athelstan, I do not have the best opinion of your fellow clerics. However, Parson Reynaud was a priest who knew all about sin for all the wrong reasons and in all the wrong ways. A man sworn to celibacy, Parson Reynaud was well known to the Daughters of Joy.' Cranston grinned. 'Ladies of the night to you, my little friar. Courtesans, young women who regard themselves as a cut above the common street whore. They have a mansion in Reynaud's parish which they call the House of Delights, in Grape Street. Our good parson was a frequent visitor, a man who strove to live life to the full. Parson Reynaud, like his ally the Flesher, was a former soldier; he served as a chaplain in the royal array in the old King's forays through France. Accordingly, Reynaud would have seen sights which would whiten anyone's hair. Perhaps that's where he left the path of righteousness. I doubt very much if Reynaud took the Scriptures seriously, except for one verse, "Do not worry about tomorrow." Parson Reynaud certainly didn't.'

'But he performed his priestly commitments, shriving his parishioners and celebrating Mass?'

'Oh, of course, he had to. Parson Reynaud was well known to the Bishop of London and his formidable archdeacon, Master Tuddenham. They would have pounced like a hungry cat on a mouse if Reynaud did not fulfil his priestly duties to justify his income, and his house, as well as all the other comforts such priests insist on.' Cranston nudged Athelstan. 'Present company excepted, of course?'

'Of course.'

'Now the advowson, the right of appointing both parson and curate to St Benet's Woodwharf, is held by the Fitzalans, the Earls of Arundel. The present lord is well known, even notorious for his meddling in matters politic. The Earl of Arundel would love nothing better than to topple our self-proclaimed regent, uncle to the King. Now Fitzalan has granted all rights of advowson to his henchman and former comrade in the King's array, Master Simon Makepeace, also known as the Flesher.

'Let me tell you a little more about that sinner.' Cranston took a deep gulp of wine. 'Simon Makepeace is probably one of the greatest villains under God's sun. We are not too sure of his origins. Born in Queenhithe, he served with Fitzalan's retinue in France, where he excelled himself as a killer and a thief. Indeed,' Cranston wagged a finger, 'I have heard it on good authority that the Flesher committed such heinous crimes that the mayor and citizens of Rouen placed a generous bounty on his head, dead or alive. Apparently, Makepeace became an écorcheur, a flayer who liked nothing better than to peel the skin of his victims till they confessed where they had hidden any treasure.'

'Heaven forfend.' Athelstan breathed. 'A flayer? I've heard about them, devils incarnate. The most violent of men; criminals freed from jail on condition that they fought in the King's array.'

'Such as Master Makepeace, Brother. Anyway, about nineteen

to twenty years ago, our killer returned to London and settled in Queenhithe. He soon won a reputation for ruthless ferocity. He became a leader amongst the rifflers, a lord of the mob who would not be challenged or checked. One man tried to oppose him, a merchant, Gilbert Croyland. Do you know what the Flesher did? He provoked Croyland and his son into a fight; he killed them both, then took their severed heads to every tavern in Queenhithe and beyond. The Flesher claimed self-defence. He could produce a score of witnesses who would swear to that, whilst no one would dare gainsay him. The Flesher insisted that Croyland's wife and daughter carry the severed heads before him on a tray.'

'But the sheriff, the Guildhall?'

'Too frightened, Brother – not only of Makepeace, but the ominous dark shadow behind him.'

'Arundel?'

'In a word, yes. The Earl of Arundel openly proclaims that Makepeace is an honest citizen and a valued member of the Fitzalan household. You see, the Flesher is the mailed gauntlet, Arundel is the fist within. He needs Makepeace to control the London gangs, the mob, that many-headed monster which lurks in the dark, nightmare corners of this city. Over the years, the Flesher's powers have increased. True, in the months leading up to the Great Revolt, the Flesher became more discreet. He did not wish to cross swords with the Upright Men and their ferocious street warriors, the Earthworms. Makepeace kept to the shadows, paying lip service to the Crown and city council, whilst offering secret support to the Upright Men or, at least, the illusion of support. Once the revolt was crushed, the Flesher continued to extend his power.'

Cranston rose and stretched. He walked to the door, opened it and then came back. 'I thought as much,' he murmured, retaking his seat. 'The Weasel has arrived, one of the Flesher's street spies. He controls a veritable horde of them. The Weasel is one of the best, and he is called that because of his skill at twisting his way through this city. Nevertheless, he is an ugly bugger and, despite his best efforts, stands out in a crowd.' Cranston scratched his head. 'I am sure there are others of his tribe lurking in the taproom, but Mine hostess, a most redoubtable woman, will keep them away from the keyhole. So,' Cranston rubbed his hands together, 'to return to my indictment. Arundel controls Makepeace, who controls the rifflers, exercising his authority and power from his hellish tavern, the Devil's Oak, close to the river. He has fingers and thumbs in every pie, be it crooked dice-throwing or our red-wigged ladies of the night. He can call up the legion of the damned and field a mob within the hour. He also controls St Benet's and Parson Reynaud. God knows what mischief those two got up to before the good parson went to join the choir invisible. You see, Athelstan,' Cranston wetted his lips, 'London's full of villains. The whores do a roaring trade, Parson Reynaud was certainly not celibate, but the Flesher is different. According to gossip, Master Makepeace likes to become violent with his women. Those skeletons Flaxwith unearthed in the crypt, whatever Sexton Spurnel's claims, were the victims of the Flesher's murderous lust. A cleaver blow to the face or the back of the head would account for the violence we saw. Of course, I haven't a shred of evidence to substantiate my allegation. Nothing to prove my suspicions, except on one night there was a pretty whore and the next, after she had visited the Devil's Oak, there wasn't. She'd vanished and remained vanished like the dew on a hot summer's day. Oh yes, our Flesher is a truly sinister soul who rules by fear and that, one day, might be his undoing.'

'Sir John, what do you mean?'

'Oh, I will come to it in a while. Just mutterings, grumbles, a growing tide of discontent with the Flesher, even though he still controls through terror. Let me explain.' Cranston leaned back on the settle. 'Close to the Devil's Oak stands a most forbidding, sinister, even macabre dwelling. The night-walkers and shadow-shifters call it the Mansion of Murder. It stands in its own grounds, about three storeys high. To all intents and purposes it is well kept, but still a very empty building. However, according to what I have learnt, the Flesher uses this mansion to terrorise all of Hell's buttery, that stretch of cramped, rotting, fetid tenements along Queenhithe's wharf. People who cross the Flesher, who fail to do what he orders, are locked up in that dreadful mansion and exposed to great war dogs. They are savaged, mauled and cruelly killed; their corpses, nothing more than mangled remains, are thrown into the Thames.'

'In God's sweet name,' Athelstan breathed, 'wickedness incarnate. Sir John, surely you can intervene?'

'Can we, Brother?' Cranston declared moodily. The coroner used his fingers to emphasise his points. 'First, we have no complaint, no evidence of a crime, nothing to link the Flesher to the death and disappearance of anyone. Secondly, the Flesher is the leader of the most powerful gang of rifflers in London. He is a true robber who wields complete authority over his tribe of thieves. As I have said, they used the Great Revolt for their own purposes. Now it is over. The King's peace has been restored, the common enemy has disappeared. The great lords gather in Parliament and the gangs have re-emerged, flexing their muscles, and the Flesher is foremost amongst these. He takes his orders from Fitzalan of Arundel, who absolutely hates Gaunt and would love to see our regent's head lopped off on Tower Hill. Now Gaunt has had a stroke of great fortune.'

'Sir John?'

'Gaunt has a great ally, no lesser person than our young King. Richard has a particular detestation for Richard Fitzalan, Earl of Arundel. Our King, God bless him, believes that foxy-faced Earl is a born traitor, an intriguer who does not wish him well.'

'Why?'

'Brother, you must never tell this to anyone but, remember after the revolt, our young King decided to stage a series of ceremonies where he would sit in cloth of gold wearing the Confessor's crown and carrying the orb and sceptre? Around him would gather the leading officers of state and the Knights of the Body?' Cranston smiled. 'I am both a royal officer and a Knight of the Body. I am allowed to wear weapons in the King's presence.'

'Yes, yes, I remember those ceremonies,' Athelstan murmured. 'They were staged in Westminster Abbey, Canterbury, and other great cities.'

'On one such occasion,' Cranston continued, 'I was helping the King to divest in the sacristy. Fitzalan of Arundel came in, but young Richard snapped his fingers and indicated he should leave. Fitzalan, his cunning face twisted into a smirk, bowed mockingly and sauntered off. Once the door closed behind him, the King confided in me that he had a dream, in which Arundel took both his crown and his life. Richard truly believes Arundel wishes him ill.'

'But that's only a nightmare?'

'Brother, young Richard is deeply sensitive in nature. He is vulnerable. Think of him as a foal surrounded by wolves. They slope either side of him and they watch as they snarl at each other. Arundel is a leader of the pack. Athelstan, you must have met someone you take an immediate and intense dislike to?'

'Yes,' Athelstan smiled, 'God forgive me I have, and most of them are priests. But, you are correct, I have met people whom I dislike immediately, and never change my mind about them.'

'Well, that's our young King's attitude towards Arundel. According to Master Thibault, Richard has instructed his beloved uncle John of Gaunt to watch Arundel closely. As you can imagine, our noble regent needs little encouragement: the two lords are at daggers drawn, and wage their bitter feud at court, in Parliament and, above all, across the city.' Cranston beat his fingers against the goblet, clattering it with his nails. 'Gaunt controls gangs such as The Master of the Minions, whom you have met, Mine host at The Tavern of Lost Souls. Arundel, however, has his leash on the Flesher and his gang the Sycamores who lurk at the Devil's Oak tavern. To cut to the quick, Gaunt and his Master of Secrets Thibault want the Flesher and his power to be utterly destroyed. They believe Arundel is plotting against the Crown and intends great mischief when Parliament meets after the feast of All Hallows.'

'What!'

'They don't know for certain, but they suspect Arundel may try to overawe Parliament with the mob.'

'But that can be countered.'

'Oh, the Flesher will whistle up his rifflers and summon all their scurriers from the alleyway. But Gaunt is also very apprehensive that Arundel, who is hiring mercenaries, may try to bring liveried troops into the city and lay siege to Westminster.'

'But I thought that was strictly forbidden. You can only quarter troops in London on land which is yours. Arundel may own a house along the riverside, as do many of the lords, but these residences are not extensive enough for troops to pitch camp. Sir John, you told me this yourself, did you not?'

'Yes, yes. I did.' Cranston scratched his chin. 'Nevertheless, I am certain that Arundel and the Flesher are plotting some mischief; something to do with the coming Parliament, though God knows what. And so we come to the Sicarius.'

'The dagger man? It was apparent that you and Raquin had a bitter feud over him. Who is he?'

'Eudo Ingersol,' Cranston replied, grasping his wine cup and making himself more comfortable on the settle. He paused at the shouting and yelling from outside, followed by the strident wail of bagpipes and the blowing of horns. 'They are taking a group of whores down to the stocks,' Cranston murmured, 'to be ridiculed until sunset. Now, Brother, the Sicarius, the dagger man.' Cranston paused to collect his thoughts. 'Master Thibault and I have grown deeply concerned at the growth and the power of the riffler gangs throughout London. They are a plague that spreads and taints everything. We decided in secret council to confront and destroy the greatest . . .'

'The Flesher and his so-called Sycamores?'

'Brother, in a word, yes. We recognise that Master Makepeace has a fearsome reputation as the Flesher. He is a killer to the bone and a vile abuser. We know he has slaughtered prostitutes for his own pleasure and barbarously removed any threat to himself or his interests. We decided to suborn his hideous coven by stealth rather than open attack.'

'Why now?'

'Why not?' Cranston testily retorted, then grimaced his apology. 'It's a matter which infuriates me, Athelstan. I would love to invoke the law against the Flesher and his coven. But, if I take him to court, what evidence can I bring? Whilst he will hire the sharpest lawyers to be found in the Inns of Court, they would swoop like a host of ravens on any indictment we lay against the Flesher. So, Master Thibault and I prayed for an opening, a secret way into the Flesher's world of wickedness. Brother, I have lit candles and tapers before the lady altar in many London churches with one prayer: let me send the Flesher to judgement. The good Lord did not let me down. On the eve of the feast of the Assumption, I was sitting here in this solar when I had a visitor. He slipped through that door, a swift shadow, cowled and masked, hidden by a heavy military cloak from chin to toe. He took this off and sat down opposite me. A youngish man, well educated – a mailed clerk, no less. He had served in the King's army and worked for a while in the chancery offices of one of the guilds. About five years ago, life changed dramatically when he entered the Flesher's household.'

'No!'

'Oh yes. Eudo Ingersol, otherwise known as the Sicarius, was one of the Flesher's leading henchmen. A very valuable retainer, a man of experience, schooled in the halls of Oxford as well as on the battlefields of France. A soul who knew many of the Flesher's secrets and, to put it bluntly, where the corpses were buried.'

'What did he want?'

'A free pardon for all crimes, certain monies and licences for himself and one other, yet to be named, to go abroad under the protection of the Crown.'

'So he wanted to betray the Flesher?'

'Yes, he was willing to sell his master and be admitted with honour into the King's peace.'

'And the other person?'

'We do not know and, perhaps, never will.'

'So why did this sinner seek repentance?'

'Oh, he cited the Flesher's cruelty, as well as his own desire for peace. I think he meant it. He wanted to escape, as he put it, the world of the knife and the garrotte. Ingersol was also brutally honest. He believed the Flesher's days were numbered, that the riffler leader had overstretched himself and was ripe for a fall. In the end, he promised to bring the Flesher and his ilk to due process of law, but he would do so gradually. He would not turn King's approver, but weaken the Flesher as much as he could from within by providing valuable infor-mation. He also believed the Flesher and Arundel were deep in some mischief, though he could tell us little about that. However, the information he did provide about robberies, housebreakings and assaults on different persons proved to be priceless and helped us frustrate him. Our bailiffs could never finger the Flesher's collar, or those of his henchmen, but a good number of Sycamores are either rotting in Newgate or hanging from the gallows.'

'Sir John, why did he have the name Sicarius?'

'Because he was a dagger man, a very skilful one. He carried a rather unique weapon, daggers especially fashioned in Italy. A craftsman in Rome created something quite unique for him.' Cranston turned and drew out his own dagger with its ornamented hilt and Toledo steel blade. 'Brother, what you see is obvious, a dagger, a knife. The Sicarius carried what looked like a small, black ivory rod. Press the hidden catch, however, and a deeply embedded blade sprang out – long, deadly, pointed and serrated on each side, sharp as a polished razor. He sat in this solar and showed me it. You could actually hide it in your hand; perhaps tuck it under the cuff of your jerkin. You wouldn't know he had it until the blade appeared. Moreover, the Sicarius was very fast, swift and skilful.' Cranston grinned. 'Even I became wary of him.'

'Could such a dagger have been used in the slayings at St Benet's?'

Cranston shrugged. 'Perhaps. The wounds were deep slits. Ingersol, however, never let that dagger out of his sight.'

'Could he be responsible for the killings?'

'A very remote possibility. In the end, Ingersol did betray the Flesher. He provided us with names and places, all the secret chambers and hidden dens along Hell's buttery. We netted many a rogue, seized malefactors and, as I have said, fingered wicked collars. It was harvest time for us; we were doing great damage to the Flesher and his coven. Then about ten days ago, everything ended. Nothing. No further information.' Cranston blinked, his face now solemn. 'I feel . . .'

'What, Sir John?'

'I don't think Ingersol was responsible for the murders at St Benet's. I have a feeling he is dead. Do you know, Athelstan, I truly liked him. Oh, he was a rogue, a true dagger man but he had a soul. He felt guilty about what he'd done. He wanted forgiveness. Above all, he wanted to start a new life. We would meet in shadowy ruins, places where no one could follow either of us, no spy, no eavesdropper. We would talk. I liked him. We also agreed that if something went truly wrong, he must come here to the Lamb of God, cloaked and hooded. Mine hostess would send one of her spit boys for me. But that never happened . . .' Cranston wiped his eyes. 'God have mercy on him. I am sure the Sicarius has been murdered, and cruelly so, either in the Flesher's Mansion of Murder, or in the gloomy vaults of the Devil's Oak.'

'So he must have been discovered or betrayed?'

'No, he probably made a mistake. The Flesher may look like Flaxwith's Samson, but his mind twists and turns as any rat in the sewer and his wits are razor sharp; that's why he's survived for so long.' He paused. 'Ingersol was giving us information. We were inflicting great damage on the Flesher and his coven. Now, we always prayed that the Flesher would put this down to circumstances. I know he plays hazard. He must have seen the cup cast the wrong dice but, on reflection, he and Raquin must have realised a traitor lurked deep in their household. If they did, and Ingersol made a mistake, that precious pair would close the trap and kill him. He would be shown no mercy, given no second chance. In the end they must have done, that's why Raquin was baiting me.'

Cranston cooled his face with a scented napkin. 'The Fisher of Men came to Queenhithe at my request. I am making discreet enquires. I want to discover if the mangled corpse of a fairly young man has been found floating in the river or along its banks, but there's nothing. Flaxwith has questioned the collectors of corpses, but again, nothing.' Cranston rose and stretched. Athelstan could detect the tension in his great friend's soul. 'I am going to settle scores,' the coroner hissed. 'I swear on all that's holy, I am going to settle with the Flesher and his kindred spirit, his filthy familiar Raquin. So, friar, we might as well begin now. I think we'll visit the Mansion of Murder and the Devil's Oak.'

Athelstan hid his disquiet. Cranston had a fiery temper, and the friar was worried about his present mood: the coroner could be easily provoked to do something stupid. 'You have warrants?' Athelstan asked.

Cranston strapped on his warbelt, fastened the buckle and tapped the hilt of his sword. 'This is my warrant. Listen, little friar, if I approached the justices at the Guildhall and asked for warrants to be sworn out, the Flesher would know within the hour. He has a myriad of spies, clerks, scriveners – yes, perhaps even justices. As far as the Flesher is concerned, the walls do have ears, and eyes as well. No, we will surprise him. And you will come with me?'

'Most reluctantly,' Athelstan agreed, getting to his feet. Secretly he prayed that Cranston's temper would dissipate and his common sense prevail. The friar shook his robe and picked up his chancery satchel. 'I am in all things, Sir John, your faithful scribe, but I would like you to reflect and use your sharp wit, not your hot temper. First, let us go back to St Benet's. I need to view that place of murder. I am sure there is something amiss, a morsel of evidence I can discover and, above all, I need to revisit that church, scrutinise the corpses and question our leading parishioners.'

They left the Lamb of God, battling their way through the surging crowd. The day had drawn on. The trading along the broad swathe of Cheapside was now totally frenetic. Traders were desperate to move goods and make a profit before the market bell tolled to mark the end of business. Stalls had been totally uncovered to display all their wares. Journeymen stood on boxes, shouting a description of their goods and the prices 'much reduced'. Apprentices slipped like lurchers through the crowd, snatching at sleeves, belts or cloaks to compel would-be customers closer to their masters' stalls. Dung carts tried to clear the stinking midden heaps where children scrambled, screaming as they chased the dogs and cats which haunted that place. The stiffening breeze carried all the flavour of this great trading area: the salty reek of fresh blood from the slaughter pens; the stench of innards dragged out from the slit bellies of poultry and other stock. All these mingled with the fragrances of the perfume sellers, as well as the sweet flavours of the cook shops and the strong fumes drifting from the countless ale houses in whose doorways the orange-wigged whores clustered to solicit for custom. Tale tellers and relic sellers touted for business. A wild-eyed, sunburnt preacher held up a bottle with a red-painted stopper. He claimed that the swarm of flies buzzing angrily inside were in fact a host of demons he'd captured under a gallows on the Oxford road. Funeral processions with bell, book and candle jostled alongside wedding marches. Two such cortèges, its members much the worse for drink, had now merged together, with the bride sitting on top of the coffin, held by a line of laughing mourners and wedding guests. Bailiffs led a line of chained prisoners, most of them in rags, down to different stocks, thews, pillories and compters. Cranston was recognised, but the coroner ignored both the greetings and the insults, except for two grotesques who, faces hidden behind garish visors, began to dance in front of them. Cranston half drew his sword and both tormentors disappeared.

They turned off the busy thoroughfare and along the needle-thin alleyways into Queenhithe. They followed the trackways which twisted into Hell's buttery, strangely silent and desolate, though Athelstan was aware of figures swiftly disappearing at their approach, as well as hollow-sounding cries and shouts which proclaimed who was passing by. Cranston apparently was tolerated; no abuse was offered, nor did he suffer the rain of missiles which would greet many a city official. At last they reached St Benet's Woodwharf and began striding across the concourse towards the church. Flaxwith had left his bailiffs on guard just within the main doorway. These assured Cranston that the corpses had been removed to the death house. One bailiff escorted them across the cemetery, whilst another was despatched to fetch the people Athelstan wished to question, the friar adding that he would meet these in the priest's house.

St Benet's mortuary chamber was a long, dismal building. Its outside whitewashed walls were smeared with dirt, its tiled roof patched, whilst the windows were roughly hewn squares with shutters pushed between the wooden frames. The painted double door hung off its latch. Athelstan pulled this open and walked into the dank, cold mortuary room. This was no better than the outside: dismal and rather squalid; a dirt-packed floor with tables standing at either side and – on the two end walls

– black, wooden crucifixes, no more than pieces of wood nailed together. The rusting, corroding braziers had been lit, and the herbs strewn above the crackling charcoal did something to offset the horrid reek of corruption.

Daventry and Parson Reynaud lay naked on two of the tables. Cranston, at Athelstan's request, took a tinder and lit the tallow corpse candles. Athelstan used these to inspect both cadavers, studying the dead flesh from chin to crutch, in particular the death wounds on each of the victims.

'You see, Sir John,' Athelstan pointed to the wound in the left side of Daventry's chest, 'a blow direct to the heart. The wound is now congealed but look at its shape, like that of a leaf. The entry is a mere slit, but then the blade was pushed in and twisted up. I suspect the killer knelt before both of his victims, or just to their side. Now with Parson Reynaud I would understand that, if the assassin was pretending to be a penitent wanting to be shrived, but why kneel next to Daventry?'

'Unless he wished to whisper something.'

'In a deserted church, Sir John?'

'True, but that brings us to the problem of who was where and when? Were Daventry and Reynaud together in the church? Did the assassin creep from one victim to another, or did the killer deal with Parson Reynaud, then wait for Daventry to arrive and kill him?'

'My friend, all this is speculation, but both men must have been dead before their assassin removed the corpse of that old lady, unlocked the arca and stole its contents.' Athelstan paused. 'But as you say, it is speculation. Let us recite what happened, as if it is a mummer's play. So, Sir John, why should anyone steal that old woman's corpse?'

'First, she was the only person the Flesher loved. Isabelle Makepeace reigned at the Devil's Oak like an empress and, if the gossip is true, Isabella Makepeace was as cruel and as vicious as her son.'

'So she would have enemies?'

'Does a dog have fleas?'

'And secondly?'

'Profit. A demand has been made, a veritable treasure to

have the corpse returned. However,' Cranston brushed some crumbs from his cloak, 'that means our assassin must reveal something of himself, which would be extremely dangerous, dealing with the likes of the Flesher.' Cranston peered at his companion, who was lost in thought. 'There is something else, Athelstan?'

'Yes, yes, Sir John, but at the moment I cannot place it. It was something I saw on the corpses.' Athelstan shrugged. 'Or was it something else? Anyway, for the moment let us put those matters aside and return to the church.'

They left the death house and took the winding, weed-strewn path, which cut like a twisting snake through the sprawling, neglected cemetery. The ground was peppered with funeral stones and requiem crosses, nothing more than a tangle of decaying wood and stone, most of it hidden by the sprouting briar and bramble. Athelstan paused and stared across the cemetery, noting the neglect, the crumbling burial mounds and half-dug pits.

'Sir John, what is happening here?'

'I have asked the same. According to Flaxwith, who has had words with Sexton Spurnel, Parson Reynaud was keen to clear the cemetery, empty as many graves as possible and so start anew.'

'Why? I mean Parson Reynaud, God rest him, seemed more interested in his comfortable house, amenable whores, his expensive robes and jewellery than God's Acre. Indeed I do wonder, Sir John, if Parson Reynaud went into the church yesterday evening not so much to shrive a penitent but meet someone, a person he did not want others to see.'

'Such as?'

'Sir John, for the time being, that's mere speculation. So let us begin. Now,' Athelstan turned and pointed back to the death house, 'yesterday afternoon, Isabella Makepeace's corpse was taken by the sexton and others to be churched in St Benet's, the Flesher and possibly his henchmen being present for the ceremony?'

'According to Sexton Spurnel, yes. But by then,' Cranston continued, 'the coffin was sealed. They brought it through here.' Cranston reached the shattered devil's door and he helped

Athelstan step over the debris which still littered the entrance. They entered the damp, chilly nave. Athelstan opened the candle chest just within the entrance. They took out and lit the squat, tallow tapers, as well as others fixed on their spigots in the Lady Chapel and elsewhere. The candlelight glowed, casting circles of golden warmth in what Athelstan now regarded as one of the most eerie churches he had ever entered. The nave seemed to create its own darkness, a presence with a life of its own. The silence was oppressive, as if it housed beings of the night who'd gathered to watch and, if necessary, intervene to provoke nameless fears. Athelstan tried to shrug off this chilling of the soul as he stood before the empty coffin.

'So, Sir John, we have the problem.' Athelstan just wished his voice did not have that sepulchral echo. 'Yesterday afternoon, this coffin, with Isabella Makepeace's corpse inside, was brought into this nave to be blessed. Later on two men entered. First Parson Reynaud, who sat in the mercy chair in the entrance to the chantry chapel, whilst his visitor Daventry, an emissary from my Lord of Arundel, also came here. We do not know Daventry's business, perhaps we never shall. Nor, at this time, do we truly know if the priest and the messenger were aware of each other. In the last resort they both came in here. They sat down quite apart. Daventry in the sexton's chair near the main door, Parson Reynaud in the entrance to that chantry chapel. I have noticed that they would not have been able to see each other. The assassin then enters; he approaches one, then the other. Both men are murdered. The coffin lid is ripped off and the old woman's corpse plucked out. How that cadaver was removed from the church is also a mystery.'

'Brother?'

'Well, it must have been dark or at least dusk. Autumn is drawing on, and to leave a church carrying an old, dead woman is fairly singular. There is the danger that the assassin might meet someone, or be seen by parishioners, or indeed anyone passing the church. Curate Cotes, Mistress Martha, Sexton Spurnel, Cripplegate, or one of the Flesher's vast retinue might visit St Benet's, though perhaps not for matters spiritual.'

Athelstan walked back, measuring his steps carefully. 'They must be gathering,' he murmured, 'perhaps when we meet we might learn more, but other mysteries remain. Sir John, the arca? A heavy, stout, reinforced money chest. It has two different locks with unique keys carried only by those who own the arca. Parson Reynaud's was still hanging about his neck when we examined his cadaver this morning. Of course, it could have been taken, used, then put back. But the Flesher was wearing his around his neck. Unless it was the Flesher who carried out the killings for his own secret purposes; that seems a logical explanation, at least superficially.'

'Yes, yes,' Cranston rubbed his hands together. 'If I empanelled a jury to sit at Westminster, they might rule there is a case to answer.'

'Precisely, Sir John.' Athelstan chuckled. 'Such an explanation sounds fine but signifies nothing.'

'Oh I know,' Cranston murmured, 'my impatience is getting the better of me.' The coroner shrugged. 'Why should the Flesher murder his own henchmen? Why should he abuse his own beloved mother's corpse then steal his own money? Finally, as God made little apples, if I summon the Flesher before any jury, he would terrorise its members, as well as turn up with a host of witnesses: they would swear the most solemn oath that yesterday evening the Flesher spent every second of his time praying in his own private chapel at the Devil's Oak. Oh no! So, back to the mysteries. How were money sacks, heavy pouches of coin removed from the church so no one can witness it being done? I cannot imagine Mistress Martha, Curate Cotes, Cripplegate or Sexton Spurnel, or indeed any other suspect, staggering through the cemetery at twilight with heavy sacks of clinking coins. And where could that be hid?'

'And of course,' Athelstan grasped Cranston by the wrist and took him back to the devil's door, 'the final mystery.'

'The doors were left locked and bolted from the inside.' Cranston waved around. 'This was broken into because, unlike the rest, it is not of solid oak but heavy panelling. According to all the witnesses, Sexton Spurnel smashed the slats and was able to stoop in to draw the bolts as well as turn the key in the lock. The evidence indicates that all the other doors were locked and bolted from within and, like this one,' Cranston pulled the door backwards and forwards, 'the keys were still in the locks. That includes every door to this church, a building with narrow windows and no secret entrances. For the love of God, Athelstan, can you imagine it? Each door has a lock and two bolts. But can an assassin pass through solid stone carrying the corpse of an old woman and heavy sacks of coin?'

'A maze of murderous mystery,' Athelstan agreed. 'Ah well, Sir John, let us meet our parish worthies and see if further light can be shed.'

They left through the devil's door and stood on the pebble-dashed path that surrounded the church. Athelstan stood kicking at this with the toe of his sandal. Many churches had such paths, and he had been advised to lay the same at St Erconwald's. Athelstan had been informed that a pebble path around the church helped to soak up and retain the rainwater when it poured down the church walls or through the gullies. Athelstan crouched and sifted through the pebbles with his fingers before he and Cranston continued their scrutiny of the entrances to St Benet's. They went round to the corpse door. Athelstan inspected its heavy, oaken frame, a thick wedge of wood hinged securely to the lintel; its bolts were slightly rusty but workable, and the friar could see they had not been inter-fered with. The same was true of the lock, its key still hung on the inside and, again, they could detect nothing amiss with the key or the large keyholes either side of the door. He and Cranston continued their way along the pebble-dashed path around the church. Again they were struck by how desolate and derelict the cemetery had become. On closer inspection, a good many of the ancient crosses and headstones had been removed; shallow graves very close to the church showed where the harrowing of the dead had taken place. Empty burial pits from where the skeletons had been plucked and flung into that great, cavernous charnel house which filled the crypt beneath the church. Athelstan felt he was walking the blighted moorlands of Hell. He truly believed the cemetery was not God's Acre. Indeed, this graveyard, together with that macabre crypt, were no more than murder pits used by the Flesher with the full connivance of a wicked priest to hide the victims of his crimes; be it whores, rivals, or anyone who dared to oppose

him. They would be slaughtered, their corpses deliberately
lost here in shallow graves, to be later dug up and hidden in
the monstrous tangle of bones beneath the church.

'A fitting home for demons,' Cranston murmured.

'I agree. Look around you, Sir John, sniff the air – to me
it reeks of wickedness. I will leave it for a while but, Sir John,
when all this is over, I intend to seek an audience with the
Bishop of London. This church should be razed to the ground,
its cemetery reconsecrated and stripped. Let the grass grow,
plant gardens. Allow this morbid, sombre place to flourish so
as to reflect God's smile.'

They walked on, pausing to scrutinise the locks on the other
doors, the main entrance, its postern gate and, finally, back to
the devil's door. Athelstan could see how the parishioners had
broken in, removing the slats before pulling at the bolts and
turning the key.

'We have seen enough,' Athelstan declared, walking back
on to the pebble-dashed path. 'Oh yes, for the moment, we
have certainly seen enough.'

Sexton Spurnel, Mistress Martha, Cripplegate and Cotes
were waiting for them in the oak-panelled solar of the priest's
house, a truly comfortable chamber with its gleaming oak
and pink plaster, whilst thick, heavy turkey rugs covered the
polished floor. Triptychs and other devotional paintings
exuded their own brightness in a wide array of vivid colours
to portray scenes from scripture. Warmed by a magnificent
dragon-mouthed hearth, as well as merrily burning braziers,
the solar was as comfortable and luxurious as any Athelstan
could recall in the great mansions of London or the bright-lit
chambers of the court. Candles glowed in silver spikes
along the rim of wheels lowered from the timber-beamed
ceiling. The air was fragranced by the sweet smell of baking
from the kitchen. A place of rest and relaxation. Athelstan
felt the cloying warmth of the house lull his wits and soothe
his humours.

The friar shook himself and sat up straight, staring about
as Sir John and all the company gathered around the solar's
polished chancery table. Mistress Martha offered ale and
freshly baked scones covered in butter and a sweet sauce.

Cranston eagerly accepted, but Athelstan shook his head and opened his chancery satchel.

'You are to question us again?' Martha asked, squeezing herself into a chair pulled close to the table. Athelstan smiled at her. He was grateful for her kindness, and intrigued by this good-looking woman who had not been Reynaud's leman or doxy. Athelstan could well understand why both the parson and his curate had lusted after such a woman.

'As Martha said, you are to question us again?' Cripplegate rested his elbows on the table. Athelstan studied the locksmith more closely. He did not look so composed or assured as he had earlier in the day. Was the locksmith innocent? A member of the guild, leader of this parish council who, like so many in life, just looked the other way? He and others had done no harm, which was as true as its hidden twin, that they had also done no good? Cripplegate held Athelstan's gaze then blinked, wetting dried lips and scratching at his grey beard. 'What more can we say?' Cripplegate's voice held a hint of desperation.

'I have certainly nothing to add.' The curate had apparently not changed his clothes and looked as bleary-eyed and sottish with drink as he had earlier.

'I have thought and thought again,' Sexton Spurnel waved a hand. 'I cannot recall anything amiss.'

'Is that true?' Cranston retorted. 'Two men murdered, one corpse stolen and a treasure chest robbed, and you still can recall nothing out of place?'

Athelstan felt a twinge of cramp. He murmured his apologies, stood up and walked around the solar, going into the small buttery, a pantry chamber where jugs of wine and water were held. Athelstan filled a beaker and drank the water greedily. He glanced around and marvelled at the small tuns of Bordeaux which he recognised as the best, the kind Prior Anselm served royal guests. He also noticed the altar wine casks, which had been removed from the sacristy, all six of them lined up against the wall. Athelstan went over, each of them was empty, waiting for the next purveyance cart. He went back into the solar and smiled at the company who were staring fixedly at him.

'I am sorry,' he declared. 'Mistress Martha, your ale is very tasty, but I find water is best for my thirst. Tell me something, have you searched the church and this house, not to mention the mortuary and cemetery for any sign of a corpse or the stolen monies?'

'We have searched.' The sexton gestured at Cripplegate and Cotes. 'And of course Master Makepeace has sent down his men as well, but we can find no trace. As Mistress Martha declared those responsible are hardly going to hide what they have stolen under our very noses.'

'Very well.' Athelstan retook his seat and rapped the table top. 'Let us quickly recall what happened yesterday evening.' He smiled around. 'A long enough day, whatever that means in St Benet's. Isabella Makepeace is placed in a coffin in the death house, her son Simon is present and places a bouquet of red roses in the casket, which is then sealed. The coffin is lowered on to a sled and carted over to St Benet's, where it is placed before the rood screen, blessed and churched.' Athelstan shrugged. 'And so on and so on.' Everyone murmured their agreement. 'Once the reception of the corpse is completed, Compline is chanted by Parson Reynaud and Curate Cotes. Parson Reynaud adjourns to his house, Curate Cotes leaves to visit certain parishioners before arriving at the Devil's Oak. Yes?' Again there was agreement. 'Parson Reynaud, according to you, Martha, meets Daventry in his chancery chamber here in the priest's house. God knows what they talked about or what messages Daventry brought. According to you, Sexton Spurnel, both men were seen walking towards the church; that's the only proof we have that they entered it together.' Athelstan pulled a face. 'After that, darkness falls in the full sense of the word. Night passes. Uneventful in itself, except for the dreadful happenings in St Benet's. Mistress Martha, you awake the following morning, you find neither Parson Reynaud nor the curate in their beds, so you hurry down to the devil's door carrying its key. You are joined by Masters Spurnel, Cripplegate and Cotes. You break in through the devil's door, only to find a true hall of abomination.' Athelstan paused. 'Oh, by the way, Parson Reynaud's papers, manuscripts and chancery coffers?'

'Master Makepeace has already taken those – or rather his familiar Copping has,' Martha replied.

'Of course they have,' Athelstan murmured. 'I am sure that anything that was written down has now vanished, so we will make little progress in that quarter.'

'Brother Athelstan,' Martha smiled, 'even if certain manuscripts hadn't been taken away, and my companions can vouch for this: the Flesher and Parson Reynaud were loath to put anything in writing.'

'So they kept everything in the dark, concealed?'

'What do you mean?' Cripplegate demanded.

'I mean, we mean,' Cranston brought his hand down on the table, 'that this church and its dead priest were involved in all kinds of iniquity.'

'Sir John, that is not fair,' the curate protested.

'Master Cotes, that's the truth,' Cranston riposted.

Athelstan sat back in his chair. He agreed with Cranston: these worthies needed to be confronted with the truth they had ignored over the years.

'Why,' Athelstan demanded, 'was the cemetery being cleared? Why has it not been properly fenced off? Why does the crypt lie open? I shall answer my own questions.' Athelstan got to his feet, one hand raised, as if taking an oath. 'I agree with the Lord High Coroner, all kinds of wickedness were carried out in St Benet's, positioned so close both to the river and the Devil's Oak tavern: smuggling, the purchasing and selling of whores in both this kingdom and abroad, the handling of stolen goods, the protection of felons fleeing from the law and the murder of those the Flesher grew tired of. This is not a parish,' Athelstan's voice rose, 'it's nothing but a house of sin.'

'How dare you!' Cripplegate rose.

'He dares and so do I.' Cranston got swiftly to his feet, half-drawing his sword in a rasp of glittering steel.

'This is not true,' Cripplegate shouted, retaking his seat.

'I am a priest here too,' the curate yelled.

'And shame on you for that,' Cranston retorted. 'You followed one line from scripture?'

'Which is?'

'You certainly looked the other way.'

The shouting and the protests continued. Athelstan waited till the hubbub had died; only then did he retake his seat.

'He is right. The friar speaks the truth,' Martha declared, her voice harsh and carrying. 'Why should we defend Parson Reynaud? We may not have done anything wrong, but did we do anything right?' She let her question hang in the air as she stared around at her companions.

'Oh yes.' Cripplegate gave a deep sigh. 'What's the use? Martha is correct, we all know she is. Sir John, Brother Athelstan,' Cripplegate held up his hand, forefingers intertwined, 'you know it's the truth. Parson Reynaud and the Flesher were—'

'Thick as thieves,' the curate jibed.

'Yes they were,' Cripplegate declared. 'What could we do? We accept they are sinners to the core, but what they did was simply a matter of much suspected and nothing proved. Moreover, Sir John, the people grouped around this table are indebted to the Flesher: he loaned me money when I left the company of the Tower archers. I used that to finance my progress from an apprentice to journeyman, to full member of the locksmith guild.' Cripplegate spread his hands. 'The same could be said—'

'Of me and Sexton Spurnel,' Cotes interjected. 'And I am glad you've raised it, Nathaniel, aren't you?' The curate turned to the sexton.

'Yes, yes,' Spurnel whispered, 'it's time we summoned up the ghosts.'

PART FOUR

Psalm-singer (**Old English**): an informant

A deep silence descended on the solar. Athelstan felt a shiver as he looked at their faces, Cranston included. He sensed the past was breaking through.

'We have to speak about it,' Cranston murmured. 'Eighteen years since that night on board *The Song of the Sword*. The Twelve Apostles and the Rose Casket mysteriously taken. Good comrades slaughtered. Somebody betrayed us, yes?' A wall of silence greeted his question. 'Yes,' Cranston roared, slamming the table with his fist.

'Yes, yes, yes,' Cotes conceded. 'But who? Eighteen years on and we all ask the same question. And yes,' the curate now became quite heated, 'unlike you, Sir John, we were trapped by what happened. The old King and his son the Black Prince excused you, they pardoned you, they did not hold you to account, but we were summarily dismissed from the Tower guard. We are Queenhithe's men. Who could we turn to? Like others, we were swept into the Flesher's bloody embrace. He gave us money, smoothed the way here and smoothed the way there. He helped us – and I know why.' The curate stopped, breathing heavily.

'Why?' Athelstan asked softly.

'The Rose Casket, the Twelve Apostles,' Cotes blurted out. 'I am sure the Flesher helped us so as to keep us under close watch. The Flesher suspects that the precious stones are still in London, hence he watches us just in case we know something about their disappearance. Such scrutiny is not difficult,' he added bitterly. 'Spurnel, your post gives you a house, food on your table and, like me, enough to drink. Cripplegate, you are now a member of a guild but you are also in the Flesher's debt. You are a man with skills and knowledge he finds useful.'

'Yes, yes,' Cripplegate shrugged, 'I accept what you say.'

'And I am what you see,' the curate continued mockingly, 'a man who entered the church because he had nowhere else to go. I was given a benefice here because no other parish priest would accept me.'

'And you, Mistress?' Athelstan turned to Martha, who still sat serenely staring at the wall.

'I am what you see, Brother,' she replied. 'A widow, forced to accept the kindness and patronage of the Flesher, Parson Reynaud and their ilk. But I have no complaint. I sit, wait, watch and pray,' she smiled thinly, 'that the new parson, even if it's you, Curate Cotes, will allow me to continue in the post I have held for so many years.'

Athelstan smiled understandingly, though he quietly promised himself to interview the housekeeper separately. Such a sharp-witted, keen-eyed woman may know more than she had revealed.

'Brother,' Martha had her head down, playing with the bracelets on her wrists, 'so far I have not told anyone about this, but when you met the Flesher earlier today, three of his bullyboys were outside. Apparently they'd been with Lawyer Copping down to the execution scaffold at the Elms. Afterwards they visited St Bartholomew's Hospital and talked to its keeper, Brother Philippe.'

Athelstan caught his breath. 'And?'

'They mentioned something about a precious jewel, how it had been sold by Brother Philippe to a Cheapside goldsmith; that's all I could learn. However, once the Flesher was informed, he became deeply excited.'

'In God's name, I can see why!' Cranston exclaimed.

The others lost their sullen looks, all attentive, the years now rolling back as the great mystery which both bound them together, and yet divided them so bitterly, re-emerged from the darkness of the past.

'The Twelve Apostles!' Sexton Spurnel exclaimed. 'Impossible! It cannot be! They are back after eighteen years. So they were stolen and hidden! The person with one must have the others.' Spurnel paused and glanced sideways at Cripplegate and Cotes.

'God help anybody,' Cripplegate murmured, 'who the

Flesher suspects holds that casket. Sir John, Brother Athelstan, I give you good counsel: the Flesher will tear London apart to find that treasure; he will kill and kill again.'

'You seem to know a great deal about what the Flesher will do?' Athelstan retorted.

'Brother Athelstan, over the years I have studied the Flesher. I have never mentioned the Twelve Apostles to him, nor he to me, yet I tell you this.' Cripplegate leaned closer. 'Firstly, if the Flesher discovers who killed Parson Reynaud, abused his mother's coffin, killed Daventry and broke into that arca, then that person will take days to die. Secondly, anyone who prevents the Flesher seizing the Rose Casket and its precious contents will perish just as miserably.'

'But none of you,' Athelstan demanded, 'has heard anything about the whereabouts of these jewels since that fateful night?'

'Not until now,' Cripplegate replied.

'I often wonder,' Sexton Spurnel murmured, 'when I am deep in my cups, who betrayed us.'

'You say all this,' Athelstan countered, 'yet you still ally yourself to the likes of the Flesher, the very felon who could have organised the attack on the royal barge *The Song of the Sword*?'

'Oh for God's sake,' Cripplegate retorted, 'he helps us and he terrifies us. He treats us like he does his ferocious dogs. As long as we obey him and humour his whims, we are kept safe.'

'We have already explained our situation,' Cotes sneered. 'What choice do any of us here have? Oh, by the way,' Cotes's voice turned mocking, 'Sir John, you are the Lord High Coroner of London. The Flesher is a dyed-in-the-wool villain. Why has his collar never been fingered by you?'

'We grow old,' Cripplegate declared. 'Sir John, Brother Athelstan, we really have no choice about who we deal with. We are the little men. We have our narrow houses, a few treasures but,' he snapped his fingers, 'who would mourn for me if the Flesher decided that I should go? Curate Cotes is correct, if the King's coroner in London cannot check the Flesher – what chance do we have?'

Athelstan nodded understandingly. Deep in his heart, he felt sorry for these people: they were trapped. He could sense their intense dislike, even hatred, for the Flesher, but they were caught in his malignant web. 'Tell me,' Athelstan took a deep breath, 'does the name Grenel mean anything to you?'

'Of course,' Sexton Spurnel replied. 'You know it does. The Grenels were also Tower archers. They were killed, probably drowned, when *The Song of the Sword* capsized during the attack.' Sexton Spurnel's face was now flushed, and Athelstan suspected the sexton had been drinking for most of the day.

'And,' Athelstan demanded, 'what were they like? Good comrades?'

'Father and son,' Curate Cotes retorted. 'Decent men, skilled archers. They kept to themselves. I mean, we hailed from Queenhithe, they were from Southwark.' The curate narrowed his eyes. 'In fact, I think they were in your parish of St Erconwald's?'

'Long before my time.'

'As I said, they kept to themselves. The father was married to some local woman. Walter, the son, was a bachelor. One day whilst practising at the butts I asked Walter if he had a sweetheart. The lad just grinned and replied how he had found happiness in the House of Bethany – that's all he said.'

'Bethany, what's that?'

'Brother, this was years ago. Perhaps it was some brothel or house of pleasure, but more than that . . .' Cotes's voice trailed away.

'Let's return to the matter in hand,' Cranston demanded. Athelstan looked towards the mullioned glass window, a small square of light now darkening as dusk set in. Athelstan pulled his chancery satchel closer. It had been a long day; it was time to return to his parish. He was curious to find out about Brother Philippe and that precious stone. Athelstan again wondered about the cellar beneath Margo's house and those two mummified corpses.

'And Daventry?' Cranston asked. 'Do you know why Arundel's man came here?'

'Sir John,' Martha replied, 'I have told you: Daventry was closeted with Parson Reynaud. I know nothing of what passed between them, and that is true of all of us.' A murmur of agreement echoed her words. Athelstan could see that the three men were still distracted about the possibility that the Twelve Apostles had reappeared in London.

'And Ingersol, the Flesher's henchman commonly known as the Sicarius, the dagger man?'

'Oh yes, we glimpsed him coming and going between here and the Devil's Oak.' Cotes replied. 'A secretive soul. A man of the shadows.'

Martha shook her head as she repressed a shiver. 'God forgive me,' she whispered, 'but I felt like a mouse that lived constantly in the shadow of the cat. Ingersol was a dangerous man; he gave me that impression. A constant visitor here, the go-between used by the Flesher to bring messages to and from Parson Reynaud. He rarely spoke or met your eye. He dressed most soberly. You would think he was a priest more than an assassin, a true thief of the night. Brother Athelstan, Ingersol would come and go, one menacing shadow flitting amongst the rest.'

'Do you think he brought messages about the cemetery outside, its clearance, the work being done? Was that the decision of Parson Reynaud, the Flesher or both?'

'Sir John,' Sexton Spurnel shook his head, 'I – we – cannot say.' He blew his cheeks out. 'The dagger man came and went. A forbidding enough character; in fact I haven't seen him for the last two weeks or so.'

Athelstan sat in silence as the parishioners scraped back their chairs, whispering to each other. The friar was baffled by the fog of mysteries which swirled about this parish and its church: murder, theft, sacrilege. Athelstan rubbed his face and lifted his head.

'Master Cripplegate?'

'Yes, Brother?'

'We have touched on this before. I ask you not because I accuse you, I am just deeply curious.'

'Brother?'

'The arca.' Athelstan pointed at the coroner. 'I want that empty arca taken to Sir John's chamber in the Guildhall.'

'Why?'

'Because I am the Lord High Coroner and I want it so,' Cranston snapped.

'Very good, Sir John.' Cripplegate turned back to the friar. 'So, Brother, your question – though I can hazard a guess.'

'Can the keys to the parish arca, whether they be the work of a craftsman or not, be copied precisely and accurately?'

'The blunt answer is yes. Sir John, Brother Athelstan, there's not a key under heaven which cannot be copied accurately and most skilfully.'

'And how?'

'Ideally, a piece of pure Castilian soap. It captures every little twist and cast of a key pressed into it. I have seen it done. A cast is made of both sides of the key, particular attention being paid to what we call the teeth, which fit snugly into the lock to turn it. Of course,' Cripplegate spread his hands, 'I am sure the Fl . . .' He caught himself in time and smiled. 'Master Makepeace, like Parson Reynaud, never let that key out of sight.'

'We'd all swear to that,' Spurnel added.

'And Isabella Makepeace? Mistress Martha, we have spoken of this before, but I would value your opinion.'

'The truth? Isabella Makepeace was of the same evil substance as her son.' Martha's voice trilled with hatred. 'No one will gainsay me.' She paused and stared around. 'Brother, Sir John, I speak honestly, Isabella Makepeace was hated. She ruled from her chamber in the Devil's Oak like any tyrant. Ask anyone who had dealings with her.'

'I have,' Cranston interjected.

'Then you will know all about her.' Martha half smiled. 'Oh, Mistress Makepeace could act the part of the great lady but, when she wanted to, she would cruelly inflict her anger on some poor unfortunate.'

'As she did to many, including myself,' the curate declared. 'The wrong word, the awkward glance, the failure to jump when she whistled were, in her eyes and her son's, heinous crimes. But Sir John, Brother Athelstan, the day draws on, the hour is late. I am sure I speak for the rest, but I have no more to say.'

Cranston glanced at Athelstan who nodded. The meeting ended, though the friar beckoned to Martha and asked her to stay for a while. They waited until the steps of the rest faded and the main door closed.

'Brother?' Martha sat on the chair closest to him. He could smell her fragrance, a sweet herbal essence.

'You do not like the Flesher or his mother?'

'Nobody does or did.'

'And you can cast no light on these mysteries?'

'Brother Athelstan,' she glanced across at Cranston, 'Sir John, you heard the Flesher's filthy remark to me this morning. Like many in St Benet's parish, I have to tolerate insults because I have no choice.' She paused, glancing down at the table top, and when she lifted her head, tears brimmed in her eyes.

'I married very young, my husband was sickly. He'd hardly made any profit from his work and, when he died, he left a mountain of debts. I buried my husband here, Brother Athelstan, and three months later found myself in the House of Delights. It was either that or whoring along the streets of Queenhithe, pandering to the sailors or working in the sweatshops of the squalid stews along the river. In the House of Delights the Flesher provided me with a chamber, food, clothes and a few coins. I was careful about who I went with.' She shrugged prettily. 'Brother Athelstan, Sir John, go through this city tonight and you will find many a woman with a similar tale.'

'Yes, yes,' Cranston agreed. 'What you say is true. You had no kin?'

'I had no kin and I had no choice,' she replied fiercely, 'until you can create that choice. I was most prudent with my monies. I counted and hoarded the coins and eventually I bought myself out.' She dabbed at her sweat-soaked brow. 'At the House of Delights I had entertained Parson Reynaud. I approached him after he made it obvious that he wanted a housekeeper. I replied that I would serve him as a good housekeeper, but I made it very clear that this would be in his house and not in his bed.'

'And he agreed?'

'Brother Athelstan,' she grinned, 'he had to. I am an excellent cook. I am also discreet, clean, and I knew Parson Reynaud in every sense of the word.' She waved a hand. 'So here I am and, if God is good, here I stay. You would think I might know of all Parson Reynaud's dealings – after all, I did share the

same house as him. The blunt answer is no! I served him and
his sinister, shadowy visitors their food and drink. I ran errands
and delivered messages, but Brother Athelstan, I am not a fool.
I was accepted, even favoured, because I knew my place. I
did not want to know what was going on. I made no attempt
to find out, to spy, to eavesdrop – in fact the opposite. Brother
Athelstan, that is how you survive in the Flesher's world. Keep
to the straight and narrow, and all will be well. Make a mistake
and you pay dearly for it. You can put me on oath; you can
go through Parson Reynaud's manuscripts,' she pulled a face,
'though the Flesher or his lawyer Master Copping have
collected these, for what they are worth. However, if you
scrutinise Parson Reynaud's world, you will find that I was
his housekeeper – nothing more, nothing less . . .'

A short while later, Cranston and Athelstan left St Benet's
and stood in the empty concourse before the church. The friar
stared up at the ancient stone front of St Benet's and wondered
how such a house of prayer could become a mansion of murder.

'Sir John, Sir John?'

Athelstan turned as Tiptoft slipped out of the darkness.

'Sir John, Brother Athelstan.' He hastened across the
cobbles, wiping the sweat from his face. 'A thousand pardons,
but I bear urgent messages from Brother Philippe and
Benedicta, not to mention Mauger and the rest. You must return
to St Erconwald's.'

'Why, what has happened?'

'Rifflers attempted to rob your cottage and that of Margo.
Benedicta was threatened—'

'No injury surely?' Athelstan clutched his stomach at a
spasm of cold fear.

'Oh no, all are safe, but they wrecked your house, or tried
to, and they dug up poor Margo's coffin. Anyway, all are safe.
Brother Philippe has closely examined the corpses.' Tiptoft
scratched his spiky red hair, 'Although I am not too sure what
that means, but that's what Benedicta said: that he has examined the corpses and has much to say. Brother Philippe hasn't
returned back across the river. Benedicta has lodged him in
the Piebald. Mine host Jocelyn says he will look after him
until our good brother returns.'

'Sir John, we should . . .'

Cranston, however had walked away, staring at the mouth of an alleyway across the concourse, one of those thread-thin ribbons of utter darkness where the night-walkers swarmed ready for the hunt.

'I am sure I heard the clatter of steel,' the coroner murmured. 'Oh heaven and all its angels, Tiptoft, Athelstan!'

The friar stared in horror as figures carrying cresset torches, their leaping flames glittering in an array of drawn steel, debouched out of the alleyway. Athelstan counted at least seven in all, each hooded and visored. They carried sword and dagger, whilst an eighth trailing behind them had a powerful arbalest, primed and ready to loose. Cranston threw his cloak back and whistled shrilly, hoping that Flaxwith or some of his bailiffs were still in the vicinity.

'*Pax et bonum.*' The leading figure placed his sword and dagger on the cobbles and held up both hands. 'Sir John, Brother Athelstan, I repeat, *pax et bonum*. We wish you no ill but we need to converse.'

'French,' Athelstan whispered, 'he has the tongue of Paris.'

'I repeat,' the man called, 'we wish you well.'

'You choose your time and place unwisely,' Cranston shouted back. 'Couldn't we meet in the full light of day in my chambers at the Guildhall?'

'That may suit you, Sir John.' The stranger gestured at his company to stay where they were whilst he, hands outstretched, walked slowly towards Cranston and Athelstan. 'I agree, Sir John, but there are some things which are best said in the dark rather than in the brightness of God's day.'

'Dark, light, day and night mean nothing here in Hell's buttery. Indeed,' Cranston continued, 'in this valley of sin the night has both eyes and ears and, at times, even hands which carry sword, dagger and every other weapon known to man.'

'Be that as it may . . .' The stranger pulled back his hood and lowered the visor concealing the bottom half of his face. 'Time passes,' the stranger murmured, 'the hours flit. I need to speak to you urgently,' he turned to the friar, 'Brother Athelstan especially.'

'And you are?' Athelstan demanded.

'Wait.' Cranston held a hand up and turned back to where Tiptoft stood. 'Search out Flaxwith and my bailiffs. Tell them to find me wherever I go.' The coroner pointed at the alleyways. 'There will be people watching who, for a coin, will lead Flaxwith through that hellish maze. Now sir,' Cranston turned back to the Frenchman, 'you are?'

The stranger scratched his black, tousled hair, his cheerful face breaking into a grin, his eyes wrinkling in amusement. A mailed clerk, Athelstan concluded, educated in the chancery and the tiltyard. Skilled in weaponry, with a sharp mind and a keen wit.

'I am Hugh Levigne.'

'And who is Hugh Levigne?' Cranston mocked.

'I am the Candlelight-Master. My companions are members of a cohort known as the Luciferi. We lodge with the French ambassador, Monseigneur Derais, in his house—'

'La Maison Parisienne.' Cranston finished his sentence. 'The official residence of the French King's principal envoy to the English court.'

'And a close friend of your King Richard,' Levigne added quickly. 'Who, I understand,' he grinned, 'adores everything French.'

'As did his father and grandfather,' Cranston retorted. 'They certainly took enough armies to France to seize and hold it as their own.'

Levigne elegantly raised a gauntleted hand. 'Those days are over. We now talk peace to each other. Heart speaks to heart. King Richard, my Lord of Gaunt and Monseigneur Thibault, your regent's Master of Secrets, all seek amity and reconciliation – Monseigneur Thibault in particular.'

'A truly delightful man,' Cranston declared drily. 'I wondered if he would appear in the masque now being staged.' Cranston tapped his warbelt. 'A very murderous play,' he murmured.

'Sir John?'

'The Twelve Apostles,' Cranston declared. 'I have more than a feeling that this is about the Twelve Apostles.'

'Sharp as sharp can be,' Levigne declared. 'More cutting than the hydra's tooth. Bluff old Jack is never what he seems to be.' Levigne, head to one side, studied Cranston from head to toe before his gaze shifted to Athelstan. 'And your constant little shadow.'

'Some shadow,' Cranston retorted.

'Bluff Jack, merry Jack,' Levigne leaned closer, 'please, I shall resheath my sword and dagger, then let us talk.' He gestured around. 'There are taverns enough here?'

'Taverns indeed, hostelries and alehouses,' Cranston declared, then paused at a whistle which cut sharply across the concourse. Athelstan glanced over his shoulder as Flaxwith and his cohort of bailiffs walked out of the darkness around St Benet's.

'We fashioned a few torches and were looking in the crypt behind the church,' Flaxwith called out. 'We have also been watching your visitors.'

'Not visitors, but friends yes?' the Candlelight-Master called out.

Cranston turned back and smiled at Levigne. 'Oh yes, our new-found friends. So Master Hugh, pick up and put away your weapons; the same goes for your companions. Once I am satisfied that they have done as I ask, we shall adjourn to a hostelry I have always wanted to visit, the Devil's Oak.'

'Sir John,' Athelstan warned, even as he noticed how Levigne was also taken aback.

'Why not?' The coroner chuckled. 'I want to show the Flesher that the King's law, the King's peace and the King's Lord High Coroner cannot be checked, curtailed or controlled but, like the spirit, we can go where and when we will. I want to visit the Devil's Oak, and now is as good a time as any. So, my friend, tell your company to follow close behind Master Flaxwith. Tiptoft,' he bellowed, 'you too stay close. Right, my beloveds, let's go sup with demons.'

The Devil's Oak was, despite its age and use, still a magnificent, if malevolent, hostelry, boasting three gables, sloping red-tiled roofs, protuberant chimney stacks and walls of ashlar stone. The front of the tavern spread out behind a porticoed entrance, its columns of pure oak painted and picked out in brilliantly garish colours; these caught the light of the many sconce torches flickering in their cressets. The entire tavern was surrounded by a battlemented wall and entered through

a fortified double gateway, where some of the Flesher's liveried
retainers stood on guard. They tried to stop Cranston, but the
coroner yelled at them to be damned, and swept into the large
cobbled bailey which stretched either side of the gateway. This
great stabling yard echoed with noise and tumult: people
shouted, sang, cursed and yelled; horses neighed shrilly as
they kicked at their stalls behind the tavern; dogs barked. A
sow, which had escaped from the piggery, lumbered into the
yard, where it was swiftly slaughtered by a cleaver, its massive
head split clean as an apple, the rich-red blood spouting out
to bring in the kennel dogs eager to lap, wary of the fists and
boots of the slaughter boys. Numerous carts loaded with provisions stood about. Travelling tinkers, chapmen and all kinds
of river people made their way up through the grand entrance
into the welcoming warmth of the spacious taproom. On either
side of the steps perched two long arrow chests. Each contained
a corpse, black as soot from head to toe, though some effort
had been made to cleanse their faces. One of the Flesher's
henchmen, his jerkin displaying the Sycamore insignia,
proclaimed how these two corpses were those of thieves;
malefactors who had tried to burgle the house of one of Lord
Makepeace's friends by breaking through a chimney stack.
Both felons had been trapped and killed by crossbow bolts,
so anyone who recognised them should say so now under pain
of forfeiture. The customers simply averted their gaze from
the gruesome sight of the barbs, still deeply embedded in the
dead men's bellies, and hurried on.

   Cranston's arrival in the courtyard soon made itself felt.
The noise subsided. People turned, hands going for knives and
daggers, or they picked up cudgels close to the arrow chest.
A horn brayed and a door to the side of the main entrance
opened in a gust of steam, which carried the reek of burning
oil and other cooking smells. The Flesher appeared, flanked
by Raquin and Copping. The riffler leader hurried down the
steps, his ugly face twisted in a smile, though he was clearly
surprised to see the coroner grace his premises.

   'Sir John, Sir John,' he blustered, 'you are most welcome.
You have news of my beloved mother, Master Daventry—'

   'And your gold and silver?'

'My rightful property.'

'No news, Master Makepeace; my apologies but no news.' Cranston stepped back, as if surveying the Devil's Oak from the top of its pointed gable to the pricks of light just above the ground, the soft glow of candles and torches burning in the cellars beneath the tavern. 'Do you know something, Master Makepeace? One of these days I am going to come back here, perhaps even tonight, and do a truly thorough search.'

'For what?' Raquin demanded.

'For whatever I find.'

'And this evening, Sir John?' The Flesher peered over Cranston's shoulder at Levigne. 'The Candlelight-Master, the Luciferi,' he murmured. 'You keep strange company, Sir John.'

'Bearing in mind who I am now talking to, that's probably the most truthful thing you've said in decades, Master Makepeace.' Cranston clapped his hands. 'But enough of the pleasantries. I want my retinue here entertained in your taproom. I also need a secure chamber, one of your best, guarded by Master Flaxwith and two of my good friend's escort. So,' Cranston again clapped his hands. The Flesher glanced at Raquin, shrugged, and led Cranston and his party up the steps and into the spacious taproom.

Athelstan gazed around in silent wonderment. If any chamber was heavily tainted with sin, this one certainly was. A yawning, cavernous place, the taproom had a high-beamed ceiling; its floorboards were covered in sawdust stained by food, drink and, Athelstan peered at one large blotch, what looked like congealed blood. The noise was raucous and never-ending: singing; carousing bagpipes wailed and trumpets blared. Two drunks, naked except for their muddy boots, danced grotesquely to the merriment of other customers. Three women tied to each other were boxing and wrestling whilst the onlookers laid wagers. A young whore disported herself on a mattress in one corner whilst her companions tried to persuade a sottish city fop to join them in the darkness beneath the stairs. Smells of cooking billowed from the kitchen behind the great serving board. Cries, moans, calls and shrieks of pleasure and pain echoed on all sides. A rat pit, built just beneath one of the shuttered windows, was being prepared for

the usual slaughter and the betting which accompanied it.
Close by, wiry-haired dogs, eager to be at their prey, threw
themselves against their cages. Levigne swore loudly. Cranston
just turned and clapped the Frenchman on the shoulder.

'I've seen worse – a rare event, but I have seen worse.'

The Flesher took them up on to the first gallery and showed
them into a chamber warmed by braziers and well lit with
candles placed along the oaken polished table and the broad
windowsill. Herb branches hung from the rafter beams to
perfume the air. The floorboards, polished and gleaming, were
covered in soft black turkey rugs, whilst leather-backed cush-
ioned chairs were placed around the long table; this sported
a small, silver nef which glowed in the dancing light. The
Flesher bowed mockingly and left, saying he would send up
a carafe of wine, fresh bread and platters of minced pork.
Cranston thanked him, shouting in a sarcastic tone that all
expenses and bills should be sent to the Exchequer at
Westminster for payment, before slamming the door shut. He
gestured at Levigne and Athelstan to sit down, but then he
tiptoed back to the door, swiftly opened it, looked out and
closed it with a sigh.

'Good,' he murmured. 'Flaxwith and two of your company,
Monseigneur Levigne, will guard the gallery. I believe these
walls are solid enough, there is no room on either side whilst,'
the coroner peered up at the ceiling, 'all above seems safe
enough . . .' He broke off at a tap on the door and Tiptoft
pushed his head through.

'Sir John, do I stay?'

'No.' The coroner sat down on a chair, beckoning the
messenger in. 'Go to Southwark, yes Brother?' Cranston didn't
wait for an answer. 'Ask Brother Philippe the physician to
stay in the parish until Athelstan and I return. Good, good.'
Cranston ushered Tiptoft out and they all waited while the
cheeky-eyed slattern came in to serve both wine and food.
Cranston ate as if starved, Levigne picked at his platter, whilst
Athelstan, lost in his own thoughts, sipped at his wine and
wondered what the Frenchman really wanted. The friar rose
and walked across to stare at the wall paintings. On their way
up to this room, the Flesher had offhandedly referred to it as

'the devil's chancery', and the crudely painted wall paintings reflected this: vigorous depictions of Hell which recalled the Hangman of Rochester's work. On this particular wall the Archangel Ariel scourged the wicked across face and eyes, driving them across a meadow where black smoke curled, shot through with fire. Next to it, a cohort of demons hunted the damned, chasing them across red-hot flagstones to a bubbling, black lake.

'We are ready,' Cranston murmured.

Athelstan returned to his seat opposite Levigne, who raised his head.

'Sir John, Brother Athelstan, we should begin. I do not like this place much.'

'I agree.' Cranston put his horn spoon away. 'Brother Athelstan, let me formally introduce Hugh Levigne, Candlelight-Master and leader of the Luciferi – the Light Bearers who are information gatherers for His Catholic Majesty the King of France and Monseigneur Derias, his envoy to England. They all reside in La Maison Parisienne, the Paris House, in Lothbury. They collect information, but also work quietly and secretly to advance their master's cause.' Cranston pushed his platter away. 'Sometimes they are our enemies; sometimes they are our allies. On the rare occasion, they could even be our friends. So,' the coroner turned to Levigne, 'what is it this time?'

'Your friend, Sir John. Let me be precise and to the point. Eighteen years ago, the French Crown, much against its better judgement, though at the time it had little choice, handed over to the English court so-called reparation for war damages.' Levigne shrugged and spread his hands. 'It was really a bribe to keep Edward of England and his brood of falcons out of France. We had no choice but to surrender the Twelve Apostles, exquisitely beautiful jewels, in their container, the Rose Casket. This coffer was regarded as equally costly, fashioned out of rare wood with golden, silver-stemmed roses.' Levigne sipped at his wine. 'At the time the French Crown was determined, as it still is, to recover this unique sacred treasure. The Rose Casket and all it contained was handed over to the Hanseatic merchants to be taken to Queenhithe on one of their ships,

The Glory of Bremen. We kept our word and stayed out of the proceedings; then we heard about the attack on you, Sir John, and your war barge, *The Song of the Sword.*' Levigne toasted Cranston with his goblet. 'We also learnt you had been injured and pulled from the river, but that the Rose Casket and the Twelve Apostles had vanished. Like the English Crown, we thought it was only a matter of time before such a gorgeous casket, with its truly precious stones, emerged on the London market or, indeed, anywhere else.' He paused. 'And yet, nothing. We know that your King's ministers searched high and low, and we certainly did. Time passes, but the Luciferi do not forget. We pay for those who act as our eyes and ears along the thoroughfares and waterfronts of your city. We are always interested in what is being offered for sale, be it a secret or a sapphire.' Levigne cleared his throat. 'Then, about two months ago – yes, about the feast of the Magdalene, we heard a most curious story. A woman, fairly old, poor and decidedly unwell, had approached London merchants, cabinet-makers and casket craftsmen. She was offering the most beautiful coffer for sale. From the description given, we realised it was the Rose Casket, but who the woman was remained a mystery until now.' Athelstan glanced warningly at Cranston to remain silent on what they already knew. 'No matter, Brother,' Levigne leaned across the table and gripped Athelstan's wrist, 'we have learnt a great deal and – how do you put it? – we are ahead of the game. We understood that a woman from your parish took a precious stone to the keeper of St Bartholomew's Hospital. She apparently offered it in return for treatment. We believe the keeper did not realise what he had received and sold it to the Cheapside merchant Blundel.' Levigne, his face all excited, leaned across the table. 'Brother, what is important is that the Twelve Apostles and the Rose Casket have reap-peared. It seems that this woman of your parish first offered the Rose Casket for sale and then one of its precious stones.' He held a hand up. 'Before you ask, she failed to sell the casket. From the little we gleaned, the woman became deeply concerned at the keen interest shown in the casket. She must have realised that no one would accept it was some family heirloom but part of a treasure stolen from a royal barge. We know that the London merchants were given a description of the casket and its contents eighteen years ago.' He shrugged. 'Merchants never forget, especially when they have received a warning from the Crown and, correct me if I am wrong Sir John, but anyone caught handling that casket, be it a seller or a customer, could face a charge of high treason?'

'Correct.' Cranston wiped his mouth on a napkin. 'Monseigneur Levigne, we know a little about what has happened. We are now hastening back to St Erconwald's. I concede that you have learnt a great deal; indeed you must also realise that the owner of this hostelry, Master Makepeace, popularly known as the Flesher, may have had a hand, and I suspect he did, in the attack on the royal barge when the Rose Casket was stolen.'

'Yes, yes, I accept that.'

'And you must also accept that the Rose Casket and the Twelve Apostles are the legitimate property of the English Crown?'

'Ah yes.' Levigne opened the buttoned pocket of his doublet and handed a cream-coloured scroll of costly parchment to Cranston, who broke the seal, read its contents, sighed dramatically and passed it to Athelstan. The message written in the clerkly hand of Thibault's Secret Chancery, asked Cranston and his '*nobilis secretarius*' Brother Athelstan 'to cooperate fully with Monseigneur Levigne in the discovery and seizure of the Twelve Apostles and their coffer the Rose Casket, feloniously taken by an act of the most heinous treason.'

Athelstan studied the signature and seal of Thibault, Gaunt's enigmatic Master of Secrets, then tapped it with his fingernails. 'Thibault,' he declared slowly, 'wants these precious stones, but he also wants to give them back to the French Crown, that is obvious.' Athelstan smiled at Levigne. 'Otherwise he wouldn't ask us to cooperate with you. In return for what, Monseigneur?'

'Gold,' Cranston whispered. 'French gold, French troops, French assistance if needed here in this kingdom. Young Richard is famous for his love of all things French and it is equally well known that the English Exchequer is empty.'

'What you say may well be correct.' Levigne rose. 'But

now you know why we have and will continue to take a great interest in you, Sir John, and the worthy Athelstan. Now we must go.'

They all left the Devil's Oak. The tavern was, as the hour grew late, the true home of all creatures of the dark. Athelstan felt wary as he followed Cranston through the throng of garishly dressed night-walkers, be it the tribe of thieves or the world of the whore. The noise was raucous in the extreme. The rough music strident. The air perfumed with all kinds of smells, both rank and sweet. Cranston did not bother to clasp the Flesher's hand but brushed it aside as he led his group out across the yard and through the massive double gates. Here Levigne and his cohort made their swift farewells and left. Cranston turned, leading Athelstan, Flaxwith and his comitatus of bailiffs along the waterfront towards London Bridge. The coroner had decided that crossing the Thames by barge was too dangerous. Athelstan agreed. The night was pitch dark, whilst a stiff easterly wind buffeted the river, making any crossing extremely perilous. Conversation was difficult. Cranston and Flaxwith were also very wary. They might well be King's men, buckled for war and vigilant, but they were, as the coroner remarked, in the kingdom of the damned. Here human wolves sloped through the darkness and demons crouched on rooftops behind sills and in the filthy enclaves, their knives sharp, eyes bright, and wits ready for any mischief which might bring them profit or the twisted merriment of hurting another soul. Eerie chanting and echoing cries cut the night air. Shouts and curses dinned the ear. They passed through the occasional pool of light, thrown by crossroads lanterns, or by bonfires where the city rubbish was burnt. The dispossessed flocked to these to warm themselves, as well as to cook the food they'd filched earlier in the day from the butchers' bins and bakers' trays. Dogs fought the feral cats and both confronted the long, grey rats that infested the alleyways leading down to the river. They passed gallows and gibbets well stocked with the ripening flesh of malefactors hanged earlier that day. Occasionally they would glimpse a furtive funeral party, pushing a corpse in a barrow to one of the many cemeteries, and Athelstan recalled that bleak wasteland around

St Benet's. The friar was even more convinced that the grave-yard and crypt of that sinister church had been used by the Flesher to hide the victims of his murderous rage. Athelstan just wondered how many corpses lay there unknown, and why the Flesher and Parson Reynaud were so intent on clearing God's Acre – for what?

At last they reached the approaches to London Bridge, where Cranston made his farewells of Flaxwith, telling his chief bailiff to inform the Lady Maude where he was going and that he would return to her on the morrow. The coroner then used his passes and seal to gain entrance, through the postern door and on to the moon-washed strip which cut across the bridge, with houses, storerooms and warehouses built on either side. The bridge lay silent, doors and shutters had been pulled closed and locked. Here and there, patches of candle glow or lantern light broke the darkness. All sound was hidden by the constant thunder of the river now in fast flow, hurling itself against the struts and starlings below, whilst the fish-tainted breeze whipped away any words he or Cranston tried to exchange. They hastened past the ancient, small chapel dedicated to St Thomas a Becket, towards the towering mass of Southwark gatehouse: here its keeper Burdon and his ever-growing brood of children kept close watch over the severed heads of traitors brought to be tarred and poled above the railings of the bridge. At last they reached the other side. They passed through the wicket gate, across the execution yard, where the corpses of malefactors still dangled either at the end of a gallows rope or gibbeted in a metal cage. Athelstan murmured a hasty prayer, then they were through, on to the alleyway leading up to St Erconwald's. Athelstan paused to bless both himself and Cranston in thanksgiving for being safely home.

'Excellent oatmeal,' Cranston declared to the agreement of others gathered around Athelstan's great table in the stone-flagged kitchen of his priest's house. Athelstan smiled, gesturing in welcome at those who'd joined him and Cranston to break their fast; Brother Philippe, Benedicta and Mauger. Sir John had lodged at the Piebald in the chamber next to Brother Philippe's and enjoyed a good night's rest. Both the coroner and the physician had risen early and attended Athelstan's Jesus Mass just after dawn. Once Athelstan was finished in the church, they'd assembled here in the priest's house to feast, as Cranston put it, on the sweetest oatmeal, the freshest bread and creamiest butter from Merryleg's pie shop.

Athelstan stared around the kitchen. On his return the previous evening he'd become very angry when he had learnt about the attack on his house, the desecration of Margo's grave and, above all, the nasty threats issued to Benedicta. Nevertheless, all had been put right. Margo rested peacefully in her coffin. Benedicta assured Athelstan that she was fully recovered, and took great pride in how other parishioners, Crispin the carpenter especially, had gathered to put matters right so even the marks of the break-in could scarcely be detected.

'Once again,' Athelstan picked up his tankard of light ale and toasted Benedicta's lovely smiling face, 'once again my profound thanks. But let us move swiftly to what brings us here.'

'It would appear, Athelstan,' Brother Philippe broke in, 'before you continue any further, well . . .' The physician scratched his cheek and blinked. 'I am sorry, but I am a little bit confused. I know from Benedicta about the conclusions you may have reached, about the two corpses found in that cellar. However, I urge you first to inspect them as I have my own theories.'

'Then let us finish eating,' Cranston urged. 'I do want to see this.'

Once the meal was over, cloaks were collected and they hurried out into the cold, misty morning, down the path, through the lychgate and across God's Acre. Here the wisps of a thick river fog, which had rolled in the previous evening, now thinned, parting and shifting like ghostly curtains. Godbless was standing outside his cottage and greeted them all before proclaiming how the demons were back. Fluttering figures, shadowy people shrouded in knotted glass; how these stalkers of the sky walked the wind and rode the clouds. Athelstan stopped to bless both beggar man and goat, then they hurried on. Mauger went ahead to unlock the death house, a grim, cold place despite the glowing braziers, the nosegays hanging from the rafters and the bowls of crushed aromatic herbs placed around that long, cold, barn-like chamber with its whitewashed walls and earth-beaten floor. Two of the mortuary tables were covered with coffin cloths. Mauger pulled these back so Brother Philippe, standing between the tables, could explain his conclusions. Athelstan stared pityingly at the two cadavers, father and son locked in their mysterious deaths. The bearded faces looked at peace, eyes and mouths closed, arms across their chests, legs together. The skin of both corpses now exuded a strange, glossy, yellow-white tinge, and Athelstan glimpsed the horrid, purple-red cuts to the chest, belly and, when he moved both corpses, the lower back.

'Death wounds,' Brother Philippe explained. 'Very serious injuries. I suspect both men were attacked by assailants carrying both sword and dagger. The victims were standing close together. They were struck from behind, they turned to face their attackers and received further wounds to the front.'

'Would they have been killed immediately?'

'No, Athelstan, Sir John will be my witness. Men in battle can and do sustain savage injuries yet still fight on. Yes, my Lord Coroner?'

Cranston stood, eyes closed, rocking backwards and forwards on his booted feet. Athelstan sensed he was going back in time. 'The attack,' Cranston murmured, 'was ferocious and swift. They overran *The Song of the Sword*, our men were struck; I saw some of them stagger about, archers going overboard—'

'Tell me,' Athelstan asked, 'where were you exactly? Were you off Southwark side?'

'Yes, yes we were. I remember glimpsing the beacon light in the steeple of St Mary Overy. The captain of our barge had moved his craft across river to confuse anyone who might be following us. *The Song of the Sword* went backwards and forwards. Eventually the captain pronounced himself satisfied and so he turned, aiming like an arrow for the north bank of the Thames. I recall the river fog parting and the wolves were upon us.'

'You were knocked unconscious?' Athelstan asked. 'You fell overboard and were fished out of the river?'

'In a word, yes.'

'And so let us move forward eighteen years,' Athelstan declared, 'and what do we have? Fat Margo, Margaret Grenel, widow of this parish, falls ill. She apparently held a great treasure. We suspect she tried to sell the Rose Casket but became frightened at the reaction of those she offered it to; that is most understandable but then matters moved on.'

'Margaret had a grievous, morbid sickness upon her,' Brother Philippe declared. 'She crossed the Thames and was admitted to the great hall at St Bartholomew's. We can only do what we have the time and money for.' The physician paused. 'So many come,' he whispered, 'one after the other. I need money, good coin to buy medicines, powders, potions and philtres. Margaret Grenel was part of the throng until she approached me. Now, I was honest with her. I could do little to assuage the humours in her belly, but she wanted opiates to control the pain and these are costly. I agreed and she gave me a jewel. Ah well,' Brother Philippe shrugged, 'I am a physician, a Benedictine monk. I know nothing about amethysts or such costly items. I took the precious stone Margo offered me in full payment for all treatment. Naturally, I wanted to be rid of it, to exchange the item for good pounds sterling, so I took it to Merchant Blundel. Looking back,' he added ruefully, 'I suppose Blundel must have been truly delighted to secure such a treasure for such a petty sum. It simply proves, as the good Lord says, that the children of this world are more astute in their dealings with their own kind than the children of the light.' He smiled. 'I am not saying I am a child of the light, just that I work for them.' The physician pulled his ave beads out of a pouch and began to sift them through his fingers. 'Athelstan,' he continued, 'what you told us this morning before Mass is truly fascinating. How the amethyst Margo Grenel gave me is part of a long-lost treasure hoard, a king's ransom now being sought by all the great, the good and the ghastly. So what will happen next?'

Cranston explained how he would visit Merchant Blundel, demand the amethyst be returned and tell the goldsmith to seek redress at the Exchequer. Athelstan let himself relax and the conversation swirl around him as he tried to impose order on his own tumbling thoughts. He and Cranston had met Brother Philippe, Benedicta and Mauger in the sacristy before mass. In hushed tones Athelstan had informed them about the history of the Twelve Apostles, the attack on the royal barge eighteen years ago, the involvement of the Flesher and their meeting with the Candlelight-Master and the Luciferi the previous evening. Both Benedicta and Mauger had explained how strangers had certainly been seen in and around St Erconwald's, on the approaches to London Bridge as well as near Haceldema, the Field of Blood, a stretch of wasteland beyond the cemetery. However, neither Benedicta nor Mauger could say if these were the Flesher's henchmen or those of the Candlelight-Master.

'We are finished here,' Athelstan declared absent-mindedly. He picked up one of the coffin sheets and draped it over the younger man's corpse. Benedicta and Mauger did the same for the other cadaver and Athelstan declared they should return to the priest's house. 'Oh,' he paused, 'where are the clothing and other effects of these two corpses? I suspect Margo must have dressed them in fresh garb and burnt what they wore on the barge.'

'Over there!' Mauger pointed to a barrel in the corner. Athelstan and Cranston walked over to this. They picked out the paltry belongings: hose, jerkin, boots, belts and other items. Cranston held up the mailed wrist guard and stared sadly at it.

'All Tower archers were given one of these,' he declared. 'Once they'd been inducted, it was a badge of office. Ah well . . .'

They left the mortuary. Mauger abruptly broke away from the group, hurrying across the burial ground, shouting and waving his hands. Athelstan glimpsed a flash of colour from behind a rather large tombstone, then Cecily the courtesan and her sister Clarissa stood up, like rabbits all alert. Athelstan was sure he glimpsed a man clad in brown and green fustian, the usual garb of a travelling chapman, scampering away as fast as he could. The chapman's swift flight was shielded by the two sisters who, all pert and dainty, blocked Mauger's rush.

'Good morning, Father,' Cecily waved. 'We were just saying farewell to one of our friends who,' she held up a tawdry necklace of white stone, 'has sold us this.'

'At this time in the morning,' Mauger scoffed, 'in God's Acre?'

'Well it's quiet here,' Clarissa retorted.

'And good for business,' Benedicta whispered.

Athelstan gestured at her and the rest to stay quiet. The friar knew from previous encounters how Cecily and Clarissa, if provoked, could give as good as they received. They could act like young ladies but, once they lost their temper, their language was extremely ripe and their tantrums uncontrollable. Mauger, however, wouldn't let the matter rest.

'What business,' he taunted, 'and how much do you charge?'

'Not as much as we would ask for you, Mauger,' Clarissa yelled. 'Not now, when you no longer have that poor widow woman kneeling before you. Gone to rest, she has, from all her troubles, and from you.'

Mauger simply waved his hand and strolled back, muttering curses to cover his deep embarrassment at Clarissa's outburst.

'Let's wash our hands,' Athelstan declared, eager to divert his companions, 'and have some more bread, honey and ale.'

Once they had gathered around the great kitchen table and the friar had served the meagre food, Cranston, who had been as fascinated as Athelstan by the sharp altercation between Mauger and the two sisters, raised his tankard in a toast. 'So, we have made some progress, yes?'

'It would seem,' Brother Philippe declared, 'that those two men, father and son, whose corpses we have just viewed were on your barge, Sir John. Grievously wounded, they both fell overboard and, I suggest, somehow reached the Southwark shore, probably not far from here. Local men, they would know the swiftest route to their house where Margo Grenel was waiting.'

'Loyal archers,' Cranston declared, 'men who took the oath and believed in it. They must have seized the casket and taken it with them.'

'I agree,' Athelstan declared. 'Margo must have learnt what had happened. She would certainly realise her menfolk were grievously wounded. She would tend their injuries but there was nothing she could really do. Both father and son died. Margo Grenel was confronted with caring for the corpses of the two men she dearly loved. She was also the most reluctant possessor of the Rose Casket and the Twelve Apostles. If she went to the Crown or any of its officers, God knows what might have happened. Would the finger of suspicion be pointed at her and her menfolk? She might be accused of high treason, of being an accomplice.'

'But surely,' Benedicta demanded, 'both men were wounded in the service of the King: they tried to save the royal casket?'

'No, no.' Athelstan shook his head. 'Sir John, you'd agree with me? The Crown lawyers would be looking for a scape-goat. They might argue that all three Grenels, or at least the bowmen, were part of a conspiracy. The two archers had betrayed the secret of *The Song of the Sword* and all the details of the treasure it held. How they had planned to steal it and simply been injured.' Athelstan paused. 'Margo might have escaped punishment, but the corpses of her beloved husband and son would have been seized, even gibbeted.'

'I would agree,' Cranston replied. 'I remember how things were after the robbery. Even I, though I nearly drowned, was closely investigated. Now,' Cranston spread his hands, 'I am a royal knight, I have influence, I am skilled in law. How could poor Margo Grenel plead? She would soon become flustered. No, no, what she did was both understandable and logical.'

Athelstan played with the crumbs on his platter. He kept thinking of Mauger, who sat with his head down; the bell clerk had not touched either drink or his food. Athelstan recalled what had happened when this business first came to light.

'Athelstan?' Cranston queried.

'For the moment we should leave the various theories which might be spun of a woman holding a king's treasure, stolen with violence, during the theft of which royal retainers were slaughtered.'

'Margo Grenel would have realised that,' Brother Philippe

offered. 'Before they died, her menfolk must have told her what had happened. After their deaths, what could she do with their corpses? If she revealed what had happened, she would bring a whole torrent of troubles down upon herself.'

'Any other woman,' Athelstan declared, 'would have panicked, tried to hide the corpses but, of course, Margo had the unique skill of being a corpse-dresser – and a very good one. She also had the cottage to herself, so she embalmed both cadavers and kept them hidden in that dry cellar beneath her house. To all intents and purposes, her menfolk had left on Crown business and never returned. Go around Southwark and you will find such a story is common. Young men, fathers, brothers,' he glanced quickly at Mauger, 'who go across the Narrow Seas and never return, not even heard of again. Those in authority, such as Sir John, who helped organise *The Song of the Sword* and its clandestine business, would conclude that both archers had been killed, drowned in the Thames. They would have no reason to think otherwise. The Twelve Apostles disappeared forever and, with no sight or sign of the Grenels, who could even suspect what had truly happened? Time soon dims memories, and so it did until Margo Grenel fell ill. I suspect the poor woman knew enough about the body to conclude that what she suffered from was deeply malignant. She had kept the Rose Casket and the Twelve Apostles well hidden. But she now decided it was time she profited from the treasure and the evil which it had brought. She tried to sell the coffer, but became frightened by the interest shown. Margo, God bless her, became truly ill. What did it matter? She took the amethyst from the chest, settled her affairs in Southwark and moved across to St Bartholomew's.' Athelstan shrugged. 'The rest we know. Interest in the Twelve Apostles would probably be quickened by the reappearance of the Rose Casket. Merchant Blundel's purchase and Roslin's attempt to steal it only proclaimed that an eighteen-year-old mystery had emerged from the darkness and the great treasure was still to be had.'

'And that's it.' Benedicta spoke up. 'That's the true problem. Where is the Rose Casket and its precious treasure now? Where could it be? Margo must have hidden it somewhere, in the church, God's Acre or elsewhere? Mauger, what do you think?'

But the bell clerk just shrugged, lost in his own thoughts. Athelstan again wondered why Mauger's confrontation with the two sisters seemed to have greatly subdued him.

'Brother Philippe,' Cranston asked, 'did Margo ever say anything about the amethyst or its origins?'

'No, no, far from it. The poor woman was very ill. She became delirious; she talked about the parish here. She mentioned you, Athelstan, on a number of occasions. She also talked about the bell and, strangely enough, how Arthur would come again.'

'Bell?' Benedicta asked. 'We have no church bells here, and who on earth is Arthur?'

'The once and future King,' Brother Philippe murmured. 'Yes, she repeated that about the bell but it was all disjointed, the utterings and mutterings of a very frenetic mind. Sometimes she would talk about her husband and son, about secrets, and she asked me if her sins would be forgiven, so I reminded her about the mercy of Christ.' Brother Philippe spread his hands. 'More than that I cannot say. Brother Athelstan, Sir John, I truly must leave.'

The meeting ended. Mauger seemed eager to be gone and slipped out of the house. Cranston and Brother Philippe made their farewells. The coroner declared he intended to visit Merchant Blundel and collect the amethyst. The physician said he would accompany the coroner as a witness. Athelstan and Benedicta watched them leave arm in arm, then returned to the priest's house. They were immediately joined by the great one-eyed tomcat Bonaventure, who strolled imperiously over to the hearth, hungrily lapped the offered bowl of milk, then threw himself down as Athelstan said, like any Roman emperor fresh from the battlefield. Benedicta and Athelstan quickly cleared the table and scrubbed the pots, tankards and platters. The widow woman asked what was to be done with the two corpses?

'We will bury them quietly tomorrow after the Jesus Mass,' Athelstan declared softly. 'Tell Mauger to prepare a grave close to Margo's. If anyone asks, tell them you are taking care of nameless corpses being buried here as an act of mercy.'

Benedicta promised she would, and left telling Athelstan not to brood too long by himself. Athelstan absent-mindedly nodded and sat on a stool before the hearth, warming himself while stroking Bonaventure, patting the great tomcat as he reflected on all that he had seen and heard. 'It's like being in a maze, Bonaventure. You twist and turn but you cannot find a path which will lead to the centre, to the heart of the mystery, though you know that path is there.' The great tomcat's response was a long, drawn-out purr of contentment. 'Quite, quite,' Athelstan whispered. 'Keep warm, my old friend, the days are closing in and the weather turns colder. I think we will have a river mist tonight, so it will be an early bed for both of us. No climbing to the top of the church tower to study the stars. The sky will be clouded, the breeze too strong and cold.' Athelstan repressed a shiver. 'Talking of church towers, my friend, I wonder what Margo meant by the bell? Even more so, the reference to King Arthur – what has that got to do with her?'

Athelstan chewed the corner of his lip. Once those two corpses were quietly buried and the grave blessed, he intended to organise a most thorough search of that cottage, as well as the parish death house where Margo had worked. Athelstan crossed himself, rose, and walked over to the lectern where his psalter was opened for the office of the day. He read the psalms, his attention caught by the words of Antiphon:

'Blessed be the Lord, my rock, who prepares my arms for battle, and readies my hands for war.'

'Do so.' Athelstan closed his eyes and fervently prayed. 'Do so now.'

Curate Cotes struggled to wake in his narrow bedchamber in the priest's house at St Benet's Woodwharf; his head pounded as if a tambour was being loudly beaten close to him; his eyes were filled with mucus, his stomach pitched with sharp, short pains. The curate felt heavy-limbed, his throat dry as dust. He heard a sound, rolled over, and stared in astonishment at the blond-haired, lissom young man, naked as he was born, pulling himself up. Curate Cotes swung himself off the bed and stared at his own clothes strewn across the floor. He heard a cough and glanced in horror at the Flesher squatting like a toad on a stool just within the doorway. This hung open and, despite his bleary eyes, Cotes glimpsed Martha, Cripplegate and the sexton staring fixedly in at him.

'Naughty, naughty boys,' the Flesher sneered. 'Curate Cotes, you are a sodomite. You visited the Devil's Oak yesterday evening and left with young Marcel here.' The Flesher assumed a mock, pious look. 'I never guessed at the truth of it till I visited St Benet's this morning.' He spread his hands. 'And so here we are.' The Flesher stooped down, picked up a heap of clothing and threw it at the young catamite. 'Swift as you can, Marcel. Dress and be gone, you naughty boy. Curate Cotes, make yourself as decent as you can and meet us all downstairs.'

Curate Cotes, now dressed in a dark nightgown, slid on to the stool in the buttery and glared at the Flesher sitting so self-satisfied and smug at the top of the table. Martha sat opposite the curate, staring in open-mouthed astonishment at him. Cripplegate and Spurnel also grouped around the table, looked highly nervous and refusing to meet his eye. The Flesher picked up his tankard of morning ale and mockingly toasted what he called, 'his guests'. Cotes grabbed his own tankard, eager to slake his burning thirst.

'I am not a sodomite,' he blurted out. 'I was drinking in the Devil's Oak, talking to people, then I staggered back here by myself. That's the last thing I remember.'

'Well, well, well,' the Flesher jibed, 'we've all seen what we saw. According to at least five witnesses, and that includes young Marcel, you, Curate Cotes, are a sodomite and, priest or not, you could face humiliation and the full rigour of the law. Being burned alive at Smithfield is a gruesome prospect, though you might die in good company because your two friends here, Cripplegate and Sexton Spurnel, certainly share your predilection for smooth-skinned youths. Don't you, gentlemen?'

'This is preposterous,' Cripplegate retorted. 'Master Makepeace, what is this all about?'

'Do not act the outraged, virtuous locksmith,' the Flesher snarled. 'You and Spurnel also visit certain houses which the mayor and his bailiffs would dearly love to raid – to search and seize the likes of you – but enough of that. You act all innocent but I, and others will agree with me, believe that the three of you must know something of the truth about the horrid events in our church.' He turned and pointed at Martha. 'I suggest, Mistress, you entertain similar suspicions?'

The housekeeper, who looked terrified, just opened and closed her mouth, then shook her head slightly. The Flesher, elbows on the table, jabbed a finger at all three men. 'I suspect you had a hand in the killing of Daventry and Parson Reynaud. I also believe that you stole my beloved mother's corpse and robbed that arca of my silver and gold.'

'You have no proof,' Cripplegate spluttered.

'I do not need proof,' the Flesher snapped. 'But if we are going to go down that path, then why did you tell fat Jack Cranston and his furtive little friar that you and the sexton were at home,' he smirked, 'in your respective beds? You weren't.'

'I was in the Devil's Oak,' Cotes declared.

'Later that night you were but, correct me if I am wrong, all three of you met in the Prospect of Jerusalem, close to St Andrews-by-the-Wardrobe? You were in a closeted window seat overlooking the tavern garden. You ate and drank till late in the evening then left. Hours later, Curate Cotes, you came to the Devil's Oak. So tell me, what did you talk about?' The Flesher moved his gauntlets, lying on the table before him, and used his stubby fingers to emphasise his points. 'It would take three to kill Daventry and Parson Reynaud. At least one of you to distract, the other to strike. And you, Master Cripplegate, did you fashion keys for that arca?'

'As the angels are my witness, how and when would I even get the opportunity to make a cast?'

'You met one of my henchmen, a fellow I truly trusted till I discovered he was a Judas. You knew him well, Ingersol; popularly known as the Sicarius.'

'I never—'

'You must have met him. He would come to St Benet's with messages from members of my household. I know, for God's sake, because I sent him. He would visit Parson Reynaud in his house. Isn't that right, Martha?'

'Yes, yes,' she whispered, 'but when he came in I left. I was very frightened of him. A dark man. He would be closeted with Parson Reynaud and, if they wished, I would serve them some refreshment.'

'Of course, of course.' The Flesher stroked Martha's hand, gripped it, then let it go.

'And Ingersol would linger to talk here, yes?'

'To me and others,' Cripplegate stuttered.

'So you did meet him?'

'Well of course but—'

'Never mind.' The Flesher was now becoming heated, his face even more flushed, the veins on his thick neck bulging in fury. No one dared move. The Flesher's hand had fallen beneath the table; his eyes – more pig-like than ever – glared at those around him who knew the Flesher's fingers were not far from the hilt of his flat-bladed cleaver. The Flesher's 'guests' also realised that all he had to do was shout, and the rifflers, who undoubtedly stood around the priest's house, would burst in with sword and mace.

'My mother's corpse, my money.' The Flesher fought back the tears of fury welling in his red-rimmed eyes. 'You would need more than one person to do all that mischief. All three of you,' the Flesher waved a hand, 'ingrates, helped by me in the past, bear some responsibility for what has happened here. Fat Jack Cranston is no help but,' the Flesher shook a fist at those seated around him, 'I want my mother's corpse as well as my money returned to me by All Hallows or, by all that you hold sacred, you shall pay for it either in the Devil's Oak or one of my other dwellings. Perhaps,' he flailed a hand, 'I should let fat Jack parade you on the public gallows at Smithfield. All three of you remember, by All Hallows or else!'

PART FIVE

Cramp Abbey (**Old English**): Newgate Prison

Athelstan sat at his kitchen table staring into the flames of the fire leaping merrily in the hearth. The day was drawing on and the friar felt slightly drowsy. The parish now lay quiet. Athelstan had walked its bounds and assured himself that all was well. The menfolk were at work, the women busy in their cottages involved in a wide variety of tasks. They always impressed Athelstan with their skill, be it the stitching of a torn cloth, the management of a spinning wheel, their expertise with the churn or the baking of different breads or pastries. He had unlocked the sacristy and checked on both the parish chest as well as the arca in its secret hole beneath the floor. He had also opened St Erconwald's chancery coffer, where important parish charters and documents were carefully stored. Once he'd satisfied himself, he moved into the sanctuary and found all was well, the Sacrament light glowing a bright red in the gathering gloom. Athelstan was scrupulous in his inspection, scrutinising the pyx, the altar, the cruets and the sanctuary furniture. The empty nave had been carefully swept, its benches, stools and leaning rods carefully stacked against either wall. The chantry chapel of St Erconwald's was Athelstan's pride and joy, a delight to sit in: its large window was filled with painted glass, and when the light poured through, it created a breath-taking vision of lovely colours. Dark blue turkey rugs softened the tread. The altar, celebrant's chair, stool and bench were of the same polished oak wood as the trellised screen which closed off the chantry chapel from the rest of the church. Athelstan just loved to sit inside, lean back in the chair and contemplate the cross of San Damiano which hung above the altar. The chantry altar was majestic, a thing of beauty covered in its royal blue coping, which protected the pure white linen cloths, the best of Cambrai, used during Mass. To the left of the altar, next to the window, hung a brilliant triptych, which recounted scenes from the life of St Erconwald, a useful foil for Athelstan when he tried to educate his parishioners on the virtues of their patron saint.

Athelstan had also tried to find Judith the mummer, after rumours he'd heard about a possible quarrel between some of the parish women over the play being prepared. However, when Athelstan visited the Piebald and nearby cook shop, neither Joceyln nor Merrylegs knew anything about the quarrel or Judith's whereabouts. Athelstan sensed they were being parsimonious with the truth but decided to leave it for a while. He believed the play was becoming increasingly divisive, and already the tensions were making themselves felt in other ways. The Hangman of Rochester, the parish painter, had decided to begin a fresco illustrating the ascent of the soul from purgatory to the gates of heaven. Each soul was depicted as a golden globe, full of light, with a little figure inside, rising through the swirling murk of smoke and flames. Nearby, dark-garbed demons crouched on burning rocks to watch the souls ascend. To the right of this was another scene depicting the souls' family and friends in life. These were divided into those who were saved and those who had sinned grievously. The hangman, out of sheer mischief, and greatly encouraged by the likes of Watkin and Pike, was placing members of the parish in one of these two groups: the identity of each person being revealed by some sign or symbol, be it Mauger with his bell or Pike the ditcher with a mattock and hoe. Parishioners were soon discovering where they would be placed and tempers were running high.

Athelstan stared down at the notes he had made as he tried to map a path through the mysterious murk of murder confronting him and Cranston. He idly wondered what the coroner was doing and quietly prayed that Sir John did not give way to the anger seething inside him and return to the Devil's Oak for a further confrontation with the Flesher or Raquin. Sir John had not forgotten that fateful night eighteen years ago, and wished to bring matters to a close. Nevertheless, the Flesher was a most vicious opponent, a powerful lord of

London's seedy underworld. More importantly, the Flesher was patronised by Fitzalan of Arundel who, by his own admission, or so Cranston reported, didn't give a fig about King or Crown, or indeed the Lord High Coroner.

'Please God keep Cranston away,' Athelstan murmured. 'Don't let him go down to the Devil's Oak.' Athelstan joined his hands, closed his eyes and quietly prayed. After all, Cranston would not be the first law officer to be provoked into a quarrel, stabbed to death and have his assailants later plead, with a host of perjured witnesses, that it was all done in self-defence.

Athelstan opened his eyes and glanced again at the memoranda. He'd tried to distance himself from the mysteries which teased and taunted his wits, and the best way to do that was to concentrate on his priestly duties. He'd continued to walk the parish bounds, returning to the church for the Angelus. After this had been recited and Mauger had rung his bell, the children of the parish gathered in the lady chapel for their religious instruction. 'His beloved scholars', as Athelstan called them, had proved to be particularly lively. Athelstan secretly compared them to a horde of busy grasshoppers, and wondered why certain children, who should go nowhere near a naked flame, being a clear danger to themselves and others, seemed to have an irresistible compulsion to light candles. The friar had been relieved to be joined by Imelda, Pike the ditcher's sharp-tongued wife. She was of valuable assistance with the children, even though she kept up a monologue about the shortcomings of her own brood. Athelstan had pointed at the statue of the Virgin and exhorted Imelda to pray for help; after all, the friar pointed out, Mary had been a mother and raised a son.

'Ah yes, Father,' Imelda had retorted tartly, 'she certainly had a boy, but she never had daughters. Now daughters, rather than sons, are hard work . . .'

Athelstan only half listened. At last the children quietened as Athelstan instructed them in the 'Ave Maria', using both the statue of Our Lady of Walsingham as well as the vivid wall paintings in the lady chapel to illustrate his lesson. He then made the children recite the 'Ave' in Latin, making them laugh at the strange sounds. Once the lesson was over, Athelstan had distributed some sweetmeats and asked the children if they had anything to tell him? Harold Hairlip, one of Hig the pigman's children, stood up and announced in his strange voice how he had seen strangers in the parish.

'Some men, Father, with a cart on the far side of the cemetery.'

'In which case, keep well away from there,' Athelstan warned. 'It's a very lonely, desolate stretch of land. God knows who wanders such a place. All right?' Athelstan stared around. 'Nobody wants to say any more?' He lifted a hand in blessing. 'Then go in peace.'

The children had fled the church back to their cottages. Most of them were under strict instruction to do so. The days were drawing in. Autumn was making itself felt and many families in the parish had to use the daylight hours to complete work both in their homes as well as their different trades – be it sewing, weaving, clearing the soil, planting vegetables or herbs, not to mention cooking and baking in the common ovens at the Piebald or Merrylegs' cook shop.

Athelstan made sure all the children had left the church, then returned to the priest's house. He'd laid out a scroll of vellum and once again began to organise what he and Cranston had discovered so far. Item: Athelstan wrote carefully, then paused to sharpen the fine quill-pen Cranston had given him from the Guildhall chancery. Item: Simon Makepeace, also known as the Flesher. A true sinner in every sense of the word. A master of mischief, a killer and a thief, who presided like an emperor over an empire of like-minded souls. Sir John was correct, the Flesher was responsible for a whole host of crimes; in particular, the attempted theft of those precious stones, the Twelve Apostles in their Rose Casket some eighteen years ago. The Flesher controlled the parish of St Benet's Woodwharf, its priest Parson Reynaud and others on the parish council: Cripplegate, its leader, Cotes the curate and Sexton Spurnel. In turn the Flesher was the cat's-paw of Fitzalan of Arundel. According to the evidence available, both of these, probably with the connivance of the parish priest, had been plotting some future mischief. In the main, the Flesher appeared to have left the church of St Benet's alone, except for the crypt and cemetery, which he had freely used to hide the victims of his macabre murders, either at the Devil's Oak or that forbidding mansion of murder.

Item: Sir John Cranston had been fervently against the Flesher and his ilk for years. Accordingly the cororner had been delighted to be approached by the Sicarius, one of the Flesher's leading henchmen, who offered to betray his master for a pardon. Athelstan lifted his head and stared at the crucifix above the hearth. God knows why the Sicarius made his decision but, there again, Athelstan reflected, he had sat in the mercy seat at the shriving pew and, over the years, listened to confessions from hundreds of people. One thing constantly surprised him. How people can change, usually due to other people: that was interesting because in his discussions with Cranston, the Sicarius had demanded a pardon not only for himself but for another – a comrade? Was it this which had changed the Sicarius, or something else?

The Flesher is as arrogant as Lucifer. Such men always overreach themselves. Was the Flesher's empire beginning to crack? Had the fear and terror he had instilled in others begun to curdle? Was an opposition forming to the nightmare he had created? Was that the reason his henchman and Parson Reynaud had been murdered, the arca plundered and Isabella Makepeace's corpse stolen? Perhaps this was not an attempt to steal the treasure or to hold a corpse for ransom, but public mockery of the Flesher? After all, the news must have seeped along the dark runnels of Queenhithe and elsewhere. The Flesher was no longer invincible. There would be hidden laughter and quiet enjoyment at the deep discomfiture and insult inflicted upon this self-proclaimed Prince of rifflers. Athelstan returned to his memorandum.

Item. The Sicarius had proved to be a man of his word: he had certainly inflicted damage on London's most notorious wolfshead. The Sicarius had supplied Cranston with a stream of invaluable information about all kinds of mischief being plotted; this had continued until about two weeks ago when the Sicarius had disappeared, making no attempt to contact Cranston or anybody else. There could only be one possible conclusion: Ingersol had been trapped by the Flesher and brutally murdered. Cranston's informant had been unable to tell the coroner what secret mayhem the Flesher and Arundel were plotting; however, that was a loose strand Athelstan could do nothing about, unless someone else decided to betray the Flesher.

Athelstan dipped his quill pen into the inkpot and continued writing. Item: the Twelve Apostles. Eighteen years ago this treasure had been taken from a Hanse ship *The Glory of Bremen*, sealed in a chancery bag and placed on board a royal barge, *The Song of the Sword*, under the command of Cranston. The barge had been attacked by two other craft as it made its way along the river on a dark, fog-bound night. Sir John had been wounded; he'd fallen overboard only to be miraculously plucked from the water. The barge had been manned by Tower archers, skilled bowmen patronised and favoured by the Crown. They included men from Queenhithe and, in particular, parishioners of St Benet's: Cripplegate, Cotes and Spurnel. Like Cranston, they had survived. Of course all three had incurred royal anger, fury and suspicion over the robbery. All three parishioners had had no choice but to accept the help of the Flesher after their dismissal from the Tower cohort. Athelstan paused. Of course, he continued writing, all three men would have fallen under suspicion not only by the Crown but the Flesher. After all, the treasure had disappeared. Had any of these been involved in its theft? According to the evidence, they had not. A clearer picture was now emerging, the real suspects being the Grenels, father and son. Both had been sorely wounded. However, during the attack on the royal barge, they must have plucked up the chancery satchel containing the treasure and either jumped or been pushed overboard. They reached Southwark shore and somehow made their way back to their own home. Both men had eventually died of their wounds. Margo, distracted by grief, was also faced with the worry of what to do with the mortal remains of her beloved menfolk, who had disappeared in such mysterious circumstances along with the royal treasure. How could she explain all that away? Margo's next decision was logical. She used her undoubted skill and experience to lovingly embalm both cadavers, turning that cellar into a family shrine. As the months and years passed, Margo would become accustomed to, and even like, the arrangement. She could take her own food down there and talk to the dead. Athelstan did not consider himself a man of sorrows, but he was acquainted with grief both as a person and as a father confessor. Occasionally, on top of the church tower or in the privacy of St Erconwald's chantry chapel, he would talk to his dead brother. He had met others who did the same. God's Acre outside was often visited: tombs, graves, headstones and crosses being carefully tended and adorned with fresh flowers or coloured ribbons. He had seen the living kneel beside the dead and speak to them. Margo Grenel would be no different. More importantly, where had she stored the Rose Casket and its precious stones? Margo must have hidden them away in some place known only to her. She would probably have left them there, but the years passed and Margo needed medical care, good physic for her malignancy. A poor woman, she had little money, so she tried to sell the Rose Casket but became deeply flustered by the keen interest shown, so she withdrew it. Margo's ill humours worsened. Now desperate, she took one of the Twelve Apostles, the amethyst, across to St Bartholomew's to buy good treatment.

'And she met,' Athelstan murmured, 'my friend Brother Philippe, who knows as little about precious stones as I do.'

The physician, a true innocent and totally unaware of what wealth or riches are, accepted the amethyst in payment, and took it down to a reputable goldsmith who would have realised its worth immediately. Perhaps that's where the rumour started; it would account for Roslin the robber breaking into Master Blundel's shop. During that affray, the amethyst becomes even more public, glimpsed by the Flesher's henchmen. 'And so,' Athelstan whispered, 'the banner is raised.' The Flesher and others, Levigne, even Master Thibault must have soon realised that if the amethyst was being sold, the Twelve Apostles must have reappeared on the London market, and so their fingers would have itched with greed. The Flesher undoubtedly sent his rifflers to search Athelstan's house, Margo's cottage and the poor woman's grave. They had discovered nothing. So where are the Twelve Apostles? Margo had left little clue, though whilst in the hospital at St Bartholomew's she had sunk into delirium and gabbled about Arthur the once and future King. But what did that mean? Was it some reference to the whereabouts of the treasure? Did her menfolk leave any hint about what they had taken from the royal barge, *The Song of the Sword*? Apart from how they died, what else was known about Henry and Walter Grenel? Good men? Skilled archers? Margo and her husband seemed an ordinary God-fearing family, though Margo never came to be shriven, even at Easter or thereabouts. Well, certainly not at St Erconwald's. Little was known about her son, Walter, except that he had been sweet on 'a woman from the House of Bethany', but what did that mean? All three Grenels were now dead, as were so many who had been involved in the transport of that treasure eighteen years ago. Sir John believed Raquin had led the attack, yet the coroner still did not know who had betrayed them. And who could that be?

Athelstan closed his eyes and tried to imagine that fateful evening, *The Glory of Bremen* berthed at Queenhithe, the barge coming down from the Tower. A spy on the quayside would soon see it approach and watch the barge's departure. The spy would then alert, if Cranston was right, the Flesher, and those two pirate craft would prepare their ambuscade. But who was that spy who had told the Flesher? One logical conclusion was that it could not have been anyone on board *The Song of the Sword*. In the middle of a fog-bound, pitch-black freezing night on the Thames, it would be very difficult, if not impossible, to distinguish between friend and foe. Moreover, Cranston was no fool and neither was the Flesher. In the weeks, months, even years following the attack, they would keep a sharp eye on the markets to see if the Rose Casket or the Twelve Apostles were offered for sale, but that did not happen. Moreover, nobody on board that barge had profited from the attack; far from it. Cotes, Sexton Spurnel and Cripplegate could not be described as being particularly wealthy. Athelstan opened his eyes and put his pen down, his mind going back to Margo mumbling about Arthur and the bell – was that a reference to Mauger? And what about the confrontation between the bell clerk and those two sisters? Perhaps it was time to question Mauger.

Athelstan sat back and dozed, only to be woken by a sharp knock on the door. He started and turned as the door was flung open and Crim the altar boy led a hooded, visored figure, garbed in black from head to toe, into the kitchen. The altar boy looked terrified, head turning against the sharp, serrated knife held against the side of his neck. Athelstan rose slowly, trying to wet his throat and lips, abruptly dry with fear.

'You must come priest! You must come now!' The voice behind the mask was low and guttural. 'Go on boy.' He shook Crim. 'Tell him.'

'They have Benedicta, Godbless and Thaddeus.'

'Where?'

'Haceldema.' The wolfshead tripped over the word. 'What you call the Field of Blood, where those hanged on the Southwark side of London Bridge are buried. You know it. Come priest!'

'Who sent you?'

'No questions, come!'

Athelstan dried his sweat-soaked hands on his robe, grabbed his cloak and keys and followed the sinister figure, one hand firmly on Crim's shoulder, out of the priest's house.

'Let him go,' Athelstan pleaded. 'He is only a child.'

'Who can run and raise the alarm. Now come before my knife slips.'

The wolfshead led Athelstan out into the cemetery. Daylight was beginning to die, the weak sun hidden by gathering clouds. The long grass and gorse, which sprouted between the grave-stones and crosses, bent under a piercing cold breeze. Athelstan was now ordered to lead the way and he hurried in front. The friar anxiously peered from left to right, desperate to glimpse any parishioner who might have wandered in on some pretext or other, but there was no one. Athelstan prayed that help would be sent. They were heading for a very lonely, desolate place. Haceldema was regarded as blighted and haunted. A stretch of wasteland peppered with stinking morasses and clumps of rough gorse, the last resting place for a legion of malefactors hanged near the bridge. Athelstan's parishioners firmly believed that it was a murky, macabre hosting ground for the ghosts of those executed and the demons who herded them.

At last they reached the wicket gate on the far side of God's Acre and followed the narrow coffin path which twisted past the wild hedges on to the wasteland bounded by a thick copse of trees. Athelstan crossed himself and again prayed for help. This place was rarely visited; it was even devoid of birdsong. Only wild pigs came to snout for the acorns from the ancient oaks, the branches of which curled up to tangle with each other. Athelstan, however, only had eyes for the two dark-clad wolf-sheads, cowled and masked, who suddenly appeared from behind one of the thick bushes. Each carried a crossbow. They beckoned at Benedicta, who cradled Bonaventure, to leave her hiding place. She was followed by a terrified Godbless, one hand on Thaddeus's neck, the other holding the goat's shabby leather leash. Both beggar and goat looked truly terrified. Godbless, like Benedicta, kept staring at the fringe of trees. Athelstan followed their gaze and glimpsed movement. Two more wolf-sheads emerged from the copse. Each of these led on a leash a ferocious war dog; huge mastiffs with bulbous heads, they were long-legged, their short-haired, tawny coats rippling with muscle. The mastiffs walked slowly but Athelstan recognised that deliberate pacing as highly dangerous. He had seen the King's great cats in their cages at the Tower; they too had that menacing stalk. The hounds were tightly muzzled yet they strained against the chained leash attached to the spiked collars around their bulging necks. Savage animals, these two strained forward, eyes blazing with fury, eager to attack. Thaddeus's and Godbless's agitation was heart-rending. Clad in his flapping rags of cloth and leather, the beggar man was now hugging the goat, which whimpered, eyes rolling back in terror.

'In God's name . . .' Athelstan stepped forward; he tried not to flinch as both war dogs lunged towards him.

'In God's name,' one of the wolfsheads mocked. 'Then tell us?'

'What?'

'The whereabouts of the Rose Casket and the Twelve Apostles.'

'I don't know.' Athelstan gestured at the mastiffs. 'What are these dogs called; why are they here?'

'They have no name, clever priest.'

'The Flesher, Master Simon Makepeace.' Athelstan was desperate to delay matters as long as possible. 'He sent you from the Devil's Oak, didn't he?'

'We know of no such person or place.' The harsh voice remained flat and incisive. 'The Rose Casket, the jewels, priest – where are they?'

'Were you involved in the attack eighteen years ago?'

'The jewels, the Rose Casket, where are they?'

Soaked in sweat, Athelstan gazed up at the grey, lowering sky. He took out his ave beads and tried to avoid Benedicta's gaze. She just stood, Crim next to her, cradling Bonaventure. The tomcat had gone strangely silent and submissive; whether he was frightened of the dogs or preparing to flee, Athelstan could not say. He stared around this sombre, god-forsaken field – well named, he bitterly thought. Would this truly become a Field of Blood?

'Priest, I asked you a question?'

Athelstan held up the ave beads. 'And I swear by the cross, I don't know where they are, and for God's sake, show mercy.' He gestured at his parishioners. 'An old man out of his wits, a poor widow woman and a child.'

'And a goat and a cat,' the wolfshead added, to guffaws of laughter from his companions. He walked over to Benedicta who was cradling Bonaventure. He grabbed the cat and pushed her away, only to scream and jump back as Bonaventure, swift as light, twisted abruptly, his front paws lashing the wolfshead's face, who promptly dropped the cat. Bonaventure, like an arrow from the bow, shot across the grass into the undergrowth. The war dogs strained forward, their handlers cursing and shouting. Athelstan stood tense, Benedicta and Crim likewise, but the beggar man jumped to his feet shouting, 'God bless Bonaventure! God bless Thaddeus!'

'The goat!' the scarred wolfshead exclaimed, nursing the deep weals on his face. 'The goat!' he repeated. One of his companions put down the crossbow, hurried over, knocked Godbless aside, seized the goat's leash and smacked it hard

on the rump. Unlike Bonaventure, Thaddeus, stricken with
fear, raced blindly toward the trees. Athelstan now realised
why the hounds had been taken there, to cast about, to recognise the terrain. Now released, they hurtled after the fleeing
goat. Godbless was screaming. Crim tried to break free of
Benedicta; both were sobbing frantically. Athelstan watched
in horror. The hounds racing either side of the goat soon caught
Thaddeus. One knocked it, the goat stumbled, and the other
hound ripped the poor creature's throat, shredding the flesh as
the blood gushed out. Godbless, now hysterical with fear,
threw himself at one of the attackers, who clubbed him on the
side of the head, knocking the beggar unconscious to the
ground. Athelstan hurried over to Benedicta. She cradled Crim
in her arms so the boy couldn't see the hounds savaging the
mangled remains of the goat, nothing more than a tangle of
skin and bone swimming in a thick puddle of blood. Athelstan
stood in front of both Benedicta and Crim, doing his best to
shield them from this gruesome sight. The hounds nosed the
remains. Now and again one of them would turn its great
bulbous head, huge jaws frothing blood and smeared with
gore. They would glare at Athelstan before returning to burrow
their massive heads into the gruesome remains.

'Perhaps the boy next, priest.' The self-appointed leader of
the wolfsheads swaggered over to Benedicta and tried to snatch
Crim from her embrace. She lunged at him, striking out with
the small knife she kept hidden in her gown; a thin, pointed,
razor-sharp blade which slashed the wolfshead's sword arm.
He screamed, staggering back to trip over the now prostate
and unconscious Godbless. The wolfshead lurched to his feet,
clutching his bloodied arm, his companions, swords and
daggers out, hurried across. Again Benedicta lunged, scything
the air with the knife, only to have this knocked aside and to
be pulled by the hair away from the screaming, terrified Crim.
Athelstan felt the red mist descend. A roaring in his ears, an
uncontrollable fury which made him shake. He screamed
and threw himself at the malefactors. The friar no longer
cared about anything but killing his opponent. Desperate to
defend Benedicta and Crim from further harm, he was shoved
and pushed back. A dagger blade cut the air. Athelstan

glimpsed this, he moved to one side and, as he did so, the wielder of the knife screamed and staggered back. The man's face seemed to collapse into a bloody pulp as the crossbow bolt struck him deep in the forehead. Other voices were raised and Athelstan wondered at the cries of 'Saint Denis, Saint Denis!' Shaken and confused, Athelstan realised the struggle had abruptly changed. He stood, sweat-soaked, trying to clear his head. Benedicta and Crim crouched on the ground beside him, hugging each other.

'In God's name,' Athelstan whispered, 'what on earth, what on earth?' He glimpsed the two great mastiffs, both killed, sprawled on the ground, massive jaws half-open, eyes all glazed, their corpses stiffening in widening puddles of blood. The five wolfsheads had suffered a similar fate; crossbow bolts had smashed into faces, necks, bellies and chests. Benedicta's assassin sat half sprawled, quietly moaning. One of the shadowy, cowled figures, who had abruptly appeared in Haceldema and were milling around them, walked over, yanked the wolfshead back by the hair and slit his throat. Athelstan felt both hot and cold. He was trembling, fearful that he might faint. Desperate to control his breathing, he moved slowly, hands out, staring at his saviours. Athelstan reckoned there were about eight in number.

'Who are you?' he called. 'Who are you?'

One of the strangers hurried forward, pulling back his hood, and Athelstan stared into the smiling face of Hugh Levigne the Candlelight-Master. '*Benedicat te Dominus.* May the Lord bless you, Brother Athelstan.'

'And may the Lord bless you too, Monseigneur.' Athelstan clasped the Frenchman's hand.

'God sent you,' he murmured, moving over to join Benedicta; she and Crim were now trying to help an injured, confused Godbless. The widow woman had taken one of the dead malefactors' cloaks and covered the pathetic remains of Thaddeus. 'Evil men,' Athelstan whispered. 'Yet the Lord delivered us. How come such deliverance occurred?'

Levigne stood watching his men move from one corpse to another. 'Brother Athelstan, we know what happened to the Twelve Apostles. Like your good friend Sir John, we strongly suspect that the attack on him eighteen years ago was planned, plotted and perpetrated by the Flesher. Now we know him by reputation. Over the years, we have kept close watch on him.'

'Of course,' Athelstan breathed, 'Sir John told me how the mayor of Rouen fixed a price on the Flesher's head for the atrocities he committed in France.'

'I have seen the indictment, Brother. It is a litany of cruelty and horror. You wouldn't think any human soul could inflict such suffering on so many innocents. Once we knew that the Twelve Apostles had emerged on the London market and that you were somehow involved in it, we decided to mount a discreet but careful watch. The Flesher is not as intelligent as he thinks. We know all about his use of war mastiffs in his Mansion of Murder.'

'So you watched the bridge?'

'We watched the Devil's Oak and the bridge.' The Candlelight-Master nodded towards the trees. 'I am sure we will find the cart with two cages and all the necessary paraphernalia for the keeping of two war dogs. We saw them arrive earlier. We had to make sure. Of course I am sorry we could not save the goat but, at least and most importantly, we have saved you, the woman and the boy. Brother Athelstan, whether you like it or not, we will continue to keep you under close watch.'

'And thank God for that, Monseigneur. So come, let's go to my house.'

Sir John Cranston stood, booted feet apart, and stared down at the corpses. 'Five men, two beasts!' he exclaimed.

'Seven beasts in all,' Athelstan remarked, standing next to the coroner.

Cranston pulled his beaver hat further down on his head and threw back his cloak to reveal his resplendent warbelt; he then glanced over his shoulder at the parishioners who'd crowded into Haceldema to see the effects of the gruesome slaughter which had occurred yesterday. Indeed their priest had done nothing to prevent them. Once Athelstan had recovered his wits and shared a deep-bowled goblet of wine with Levigne, he'd thanked the Frenchman and asked him to mount guard over the corpses until the parish watch was summoned. Levigne quickly agreed. The Luciferi searched the dead men's wallets and purses. They stripped the cadavers completely, keeping the clothes, weapons and any coins for their own use. The Frenchmen were thorough. They also found the cart and cages as well as a dray horse, hidden away deep in the copse of trees. Athelstan ruefully reflected that he should have paid more attention to what young Harold Hairlip had told him – strangers in St Erconwald's parish usually meant trouble. The parish watch was eventually organised just before Compline. Athelstan briefly explained what had happened and how they would have to set up a watch until the following morning when Sir John Cranston would decide what to do with the dead. Levigne came and made his farewells late in the evening. Athelstan was resting with Benedicta and Crim, Godbless being fast asleep in the bedloft. Levigne assured the friar that he and his retainers had searched all the attackers' belongings. They could not find a shred of evidence about who they were or who had sent them which, Cranston now declared, was a sure mark of the Flesher.

'He hides his tracks very well,' the coroner declared. 'Cunning, subtle and devious he is. Now you know, Brother, why he has never been fingered.'

Most of the parishioners believed all five wolfsheads had been despatched by the Flesher. They'd heard rumours about their little priest being involved in that heinous business at St Benet's Woodwharf, and how he had visited the Flesher's lair at the Devil's Oak. There were also whispers about a certain treasure being found, though such wild stories often ran rife throughout the parish. They'd certainly heard about the attack on Godbless and the utter destruction of Thaddeus. The mauled remnants of that four-legged parishioner had been wrapped in a coffin cloth and taken to the death house. After the Jesus Mass, just before dawn that morning, Athelstan had given a pithy description of the attack and, despite all the suspicions being voiced, he refused to name who could have been responsible for such wickedness. Athelstan had certainly glimpsed Watkin and Pike out of the corner of his eye, deep in discussion. Both of these parish worthies stood just inside the rood screen, immersed in an argument which seemed to have lasted throughout morning Mass. Watkin appeared to want to have words with his priest, but Pike tugged at the dung-collector's sleeve and led him down the nave, whispering heatedly at him. Athelstan wondered what the issue was but then became distracted when he learnt that Sir John Cranston had arrived and had been taken straight to Haceldema, where the parish watch, under Beadle Bladdersmith, had set up guard. Athelstan joined them and immediately informed Cranston about exactly what had happened the previous day.

'Yes, that's all logical,' the coroner murmured. 'A fine example of Makepeace's malevolence. Do you know, Athelstan, sometimes I feel like kidnapping the Flesher, putting him aboard a war cog and taking him to Rouen myself to watch the bastard hang.'

'Oh, he'll hang all right.'

'Do you want his death, Athelstan?'

'No, Sir John, God does.' Athelstan struck his breast. 'I have a feeling here, deep in my heart, that the Flesher's cup of wickedness is brimming over. Somewhere beyond the veil, the books are being opened and a court is being set up. The sheer terror and horror he has inflicted upon total innocents must be paid for.' Athelstan gestured at the corpses. 'This is only the beginning. I have given the dead a simple blessing. I cannot see my way to delivering absolution for sinners intent on such sheer malice.'

'And Bonaventure?' Cranston asked.

'Hale and hearty, Sir John. He did what damage he could and fled, cunning cat.'

'Very well,' Cranston whispered. 'But, Brother, let us dispense with the audience.' Cranston turned and walked back to the parishioners. 'I need to have words with your priest,' he bellowed, 'so apart from Master Flaxwith and his bailiffs,' Cranston pointed across Haceldema, where his henchmen had gathered, 'it's time all of you went about your lawful business. Master Joceyln, Master Merrylegs, I give you an invitation. All upright members of this parish may break their fast at your worthy establishments. The Guildhall Exchequer will honour all reasonable bills.' Athelstan had rarely seen his parishioners move so fast. Joceyln and Merrylegs, delighted at the prospect of such profit, led the charge from Haceldema, streaming across God's Acre to feast on fresh bread, spiced meats and strong ale. Cranston and Athelstan watched them go. The friar then turned back and stared at the corpses, as well as those of the mastiffs brought low by crossbow bolts to their heads. Athelstan felt a pang of sorrow at the pathetic sight.

'Magnificent beasts,' he whispered, 'abused by wicked men for their own evil purposes.' He shifted his gaze to the dirty, white corpses which, naked as they were born, sprawled gruesomely, their purple-red death wounds clear to see.

'Who would have thought,' Athelstan exclaimed, 'the death of poor Margo would provoke such murderous fury?'

'The Flesher is responsible.' Cranston's face and voice was sullen and, tired though he was, Athelstan felt a prickle of cold agitation.

'Sir John,' he warned, '*tace atque vide*: stay silent and watch. We do not have a shred of evidence to place these horrors at the Flesher's blood-soaked feet, even though we know he is the *fons et origo*.'

'Oh, he certainly is the fount and origin of all this wickedness,' Cranston intervened. 'God knows he is, yet even the heaviest stones crack.' Cranston gestured at the corpses. 'When I received your message last night, I ordered Flaxwith to seize the remains of both man and beast. They can be exposed on the steps of St Benet's, with a proclamation pinned to the church door as well as at the cross in St Paul's churchyard. Anyone who recognises any or all of these corpses should immediately present themselves before me and my fellow justices at the Guildhall.'

Athelstan clutched Cranston's arm. 'My friend, I understand your anger but, again I repeat, do not do anything imprudent. I have been thinking, reflecting, puzzling: there are other paths to be followed.'

'Such as?'

'A visit to the House of the Delight. Oh, by the way, talking of visiting, have you dealt with Merchant Blundel?'

'Oh yes. He demonstrated all protest and outraged

righteousness, yet Merchant Blundel knows he cannot keep the property of the Crown. He also is fully aware of the ordinances of the city council and his own guild.'

'And where is the amethyst now?'

'In my arca at the Guildhall.'

'Which brings us back to the question of the arca at St Benet's.' Athelstan patted Cranston on the arm. 'A thought has occurred to me, but first I need to deal with our bell clerk.'

They found Mauger busy in the death house. At Athelstan's instructions he, helped by Watkin and Pike, also sworn to silence, had quietly and secretly buried the Grenels in a grave close to Margo's. Now he was tidying up before hurrying off to join the rest breaking their fast free of charge at the Piebald and the adjoining cook shop. Athelstan closed the door to the death house behind him and, beckoning at Cranston, walked over to where Mauger was washing down one of the corpse tables. Athelstan always insisted that this take place once a cadaver was removed, whilst Mauger was well paid for such services. The friar stood at the head of the table. Mauger kept scrubbing, although Athelstan could see that the bell clerk was so agitated he was almost scrubbing the table with his eyes closed. At last Mauger threw the brush down on to the ground and went over to sit on a three-legged stool in the corner. He put his face in his hands and began to quietly sob.

'Satan's tits,' Cranston breathed. 'What is wrong with the man?'

Athelstan went to crouch by Mauger. He gently prised away the bell clerk's hands. 'Look at me, Mauger.' The man raised his long, tear-streaked face. 'Now,' Athelstan brought across another of the mortuary stools and sat as close as he could to the bell clerk, aware of Cranston standing just behind him. 'I shall tell you what I think, Mauger, then you can tell me if I have spoken the truth. Very well?' Mauger nodded.

'When the facts behind Margo Grenel's secret life began to emerge,' Athelstan continued, 'on the morning of her funeral, I noticed you were most attentive to where both Benedicta and I went that day. Benedicta had discovered the secret of Margot Grenel's cellar and came to fetch me from the church.

Now Benedicta did not wish for the hue and cry to be raised, for shouts of "Harrow! Harrow!" to rouse the parish watch. No, Benedicta is prudent. She came to me discreetly, even secretly. But, of course, you were watching and waiting most attentively. You followed us to Margo's house and, acting all innocent, stumbled in, as if as surprised as anyone else. You blurted out the story about the Grenels joining the royal array on a chevauchée across the Narrow Seas, some military expedition under the old King. Of course, that's utter nonsense. Even at the time, I thought it came too glib, too fast, too polished, as if you had been preparing it for some time. Now,' Athelstan paused, 'before I continue, Mauger, do you know anything about the whereabouts of the Rose Casket or the precious stones known as Twelve Apostles?'

'No, no, no,' Mauger mumbled, 'no I don't. Brother Athelstan,' he moaned, 'do not judge me harshly.'

'You are the bell clerk at St Erconwald's, Mauger: you have access to the parish chest where Margo left her keys before going across to St Bartholomew's. You took these. You searched that poor woman's house. What were you looking for? The treasure?'

'I found nothing. I took nothing, please believe me.'

'I do and I am grateful, Mauger, that you have not challenged me. I thought your explanation was too glib. Then we had Margo's ramblings when she was in a delirium, sleeping under the influence of an opiate in St Bartholomew's. She muttered disjointedly about a bell. Now, we do not have a church bell in the steeple, but we do have you, Mauger, our bell clerk. Why should she mention you? What was your true relationship with that dead woman? What did Cecily and Clarissa mean about Margo kneeling before you? What did she do for you, Mauger, and why?'

'Yes, why?' Cranston echoed.

'Come on,' Athelstan urged, 'your intervention on the morning of Margo's burial? What did those two sisters see? Clarissa and Cecily have their own peculiar trade, they carry it out in the most hidden places, which is why they are in the cemetery almost as often as you are. That's where you met Margo, wasn't it?'

Mauger nodded.

'So, Mauger, how did that come about? Why should Margo – and she did – perform sexual favours for you, with her mouth or her hands? I am sure that's what Cecily and Clarissa were referring to. Yet Margo was a respectable widow with a good name in the parish.' Athelstan sighed and tapped his feet. 'Of course, Mauger,' he breathed, 'you could meet Margo in the cemetery but, bearing in mind your parish duties as well as Margo's, you would have every excuse to be seen together, even in her cottage.' Athelstan looked around, 'Or even in here, the death house.'

'And those two doxies,' Cranston observed, 'are experts at peering through keyholes or cracks. So tell us, clerk, how did this situation come about?'

'Eighteen years ago . . .' The bell clerk straightened up, resting his hands on his knees as if he were a minstrel or troubadour sitting in the inglenook to recite a poem or story. 'Eighteen years ago,' he repeated, 'I was not a bell clerk, but a watchman like Beadle Bladdersmith is, but better,' he added warningly. Mauger half closed his eyes. 'A bitterly cold night. A river mist had rolled in like the thickest steam, hiding everything in sight and dulling all sound. I was trying to keep warm, sheltering in an enclave against the bitterness, when I glimpsed lights along the river and muffled sounds. Then I heard a crack carry across the water. Yes, that's it, a sharp, horrid crack of something deadly, followed by the cries of men in mortal agony and the blood-chilling shrill of battle, of sword against sword, knife against knife. Only then did I realise some bloody affray was raging along the Thames. I wondered if the French had brought their galleys up, but there again, those were the stirring days where no enemy would dare bait the old King.' He paused. 'Even an angel from heaven couldn't have guided St Peter up the Thames in such weather; a thick, cloying mist hung over the water. I then thought it might be pirates.'

'Didn't you think of raising the alarm?'

'Of course, Sir John. There was the crack, the cries and the clash of steel, but then it all faded away. You must remember the season. I even wondered if I'd heard the echoes of some ghastly conflict from a long time ago, ghosts from the past, a haunting over the Thames. Strange things do happen along the river.'

'They certainly do,' Athelstan remarked. 'But you realised it was no ghostly conflict because of the Grenels, Henry and Walter. They came staggering ashore, one of them carrying a blue and red chancery bag. Mauger, you said you were standing in an enclave. You were a watchman. You were carrying a lanternhorn, weren't you?'

'Brother, Brother,' Mauger held up a hand, 'of course I carried a shuttered lantern and I used that – the notion of some haunting was just a passing thought. I left the enclave, climbed the barrier wall and walked across the shale. I saw two men, helping each other, crawl out of the water. They were soaked, shivering, finding it hard to keep upright. I raised my lantern and realised they were dressed in the garb of Tower archers; the royal insignia decorated their right shoulders. As I drew closer, I recognised Henry and Walter Grenel.' The bell man paused, eyes closed, breathing noisily through his nose. 'The Grenels.' He murmured. 'I'd greeted them in the parish and along the quayside. I was shocked to see them wounded so grievously. Henry carried a bag sodden with blood. They were on the point of collapse. I am not too sure if they recognised me but, to cut the quick, I helped them back to their cottage. Margo was beside herself.' Mauger lifted a hand. 'Sir John, Brother Athelstan, I swear I did not realise at the time what that chancery satchel contained. It just looked stained, soaked in both blood and river water.' He paused.

'Continue,' Athelstan gently insisted, 'tell us the truth. I can guess what it is, but we need you to describe what actually happened, to confirm our suspicions.'

'Brother, both men were mortally wounded. I had nothing to do with their deaths. Margo begged me to help her. I did, but there was little even the most skilled physician could achieve.' He sniffed noisily. 'I have served in the King's array. My duty was to help the leeches and the physicians of the royal army in the hospital tents. I can recognise a deadly wound when I see it. Henry and Walter Grenel had sustained hideous injury. They were dead within the day. When I met you that morning, I intimated that perhaps Margo had killed her husband and son; that was very wrong of me. A pernicious lie. I must put that right. Henry and Walter died because of wounds inflicted by others. Both Margo and I did our very best to help them but there was nothing we could do.'

Athelstan stared at Mauger and realised the bell clerk was probably terrified of being indicted for murder. The friar stretched out and clasped the man's mittened hands. 'Mauger, I believe you but, before those men died, did they speak?'

'Henry gasped about being attacked on the river, of dark shapes hurtling through the night. How he and Walter had grabbed the chancery satchel and fought their way through, only to be surrounded and receive grievous wounds. Henry was in deep pain. I believe Margo fed both husband and son heavy wine soaked with opiate.' Mauger wiped his face. 'As I said, they were dead within the day.'

'And after that?'

'Well, over the weeks following, rumour ran rife along the riverside about a furious night battle on the Thames. Apparently a great slaughter had taken place—'

'It certainly did,' Cranston interjected. 'I was there.'

'Corpses, weapons and clothing were swept ashore. Only then did I realise what had truly happened. I returned to question Margo but she had become tight-lipped, obdurate: she refused to talk about what had happened or what she'd done that fateful evening. The weeks passed. Stories about a treasure being stolen during the affray were repeated in the alehouses and taverns along both banks of the Thames, especially in Queenhithe. People wondered if the Flesher had had a hand in that hideous mischief.'

'And then?'

Mauger swiftly crossed himself. 'Father, I am a sinner. I always did like Margo. In her prime she was plump and comely. As Scripture says, I lusted after her in my mind's eye. I am a lonely man, Father. My woman died decades ago. I have been with Cecily and Clarissa but . . .' He shook his head.

'You threatened Margo, didn't you?' Athelstan insisted. 'That's what those two sisters were referring to, sexual favours in return for your silence. You wore her down. Margo may remain obdurate but, as time passed, she realised that she could never allow anyone into that cellar, and God help her if the Twelve Apostles and the Rose Casket were found upon her. Margo was a working woman. She had dressed enough corpses for burial, including those executed. Little wonder that she gave in to you and offered sexual favours in return for your silence.'

Mauger just nodded.

'And, of course,' Athelstan continued, 'that's why she would not come to be shrived at the mercy pew. She could not come to confession, at least not here. She was ashamed, frightened that I might recognise her voice. More importantly, it might make me wonder with whom she was consorting. If she had confessed, I might well have asked her, or she might have given me the name freely. She would also have to confess that she was being forced and that might lead to the reasons why. God rest the poor woman.' Athelstan smiled thinly. 'So many souls whisper their sorrow and pain to me. I cannot, I do not and I never shall remember or recall what is confessed to me at the shriving stall, whilst the seal of confession is the most solemn and sacred in our church.' Athelstan leaned over and gently nudged Mauger. 'Bell clerk, you must be shriven very soon yourself. You must confess and be absolved by me or another priest. You do understand? So, to return to that evening when the royal barge was attacked. You were in Margo's cottage with those two dying men, Henry and Walter? You must have heard what they said.'

'Henry was the clearest. His son Walter seemed to be in a delirium, a fever. He kept babbling about the House of Bethany and, like Lazarus, he must go there. Margo did her best to soothe him. Both men fell unconscious and drifted away.' The bell clerk flapped a hand. 'Brother Athelstan, Sir John, more than that I cannot say, I am sorry.'

Athelstan stared hard at this solemn, morose man, steeped deep in his shame. 'Come, Mauger,' Athelstan patted the bell clerk gently on the arm, 'when you are ready, you may come back and talk to me. In the meantime, here is your penance.' Mauger raised his head. 'Go into the church, spend an hour there, just sit in the warmth of the chantry chapel and pray for the souls of all three Grenels. And, when you have finished, present yourself before the lady altar and light a candle for each of them, a prayer that their journey into the light be peaceful.'

'I will, Father.' Mauger got to his feet, clearly relieved. 'But do you know, I have been thinking about what young Walter said. I mean, about Lazarus: didn't he come back from the dead? Isn't that what happened in the Scriptures?'

'Yes, yes,' Athelstan agreed. 'And we also have the story about Lazarus the poor man; that when he died he went to heaven, whilst the rich man Dives was buried in Hell because of his lack of care. But go, Mauger, we are finished here.'

Once the bell clerk had left, Athelstan closed and bolted the door behind him. He took out another tallow candle from the chest and handed it to the coroner to light.

'Brother?'

'Think, my fine friend,' the friar urged, 'you are Margo Grenel. You hold a great treasure which makes the world itch when it hears about it. She has to hide it. A coffer with twelve beautiful, precious stones. Now, where would she conceal it? Where are those places people do not want to go?'

Cranston held the candle up, admiring the flame. 'Well, she is not going to hide it in her cottage, is she? We have already seen what happened, and Margo would have recognised the danger. I understand she dressed corpses for burial, so she could hide those jewels amongst the dead, but that's dangerous. She has to wait for a certain funeral and there is always the risk of being discovered. She could conceal it in a privy, jakes or sewer but, there again, these are cleaned and swilled – though not as often as I would wish.' Cranston stamped his foot on the earth-beaten floor. 'You think she could have hidden it here, in the death house, a place everyone avoids?'

'Precisely,' Athelstan agreed. 'Sir John, let's search this place as carefully as we can.'

Both coroner and friar did. Athelstan scrutinised the ground, especially where it met the wall, but he could find no trace, no evidence which would suggest a treasure had been buried or concealed in the mortuary.

'So if it's not here, where?' Athelstan murmured. 'Sir John, let us leave this for the moment. We have certain ladies we must talk to.'

Cranston and Athelstan left the death house and were making their way through the cemetery when Benedicta called their names and hurried out of Godbless's cottage. The widow woman was followed by Bonaventure, the great tomcat walking proudly, as if a victor in a tournament; as Athelstan remarked, 'Not a whit the worse for his brush with savage death the previous day . . . Cunning, cunning cat,' Athelstan declared, and sketched a blessing over his constant dining companion before turning to Benedicta, who looked pale and drawn.

'You should rest.' Athelstan grasped her hands; they felt cold. He gently squeezed her fingers. 'Sleep,' he urged. She smiled and gestured with her head back at Godbless's cottage.

'Our poor friend sleeps, thank God. I gave him some wine mixed with a little poppy powder. He wants Thaddeus's remains, pathetic and as few as they are, to be buried in the sacred soil of God's Acre. Godbless insists on this. He claims it is only right – after all, the previous priest buried a bear here.'

'A bear?'

'Yes,' she smiled. 'A bear called Tori.' She stumbled over the name. 'I think it was that. Anyway, I was a mere slip of a girl. A dancing bear, and its keeper visited the parish one May Day and joined in our festivities. Oh yes,' Benedicta's smile widened, 'that bear could dance a merry jig, and he did until he fell sick and died. The parish priest at the time was petitioned by the council, on one of the few occasions when he wasn't drunk. Anyway, he agreed, and the poor animal was buried here. I am sure a headstone was erected in its memory. I hope so; after all, it truly was a merry dancer. Now Father, Godbless?'

'Benedicta, please take him to your cottage. Cast around the parish, see if you can find, purchase or borrow a baby kid, a young goat.' He answered Benedicta's quizzical look. 'Let us see if we can find Thaddeus the Younger. Right, Sir John . . .' Athelstan watched Benedicta hurry back along the coffin path to Godbless's cottage.

'Where to now, Brother?'

'Not the Devil's Oak, my Lord Coroner, oh no! I suggest we visit the House of Delights in Grape Lane. I'll tell Benedicta where we are going and then we will be gone.'

Athelstan was genuinely surprised when he and Cranston stopped before the glossy, painted door of the narrow three-storey house in Grape Lane. He glimpsed the bell under its coping, on which a bronze angel nestled all coy, its wings decently covering its breast. The door and its latch were highly polished, its white-stone steps scrubbed clean. When he stepped back and stared up, Athelstan could see how the windows were filled with painted glass rather than horn, whilst all the shutters, neatly thrown back, were painted to gleaming.

'A true place of joy,' Cranston murmured. 'There's a number of these houses across the city and, unless you thought otherwise, you would think they were rich, comfortable nunneries.' Cranston rubbed his hands gleefully, icy blue eyes full of mischief. 'So, Monk?'

'Friar, Sir John.'

'Brace yourself against a tide of beauty, my little ferret.' Cranston pulled on the bell and, within a few heartbeats, the door swung back on its well-greased hinges. A young woman stepped out. She was dressed soberly in a brown gown from neck to foot, with white bands at cuff and neck; the maid's raven-black hair was pinned neatly under a white gauze veil, her pretty face framed by a starched wimple. She stood on the threshold and looked them up and down from head to toe; she grinned, stepped back, and beckoned them in with a cheeky wink at Cranston.

'Enough of that, young Ursula,' the coroner growled. 'Just let me clap eyes on the domina of the house, the Lady Beatrice.'

'I am here, Jack Cranston.' A voice further along the passageway, behind the maid, called mockingly. 'Come in Jack, the weather is turning cold.' Ursula ushered Athelstan and Cranston into a well-furnished, opulently decorated waiting room, just inside the front entrance. Athelstan was aware of comfortable turkey rugs on the polished floor, perfume pots in wall niches, candles with their darting flames illuminating the carefully etched frescoes. Both coroner and friar sat on a comfortable settle as Lady Beatrice swept in. The domina was garbed like Ursula. She was old, lean and sinewy, her good-looking face marred by a cynical twist to what was now faded beauty. She eased herself on to a chair opposite them, Ursula standing beside her. Beatrice carefully folded back the cuffs of her gown, lifted her head and smiled at Cranston.

'So, Jack, this is an official visit?'

'As it always was and always will be, Mistress Beatrice. You know that. You also know that I, Jack Cranston, have more than a soft spot for you because our pasts are closely entwined.' The domina blushed and glanced away. 'The Flesher,' Cranston abruptly declared. 'Simon Makepeace. Does he come here?'

On their journey across the river, Cranston and Athelstan had discussed what path they would follow during their investigation at the House of Delights. The friar had insisted that they seek confirmation of a growing suspicion he had carefully nourished.

'The Flesher?' Cranston repeated gently. 'What does he do here? How does he act? Where does he go? I need answers to these questions.'

'And so you shall.' The Lady Beatrice was trying hard to control the fury seething within her. 'Jack, I can see you and the redoubtable Brother Athelstan are here about a man I loathe. I appreciate you are in a hurry.' She smiled dazzlingly at Athelstan, who realised that – in her youth – this domina must have been a truly beautiful woman.

'Lady Beatrice,' Cranston declared, 'you are correct, we are in a hurry.'

'I will only say this in your presence and yours alone.' Beatrice's face became drawn and fierce. 'I truly detest the Flesher. He repels me. He is a devil incarnate. I hate him, his coven and all that he does. I would do anything, pay any sum, to bring him down.' She leaned closer; her voice now hissed with a deadly rancour. 'Jack, I sit here like a cloistered nun but, as Ursula will tell you, I listen carefully to all the chatter and gossip which trickles through London's underworld like filth seeps along a sewer. I keep an eye on the Flesher and his horde of rats at the Devil's Oak. I am of the mind that the

Flesher is riding for a fall. Oh yes, in my green and salad days, I studied the classics. The ancient Greeks talk of "hubris", an arrogance which contains the seeds of its own hideous destruction. The Flesher is guilty of great hubris. He is as saturated in this as he is in the blood of others . . .' She wiped spittle from her lips. Despite the heavy brown robe, Athelstan could see Beatrice's body tense in spasms of violent anger.

'Lady Beatrice?'

She took a deep breath, then glanced up, all pretty and pert. 'Yes, Brother?'

'Martha Ashby, housekeeper to Parson Reynaud – or Parson Reynaud that was. In her green and salad days she worked here in the House of Delights?'

'Oh, sweet Martha,' Lady Beatrice smiled, 'she certainly did work here, but only for a short while. She was very popular and, consequently, very expensive.'

'What do you mean? I don't understand.'

'Brother Athelstan, have you ever heard about the triple crown of Venus?' Beatrice and Ursula grinned whilst Cranston coughed self-consciously. Athelstan, colouring slightly, shook his head, even as he half suspected what he was about to be told.

'The triple crown of Venus? Well,' the domina was clearly enjoying herself, 'in the act of love, as described by the Roman poet Ovid, in his *Ars Amandi, The Art of Loving*, some women just use their bodies, a few use their hands and, fewer still, their lips, all with the greatest skill. This is the triple crown of Venus worn by only a few women. Young Martha was certainly one of these. If you want,' she added impishly, 'Ursula here can demonstrate what I mean.'

'And if you want,' Athelstan countered, 'I am prepared to lead you in reciting fifteen decades of the rosary on your knees on the cobbles outside.' Beatrice and Ursula laughed, both raising their fingers coquettishly to cover their mouths. 'Seriously, and this is serious,' Athelstan's smile faded, 'why did Martha leave; I mean, if she was so skilled?'

Beatrice replied: 'Sir John here is, I understand, a superb swordsman, but only when he has to be. So it was with Martha. For a time she had to but, when she no longer had to, she left. Brother Athelstan, I have heard of you and your work amongst the poor. You know this world and how it is if you are a woman alone in this city, you are highly vulnerable. Visit the nunneries, be it in Farringdon ward or Queenhithe, you'll find these houses throng with young women who are there not because they wish to serve God, but because they are desperate to escape the cruel world of men. If a woman has money or, better still, wealth and menfolk, she is safe. If she is cloistered by Holy Mother Church, she is protected. But, as for the rest, they are lambs wandering through the wolf pack.'

Athelstan closed his eyes. For a brief moment he recalled poor Thaddeus being torn to pieces by those war mastiffs.

'Why are you interested in Martha?' Ursula asked. 'We have all heard what happened at St Benet's.'

'I suspect Martha knows more than she has told us,' Athelstan replied. 'She is a good woman but prudent. I think she is very much afraid of the Flesher. Now, listen, when she stayed here, did the Flesher frequent her?'

'Yes, but Martha often pleaded to be excused. She was quick to seize on any pretext, be it her monthly courses or some malignancy in her humours. She did not like him, as many of our girls did not and do not like him.'

'He is violent?'

'Sir John, you speak the truth, very violent. I am also afraid of him, yet I have had occasion to warn him. My ladies are not the doxies and common whores to be found along Queenhithe quayside. I have heard the rumours about what he does to them. Oh yes, the stories are rife about young women who disappear and whose remains are hidden in that great catacomb at St Benet's.'

'And when the Flesher comes here?'

'Oh, the Flesher wants to bathe. He just loves hot, fragranced water. He strips naked and wallows like a pig in the mud. He climbs into our large, iron-bound tub with small tables just within reach so he can help himself to wine, sweetmeat, napkins and anything else he needs.' She shrugged. 'Of course, he is joined by two or three of our ladies, naked except for their headdresses.'

'Headdresses!'

'That's what he wants. Strange sight, Sir John, a young

woman like Ursula naked except for her wimple and headdress.
I have heard stories about what he did at a nunnery outside
Rouen; he made the good sisters parade naked except for their
veils. The Flesher is a man who likes to humiliate women at
every turn and twist. But, of course, you would be surprised,
Brother, at what our customers demand.'

'I am sure I would, though I have heard a number of interesting confessions. Now tell me, the Flesher, when he stripped
off naked: did he take off the key which hung on a chain
around his fat neck?'

'Oh yes. He took it off. He was concerned that during his
water frolics with our young maids, the chain would snap and
the key might fall off. Oh no, he undid the chain and stepped
into the tub, naked as he was born.'

'And the key?' Cranston demanded.

'Let me guess,' Athelstan declared, 'he took it off and left
it with his clothing, warbelt and purse in a small antechamber
just within sight of the bath? These belongings were guarded
by one of his leading henchmen, the creature Raquin or a man
called Ingersol, popularly known as the Sicarius.'

'Brother Athelstan, you have the second sight!'

'No, just a student of what is possible, so I can work out
what is certainly probable. I will go even further. Recently
the Flesher has changed, has he not? He has taken to keeping
his key and chain under the most careful scrutiny. Am I
right?'

'Brother Athelstan, you are correct. Until a short while ago,
a few weeks at the very most, the Flesher would strip and
climb into the tub. This abruptly changed. The Flesher insisted
on putting the chain and key on one of the tables close to the
bathtub.'

'And at the same time,' Athelstan declared, 'Ingersol
the Sicarius has completely vanished; he is no longer in the
Flesher's retinue?'

'In a word, Brother Athelstan, yes.'

'What did you think of the Sicarius?'

'A shadow, a dark presence, much trusted by the Flesher.
He would stand guard while his master went about his frolics.
As I said, his job was to guard the devil's property.' She

shrugged. 'Ingersol disappeared and the Flesher took to guarding his own precious items.'

'Tell me, Mistress, you have Castilian soap here?'

'Yes, and it is very expensive. Small tablets bought from a merchant on Cheapside. He imports them from Spain, a very profitable trade.'

'Lady Beatrice,' Athelstan took out his ave beads and sifted them through his fingers, 'you want to bring the Flesher down, that is most obvious. I also recognise that you are in considerable danger. If the Flesher knew what you are telling us, he would exact a terrible revenge.'

'Brother Athelstan, I trust you and Sir John, but you will find others are becoming tired of the Flesher and his wicked ways.'

'Tell me,' Cranston intervened, 'did Parson Reynaud come here?'

'Not as often as he used to, Jack – age can take care of a man's lusts.'

'And Daventry, Arundel's man. He visited St Benet's to meet the parson and was murdered there?'

'Yes, so I have heard. Daventry came here on one occasion. He was a mailed clerk, a man who kept close counsel; the lady he hired claimed he spent most of his time studying a chart depicting all the streets and alleyways of Queenhithe.'

'And the others?' Athelstan asked. 'Master Cripplegate, Sexton Spurnel, Curate Cotes?' Lady Beatrice's head went down and Athelstan could see she was smiling. 'Mistress?' She raised her head.

'Brother Athelstan, Cripplegate may have been married but his wife had no children. From the little I know, all three men prefer a different meal from that which we serve here.'

'You mean they like other men, or should I say lust for other men?'

'Brother Athelstan, so the rumour goes. But you asked about Castilian soap?'

'Yes, I did. Lady Beatrice I will take you into my confidence, as even Sir John must be wondering where this path is leading. The arca at St Benet's was opened and robbed. I am sure you can appreciate the mystery. The arca had two distinct locks,

each with a unique key. One was held by Parson Reynaud and
the other by the Flesher. Now we found Parson Reynaud's,
but the Flesher, according to reports, never lets that key out
of his sight. That must be wrong. Somebody got hold of that
key, just for a short while, and made an impression. I reflected
where and when would this great lecher take off that chain
and key? And then I asked where and when could a replica
of it be cast?' Athelstan spread his hands. 'And so here we
are, and that's why I am asking you to bring me a tablet of
Castilian soap.'

'Of course!' Ursula left the chamber and Lady Beatrice began
to chat with Sir John about mutual acquaintances in the city
and court: who was rising, who was falling, all the petty scandals
and gossip. Listening carefully, Athelstan realised that this
woman had once been part of the merry dance Cranston had
led as a young man, long before he met the Lady Maude.

Ursula returned with a small cake of purest Castilian. The
fragrance was so sweet it filled the antechamber, its colour
like that of the purest alabaster. Athelstan carefully picked the
soap out of its silver dish and smiled at the Lady Beatrice.
'Can I trouble you further? Do you have a coffer key?' He
held up a hand, 'I just want to make an impression. I shall do
it here and give both soap and key back to you.'

Again Ursula was despatched and returned with a small
casket key, which Athelstan carefully scrutinised. He pulled
back the sleeves of his gown, positioned the soap in its silver
dish and pressed the key gently in it. He left it for a while
then, with a thin-tipped chancery knife, carefully extracted
the key from the soap. Both he and Cranston examined the
makeshift cast made, especially the fine copy of the teeth at
the end of the coffer key.

'But what then?' Cranston asked.

'Sir John?'

'I understand your argument. You would have us believe
Ingersol took the Flesher's key, along with a fine piece of
Castilian soap, and a cast was made.'

'Once he'd done that, he would have to put the key back
as well as the . . .' Cranston grinned and shook his head. 'My
apologies, my wits are not as sharp as they should be. Of

course,' he turned to Lady Beatrice, 'the Sicarius would be in the antechamber guarding the Flesher's belongings, including the key.'

'Yes. He wouldn't use your soap,' Cranston chewed the corner of his lip, 'but his own.'

'Or some wax,' Athelstan interjected. 'You have candles burning, Mistress, of course you have. A piece of pure beeswax could provide excellent material for a cast, as it soon melts and then quickly hardens. It would keep the cast in all its detail. After all, it's the teeth of the key which matter. Mistress, Sir John and I are openly debating a matter which, if the Flesher learnt about, could place you and yours in great danger, not to mention ourselves. Sir John and I are hunting the Flesher, as we are the assassin who committed those horrors at St Benet's Woodwharf. So what we debate here is strictly *sub rosa* – a secret protected by the King's writ.'

'Yes, Brother.'

'So I ask you, from what you have heard and seen of the Flesher, his visits here, the way he trusted the Sicarius. Do you think the Sicarius had the time to make a cast of that key to the arca, the only occasion we believe the Flesher ever became separated from it?'

'Yes, Brother Athelstan, it is possible, even probable because—'

'Because what?'

'Because a few weeks ago, the Sicarius disappeared, and has never been seen since, at least not by us here in this house. Naturally, I was curious. I asked the Flesher where the Sicarius was. All I received back in reply was the most repulsive scowl. Raquin, who was with him at the time, laughed as he always does, high and piercing, like the neigh of a prancing palfrey. Moreover, I'd heard the rumours – even the Flesher himself had mentioned this – that there could be a traitor in his comitatus.' She shrugged prettily. 'And it would appear that perhaps the Sicarius was the guilty one, hence his disappearance. After all, that's what happens when you offend, alienate or obstruct the Flesher: you simply disappear. But at the end of the day, I might be wrong. Jack, I do what I am and I am what I do.' She waved a hand. 'People dismiss me as a common whore, but I have a sharp wit and a keen mind. I watch the filthy politic of the Flesher. His world repels me but it's a world which taints mine.'

'And the Sicarius?'

'As I have said, a brooding, dark presence. Fairly handsome, taciturn and watchful. He rarely talked and, when he did, he was a man of few words. A strange, eerie character. Sometimes I'd catch him staring at me sadly.'

'Why do you call him strange?' Cranston leaned over and grasped Lady Beatrice's hands and kissed the tip of her fingers. She immediately acted all coy, eyelids fluttering, hand beating gently against her chest.

'Oh Jack,' she whispered, 'we have seen the days.'

Athelstan fought to keep his face straight and impassive.

'We certainly have, my lady,' Cranston retorted. 'And so I trust your judgement about men, be it the Flesher or Ingersol. What was strange about him? Why was he sad?'

'In a word, Jack, he seemed to be a man deeply uncomfortable in his own skin.'

'And?'

'As I've said, Jack, the Flesher is riding for a fall. Perhaps Ingersol was the traitor. Perhaps he was just one of many who are beginning to grow tired of the filthy, treacherous, murderous world of Master Simon Makepeace.' Lady Beatrice smoothed her long white fingers down her gown and glanced up sharply. 'Do you think the same?' she asked.

'What I suspect,' Athelstan told her, 'is that weeks ago the Flesher came here with the Sicarius, his personal retainer and henchman. We now know the Sicarius had decided to betray the Flesher.' He smiled thinly at Lady Beatrice. 'That too is a secret, but one that will not help the poor man who has probably paid with his blood for his change of mind. Now I suggest that Ingersol was intent on a killing blow against his murderous master. He would break into the Flesher's arca at St Benet's and steal everything. How he planned to obtain the key held by Parson Reynaud is still a mystery. Anyway, on that particular day, the Flesher comes here for his water frolics, well served by the ladies of the house. He strips in the ante-chamber and, intent only on his pleasure, takes off the key chain from around his neck. Meanwhile the Sicarius sits in a small antechamber or enclave. He is by himself.' Lady Beatrice nodded in agreement. 'He has a piece of pure beeswax or a small tablet of Castilian soap; he may well have had both. He takes an impression of the key to the arca, concentrating as we did on the teeth of the key.' Athelstan paused, eyes narrowed. 'We know very little of the provenance of the Sicarius. He styled himself the dagger man. He is silent and taciturn, of a secretive disposition. He may have been well versed in forging keys or picking locks.'

'That's true,' Cranston intervened. 'Many felons, like scholars in the schools, graduate from one profession to another. Moreover, he was a clerk, a mailed clerk. He may have had a skill for picking the locks of chancery chests.'

'He was definitely sure of himself,' Athelstan agreed. 'And I am almost certain that he knew the only time he could get to that key is when the Flesher visited the House of Delights which, of course, explains our presence here today. Now he must have been successful on that particular occasion. If the Flesher had caught him, then there would have been a rather violent confrontation between the riffler and his henchman.'

'Nothing like that ever occurred here,' Lady Beatrice intervened. 'But how did the Flesher discover Ingersol was the traitor?'

'And that's my final conclusion,' Athelstan continued. 'Even though, I concede, it is mere supposition, a theory with no hard evidence. I suspect the Sicarius made a hideous mistake. Once he had finished fashioning the cast or casts, he hid these away in his wallet and put back the key. I suggest that he never examined it carefully. The soap of Castile and beeswax candles exude a beautiful fragrance. However, when they harden, any traces become small globules, rather difficult to remove. In other words,' he sighed, 'for some reason the Flesher examined that key. He smelt it, scrutinised it and, being the cunning viper he is, reached the conclusion that someone had tried to make a cast of his key. He would also realise that the only person who could have done so was the Sicarius, here in the House of Delights. The Flesher would consult with his evil familiar, Raquin. Both men would conclude that the

Sicarius intended great mischief and was undoubtedly the
traitor in the Flesher's camp. A violent confrontation must
have taken place. Ingersol was then executed, his corpse hidden
God knows where.' Athelstan crossed himself. 'I concede
this is pure conjecture, but a logical possibility.' He smiled.
'Was it the key which led to Ingersol's downfall? If not – what?
If it was—'

'The Flesher would have been alerted; he would have
protected the arca better,' Cranston declared. 'Surely?'

Athelstan pulled a face. 'True, true,' he murmured. 'One
thing, however, I am sure of: a cast was made of the Flesher's
key here in the House of Delights – whether the Flesher
realised what had happened is the hypothesis we cannot
definitely prove.'

They sat in silence for a while, until Lady Beatrice leaned
across and nipped Cranston's wrist. 'Jack, the hour is passing,
is there anything else?'

The coroner glanced at Athelstan who just shook his head.

'In which case . . .' Lady Beatrice rose, Cranston and
Athelstan likewise. They made their farewells. The friar was
about to follow the coroner out of the room when his gaze
was caught by one of the frescoes on the wall close to the
door. Athelstan peered closer and realised the painting was an
artist's impression of the heavenly constellations, each titled
in Latin on a silver scroll: 'Pleiades', 'Stella Matutina',
'Magnus Artorius'. Athelstan stared at these, mouthing the
words, remembering something Benedicta had told him.

'Brother?'

Athelstan kept staring at the painting as his mind began to
wonder. He recalled what he'd learnt earlier that day and shook
his head in surprise once again, mouthing the words quietly
time and again.

'Brother?' Cranston came back to fetch him. 'Athelstan, are
you well?'

'I am amongst the stars, Sir John, and a thought has occurred
to me. Logic dominates our lives, whether we like it or not,
yet we always have to test the conclusion. So, let us leave.'

PART SIX

Sneaksman (**Old English**): a thief

They left the House of Delights and were halfway down Grape Street when Cranston abruptly turned and strode back to the shadow-filled mouth of an alleyway.

'You'd best come out,' he shouted. 'You have been following us since we left that house, hugging the wall. Come on! Enough deceit. Either show yourselves or I will go fetch you myself.'

Two figures sloped out of the murk and hurried towards them.

'Watkin and Pike!' Athelstan exclaimed. 'In God's name what are you doing here?'

'Benedicta told us. So we hurried across and were waiting for you to leave.'

'And why did you want to know where we were going? Come on,' Athelstan urged. 'You are the leaders of my parish council. You must have good reason to follow your priest across the Thames and into this maze of alleyways. Oh, for the love of Mary.' Athelstan pointed at a shabby alehouse further down Grape Street. 'We will set up camp there and you can tell us.'

'It is important,' Pike declared, his thin, choleric face all flushed. 'Watkin and I have been in discussion about what we should do and it's time we told you. It's about the Flesher, St Benet's, and Watkin's dung cart.'

'Now that does sound interesting,' Athelstan murmured. 'But come, let's make ourselves more comfortable.'

The alehouse consisted of a long, low-beamed hall where barrels, tubs and boxes served as tables and stools. A dark place, the gloom lit by a cluster of rush lights and smelly oil lamps. The stench of burning almost masked the rank, wet odour of the bedraggled chickens that pecked at the floor, scrabbling furtively away as a rat slithered through the wet rushes, snouting for morsels or scraps. The greasy-aproned slattern ushered them to what she grandly described as 'the window seat': four overturned barrels around a trestle table under a square-cut window, its shabby shutters thrown back. Athelstan peered out at the garden with its flowerbeds, herb plots, stew ponds and grassy fringes, all gaunt and stark under the tightening grip of a cold autumn. Athelstan refused the offer of a drink. Cranston ordered ale for himself and 'his two friends', bellowing at the serving girl that he wanted the tankards clean and the ale thoroughly brewed. Once the black jacks were served, Athelstan tapped the stained barrel top.

'Gentleman,' he declared, 'you have brought us here, it must be urgent, so what?'

'The business in Haceldema,' Watkin declared, indicating with one dirty hand for Pike to remain silent. 'We believe it's the work of the Flesher and it has proved too much. Oh, we've heard stories about him before, but to witness such villainy! The savage destruction of poor Thaddeus, the grave injuries inflicted on Godbless, not to mention you, Benedicta and Crim being threatened with steel and hell-hounds – these are injuries too great to bear.' Watkin drew himself up, his broad, florid face bright with anger. 'The Flesher truly is a human dung cart, full of every kind of shit, and reeking like the filthiest midden heap. He's like the river Fleet – wherever he goes, muck and dirt follow. I confess,' Watkin was now becoming more dramatic and Athelstan hid a smile. He now realised why Judith the mummer always gave Watkin a lead role in the mystery plays. 'I confess,' Watkin repeated, 'Pike and I have been supping with wolves. It's time we left the banqueting table and made our peace. Isn't that true, Pike?'

'I agree with Watkin,' the ditcher declared. 'I would love to dig the deepest pit, throw the Flesher in and bury him beneath the reeking mess of London's filthiest lay stall.'

'Look, gentlemen,' Cranston intervened, 'your detestation of the Flesher is most laudable. But what is this all about?'

'As you know, Brother Athelstan,' Watkin told him, 'I have bought a new dung cart, thanks to a loan from the Flesher. I arranged it through family kin I have in Queenhithe. The Flesher's lawyer, Master Copping, called it an investment.'

Watkin stumbled over the word and gave a broad, gap-toothed smile. 'The Flesher loans money to people like me, so I bought that cart. From what was left of the money, I had a secret place constructed, well sealed off with oaken wood which had been heavily coated with the thickest pitch.'

'Why did you do that?'

'Brother Athelstan, that's what Master Copping told us to do. The Flesher would advance us the money, I was to buy a new cart with a secret compartment.'

'And you didn't ask why?'

'Sir John, you know full well that half the coffins carried across London often contain more smuggled goods than corpses. Taxes are high. The custom collectors are sharp and ruthless. Anyway, the Flesher has similar carts all over London. We thought we'd be involved in a little smuggling.'

'And if you are caught,' the coroner warned, 'your cart would be confiscated and you would face heavy fines. You would also be led through the city to the sound of bagpipes to stand in the Pillory of Purgatory near the Great Conduit in Cheapside.'

'Oh, we know all that. But this was different.' Pike again grinned. 'Nothing illegal – or immoral, like smuggling whores. We were simply told to bring our cart to the Devil's Oak on the eve of the feast of St Cecilia.'

'Twenty-first of November,' Athelstan exclaimed. 'Cecilia was a virgin martyr executed in Ancient Rome. She is the patron saint of church music.'

'And on her feast day, 22 November,' Cranston declared, 'Parliament has been summoned to meet at Westminster, both the Lords and the Commons. The King intends to seek formal approval for his uncle John of Gaunt to act as regent, not to mention a new tax to fill the royal coffers.' Cranston fell silent, staring across at Athelstan, his blue eyes all fierce as he pondered the possibilities. 'Do you know, Pike and Watkin, when we left the House of Delights I realised we were being followed. I thought it was the Candlelight-Master and his Luciferi. A group of Frenchmen.' He answered their puzzled look. 'They are the ones who rescued Athelstan and the others in Haceldema. I now regard them as the messengers of God, as I do you.'

'Sir John, what do you mean?'

'I just wonder, I truly do, my friends.' Cranston stared around the dirty alehouse, then he abruptly leaned forward, seizing Watkin and Pike by the front of their shabby jerkins. He pulled them forward, giving each a short shake as they protested. 'Don't worry,' he growled, 'you are my friends not my foes. Raise your right hands, go on. Raise them,' he urged. They did so, eyes all anxious. 'By the power invested in me,' Cranston intoned, 'as the King's Lord High Coroner in London, I swear you to be officers of the law and members of my comitatus within the city and beyond. You so swear?'

Both men nodded, Pike gulping back his fear, Watkin slightly trembling. Both men regarded Cranston as a most fearsome figure, who sat at the right hand of the power, whatever that was. 'Brother Athelstan,' Cranston released both men, 'you are their parish priest and you've witnessed their oath of office, so give us your most powerful blessing.'

Athelstan, biting his lip to hide his smile, did so, and both parishioners, heads bowed, crossed themselves. 'Right,' Cranston waved a stubby finger at them, 'you are to remain silent about what you have learnt and might learn in the future. You are to act as upright officers, which is why I will divulge my secrets to you.' Cranston produced the miraculous wineskin and took the most generous gulp before sharing it with Pike and Watkin; the latter went to take a second mouthful, but Cranston snatched it away.

'Fitzalan Earl of Arundel,' the coroner began.

'We've heard of him,' Pike declared.

'A fearsome lord,' Watkin added. 'Very cruel to the Upright Men, a great killer of our company and our comrades.' Watkin abruptly paused, hand over his mouth. 'I shouldn't have said that, should I?'

'Never mind.' Cranston waved a hand. 'That's in the past. I deal with the future. I suspect Fitzalan of Arundel intends to overawe the Parliament summoned to meet at Westminster on the feast of St Cecilia. Now, I know the King and his council, in particular my Lord of Gaunt and Master Thibault, also believe that. They also recognise that Arundel cannot bring troops, in this case mercenaries, either into the city or

Westminster, the latter being royal property, whilst every inch of this city is owned by someone else . . .'

'Except for St Benet's Woodwharf,' Athelstan interjected. 'A large, cavernous church with a broad, sprawling cemetery which Parson Reynaud was intent on clearing. He intended to make it into a campsite, didn't he? What with that church and that wasteland of a graveyard, Arundel could easily quarter a thousand, perhaps two thousand mercenaries there. Oh yes,' Athelstan took his ave beads from his pouch, threading them through his fingers to soothe his excitement, 'moreover, St Benet's stands close to the Thames. Can you imagine troops encamped and, when Arundel decides, a fleet of war barges could ferry these soldiers to Westminster to lay siege to the palace – the abbey as well as the great offices of the Exchequer and Chancery. But can he do that? I mean, bring troops on to church property?'

'Brother, Arundel could and will. He holds the advowson of St Benet's. He possesses all the power of a manor lord. He can appropriate buildings and assemble whomever he wants. Oh yes,' Cranston exclaimed, 'that's what Arundel intends, and he brought the Flesher into his plot. That is the secret they have been preparing; that's why Daventry was sent to Parson Reynaud, probably to push matters ahead. Arundel is plotting to turn the entire church and its land into a fortified enclave, with war barges on the Thames and a few mounted hobelars to guard the approaches. They could stable their horses in the death house. Arundel may well turn Mistress Martha out and use the priest's dwelling as his own. They will have weapons enough. The main problem will be purveyance, fresh food and water for soldiers who might be quartered there for ten to fourteen days, as long as the Parliament lasts. Now gentlemen, that is the reason why –' Cranston pointed at Athelstan's two parishioners, who sat, faces all startled, staring at the coroner like frightened rabbits – 'he needs you and others, not to mention the Flesher, whose cellars at the Devil's Oak will be crammed with purveyance ready for the arrival of the mercenaries. Remember, Athelstan, when we visited that tavern? All those provision carts in the courtyard, the casks, the barrels? Once Parliament sits, I am certain that the

kitchens, butteries and bakeries at the Devil's Oak will become
very busy. The tavern also owns a stew pond, not to mention
a well with plenty of fresh water. And so we have it. Oh yes,
most cunning! Arundel will arrive and move amongst the lords
with his henchmen whilst his troops stand off Westminster.
He will have one aim in mind, to compel our young King to
hand over the royal council to the Fitzalans and their ilk. Once
he has this, Arundel will move for the impeachment of John
of Gaunt. Our noble regent will realise what is coming and
take ship to foreign parts, go into exile, leaving the King, the
court, the council, the city and the kingdom to Arundel and
his faction. Arundel will topple Gaunt and, who knows in time,
may even move against our young King.'

'Sir John, you think so?'

'Brother Athelstan, I know so.'

'So, what can be done?'

'These . . .' Cranston picked up his tankard and toasted Pike
and Watkin. 'Brother Athelstan, our two companions – along
with others of their kind – will be our saviours. So, Brother,
look to the dung collectors from where our salvation comes.
I swear that I, Sir John Cranston, will invoke something much
more ancient and powerful than a manor lord's right to
advowson. I shall summon up all the Crown's power and ritual
surrounding the crime of murdrum.'

'Sir John?' Watkin queried.

'Murder, the unlawful slaying of another human being. Now
we know that has taken place at St Benet's and, by the way,
I am not talking about the killing of Parson Reynaud or
Daventry. Oh no, St Benet's is a house of grievous ill-repute.
We suspect that the church, its cemetery and crypt are in fact
a mausoleum of murder. They contain the corpses, many of
these innocents, maliciously slain, their corpses hidden away.
Accordingly, I am going to issue a writ under statute law and
search the entire area: church, cemetery and crypt. Sooner or
later I will find victims of murder. So Watkin, Pike, as duly
sworn officers of both the Crown and city council, have words
with your respective guilds and fraternities, the diggers and
the dung collectors of London. Tell them I am going to
use the law to summon them in haste to assemble under the

royal standard in the cemetery at St Benet's. Tell them that the usual writs will be issued, proclamations will be posted on the Cross at St Paul's churchyard, the Standard in Cheapside, as well as the gates to London Bridge. I expect them to be there in the next three days.'

'Sir John?'

'Yes, my little friar?'

'If Arundel is plotting to do what you say, and I think he is, is it possible that the murders of Daventry and Parson Reynaud were perpetrated to thwart this? The work of some opponent of the Fitzalans?'

'Perhaps. But we have no evidence.' Cranston again took a generous swig from the miraculous wineskin and shared it with Pike and Watkin, warning them to take only a mouthful. Cranston then leaned back, beaming at Watkin and Pike as if they were long-lost brothers. He dug into his purse and plucked out two coins, pushing these towards the ragged, mittened hands of both men. 'Go, and as Scripture says,' he intoned, 'spread the word.' Cranston clapped his hands in glee. 'Arundel and the Flesher may well try to protest but, rest assured, I have the right and the law is on my side. So,' Cranston rose, 'you gentlemen be about your business. Brother Athelstan, let us adjourn to my chantry chapel at the Lamb of God.'

The church bells of Cheapside were tolling the appeal for the members of all guilds and fraternities to remember their promises to pray and provide for the poor. A preacher standing on a barrel also reminded the crowds of Christ's words, 'The poor you will always have with you.'

'True enough,' Athelstan murmured, staring round at the horde of beggars who gathered at the mouth of different alleyways or runnels. Now and again Athelstan would pause to distribute a little from his alms pouch but, for the rest, he had to follow Cranston as the coroner pushed his way through the colourful, noisy throng. Cranston had made it very clear that he had his eagle eye on one thing and one thing only, his favourite tavern's brilliantly hued, beacon-like sign, beckoning them into the comfortable and luxurious warmth of the solar, a fitting harbour against the cold, misty autumn day. The coroner and friar dodged barrows and carts. They paused to allow coffin cortèges make their mournful way by, wished well to wedding parties, and walked on, trying to ignore the apprentices tugging at their sleeves to visit this stall or that, as well as a legion of cooks desperate to sell their pies and potages before the market bell sounded the end of trading. At last they approached the Lamb of God. Cranston was openly debating whether to have chicken cooked in white wine or a minced beef pie when he stopped, cursing volubly, as he glimpsed Tiptoft surging through the crowd like a war barge along the river.

'Sir John,' Tiptoft proclaimed dramatically, 'My Lord Coroner, Brother Athelstan, you must come.'

'Where?' the friar demanded.

'St Benet's Woodwharf. Flaxwith is assembling his bailiffs. Sir John, more murder and mayhem and,' the courier lowered his voice to a whisper, 'the Flesher is trapped and awaits arrest.'

Cranston and Athelstan arrived to find St Benet's Church under siege. All the doors were locked and bolted, whilst a strong guard of Flaxwith's cohort had set up watch on the devil's door, still not fully repaired. Cranston's chief bailiff had brought the corpses from Southwark. The cadavers of the wolfsheads and the two war hounds now sprawled gruesomely on the church steps. Athelstan took his ave beads out and threaded them through his fingers to pray and soothe his nerves. The public display of slain outlaws was common practice, but Athelstan found it barbaric even though it was necessary. The bellies of the dead were now beginning to swell and the reeking stench of putrefaction hung heavily in the air. A garishly written proclamation, the letters etched in red ink, had been pinned to the church door. It declared how these malefactors were guilty of grievous crimes, including murderous assault on citizens as well as on an anointed priest. Accordingly, the proclamation insisted, anyone who recognised the dead, be it man or beast, should, under the pain of forfeiture and imprisonment, present themselves immediately before the justices at the Guildhall.

A crowd had been drawn in by the display of the dead and the dire words of the proclamation. They were quite certain that the dead men were rifflers from the Devil's Oak; such cries of recognition were sudden, shouted comments, though no one came forward to state the truth. Athelstan noticed how many of the crowd either spat on the corpses or made gestures against the evil eye to protect themselves against the spirits of the dead men. Here and there, someone would step forward and kick one of the corpses with the toe of his boot. Indeed, the only mercy shown to the dead was that someone had draped dirty cloths over their private parts, whilst bailiffs armed with clubs tried to drive away the mangy street dogs eager to nose the dead, lips curled back, sharp teeth ready to tear cold flesh. Flaxwith appeared. He nodded at Cranston. The bailiff winked, tapped the side of his nose knowingly and made his way to the top step where he turned to address the crowd.

'I have sent a messenger to fetch Master Makepeace from the Devil's Oak and asked him to come here as soon as possible.' Flaxwith then pointed down to Cranston. 'However, the Lord High Coroner is now present. Rest assured all is in good order. In accordance with the law, the corpses of these outlaws and their savage dogs have been displayed and you know the reason why. If you recognise the dead, you know what you must do. Now disperse. Anyone who remains will be held and sworn as members of my comitatus and assist our guard over these corpses.'

The crowd thinned and disappeared like snow under the sun. Flaxwith, all pleased, tripped down the steps, followed by Samson, who immediately tried to lick the coroner's leg, until his master hastily tightened his collar leash, pulling the dog back and ordering him to behave. He then gestured at Cranston and Athelstan to follow him into the shadow of the church porch.

'Satan's tits,' Cranston breathed. 'Flaxwith, what is this all about?' The chief bailiff stared around, then beckoned Cranston and Athelstan to draw even closer. 'Sir John,' he whispered, 'Raquin and Copping accompanied their master to St Benet's this morning. Apparently the Flesher went into the priest's house; his two henchmen visited the church.' Flaxwith pulled a face. 'All seemed well enough, Sir John, no alarm was raised. Peace reigned, until myself and the others arrived with the carts carrying the corpses. We laid them out and I thought we should, as a courtesy, visit Mistress Martha to inform her about what we had done. When I received your instructions yesterday evening, I did send a confidential message to the housekeeper about what was planned for today. Anyway, when I reached the house, I could hear moans and groans as well as shouted curses, followed by a pounding as if someone was imprisoned in a chamber, desperate to be released. The main door was not locked or bolted. Well, you'd best see for yourself.'

Flaxwith led Cranston and Athelstan from the church, through God's Acre and up the slight rise to the priest's house. As soon as they drew close, Athelstan could hear the shouts and strident curses. They went in. Athelstan hastened to the stairs to the left of the entrance hall and stood listening to the cursing and pounding from above.

'That's the Flesher,' Flaxwith declared cheerily. 'He's locked in Mistress Martha's bedchamber. The door is of the heaviest oak. Martha has the key: the window looks out over the back of the house and is far too small to crawl through. His victim is in here.'

Flaxwith led Cranston and Athelstan into the solar. Martha, her gown bloodied, her hair hanging in a tangle down to her shoulders, sat on a stool staring into the fire. She turned, smiled wanly, and rose to meet them. Athelstan hastened forward as the woman swayed on her feet.

'God in heaven,' the friar whispered, staring at her bruised face, the weals on her shoulders, neck and chest as the torn gown she wore slipped before she pulled it up again. Again Martha tried to smile, but the corner of her mouth was bruised whilst her lips were puffy and swollen.

'Mistress?' Athelstan led her across to a chair while Cranston poured a goblet of wine, which she gratefully accepted, sipping it. Now and again she would tenderly touch one of the bruises on her face. 'What happened, Mistress?'

'A normal enough morning,' she slurred. 'I was alone. Sexton Spurnel, Cripplegate and the curate were away, busy elsewhere. I mean, that's understandable as the church is sealed.' She pointed to the hour candle on its stand in the far corner. 'They are late; they should be here already. They always come in the late afternoon to ensure all is well.'

'Where are they?'

Athelstan glanced at Flaxwith, who just shrugged.

'Go out,' Cranston ordered. 'Send some of your lovely boys to take up all three of them. But do it quietly and secretly and bring them here. If they object, arrest them. But Flaxwith,' Cranston, cradling the miraculous wineskin, lifted it as if in toast, 'you have done very well. The Flesher is imprisoned upstairs. No one knows. Yes?'

'And Copping and Raquin?' Athelstan asked.

'Sir John, Brother Athelstan, they lie slain in St Benet's.'

'In God's name!' Athelstan exclaimed.

'Satan's tits!' Cranston breathed. 'Flaxwith, you didn't tell us that.'

'Sir John, I am wary of eavesdroppers – that's why there is a strong guard on the devil's door, the only entrance to St Benet's. There's nothing we can do about those two felons. Stabbed to the heart, they are. I left them as I found them. Of course I have not sent any message to the Devil's Oak – that was just a pretence.'

'Yes, yes, I can see.' Cranston put the miraculous wineskin away. 'It must stay like that or we will have rifflers gathering here like flies on a turd. So, Flaxwith, take up those three parish worthies, they may well be arriving very soon. Tiptoft, whom I have left with the corpses, must be despatched urgently to the Tower. I want a cohort of Cheshire archers here as soon as possible.' Cranston fished in his wallet and handed Flaxwith a waxen copy of his seal. 'Tiptoft is to show that to the constable at the Tower. He is to insist that the archers are needed urgently on King's business. Once you have done that, come back.'

Cranston and Athelstan then turned to Martha, who sat leaning against the table, gently sipping at the goblet. Now and again a jab of pain would make her close her eyes.

'Mistress,' Athelstan murmured, 'I appreciate you are in great distress but, as you can imagine, we need to know what happened. We must seize your attacker and take him to a place where he can be closely guarded.'

'The perpetrator,' Cranston urged, 'is guilty of house-breaking, damage to church property and, from what I can gather, the most horrific rape. We have the proof. You are both victim and witness. Mistress, you may not know this, but such crimes are felonies which carry the death sentence. Moreover, justice is swift in these matters, so I need to lay an indictment before the King's justices as soon as possible.'

'I was busy about the house,' Martha murmured, as if she was talking to herself. 'The door was off the latch. The Flesher – yes, that beast with no soul. Anyway, he swaggered in with Raquin and Copping, his lapdogs. He said they wished to survey both church and cemetery. I just shrugged and left them to it. Sir John, I don't like him or his coven, I never have and I never will. I went up to my own chamber.' She paused as Flaxwith came back into the house. She smiled at him, then listened to the Flesher's curses. 'I was in my chamber standing near the window.' She continued with a sigh. 'I was wondering what I should do now Reynaud was dead.' She drew in a sharp breath. 'I heard voices, footsteps below. I thought the Flesher and the others had left for the church; you can still enter through the devil's door. Anyway,' she gulped from the goblet, 'I heard a sound and turned. The Flesher was in my bedchamber. He kicked the door shut, turned the key and drew the bolts close.' She blinked. 'I knew what he wanted; he was always greedy for me. I begged him not to touch me, not to hurt me. I tried to explain that those days were over.'

'So he broke in here and assaulted you?' Cranston tenderly clasped the woman's hand. 'Mistress I realise you are deeply hurt, but your remedy is in the law. I must ask you these questions and you must give me the truth as if you are on oath. Did the Flesher break into your bedchamber? Was he in any way welcome there? Did you intimate that you wanted him?'

'No, no, no,' she retorted. 'I did not want him anywhere near me. I never have and I never will.'

'And he assaulted you?'

'Yes he did.'

'And he raped you?'

'Yes he abused me.' She turned on the chair and hitched

up her gown. Athelstan saw her torn stockings, as well as the bruises and cuts along her legs. 'I could pull this up to show more injury, as well as the stain of his seed. Yes, he raped me.' She paused to let the silence deepen, until the cursing and banging in the gallery above broke out again. 'I admit I acted,' she gasped, 'once the assault began. I tried to pretend, as I used to, that I loved to be ravished. I wanted it over as quickly as possible. He spent his seed then lay back on the bed. I got up and fled the chamber. I took the key from the lock and turned it. He didn't realise what was happening. He was, as usual, like a man mawmsy with ale. I came down stairs and sat here till Flaxwith arrived.'

'Mistress, I will have you taken from here,' Athelstan declared. 'Sir John will provide an escort to accompany you to Benedicta, a widow woman in my parish at St Erconwald's. She has all the skills of a leech; she will tend to your injuries. Perhaps we should confront the Flesher . . .' Athelstan broke off as Flaxwith intervened.

'Sir John, Brother Athelstan, I do urge you to view the corpses in St Benet's. Sir John, once you have as coroner—'

'The corpses belong to me,' Cranston declared, 'and can't be removed without my permission. Yes, yes, it's time we viewed these worthies . . .'

Athelstan and Cranston, followed by Flaxwith, went into the sombre, mildewed nave of St Benet's, gloomy, cold and deeply oppressive. Athelstan wondered if all the beings of light had fled this accursed parish, a sanctuary of sin, violence, murder and now rape. Before they left the priest's house, Cranston had summoned two of Flaxwith's bailiffs to lock and bolt the priest's house behind them and mount the most careful guard over Martha and the Flesher, still trapped in the house-keeper's chamber. They had found more bailiffs guarding the devil's door, the only entrance into a church sealed shut because of the terrible sacrileges perpetrated there. Cranston urged these to be most vigilant. He quietly murmured how he hoped the cohort of Cheshire archers would arrive soon – before the rifflers who thronged the Devil's Oak realised something was wrong and came searching for their master. The coroner took out his tinder and lit three of the large tallow candles, which threw moving circles of golden light as they followed Flaxwith into the same chantry chapel where Parson Reynaud had been stabbed. Raquin's corpse lay slumped in a corner at a half-crouch. The henchman's ugly face was contorted by the sudden, violent death which had snatched his soul as swiftly as a falcon would its prey: his eyes half open in an empty, glassy stare, a bloody froth on his gaping lips, hands hanging down either side. Raquin's dagger had slipped from the fingers of his left hand, though the other still half held his sword.

'Satan's tits!' Cranston crouched down, staring at his dead enemy. 'So your soul has been seized for judgement? I thank Heaven your blood is not on my hands, nor the fate of your soul dependent on my actions. God have mercy on you, though God knows he will have a veritable litany of sin to forgive.' The coroner glanced over his shoulder at Flaxwith. 'You found him like this?'

'Yes, Sir John. I viewed both him and Copping, then I left a close guard on the devil's door. Nobody has been here. Sir John, I know of Raquin – his death will shake many trees; there will be Hell to pay.'

'But not in this life,' Cranston retorted, 'not if we are cunning enough. Athelstan, what do you think happened?'

The friar stood, eyes closed, swaying slightly on his feet. 'The Flesher,' he began, 'undoubtedly arrived at St Benet's. He decided he would have his pleasure of Martha and sent his two dogs in here. I can imagine them swaggering around. Raquin was sure of himself. Copping knew that he was protected. By the way, where is Copping's corpse?'

'In the sacristy,' Flaxwith replied.

'Raquin's killer came in here.' Athelstan squatted down beside the coroner, pulling at Raquin's jacket so he could scrutinise the soaking-wet heart wound. 'Raquin adopted the stance of a veteran street fighter. Perhaps there was more than one assailant, which is why Raquin retreated into a corner to protect his back. He draws sword and dagger but, and this is the strange thing, his weapons show no sign of inflicting a wound.' Athelstan shook his head. 'Raquin was an experienced brawler, a skilled killer. Yes?' Cranston grunted his agreement. 'Yet look around, Sir John, can you detect any sign of disturbance?'

The coroner rose, peering at the floor, walls and different pieces of chapel furniture. 'Nothing!' he exclaimed. 'Nothing to show that the most deadly confrontation took place here. Nothing except a man who drew his weapons but never used them and suffered a fatal blow to his heart.'

'And the wound itself?'

Cranston crouched down again and peered at the blood-encrusted jerkin. He loosened this and raised the sopping shirt beneath to reveal a deep, bloody slit just beneath the left breast. 'Very similar to that inflicted on Parson Reynaud and Daventry,' Athelstan observed. 'Well,' he straightened up, 'Master Flaxwith, let us view Copping's corpse.'

The bailiff led them back up the nave, across the bleak, empty sanctuary and into the sacristy. Copping lay on his back, arms flung out. He'd drawn his dagger, which lay just beyond his right hand. Again Cranston and Athelstan noticed no disturbance, nothing but a dead-eyed victim with blood crusting his mouth and congealing either side of his corpse. Cranston and Athelstan crouched down to scrutinise the wound, swiftly drawing the conclusion that Copping's death almost mirrored that of Raquin. An armed, fairly vigorous man, taken by surprise and killed by a knife thrust straight to the heart.

'A skilled dagger man,' Cranston murmured, getting up and walking slowly around the corpse. 'I do wonder if the Sicarius is truly dead. But what fascinates me, Athelstan, is how this assassin can get so close to his victim and strike so swiftly that his opponent has no chance to resist. There is no sign, as with Raquin and the rest, of even the slightest struggle,' he shrugged, 'apart from weapons being drawn by these two last victims. There is something else, Brother. Have you noticed how this church has virtually become a slaughter's yard, a butcher's pen?'

'Yes, yes I agree,' Athelstan declared. 'Does the assassin choose this church because of some macabre, sinister reason? There again, Sir John, look around, this is a hall of shadows, a place which lends itself to murder.'

'True, true.' Cranston walked to the sacristy door and stared across the sanctuary. 'In my life, Brother, I have dealt with assassins, soft footed and skilful. They move like a hunting cat. I just wonder who this one is.'

'Could it be the Flesher? Has he decided to rid himself of all his henchmen?' Athelstan murmured. 'Or those three other upright members of this parish, Cotes, Cripplegate and Spurnel. Sir John, all three served in the royal array. If they were members of the Tower cohort, they would be experienced, skilled men-at-arms. Perhaps they had formed their own confederation? But it is proof we need, yet our killer leaves very little, and that's strange . . .'

'What do you mean, Brother?'

'Well, Mistress Makepeace's corpse was brutally torn from its coffin and vanishes like smoke in the air. The person who stole it left that note saying the remains would be returned at a given time, in a given place, for a substantial sum of money.'

'And yet no demand has been made?' Cranston declared. 'Not a jot, not a tittle. What do you think, Brother?'

'At this time, in this place, Sir John, I do begin to wonder. Was the corpse stolen, not to be held for ransom but simply as a heinous insult to the Flesher? The culprit has no intention of returning the corpse. He simply wants to bait his victim, taunt him and prolong the agony. The Flesher has been condemned to wait and to receive no response. Can you imagine, Sir John, how the Flesher must feel as days turn into weeks and weeks into months? No, I suspect his mother's corpse will never be returned. Well, not until we unmask this most skilled assassin. Now, back to the matter in hand. Raquin and Copping came in here and they parted. Copping wandered into the sacristy; perhaps he was looking to see if anything precious or valuable remained. I notice how the pyx, sanctuary lamp, cruets, cloths, vestments and sacred vessels have all disappeared. The Flesher would order Cripplegate, Cotes and Spurnel to keep them under close guard before Arundel's mercenaries arrive.' Athelstan stared down at the corpse. 'Is the killer someone we don't really know? Talking of which, Sir John, I wonder where the Candlelight-Master and his Luciferi are.'

'Could they be the assassins?'

'They are certainly skilled enough and nurse a powerful grievance against the Flesher from his days in France. They also suspect he was responsible for the attack on the royal barge eighteen years ago. They have already demonstrated their skill and stealth. Did they enter this church and surprise Raquin and Copping?'

'I am not too sure, Brother, even though I know they keep careful watch but only from afar, little friar. They prefer to keep your parish under keen scrutiny. After all, that's where the Rose Casket and its precious contents emerged after eighteen years.'

'True, true,' Athelstan murmured.

'Brother?'

'Nothing for the moment, Sir John,' Athelstan declared briskly. 'So, Copping and Raquin enter here and part, their assassin or assassins strike. If there was more than one, did they deal with their victims singularly or at the same time?'

Cranston walked over to Athelstan and, pretending to be the assassin, gently pressed his fist against Athelstan's left side before gripping the surprised friar by the shoulder. 'My little friar, that's how swiftly it could happen and how quickly I have seen it done. I once watched a Florentine merchant grip his opponent's hand as if to clasp it, but then he pulled him close, driving a dagger deep into his heart. There are three wounds which are deadly. The first is to the head, usually between the eyes and into the brain. Secondly, to the throat, which severes both the breath and the blood cords, whilst the third is a direct thrust to the heart. The victim has no time to respond. He or she stands in deep shock and then collapses. I'll wager that's what happened here.'

'True, true, Sir John, but remember both men had drawn their weapons. When you approached me, I did not expect you to do what you did. But, according to the evidence, Raquin and Copping had armed themselves. So how did their assailant manage to get so close?'

'Sir John!'

Cranston and Athelstan left the sacristy. Flaxwith stood in the entrance to the rood screen. 'Cripplegate, Cotes and Spurnel have arrived, Sir John. I understand they were expected to make a visit here.'

'Take them over to the priest's house,' Cranston ordered. 'Keep them separate from Martha. And, once we leave this church, set up a close guard. No one is allowed in here.'

Flaxwith nodded and left. 'Sir John, you'd best follow him,' Athelstan declared. 'Just make sure all is well. As for me, I want to walk this macabre church. I really believe it is a hosting ground for evil spirits rather than God's own house and the Gate to Heaven.'

Cranston said he would return. Athelstan watched him go then walked down the sanctuary steps. He paused to pray for a while, before making his way along the transept, peering into the shabby chantry chapels and the shadow-filled enclaves with their crumbling sills and weather-beaten frescoes. Undoubtedly the paintings he glimpsed had been the work of some long-dead artist, who had skilfully depicted scenes from the Scriptures, especially the Gospel of St John. Now, due to water running down the walls, these were beginning to decay and flake and Athelstan wondered how much money, if any, had been spent on the maintenance of this church. He walked closer; one of the paintings caught his eye. Athelstan just stood scrutinising the fresco very carefully, trying to curb the spurt of excitement within him. What he saw in that painting matched other scraps of information he had collected, as well as the half-formed suspicions he had sifted. Athelstan crouched down and studied that particular wall painting even closer. The artist had been keen to delineate the story of Lazarus whom Christ had raised from the dead. Jesus loved to relax in the house of Lazarus and his two sisters. 'You should have realised this before, stupid friar,' Athelstan murmured to himself. 'A scene from the Gospels which you have studied many a time.'

'Athelstan, Athelstan?'

Cranston came marching down the nave. The friar left the shadowy transept to meet him.

'Come my friend,' Cranston urged. 'Master Thomas Chaucer, captain of the Cheshire archers at the Tower, has arrived with his cohort, all resplendent in their livery. They sport young Richard's personal emblem of the white hart. No mob of rifflers would dare quarrel with such lovely lads.'

They left the church; the strengthening breeze buffeted their faces. Athelstan flinched at the dirt carried from the mounds of loose soil heaped near the shallow pits. The cemetery, however, had been transformed by the arrival of the Cheshire archers, garbed in their green and brown tunics, similar to the livery of the royal foresters. They also wore tabards displaying all the rich colours of the Plantagenet royal house, red-blood and gold, whilst the King's personal emblem of the 'whyte harte couchant' decorated their right shoulder. Recruited from the Welsh Marches, these were the kingdom's most skilled bowmen. They thronged about, bow staves unstrung, with quivers of goose-filled shafts hanging down by their right side. Their captain, Thomas Chaucer, was pleasant faced and red-cheeked, like some healthy plough boy. He hurried across to introduce himself, as well as to receive Cranston's orders about deployment around the church, to guard every entrance both to that and the priest's house.

'Now for the Flesher,' Cranston declared, 'and for that, Master Chaucer, I need you and three of your finest.'

Chaucer hurried to obey and, escorted by Flaxwith and the cohort, Cranston hammered on the door of the priest's house. The bailiff inside drew the bolts and Cranston swept through into the solar, where Martha lay sleeping on a settle wrapped tightly in blankets. Cranston and Athelstan inspected her care-fully, then climbed the stairs, preceded by the four archers, weapons at the ready. They reached the first gallery and Cranston was ushered towards the chamber where the Flesher was imprisoned. The coroner pushed the door open and gestured at Chaucer and his men to help Flaxwith and his bailiffs. At first all was confusion, shouts and cries, furniture kicked and thrown as the Flesher tried to resist. At last he was secured, wrists and ankles lashed with cords. The riffler was then pushed on to a high stool beneath the window, whilst Athelstan and Cranston inspected the bedchamber. The room had been wrecked: caskets and coffers overturned. Small tables and stools smashed. Drapes pulled from the wall. Blankets, coverlets and the tester from the small four-poster bed lay tossed on the floor. The chamber reeked of a fragrant perfume as a table of soaps, oils and creams had been overturned, the jars and dishes crudely stamped on. Athelstan swiftly studied everything. The Flesher, now bound and gagged, eyes bulging with fury, had wrecked the room. Nevertheless, despite all the damage, Athelstan concluded this was a true lady's chamber, with its little-fringed cushions, embroidered cloths, a delicate figurine depicting St Martha and a tray of small painted scent bottles. Athelstan noticed the other items lying around, a pair of leather gloves, a studded wrist guard, and other personal possessions. He picked up the face-cloth smeared with cream and powder, shaking away the crushed shards of the goblets and jug which had been smashed and ground underfoot, the wine snaking its way through the mess which covered the floor.

Cranston, however, was more concerned with the prisoner and, flanked by the captain of archers and one of his men, the coroner crouched down before the Flesher. Athelstan, standing behind Sir John, watched the hideous anger flare in the prisoner's face. Cranston leaned over, took the gag from the riffler's mouth, then held up a gauntleted hand.

'This chamber,' he declared, 'is not the Devil's Oak. It is now part of my court. This is where you committed your hideous crimes and, because of that, you are well and truly trapped. Do you understand?' Cranston hissed. 'You broke into this house, you ravaged and ransacked it, then raped the woman living here.'

'I was welcomed here. Copping will—'

'Copping lies slain in St Benet's, as does Raquin. Both stabbed to the heart like Parson Reynaud and Daventry.'

The Flesher's jaw fell slack and, for the first time, Athelstan glimpsed fear in the riffler's small, crafty eyes.

'How is this?' he whispered.

'Your henchmen are dead, Master Makepeace. Parson Reynaud, Daventry, Raquin and Copping, as is Ingersol.'

'Never heard of him.'

'A stupid reply,' Cranston countered. 'Ingersol was one of yours until he became one of mine. You had him murdered and now, Master Makepeace, see the archers around me, you are under arrest for divers, dire felonies. You will be indicted before the justices at the Guildhall and, believe me, retribution shall be swift.' Cranston edged a little closer. 'Flesher,' he whispered, 'when you are alone in the dungeon beneath the Guildhall, close your eyes, breathe in deeply and wait.'

'For what?'

'The ghosts, Master Makepeace! All the ghosts of those you have barbarously slain over the years. You will see them gather, cluster in the corners, or crawl along the floors and across the ceilings. Flitting dark shapes, hungry for justice to be done. I will even put a lighted candle in the cell; its flame all glowing will lose its golden ring, turning to a dark blue as fire does when the dead draw close.'

The captain of archers glanced quizzically at Athelstan, who just shook his head and raised a finger to his lips. Cranston was giving vent to eighteen years of uncontrolled fury, of a deep, curdling resentment against this devil in human flesh.

'All those ghosts, killer,' Cranston continued, 'trooping into confront you and, once they've gone, Hell's own demons, a horde of them ready to welcome you. What I hope will lead this spectral visitation are the ghosts of those good men killed on *The Song of the Sword* so many years ago.' The Flesher lunged forward, but the cords that Flaxwith's bailiffs had tied so expertly made him wince, so he fell back.

'Now,' Athelstan brought a stool and sat beside Cranston, determined to divert the coroner's rage, 'what did happen this morning? What defence can you offer?' The Flesher, trying to control his breathing, brought his head back as if he was about to spit. 'I wouldn't,' Athelstan warned. 'Tell us what happened today; in return I will do something to ease your confinement, even if it is only a goblet of wine.' The Flesher glared at the friar. 'It's the only way open to you,' Athelstan insisted softly. 'Copping and Raquin do lie dead. In a very short while, the Devil's Oak will be surrounded by royal archers, a cohort of whom now ring St Benet's, its cemetery and this house.' The Flesher's face sagged. 'Come on now,' Athelstan urged. 'Your power is finished. For the first time in your life, someone has held you to account for a great crime. I am no lawyer, but you broke into this house, you ransacked it and you raped an honourable woman, housekeeper to a priest, whatever she may have been in the past. This is someone whom you cannot frighten, silence, or despatch your killers to take care of. So?'

The Flesher took a deep breath. 'I was at the Devil's Oak,' he blurted out. 'Copping said he'd received an urgent message from some street swallow.' The Flesher wetted his lips. 'The urchins whom we hire to take news or a short message. According to him, something had been found here at St Benet's. I was to come most discreetly. The urchin had learnt it by heart. I thought something had been found in the church. So we arrived. Cripplegate, Cotes and Spurnel were not to be seen, so I came up to the house. I asked Martha what was the matter. She acted all flirtatious. She said she had no reason to send any message, that it could be the work of others, but if I wanted to wait for them I was most welcome. She was the Martha of yesteryear, all coy and simpering, and I recalled how she was always a bundle of joy in bed. When the others went across to the church, I joined Martha here in the chamber.'

'And then you raped her?'

'No, she acted all difficult and resisting as she used to when playing the game.'

'Does that include the grievous injuries, scars, weals and welts, not to mention the hideous bruises on her face, and her clothes all torn?'

The Flesher just glared back.

'And the Twelve Apostles?' Cranston grated.

'I know nothing of them or that royal barge.'

Cranston drew his hand back and, before Athelstan could intervene, struck the Flesher a stinging blow across the face. The friar seized the coroner's arm and gently squeezed. 'Yes, yes, I have had enough.' Cranston scraped back the stool. 'Master Chaucer, have the prisoner hooded and masked. He is to be taken immediately to the Guildhall dungeons, where you personally will guard him until my arrival. Oh,' Cranston picked up the gag from the floor and pointed to the Flesher, 'keep him silent, and let none of your escort speak to him or about him.'

Having taken the captain of archers' assurances that all would be as he had ordered, Cranston beckoned Athelstan to follow him down to join the three parishioners seated around the solar table, Flaxwith standing just within the door. Cranston took a generous slurp from the miraculous wineskin, offered it to Athelstan who refused, and then to the chief bailiff who drank and handed it back.

'Congratulations, Sir John.'

'Thank you, Flaxwith. Leave one of your lovely lads to keep an eye on things here. What I want you to do is wrap Mistress Martha in blankets, commandeer a barge and take the poor woman cloaked and cowled across to Benedicta at St Erconwald's. You will do that?' Flaxwith nodded and left.

'Well, gentlemen?' Cranston moved in his chair. 'I shall be blunt and you will return the compliment. Mistress Martha was attacked and raped by the Flesher. She is now being taken to a more restful, safe place. Raquin and Copping have also been despatched, but to their eternal rest. Oh yes,' Cranston nodded at their exclamations of surprise, 'both men were murdered in your church, stabbed to the heart like Parson Reynaud and Daventry. So, sirs, where were you this day?' He leaned over, poking a finger at all three. 'I asked you a question, I demand a reply.'

'We gathered in the taproom of the Golden Boy.'

'Oh, I know the place well,' Cranston grinned. 'A tavern frequented by handsome young men who are also desirous of meeting other handsome young men. And so, why were you there?'

'We were discussing what was to be done here,' Cripplegate sighed. 'And we decided there was, in truth, little we could do.'

'Except now,' Curate Cotes declared, his face all flushed with excitement as well as the after-effects of copious tankards of ale. 'The Flesher has been arrested, hasn't he? Sir John, you are going to indict him and you will need all the witnesses you can gather. Well,' the curate tapped his chest, 'I will be one. I'll take the oath and swear what a true malefactor the Flesher really is.' Cotes shook his fist. 'He's guilty of every sin listed and a few that aren't. He made a mistake, didn't he? He trapped himself. Breaking and entry, ravaging a house and raping a woman; these are felonies worthy of death.'

'Oh, you'll do more than that.'

'Sir John?'

'You will join me in my foray, together with a strong comitatus of archers, to the Devil's Oak. You will be my witnesses. It's time we informed the wolf pack that their leader is caged and bound for death, whilst his lair is about to become mine.'

Athelstan sat at his kitchen table, staring down at the memo-randum he'd drawn up for his own reflection. The sudden arrest of the Flesher was now two days old and the news had swept the taverns, alehouses, brothels and stews along the Thames. Already other gang leaders, riffler chieftains such as the Master of the Minions at the Tavern of Lost Souls, were flexing their muscles. The London gangs were on the hunt, sloping through the darkness to see what pickings they could seize. The Flesher's fall had been swift and sudden.

'Like Lucifer,' Athelstan murmured to himself, 'being hurled down, never to rise again. Oh yes, like lightning which strikes in one corner of heaven and lights up the other.'

Athelstan realised that the brutal murders of Parson Reynaud, Daventry, the disappearance of Ingersol, the damage that henchman had wreaked before he was discovered, and now the brutal slayings of Copping and Raquin had greatly weak-ened the Flesher's mob of malefactors. Moreover, the riffler leader had been taken up and committed to the Guildhall. Any influence he had with the likes of Fitzalan of Arundel or any of the leading citizens of the city faded like snow under the sun. Nobody wished to be associated with a man bound for the gallows. Cranston had proclaimed this message when, escorted by a company of Cheshire archers, he had swept into the great stableyard at the Devil's Oak. Cranston, using all his power as Lord High Coroner, had set up court in the tavern's spacious taproom and issued his proclamations. How the Flesher had been taken up and arrested for the most heinous felonies and that he would soon be indicted before the justices at the Guildhall. Only then did Cranston loose his most deadly arrows. Standing on a stout table, booted feet apart, cloak thrown back so all could see his warbelt, Cranston had warned all and sundry that if an individual associated with the Flesher was named and proclaimed as being involved in any felonious act, he or she would also face indictment and, Cranston cheer-fully added, 'a swift ride to meet the hangman at Smithfield. Indeed,' the coroner had continued, 'there was no statute of limitations. The Crown was deeply interested in any information about the treasonable attack on the royal barge *The Song of the Sword* some eighteen years previously. On the other hand,' Cranston had bellowed, 'anyone who turned King's approver and brought information against Simon Makepeace, commonly known as the Flesher, such a person would receive a full and comprehensive pardon for all crimes committed. Finally,' Cranston had paused and beamed around, 'because Simon Makepeace, also known as the Flesher, was a notorious suspect of ill-repute, all his property was now seized and sealed as forfeit to the Crown, which included the Devil's Oak and all it contains.' Cranston stamped his foot. 'Accordingly,' he bellowed, 'I will be leaving a cohort of archers in this tavern to escort everyone from the premises, as well as to ensure you take nothing but your personal property with you.'

Cranston's blunt declaration had provoked uproar, but the coroner didn't give a fig. He stood on the taproom table stamping his foot and gesturing towards the door. The rifflers, leaderless, disorganised and now very fearful, had no choice but to obey. Athelstan had watched them stream out of the tavern before joining Cranston, escorted by two archers, who began a thorough search of the cellars beneath the taproom. The search soon confirmed their suspicions about Fitzalan and the coming Parliament. The cellars were cavernous and crammed with barrels of dried pork, bags of flour, rolls of bacon all cured and spiced, sacks of oatmeal, vats of ale and tuns of wine, all in preparation for Fitzalan's troops occupying St Benet's. In more secret places they also discovered precious items: pouches and purses bulging with good coin; caskets of jewellery and canvas bags containing rolls of precious cloth. Most of these, Cranston wryly observed, were probably the ill-gotten plunder of some robber in the Flesher's pay. Documents, indentures, household books, buttery bills and taproom ledgers were seized. Cranston was almost beside himself with glee, saying he was sure he had enough evidence of crimes and felonies to hang the Flesher a hundred times over, whilst Fitzalan's great scheme, planned and plotted around St Benet's, was nothing more than smoke in the wind. The plot to overawe the November Parliament was completely frustrated. Royal troops would soon occupy St Benet's, whilst Fitzalan would be ordered to appear before the King with the smallest of escorts.

'Of course he won't come,' Cranston murmured, rubbing his hands. 'He'd be too frightened; too wary of falling into Gaunt's hands, of being trapped by Master Thibault.'

Athelstan had returned to Southwark, leaving Cranston very busy at the Guildhall. In the meantime Tiptoft kept appearing in the parish, bringing messages from Cranston. How a number of the Flesher's principal rifflers had become King's approvers, each citing a litany of horrid crimes against their master. One item, however, remained unmentioned. No one had offered even a scrap of information about the attack on *The Song of the Sword*.

'My Lord Cranston,' Tiptoft intoned, 'believes most of those involved are now dead, perhaps even silenced by the Flesher, whilst the prospect of reward and a royal pardon are not viewed as the best protection against the charge of high treason and all that entails. However, Sir John does live in hope—'

'As do I,' Athelstan murmured, pushing away the memorandum and staring at the hour candle. Athelstan was sure the Candlelight-Master and the Luciferi still kept him and his parish under close scrutiny, so what he planned to do within the next hour was fraught with some danger. He pulled across his psalter and opened up at the office of the day. Athelstan read the psalm and recited the prayers until he heard a sound outside. He stood up, crossed himself and walked to the door. Just as he opened it, Mauger appeared with a barrow containing a spade, mattock, hoe, and the pathetic remains of Thaddeus the goat, carefully sewn up in a canvas sheet soaked in pine juice. Benedicta and Crim, each carrying a capped, lighted candle, would act as mourners. Godbless had declared himself too weak and frail for the ceremony.

'Good morrow,' Athelstan smiled. 'Benedicta, how is Mistress Martha?'

'She has now bathed and tended her wounds. Tiptoft brought some fresh clothing from the house, as well as the personal items, caskets and coffers she had asked for.'

'And has she commented on the Flesher's allegations that she acted all flirtatious and coy?'

'She dismisses them as lies. She hates the Flesher and all his kind. She pointed out that Copping and Raquin went down to the church. She thought the Flesher had gone with them and went up to her chamber.'

Athelstan raised a hand. 'Very good. Thank you.' He hurriedly blessed the pathetic remains, slipped back into the house, put on a purple stole and joined the small funeral cortège. The friar led them into the cemetery, along the ancient coffin paths, into a neglected area of God's Acre. Once they'd reached this desolate spot, Athelstan walked beside Benedicta, whispering at her to remain vigilant for the Candlelight-Master or his henchmen. Nevertheless, the cemetery seemed deserted on that deeply autumnal afternoon, with its lowering grey skies, its sharp breezes whipping up the dry leaves into a frenetic dance.

'Father, I think we will deceive anyone who is watching us. We are just a small funeral party carrying out some pathetic burial, but Father, do you know where we are going?'

'I certainly do.' Athelstan urged Crim to turn right, leading them through a mess of gorse which had overgrown the narrow trackway into a small clearing. At the far end stood a grey headstone, weathered and covered in thick, green lichen; some of this had been peeled away to reveal the name 'Artorius'.

'Here we are,' Athelstan declared. Mauger positioned the wheelbarrow, took out the spade and looked at his parish priest expectantly. 'Artorius,' Athelstan repeated, 'the Latin name for a bear. In this case, a poor dancing bear who came with its master to our parish so many years ago and unfortunately died. People thought its name was "Tori"; as you did Benedicta – remember? Of course the lichen hid the full name "Artorius". I discovered this after examining the Book of the Dead, the parish record of who lies buried where.' Athelstan nodded with his head. 'I discovered the headstone, but Margo also knew of it because she spent a great deal of time in God's Acre, be it dressing corpses in the death house or helping at funerals. Of course Margo was also looking for a place to hide a certain treasure. If she chose someone's grave, there was always the danger of that grave being reopened to receive the corpse of a friend or relative. Margo had a sharp mind and a keen wit.

Our God's Acre is broad and sprawling. She did not want to bury the treasure in some unmarked spot and later find she was unable to place it. This, of course, is different.'

'Clever, clever,' Benedicta murmured.

Athelstan gripped the widow woman's arm.

'I believe,' he pointed to the overgrown crumbling earth, 'that this grave contains more than the pathetic remains of a dancing bear.' Athelstan crouched down, sifting the loose soil through his fingers. 'This has been disturbed since our poor bear was buried. Of course when Margo fell into a delirium at St Bartholomew's, she started to think about the treasure and, in her muddled way, made references to the legendary King Artorius, the Latin version of King Arthur, "The once and future King." In her fever, she must have recalled what happened eighteen years ago. Perhaps she was trying to tell us but, never mind . . .'

He got to his feet and raised his voice. 'We shall now commit the remains of poor Thaddeus to the soil and his memory to God. Mauger, start digging,' he lowered his voice to a whisper, 'and be prepared for a surprise.'

The bell clerk began to shovel at the earth, Athelstan advising him to do so most carefully, whilst Crim was ordered to blow out his candle, scamper through the grass and raise the alarm if anyone approached. Mauger sifted away the dirt, the loose soil and gravel and, as he watched, Athelstan recalled God's Acre at St Benet's, those shallow pits with their dirt and fine pebbles. Athelstan closed his eyes as he wondered how that skilled assassin must have worked, using that blighted cemetery to hide what had been done.

'Father?' Athelstan opened his eyes. Mauger was leaning on his spade. 'I've hit something hard.'

Athelstan took off his stole, put down the holy water stoup and the asperger's rod, then joined Mauger in sifting back the dirt. The friar murmured a swift ave as his fingers brushed a piece of leather. Now digging with his hands, Athelstan eagerly pulled at the rotting chancery satchel, battered and fading, the leather now chipped and peeling, its bronze clasps rotten and broken. Athelstan quickly looked inside, then put the satchel on to the wheelbarrow. He asked Mauger to swiftly bury

Thaddeus's remains, fill in the grave, cover what they had discovered and go back to the priest's house.

Once they'd arrived, Athelstan ushered them in. He ordered Mauger to place the chancery satchel on the table, whilst Benedicta made sure the door was locked and bolted. Athelstan then opened the chancery satchel to reveal an exquisitely carved casket which, even under its coating of clay, exuded a unique beauty, with its beautifully worked golden roses and finely etched silver stems. Athelstan took a deep breath and opened the casket. The purple samite cushion inside was stained and dirt-engrained, but even this did not diminish the sheer, brilliant beauty of the eleven different precious stones embedded in the cushion, each with its distinctive shape and colour. Athelstan gently moved the casket and the light piercing the shuttered window made it seem as if the coffer contained its own secret power. Mauger gasped, hand going out to touch the precious stones. Benedicta exclaimed in surprise, whilst Crim danced around the table like a march hare.

'Wealth,' Mauger hissed, 'wealth like I've never seen.'

Athelstan glimpsed the greed flare in the bell clerk's face and abruptly snapped the coffer shut. 'Mauger, on your soul's salvation, do not tell anyone what you've seen. Go fetch Sir John immediately. Ask him to bring a cohort of archers. Benedicta, take Crim and ensure Mistress Martha is resting and recovering.'

'And you?'

Athelstan took the casket and placed it under his chancery chair. 'Once you have all gone, Benedicta, I am going to lock and bolt that door, secure the window shutters, sit on that chair and not move until Sir John arrives!'

Once they'd gone, and Athelstan believed he and the treasure were as safe and secure as could be, he leaned back in his chair, closed his eyes and began to meditate, forcing his mind, his heart, his very soul into that sombre, macabre church. 'May the angel who once guarded St Benet's Woodwharf,' he prayed, 'return, lift the darkness and reveal the truth.' Athelstan had written and rewritten his memorandum on the murders and, in doing so, he had fashioned what he called 'certain candles' to lead him deeper into the darkness, to drive back the encroaching gloom of that sinister church and its malevolent mysteries. In his mind's eye Athelstan drifted into St Benet's nave. 'No, no,' he murmured to himself, 'first I must look outside.'

Athelstan recalled those shallow, dirty pits on either side of the church, studying them carefully using the power of his imagination, before moving back into the nave. Athelstan had developed this method when reflecting upon the life of Christ. He would try to picture himself in Pilate's hall or Calvary, where Christ had been crucified. He tried to recreate the scene, the season of the year, the hour of the day and the people who might be present. He did the same now as he entered St Benet's nave and imagined Parson Reynaud sitting on that mercy seat waiting for some parishioner to approach the shriving stool. Or was the parson really waiting for Daventry? Why had Fitzalan's man been found murdered at the other end of the nave? Distant, apart, yet both had been killed by a deep stab wound to the heart. Was this the work of a professional assassin, a man like the Sicarius, Ingersol? What role did he really play in all this? That shadowy, enigmatic figure who drifted in and out of these mysteries as he had the parish of St Benet's? Athelstan imagined the assassin slipping into the nave and felt a shiver of excitement. Was it the Sicarius? Did he survive? Did he have a copy of the Flesher's key ready for use that night? Both that key and the one held by the parson were needed to open the arca, but how did they come together on that particular evening, at that particular time and place? And once the arca was opened, where did such a large amount of money go? How was it moved out? And the corpse of Isabella Makepeace? Again Athelstan recalled that long nave and the line of the cemetery which ran past the devil's door. He must ask Flaxwith to take his ugly mastiff Samson and walk up and down that strip of God's Acre. 'I am sure the solution is there,' Athelstan murmured to himself.

He was still sifting the possibilities when he drifted into a deep sleep, rudely woken by the arrival of a rather boisterous coroner, who swept into St Erconwald's accompanied by a group of knight bannerets of the royal household, resplendent in their gorgeous livery. They led a cohort of Cheshire archers, some Genoese mercenaries skilled in the use of the arbalest, as well as Flaxwith and his comitatus of bailiffs. Cranston, however, would allow no one but himself to enter Athelstan's small house. Athelstan let the coroner stride in then locked and bolted the door behind him. Athelstan put the Rose Casket on the table and pulled back the lid. Cranston gasped in surprise.

'Satan's tits!' he whispered, leaning over and slamming the casket shut. 'The sight of that would tempt the honesty of any man. And the first thing I must do, Athelstan, is get it out of here.'

For a while Cranston busied himself. A steel-bound arca with three intricate clasp locks was unloaded from the cart Cranston had requisitioned. The Rose Casket was placed in the arca, which was locked and sealed, the treasure chest being guarded by the royal knights. Cranston bellowed he would personally ride next to the arca whilst his war horse could trail behind. Of course the arrival of Cranston and his powerful escort turned the parish into a beehive of gossip and constant scurrying about. This was aided and abetted by Jocelyn and Merrylegs, who set up stalls in God's Acre to sell hot, highly spiced pastries and frothing tankards of St Erconwald's ale. Athelstan allowed the eating, drinking and good-natured revelling in God's Acre, though he asked Benedicta to keep a sharp eye on both that and Mistress Martha. Once the arca was loaded and chained securely, Cranston invited himself back into the house, standing by the unshuttered window so he could keep an eye on the cart and its escort. For a while the coroner just stared through the open window, as if obsessed by the arca and all it contained. Athelstan guessed that the coroner was going back to that turbulent, dark night on the Thames when *The Song of the Sword* had been so savagely attacked. At last the coroner gave himself a shake and glanced across at Athelstan.

'The Flesher,' he declared, taking a gulp from the miraculous wineskin, 'Master Thibault had him swiftly arraigned before the justices, and a chorus of King's approvers sang that bastard to his death. He is to hang tomorrow morning at Smithfield.'

'Good lord,' Athelstan whispered, 'so swiftly?'

'Brother, the old King used to dispense justice from horse-back, one hand holding the reins, the other the cross-hilt of his sword. I assure you the condemned were still kicking against the noose as old Edward left. Master Thibault and, of course, my Lord of Gaunt are insistent that judgment be carried out forthwith. They have ordered your parishioner, the Hangman of Rochester, to officiate on the Smithfield gallows.' Cranston paused. 'And they asked you to act as the scaffold priest. I think that would be fitting.' The coroner laughed sharply. 'Moreover, there is no other priest who wants to be even associated with the Flesher. Parson Reynaud was notorious, and no cleric wishes to be painted or tainted with the same brush.'

Athelstan held up a hand staring across the room. 'Yes, yes,' he whispered, 'on one condition.'

'Brother?'

'When the Flesher is brought out to be hanged, he is to be closely shaved and shorn before he is placed in the gallows cart.'

PART SEVEN

Cage-bird (**Old English**): a prisoner

The execution ground at Smithfield heaved with a throng rarely seen before. The crowd, surging backwards and forwards, had become highly excited, eager to witness what was about to happen. Even the horse traders and cattle sellers had decided there would be no business that day so they had taken down their signs. All of London seemed to have emptied to witness the Flesher hang. The great three-branched scaffold, commonly known as the Elms, the principal gallows, had been well prepared: the long, dark hanging tree rearing up stark against the sky. Braziers flared, their flames leaping greedily. All eyes were on the long, thin ladder propped against the execution post, the 'Judas steps' leading up to the noose, which hung down like some deadly garland at the end of its long rope. The Hangman of Rochester, garbed in black from head to toe, was ready to act as high priest at this grue-some, macabre ceremony. The executioner stood on the edge of the high platform, watching like some tavern host for the arrival of his one and only guest that day.

A sharp, grey morning. The rain had ceased its constant patter, though everything remained wet and slippery. Nevertheless, the grim, grey weather had certainly not curbed either the enthusiasm of respectable citizens or that of the horde of dark-dwellers from the Kingdom of Chaos and the Mansions of Midnight which the Flesher had once ruled. All of London had swarmed out for what was called an 'unholy day'. Miscreants of every kind were eager to watch the hanging of one of their own dark lords: the garishly painted whores in their flame-red wigs and white-plastered faces were hungry for business. These ladies of the night were shepherded by their pimps, garbed in garish rags, sharp, pointed knives pushed through their rope belts, each carrying a small bucket ready to collect the coins of anyone desperate enough to hire a common whore. The conjurors also sought business, clacking their boxes of runes so they could tell the future of anyone stupid enough to believe them. Meanwhile the heralds of the night declared themselves ready to recount blood-chilling stories about the man set to be hanged. Swarms of rifflers ignored these as they pushed their way through, desperate to watch a rival they hated dance in the air as he choked to death. Of course, a hanging whets every appetite, and the itinerant cooks, water-carriers, ale-sellers and wine-carriers bustled about to do business. Guilds and fraternities were also present, chanting psalms and hymns of mourning. The air was riven by chanting, jeering, praying and catcalling. Smoke drifted up from the moveable stoves to mingle with the stench of human sweat and other odours; roasting meat well past its prime, crackling rancid fat, as well as the sweet incense gusting up from thuribles and herb pots. This mass of Londoners could, in the blink of an eye, become an unruly mob, which is why they were cowed by the massed presence of archers and men-at-arms who ringed the scaffold site.

Athelstan, standing behind the Hangman of Rochester, stared out over this surging mass, watching the prisoner and his escort wend their way through the crowd. 'The devil's own carriage,' as the execution cart was called, was surrounded by a screen of men-at-arms, its horses led by the red-garbed custodians of the condemned.

The cart trundled slowly forward and stopped before the steps. The Hangman of Rochester moved back to stand by the ladder. The Flesher, his arms bound, was dragged out. He struggled as he was pushed up the steps, but the archers would take no opposition. The Flesher, shorn and shaved, his ugly face bulging with fury, soon stood in his hanging shroud on the lofty platform. The archers pushed him close to the edge so the condemned man could be seen by the mob, which surged and swirled about like water boiling in a cauldron. All the other riffler leaders, led by the Master of the Minions, had secured the best places beneath the gallows; their henchmen, grouped behind them, screamed a litany of curses, whilst the crowd bellowed its own insults. The Fraternity of the Hanged and the Brotherhood of the Noose tried to chant fresh songs of mourning. Some Friars of the Sack recited the '*De Profundis* – Out of the depths have I cried to you, oh Lord,' but their words were swept away by the raucous noise. The roar of the mob was now constant. The rifflers surged backwards and forwards. A coven of witches, wizards and warlocks fought to get closer, eager to creep beneath the platform, daggers and blades at the ready, for the flesh and clothing of a condemned man were said to contain magical properties, the Flesher's corpse being regarded as a great prize.

The hangman now moved a second thin ladder to rest against one of the gallow branches. He lifted his mask and shouted at the sheriff's men, 'We must do this now or there could be a riot.'

Suddenly a great roar erupted, mingled with curses, jeers and catcalls. Sir John Cranston, who had been overseeing matters at the foot of the scaffold, climbed the steps on to the execution platform. The coroner also sensed the danger. He clapped his hands, shouting at the heralds, who raised their trumpets with a flourish and blew a shrilling fanfare time and time again, until a deep and brooding silence descended like a cloud over Smithfield. A sinister, danger-fraught stillness, as if the milling mob had withdrawn for a moment but was watching, waiting, ready to spring. The trumpet fanfares trailed off. One of the sheriff's men, in a bellowing voice, proclaimed, 'How Simon Makepeace, also known as the Flesher, had been judged guilty of heinous felonies and was worthy of death with no hope of pardon so sentence should be carried out immediately.'

The hangman moved with alacrity. Grasped by the archers, the Flesher was pushed up one ladder whilst the hangman scaled the one next to it. He reached the top rung and, balancing himself carefully, fitted the noose around the Flesher's neck, positioning the knot carefully behind the left ear. He then checked the rope. Once satisfied, the hangman hurriedly descended, the archers likewise, leaving the condemned man, his hands tightly bound, perched on the top rung. A drum began to beat. The hangman seized the ladder the Flesher was perched on and abruptly twisted it. The Flesher fell like a stone and the crack of his breaking neck could be clearly heard. A great sigh echoed from the crowd, a prolonged gasp of breath as this mass of people marked the end of the Flesher's notorious, sinful life. For a few moments total silence, eventually broken by desultory jeering and catcalling. Such insults soon faded as the crowd broke up, now interested in what else might be going on. Athelstan asked the hangman to cut the corpse down.

'I think it's to be gibbeted on the approach to London Bridge, Father.' The hangman lifted his sweat-soaked mask. 'Anyway, those were the orders given to me.'

'Let the friar bless the corpse.' Cranston walked over. 'And I want to scrutinise it. I just want to make sure this sinner has truly gone to God; though,' the coroner added ruefully, 'I heard his neck crack. It was a great mercy for him.' He tossed a coin at the hangman who deftly caught it. 'You showed him more compassion than he did his victims.'

Cranston turned away as a disturbance broke out close to the steps leading up to the execution platform. A coven of warlocks and witches, garbed in their dusty black robes, knives at the ready, were once again trying to creep beneath the scaffold, determined to reach the Flesher's corpse which was being laid out for inspection and blessing. The coroner frightened these away. Athelstan went over and knelt by the cadaver. The Flesher's head was strangely twisted, his ugly face, mottled red and blue, seemed even more grotesque. Athelstan blessed the dead man's body, then asked the hangman to lift the grey linen shroud cloth. Athelstan tried to ignore the sheer ugliness of the corpse as he inspected the dead Flesher's hands, arms, chest, back and face. At last he pronounced himself satisfied. However, he continued to kneel by the corpse, lost in his own thoughts, until a black, glossy-winged raven floated down, only to be beaten off by the hangman. Athelstan crossed himself, rose and told the coroner he was finished. He walked to the edge of the scaffold, watching the crowd disperse as well as half listening to Cranston's instructions. How the Flesher's corpse was to be gibbeted not on the approaches of London Bridge, but in the stableyard of the Devil's Oak tavern.

'A warning,' Cranston grated, 'and a clear proclamation of what has happened.'

'And the Rose Casket? The Twelve Apostles?' Athelstan asked.

'Don't you worry about them, little friar, they are in the kingdom's strongest arca, the Tower of London, guarded by men of the royal household. The Candlelight-Master and the Luciferi have already made their presence felt. Discussions have opened, but those do not concern either you or me, my friend.'

'Sir John, I agree. However, we are not yet finished our business. I need your help. So listen and do so carefully.'

Two days after the Flesher's execution, Athelstan convened what he called 'his own Inquisicio' or Inquisition, after the Jesus Mass in St Erconwald's. Cranston and Benedicta had been invited; Martha the housekeeper, Cripplegate, Curate Cotes and Spurnel were also summoned. Flaxwith and his bailiffs guarded all entrances to the church, in particular the sanctuary where Athelstan had set up this 'Inquisicio'.

He slouched on a stool with the heavy, intricately carved sanctuary chair set before him. Cranston and Benedicta sat on one wall bench, the parishioners of St Benet's on the other. Athelstan intoned the '*Veni Creator Spiritus* – Come Holy Spirit;' he blessed all assembled and invited Martha to sit on the spacious sanctuary chair. The housekeeper, garbed in a simple Lincoln-green gown, her lustrous hair covered by a white gauze veil, walked across. She sat down carefully, looking pale and nervous. Her face still bore the effects of the Flesher's attack.

'Brother Athelstan,' she sat rigid in the chair, 'why have you summoned me? Why am I placed here?'

'I have not, Mistress, you have brought about this confrontation. You are a murderess. You have slaughtered four men and, although I admit they may have been worthy of death, you are still a killer. You are an assassin.' Athelstan raised a hand to still her protests and those of others. 'Mistress Martha, you are bruised from head to toe, the work of the Flesher. However,' Athelstan leaned forward, 'two days ago I scrutinised the Flesher's corpse. He attacked you, yes?' She nodded. 'You resisted, yes?' Again the nod. 'Then tell me, Martha, you are still fairly young and vigorous, you have sharp teeth and even sharper nails. You claimed to have fought furiously, yet I could find no cut or mark on him. Why not?'

Martha just stared back. 'A man attacked you,' Athelstan insisted, 'a veritable brute, a wild animal. You resisted, so you said. But again, there's no sign of that on him. I asked for him to be shorn and, after he was hanged, I inspected the Flesher's corpse from head to toe. I found nothing.'

'He was violent—'

'And you could have been equally violent back, but you weren't. You calculated, quite rightly, that if you laid your allegations swiftly, the law would act, the Flesher would be exposed and left vulnerable. After all, his lawyer Master Copping and his henchman Raquin were dead, murdered by you, of course; whilst he'd been caught red-handed in a crime, the victim of which could not be frightened or cowed. The Flesher had no real defence whatsoever. You planned it carefully, Mistress, as you planned so many things.'

'This is preposterous,' Curate Cotes spluttered.

'You will remain silent,' Cranston snapped. 'Brother?'

'Martha Ashby,' Athelstan continued, smiling gently, 'married as a young girl to a sickly locksmith. He died, and you had no choice but to enter the House of Delights some nineteen years ago. Whatever your gifts or talents, you worked there most reluctantly. You were looking for a way out when you met a young soldier, a Tower archer named Walter Grenel. Both of you fell in love, but there was a problem. Walter was from a respectable family, yet he was consorting with what others would call a common whore. Accordingly, his meetings with you were kept secret. Walter would leave the Tower, or his mother's cottage in Southwark, and go into Queenhithe. I suspect both of you met in the darkness of St Benet's nave, a most suitable place to hide, to talk, to kiss and caress. During one of these meetings, he probably saw the same wall painting I did. The paint is now faded, but it's still a vivid celebration of the story of Lazarus, Jesus' friend, who lived in the small village of Bethany outside Jerusalem with his two sisters—'

'Mary and Martha,' Cotes interjected. 'That's your name, Mistress, but Walter used that painting to hide your true name and calling: Martha from the House of Bethany. He was talking about you. It was his way of hiding the fact that his sweetheart was a—'

'Enough!' Athelstan snapped. 'Mistress Martha may be many things, but she was not, is not, a whore. Young Walter was deeply smitten, wasn't he Martha? And you,' Athelstan pointed a finger, 'had an unwilling hand in what later happened. I say unwilling, because anything else would be truly heinous. You learnt from Walter how a company of Tower archers, himself included, had been summoned to collect something very valuable.'

'Oh Lord and his angels.' Cripplegate got slowly to his feet and walked towards Martha. Sexton Spurnel made to follow, but Cranston shouted at both men to sit down, which they did so hurriedly.

'We were given orders that we were to man the royal barge *The Song of the Sword* on the morning before that night attack. The only other piece of information,' Cripplegate waved a hand, 'is that we were to collect something from a Hanseatic ship.'

'*The Glory of Bremen*?'

'True, true,' Cranston interrupted. 'Only I knew what we were actually receiving, that was made known to me under the Secret Seal. But the Flesher, and I am sure he was responsible for the attack, would have received information from other quarters, some Judas eager for his thirty pieces of silver. The Flesher must have heard how the French had been forced to hand over the Rose Casket and the Twelve Apostles and he would plot their robbery. A scrap of information here, another scrap there and, of course, you don't have to be a brilliant master of logic to see what was happening. A royal barge, manned by myself and a select cohort collecting something valuable from a Hanseatic ship at the dead of night on the Thames?'

'You, you . . .' Spurnel waved a fist at Martha.

'You ruined our lives!' Cotes snarled.

Martha just sat, head down.

'I truly believe,' Athelstan continued, 'you did not act in malice. You simply made a most dreadful mistake. Walter did the same. A young, romantic archer. He wished to show off. He wanted to demonstrate how important he truly was. He probably told you that he could not meet you. How he was unable to keep an assignation with his sweetheart from the House of Bethany because he'd been summoned to serve on board a royal barge, despatched to receive something precious from a Hanseatic ship. You, Martha, a young woman, unaware of the encroaching darkness, must have informed someone in the Flesher's household. Simon Makepeace would simply match that information with what he'd received elsewhere, hence the attack.'

'I would agree,' Cranston spoke up. 'The English Crown's demand for the Rose Casket and the Twelve Apostles was public knowledge. You've seen them, Athelstan, truly beautiful. Every one of them is worth a king's ransom.'

'You now know that, Martha,' Athelstan returned to his indictment. 'You later realised the hideous mistake you'd made. The great battle along the river became common knowledge. I am sure it was discussed in the House of Delights, as it was in the ale booths and taverns both sides of the Thames, but what could you do? You secretly mourned your love. You hid your most grievous hurt. You accepted the hideous damage which you had unwittingly inflicted, but what else? Admit that you were involved in a treasonable act? Who would believe your innocence? You would have been accused of sending your lover to his death, as well as a litany of other heinous crimes. You probably sensed that young Walter would never be returning, that his corpse either lay in the muddy roots of the Thames or was swept out to sea. Within the year you left the House of Delights. You tried to compose yourself as the respectable housekeeper to the priest of your parish. A humdrum existence, yet during it your resentment and hatred for the Flesher only deepened. You mourned. You lusted for revenge, but you could do nothing until Eudo Ingersol, the Sicarius, broke into your life.'

Athelstan paused. Martha was sitting rigidly, yet deeply agitated, fighting to control her tears. 'Ingersol was the

Flesher's emissary to St Benet's. A dark shadow of a man who slipped in and out until he met you. Once again you fell in love. You hated the Flesher. You wanted to be free of his world and so did Ingersol. This only deepened the bond between you. As you know, Ingersol turned traitor, asking Sir John here for a pardon and licence, the opportunity to be free of London and Queenhithe, permission to go where he wished, protected by the Crown. He wanted this for himself and one other – that was you. Yes?' Athelstan paused, staring at Martha who was lost in her own world. 'You both contrived a plot to injure the Flesher and inflict great damage on him. You would rob the arca and take the Flesher's ill-gotten gains to support your new life. Of course, the real obstacle was the arca and its unique locks, one key being held by the Flesher and the other by Parson Reynaud. Eventually you made a decision. You knew the House of Delights, the Flesher's love of bathing in a tub of hot water, his skin cleaned with precious tablets of Castilian soap. You would use that and perhaps the soft, pure beeswax candles which illuminated the bath chamber. After all, both you and Ingersol knew exactly what happened there. You would seize your opportunity and use the candles or the soap to create a duplicate key. And then, by some means, fair or foul, also seize that held by Parson Reynaud. The old priest would not be so difficult.'

'If Copping was here,' Martha glanced up, 'that lawyer would argue that you have words but no proof.'

Despite Martha's paleness, her obvious anxiety and fear, Athelstan caught the mockery in the woman's voice.

'Oh, we shall come to that by and by, Mistress. But to repeat, we were talking about Ingersol. You fell in love for the second time in your life. And, for the second time, your beloved was destroyed by the Flesher. Simon Makepeace was a cunning bastard, well served by Copping and Raquin. At some time, Ingersol made a dreadful mistake and the Flesher discovered that his loyal henchman was hand in glove with Sir John here.'

'And he certainly was,' Cranston interjected.

'Of course,' Athelstan continued, 'Ingersol paid the price, killed barbarously. Another great love of your life snuffed out

swift as a candle flame. Somehow you knew Ingersol would
never return, so you plotted a most hideous revenge. You
would use all the skills you'd been taught. Ingersol, an
experienced street fighter, would have feared for your safety.
He gave you one of his weapons: an Italianate dagger of subtle
design, bone-handled with a cleverly disguised lever to press
so that a blade, long, pointed and serrated, would leap out like
a dancing flame. He would instruct you on how to draw close
to your victim. On reflection you needed little education after
your stay in the House of Delights, which honed all the skills
necessary for the bedchamber. You watched and you waited.
You had the dagger as well as a copy of the Flesher's key to
the arca. I suspect he never discovered what had happened.
He probably thought that by murdering Ingersol he had nipped
any future problem in the bud . . .'

'Lord save us.' Cripplegate would have sprung to his feet,
but Cranston growled and he hurriedly sat down.

'On the night of the murders,' Cripplegate exclaimed, 'we
left the parish. No one else was expected, either at the church
or the priest's house. The only other person beside Martha
were the parson and Daventry.'

'She had certainly planned a harvest of vengeance,' Athelstan
agreed. 'She chose the night Isabella Makepeace was churched
because that woman's corpse was part of her vengeance.'
Athelstan pointed at the three parishioners. 'You gentlemen
left the church precincts. Thanks to Sir John, we know where
you were that night and who you were with, but not you,
Mistress. Forget the story of retiring early to bed; you were
plotting furiously. You are a mummer, Martha, and you can
change your appearance and your manner. A bright gown, a
painted face, ready to act all coy and welcoming for the parson
and Daventry. I am sure that you promised them sexual favours,
taking each man carefully aside. However, not in the house
where Curate Cotes or someone else may visit. What better
place than a lonely, dark church? Parson Reynaud would act
as if he was to shrive penitents, Daventry would be told to
wait in the shadows. I doubt if either of them knew what was
really happening. You are a consummate lover, Martha, a
skilled practitioner in bedroom skills, a wearer of Venus's

triple crown. You separated Daventry from the parson. You promised to confer your favours on both of them and they were to wait for you in the church. We know that Parson Reynaud was hot and lecherous for you, whilst a man like Daventry would never refuse such a gift.'

'Unbelievable—' Sexton Spurnel interjected.

'Oh, most logical,' Athelstan cut across the sexton. 'On that night Mistress Martha moved most swiftly. She'd made other preparations but first she had to deal with the living before she dealt with the dead. She crept into the church and softly knelt in front of Parson Reynaud. He expected to fully enjoy her. Martha all smiling and charm, drew very close. In her right hand the Sicarius's dagger. She lifts her head up and, as she does, presses the lever and drives the blade in one swift, killing blow into the parson's heart. Any of you who has served in battle knows such a direct blow kills instantly. No protest, no screaming. Who knows, perhaps Martha covered the parson's mouth as she watched the life glow in the priest's eyes turn to the dull, glassy stare of the dead.

'Martha is well prepared. She wipes the blade on a cloth and hurries, quiet as a shadow, down the nave, where she has told Daventry to sit on the sexton's chair just inside the main door. The nave is long and dark; night is creeping in. Daventry had not seen or heard what had happened at the far end of the church. He would not even imagine it. All he sees is this lovely woman, who has been furtively flirting with him, hurry through the murk to gladden his evening. He is ready, he has unstrapped his warbelt and it lies on the floor beside him. He squats, legs apart, and allows Martha to kneel before him. Martha, you undo the points on his hose. Daventry leans towards you and you strike as fast and fatal as any viper. The Sicarius had taught you well. Another thrust to the heart. You clean the knife, you refasten the points on Daventry's hose, but you are hurrying and you do not do it correctly, I noticed that.'

Athelstan rose to his feet, walking backwards and forwards across the sanctuary. He pointed at Martha. 'Now you turn on the dead. You have Parson Reynaud's keys. You lock that church, make it secure except for the corpse door. You wrench the coffin open and, armed with both keys to the arca, you enter the sacristy and remove the sacks of coins from the chest. Night has fallen. You then do something very subtle and devious. I forget the actual Latin tag, but when translated it reads, "to hide in full view".'

'What!' Curate Cotes exclaimed.

Athelstan just shook his head as he retook his seat. 'Now, it's logical to assume,' he continued, 'that if you have stolen a corpse and intend to hold it for ransom, you would take it to your own very secret place, a stratagem emphasised by reading that note pinned to the empty coffin. Of course, the ransom never happened. You just wanted to hide Isabella Makepeace's corpse and you did so in full view.'

'Where?' Cripplegate demanded.

'Why in God's Acre at St Benet's . . . I noticed,' Athelstan cleared his throat, 'all those pits with mounds of earth beside them. You used one of those many barrows or handcarts which stand around the cemetery to take both the remains and the coins to pits nearest the corpse door: that's where Sir John found them. You buried them there and then returned to the church, locking the door behind you, as you had sealed every other entrance to that benighted church.'

'It's not possible!' Cripplegate declared.

'Oh yes it is,' the sexton interjected.

'You are right,' Athelstan agreed. 'Martha knows that cemetery like the back of her hand. She may have even prepared the pits earlier in the day, only a few yards from the corpse door. To all appearances, just another two mounds amongst many. Who would even think the robber, the violator, would hide his plunder so close?'

'Brother . . .' Cripplegate made to get up, but Cranston loudly coughed and he sat back down.

'Master Cripplegate?'

'Brother, is it true Sir John has found both corpse and coins?'

'Not me personally,' Cranston answered cheerfully. 'Samson, Flaxwith's dog, he has a nose for corpses. Brother Athelstan had a suspicion and Samson proved him correct. Admittedly,' Cranston shrugged, 'it took some time. The corpse was covered in roses which had rotted; their pungent smell masked that of decay, but Samson has the keenest nose . . .'

'And the money?'

'A matter of logic,' Cranston replied. 'If the corpse was buried beneath one of those mounds, why not the money? We searched and we found.'

'Very cunning,' Cotes called out. 'Remember, Mistress, you were the one who claimed it would be highly unlikely that the thief, the assassin, would hide the corpse and coins in or around St Benet's.'

'Hidden in full view,' Athelstan agreed. 'Martha, you didn't really care. You just wanted to hurt the Flesher, inflict as much injury as possible. You were determined he would never recover either his treasure or his mother's corpse.' Athelstan paused as Martha smiled to herself.

'He was hurt,' she whispered, 'grievously so. But what proof do you have that I was responsible?'

'In a while,' Athelstan retorted. 'But on that night you have slain Reynaud and Daventry and stolen both the coins and the corpse. You now move back into the church to set your seal of mystery on those gruesome events. All the doors are locked and bolted. You have replaced one of the arca keys back on the chain around Reynaud's neck. You hold the ring of keys taken from the pocket of his robe. All is finished. You leave the church by the corpse door. You lock it, then insert a pebble you have picked up from the path that will obstruct any attempt to open it in the morning. Only then do you retire to bed.' Athelstan paused, staring down at the ground. 'Clever,' he murmured. 'Oh so very clever. Martha, you are a woman of so many talents.'

'Only in love,' Martha told him. 'Only in love.'

'And so the next morning,' Athelstan continued, 'Martha rises and robes herself. In her pocket she holds the keys and a small metal rod. She prepares herself and hurries out. She has to be first at the devil's door; she carries the key to that.' Athelstan shrugged. 'You know what happened next . . .'

'We broke into the church through the devil's door,' the curate declared. 'We did that at Martha's behest; it was the most logical thing to do. The other doors were of solid oak.'

'The devil's door was panelled, slats of wood easy to remove,' Athelstan agreed. 'And so you break in. You know what you saw. Martha, however, moved swiftly. She hurries to the corpse door and, hidden in that shadowy transept, she draws across the bolts and pushes in the small rod to remove the pebble. She then hastens across to the chantry chapel where Parson Reynaud sits stabbed to the heart, and slips the ring of keys into the pocket of his robe.'

'Yes, yes,' the sexton broke in, 'when we entered the church, all was confusion and scurrying about. Martha, you were flitting here and there like a bat caught in the light.'

'So easy,' Athelstan agreed, 'that long, dark, shadow-filled nave. You three men were startled and shocked out of your wits. Martha, of course, knew exactly what she had to do. Not much: draw across well-oiled bolts, push a pebble out of a lock and slip keys into the pocket of a dead man's robe.' Athelstan pointed at Martha, sitting pale-faced but still composed. 'You'd inflicted grave injury, but were eager to deliver the killing blow when circumstances were in your favour. The Flesher was responsible for the murder of the two great loves of your life and you were determined to settle for both. Oh, by the way,' Athelstan leaned forward, 'I must tell you; we have just given the first of your beloveds, Walter Grenel, a proper Christian burial.'

Martha abruptly lifted her head and, for a moment, swayed in the chair, until she caught its arms, pressing down against them.

'I don't know what—'

'Sir John,' Athelstan turned to the coroner, 'tell Martha what we found in Margo Grenel's cottage. Oh, by the way,' Athelstan gestured at the three men who seemed equally shocked, 'this will stay confidential. Sir John?'

In a few pithy sentences, Cranston described the last few hours of Walter Grenel's life, and how his corpse had been embalmed and hidden away. Athelstan ignored the exclamations of the three men, as did Cranston: the coroner compelled them to swear on the crucifix Flaxwith produced that they would keep this information secret as if it was a matter for the confessional. Athelstan concentrated on Martha, and any doubts about his indictment against her crumbled away. The housekeeper sat back in the sanctuary chair truly shocked, eyes staring wildly, mouth gaping. She had lost all her poise, that calm demeanour which constantly masked her every glance and word. She tried to speak but the words caught in her throat. She blinked furiously, shaking her head, as if trying to concentrate on what Cranston had told her.

'I didn't know, I never knew.' She waved a hand. 'Brother, you'd best continue.' Her voice was strained and hoarse.

'And so I shall, Martha. You were determined on the Flesher's death, but not at your hands. He was to die publicly in hideous disgrace. You'd learnt from Ingersol how many were coming to resent the riffler lord. How the cup of wickedness he'd filled was brimming over. The Flesher had committed foul crimes, but any victim who survived dared not protest. You were different. You bided your time.' Athelstan paused to sip from a beaker of water Cranston had brought over. The coroner had finished taking the vows of silence and came to stand beside Athelstan.

'Your vengeance,' Athelstan declared, 'began the night Flaxwith sent you a message that, on the morrow, he was to bring the corpses of five malefactors and two war dogs for exposure on the steps of St Benet's. Master Bailiff, that is correct?'

'It is,' Flaxwith replied, from where he stood guarding the entrance to the rood screen. 'News about what had happened at St Erconwald's had swept the city and Queenhithe ward. After all, parishioners like Watkin have kin there.'

'True, true,' Cripplegate called out. 'Everyone knew. Many rejoiced but all hid their glee.'

'Circumstances,' Athelstan continued, 'do conspire to impede but also to help. You, Mistress, recognised that the Flesher had been greatly discomfited. He would be wary of appearing publicly in St Benet's after such a setback. You sent a message with a street swallow. The urchin was to inform the Flesher that something had been discovered in St Benet's and that he should come immediately to discover what it was. The Flesher was ensnared. He was desperate for any news about both the missing corpse and his stolen monies. He had little to fear. St Benet's was boarded up, in a sense derelict, which is why he would be accompanied only by Copping and Raquin the killer. The Flesher believed he'd be safe enough. The pack at the Devil's Oak was not too far away, easy to whistle up, and what could the Flesher fear from you three sirs or pretty Martha?' Athelstan smiled at the housekeeper, who was still clearly shocked at what she had learnt. The friar suspected that she was brimming with questions, but dared not ask them, as it would prove Athelstan was correct.

'We were absent,' Cripplegate declared. 'We intended to visit the parish late that afternoon.'

'Whatever,' Athelstan went on, 'on that fateful morning, the Flesher swaggers in. You, Martha, bedecked in all your glory, and I shall come to that later, welcomed him warmly; it was just like the old days. You flirt using all your undoubted skill, charm and experience. The Flesher is roused. A man with a brutal, impetuous appetite, he walks deeper into the trap. At your insistence – after all, you cannot do anything while they are present – Copping and Raquin are despatched to St Benet's; they could squeeze themselves through the devil's door. The Flesher then follows you up to your bedchamber. You are now in full flower, ever so seductive. You serve him a goblet of wine, but then claim you have something to collect from the church. You also want Copping and Raquin to stay there, as they are marked down for slaughter. You ask the Flesher will he wait? And, of course, he is only too eager. You slip out of the house, in your hand the dagger Ingersol gave you. Once in the church, Raquin and Copping think you are on some errand for their master.'

'And by chance I found them separate? I deal with them one after the other?' Martha paused, realising what she had conceded.

'Separate?' Athelstan queried. 'Who told you that they were separated when they were killed? Did I? Did Sir John or Flaxwith?'

'I learnt later.'

'Nonsense, Martha. You've been here in St Erconwald's since we brought you from St Benet's that morning.' Athelstan turned to the three parishioners. 'Have any of you discussed the deaths of Raquin and Copping with Martha?'

They shook their heads, grunting their denials. 'So back to that church, Martha. You are confident and flirtatious. You tell Copping that the Flesher wants the sacristy searched just in case something can be found.' Athelstan pulled a face. 'A message, or something similar to that, which at the time would make sense. No matter. Those two men wouldn't have the slightest suspicion about what you intended. Copping goes off to the sacristy, you lead Raquin into that chantry chapel. You flirt and tease. Raquin cannot believe his good fortune: this lovely woman acting so welcoming. You draw close. Raquin is seduced and distracted. You drive that dagger straight into his heart, swift as a lunging cat. Copping is in the sacristy. He has not seen or heard anything untoward. Again, you draw close, any excuse. Then you strike. Copping collapses, dying almost immediately. To confuse matters further, you draw Copping's knife and place it near his hand. Once satisfied, you hurry back to Raquin, huddled in that corner. You unsheathe both sword and dagger, and position them as if Raquin had at least armed himself against his killer. Of course, it was all pretence, a way of diverting suspicion, indicating that both men had the opportunity to confront their assassin before they died.'

Athelstan shrugged. 'Who would ever have dreamt that their opponent was the sweet, docile Martha?' Athelstan stared at the housekeeper. 'So it was, so it was,' he murmured. 'You'd slaughtered the Flesher's henchmen and returned to the priest's house, where you accepted the Flesher's violent embraces. Painful, humiliating, but the reward was great. Your bedchamber makes an excellent prison: its window is narrow and the door of solid oak. You escape and wait. Flaxwith is coming and you know these three gentlemen here will also be arriving. Meanwhile, at the Devil's Oak, none of the wolf pack would ever dream about what was happening to their master. Moreover, they would be fearful of approaching St Benet's whilst those corpses were being exposed.'

Martha stretched out her hands as if closely studying them, then she lifted her head. 'And the proof for all this, Brother Athelstan?'

'Proof? Oh, I concede you will have to be put to the

question in the press yard at Newgate.' Athelstan steeled
himself as the woman flinched in fear. 'Sir John believes there
is enough to draw up and present a bill of indictment before
King's Bench at Westminster. I am sure the Justices of Oyer
and Terminer, not to mention the specially convoked jury, will
rule there's more than a case to answer. As for proof? Well,
on the night Daventry and the parson were murdered, you
were the only one in St Benet's. Our three worthies over there
were ensconced in another tavern. We now know that. Ingersol
is dead. None of the Flesher's coven had a hand in these
mysteries.' Athelstan pointed directly at her. 'You were the
only one there. You had the keys, the means, as well as
extensive knowledge about St Benet's and its cemetery.
Moreover, only someone like you could get close to Parson
Reynaud and a fighting man such as Daventry, whose points
you were undoing as you edged nearer to stab him. Martha,
you also had the motive. By your own admission, you hated
the Flesher and all his works—'

'And the next day,' Cripplegate shouted, 'you led us all by
the nose.'

'Yes, I think she did,' Athelstan agreed. 'On the morning
after, Martha was waiting for you at the devil's door ready to
give advice on what to do. The same proof covers the murders
of Raquin and Copping. Who else was there? St Benet's was
totally deserted, indeed shunned by others. Martha,' Athelstan
was determined to bluff his way forward if that was the only
path to the truth, 'Sir John, with the help of Flaxwith, has
found the street swallow who took your message to the Flesher.'

'I didn't, I . . .' Her voice faltered.

'Yes you did,' Athelstan retorted. 'Let us move on. Copping
and Raquin? Who would they allow to draw so close? Who
was there to make that approach?'

'Surely they drew their weapons?' she whispered, 'I mean,
Raquin was a dagger man.'

'I have asked you this before,' Athelstan replied. 'How do
you know those two men were found separate? You have given
no satisfactory answer.'

'And you made another mistake.' Cranston took up the
questioning as Athelstan drank from the beaker.

'Sir John?'

'When we were comforting you in the priest's house after the Flesher's attack, Flaxwith informed us that Copping and Raquin lay murdered in St Benet's. Brother Athelstan and I were shocked, surprised. You said nothing at all about such startling news. On reflection, little wonder: you already knew. You were responsible for their deaths.'

'I have already referred to further proof,' Athelstan continued. 'I found no signs, no marks, no bruise on the Flesher's corpse, not even a scratch. No sign, no indication that you tried to defend yourself from his brutal assault. Moreover, when I first met you after the Flesher's attack, your face was unpainted. However, when I went into your chamber, I noticed face-cloths smeared with fresh creams and powder. You used those cloths to remove the paint you carefully applied when you were preparing to seduce the Flesher. I also noticed the jug of rich claret and the two goblets lying smashed on the bedchamber floor. Why should there be a jug and two wine cups in your bedchamber? Of course, that was all part of your plot to provoke the Flesher's lust for you. Then,' the friar added softly, 'there's your reaction to our discovery of Walter Grenel's corpse. You were lovers, weren't you? He gave you his wrist guard, the insignia of a Tower archer as a keepsake. Martha, we found it in your chamber. We have it now and it's only a matter of time before our searchers discover the dagger Ingersol gave to you, the one used to kill those four men in St Benet's. Afterwards you hid it away before we arrived. Since that day you have not returned to St Benet's. Consequently that dagger must be hidden, concealed somewhere in the priest's house. Rest assured, we shall find it.'

'You will be arrested,' Cranston intoned, 'taken to the condemned hold at Newgate, the justices will question you closely. Or,' he paused, 'the money stolen from the arca has been recovered. The four men you killed were either felons, associates of notorious felons, or involved in plotting serious felonies against the King's peace. Mistress Martha, in return for your full and truthful confession, there will be no trial, no questioning. You will be despatched to a convent and immured there for life. A comfortable enough existence. You will be well looked after and cared for, but you will never leave that convent alive. Mistress,' Cranston walked across and patted Martha on the shoulder, 'the choice is yours.'

Athelstan remained silent. Cranston and he had agreed to allow Martha a path to the truth by her own confession. She would be given the choice to escape brutal imprisonment and the full rigour of the law at the Elms in Smithfield. The silence deepened. Curate Cotes made to speak but Cranston snapped his fingers and shook his head.

'Can I visit his grave?' Martha lifted her head. 'Can I visit Walter's grave? I would love to. I need to say farewell to at least one of my loves.'

'Of course.'

'And Brother Athelstan,' she raised her head, her face all tear-streaked, 'what Sir John promised?'

'It will be that way.'

'I confess.' Martha crossed herself. 'I confess to a deep,' her voice turned brittle hard, 'lasting detestation and hatred for that devil incarnate Simon Makepeace.' She drew a deep breath. 'I loved Walter Grenel, he loved me. He even gave me his precious wrist guard as a token. He told me, on the morning before he disappeared, how he had been chosen for a very important but secret task, the removal of something precious from a Hanseatic ship, *The Glory of Bremen*. He and others, under Sir John Cranston, were to transport it by barge to the Tower. I was young, immature and stupid. I babbled like a brook and the news must have been passed on to the Flesher. Only long afterwards did I fully realise the effect of what I'd done. But it was too late for anything but grief.' She raised a hand. 'You know the rest. I felt I was in a nightmare but I hid my sorrow, my love, as I did my growing hatred for the Flesher. I kept myself as free as I could from his filthy world. Then Eudo Ingersol entered my life. To put it bluntly, I fell deeply in love with him.'

'You fooled us,' Cotes sang out.

'That was and still is very easy,' Martha retorted. 'We would meet down in that ghostly crypt. Parson Reynaud was correct, no one ever went there.'

'And you plotted your escape?'

'And our revenge, Brother. Eudo would secretly become a King's approver, betraying the Flesher at every twist and turn. I encouraged him to approach you, Sir John. I had learnt how the Flesher and Raquin hated you but also greatly feared you.'

'Good,' Cranston grunted. 'They had good cause to.'

'You know what happened, Sir John. Eudo handed over valuable information. Both of us prayed, desperate to get the Crown's protection and licence to go abroad. Of course we needed money and we dreamed of robbing the arca at St Benet's. I know I could inveigle Parson Reynaud, use my skills to seize his key, at least for a while. The Flesher's was a different matter . . .'

'Eudo made a cast of it at the House of Delights?'

'No, Brother, he made two. One with soap of the purest kind, the second with beeswax. Eudo acted all dark and secretive but, in truth, he was a merry soul. He thought it was highly amusing that whilst the Flesher disported himself in candlelight, being bathed with the purest soap, we would use both to cast a key and so rob his arca. Eudo was successful, he travelled to Colchester to get this fashioned.'

'But the Flesher discovered what his henchman had done?'

'No, Brother, he did not. Eudo was very careful. Of course the Flesher and Raquin realised they were being betrayed. They believed you, Sir John, was closely involved. For a while they watched their retainers, the Sycamores, but eventually, from the little I learnt, they turned their attention to you.'

'Oh Lord save us,' Cranston murmured.

'He may well do, Sir John, but not Eudo. They watched you meet him and that was it. One day Eudo was supposed to visit me, then he didn't. Nothing at first but, as the days passed, I heard rumours. On more than one occasion I eavesdropped on Parson Reynaud, the Flesher and Raquin. I realised what had happened. My hatred became more acute, my desire for vengeance more sharp. I just waited for the opportunity. Eudo had told me how the Flesher was ripe for a fall. He'd also given me his second dagger and showed me how to use it.' She smiled thinly. 'I had all the skills and experience necessary to draw close to a man.' Her grin widened, as if she were talking to herself. 'Eudo was correct. It was so very, very easy.

One deep thrust, then step back and watch them die.' She shrugged. 'For the rest, Brother Athelstan, what you've said is true. I can add very little to it. You'll find the dagger in a pouch in the mattress of my bedchamber.' Martha rose unsteadily to her feet. 'You have what you need. I cannot answer any more questions. I must see Walter's grave, please?'

Athelstan nodded at Cranston, who told Flaxwith to take his bailiffs and follow Benedicta. The widow woman would show them where Walter was buried. The coroner also dismissed Cripplegate and his two colleagues, warning them to keep away from St Benet's. At last the church emptied, the silence deepening. Cranston walked over to the lady chapel to light a taper. Athelstan knelt beneath the pyx. He was deep in prayer when the main door was abruptly flung open. Athelstan scrambled to his feet and turned. Godbless came hurrying up the nave, almost dragging a young goat by the leash around its neck.

'Brother Athelstan, Brother Athelstan, Sir John, God bless you! A miracle! Thaddeus has come back from the dead.'

AUTHOR'S NOTE

*T*he Mansions of Murder *is a work of fiction, but I suggest it accurately reflects the political situation in the late autumn of 1381.* The gangs of the underworld, the rifflers, did exercise their own authority and could be highly dangerous. One example will suffice. In 1326 Queen Isabella and her lover Roger Mortimer landed at Walton-on-Naze in Essex with the avowed aim of toppling Edward II. Roger Mortimer, through his friends in the city, could summon up the rifflers, and he did so within a matter of days. The London mob surfaced so quickly and so savagely they even surprised Edward's own Treasurer, the Bishop of Exeter, as he rode past St Paul's. Exeter and two of his squires were pulled from their horses, decapitated, their corpses stripped and left to public exposure. The London mob continued to be such a threat for centuries. Indeed, we must remember, that the Tower was built not so much to defend London but to overawe it!

The preservation of corpses, especially the embalming of soldiers killed on the eastern marches, did reach a high level of sophistication, as the knight found at St Bees in Cumbria will attest. The mummification of the dead was not just the monopoly of ancient Egypt. By the fourteenth century, the art of embalming had developed so corpses could be carefully preserved and transported for burial wherever the deceased's relatives decided. Finally, Richard Fitzalan, Earl of Arundel, and his namesake the young King, deeply hated each other. Indeed, during the funeral obsequies of King Richard's beloved Queen Anne of Bohemia, Fitzalan arrived late for the ceremony. The King took this as a deliberate insult, a slur on his wife's memory. He marched down the church and attacked Fitzalan in full view of both court and people. Naturally Fitzalan's opposition to the King deepened and, in 1397, he paid for this with his life. Politics during the reign of Edward II truly was a matter of survival.